Developing & Managing

Your School Guidance & Counseling Program

⤚ Fifth Edition ⤙

by

Norman C. Gysbers
Patricia Henderson

AMERICAN COUNSELING ASSOCIATION
5999 Stevenson Avenue
Alexandria, VA 22304
www.counseling.org

Developing & Managing

Your School Guidance & Counseling Program

 Fifth Edition

10   9   8   7   6   5   4   3   2   1

American Counseling Association
5999 Stevenson Avenue
Alexandria, VA 22304

Director of Publications
Carolyn C. Baker

Production Manager
Bonny E. Gaston

Editorial Assistant
Catherine A. Brumley

Copy Editor
Kathleen Porta Baker

Cover and text design by Bonny E. Gaston.

Library of Congress Cataloging-in-Publication Data
Gysbers, Norman C.
   Developing & managing your school guidance & counseling program / Norman
C. Gysbers, Patricia Henderson.—5th ed.
       p.   cm.
   Includes bibliographical references and index.
   ISBN 978-1-55620-312-1 (alk. paper)
   1.   Educational counseling—United States.   I.   Henderson, Patricia, Ed.D.   II.   Title.
III. Title: Developing and managing your school guidance and counseling program.

LB1027.5.G929 2012
371.4'220973—dc23   2011023182

To School Counselors and Their Leaders

Table of Contents

⌒ Part I ⌒

Planning

⌒ Part II ⌒

Designing

⌒ Part III ⌒

Implementing

☞ Part IV ☜
Evaluating

☞ Part V ☜
Enhancing

Appendixes

Preface

☞ One of the most fundamental obligations of any society is to prepare its adolescents and young adults to lead productive and prosperous lives as adults. This means preparing all young people with a solid enough foundation of literacy, numeracy, and thinking skills for responsible citizenship, career development, and lifelong learning. (Harvard Graduate School of Education, 2011, p. 1)

As we enter the second decade of the 21st century, the United States continues to undergo substantial changes in its occupational, social, and economic structures. Occupational and industrial specialization continue to increase dramatically. Increasing size and complexity are the rule rather than the exception, often creating job invisibility and making the transition from school to work and from work to further education and back again more complex and difficult.

Social structures and social and personal values also continue to change and become more diverse. Emerging social groups are challenging established groups, asking for equality. People are on the move, too, from rural to urban areas and back again and from one region of the country to another in search of economic, social, and psychological security. Our population is becoming increasingly diverse.

All of these changes are creating substantial challenges for our children and adolescents. A rapidly changing work world and labor force; violence in the home, school, and community; divorce; teenage suicide; substance abuse; and sexual experimentation are just a few examples. These challenges are not abstract aberrations. These challenges are real, and they are having and will have a substantial impact on the personal–social, career, and academic development of our children and adolescents.

Responding to Challenges

In response to these and other continuing societal and individual needs and challenges, educational leaders and policymakers are in the midst of reforming the entire educational enterprise (National Association of Secondary School Principals, 2004; No Child Left Behind Act of 2001; Race to the Top, 2011; Zhao, 2009). Guidance and counseling in the schools also continues to undergo reform, changing from a position-services model to a comprehensive program firmly grounded in principles of human growth and development. This change makes guidance and counseling in the schools an integral part of education and an equal partner with the overall instruction program, focusing on students' academic, career, and personal–social development.

Traditionally, however, guidance and counseling was not conceptualized and implemented in this manner because, as Aubrey (1973) suggested, guidance and counseling was seen as a support service lacking a content base of its own. Sprinthall (1971) made this same point when he stated that the practice of guidance and counseling has little content and that guidance and counseling textbooks usually avoid discussion of a subject matter base for guidance and counseling programs.

If guidance and counseling is to become an equal partner in education and meet the increasingly complex needs of individuals and society, our opinion is that guidance and counseling must conceptually and organizationally become a program with its own content base and structure. This call is not new; many early pioneers issued the same call. But the call was not loud enough during the early years, and guidance and counseling became a position and then a service with an emphasis on duties, processes, and techniques. The need and the call continued to emerge occasionally thereafter, however, but not until the late 1960s and early 1970s did it reemerge and become visible once more in the form of a developmental comprehensive program.

This is not to say that developmental guidance and counseling was not present before the late 1960s. What it does mean is that by the late 1960s the need for attention to aspects of human development other than "the time-honored cognitive aspect of learning subject matter mastery" (Cottingham, 1973, p. 341) had again become apparent. Cottingham (1973) characterized these other aspects of human development as "personal adequacy learning" (p. 342). Kehas (1973) pointed to this same need by stating that an individual should have opportunities "to develop intelligence about his [or her] self—his [or her] personal, unique, idiosyncratic, individual self" (p. 110).

Reconceptualization of Guidance and Counseling

The next step in the evolution of guidance and counseling was to establish guidance and counseling as a comprehensive program—a program that is an integral part of education with a content base and organizational structure of its own. In response to this need, Gysbers and Moore (1981) published a book titled *Improving Guidance Programs*. It presented a content-based, kindergarten through 12th-grade comprehensive guidance and counseling program model and described the steps to implement the model. The first, second, third, and fourth editions of our current book built on the model and implementation steps presented in *Improving Guidance Programs* and substantially expanded and extended the model and implementation steps. This fifth edition expands and extends the model and steps even further, sharing what has been learned through various state and local adoption and adaptations since 2006.

Organization of This Book

Five phases of developing comprehensive guidance and counseling programs are used as organizers for this book. The five phases are planning (Chapters 1–4), designing (Chapters 5 and 6), implementing (Chapters 7–9), evaluating (Chapter 10), and enhancing (Chapter 11). In several chapters, ways to attend to the increasing diversity of school populations and the roles and responsibilities of district- and building-level guidance and counseling leaders are highlighted. The appendixes offer examples of forms and procedures used by various states and school districts in the installation of comprehensive guidance and counseling programs. Also included as an appendix are the ethical standards of the American School Counselor Association (ASCA) and the Multicultural Counseling Competencies of the Association for Multicultural Counseling and Development (Arredondo et al., 1996; Sue, Arredondo, & McDavis, 1992).

Part I: Planning

Chapter 1 traces the evolution of guidance and counseling in the schools from the beginning of the 20th century. The changing influences, emphases, and structures from then until now are described and discussed in detail. The emergence of comprehensive guidance and counseling programs is highlighted. Having an understanding of the evolution of guidance and counseling in the schools and the emergence of developmental comprehensive programs is the first step toward improving your school's guidance and counseling program. Chapter 2 is based on this understanding and focuses on the issues and concerns in planning and organizing for guidance and counseling program improvement. Chapter 3 then presents a model guidance and counseling program based on the concept of life career development; it is organized around four basic elements. Chapter 4, the last chapter in the planning phase, discusses the steps involved in finding out how well your current program is working and where improvement is needed.

Part II: Designing

Chapter 5 begins the designing phase of the program improvement process and focuses on designing the program of your choice. Issues and steps in selecting the desired program structure for your comprehensive program are presented. Chapter 6 describes the necessary tasks required to plan the transition to a comprehensive guidance and counseling program.

Part III: Implementing

Chapter 7 presents the details of beginning a new program in a school or district, and Chapter 8 emphasizes the details of managing and maintaining the program. Chapter 9 first looks at how to ensure that school counselors have the necessary competence to develop, manage, and implement a comprehensive guidance and counseling program and then highlights counselor supervision procedures.

Part IV: Evaluating

Comprehensive guidance and counseling program evaluation is discussed in detail in Chapter 10. Program evaluation, personnel evaluation, and results evaluation are featured, with attention given to procedures for each.

Part V: Enhancing

Chapter 11 focuses on the use of data gathered from program, personnel, and results evaluation and from needs assessments to redesign and enhance a comprehensive guidance and counseling program that has been in place for a number of years. The chapter uses actual data gathered in a school district and describes in detail the way this school district built on the guidance and counseling program foundation it had established in the early 1980s to update and enhance its program to meet continuing and changing student, school district, and community needs.

Who Should Read This Book

A goal of this book is to inform and involve all members of a kindergarten through 12th-grade guidance and counseling staff in the development and management of comprehensive school guidance and counseling programs. Although specific parts are highlighted for guidance and counseling program leaders (central or building-level directors, supervisors, coordinators, department heads) and school administrators, the information provided is important for all to know and use. In addition, this book is designed for practitioners already on the job as well as for counselors-in-training and administrators-in-training. It can and should be used in preservice education as well as in-service education.

The Fifth Edition: What Is New?

All of the chapters in the fifth edition have been reorganized and updated to reflect current theory and practices. A more complete theory base for comprehensive guidance and counseling programs is provided, along with updated examples of the contents of various components of comprehensive guidance and counseling programs drawn from many state models and from the ASCA (2005) National Model. New information and practical ideas and methods have been added to assist school counselors and school counselor leaders in better understanding the issues involved in developing and managing comprehensive school guidance and counseling programs.

Increased attention is given in this fifth edition to the important topic of diversity. Increased attention is also given to expanded discussions of whom school counselors' clients are and the range of issues they present. Also, increased attention is given to helping school counselors and their leaders be accountable for the work they do and for evaluating and reporting the impact of their programs' activities and services on students' academic, career, and personal and social development. In addition, increased attention is given to the issues and challenges that the leaders of comprehensive guidance and counseling programs face in an increasingly complex educational environment.

Finally, a new section, Your Progress Check, is found at the end of each chapter. This feature allows you to check the progress you are making as you move through the planning, designing, implementing, evaluating, and enhancing phases of change.

Concluding Thoughts

Some readers may think that guidance and counseling program improvement is a simple task requiring little staff time and few resources. This is not true. Substantial work can be completed during the first several years but, with the necessary resources available to ensure successful implementation, at least 4 to 5 years are usually required. To carry the program through the enhancement phase may require an additional 5 years. Then we recommend an ongoing program improvement process.

Moreover, the chapter organization may lead some readers to think that guidance and counseling program improvement activities follow one another in a linear fashion. Although a progression is involved, some of the activities described in Chapters 2 through 10 may be carried out concurrently. This is particularly true for the evaluation procedures described in Chapter 10, some of which are carried out from the beginning of the program improvement process throughout the life of the program. The program enhancement process follows evaluation and connects back to the beginning, but at a higher level, as program redesign unfolds. Thus, the process is spiral, not circular. Each time the redesign process unfolds, a new and more effective guidance and counseling program emerges.

Finally, it is important to understand that a comprehensive guidance and counseling program, as described in the chapters that follow, provides a common language for the program elements that enable students, parents, teachers, administrators, school board members, and school counselors in a school district to speak with a common voice when they describe what a program is. They all see the same thing and use the same language to describe the program's framework. This is the power of common language, whether the program is in a small or large rural, urban, or suburban school district. Within the basic framework at the local district level, however, the guidance knowledge and skills (competencies) students are to learn, the activities and services to be provided, and the allocations of school counselor time are tailored specifically to student, school, and community needs and local resources. This provides the flexibility and opportunity for creativity for the personnel in every school district to develop and implement a comprehensive guidance and counseling program that makes sense for their districts. We are convinced that without the common language for the program elements and the obligation to tailor it to fit local school districts, guidance and counseling and the work of school counselors will be lost in the overall educational system and, as a result, will continue to be marginalized and seen as a supplemental activity that is nice to have, but not necessary.

References

American School Counselor Association. (2005). *The ASCA National Model: A framework for school counseling programs* (2nd ed.). Alexandria, VA: Author.

Arredondo, P., Toporek, R., Brown, S., Jones, J., Locke, D. C., Sanchez, J., & Stadler, H. (1996). Operationalization of the multicultural counseling competencies. *Journal of Multicultural Counseling and Development, 24,* 42–78.

Aubrey, R. F. (1973). Organizational victimization of school counselors. *The School Counselor, 20,* 346–354.

Cottingham, H. F. (1973). Psychological education, the guidance function, and the school counselor. *The School Counselor, 20,* 340–345.

Gysbers, N. C., & Moore, E. J. (1981). *Improving guidance programs.* Englewood Cliffs, NJ: Prentice-Hall.

Harvard Graduate School of Education. (2011). *Pathways to prosperity: Meeting the challenge of preparing young Americans for the 21st century.* Cambridge, MA: Author.

Kehas, C. D. (1973). Guidance and the process of schooling: Curriculum and career education. *The School Counselor, 20,* 109–115.

National Association of Secondary School Principals. (2004). *Breaking ranks II: Strategies for leading high school reform.* Reston, VA: Author.

No Child Left Behind Act of 2001, Pub. L. No. 107-110, 115 Stat. 1425 (2002).

Race to the Top. (2011). In *Wikipedia.* Retrieved from http://en.wikipedia.org/wiki/Race_to_the_Top

Sprinthall, N. A. (1971). *Guidance for human growth.* New York, NY: Van Nostrand Reinhold.

Sue, D. W., Arredondo, P., & McDavis, R. J. (1992). Multicultural counseling competencies and standards: A call to the profession. *Journal of Counseling & Development, 70,* 477–486.

Zhao, Y. (2009). *Catching up or leading the way.* Alexandria, VA: Association for Supervision and Curriculum Development.

Acknowledgments

⌒ With this fifth edition, we gratefully acknowledge the substantial contributions of school counselors as they work with children, young people, parents, teachers, administrators, and community members throughout the United States. It is to school counselors and their leaders that we dedicate this book. At the same time, we also gratefully acknowledge the assistance of those individuals who helped us make all five editions of this book possible. Unfortunately, it is impossible to list them all, but know that we appreciate their support and encouragement. We particularly acknowledge the work of the counselors, head counselors, and administrators from Northside Independent School District, San Antonio, Texas. We appreciate the district's willingness to host visitors who come to see a comprehensive guidance and counseling program at work. Thanks also to Linda Coats who typed a number of the revised chapters and helped assemble the revised chapters into the final book form. Finally, thanks to Carolyn Baker, director of publications at the American Counseling Association, for all of her help.

About the Authors

☞ **Norman C. Gysbers** is a Curators' Professor in the Department of Educational, School, and Counseling Psychology at the University of Missouri—Columbia. He received his BA from Hope College, Holland, Michigan, in 1954. He was a teacher in the Muskegon Heights Michigan School District (1954–1956) and served in the U.S. Army Artillery (1956–1958). He received his MA (1959) and PhD (1963) from the University of Michigan. He joined the faculty of the College of Education, University of Missouri, in 1963 as an assistant professor. In addition to his duties as an assistant professor, he also served as the licensed school counselor at the University Laboratory School until 1970.

He was awarded a Franqui Professorship from the Université Libre de Bruxelles, Brussels, Belgium, and lectured there in February 1984. He was a visiting scholar at the University of Hong Kong in May 2000, 2002, and 2004 and at the Chinese University of Hong Kong in January 2001; a Scholar in Residence at the University of British Columbia in July–August 2000; and a Visiting Scholar at National Taiwan Normal University in January 2011.

His research and teaching interests are in career development, career counseling, and school guidance and counseling program development, management, and evaluation. He is author of 90 articles, 38 chapters in published books, 15 monographs, and 22 books, one of which was translated into Italian, Korean, Japanese, and Chinese.

He has received many awards, most notably the National Career Development Association's Eminent Career Award in 1989, the American School Counselor Association's Mary Gehrke Lifetime Achievement Award in 2004, the William T. Kemper Award for Excellence in Teaching in 2002, the Governor's Award for Excellence in Teaching in 2004, the Faculty/Alumni Award from the University of Missouri in 1997, and the Distinguished Faculty Award from the University of Missouri in 2008.

Gysbers was editor of *The Career Development Quarterly* from 1962 to 1970; president of the National Career Development Association, 1972–1973; president of the American Counseling Association, 1977–1978; and vice president of the Association of Career and Technical Education, 1979–1982. He was the editor of *The Journal of Career Development* from 1978 until 2006.

☞ **Patricia Henderson** is a former director of guidance at the Northside Independent School District in San Antonio, Texas. She received her AB in English from Mount Holyoke College in 1962, her MA in guidance from California State University, San Jose, in 1967, and her EdD in educational leadership from Nova University in 1986. She is certified as a school counselor and midmanagement administrator by California and Texas. She has been a teacher, counselor, and administrator in public schools. She has been an adjunct professor at California State University, Fullerton; California State University, Long Beach; Our Lady of the Lake University in San Antonio; and the University of Texas at San Antonio and is currently at Texas A&M University—San Antonio.

Henderson consults with school districts and has conducted workshops at numerous professional meetings. Her professional interests are in school guidance and counseling; program development, management, implementation, evaluation, and improvement; enhancing roles of school counselors through supervision, staff leadership, and meaningful school counselor performance evaluation; creating systemic change through collaborative program development; and counselor supervision. She and Dr. Gysbers have also coauthored *Leading and Managing Your School Guidance Program Staff* (1998), *Comprehensive Guidance Programs That Work—II* (1997), and *Implementing Comprehensive School Guidance Programs: Critical Issues and Successful Responses* (2002). She wrote "The Theory Behind the ASCA National Model," included in *The ASCA National Model* (2nd ed.). She is coauthor with Larry Golden of *Case Studies in School Counseling* (2007). She is the author of *The New Handbook of Administrative Supervision in Counseling* (2009). She has authored or coauthored 30 articles or chapters. She wrote *The Comprehensive Guidance Program for Texas Public Schools: A Guide for Program Development, Pre-K–12th Grade* (1990, 2004, in press) under the auspices of the Texas Education Agency and the Texas Counseling Association and *Guidelines for Developing Comprehensive Guidance Programs in California Public Schools* (1981) with D. Hays and L. Steinberg.

She has received awards from professional associations for her writing, research, and contributions to professional development and recognition as an outstanding supervisor at the state and national levels. She received the Texas Association for Counseling and Development Presidential Award in 1990, an Honorary Service Award from the California State PTA in 1978, and Lifetime Membership in the Texas PTA in 1999. She received the William Truax Award from the Texas Counseling Association in 2005, the Mary E. Gehrke Lifetime Achievement Award from the American School Counselor Association in 2006, and the 2010 Lifetime Achievement Award from the Association for Counselor Education and Supervision.

Henderson has been a member or chair of numerous committees and held leadership positions within the California Counseling Association, Texas Counseling Association, American School Counselor Association, Association for Counselor Education and Supervision, and American Counseling Association. She has been president of the Texas Counseling Association (1992–1993), Texas Association for Counselor Education and Supervision (1988–1989), and Texas Career Development Association (1995–1996).

~ Part I ~

Planning

Evolution of Comprehensive Guidance and Counseling Programs: From Position to Services to Program

Planning—Building a Foundation for Change

- Study the history of guidance and counseling in the schools.
- Learn about the people, events, and societal conditions that helped shape guidance and counseling in the schools.
- Understand the implications of the shift from position to services to program in the conceptualization and organization of guidance and counseling.

☞ By the beginning of the 20th century, the United States was deeply involved in the Industrial Revolution. It was a period of rapid industrial growth, social protest, social reform, and utopian idealism. Social protest and social reform were being carried out under the banner of the Progressive Movement, a movement that sought to change negative social conditions associated with the Industrial Revolution.

These conditions were the unanticipated effects of industrial growth. They included the emergence of cities with slums and immigrant-filled ghettos, the decline of puritan morality, the eclipse of the individual by organizations, corrupt political bossism, and the demise of the apprenticeship method of learning a vocation. (Stephens, 1970, pp. 148–149)

Guidance and counseling was born in these turbulent times as vocational guidance during the height of the Progressive Movement and as "but one manifestation of the broader movement of progressive reform which occurred in this country in the late 19th and early 20th centuries" (Stephens, 1970, p. 5). The beginnings of vocational guidance can be traced to the work of a number of individuals and social institutions. People such as Charles Merrill, Frank Parsons, Meyer Bloomfield, Jessie B. Davis, Anna Reed, E. W. Weaver, and David Hill, working through a number of organizations and movements such as the settlement house movement, the National Society for the Promotion of Industrial Education, and schools in San Francisco, Boston, Detroit, Grand Rapids, Seattle, New York, and New Orleans, were all instrumental in formulating and implementing early conceptions of guidance and counseling.

Brewer (1942) stated that four conditions, acting together, led to the development of vocational guidance. He identified these conditions as the division of labor, the growth of technology, the extension of vocational education, and the spread of modern forms of democracy. He stated that none of these conditions alone were causative but all were necessary for the rise of vocational guidance during this time period. To these conditions, J. B. Davis (1956) added the introduction of commercial curriculums, the increase in enrollment in secondary schools leading to the introduction of coursework such as practical arts, manual training, and home economics and child labor problems.

This chapter traces the history of guidance and counseling in the schools from the beginning of the 20th century through the first decade of the 21st century. It opens with a review of guidance and counseling during the first two decades of the 1900s, focusing on the work of Frank Parsons and Jessie Davis, the early purposes of guidance and counseling, the appointment of teachers to the position of vocational counselor, the guidance and counseling work of administrators, the spread of guidance and counseling, and early concerns about the efficiency of the position model. The chapter continues with a discussion of the challenges and changes for guidance and counseling that occurred in the 1920s and 1930s. The changing purposes of guidance and counseling, as well as the emergence of the service model, are described. Then, two important federal laws from the 1940s and 1950s are presented and described. This discussion is followed by a focus on the 1960s, a time of new challenges and changes, a time when pupil personnel services provided a dominant organizational structure for guidance and counseling. It was also a time when elementary guidance and counseling emerged and a time when calls were heard about the need to change the then dominant organizational structure for guidance and counseling.

The next sections of the chapter focus on the emergence of comprehensive guidance and counseling programs in the 1960s and their implementation in the 1980s, 1990s, and the first decade of the 2000s across the United States. Attention is paid to the importance of federal and state legislation. The chapter continues with an emphasis on the promise of the 21st century: the full implementation of comprehensive guidance and counseling programs in every school district in the United States. The American School Counselor Association (ASCA) National Model is described, along with pertinent state and federal legislation. The chapter closes with a presentation of five foundation premises that undergird comprehensive guidance and counseling programs.

Beginnings of Guidance and Counseling in the Schools: The First Two Decades of the 1900s

Work of Frank Parsons

The implementation of one of the first systematic conceptions of guidance and counseling in the United States took place in Civic Service House, Boston, Massachusetts, when the Boston Vocation Bureau was established in January 1908 by Mrs. Quincy Agassiz Shaw, based on plans drawn up by Frank Parsons, an American educator and reformer. The establishment of the Vocation Bureau was an outgrowth of Parsons's work with individuals at Civic Service House. Parsons issued his first report on the bureau on May 1, 1908, and according to H. V. Davis (1969, p. 113), "This was an important report because the term *vocational guidance* apparently appeared for the first time in print as the designation of an organized service." It was also an important report because it emphasized that vocational guidance should be provided by trained experts and become part of every public school system.

Parsons's conception of guidance stressed the scientific approach to choosing an occupation. The first paragraph in the first chapter of his book, *Choosing a Vocation,* illustrated his concern:

No step in life, unless it may be the choice of a husband or wife, is more important than the choice of a vocation. The wise selection of the business, profession, trade, or occupation to which one's life is to be devoted and the development of full efficiency in the chosen field are matters of deepest movement to young men and to the public. These vital problems should be solved in a careful, scientific way, with due regard to each person's aptitudes, abilities, ambitions, resources, and limitations, and the relations of these elements to the conditions of success in different industries. (Parsons, 1909, p. 3)

Work of Jessie B. Davis

When Jessie B. Davis moved from Detroit, Michigan, to Grand Rapids, Michigan, to assume the principalship of Central High School in 1907, he initiated a plan "to organize an entire school for systematic guidance" (J. B. Davis, 1956, p. 176). He used grade-level principals as counselors to about 300 students each. Interestingly, he did not see vocational guidance as a new profession. According to Krug (1964), he saw it as the work of school principals.

As part of Davis's plan to provide systematic guidance to all students, he convinced his teachers of English to set aside the English period on Fridays to use oral and written composition as a vehicle to deliver vocational guidance. The details of his plan are described in his book *Vocational and Moral Guidance* (J. B. Davis, 1914) and are outlined briefly here. Note that vocational guidance through the English curriculum began in Grade 7 and continued through Grade 12. Note, too, the progression of topics covered at each grade level. School counselors today will understand and appreciate the nature and structure of Davis's system.

- *Grade 7:* vocational ambition
- *Grade 8:* the value of education
- *Grade 9:* character self-analysis (character analysis through biography)
- *Grade 10:* the world's work—a call to service (choosing a vocation)
- *Grade 11:* preparation for one's vocation
- *Grade 12:* social ethics and civic ethics

Early Purposes of Guidance and Counseling

In the beginning, the early 1900s, school guidance and counseling were called *vocational guidance.* Vocational guidance had a singular purpose. It was seen as a response to the economic, educational, and social problems of those times and was concerned with the entrance of young people into the work world and the conditions they might find there. Economic concerns focused on the need to better prepare workers for the workplace, whereas educational concerns arose from a need to increase efforts in schools to help students find purpose for their education as well as their employment. Social concerns emphasized the need for changing school methods and organization as well as for exerting more control over conditions of labor in child-employing industries (U.S. Bureau of Education, 1914).

Two distinctly different perspectives concerning the initial purpose of vocational guidance were present from the very beginning. Wirth (1983) described one perspective, espoused by David Snedden and Charles Prosser, that followed the social efficiency philosophy. According to this perspective, "the task of education was to aid the economy to function as efficiently as possible" (Wirth, 1983, pp. 73–74). Schools were to be designed to prepare individuals for work, with vocational guidance being a way to sort individuals according to their various capacities, preparing them to obtain a job.

The other perspective of vocational guidance was based on principles of democratic philosophy that emphasized the need to change the conditions of industry as well as assist students to make educational and occupational choices. According to Wirth (1980), "The 'Chicago school'—[George Hubert] Mead, [John] Dewey, and [Frank] Leavitt—brought the perspective of democratic philosophy to the discussion of vocational guidance" (p. 114). Leavitt (1914), in a speech at the founding meeting of the National Vocational Guidance Association in 1913 in Grand Rapids, Michigan, stressed the need to modify the conditions and methods in industry. He stated,

> It is well within the range of possibility that vocational guidance, when carried out in a compre-hensive, purposeful, and scientific way, may force upon industry many modifications which will be good not only for children but equally for the industry. (p. 80)

Position of Vocational Counselors

The work of Frank Parsons and the Vocation Bureau soon became known across the coun-try. Out of it grew the first National Conference on Vocational Guidance, held in Boston in 1910, followed by a similar conference in New York in 1912 and the formation of the National Vocational Guidance Association in Grand Rapids in 1913 (W. C. Ryan, 1919). It also had a direct impact on Boston public schools because in 1909 the Boston School Committee asked personnel in the Vocation Bureau to outline a program of vocational guid-ance for the public schools of Boston. On June 7, 1909, the Boston School Committee approved the bureau's suggestion and "instructed the Superintendent of Schools to appoint a committee of six to work with the director" (Bloomfield, 1915, p. 34). Upon comple-tion of its work, the committee issued a report that identified three primary aims for vo-cational guidance in the Boston schools:

> Three aims have stood out above all others: first, to secure thoughtful consideration, on the part of parents, pupils, and teachers, of the importance of a life-career motive; second, to assist in every way possible in placing pupils in some remunerative work on leaving school; and third, to keep in touch with and help them thereafter, suggesting means of improvement and watching the advancement of those who need such aid. (Bloomfield, 1915, p. 36)

These aims were implemented by a central office staff and by appointed vocational counselors in each elementary and secondary school in Boston. Teachers were appointed to the position of vocational counselor often with no relief from their teaching duties and with no additional pay (Brewer, 1922; Ginn, 1924). The vocational counseling duties these teachers were asked to perform in addition to their regular teaching duties included

1. To be the representative of the Department of Vocational Guidance in the district.
2. To attend all meetings of counselors called by the Director of Vocational Guidance.
3. To be responsible for all material sent out to the school by the Vocational Guidance Department.
4. To gather and keep on file occupational information.
5. To arrange with the local branch librarians about shelves of books bearing upon educational and vocational guidance.
6. To arrange for some lessons in occupations in connection with classes in Oral English and Vocational Civics, or wherever principal and counselor deem it wise.
7. To recommend that teachers show the relationship of their work to occupational problems.
8. To interview pupils in grades six and above who are failing, attempt to find the reason, and suggest a remedy.

9. To make use of the cumulative record card when advising children.
10. To consult records of intelligence tests when advising children.
11. To make a careful study with grades seven and eight of the bulletin A Guide to the Choice of Secondary School.
12. To urge children to remain in school.
13. To recommend conferences with parents of children who are failing or leaving school.
14. To interview and check cards of all children leaving school, making clear to them the requirements for obtaining working certificates.
15. To be responsible for the filling in of Blank 249, and communicate with recommendations to the Department of Vocational Guidance when children are in need of employment. (Ginn, 1924, pp. 5–7)

Vocational Guidance Spreads Across the Country

At about the same time that the Boston schools were establishing a vocational guidance program, a group of New York City teachers, called the Student Aid Committee of the High School Teachers' Association, under the leadership of E. W. Weaver, was active in establishing a program in the New York City schools. A report issued in 1909 by the committee indicated that they had passed the experimental stage and were ready to request that

(1) the vocational officers of the large high schools be allowed at least one extra period of unassigned time to attend to this work; (2) that they be provided with facilities for keeping records of students and employment; and (3) that they have opportunities for holding conferences with students and employers. (W. C. Ryan, 1919, p. 25)

Vocational guidance was also being introduced into the public schools in other parts of the United States. In Chicago, it first took the form of a central office to serve students applying for employment certificates, to publish vocational bulletins, and for placement. In other cities such as Buffalo, New York; Cincinnati, Ohio; DeKalb, Illinois; Los Angeles; Milwaukee, Wisconsin; New York; Philadelphia; Rochester, New York; and San Jose, California, vocational guidance took several different forms but relied mostly on disseminating occupational information and on conducting occupational surveys, placement activities, and life career classes.

According to W. C. Ryan (1919, p. 26),

by April 1914, approximately 100 public high schools, representing some 40 cities, were reported to the U.S. Bureau of Education as having definitely organized conscious plans of vocational guidance, through vocation bureaus, consultation committees, trial vocational courses, or regular courses in vocations.

Titles of these offices varied and included, for example, the Division of Attendance and Vocational Guidance in Minneapolis. This expansion continued throughout the next 4 years, so that by 1918, 10 years after the establishment of the Vocation Bureau by Parsons in Boston, "932 four-year high schools reported vocation bureaus, employment departments, or similar devices for placing pupils" (W. C. Ryan, 1919, p. 36).

Challenges to Vocational Guidance

At the same time that progress was being made in institutionalizing vocational guidance in the schools, substantial challenges to this process were also present. Brewer (1942), in his history of vocational guidance, described a number of these challenges. One challenge he noted was high interest followed by a loss of that interest because of personnel changes. Another challenge was from conservatives "who began their barrage of criticism when the traditional curriculum was in any way endangered" (p. 87).

In addition to these challenges, other challenges included a lack of a practical plan to develop and implement vocational guidance, a lack of adequate preparation of teachers to carry out vocational guidance work, and a lack of resources and equipment. Two quotes from Brewer's history illustrate these challenges and their consequences.

> Vocational guidance is not a job for amateurs, to be assigned to a person because he or she has a warm heart. It should not be regarded as an adjunct to the teaching of English or mathematics. It is not a side issue of the work of deans of men or women. It is not a pastime to be indulged in during odd moments by a school principal, vice-principal, placement officer, registrar, or atten-dance officer. Vocational guidance is a distinct profession, just as independent as the work of the physician, the lawyer, the nurse, or any other highly specialized worker. (Brewer, 1942, p. 88, quot-ing Harry D. Kitson)
>
> Another common reason for abandoned plans was because the vocational counselor had noth-ing but an office and his mental equipment behind him. Vocational training, on the other hand, had back of it an investment of thousands of dollars in machines and equipment and could not so easily be "folded up." It was simple enough in times of financial stress, or for other reasons, to assign a vocational counselor back to a "more important" teaching or administrative position. (Brewer, 1942, p. 88)

Early Concerns About the Position of Vocational Counselor

By the 1920s, as the guidance and counseling movement (vocational guidance) was spread-ing across the United States, concerns were already being expressed about the way guid-ance and counseling was organized, was being perceived by others, and was being practiced. In a review of the Boston school system, Brewer (1922) stated that the work was "com-mendable and promising" (p. 36). At the same time, he expressed concern about a lack of effective centralization and supervision. What was done and how well it was done were left up to individual principals and counselors. Myers (1923), in an article titled "A Critical Review of Present Developments in Vocational Guidance With Special Reference to Future Prospects," also expressed concern:

> The first development to which I wish to call attention is a growing recognition of vocational guid-ance as an integral part of organized education, not as something different and apart from edu-cation that is being wished upon the schools by a group of enthusiasts because there is no other agency to handle it. . . . Second, vocational guidance is becoming recognized as a specialized ed-ucational function requiring special natural qualifications and special training. . . . A third devel-opment that claims attention is an increasing appreciation that a centralized, unified program of vocational guidance for the entire school system of a city is essential to the most effective work. We are rapidly passing out of the stage when each high school and junior high school can be left to organize and conduct vocational guidance as it sees fit. (pp. 139–140)

In expressing these concerns, Myers was calling attention to problems associated with the position model in which teachers were designated as vocational counselors with no struc-ture to work in and little or no released time from their teaching duties. Apparently, the position model for guidance and counseling caused it to be seen as an ancillary activity that could be conducted by anybody. In contrast, he stressed the need to view guidance as an integral part of education that required trained personnel working in a unified program of guidance. Myers's words were prophetic. These words are the same as those we use today to describe the importance, personnel requirements, and structure of comprehensive guidance and counseling programs in schools.

Myers (1923) made another astute observation about some unanticipated outcomes the prevailing way of organizing guidance and counseling (the position model) was causing in the schools:

> Another tendency dangerous to the cause of vocational guidance is the tendency to load the vocational counselor with so many duties foreign to the office that little real counseling can be done. The principal, and often the counselor . . . [have] a very indefinite idea of the proper duties of this new officer. The counselor's time is more free from definite assignments with groups or classes of pupils than is that of the ordinary teacher. If well chosen he [or she] has administrative ability. It is perfectly natural, therefore, for the principal to assign one administrative duty after another to the counselor until he [or she] becomes practically assistant principal, with little time for the real work of a counselor. In order to prevent this tendency from crippling seriously the vocational guidance program it is important that the counselor shall be well trained, that the principal shall understand more clearly what counseling involves, and that there shall be efficient supervision from a central office. (p. 140)

Myers's (1923) words were again prophetic. They pointed directly at the heart of the problem with the position model, that is, the ease at which "other duties as assigned" can become part of guidance and counseling and the work of school counselors, a problem that continues to plague school counselors even today.

Guidance and Counseling in the 1920s and 1930s: Challenges and Changes

Changes in Purpose of Guidance and Counseling

The 1920s witnessed the continued expansion of guidance and counseling in the schools. During this period of time, the nature and structure of guidance and counseling were being influenced by the mental hygiene and measurement movements, developmental studies of children, the introduction of cumulative records, and progressive education. In effect, "Vocational guidance was taking on the new vocabulary present in the culture at large and in the educational subculture; the language of mental health, progressive education, child development, and measurement theory" (A. H. Johnson, 1972, p. 160). As a result, additional purposes for guidance and counseling were identified.

Educational Purposes

The addition of an educational purpose for guidance was a natural outgrowth of a change that was taking place in education itself. With the advent of the Cardinal Principles of Secondary Education (National Education Association [NEA], 1918), education, at least philosophically, began to shift from preparation for college alone to education for total life.

> This was a life to be characterized by an integration of health with command of fundamental processes, worthy home membership, vocational competence, civic responsibility, worthy use of leisure time and ethical character. . . . Given these Seven Cardinal Principles, an education now appeared equally vocationally relevant—from this one could construe that all of education is guidance into later vocational living. (A. H. Johnson, 1972, pp. 27–28)

This change occurred partly because the leadership of guidance and counseling, particularly on the part of people like John Brewer (1922), was increasingly more educationally oriented. It also occurred, according to Stephens (1970), because the NEA's Commission on the Reorganization of Secondary Education (CRSE) "had so broadened the definition of vocation as to soften it, if not to virtually eliminate it as a cardinal principle of secondary education" (p. 113). This move by the CRSE, together with the more educationally oriented leadership of guidance, served to separate what had been twin reform movements of education—vocational education and vocational guidance, as Stephens called them—leaving vocational guidance to struggle with its own identity. This point is made in a similar way by A. H. Johnson (1972):

> The 1918 report of the NEA's Commission on the Reorganization of Secondary Education construed almost all of the education as training for efficient vocational and avocational life. No element in the curriculum appeared salient after the CRSE report. This was no less true of vocational education. Thus, as a "cardinal principle" vocational education was virtually eliminated. The once correlated responsibility of vocational guidance lost its historical anchorage to vocational education and was set adrift in the public school system to be redefined by the logic of the education subculture. (p. 204)

Personal Adjustment Purposes

During the 1920s, it was clear that less attention was being focused on the social, industrial, and national and political aspects of individuals, whereas considerably more attention was being given to the personal, educational, and statistically measurable aspects of individuals. More specifically, at least within the school setting, there apparently was a "displacement of the traditional vocational, socioeconomic, and political concerns from the culture at large to the student of the educational subculture whose vocational socialization problems were reinterpreted as educational and psychological problems of personal adjustment" (A. H. Johnson, 1972, p. 221).

As a result of this displacement of concerns, vocational guidance practices began to emphasize a more personal, diagnostic, and clinical orientation to students, with an increasing emphasis on psychological measurement.

> Content to explore with yet greater precision the psychological dimensions of the student, and guaranteed a demand for testing services in the public school system, the guidance movement defined its professional role to meet the expectations of its institutional colleagues. Thus there developed a mutual role expectation that requires analysis and synthesis (gathering and organizing personal data), diagnosis (comparing personal data to test norms, and occupational or professional profiles), prognosis (indicating available career choices), and counseling (or treating, to effect desired adjustment then or in the future). This formed the basis for the clinical model. Testing had created the demand for a unique technical skill around which the clinical model could develop, and around which vocational guidance had established a professional claim. (A. H. Johnson, 1972, p. 138)

Further evidence of this can be seen in the 1921 and 1924 statements of the Principles of Vocational Guidance of the National Vocational Guidance Association (Allen, 1927). These principles emphasized testing, the use of an extensive cumulative record system, information, the study of occupations, counseling, and case studies. Between 1925 and 1930, as the personal adjustment purpose of vocational guidance emerged, counseling became of primary concern. "Vocational guidance became problem oriented, centering on adjustable psychological, personal problems—not social, moral, religious, ethical, or political problems" (A. H. Johnson, 1972, p. 201).

What Should Be the Duties of the Counselor?

One of the tasks of the profession in the 1920s and early 1930s was to establish the preferred list of duties to be carried out by individuals filling the position of counselor. The task was to decide which duties would constitute a complete program or, as Proctor (1930) stated, the standard setup for guidance and counseling. Myers (1931) prepared a list of actual counselor duties. There were 37 items on the list. After reviewing the list, Myers stated,

> Here is, indeed, a formidable list of things which counselors do. It is obvious that many of these are essential to an effective guidance program and may properly be expected of a counselor. It is equally obvious that some of them are routine administrative or clerical matters which have nothing whatever to do with counseling. Evidently, under the guise of setting up a counseling program, some junior and senior high school principals have unloaded a large number of their office duties upon the counselor. (p. 344)

In the same article, Myers (1931) classified the preferred duties into the following categories:

- Interviewing or conferring with individual pupils
- Meeting with pupils in groups
- Conferring with teachers and other members of the school staff
- Conferring with special officers of the school system
- Conferring with parents
- Conferring with representatives of industry, business, and the professions
- Working with social agencies of the community. (pp. 345–347)

As guidance and counseling was becoming institutionalized in schools and was in the process of being defined and implemented, the expectations of other educational personnel concerning guidance and counseling were also being shaped. This seemed to be particularly true for school administrators. A. H. Johnson (1972) underlined this when he pointed out that administrative obligations were a substantial part of the new professional responsibilities. In fact, many suggested vocational guidance responsibilities delineated by the profession became administrative obligations when incorporated into the school settings. "Professional responsibilities became in fact administrative obligations for which guidance would be held accountable not to professionally determined values but values of the education subculture interpreted through its administrative structure" (A. H. Johnson, 1972, p. 191).

Services Model of Guidance and Counseling

By the late 1920s and early 1930s, various specialists, in addition to counselors, had joined the staffs of schools. These specialists included personnel such as attendance officers, visiting teachers, school nurses, and school physicians. Myers (1935) suggested that the phrase *pupil personnel work* be used to coordinate the work of these specialists and that someone from central office be given the responsibility for overseeing their work. Myers went on to point out that "probably no activity in the entire list suffers as much from lack of a coordinated program as does guidance, and especially the counseling aspect of it" (p. 807).

Given Myers's (1935) point about the lack of a coordinated program for guidance (remember that the prevailing organization for guidance and counseling at that time was a position with a list of duties), what would be the best way to provide a more coordinated program for guidance and counseling? The concept that emerged was *guidance services.* Five services were typically identified: individual inventory, information, counseling, placement, and follow-up. According to Roeber, Walz, and Smith (1969),

> This conception of guidance services was developed during a period in the history of the guidance movement when it was necessary to have some definitive statement regarding the need for and nature of a more organized form of guidance. This delineation of guidance services generally served its purpose and gave the guidance movement something tangible to "sell" to state departments of education and to local schools. (p. 55)

Counseling Service Predominates: Student Adjustment Is the Focus

Although all of the services of guidance were seen as important, one service, counseling, began to predominate over the other services in the 1930s. The emergence of the importance of counseling had begun earlier in the 1920s as a result of the more personal, diagnostic, and clinical orientation to students that was occurring during that time period. By the 1930s, attention to a more personal, diagnostic, and clinical orientation to students intensified. As a result, counseling, with its increasing attention on the personal adjustment of students, began to be seen as something separate and distinct from vocational guidance.

> Up to 1930, . . . not much progress had been made in differentiating this function [personal counseling] from the preexisting programs of vocational and educational guidance. After that date, more and more of a separation appeared as guidance workers in the high schools became aware of increasingly large numbers of students who were troubled by personal problems involving hostility to authority, sex relationships, unfortunate home situations, and financial stringencies. (Rudy, 1965, p. 25)

Bell (1939), in a book on personal counseling, stated that the goal of counseling was student adjustment through personal contact between counselor and student. Adjustment in his thinking included all phases of an individual's life: school, health, occupational, motor and mechanical, social, home, emotional, and religious. Koos and Kefauver (1937) also noted the theme of adjustment when they stated that guidance had two phases, the distributive and the adjustive. The goal of the first phase was to distribute students to educational and vocational opportunities. The goal of the second phase was to help students make adjustments to educational and vocational situations. M. E. Campbell (1932) added that guidance needed to focus on "problems of adjustment to health, religion, recreation, to family and friends, to school, and to work" (p. 4).

Vocational Guidance Continues to Be Defined

According to M. E. Campbell (1932), vocational guidance was defined as

> the process of assisting the individual to choose an occupation, prepare for it, enter upon and progress in it. As preparation for an occupation involves decisions in the choice of studies, choice of curriculums, and the choice of schools and colleges, it becomes evident that vocational guidance cannot be separated from educational guidance. (p. 4)

Campbell went on to distinguish between vocational guidance and vocational education (career and technical education) and to emphasize that vocational guidance was a process that helped students explore all occupations, not just those for which vocational education provided training.

> As vocational guidance and vocational education are linked together in many minds, a statement about this relationship may clarify the situation. Vocational education is the giving of training to persons who desire to work in a specific occupation. Vocational guidance offers information and assistance which leads to the choice of an occupation and the training which precedes it. It does not give such training. The term *vocational* refers to any occupation, be it medicine, law, carpentry, or nursing. Preparation for many occupations and professions must be planned in the secondary school and in college by taking numerous courses, which are not usually known as vocational. Vocational guidance concerns itself, therefore, with pupils in the academic courses in high school or students of the liberal arts in college, as well as with the pupils in the trade and commercial courses, which have become known as vocational education. (p. 4)

This distinction is important because, from the 1930s to the present, this was and is a point of contention in defining the focus and scope of guidance and counseling in career and technical education legislation. Some individuals contend that vocational guidance is guidance and counseling for career and technical education students only, and that if money was made available, it should be spent only for the guidance and counseling of students in these programs.

Federal Initiatives Begin

Although the educational and personal adjustment themes for guidance continued to play a dominant role in guidance and counseling practice in the schools during the 1930s, the vocational emphasis also continued to show strength. In February 1933, the National Occupational Conference, funded by a Carnegie grant, opened its doors. The activities of the National Occupational Conference included studies and research related to the problems of occupational adjustment, book publication, and the development of a service that provided information and consultation about vocational guidance activities. The National Occupational Conference for a time also provided joint support for *Occupations,* the official journal of the National Vocational Guidance Association.

In 1938, a national advisory committee on education, originally appointed in 1936 by President Franklin D. Roosevelt, issued a report that pointed to the need for an occupational information service at the national level as well as for guidance and placement services as a part of a sound program of vocational education. As a result of these recommendations, and with funds from Vocational Education and from the Commissioner of Education (Studebaker, 1938), the Occupational Information and Guidance Service was established in 1938 in the Vocational Division of the U.S. Office of Education. Richard Allen served for a few months as the chief of the unit before Harry Jager assumed the post (Wellman, 1978). Although the service was located in the Vocational Division, it was not designed to be exclusively vocational in nature. This point was made clear in a document, "Principles Underlying the Organization and Administration of the Occupational Information and Guidance Service," issued by the U.S. Office of Education in 1940.

> The functions to be performed by the Occupational Information and Guidance Service are to be as broad and complete as it is practicable for the Office to provide for at any given time within the limits of funds, cooperative assistance from various organizations, both within the government

and outside, and other assets. The activities in which the service will be interested will include such phases of guidance as vocational guidance, personal guidance, educational guidance, and placement. While, with respect to personnel, no service in the Office can now be said to be complete, the various divisions or services go as far as possible in their respective fields in meeting needs or requests for service. Thus, for example, in the field of education for exceptional children, a service which would require 15 or 20 professional workers in the office if it were even to approximate completeness in numbers and types of persons needed, we have only one specialist. Yet this specialist is responsible for representing the Office in handling all problems and service in this particular field. (Smith, 1951, p. 66)

Of particular importance was the statement that "the activities in which the service will be interested will include such phases of guidance as vocational guidance, personal guidance, educational guidance, and placement." Not only did the statement clearly outline the broad mission of the service and, as a result, of guidance and counseling in the schools, but it also described a currently popular way of describing guidance and counseling as having three phases: vocational, personal, and educational. Once the Occupational Information and Guidance Service was established at the federal level, it also became possible to establish guidance offices in state departments of education. Such funds could be used only for state offices, however. No funds could be used to support guidance and counseling at the local level.

Reimbursement was provided for state supervision under the George Dean Act [an Act to Provide for the Further Development of Vocational Education in the several states and territories; Pub. L. No. 673] and the number of states with a state guidance supervisor increased from 2 to 28 between 1938 and 1942. The Occupational Information and Guidance Service was instrumental in initiating conferences of state supervisors to consider issues in the field. This group subsequently became the NAGS (National Association of Guidance Supervisors), then NAGSCT (National Association of Guidance Supervisors and Counselor Trainers), and finally the current ACES (Association for Counselor Education and Supervision). (Wellman, 1978, p. 2)

A Growing Interest in Psychotherapy

As the 1930s ended, the services model of guidance and counseling with its position of counselor continued to evolve and flourish, assisted by a growing interest in psychotherapy. Of particular importance to guidance in the schools was the work of Carl Rogers, beginning with the publication of his book *Counseling and Psychotherapy* in 1942.

The years following its publication in 1942 saw a growth in interest in psychotherapeutic procedures, which soon became even greater than interest in psychometrics. This movement, and the numerous research and theoretical contributions which have accompanied it, has had its impact on vocational guidance. (Super, 1955, p. 5)

Aubrey (1982) used the expression "steamroller impact" to describe the full effect of this book as well as Rogers's later works on guidance and counseling in the schools.

The impact of psychotherapy on vocational guidance and the testing movement precipitated a new field: counseling psychology. This field, in turn, had a substantial impact on the professional development of school guidance and counseling and the work of school counselors in the 1950s, 1960s, and 1970s, particularly in terms of the training counselors received and the role models and professional literature available to them.

An important outcome of the merger of the vocational orientation, psychometric, and personality development movements has been a changed concept of the function and training of the person who does the counseling. He [or she] was first either a teacher who helped people explore the world of work or a psychologist who gave and interpreted tests. Then he [or she], who might or might not have been a psychologist, was a user of community resources, of occupational information, and of psychological tests. He [or she] has now emerged as a psychologist who uses varying combinations of exploratory experiences, psychometric techniques, and psychotherapeutic interviewing to assist people to grow and to develop. This is the counseling psychologist. (American Psychological Association, 1956, p. 284)

Important Federal Legislation in the 1940s and 1950s

Vocational Education Act of 1946

In 1946, an event occurred that was to have substantial impact on the growth and development of guidance and counseling in the schools. This event was the passage of the Vocational Education Act of 1946, commonly referred to as the George–Barden Act, after the two legislators who sponsored the legislation. As a result of the act, funds could be used to support guidance and counseling activities in a variety of settings and situations. More specifically, the U.S. Commissioner of Education ruled that federal funds could be used for these four purposes:

1. the maintenance of a state program of supervision
2. reimbursement of salaries of counselor-trainers
3. research in the field of guidance
4. reimbursement of salaries of local guidance supervisors and counselors. (Smith, 1951, pp. 67–68)

For the first time, because of the ruling of the U.S. Commissioner of Education, guidance and counseling received material, leadership, and financial support. The result of such support was a rapid growth of guidance and counseling at state and local levels. It also signaled to all concerned the need for attention to the preparation of counselors. This problem had been of concern for some time but had not been given extensive consideration. The passage of the Vocational Education Act of 1946, which made it possible to use state funds to reimburse counselor training, made the constantly reoccurring question "What should constitute a counselor training program?" of extreme importance. How this question was answered set the pattern for the practice of guidance and counseling in the schools for many years to come.

In Spring 1948, the Occupational Information and Guidance Service staff called a meeting of state guidance supervisors and counselor trainers in cooperation with the Division of Higher Education of the U.S. Office of Education. The question was, "What should be the preparation of counselors?" Eight major subtopics were identified, and subcommittees were established to study each subtopic. Reports were presented for consideration at the National Conference of State Supervisors of Guidance Services and Counselor Trainers held in Washington, DC, on September 13 to 18, 1948. These reports were then revised with others participating in the work. Six of the seven were then published between 1949 and 1950 by the Federal Security Agency, Office of Education. These reports (and the one not published) were as follows:

1. "Duties, Standards, and Qualifications for Counselors," February 1949, cochairpersons, Eleanor Zeis and Dolph Camp

2. "The Basic Course" (never published)
3. "Counselor Competencies in Occupational Information," March 1949, chairperson, Edward C. Roeber
4. "Counselor Competencies in the Analysis of the Individual," July 1949, chairperson, Ralph C. Bedell
5. "Counselor Competencies in Counseling Techniques," July 1949, chairperson, Stanley R. Ostrom
6. "Administrative Relationships of the Guidance Program," July 1949, chairperson, Glenn Smith
7. "In-Service Preparation for Guidance Duties, Parts One and Two," May 1950, Chairperson, John G. Odgers

An additional report had been issued on supervised practice at the eighth National Conference but was referred back to committee. After revision, it was considered at the ninth National Conference in Ames, Iowa, September 11 to 15, 1950, and with subsequent revision, was released as the eighth report in the series:

8. "Supervised Practice in Counselor Preparation," April 1952, chairperson, Roy Bryan

All of the published reports were edited by Clifford P. Froehlich, specialist for the training of guidance personnel, under the general direction of Harry A. Jager, chief, Guidance and Personnel Services Branch.

During the early and middle 1950s, a major change occurred in the organizational structure of guidance and counseling at the federal level. On May 16, 1952, the Guidance and Personnel Branch of the U.S. Office of Education was discontinued under the Division of Vocational Education. Then, on October 27, 1953, a Pupil Personnel Services Section was established in the Division of State and Local School Systems with Harry Jager designated as chief, but this work was halted with Jager's death the following year. However, in 1955, a Guidance and Personnel Services Section was once again established, with Frank L. Sievers as the first chief (Miller, 1971).

These changes reflected the shift that had begun in the 1930s—the shift to guidance and counseling organized as a set of services within pupil personnel services with its continued emphasis on the position of counselor. As we will see, the pupil personnel services model was to become the dominant organizational framework for guidance and counseling in the 1950s and 1960s.

National Defense Education Act of 1958

In 1958, another important event occurred that had substantial impact on guidance and counseling in U.S. schools throughout the 1960s and 1970s. The event was the passage of the National Defense Education Act (NDEA) of 1958. Under Title V, the guidance and counseling title in the act, funds were provided for two major programs: Part A provided funds in the form of grants to states to establish statewide testing programs; Part B provided funds for training institutes to prepare individuals to be counselors in secondary schools. In the 1960s, the provisions in Part B were expanded to include support for guidance programs, testing, and training at the elementary and junior high school levels as well.

Our purpose here is not to report fully on the overall impact of the NDEA but rather to focus briefly on the act's impact on how school guidance and counseling and the work of school counselors were further conceptualized and institutionalized as a result of its implementation. Of particular importance was the nature of the training school counselors received and the major professional issues addressed during the courses provided for institute participants.

Pierson (1965) described five issues that seemed to be central to the training of school counselors in NDEA institutes:

1. determinism and a free society
2. mental health and individual responsibility
3. basic science and supervised practice
4. teaching and counseling
5. the role of the school counselor

Of these, Issues 4 and 5 related most directly to how counselors functioned in schools. The teaching and counseling issue was resolved, according to Pierson (1965), by counselor educators who promoted the idea "that the services of the high school counselor are adjunct to the services of the classroom teacher" (p. 40). The role definition issue was handled by saying that the role of the counselor cannot be predetermined. Counselors were taught to develop their own role definition. "The adequately trained school counselor develops his [or her] own role, a role that tends to be unique with him [or her] and unique to the situation in which the role is developed" (p. 39).

Further analysis of NDEA institutes also makes it clear that there was a heavy emphasis on individual and group counseling through counseling practica and group procedures courses. Placement and traditional educational and occupational information procedures (collecting, classifying, and using information) as well as philosophy and principles received relatively less attention. Pierson (1965) summarized curriculum offerings in institutes by pointing out that

> the curriculum in regular session institutes has placed great stress upon practicum; about one third of an enrollee's time has been spent in supervised practice in counseling. At the same time, institutes have strengthened their instruction in psychology, particularly in the areas of personality, learning, growth and development, and mental health. (p. 46)

Another aspect of the counselor role dilemma was identified by Tyler (1960) in her review of the first 50 institutes. She described it as follows:

> Before one can really define the role of the counselor, it will be necessary to clarify the roles of all workers who make up guidance staffs. It may be desirable to replace the ambiguous word *guidance* with the clearer term *pupil personnel work.* (p. 77)

New Challenges and Changes: Guidance and Counseling in the 1960s

Pupil Personnel Services Become Dominant

Concurrent with the influence of the NDEA on the development of guidance and counseling in the schools was the influence of the pupil personnel services movement in the 1960s. What began in the 1930s, and was nurtured in the 1940s and 1950s, finally matured in the 1960s. What were those services? The Council of Chief State School Officers (1960) stated that pupil personnel services included "guidance, health, psychological services, school social work, and attendance" (p. 3). Thus, guidance and the position of school counselors were conceptualized among several services that sought to "facilitate pupil learning through an interdisciplinary approach" (Stoughton, McKenna, & Cook, 1969, p. 1).

Of particular importance to the development of the pupil personnel services concept was the creation in 1962 of the Interprofessional Research Commission on Pupil Personnel Services. This commission was created by the U.S. Office of Education and financed by the National Institute of Mental Health. It was composed of 16 professional member associations. The aims of the commission were threefold:

1. to provide through research a body of knowledge that will increase the effectiveness of all professions and services collaborating to provide the total learning experience
2. to demonstrate efficient programs of pupil personnel services for various sizes and types of communities
3. to carry on and stimulate research on preventative mental hygiene related to the schools. (Eckerson & Smith, 1966, p. 4)

In the Interprofessional Research Commission on Pupil Personnel Services' conception of pupil personnel services, guidance and counseling were viewed "as a lifetime service, from preschool to retirement, with the goal of increasing each individual's capacity for self-direction" (Eckerson & Smith, 1966, p. 24).

As the 1960s continued to unfold, the impact of the pupil personnel services movement on guidance and counseling became increasingly apparent. Many state departments of education and local school districts placed guidance and counseling and the positions of school counselors administratively under the pupil personnel services umbrella. In addition, textbooks written in the 1960s on the organization and administration of guidance and counseling adopted the pupil personnel services model as the way to organize guidance in the schools. This fitted nicely with the service model of guidance and counseling with its position orientation that had been evolving since the 1920s. As a result, guidance and counseling became a subset of services to be delivered by school counselors who occupied positions within the broader framework of pupil personnel services. The number of these guidance services varied depending on the authority quoted, but there were usually six: orientation, individual inventory or appraisal, counseling, information, placement, and follow-up. Also, as a result of the services model of guidance and counseling and the focus on personal adjustment discussed earlier in this chapter, the counseling service emerged as the central service.

Stripling and Lane (1966) stressed the centrality of counseling—both individual and group. A second priority area was consultation with parents and teachers. Other traditional guidance functions such as appraisal, placement, and evaluation were seen as supplementary and supportive to counseling, group procedures, and consultation. Ferguson (1963) emphasized the same theme that counseling was the core service: "No longer is it viewed merely as a technique and limited to vocational and educational matters; counseling is regarded as the central service in the guidance program" (p. 40).

This emphasis on counseling during the 1960s had deep historical roots. It began to emerge in the 1920s under the services model and the intense interest in personal adjustment that followed. It was reinforced further, according to Hoyt (1974), by the NDEA Title V-B training institutes whose enrollees by law were either counselors or teachers and by the standards used by the U.S. Office of Education to judge whether a proposed training institute was acceptable for funding. These factors, Hoyt suggested, led the training institutes to place "a heavy emphasis on the counseling function. . . . The emphasis was on counseling and counselors, not on guidance and guidance programs" (p. 504).

Focus on School Counselors, Not on Guidance and Counseling

During this time, the services model for guidance and counseling, with its position orientation within pupil personnel services, focused heavily on the role and functions—the positions—of school counselors. In fact, to many individuals, what school counselors did became the program. Literally hundreds of articles were written about the role and functions of school counselors. The need for such statements was heightened considerably by competition from other pupil personnel workers as they too sought to establish themselves and their roles in the schools, particularly when the Commission on Guidance in American Schools proposed that

> the confusing term *guidance services* be abandoned and that pupil personnel services be seen as the activities of the school counselor, the school psychologist, the school social worker, the school health officer, and the school attendance officer. Pupil personnel services thus became broader than any so-called guidance services and yet a central function of such services is the work of the school counselor. (Wrenn, 1962, p. 142)

In his landmark work, *The Counselor in a Changing World*, Wrenn (1962) also emphasized the work of the counselor. He delineated four major functions for the school counselor:

> It is recommended that the professional job description of a school counselor specify that he [or she] perform four major functions: (a) counsel with students; (b) consult with teachers, administrators, and parents as they in turn deal with students; (c) study the changing facts about the student population and interpret what is found to school committees and administrators; (d) coordinate counseling resources in school and between school and community. From two thirds to three fourths of the counselor's time, in either elementary or high school, should be committed to the first two of these functions. (p. 137)

In a similar fashion, Roeber (1963) outlined proposed school counselors' functions. He suggested that counselors engage in helping relationships, including individual counseling, group procedures, and consulting. In addition, the counselor should have supporting responsibilities, including pupil-environment studies, program development, and personal development. This emphasis on the counselor during the 1960s came at a time when some individuals were calling for "the abandonment of the term *guidance* as it is associated with services provided by a counselor" (Roeber, 1963, p. 22).

Search for Identity: Educator or Psychologist?

Up until the 1950s many school counselors were teachers or administrators serving as school counselors part-time. Thus, it was not surprising that the general wisdom was that anybody serving as a school counselor should have an educational background; they should be teachers first. As more and more school counselors became full time in the 1950s, but particularly in the 1960s and 1970s, the question "Is teaching experience necessary?" was being asked more frequently. This question raised the question, "If school counselors aren't teachers first, who are they?"

The 1960s and 1970s saw intense debate in the literature concerning the school counselor identity issue. As we will see, some writers identified school counselors as educators so they felt that teaching experience was necessary to become a school counselor. Other writers identified school counselors more with psychology and psychologists so they questioned the necessity of teaching experience as a prerequisite to becoming a school counselor in the schools.

An interesting exchange occurred between Brammer (1968) and Felix (1968) on this issue. Brammer stated the field should drop the guidance model and adopt a counseling psychologist model for school counseling: "Where will school counselors play ball? I have suggested the counseling psychology ball park, not as an ideal solution, but as the possibility most compatible with evolving school counseling functions" (p. 8).

Felix (1968) disagreed sharply with Brammer in a rejoinder to Brammer's (1968) article. Felix strongly defended the guidance model for school counseling. He ended his rejoinder with the following statement using the same ball park analogy that Brammer used:

> We have let some psychologists come into our park, even though the place is not really suited to the game at which they excel. They have put down the floor they brought with them. Now they want us to change the way we train and practice, and even change the name of our team. Next thing you know, they will want to rename the park. (p. 11)

Elementary Guidance and Counseling

The 1960s also witnessed the birth of elementary school guidance and counseling, after a gestation period of more than 50 years. Professional literature indicated that teachers were appointed as elementary counselors as early as 1910 in the Boston schools. Apparently, however, the secondary school emphasis was so strong during the early years that little attention was paid to the work of counselors in elementary schools. What attention there was proved to be heavily occupational in nature. Witness, for example, the publication of a book by McCracken and Lamb in 1923 titled *Occupational Information in the Elementary School*.

Faust (1968) divided the emergence of elementary school counselors into three time periods. The first period, which he titled *traditional,* stretched from the beginnings of the guidance and counseling movement in 1908 through the 1940s. During this period, elementary guidance and counseling borrowed methods and techniques extensively from secondary school guidance and counseling practice. For the next 15 years, from 1950 to 1965, elementary guidance and counseling began to change. Faust called this the *neotraditionalist* period. It was characterized by a deemphasis on traditional secondary methods coupled with more emphasis on group counseling and learning climates. In the middle 1960s, according to Faust, the *developmentalist* period emerged. Elementary school counselors had arrived and had an identity of their own. The emphasis now was developmental, not crisis centered. Individual and group work were stressed.

The developmental emphasis was reinforced by a preliminary report of the Joint Association for Counselor Education and Supervision and American School Counselor Association (ACES–ASCA) Committee on the Elementary School Counselor that appeared in the February 1966 issue of the *Personnel and Guidance Journal*. Its central focus was "on the child and teacher in the educative process" (Faust, 1968, p. 74). Effective learning climates were to be central to the work of school counselors.

Calls to Change the Position–Services Model

Beginning in the 1960s, but particularly in the 1970s, the call came to reorient guidance and counseling from what had become an ancillary position organized around a set of services within pupil personnel services to a comprehensive developmental program. The call for reorientation came from a number of diverse sources. They included a renewed interest in vocational-career guidance and its theoretical base career development, concern about the efficacy of the then-prevailing approach to guidance and counseling in the schools, and a renewed interest in developmental guidance and counseling.

Vocational-Career Guidance

The resurgence of interest in vocational-career guidance that began in the 1960s was aided, in part, by a series of national conferences on the topic. These conferences were funded through the Vocational Education Act of 1963 and later amendments. Hoyt's (1974) account of these conferences makes it clear that they contributed substantially to the renewed interest in the term *guidance* and its practice in the schools.

The resurgence of interest in vocational-career guidance was also aided by a number of career guidance projects begun in the 1960s. Among them was the Developmental Career Guidance Project, begun in 1964 in Detroit to provide career guidance for disadvantaged youths. It was one of the early developmental career guidance programs, one that accumulated sufficient evaluative data to support the further development of comprehensive guidance programming in schools (Leonard & Vriend, 1975).

Concern About the Prevailing Position–Services Model

Paralleling the resurgence of interest in vocational-career guidance was a growing concern about the efficacy of the services model with its emphasis on the role and function—or the position—of the school counselor. Particular concern was expressed about an overemphasis on the one-to-one relationship model of counseling and the tendency of counselors to focus mainly on crises and problems to justify their reason for being in a school.

> The traditional one-to-one relationship in counseling which we have cherished and perhaps overvalued will, of course, continue. But it is quite likely that the conception of the counselor as a room bound agent of behavior change must be critically reappraised. The counselor of the future will likely serve as a social catalyst, interacting in a two-person relationship with the counselee part of the time, but also serving as a facilitator of the environmental and human conditions which are known to promote the counselee's total psychological development, including vocational development. (Borow, 1966, p. 88)

During the 1960s, concern was also expressed about the potency of the guidance services model and the need for more meaningful reconceptualizations for guidance and counseling so that guidance and counseling could reach higher levels of development (Roeber et al., 1969). This same theme was echoed by Sprinthall (1971):

> It is probably not an understatement to say that the service concept has so dominated guidance and counseling that more basic and significant questions are not even acknowledged, let alone answered. Instead, the counselor assumes a service orientation that limits and defines his [or her] role to minor administrative procedures. (p. 20)

Developmental Guidance

In the 1960s, the term *developmental guidance* was heard with increasing frequency. Mathewson (1962), in discussing future trends for guidance, suggested that although adjustive guidance was popular, a long-term movement toward developmental forms of guidance would probably prevail:

> In spite of present tendencies, a long-term movement toward educative and developmental forms of guidance in schools may yet prevail for these reasons: the need to develop all human poten-

tialities, the persistence and power of human individuality, the effects of dynamic educative experience, the necessity for educational adaptability, the comparative costs, and the urge to preserve human freedom. (p. 375)

Similarly, Zaccaria (1966) stressed the importance of and need for developmental guidance. He pointed out that developmental guidance was a concept in transition, that it was in tune with the times, but that it was still largely untried in practice.

Comprehensive Guidance and Counseling Programs Emerge: The 1970s

In the early 1970s, interest in career development theory, research, and practice as well as in career guidance and career education, their educational manifestations, increased. Other educational movements, such as psychological education, moral education, and process education, emerged as well. In addition, interest in the development of comprehensive systematic approaches to guidance and counseling program development and management continued to increase. The convergence of these movements in the early 1970s served as a stimulus to continue the task of defining guidance and counseling developmentally in measurable student outcome terms—as a program in its own right rather than as services ancillary to other educational programs.

Basic Ideas, Vocabulary, and Systems Thinking

By 1970, a substantial amount of preliminary work had been done in developing the basic ideas, vocabulary, and constructs to define guidance and counseling in comprehensive developmental outcome terms. As early as 1961, Glanz identified and described four basic models for organizing guidance because of his concern about the lack of discernible patterns for implementing guidance in the schools. Tiedeman and Field (1962) issued a call to make guidance an integral part of the educational process, and they also stressed the need for a developmental, liberating perspective of guidance. Zaccaria (1965) stressed the need to examine developmental tasks as a basis for determining the goals of guidance. Shaw and Tuel (1966) developed a model for a guidance program designed to serve all students. At the elementary level, Dinkmeyer (1966) emphasized the need for developmental counseling by describing pertinent child development research that supported a developmental perspective.

Paralleling the preliminary work on ideas, vocabulary, and constructs was the application of systems thinking to guidance and counseling. On the basis of a nationwide survey of vocational guidance in 1968, a systems model for vocational guidance was developed at the Center for Vocational and Technical Education in Columbus, Ohio. This model focused on student behavioral objectives, alternative activities, program evaluation, and implementation strategies (R. E. Campbell et al., 1971). T. A. Ryan (1969), and Hosford and Ryan (1970) also proposed the use of systems theory and systems techniques for the development and improvement of comprehensive guidance and counseling programs.

Beginning Models for Guidance and Counseling Programs

On the West Coast, McDaniel (1970) proposed a model for guidance called Youth Guidance Systems. It was organized around goals, objectives, programs, implementation plans, and designs for evaluation. The primary student outcome in this model was considered to be decision making. Closely related to this model was the Comprehensive Career

Guidance System developed by personnel at the American Institutes for Research (Jones, Hamilton, Ganschow, Helliwell, & Wolff, 1972; Jones, Nelson, Ganschow, & Hamilton, 1971). The Comprehensive Career Guidance System was designed to plan, implement, and evaluate guidance programs systematically. Systems thinking also undergirded T. A. Ryan and Zeran's (1972) approach to the organization and administration of guidance services. They stressed the need for a systems approach to guidance to ensure the development and implementation of an accountable program. A final systematic approach to guidance was advocated in the Program of Learning in Accordance With Needs System of Individualized Education (Dunn, 1972). Guidance was seen as a major component of the Program of Learning in Accordance With Needs and was treated as an integral part of the regular instructional program.

Integrating Career Development Into the Curriculum

The task of defining guidance and counseling in comprehensive developmental outcome terms received substantial support from these approaches that applied systems thinking to guidance. Additional support was provided by the development in a number of states in the early 1970s of state guides for integrating career development into the school curriculum. One such guide was developed in August 1970 by the state of Wisconsin (Drier, 1971) and another, the California Model for Career Development, in Summer 1971 (California State Department of Education, 1971).

The idea of implementing career development through the curriculum did not, of course, originate with these models. As early as 1914, J. B. Davis had outlined such a curriculum. Of more immediate interest, however, are Tennyson, Soldahl, and Mueller's (1965) *The Teacher's Role in Career Development* and the Airlie House Conference in May 1966 on the topic "Implementing Career Development Theory and Research Through the Curriculum," which was sponsored by the National Vocational Guidance Association (Ashcroft, 1966). Later in the 1960s and early 1970s came the work of such theorists and practitioners as Gysbers (1969), Herr (1969), Hansen (1970), and Tennyson and Hansen (1971), all of whom spoke to the need to integrate career development concepts into the curriculum. Through these efforts and others like them, career development concepts began to be translated into individual outcomes and the resulting goals and objectives arranged sequentially, kindergarten through 12th grade.

A National Project to Develop State Models

Concurrent with these efforts, a national effort was begun to assist the states in developing and implementing state models or guides for career guidance, counseling, and placement. On July 1, 1971, the University of Missouri–Columbia was awarded a U.S. Office of Education grant, directed by Norman C. Gysbers, to assist each state, the District of Columbia, and Puerto Rico in developing models or guides for implementing career guidance, counseling, and placement programs in local schools. This project was the next step in a program of work begun as a result of a previous project at the university, a project that conducted a national conference on career guidance, counseling, and placement in October 1969 and regional conferences across the country during the spring of 1970. All 50 states, the District of Columbia, and Puerto Rico were involved in the 1971 project, and by the time the project ended in 1974, 44 states had developed some type of guide or model for career guidance, counseling, and placement. As a part of the assistance provided to the states, project staff conducted a national conference in January 1972 and developed a manual (Gysbers & Moore, 1974) to be used by the states as they developed their own guides.

Model Development Continues

As the movement toward planning and implementing systematic developmental and accountable guidance and counseling programs in the early 1970s became more sophisticated, theoretical models began to be translated into practical, workable models to be implemented in the schools. Many of these translations were based on an expanded conception of career guidance. For example, when the guidance staff in Mesa, Arizona, felt the need to reorient their guidance program to make it more accountable in 1972, they chose a comprehensive career guidance program that included needs assessment, goals, and objectives development and related guidance activities (McKinnon & Jones, 1975). To train the staff in program development and implementation methods and procedures for the new system, they wrote competency-based training packages in cooperation with the American Institutes for Research. For another example, guidance personnel at the Grossmont Union High School District in California chose the California Model for Career Development (California State Department of Education, 1971) to supply the content of their program and then proceeded to lay out a systematic, developmental career guidance program (Jacobson & Mitchell, 1975). For yet another example, the Georgia State Department of Education initiated a project funded by the U.S. Office of Education to coordinate the efforts of several Georgia school systems in planning and implementing comprehensive career guidance programs. The goal of the project was to develop a career guidance system that was based on student needs and focused on a team approach and curriculum-based strategies (Dagley, 1974).

On July 1, 1974, the American Institutes for Research began work on bringing together program planning efforts previously undertaken by the Pupil Personnel Division of the California State Department of Education and their own Youth Development Research Program in Mesa, Arizona, and elsewhere (Jones, Helliwell, & Ganschow, 1975). This resulted in the development of 12 competency-based staff development modules on developing comprehensive career guidance programs from kindergarten through 12th grade. As a part of the project, the modules were field tested in two school districts in California in the summer of 1975 and in a preservice class of guidance and counseling majors at the University of Missouri–Columbia in Fall 1975. A final report on this project was issued by the American Institutes for Research in January 1976 (Dayton, 1976). Jones, Dayton, and Gelatt (1977) subsequently used the 12 modules as a point of departure to suggest a systematic approach in planning and evaluating human service programs.

The work that began in the early 1970s on various guidance program models was continued and expanded. "Career Development: Guidance and Education," a special issue of the *Personnel and Guidance Journal* edited by Hansen and Gysbers (1975), contained a number of articles describing program models and examples of programs in operation. The American College Testing Program (1976) published a programmatic model for guidance in *River City High School Guidance Services: A Conceptual Model.*

Putting Comprehensive Guidance and Counseling Programs Into Practice in the 1980s and 1990s

Comprehensive Programs Gain Acceptance

As the 1970s ended, examinations of the traditional way of organizing and managing guidance and counseling in the nation's schools continued, and recommendations for a new way increased (Herr, 1979). The idea of comprehensive developmental guidance programs was gradually enveloping the services model and its position orientation. This movement was first endorsed by ASCA in a 1974 position statement, *The School Counselor and the Guidance and Counseling Program,* and then in a review and revision of the statement in 1980. The movement was further endorsed in ASCA's 1978 position statement, *The School Counselor and Developmental Guidance,* and in that statement's 1984 review and revision (see ASCA, 1984). As Shaw and Goodyear (1984) noted, guidance specialists needed to "make concrete, written, and reasonable proposals for the delivery of primary preventive services so that some of their less professional and highly scattered responsibilities can be diminished" (p. 446).

The work of putting comprehensive guidance and counseling programs into place in the schools continued throughout the 1980s. Gysbers and Moore (1981) provided a theoretical base as well as a step-by-step process for developing and implementing comprehensive school guidance programs in a book titled *Improving Guidance Programs.* This publication grew out of earlier work (Gysbers & Moore, 1974) in the University of Missouri project to assist states in developing and implementing models or guides for career guidance, counseling, and placement. In addition, Hargens and Gysbers (1984) presented a case study of how one school district had remodeled and revitalized its school guidance and counseling program so that it was developmental and comprehensive.

The state of Missouri published a draft version of *Missouri Comprehensive Guidance* (1986) that presented the state's plan to help school districts to develop, implement, and evaluate comprehensive, systematic school guidance programs begun during the 1984 to 1985 school year. Wisconsin published *School Counseling Programs: A Resource and Planning Guide* (Wilson, 1986), the result of work begun in 1984 to reexamine the school counselor's role. The National School Boards Association (1986) passed a resolution that supported comprehensive programs of guidance and counseling in the schools. The College Entrance Examination Board (1986) issued *Keeping the Options Open: Recommendations,* a report with direct relevance to comprehensive guidance and counseling programs in the schools that was based on work of the Commission on Precollege Guidance and Counseling begun in 1984. Recommendations in the report urged schools to establish comprehensive and developmental guidance programs for kindergarten through 12th grade. Henderson (1987), in "A Comprehensive School Guidance Program at Work" and "How One District Changed Its Program" (Henderson, 1989), described how a comprehensive guidance program was designed, the program's content, how the program was being implemented in a large school district in Texas, and the process used to implement it. Myrick (2003) discussed a developmental guidance and counseling model and its implementation in detail.

The 1980s also witnessed the development of an approach to comprehensive guidance and counseling programs called *competency-based guidance.* S. K. Johnson and Johnson (1991) described this approach as the new guidance, a concept they defined as

> a total pupil services program developed with the student as the primary client. The program is designed to guarantee that all students acquire the competencies to become successful in school and to make a successful transition from school to higher education, to employment or to a combination of higher education and work. (p. 6)

Importance of Legislation

As described previously, in the 1940s and 1950s, Congress passed the Vocational Education Act of 1946 and the NDEA. Each of these acts had a substantial and long-lasting impact on the nature, structure, and availability of guidance and counseling in the schools. In addition to these two pieces of legislation, the 1960s witnessed the passage of the Elementary and Secondary Education Act of 1965 and later amendments that provided some funding for school guidance and counseling (Herr, 2003).

Vocational education (career and technical education) legislation has continued to provide support for guidance and counseling in the schools through the reauthorization of such legislation in the 1930s, 1940s, 1950s, 1960s, and 1970s. Beginning in the 1980s, this legislation was named after Carl D. Perkins, a legislator from Kentucky, and was called the Carl D. Perkins Vocational Education Act of 1984. Subsequent reauthorizations occurred in 1990 (Carl D. Perkins Vocational Education and Applied Technology Education Act Amendments of 1990) and in 1998 (Carl D. Perkins Vocational Technical Education Act Amendments of 1998).

Several other federal laws are worth noting. In 1994, the School-to-Work Opportunities Act of 1994 was passed. It had the same definition of guidance and counseling as the 1990 Carl D. Perkins Vocational Education and Applied Technology Education Act. The same year the Elementary School Counseling Demonstration Act of 1994 was passed and provided funds for guidance and counseling in the schools.

State Models Are Developed

In the late 1980s and the 1990s, state program models were being developed and put into operation as a result of the work of guidance leaders at the state level and the work of counselors, administrators, and boards of education at the local level. A nationwide survey conducted by Sink and MacDonald (1998) revealed that approximately one half of the states had developed models for comprehensive guidance and counseling programs, and the authors speculated that by the end of the 1990s this number would increase to 34 or more states. With the increased recognition of guidance as a unique program within schools, and the advancement of supervision and administration in the counseling field, new models for providing leadership to school guidance programs and counselors were evolving (Gysbers & Henderson, 1997; Henderson & Gysbers, 1998).

Moving Toward Full Implementation of Guidance and Counseling Programs: The Promise of the 21st Century

In the first decade of the 21st century, work on developing, implementing, and evaluating comprehensive guidance and counseling programs continued to intensify and expand. During this time period, a number of states developed or revised their state models. ASCA developed a National Model. Work on federal legislation for guidance and counseling continued, and a number of states passed legislation or rules that support the development, implementation, and evaluation of comprehensive guidance and counseling programs in their local school districts. Finally, models for leadership and management of school guidance and counseling programs and staff members continued to be refined.

ASCA National Model

In 1997, the ASCA published *Sharing the Vision: The National Standards for School Counseling Programs* (C. A. Campbell & Dahir, 1997), which was followed by the publication of *Vision Into Action: Implementing the National Standards for School Counseling Programs* (Dahir, Sheldon, & Valiga, 1998). These national standards are now called *content standards for students*. In 2001, ASCA's governing board agreed that the development of a national school counseling program model was the next necessary step because what

ASCA had developed up to this point had been only content standards for students' academic, career, and personal–social development. What was needed was a framework for a total school counseling program.

On the basis of ASCA's governing board's decision to move forward to develop a national model, a committee of national leaders and practicing school counselors met in Tucson, Arizona, in June 2001. A draft of the model was prepared in Fall 2001. Two subsequent meetings of the committee took place in 2002, and the model was officially unveiled at the ASCA National Conference in Miami in June 2002. Additional revisions were undertaken, and in 2003, *The ASCA National Model* was officially released by the association.

The National Model was based on the work of Gysbers and Henderson (2000), Myrick (2003), and C. D. Johnson and Johnson (2001). It contains four elements: foundation, delivery system, management system, and accountability. It is comprehensive in scope, preventative in design, and developmental in nature and is an integral part of the total educational program. It is implemented by certificated school counselors. Conducted in collaboration, it monitors student progress and is driven by data. A workbook was published in 2004 (ASCA, 2004), and a second edition of the National Model was published in 2005 (ASCA, 2005).

In the second edition of *The ASCA National Model,* Henderson (2005) added a section titled "The Theory Behind the ASCA National Model." In it, she defined what constituted a theory and presented a brief history of school counseling theory. Then she outlined seven questions to be answered by theory. She answered them by presenting 27 major principles and 15 subprinciples to represent the theoretical base of the ASCA National Model.

The publication of the ASCA National Model served to further stimulate the movement begun in the 1970s to develop, implement, and evaluate comprehensive guidance and counseling programs in all of the states and school districts in the United States. As a result of its publication, some states that did not have models developed them. For those states that had models, aligning them with the ASCA National Model became a priority.

Comprehensive Programs: Direct or Indirect Services

The development and implementation of comprehensive guidance and counseling programs increased rapidly across the country. Martin, Carey, and DeCoster (2009) found that "17 states have established models, 24 are progressing in model implementation, and 10 are at a beginning stage of model development" (p. 378). The purposes of these programs and how those purposes should be achieved received a great deal of attention in the literature. Some writers suggested that school counseling should consist mainly of direct services to students, with school counselors spending most of their time (80% or more) providing direct services (Gysbers & Henderson, 2006). Other writers recommended that school counseling focus more on indirect roles such as consultation, advocacy, coordination, and collaboration (Green & Keys, 2001; Paisley & McMahon, 2001).

Whiston (2002) expressed concern about a move to making guidance and counseling a primarily indirect program:

> My concerns about the increasing focus on collaboration should not be construed as being uncooperative or opposed to collaborative activities. However, I am concerned that some of the systemic problems in school counseling cannot be addressed through typical collaborative activities. Some collaborative efforts are short-lived and fade away after the initial excitement dissipates or there are personnel changes within the cooperating organizations. My concern is with stu-

dents and the belief that unrealistic caseloads keep school counselors from providing the assistance students need. Although collaboration can often be an important activity, it may be time for the field to place more emphasis on increasing the number of school counselors and providing more effective programs to students rather than on initiating collaborative programs (p. 152).

Even individuals who favored the direct services approach, however, had differing opinions as to what direct services should be provided. Some felt that too much attention was being given to academic issues and concerns at the expense of providing individual and small-group counseling, in light of students' increasing mental health needs. Others felt the opposite, stating that students' academic achievement should be the priority for direct services.

What do school counselors say about the direct versus indirect services debate? In a survey of Arizona school counselors, Kolodinsky, Draves, Schroder, Lindsey, and Zlatev (2009) found that their greatest job satisfaction came from directly serving students.

> While the ASCA National Model points to an increase in accountability, data collection, and program evaluation by school counselors (Dollarhide & Saginak, 2008; Poynton & Carey, 2006), it is interesting to note that the vast majority of respondents in this study reported that their greatest feeling of job satisfaction came in interactions where they had greater freedom to directly serve and interact with students. (p. 198)

Selection and Training of School Counselors

Concern about the selection, background, education, and supervision of school counselors, first expressed many years ago, continues today. The teaching certification and experience debate, at times heavy in years past, seems to have diminished as more and more states have dropped these requirements from their school counselor certification standards. Although some states dropped them, they still recognize the need for some exposure to schools by requiring education coursework and educational internships.

In 1996, the Education Trust, supported by the DeWitt Wallace–Reader's Digest Fund, initiated a 5-year project to change the preparation of school counselors and the practice of school counseling. The goal was to help low-income and minority youth improve academically and to close the academic achievement gap for these youth (P. J. Martin, 2002).

In June 2003, the National Center for Transforming School Counseling was established. The goal of this organization was to ensure school counselors are trained and ready to help all groups of students reach high academic standards. School counselors are seen as assertive advocates, leaders, and team members to help each student succeed.

The goal of the National Center for Transforming School Counseling, academic achievement, was questioned by some, however. For example, Galassi and Akos (2004) reviewed current school counseling models, including the one being proposed by the National Initiative for Transforming School Counseling. They pointed out that this initiative was a shift from a mental health focus to an academic achievement focus and expressed their concern about this as follows:

> The Transforming School Counseling Initiative, in response to educational reform, has focused almost entirely on academic achievement and narrowing the minority achievement gap. Although these are laudable goals, they seem to minimize the role of the other developmental needs (personal and social) in academic achievement and career development in the lives of twenty-first century youth. (p. 149)

Federal and State Legislation

In 2001, the U.S. Congress passed the No Child Left Behind Act. In it, Part D, Subpart 2, titled "Elementary and Secondary School Counseling Programs," provided for grants to local educational agencies to establish or expand elementary and secondary school counseling programs. However, the level of money actually appropriated was not sufficient to fund the secondary portion of the act. Thus, only grants to local education agencies were available for elementary school counseling programs. In 2006, however, the Carl D. Perkins Vocational and Technical Education Act of 1998 was amended and became the Carl D. Perkins Career and Technical Education Improvement Act of 2006.

A number of states have also been active in passing legislation or rules for guidance and counseling in the schools. For example, Utah's State Board of Education passed a rule (R277–462) that defined a comprehensive guidance program and provided qualification criteria by which to distribute Comprehensive Guidance Funds. Within the same rule, school districts and charter schools in Utah are required to have a ratio of one counselor for every 350 students (Utah Administrative Code, 2011).

In another example, the Texas legislature enacted S.B. 518, which made Education Code Sections 33.003 to 33.006 applicable to all school districts ("An Act Relating to Public School Counselors," 2001). These sections stated that Texas school counselors shall plan, implement, and evaluate developmental guidance and counseling programs. Similarly, in the state of West Virginia, the Board of Education enacted a legislative rule for comprehensive developmental guidance and counseling in 2002. Finally, as a last example, the State of Florida enacted a bill titled "An Act Relating to Career Education" in 2004. In Section 5, Subsection 1006.025, it states that each district school board shall annually submit a district guidance report to the Commissioner of Education that includes the degree to which a district has adopted or implemented a guidance model program.

Leadership and Supervision Issues and Models

With rules and guidelines for comprehensive guidance programs delineated in federal and state legislation, policy, and models, effective leadership of guidance programs and school counselors is recognized as necessary to ensure compliance. A growing number of school counseling leaders are being identified at the school district and building levels. Issues identified as critical to successful implementation of comprehensive guidance programs have been successfully resolved through effective leadership (Henderson & Gysbers, 2002). Models for guidance leadership, administration, supervision, and management are being refined. Leadership of school counselors is required to ensure their competent performance (Henderson & Gysbers, 1998; Lieberman, 2004; Schwallie-Giddis, ter Maat, & Pak, 2003). Management and accountability systems have been called for throughout the history of school guidance and counseling. It is finally clear that without proper leadership, such systems cannot be implemented. Leadership by school counselors is called for not only to manage their own programs (Fitch & Marshall, 2004) but also to assist teachers and administrators with better meeting the needs of their students (ASCA, 2003; Education Trust, 2003).

What were some critical leadership issues that school counseling program leaders faced? Henderson and Gysbers's (2002) edited book, *Implementing Comprehensive School Guidance Programs,* addressed 10 critical issues in leadership. Twenty guidance leaders from around the country were chosen to show how effective leadership could be responsive to these critical issues. Their responses clearly showed that the key to success was effective leadership.

In 2009, Henderson's book, *The New Handbook of Administrative Supervision in Counseling*, was published. In it, she described administrative supervisors' responsibilities and the knowledge and skills they need to do their work effectively. She drew on the experiences of administrative supervisors as well as the theory and research of counseling leadership and supervision and related disciplines.

Comprehensive Guidance and Counseling Programs: Five Foundation Premises

As the guidance and counseling movement (then called vocational guidance) began to unfold in the United States at the turn of the 20th century, teachers, often part time or with no reduced time, and administrators were appointed as counselors and given a list of duties to perform. By the 1920s, the guidance and counseling movement had spread across the country. Educational guidance became a priority along with vocational guidance. During the late 1920s and early 1930s, efforts were made to identify what the activities of guidance and counseling should be, to establish the standard setup for guidance and counseling. During this same period of time, personal–social guidance and counseling emerged, as did the services model under the banner of pupil personnel work. Thus, by the 1930s, the three aspects of guidance and counseling (vocational, educational, and personal–social) and the services model with the position of counselor had been established. With the aid of federal legislation in the 1940s and 1950s, guidance and counseling in the schools continued to expand and became a part of overall education in the United States.

In the 1960s and 1970s, owing to concerns about the efficacy of the position–services model of guidance and counseling, the program model began to emerge. Although not a new concept, the program model has become, during the 1980s, 1990s, and the early years of the 2000s, the major way of organizing and managing guidance and counseling in the schools. The position–services model has been transformed and incorporated into a developmental, comprehensive program.

Why is an understanding of the history of guidance and counseling in the schools important? It helps us understand why and how the position–services model for guidance and counseling evolved. It also helps us understand why and how the comprehensive guidance and counseling model emerged in the 1960s and 1970s in response to dissatisfaction with the position–services model.

Just as we need to understand how guidance and counseling in our schools evolved, so too do we need to understand the five premises on which the program model is based. These premises undergird the organization and management of guidance and counseling in the schools. These premises are the point of departure for developing and managing your school guidance and counseling program.

1. *Guidance and counseling is a program.* Its characteristics are similar to other programs in education and includes
   - student standards;
   - activities and processes to assist students in achieving these standards;
   - professionally certificated personnel;
   - materials and resources;
   - program, personnel, and results evaluation.
2. *Guidance and counseling programs are developmental and comprehensive.* They are developmental in that guidance and counseling activities are conducted on a regular, planned, and systematic basis to assist students in their academic, career, and personal–social development. Although immediate and crisis needs of students are

to be met, a major focus of a developmental program is to provide all students with experiences to help them grow and develop. Guidance and counseling programs are comprehensive in that a full range of activities and services are provided.

3. *Guidance and counseling programs feature a team approach.* A comprehensive, developmental program of guidance and counseling is based on the assumption that all school staff are involved. At the same time, it is understood that professionally certified school counselors are central to the program. School counselors not only provide direct services to students but also work in consultative and collaborative relations with other members of the guidance team, members of the school staff, parents, and members of the community.

4. *Guidance and counseling programs are developed through a systematic process of planning, designing, implementing, evaluating, and enhancing.* This process ensures intentional delivery of a program designed to address established priorities.

5. *Guidance and counseling programs have established leadership.* This ensures accountability for the program and for the quality of the performance of program staff.

Your Progress Check

Now that you have completed reading Chapter 1, you have gained a more complete understanding of the evolution of guidance and counseling in U.S. schools over the past 100 years.

You have learned about

- the early beginnings of guidance and counseling in the schools, including the work of Frank Parsons and Jessie B. Davis;
- the establishment of the position model of organizing guidance and counseling in the schools;
- the changing purposes of guidance and counseling as it continued to evolve in the 1920s and 1930s;
- how the position approach was incorporated into the services model for guidance and counseling in the 1930s;
- the importance of federal legislation beginning in the 1940s and continuing till today;
- how the position approach and the services model were incorporated into the comprehensive guidance and counseling program;
- the five fundamental premises that undergird the comprehensive program approach to guidance and counseling in the schools.

On the basis of the understanding gained from this chapter's review of how guidance and counseling has been conceptualized and institutionalized in the schools over the years, you are now ready to examine a comprehensive program organization and management structure for guidance and counseling. The chapters that follow provide the philosophical foundation and practical specifics of organizing and managing guidance and counseling while using the concept of a comprehensive program. The issues involved, the procedures and methods to be used, and the resources and personnel required are presented in detail.

References

Allen, F. I. (1927). *Principles and problems in vocational guidance.* New York, NY: McGraw-Hill.

American College Testing Program. (1976). *River City High School guidance services: A conceptual model.* Iowa City, IA: Author.

American Psychological Association, Division of Counseling Psychology, Committee on Definition. (1956). Counseling psychology as a specialty. *American Psychologist, 11,* 282–285.

American School Counselor Association. (1984). *The school counselor and developmental guidance: Position statement.* Alexandria, VA: Author.

American School Counselor Association. (2003). *The ASCA National Model: A framework for school counseling programs.* Alexandria, VA: Author.

American School Counselor Association. (2004). *The ASCA National Model workbook.* Alexandria, VA: Author.

American School Counselor Association. (2005). *The ASCA National Model: A framework for school counseling programs* (2nd ed.). Alexandria, VA: Author.

An Act Relating to Career Education, Florida H.B. 0769 (2004).

An Act Relating to Public School Counselors, S.B. 518, Amends Texas Education Code, §§ 33.001, 33.005–33.006 (2001).

Ashcroft, K. B. (1966). *A report of the invitational conference in implementing career development theory.* Washington, DC: National Vocational Guidance Association.

Aubrey, R. F. (1982). A house divided: Guidance and counseling in 20th century America. *Personnel and Guidance Journal, 61,* 198–204.

Bell, H. M. (1939). *Theory and practice of personal counseling.* Stanford, CA: Stanford University Press.

Bloomfield, M. (1915). *Youth, school, and vocation.* Boston, MA: Houghton Mifflin.

Borow, H. (1966). Research in vocational development: Implications for the vocational aspects of counselor education. In C. McDaniels (Ed.), *Vocational aspects of counselor education* (pp. 70–92). Washington, DC: George Washington University.

Brammer, L. M. (1968). The counselor is a psychologist. *Personnel and Guidance Journal, 47,* 4–9.

Brewer, J. M. (1922). *The vocational-guidance movement.* New York, NY: Macmillan.

Brewer, J. M. (1942). *History of vocational guidance: Origins and early development.* New York, NY: Harper.

California State Department of Education. (1971). *Career guidance: A California model for career development K–adult.* Sacramento, CA: Author.

Campbell, C. A., & Dahir, C. A. (1997). *Sharing the vision: The national standards for school counseling programs.* Alexandria, VA: American School Counselor Association.

Campbell, M. E. (1932). *Vocational Guidance Committee on Vocational Guidance and Child Labor: Section III. Education and training* (White House Conference on Child Health and Protection). New York, NY: Century.

Campbell, R. E., Dworkin, E. P., Jackson, D. P., Hoeltzel, K. E., Parsons, G. E., & Lacey, D. W. (1971). *The systems approach: An emerging behavioral model for career guidance.* Columbus, OH: National Center for Research in Vocational Education.

Carl D. Perkins Career and Technical Education Act of 2006, Pub. L. No. 109–270. http://www2.ed.gov/policy/sectech/leg/perkins/index.html

Carl D. Perkins Vocational and Applied Technology Education Act Amendments of 1990, Pub. L. No. 101-392, 104, Pt. 2, Stat. 753 (1990).

Carl D. Perkins Vocational and Applied Technology Education Amendments of 1998, Pub. L. No. 105-332, 112, Pt. 1, Stat. 3076 (1998).

Carl D. Perkins Vocational Education Act of 1984, Pub. L. No. 98–524, Part 1, Stat. 2433 (1984).

College Entrance Examination Board. (1986). *Keeping the options open: Recommendations.* New York, NY: Author.

Council of Chief State School Officers. (1960). *Responsibilities of state departments of education for pupil personnel services.* Washington, DC: Author.

Dagley, J. C. (1974, December). *Georgia career guidance project newsletter.* Athens: University of Georgia.

Dahir, C. A., Sheldon, C. B., & Valiga, M. J. (1998). *Vision into action: Implementing the national standards for school counseling programs.* Alexandria, VA: American School Counselor Association.

Davis, H. V. (1969). *Frank Parsons: Prophet, innovator, counselor.* Carbondale: Southern Illinois University Press.

Davis, J. B. (1914). *Vocational and moral guidance.* Boston, MA: Ginn.

Davis, J. B. (1956). *The saga of a school master.* Boston, MA: Boston University.

Dayton, C. A. (1976). *A validated program development model and staff development prototype for comprehensive career guidance, counseling, placement, and follow-up* (Final Report, Grant No. OEG-0-74-1721). Palo Alto, CA: American Institutes for Research.

Dinkmeyer, D. (1966). Developmental counseling in the elementary school. *Personnel and Guidance Journal, 45,* 262–66.

Drier, H. N. (Ed.). (1971). *Guide to the integration of career development into local curriculum: Grades K–12.* Madison: Wisconsin Department of Public Instruction.

Dunn, J. A. (1972). *The guidance program in the plan system of individualized education.* Palo Alto, CA: American Institutes for Research.

Eckerson, L. O., & Smith, H. M. (Eds.). (1966). *Scope of pupil personnel services* (Catalog No. FS5.223: 23045). Washington, DC: U.S. Government Printing Office.

Education Trust. (2003). *Transforming school counseling.* Retrieved October 28, 2004, from http://www.edtrust.org

Elementary and Secondary Education Act of 1965, Pub. L. No. 89-10, Stat. 27-58 (1965).

Elementary School Counseling Demonstration Act of 1994, Title X, Programs of National Significance, Fund for the Improvement of Education, § 10102 of the Improving America's School Act of 1994, Pub. L. No. 103-382, 108 Stat. 3518-4062 (1994).

Faust, V. (1968). *History of elementary school counseling: Overview and critique.* Boston, MA: Houghton Mifflin.

Felix, J. L. (1968). Who decided that? *Personnel and Guidance Journal, 47,* 9–11.

Ferguson, D. G. (1963). *Pupil personnel services.* Washington, DC: Center for Applied Research in Education.

Fitch, T. J., & Marshall, J. (2004). What counselors do in high-achieving schools: A study on the role of the school counselor. *Professional School Counseling, 7,* 172–178.

Galassi, J. P., & Akos, P. (2004). Developmental advocacy: Twenty-first century school counseling. *Journal of Counseling & Development, 82,* 146–157.

Ginn, S. J. (1924). Vocational guidance in Boston public schools. *Vocational Guidance Magazine, 3,* 3–7.

Glanz, E. C. (1961). Emerging concepts and patterns of guidance in American education. *Personnel and Guidance Journal, 40,* 259–65.

Green, A., & Keys, S. (2001). Expanding the developmental school counseling paradigm: Meeting the needs of the 21st century student. *Professional School Counseling, 5,* 84–95.

Gysbers, N. C. (1969). *Elements of a model for promoting career development in elementary and junior high school.* Paper presented at the National Conference on Exemplary Programs and Projects, 1968 Amendments to the Vocational Education Act (ED045860), Atlanta, GA.

Gysbers, N. C., & Henderson, P. (1997). *Comprehensive guidance programs that work—II.* Greensboro, NC: ERIC Counseling and Student Services Clearinghouse.

Gysbers, N. C., & Henderson, P. (2000). *Developing and managing your school guidance program* (3rd ed.). Alexandria, VA: American Counseling Association.

Gysbers, N. C., & Henderson, P. (2006). *Developing & managing your school guidance and counseling program* (4th ed.). Alexandria, VA: American Counseling Association.

Gysbers, N. C., & Moore, E. J. (Eds.). (1974). *Career guidance counseling & placement: Elements of an illustrative program guide.* Columbia: University of Missouri.

Gysbers, N. C., & Moore, E. J. (1981). *Improving guidance programs.* Englewood Cliffs, NJ: Prentice-Hall.

Hansen, L. S. (1970). *Career guidance practices in school and community.* Washington, DC: National Vocational Guidance Association.

Hansen, L. S., & Gysbers, N. C. (Eds.). (1975). Career development: Guidance and education [Special issue]. *Personnel and Guidance Journal, 53.*

Hargens, M., & Gysbers, N. C. (1984). How to remodel a guidance program while living in it: A case study. *The School Counselor, 32,* 119–125.

Henderson, P. (1987). A comprehensive school guidance program at work. *Texas Association for Counseling and Development Journal, 10,* 25–37.

Henderson, P. (1989). How one district changed its program. *The School Counselor, 37,* 31–40.

Henderson, P. (2005). The theory behind the ASCA National Model. In American School Counselor Association, *The ASCA National Model* (pp. 79–101). Alexandria, VA: American School Counselor Association.

Henderson, P. G. (2009). *The new handbook of administrative supervision in counseling.* New York, NY: Routledge.

Henderson, P., & Gysbers, N. C. (1998). *Leading and managing your school guidance program staff.* Alexandria, VA: American Counseling Association.

Henderson, P., & Gysbers, N. C. (Eds.). (2002). *Implementing comprehensive school guidance programs: Critical leadership issues and successful responses.* Greensboro, NC: CAPS.

Herr, E. L. (1969). *Unifying an entire system of education around a career development theme.* Paper presented at the National Conference on Exemplary Programs and Projects, 1968 Amendments to the Vocational Education Act (ED045860), Atlanta, GA.

Herr, E. L. (1979). *Guidance and counseling in the schools: The past, present, and future.* Washington, DC: American Personnel and Guidance Association.

Herr, E. L. (2003). Historical roots and future issues. In B. T. Enford (Ed.), *Transforming the school counseling profession* (pp. 21–38). Upper Saddle River, NJ: Prentice-Hall.

Hosford, R. E., & Ryan, T. A. (1970). Systems design in the development of counseling and guidance programs. *Personnel and Guidance Journal, 49,* 221–230.

Hoyt, K. B. (1974). Professional preparation for vocational guidance. In E. L. Herr (Ed.), *Vocational guidance and human development* (pp. 502–527). Boston, MA: Houghton Mifflin.

Jacobson, T. J., & Mitchell, A. M. (1975). *Master plan for career guidance and counseling* (Final Report, Pupil Personnel Services). Grossmont, CA: Grossmont Union High School District.

Johnson, A. H. (1972). Changing conceptions of vocational guidance and concomitant value-orientations 1920–30. *Dissertation Abstracts International: Section A. Humanities and Social Sciences, 33,* 3292. (UMI No. 72-31933)

Johnson, C. D., & Johnson, S. K. (2001). *Results-based student support programs: Leadership academy workbook.* San Juan Capistrano, CA: Professional Update.

Johnson, S. K., & Johnson, C. D. (1991). The new guidance: A system approach to pupil personnel programs. *CACD Journal, 11,* 5–14.

Jones, G. B., Dayton, C., & Gelatt, H. B. (1977). *New methods for delivering human services.* New York, NY: Human Services Press.

Jones, G. B., Hamilton, J. A., Ganschow, L. H., Helliwell, C. B., & Wolff, J. M. (1972). *Planning, developing, and field testing career guidance programs: A manual and report.* Palo Alto, CA: American Institutes for Research.

Jones, G. B., Helliwell, C. B., & Ganschow, L. H. (1975). A planning model for career guidance. *Vocational Guidance Quarterly, 23,* 220–226.

Jones, G. B., Nelson, D. E., Ganschow, L. H., & Hamilton, J. A. (1971). *Development and evaluation of a comprehensive career guidance program.* Palo Alto, CA: American Institutes for Research.

Kolodinsky, P., Draves, P., Schroder, V., Lindsey, C., & Zlatev, M. (2009). Reported levels of satisfaction and frustration by Arizona school counselors: A desire for greater connections with students in a data-driven era. *Professional School Counseling, 12,* 193–199.

Koos, L. V., & Kefauver, G. N. (1937). *Guidance in secondary schools.* New York, NY: Macmillan.

Krug, E. A. (1964). *The shaping of the American high school.* New York, NY: Harper & Row.

Leonard, G. E., & Vriend, T. J. (1975). Update: The developmental career guidance project. *Personnel and Guidance Journal, 53,* 668–671.

Leavitt, F. M. (1914). How shall we study the industries for the purposes of vocational guidance? In U.S. Bureau of Education, *Vocational guidance: Papers presented at the organization meeting of the Vocational Guidance Association, Grand Rapids, Michigan, October 21–24, 1913* (Bulletin 14[587], pp. 79–81). Washington, DC: U.S. Government Printing Office.

Lieberman, A. (2004). Confusion regarding school counselor functions: School leadership impacts role clarity. *Education, 124,* 522–529.

Martin, I., Carey, J., & DeCoster, K. (2009). A national study of the current status of state school counseling models. *Professional School Counseling, 12,* 378–386.

Martin, P. J. (2002). Transforming school counseling: A national perspective. *Theory Into Practice, 41,* 148–153.

Mathewson, R. H. (1962). *Guidance policy and practice* (3rd ed.). New York, NY: Harper & Row.

McCracken, T. C., & Lamb, H. E. (1923). *Occupational information in the elementary school.* Boston, MA: Houghton Mifflin.

McDaniel, H. B. (1970). *Youth guidance systems.* Palo Alto, CA: College Entrance Examination Board.

McKinnon, B. E., & Jones, G. B. (1975). Field testing a comprehensive career guidance program: K–12. *Personnel and Guidance Journal, 53,* 663–667.

Miller, C. H. (1971). *Foundations of guidance.* New York, NY: Harper & Row.

Missouri Comprehensive Guidance. (1986). *The Counseling Interviewer, 18*(4), 6–17.

Myers, G. E. (1923). A critical review of present developments in vocational guidance with special reference to future prospects. *The Vocational Guidance Magazine, 2,* 139–142.

Myers, G. E. (1931). What should be the duties of the counselor? *Occupations, 9,* 343–347.

Myers, G. E. (1935). Coordinated guidance: Some suggestions for a program of pupil personnel work. *Occupations, 13,* 804–807.

Myrick, R. D. (2003). *Developmental guidance and counseling: A practical approach* (4th ed.). Minneapolis, MN: Educational Media Corporation.

National Defense Education Act of 1958, Pub. L. No. 85-864, 72, Pt. 1, Stat. 1580 (1958).

National Education Association. (1918). *Cardinal principles of secondary education: A report of the Commission on the Reorganization of Secondary Education.* Washington, DC: Author.

National School Boards Association. (1986). *Resolution on guidance and counseling.* Alexandria, VA: Author.

No Child Left Behind Act of 2001, Pub. L. No. 107-110, 115 Stat. 1434 (2001).

Paisley, P. O., & McMahon, H. G. (2001). School counseling for the 21st century: Challenges and opportunities. *Professional School Counseling, 5,* 106–115.

Parsons, F. (1909). *Choosing a vocation.* Boston, MA: Houghton Mifflin.

Pierson, G. A. (1965). *An evaluation—Counselor education in regular session institutes.* Washington, DC: U.S. Department of Health, Education, and Welfare, Office of Education.

Proctor, W. M. (1930). Evaluating guidance activities in high schools. *The Vocational Guidance Magazine, 9,* 58–66.

Roeber, E. C. (1963). *The school counselor.* Washington, DC: Center for Applied Research in Education.

Roeber, E. C., Walz, G. R., & Smith, G. E. (1969). *A strategy for guidance.* New York, NY: Macmillan.

Rogers, C. R. (1942). *Counseling and psychotherapy.* Boston, MA: Houghton Mifflin.

Rudy, W. S. (1965). *Schools in an age of mass culture.* Englewood Cliffs, NJ: Prentice-Hall.

Ryan, T. A. (1969). Systems techniques for programs of counseling and counselor education. *Educational Technology, 9,* 7–17.

Ryan, T. A., & Zeran, F. R. (1972). *Organization and administration of guidance services.* Danville, IL: Interstate.

Ryan, W. C., Jr. (1919). *Vocational guidance and the public schools* (Bulletin 1918, No. 24). Washington, DC: U.S. Department of the Interior, Bureau of Education.

School-to-Work Opportunities Act of 1994, Pub. L. No. 103-239, 108 Stat. 568 (1994).

Schwallie-Giddis, P., ter Maat, M., & Pak, M. (2003). Initiating leadership by introducing and implementing the ASCA National Model. *Professional School Counseling, 6,* 170–174.

Shaw, M. C., & Goodyear, R. K. (1984). Prologue to primary prevention in schools. *Personnel and Guidance Journal, 62,* 446–447.

Shaw, M. C., & Tuel, L. K. (1966). A focus for public school guidance programs: A model and proposal. *Personnel and Guidance Journal, 44,* 824–830.

Sink, C. A., & MacDonald, G. (1998). The status of comprehensive guidance and counseling in the United States. *Professional School Counseling, 2,* 88–94.

Smith, G. E. (1951). *Principles and practices of the guidance program.* New York, NY: Macmillan.

Sprinthall, N. A. (1971). *Guidance for human growth.* New York, NY: Van Nostrand Reinhold.

Stephens, W. R. (1970). *Social reform and the origins of vocational guidance.* Washington, DC: National Vocational Guidance Association.

Stoughton, R. W., McKenna, I. W., & Cook, R. P. (1969). *Pupil personnel services: A position statement.* Bloomfield, CT: National Association of Pupil Personnel Administrators.

Stripling, R. O., & Lane, D. (1966). Guidance services. In L. O. Eckerson & H. M. Smith (Eds.), *Scope of pupil personnel services* (Catalog No. F5 5.223:23045, pp. 25–35). Washington, DC: U.S. Government Printing Office.

Studebaker, J. W. (1938). The new national Occupational Information and Guidance Service. *Occupations, 16,* 101–105.

Super, D. E. (1955). Transition: From vocational guidance to counseling psychology. *Journal of Counseling Psychology, 2,* 3–9.

Tennyson, W. W., & Hansen, L. S. (1971). Guidance through the curriculum. In L. C. Deighton (Ed.), *The encyclopedia of education* (Vol. 4, pp. 248–254). New York, NY: Macmillan.

Tennyson, W. W., Soldahl, T. A., & Mueller, C. (1965). *The teacher's role in career development.* Washington, DC: National Vocational Guidance Association.

Tiedeman, D. V., & Field, F. C. (1962). Guidance: The science of purposeful action applied through education. *Harvard Educational Review, 32,* 483–501.

Tyler, L. E. (1960). *The National Defense Counseling and Guidance Training Institutes program: A report of the first 50 institutes.* Washington, DC: U.S. Department of Health, Education, and Welfare, Office of Education.

U.S. Bureau of Education. (1914). *Vocational guidance: Papers presented at the organization meeting of the Vocational Guidance Association, Grand Rapids, Michigan, October 21–24, 1913, Prefatory Statement* (Bulletin No. 14[587]). Washington, DC: U.S. Government Printing Office.

Utah Administrative Code, Rule R277-462, Comprehensive Counseling and Guidance Program (2011). http://www.rules.utah.gov/publicat/code/r277/r277-462.htm

Vocational Education Act of 1946, Pub. L. No. 79-586, 60, Part 1, Stat. 775-778 (1946).

Vocational Education Act of 1963, Pub. L. 88-210, 77 Stat. 403 (1963).

Wellman, F. E. (1978). *U.S. Office of Education Administrative Unit: Past, present, and future.* Unpublished manuscript, University of Missouri–Columbia.

West Virginia Board of Education Legislative Rule, Series 67, Comprehensive Developmental Guidance and Counseling, 2315 (2002).

Whiston, S. C. (2002). Response to the past, present, and future of school counseling: Raising some issues. *Professional School Counseling, 5,* 148–155.

Wilson, P. J. (1986). *School counseling programs: A resource and planning guide.* Madison: Wisconsin Department of Public Instruction.

Wirth, A. G. (1980). *Education in the technological society.* Lanham, MD: University Press of America.

Wirth, A. G. (1983). *Productive work in industry and schools.* Lanham, MD: University Press of America.

Wrenn, C. G. (1962). *The counselor in a changing world.* Washington, DC: American Personnel and Guidance Association.

Zaccaria, J. S. (1965). Developmental tasks: Implications for the goals of guidance. *Personnel and Guidance Journal, 44,* 372–375.

Zaccaria, J. S. (1966). Developmental guidance: A concept in transition. *The School Counselor, 13,* 226–229.

Chapter 2

A Comprehensive School Guidance and Counseling Program: Getting Organized to Get There From Where You Are

Planning—Getting Organized to Get There From Where You Are

- Decide that you want to change.
- Understand the necessary conditions for effective change.
- Get the program idea to stick.
- Expect resistance to change.
- Develop trust among counselors, teachers, and administrators.
- Form committees and work groups.
- Meet with the administration or district board of education.
- Provide leadership for change.
- Be active.

☞ The traditional way of organizing guidance and counseling in the schools, first as a position and then as a position in a service, is continuing to give way to the organizational framework of a comprehensive guidance and counseling program. Comprehensive guidance and counseling programs are increasingly becoming not just a promise but a reality in school districts across the United States (Martin, Carey, & DeCoster, 2009). This change is not yet complete, however, because school counselors are often unable to spend 100% of their time carrying out a fully implemented comprehensive guidance and counseling program. They are still expected to fulfill multiple, often conflicting roles. They are expected to work in the curriculum, assist students with their educational and occupational planning, and do community outreach. They are expected to do crisis counseling, small-group counseling, and teacher and parent consultation as well as referral. In addition, they are expected to coordinate the school district's testing program, develop master schedules, do assessment and case management work for special education, and be responsible for various administrative and clerical duties not connected with the guidance and counseling program.

School counselors want to respond to the needs and expectations of students, parents, and teachers. However, they often find that the press of some of their existing off-task duties interferes with or actually prevents them from doing so. Thus, they find themselves in a quandary, and role confusion, if not direct role conflict, is often the result.

How serious is the problem? Consider the findings of the following studies of how school counselors spend their time. In a 3-year study conducted in Arizona (Vandegrift, 1999), the question was asked, "Are Arizona public schools making the best use of school counselors?" The study revealed that school counselors in Arizona were spending up to 15% of their time performing nonguidance activities. To put this percentage into perspective, Vandegrift (1999) conducted a cost–benefit analysis based on 1996 median salaries:

> A simple cost–benefit analysis helps in beginning to answer these questions. The median counselor salary in Arizona is $27,000. The median salary of a school secretary is $20,600. Fifteen percent of a counselor's wages is $4,050, while 15% of a secretary's wages is $3,090—a difference of nearly $1000. If all 1,327 Arizona public school counselors (who comprise the state's counselor directory) are spending an average of 15% of their time on non-guidance activities, this represents an investment of some $5 million. Assuming non-guidance activities such as class scheduling could be performed by secretarial staff, Arizona taxpayers currently are paying 100 times more (or over $1 million) for these services to be performed by Master's-degreed professionals. Moreover, time spent on non-guidance activities clearly is time not spent working with students, faculty and staff. (p. 5)

A similar study conducted in Texas (Rylander, 2002) revealed

> that school counselors spend only about 60 percent of their time exclusively on counseling. A good portion of their time is spent on other administrative tasks. Counselors acknowledge they should not be relieved entirely of administrative duties, because all school staff must assume some measure of administrative responsibility. Most claimed, however, that excessive administrative duties hampered their effectiveness and their availability to students. One particular area of concern among counselors was their role in administering statewide tests. While counselors believe they have a role in test assessment, they argued that the role of coordinator of TAAS [Texas Assessment of Academic Skills] testing took too much time away from counseling. Many recommend shifting most or all of those duties to other staff. (Executive summary)

Two studies conducted by the Joyce Ivy Foundation in 2008 and 2009 indicated that counselor time off task continues to be a major problem. In their study of school counselor time in Michigan (Joyce Ivy Foundation, 2008), 406 Michigan high school counselors from more than 350 high schools reported that 30% of their time was "absorbed with administration and paperwork, much of it attributable to their increasing role and duties in administering tests and curriculum changes" (p. 9). In a similar study in Ohio (Joyce Ivy Foundation, 2009), 630 Ohio school counselors spent 34% of their time off task "performing administrative work, such as scheduling, test management, maintaining student records, and signing tardy slips" (p. 4).

Why does the problem exist? One possible reason is that the organizational framework for guidance and counseling in many schools is still the position–services model consisting of lists of duties. Guidance and counseling remains an undefined program in many school buildings even though a written comprehensive program may exist somewhere at the district level. As a result, school counselors continue to find themselves in mainly supportive remedial roles, roles that are not seen as mainstream by most people. And, what is worse, this organizational framework reinforces the practice of having counselors do many inappropriate tasks because such tasks can be justified as being of service to someone. The following list of off-task duties is typical. Most school counselors do not do all of them, but many school counselors do some of them.

- Counselors register and schedule all new students.
- Counselors serve as coordinators for the schoolwide testing program.
- Counselors talk to new students concerning school rules.
- Counselors change students' schedules.
- Counselors are responsible for signing excuses for students who are tardy or absent.
- Counselors teach classes when teachers are absent.
- Counselors fill in for the principal when the principal is absent.
- Counselors do senior grade checks.
- Counselors are assigned lunchroom duty.
- Counselors arrange class schedules for students.
- Counselors are responsible for discipline cases.
- Counselors send home students who are not appropriately dressed.
- Counselors compute grade point averages.
- Counselors fill out student reports and records.
- Counselors are in charge of student records.
- Counselors supervise study halls.
- Counselors assist with duties in the principal's office.
- Counselors serve as case managers for special education.
- Counselors are responsible for all of the assessments for special education.

Another possible reason for this jumble of off-task duties is that some administrators are not aware of or do not understand the comprehensive guidance and counseling program concept and, as a result, see school counselors as office people, not program people. Thus, assigning school counselors administrative and clerical off-task duties seems logical and reasonable because this is what office people do. What they may not realize is that assigning these off-task duties to school counselors has a direct impact on the number of guidance and counseling interventions available to students. When school counselors are carrying out off-task duties, they are not available to work directly with students. To illustrate, suppose school counselors are spending 20% of their time on off-task duties. On the basis of 180 seven-period days in a school year, school counselors would lose 36 days or 252 clock hours of time providing direct services to students and their parents. What direct services could be provided if school counselors had 36 more days or 252 more hours available in the school year?

Elementary school students could receive
- 200 more 30-minute classroom guidance units on academic, career, and personal/social issues;
- 100 more hours of individual and small-group counseling.

Middle school students could receive
- 75 more classroom guidance units on academic, career, and personal–social issues;
- 50 more hours to develop and begin to use personal plans of study;
- 88 more hours of individual and small-group counseling.

High school students could receive
- 50 more classroom guidance units on academic, career, and personal–social issues;
- 88 more hours to develop and begin to use personal plans of study;
- 75 more hours of individual and small-group counseling.

Given this situation, the challenge that school counselors and program leaders face is how to make the transition from the position–services model, with the wide variety of tasks involved, to a comprehensive program that is an equal partner with other programs in education. How do we take an undefined and fragmented program, improve it, and make it a clearly defined and fully operational comprehensive K–12 program?

Making the transition is complex and difficult, but doable. It means for a time carrying out the duties required by the current position–services model while at the same time planning and beginning to carry out the new comprehensive guidance and counseling program and its tasks. The experience is similar to living in your home while you are remodeling it. It can be done, but it is exacting, time consuming, and often frustrating.

A number of issues and conditions need to be considered in planning the process of change and in making the transition to a comprehensive guidance and counseling program. Thus, this chapter first gives attention to deciding to change and to understanding the necessary general and specific conditions for change. After this discussion, the focus is on how to get the program concept of guidance and counseling to stick. Then, a sample timetable of tasks that may be involved in the changeover process is presented. Possible resistance to change is discussed next, including appreciating the challenges involved in change. Developing trust among counselors, teachers, and administrators follows. Next, the need to form committees and work groups to carry out the tasks involved in change is described. The chapter ends with the issue of the leadership for change and the admonition that action is needed.

Decide That You Want to Change

The initial stimulus to move to a comprehensive guidance and counseling program may come from counselors, or it may come from parents, students, school administration, the school board, or community organizations. No matter where the initial stimulus comes from, however, the total K–12 guidance staff must be involved in responding, and the administration and board of education must be involved and provide support. The decision to change, we believe, must be made jointly by school counselors and administrators. Because this is a key decision that will change how guidance and counseling is delivered in the schools, it requires careful thought (Erickson, 1997).

In one school district, for example, the guidance and counseling staff met several times with the full endorsement of administration to assess the need to change. They compared and contrasted the activities they thought they should be providing with those they actually were providing. On the basis of this comparison, they decided to take a detailed look at their program. Once consensus was obtained among the guidance and counseling staff, the decision was shared with the administration, and support was obtained to proceed (Hargens & Fuston, 1997).

When the issue of change has been fully discussed, consensus must be reached on how to respond. School counselors and administrators may decide to maintain the program as it is and not change. Or, as with the school district just discussed, the decision to change may be made jointly. If the decision to change is made, it is imperative that a majority of staff (counselors and administrators) agree to participate fully in whatever it takes to change their guidance and counseling program, to make it comprehensive from kindergarten through 12th grade.

Understand the Necessary Conditions for Effective Change

As you are considering changing to a comprehensive guidance and counseling program, it is important to understand that there are general conditions that affect how changes are made in any setting as well as conditions that are specific to school guidance and counseling and your school district. Identifying and appreciating the roles these conditions may play in the change process is indispensable to this first phase of the planning process.

Some General Conditions to Consider

Change Is a Process, Not an Event

Too often, change is treated as a one-time event. Enthusiasm is generated about a possible change, an event is held to launch the change, but then everyday events that follow smother any follow-through. People are good at holding "first annuals" but often forget to finish the tasks. Make no mistake—change is a process, not an event. Sufficient time must be built into the change schedule if the change is to be successful. Perseverance is a virtue.

Diagnostic Approach to Change

Connor, Lake, and Stackman (2003) recommended that a diagnostic approach be used in the change process. Their approach began with formulating the problem statement ("We need to improve the way we organize and implement guidance and counseling activities and services in our school district"). They then recommended gathering information about the problem ("How are we presently organized to provide guidance and counseling activities and services?"). Next, they recommended analyzing the information ("We are not reaching all students and their parents, our activities and services are disconnected K–12, and we are not accountable"). Finally, they recommended developing suggestions for future actions ("We need to improve what we do by adopting and implementing an accountable comprehensive guidance and counseling program K–12").

Magnitude of Change

Waters, Marzano, and McNulty (2003) used the terms *first order* and *second order* to describe the magnitude of change. They defined *first-order change* as

> changes that are consistent with existing values and norms, create advantages for individuals or stakeholder groups with similar interests, can be implemented with existing knowledge and resources, and where agreement exists on what changes are needed and on how the changes should be implemented can be considered first order. (p. 7)

Second-order change, however, "requires individuals or groups of stakeholders to learn new approaches or it conflicts with prevailing values of norms" (p. 7).

What is the problem? The problem occurs when one group sees a change as first order, that is, simply an extension of the past and consistent with current values, whereas another group sees the same change as second order, a break from the past that conflicts with current values. As Waters et al. (2003) pointed out, it is important to find out whether the changes to be made are first- or second-order changes and for which individuals or groups. Is the change to a comprehensive guidance and counseling program seen as a first-order change by school counselors but a second-order change by administrators? Or vice versa? It makes a difference and will affect whether change occurs smoothly, unevenly, or not at all.

Some Specific Conditions to Consider

Mitchell and Gysbers (1978) identified a list of conditions they felt were prerequisite for successful transition to a comprehensive guidance and counseling program in a local school district. We believe these conditions are as applicable to today's situations as they were in the 1970s and 1980s.

1. All staff members are involved.
2. All staff members are committed to the common objective: total, integrated development of individual students.
3. The administration is committed to the comprehensive approach and is willing to negotiate (trade off), helping staff members identify current activities that do not contribute to priority outcomes and supporting staff members' abandonment of such activities in favor of those that do contribute to priority outcomes.
4. All staff members see the comprehensive systematic counseling and guidance program as a function of the total staff rather than the exclusive responsibility of the counselors.
5. Counselors are willing to give up such "security blankets" as writing lengthy reports of their contacts with counselees or seeing counselees individually on matters better addressed in a group.
6. Counselors are interested in acquiring competencies.
7. Staff development activities to help staff members acquire competencies needed for successful implementation of a comprehensive program are provided.
8. Time is made available for planning and designing the program and the evaluation, with all interested groups participating (students, parents, teachers, counselors, administrators, and community).
9. Program developers design an incremental transition rather than an abrupt transition that ignores the need for continuing many current activities and thrusts. (p. 36)

From the perspective of a statewide implementation effort, Jensen and Petersen (1997) identified similar conditions in describing the State of Utah's plan to implement comprehensive guidance and counseling programs in its schools. They affirmed that the model for guidance and counseling must be endorsed and supported by school and community leaders, that time must be devoted to the change process, that change requires strong support from building administrators in local school districts, and that teams of school counselors and administrators must participate in the change process. In addition, they stressed that the change process must be adequately funded.

Making the transition from guidance and counseling organized around the position–services model to guidance and counseling as a comprehensive program is not easy, automatic, or rapid. It involves changing the behavior patterns of students, parents, teaching staff, administration, community, and guidance staff. Because of this, Mitchell and Gysbers (1978) pointed out that although all nine conditions are important, none is more important than the 10th and last condition:

10. Abrupt change is difficult and anxiety-producing; it tends to cause participants in the change to build barriers against it. (p. 36)

This 10th item speaks to perceptions of change as first or second order. Thus, assessing the magnitude of change as perceived by the individuals and groups involved is important as the planning phase begins to unfold.

Getting the Program Idea to Stick

A major challenge in the getting-organized phase of planning is getting the program concept of guidance and counseling to stick in the minds of school counselors, administrators, and teachers, some of whom may not understand what a program is and how it can contribute to student success. What does it mean for the program idea to stick? Heath and Heath (2008) stated, "By 'stick', we mean that your ideas are understood and remembered, and have a lasting impact—they change your audiences' opinions or behavior" (p. 8).

How does one change one's audiences' opinions or behavior? Heath and Heath (2008) offered the following advice:

For an idea to stick, for it to be useful and lasting, it's got to make the audience:

1. Pay attention
2. Understand and remember it
3. Agree/believe
4. Care
5. Be able to act on it (p. 246).

To capture the audience's attention and make the program concept stick, we need to identify and share the single most important idea, the core of the message, that we want them to grasp and understand about the importance of the program concept for guidance and counseling. Next, we need to provide understandable and memorable concrete examples about why the program concept is needed to serve the needs of all students. The information shared about the importance of the program concept must be credible and touch the audience's emotions so that they care. Finally, we need to share ideas about how to act—how to participate fully in changing guidance and counseling from the traditional position–services model to a comprehensive guidance and counseling program (Heath & Heath, 2008).

According to Heath and Heath (2008), at least two barriers stand in the way of getting one's ideas to stick. The first barrier they called "the curse of knowledge." Sometimes, they suggested, we have too much knowledge, which leads us to translate that knowledge into language that has meaning to us. This causes us to talk as though we are the audiences. It leads us "to use language that is sweeping, high-level, and abstract" (p. 255), that has meaning to us but not to our audiences. To overcome the curse of knowledge, we need to translate our ideas into concrete language, often using stories that have meaning to audiences. We need to start where our audiences are, not where we are.

The second barrier that Heath and Heath (2008) described is the lack of common language. This is particularly true in work in guidance and counseling because its history has provided its audiences with multiple ways to describe and frame what school guidance and counseling is and what school counselors do. This has resulted in misunderstandings and confusion among its audiences about school guidance and counseling and school counselors. The comprehensive guidance and counseling program, now being implemented in schools across the country, removes this barrier because it provides all involved with common language to describe the framework and elements of the program as well as the roles and responsibilities of school counselors who work in the program.

Sample Timetable of Tasks Involved in the Change Process

Because modifying an existing school guidance and counseling program or planning and implementing a new program is complex and time consuming, it is important in the getting-organized phase of planning to understand the tasks involved in the change process fully from beginning to end as well as the amount of time that may be involved. To help you understand possible tasks and time, we have included a sample timetable of tasks, organized around the four phases of change suggested by Mitchell and Gysbers (1978): planning, designing, implementing, and evaluating. We added the fifth phase, enhancing.

The time periods and the tasks presented in this sample timetable are illustrative only. Some school districts move through the phases of change more quickly than others, whereas other districts enter at different phases depending on the nature and structure of their current program. Some tasks as presented may not fit some school districts; therefore, tasks may need to be added or subtracted depending on specific school district needs and resources.

Note that the sample timetable focuses on evaluation over a period of 5 years (a period of time chosen only for purposes of illustration). This continuing evaluation through the 4th, 5th, 6th, 7th, and 8th years allows sufficient time for program, personnel, and results data to be gathered and analyzed. The 9th and 10th years begin the program enhancement process, during which evaluation data are used to inform one about how to redesign the program. The sample timetable is designed to provide you with a clear picture, a road map, of what needs to be done during an example period of 10 years to fully install, evaluate, and enhance a comprehensive guidance and counseling program. Use it as a checklist to create a timetable for your district to follow that meets your needs in the getting-organized phase of planning.

You will also note that in Year 1, the first two points of planning include building a foundation for change and getting organized to get there from where you are. You have seen these titles with their example tasks already, because they appear at the beginning of Chapters 1 and 2 as advance organizers for these chapters. All of the chapters that follow use this format.

Year 1

Planning—Building a Foundation for Change
- Study the history of guidance and counseling in the schools.
- Learn about the people, events, and societal conditions that helped shape guidance and counseling in the schools.
- Understand the implications of the shift from position to services to program in the conceptualization and organization of guidance and counseling.

Planning—Getting Organized to Get There From Where You Are
- Decide that you want to change.
- Understand the necessary conditions for effective change.
- Expect resistance to change.
- Develop trust among counselors, teachers, and administrators.
- Form committees and work groups.
- Meet with the administration or district board of education.
- Provide leadership for change.
- Be active.

Planning—Conceptualizing the Comprehensive Guidance and Counseling Program Model
- Understand the theoretical foundation of the program.
- Learn about a perspective of student development.
- Learn about the place of comprehensive guidance and counseling programs in the educational enterprise.
- Learn about the four comprehensive guidance and counseling program elements that constitute a comprehensive program.
- Understand the power of common language.

- Understand the importance of the program concept.
- Appreciate the flexibility and adaptability of a program.
- Learn about six program imperatives.

Years 1–2

Planning—Conducting a Thorough Assessment of the Current Program
- Gather student and community status information.
- Identify current resource availability and use.
- Study current guidance and counseling program delivery.
- Gather perceptions about the program.
- Present a report describing the current program.

Years 2–3

Designing—Adapting the Guidance and Counseling Program Model
- Define the basic structure of your program.
- Identify and list student competencies by content areas and school levels or grade groupings.
- Reaffirm policy support.
- Establish priorities for program delivery (qualitative design).
- Establish parameters for resource allocation (quantitative design).
- Write down and distribute the description of the desired program.

Designing—Planning the Transition
- Specify changes needed to implement a comprehensive guidance and counseling program districtwide.
- Develop a plan for accomplishing districtwide program improvement.
- Begin building-level program improvement efforts.
- Expand the leadership base.

Years 3–4

Implementing—Making the Transition
- Develop the personnel, financial, and political resources needed for full program implementation.
- Focus on special projects.
- Facilitate building-level changes.
- Implement public relations activities.

Years 4–5 (and Thereafter)

Implementing—Managing the New Program
- Improve program activities.
- Enhance the role of the professional school counselor.
- Develop the building program plan.
- Monitor program implementation.

Implementing—Ensuring School Counselor Competency
- Implement a counselor performance improvement system.
- Support professional development.
- Address incompetence.
- Bring new counselors into the program and to the proper roles.
- Clarify roles of building guidance and counseling program staff leaders.

Years 4–8

Evaluating—Evaluating the Program, Its Personnel, and Its Results
- Evaluate school counselor performance.
- Conduct program evaluation.
- Conduct results evaluation.
- Evaluate guidance and counseling interventions.

Years 9–10

Enhancing—Redesigning Your Comprehensive Guidance and Counseling Program
- Commit to the redesign process.
- Begin the redesign process.
- Make redesign decisions on the basis of needs and evaluation data.
- Implement the new design.
- Understand that revitalization follows redesign.

Expect Resistance to Change

What Is Resistance to Change?

Connor et al. (2003) defined resistance to change as "any attempt to maintain the status quo when there is pressure for change" (p. 151). According to Connor et al., some people resist by refusing to move. Others become spectators, sitting on the sidelines criticizing but not participating. Some may even try to keep others from participating in change.

Expressing Resistance to Change

Given the preceding definition of resistance, what kind of resistance have school counselors and administrators exhibited when faced with change from their current organizational structure for guidance and counseling to that of a comprehensive program? Goodloe (1990) described the following expressions of resistance:

> *Reluctance to change:* Principals were used to a guidance service model that focused on student scheduling. Older counselors near retirement had a built-in bias for the tried and true of the "old time" service delivery model. Since many of these educators steadfastly denied that the old guidance services were "broken," they flatly refused to even consider listening to the "fixing organizers" of the CGCP [Comprehensive Guidance and Counseling Program].
>
> *Double duty:* Despite the convincing logic demonstrating the need for a new and improved organized guidance program, counselors were paralyzed by the administrators' conflicting message: "Okay, establish the new program, but continue to maintain your present list of duty assignments." Schools failed to "streamline and displace" nonguidance functions to other paraprofessionals or clerical staff. "Add-ons" continually threatened the program's successful implementation.
>
> *Time and stress management:* As the message of change worked its way through the system's tightly connected communications grapevine, and news came out that the new program demanded a greater time commitment and contributed to more job stress, the pilot expansion schools became more and more skeptical and resistant. The sentiment was, "Why trade a new model when the old one works fine?"

Killer statement: If given the chance to solidify, resistance to change blocked the road to innovation. Statements such as "Ain't it awful!" "If only. . . ." "We've tried that!" "Yes, but . . . ." "THEM vs. US" "Let's wait until. . . ." had a debilitating effect on the will and energy to change. (pp. 72–73)

Appreciate the Challenges Involved

Behind these statements may lie fears of those faced with change. This human condition of some members of the school counseling and administrative staff must be understood. The failure of some staff members to embrace a program approach can be appreciated if their original justification for existence and their current functions and operational patterns are understood. Many school counselors, for example, maintain they are trapped and can react only minimally to change; they are the victims of school rigidity and bureaucracy that place them in quasi-administrative and services functions that impede them from achieving guidance objectives (Aubrey, 1973).

It is easy to label those who resist as troublemakers and to dismiss resistance as negative and malicious acts. Connor et al. (2003) pointed out, however, that "a more constructive, and in the long run more effective, approach is to acknowledge the validity of the class of responses as a whole and respond from a position of understanding and respect" (p. 151). We need to appreciate the challenges involved in developing, implementing, and evaluating a comprehensive guidance and counseling program, and thus understand why some school counselors and administrators might resist.

The failure of some school counselors and administrators to readily embrace a comprehensive program approach to guidance and counseling can be better understood if the challenges of this approach to organizing guidance and counseling are known. Here are a few examples of these challenges:

- Guidance and counseling programs are developmental.
- Guidance and counseling programs serve all students and their parents.
- Guidance and counseling programs require school counselors to do large-group presentations, small-group counseling, individual student planning activities, consultation, and referral.
- Guidance and counseling programs facilitate students' academic, career, and personal–social development.
- Guidance and counseling program activities are aimed at explicitly stated expectations for student results.
- Guidance and counseling programs are intentionally delivered and are accountable.

Why do some school counselors and administrators consider these statements as challenges? They are challenges because they may require school staff to change their work behavior. They may also require some counselors to acquire new skills to fulfill the responsibilities of new guidance program emphases. In addition, some counselors may fear the potential loss of status and power they enjoy from being associated with the authority of the principal. New relationships with teachers and students required by the program may make some counselors uncomfortable. New demands and the need to develop new counselor competencies threaten others. The most difficult challenge most counselors face, however, may be the prospect of accepting responsibility for helping students achieve success in school. Can counselors working in a comprehensive program deliver what they propose? Can they be accountable?

Another challenge counselors face in considering change is balancing the costs involved (the personal and professional time involved, the changes in day-to-day work behavior) with the benefits to be gained. Will the benefits outweigh the costs involved in working through the transition? One school district (Davis, 2002) faced this challenge and found that the hard work involved/paid off in the following ways:

> The comprehensive guidance model provided the immediate structure to establish the program in every school. Administrators received comprehensive guidance training. A few had to be converted to a model that allocated considerable time for class curriculum. They thought a counseling program should be limited to individual and small-group counseling for identified students. Soon after the program began, principals and teachers observed positive behavior changes as students began applying the skills the counselors were teaching. They acknowledged the value of everyone receiving the curriculum. Skills were reinforced throughout the school. Siblings, friends, and school personnel reminded one another to apply the skills the counselor had taught. Data collected in each school gave evidence that violations of school rules and negative behavior were decreasing. Other districts using the curriculum also reported positive behavior changes. (p. 225)

Develop Trust Among Counselors, Teachers, and Administrators

Because of people's tendency to resist change and because of the challenges and risks involved in making the transition to a comprehensive guidance and counseling program, guidance staff may require time and privacy as they deal with the issues involved. Time and privacy are necessary to work through possible resistance to change that may not otherwise emerge and to develop trust and working relationships as a total staff. This is true particularly for school districts with personnel at the elementary, junior high or middle school, and high school levels. Current duties at these levels often do not provide time for full-staff discussions about program direction and focus. Thus, having time and privacy for open dialogue, confrontation, and the processing of attitudes and feelings during the planning process is a necessity.

Staff trust can be developed and nurtured through the full involvement of staff in the change process. In the earlier section, Decide That You Want to Change, an example was given about how the guidance staff of one school district met several times as a full staff to assess the need for change. One result of these discussions was the decision to change; to take charge of their own destiny (Hargens & Fuston, 1997). Another result, just as important, was the full involvement of the staff in the change process.

Having staff involved in the initial decision to make changes and then in the steps involved in the transition process can help bring about staff trust and commitment; everyone is in this together. It is also important that staff members realize that their advice and counsel will be put to legitimate use. Going through the frustrations and joys of making the transition to a comprehensive program can bond staff into a full-fledged guidance and counseling team. As Maliszewski (1997) remarked, a person

> can't steal second with one foot on first. . . . Change implies risk taking and hard work. . . . Personal and professional growth are rewards for counselors who develop and implement "risk taking" approaches to ensure that guidance programs produce positive results for all students. (p. 217)

Form Committees and Work Groups

Once consensus to change has been reached, the next step is to form committees and work groups to accomplish the tasks involved. Only two committees are recommended throughout the entire process: a steering committee and a school–community advisory committee. The majority of improvement tasks can be handled by forming work groups. It is desirable that the superintendent of schools or the designee of the superintendent formally appoint the members of both committees.

Steering Committee

The steering committee should be large enough to reflect a cross-section of the ideas and interests of the staff but not so large as to be unwieldy and inefficient. Ordinarily, the steering committee is composed of guidance personnel or representatives from each grade level or building involved. Building administrators and the superintendent or a member of the cabinet are essential members, as are such individuals as the directors of vocational education and special education. Sometimes teachers, parents, school board members, or students may also serve. The chairperson of the steering committee is the guidance and counseling program leader. If no such title exists, then the person who is administratively responsible for the guidance and counseling program should be chairperson.

The steering committee is responsible for managing the efforts needed to plan, design, implement, evaluate, and enhance the district's guidance and counseling program. This committee is a decision-making body and is responsible for outlining the tasks involved and making certain that the resources needed to carry out these tasks are available. It monitors the activities of the work groups and coordinates their tasks. The steering committee not only makes process-change decisions but also program-change decisions.

To carry out these responsibilities, one of the first tasks for the steering committee is to prepare a timetable of the steps it has chosen to take. Because it is the master timetable for program change, it requires careful thought and attention. Allow sufficient planning time for this phase of getting organized. Keep in mind that the timetable will probably be modified as the program improvement process unfolds. The master timetable is important because it provides those involved with an overview of the scope and sequence of the improvement process. It also shows the relationship of the steps and activities. Potential problems can be identified and therefore anticipated and dealt with in advance. Moreover, the master timetable provides those involved with an indication of the resources and materials required.

As your local timetable for tasks is being developed, consider the sample timetable for program installation presented in the first part of this chapter. This book is organized on the basis of this sample timetable so it can provide advice and counsel every step of the way and serve as a beginning point and as a checklist for all program planning, designing, implementing, evaluating, and enhancing processes.

In addition to being responsible for the steps, resources, and strategies needed to make the transition to a comprehensive program, the steering committee is responsible for developing a plan for public relations through advocacy. This development may be done later in the program improvement process, but whenever it is done, careful planning is required. Effective public relations do not just happen, nor can they be separated from the basic comprehensive program. In fact, the best public relations begin with a sound, comprehensive guidance and counseling program. The best public relations in the world cannot cover up an ineffective guidance and counseling program that does not meet the needs of its consumers.

School–Community Advisory Committee

The school–community advisory committee is composed of representatives from the school and community. The membership of this committee will vary according to the size of the school district and the community and can include such individuals as an administrator (assistant superintendent, principal); the guidance program leader; a representative of the teaching staff; a representative of the student body; representatives from business, industry, and labor; a representative from the mental health community; a representative from the parent–teacher association; and a newspaper editor or other media representative. If any of these individuals are serving on the steering committee (with the exception of the guidance program leader), they should probably not serve here.

The school–community advisory committee acts as a liaison between the school and community and provides recommendations concerning the needs of students and the community. A primary duty of the committee is to advise those involved in the guidance program improvement effort. The committee is not a policy- or decision-making body; rather, it is a source of advice, counsel, and support. It is a communication link between those involved in the guidance program improvement effort and the school and community. The committee meets throughout the transition period and continues as a permanent part of the improved guidance program. A community person should be chairperson. The use and involvement of a school–community advisory committee will vary according to the program and the community, but in all cases membership must be more than in name only. Community involvement and interaction are important, and advisory committee members can be particularly helpful in developing and implementing the public relations plans for the community.

Work Groups

To accomplish the work involved in making the transition to a comprehensive guidance and counseling program, we recommend the use of work groups. Work groups are small groups of staff members, usually counselors, but sometimes also include administrators, teachers, parents, and students who are assigned specific tasks that need to be completed as part of the transition process. Assignments to work groups will vary depending on the tasks involved. Work groups form and disband as needed.

Here are some suggestions concerning work groups:

1. Use as many work groups as possible because they reduce the overall workload and provide opportunities for as many people as possible to become involved and learn about remodeling and revitalizing the guidance and counseling program. Remember: Never use one person when two will do.
2. Some work groups should include counselors only; some should include administrators or others. Specific suggestions about work group membership are provided in subsequent chapters.
3. Work groups are responsible to the steering committee. Work group leadership is drawn from the steering committee. In fact, in the first phases of the improvement process, the steering committee's agenda will consist of work group reports.
4. Charges to work groups need to be specific and feasible. Each group exists for one purpose; when the purpose is accomplished, the work group disbands.
5. Work group membership should include cross-grade–level representation when appropriate. This enhances trust and builds knowledge among the members that will provide a foundation for the comprehensive guidance and counseling program.

Meet With the Administration and District Board of Education

Because the development and installation of a comprehensive guidance and counseling program is a school district issue as well as a building issue, the district's administration and board of education must be brought into the planning process at the very beginning. Early on, it is important for the steering committee, working closely with the superintendent, to meet with the board and inform its members about the need for the shift from the position–service model to a comprehensive program to meet the needs of students, parents, teachers, and the community more effectively. The goal of the initial meeting is to inform the board, gain its support, and secure its authorization to work toward improving the guidance and counseling program in the district.

At the initial meeting, sharing with the board the following National School Boards Association (2010) statement may be useful: "NSBA believes that every school district should consider having a comprehensive guidance and counseling program kindergarten through grade 12, staffed by professionally trained counseling personnel" (p. 20).

At the initial meeting, it is also important to obtain in writing from the board assurances concerning its authorization of the improvement process. The assurances requested by the steering committee could include those listed by the State of Missouri:

- Authorizes the administration to provide professional school counselors with the time and resources to develop and implement a comprehensive guidance program under the leadership of the steering committee.
- Receives periodic reports from the steering committee.
- Approves the program as an official program of the school district and adopts a policy that mandates the program.
- Works with the steering committee and administration to fully implement the program once it is approved.
- Works with the advisory council and school staff to publicize the program to the community.
- Provides sufficient funding to ensure continued program development, implementation, and evaluation through the program enhancement process. (Gysbers, Stanley, Kosteck-Bunch, Magnuson, & Starr, 2008, pp. 24–25)

Provide Leadership for Change

If you are the school district's guidance and counseling program leader, you will have the primary responsibility for organizing and managing the program improvement process. If you do not take the primary leadership role for these efforts, they will not get done. You must cause, lead, implement, and maintain the work accomplished during this important time of change in your school district. You are the manager of the improvement process as well as of the program.

As the manager of the improvement process, you must develop and monitor the plan for change. Specifically, you must develop the proposal to change and the time frame in which you anticipate change will take. You must form the steering committee, chair it, and plan its agendas and meeting schedule. You must also form, or cause to form, the school–community advisory committee and the various work groups as needed. You should attend as many meetings of the work groups as feasible to keep them on task, and you must attend all steering and school–community advisory committee meetings. They are, after all, steering and advising the program for which you are accountable.

[As the program leader, you not only continue your usual duties but also add the responsibilities of being the primary missionary for the improved program.] You must be very clear about the model you and your district want to adopt or adapt. The success of this project is directly linked to your conceptualization of the guidance and counseling program. For a while, you may be the only person who may grasp the new design, the student competencies, the comprehensive nature of the program, and the means for redirecting the activities of the guidance staff.]

As the school district's guidance program leader, you have responsibility not only for improving and managing the program but also for assisting the staff involved. As explained in *Leading and Managing Your School Guidance Program Staff* (Henderson & Gysbers, 1998), we use the "generic title, 'guidance program staff leader,' to connote the interconnectedness of program and staff leadership responsibilities" (p. 21). At this point, the focus is on your staff leader responsibilities. You develop mechanisms for educating and involving counselors and administrators. You bring all of the members of the steering committee along as the process unfolds. [Ultimately, the counselors on the steering committee provide peer leadership to their colleagues, under your direction]

You need to keep the purposes for changing the program in front of everyone for the duration of the change process.] Remember that you are doing all this to better facilitate students' academic career and personal–social development and parent involvement by means of more appropriate use of school counselors' unique talents and skills. We advise you to develop a support system for yourself. This system might include committed school counselors in the district, your own supervisor or supervisors who are eager for the change to come, and guidance and counseling program leaders from other districts who have embarked on similar projects. [Involvement in state and national associations for school counselors and counselor educators provides useful assistance and affiliation as well.]

Be Active

Make a Commitment to Action

It is important to remember that many systems grind along with much polarization; even some school counselors compose their worlds of grim problems to be worked through. You may be flooded with the destructive aspects of situations. You may find that some individuals with whom you work are impressed with the weaknesses of others and stereotype them with all the incompetencies they can uncover. Although you cannot ignore destructive forces, the positive prescription is to be alert for the constructive forces that are sometimes masked and suppressed in a problem-oriented system.

Some people have as great an innate capacity for joy as they have for resentment, but resentment causes them to overlook opportunities for joy. People who are locked into destructive situations often focus on their differences. [As a leader, your job is to help them discover and build on their commonalities.] [Unhappy people tend to emphasize past wrongs, and as a result, use them to destroy the present and future.] As a leader, your task is to help change the present so that there will be a new past on which to create the future (Shepard, 1974). Make a commitment to action!

Be Optimistic

The tasks in making the transition from an undefined program to a defined program are complex and difficult. They require time and perseverance. Although the time required may seem long, it does provide the opportunity for counselors (and everyone else) to learn how to master the new program. Thus, the getting-organized phase of planning should be designed to assist those involved to develop a vision of what the comprehensive program will look like and to become committed to working to make it happen. Our belief is that staff development enables people to have vision and involvement and raises their level of commitment. Staff development begins during the getting-organized phase and must be carried out throughout the entire program improvement and revitalizing process. Be optimistic!

Your Progress Check

Getting organized to get there from where you are is a major step in the overall planning phase. If you have followed the recommendations in Chapter 2, you have

- decided that your school district needs to remodel and revitalize its guidance and counseling program;
- identified the necessary conditions for effective change in your district;
- established a timetable outlining when and how your district's guidance and counseling program will be remodeled and revitalized;
- identified possible resistance to change and how to respond to such resistance;
- begun the process of developing trust among teachers, administrators, and counselors;
- formed your district's steering committee and school–community advisory committee;
- established a time to meet with your administration and board of education;
- committed to be active and involved in the remodeling and revitalization of your district's guidance and counseling program.

References

Aubrey, R. F. (1973). Organizational victimization of school counselors. *The School Counselor, 20,* 346–354.

Connor, P. E., Lake, L. K., & Stackman, R. W. (2003). *Managing organizational change* (3rd ed.) Westport, CT: Praeger.

Davis, D. (2002). Revising and enhancing the Davis School District comprehensive guidance program. In P. Henderson & N. C. Gysbers (Eds.), *Implementing comprehensive school guidance programs: Critical leadership issues and successful responses* (pp. 219–228). Greensboro, NC: CAPS.

Erickson, T. (1997). Box Elder comprehensive guidance program. In N. C. Gysbers & P. Henderson (Eds.), *Comprehensive guidance programs that work—II* (pp. 125–137). Greensboro, NC: ERIC Counseling and Student Services Clearinghouse.

Goodloe, J. P. (1990). Comprehensive guidance in Montgomery County, Maryland. In N. C. Gysbers (Ed.), *Comprehensive guidance programs that work* (pp. 63–78). Ann Arbor, MI: ERIC Counseling and Personnel Service Clearinghouse.

Gysbers, N. C., Stanley, J. B., Kosteck-Bunch, L., Magnuson, C. S., & Starr, M. F. (2008). *Missouri comprehensive guidance program: A manual for program development, implementation, evaluation and enhancement.* Warrensburg: Missouri Center for Career Education.

Hargens, M., & Fuston, J. K. (1997). Comprehensive guidance program of the St. Joseph district. In N. C. Gysbers & P. Henderson (Eds.), *Comprehensive guidance programs that work—II* (pp. 61–74). Greensboro, NC: ERIC Counseling and Student Services Clearinghouse.

Heath, C., & Heath, D. (2008). *Made to stick: Why some ideas survive and others die.* New York, NY: Random House.

Henderson, P., & Gysbers, N. C. (1998). *Leading and managing your school guidance program staff.* Alexandria, VA: American Counseling Association.

Jensen, L., & Petersen, J. (1997). The comprehensive guidance program in Utah. In N. C. Gysbers & P. Henderson (Eds.), *Comprehensive guidance programs that work—II* (pp. 89–106). Greensboro, NC: ERIC Counseling and Student Services Clearinghouse.

Joyce Ivy Foundation. (2008). *2008 Michigan high school counselor report—The eleven-month challenge: 22 recommendations for improving the transition from high school to college.* Ann Arbor, MI: Author.

Joyce Ivy Foundation. (2009). *2009 Ohio high school counselor report—Converting high school achievement into adult opportunity: The school counselor role and beyond.* Ann Arbor, MI: Author.

Maliszewski, S. J. (1997). Developing a comprehensive guidance system in the Omaha Public Schools. In N. C. Gysbers & P. Henderson (Eds.), *Comprehensive guidance programs that work—II* (pp. 195–219). Greensboro, NC: ERIC Counseling and Student Services Clearinghouse.

Martin, I., Carey, J., & DeCoster, K. (2009). A national study of the current status of state school counseling models. *Professional School Counseling, 12,* 378–386.

Mitchell, A. M., & Gysbers, N. C. (1978). Comprehensive school guidance and counseling programs. In *The status of guidance and counseling in the nation's schools* (pp. 23–39). Washington, DC: American Personnel and Guidance Association.

National School Boards Association (2010). *Beliefs and policies of the National School Boards Association.* Alexandria, VA: Author.

Shepard, H. (1974). *Rules of thumb for change agents.* Unpublished manuscript.

Rylander, C. K. (2002). *Guiding our children toward success: How Texas school counselors spend their time.* Austin: Texas Comptroller of Public Accounts.

Vandegrift, J. A. (1999). *Are Arizona public schools making the best use of school counselors? Results of a 3-year study of counselors' time use.* Phoenix, AZ: Morrison Institute for Public Policy.

Waters, T., Marzano, R. J., & McNulty, B. (2003). *Balanced leadership: What 30 years of research tells us about the effect of leadership on student achievement.* Aurora, CO: Mid-Continent Research for Education and Learning.

A Comprehensive Guidance and Counseling Program: Theoretical Foundations and Organizational Structure

Planning—Conceptualizing the Comprehensive Guidance and Counseling Program

- Understand the theoretical foundation of the program.
- Learn about a perspective of student development.
- Learn about the place of comprehensive guidance and counseling programs in the educational enterprise.
- Learn about the four comprehensive guidance and counseling program elements that constitute a comprehensive program.
- Understand the power of common language.
- Understand the importance of the program concept.
- Appreciate the flexibility and adaptability of a program.
- Learn about six program imperatives.

≈ The second phase of planning consists of conceptualizing the comprehensive guidance and counseling program, of bringing together all of the necessary and appropriate guidance and counseling interventions, and of arranging them into a program configuration. To accomplish this task, it is first necessary to have a firm understanding of the theoretical foundation of the program as well as a perspective on student development. It is also necessary to understand the place such a program has in the overall educational enterprise from kindergarten through 12th grade.

To assist you in the conceptualization process, we begin this chapter by presenting a theoretical foundation for comprehensive guidance and counseling programs (Henderson, 2005) and a perspective on student development called *life career development* (Gysbers, Heppner, & Johnston, 2009; Gysbers & Moore, 1975, 1981; McDaniels & Gysbers, 1992). Next, we present the two major education systems: the instruction program and the guidance and counseling program. Then we describe the four program elements of a comprehensive guidance and counseling program, including (a) content, (b) organizational framework, (c) resources, and (d) development, management, and accountability. The chapter closes with a discussion of the power of common language, the importance of the program concept, the flexibility and adaptability of a program, and six program imperatives.

Understand the Theoretical Foundation of the Program

According to *Random House Webster's Unabridged Dictionary* (2001), a theory "is a more or less verified or established explanation accounting for known facts or phenomena" (p. 1968). It is "a coherent group of general propositions used as principles of explanation for a class of phenomena" (p. 1967). In keeping with this definition of theory, Henderson (2005) presented a brief history of school counseling theory, identified seven fundamental questions to be answered by theory, and then described 27 major principles that provide answers to the seven fundamental questions. These 27 principles become the "principles of explanation for a class of phenomena" (p. 1967), in this case, comprehensive guidance and counseling programs from kindergarten through 12th grade, and are presented here:

Principle 1: As with other dimensions of their development, all children and adolescents benefit from assistance in accomplishing the age-appropriate tasks related to their academic, career, and personal–social development.

Principle 2: All children and adolescents can benefit from interventions designed to assist their academic, career, and personal–social development.

Principle 3: Some children and adolescents need more assistance in accomplishing the age-appropriate academic, career, and personal–social developmental tasks. These children and adolescents benefit from preventative or remedial interventions specially designed to assist them in achieving tasks appropriate to their developmental level.

Principle 4: School counselors are qualified to make contributions to all of children's and adolescents' development in the areas of academic (educational), career, and personal–social development.

Principle 5: School counselors can design and deliver interventions to meet students' developmental needs and design and deliver interventions to meet students' needs for prevention and remediation, thereby helping to close gaps between specific groups of students and their peers.

Principle 6: School counselors' interventions in students' academic, career, and personal–social development assist students to acquire and apply skills, attitudes, and knowledge that promote development in those three dimension of human growth and development.

Principle 7: School counselors can assist other adults to enhance their work with students' academic–educational, career, and personal–social development and to remove personal barriers to individual students' success.

Principle 8: School counselors work with others in the school system on behalf of students to support accomplishment of the system's mission and to assist in the removal of systemic barriers to student success.

Principle 9: The work of school counselors should be organized as a program.

Principle 10: The delivery system dividing program activities into the four program components of guidance curricula, individual student planning, responsive services, and system support is the most effective and efficient means for organizing the program.

Principle 11: The four program activity components described as the delivery system for the model school guidance and counseling program include all the means to affect students' academic, career, and personal–social development: guidance curricula, individual student planning, responsive services, and system support.

Principle 12: School guidance and counseling program activities can be designed that effectively have an impact on all students' academic, career, and personal–social development and that help those students whose healthy academic, career, and personal–social development is threatened or interrupted.

Principle 13: Intentionally designed interventions targeting identified needs or specified goals and objectives are more effective than interventions that are not intentionally designed.

Principle 14: A systematic approach to developing the school guidance and counseling program (i.e., planning and building the foundation, designing the delivery system, implementing and monitoring the program, holding program staff accountable, and evaluating the program) ensures its effectiveness and relevancy.

Principle 15: Collaborative, cooperative planning with parents or guardians, teachers, administrators, staff, and community members in developing a school guidance and counseling program results in the program being effective and an integral part of the total school mission.

Principle 16: Effective local school guidance and counseling programs are designed with awareness of local demographics and political conditions and on the basis of needs assessments based on locally gathered data.

Principle 17: Establishing priorities for and recognizing parameters within the program are critical to effective management and implementation of school guidance and counseling programs.

Principle 18: There are organizational procedures that school counselors can use to manage implementation of their programs for effectiveness, efficiency, and relevancy to the school.

Principle 19: Accountability for student results, school counselor performance, and program completeness is essential to ensuring the effectiveness and relevance of school guidance and counseling programs, and it requires the collection and use of data.

Principle 20: Leadership for school guidance and counseling programs is a responsibility shared between school counselors and school principals.

Principle 21: Having benefited from school counselors' interventions, children and adolescents are more ready to learn academically and to be successful in school.

Principle 22: Explicit statements of the results desired for students better ensure their achievement of those results.

Principle 23: Evaluation of student results, school counselor performance, and program completeness is essential to ensuring the effectiveness and relevance of school guidance and counseling programs, and it requires the collection and use of data.

Principle 24: Evaluation of student results is based on established standards for the measurement of student development, growth, and change.

Principle 25: Evaluation of school counselors' performance is based on established standards for school counseling practice.

Principle 26: Evaluation of program completeness is based on alignment with established models of comprehensive guidance and counseling programs and local program designs.

Principle 27: The purpose of evaluation is improvement.

Individually, each principle describes a determining characteristic of a comprehensive guidance and counseling program. Taken together, they constitute the guiding principles that characterize and operationalize the total program. When viewed holistically, they represent the principles for guiding the overall planning, design, implementation, evaluation, and enhancement of the program.

Learn About a Perspective of Student Development

Life Career Development

Life career development is defined as self-development over the life span through the integration of the roles, settings, and events in a person's life. The word *life* indicates that the focus of this conception of human growth and development is the total person—the human career. The word *career* identifies and relates the many and often varied roles that individuals have (student, worker, consumer, citizen, parent), the settings in which individuals find themselves (home, school, community), and the events that occur over their lifetimes (entry job, marriage, divorce, retirement). The word *development* indicates that individuals are always in the process of becoming. When used in sequence, the words *life career development* bring these separate meanings together, but at the same time a greater meaning evolves. Life career development describes total individuals, each of whom is unique and has his or her own lifestyle.

Added to the basic configuration of life career development are the influencing factors of gender, ethnic origin, spirituality, race, sexual orientation, and socioeconomic status. All of these factors play important roles in shaping the life roles, life settings, and life events of all ages and circumstances over the life span. These factors are important to the conception of life career development because we live in a nation that is part of a world economy; it is increasingly diverse racially, religiously, and ethnically and yet has common themes that connect us all. The United States continues to change its views on what it means to be female or male, educationally and occupationally. Socioeconomic status continues to play an important role in shaping an individual's socialization and current and future status (Gysbers et al., 2009).

Career Consciousness

A major goal in using the theoretical perspective of life career development is to assist individuals to identify, describe, and understand the dynamics of their own life career development, to create within them career consciousness, that is, the ability to visualize and plan their life careers. "Included within the idea of consciousness is a person's background, education, politics, insight, values, emotions, and philosophy" (Reich, 1971, p. 15). But consciousness, according to Reich (1971), is more than this. It is the whole person. It is the person's way of creating his or her own life. Thus, the challenge is to assist individuals to become career conscious. The challenge is to assist them to project themselves into future possible life roles, life settings, and life events; to realize the importance of gender, ethnic origin, spirituality, race, sexual orientation, and socioeconomic status to their development; and then to relate their projections to their present situations for consideration and incorporation into their plans to achieve their goals or resolve their problems. Contained in the concept of career consciousness is the notion of *possible selves*. What are possible selves? According to Markus and Nurius (1986), "Possible selves represent individuals' ideas of what they might become, what they would like to become, and what they are afraid of becoming, and thus provide a conceptual link between cognition and motivation" (p. 954). Why are possible selves important? "Possible selves are important, first, because they function as incentives for future behavior (i.e., they are selves to be approached or avoided) and, second, because they provide an evaluative and interpretive context for the current view of self" (p. 954).

In the definition of life career development, the word *career* has a substantially different meaning than in some other definitions. Here it focuses on all aspects of life, not as separate entities but as interrelated parts of the whole person. The term *career*, when viewed from this broad perspective, is not a new word for *occupation*. People have careers; the work world or marketplace has occupations. Unfortunately, too many people use the word *career* when they should use the word *occupation*. Moreover, the term *career* is not restricted to some people. All people have a career; their life is their career. Thus, the words *life career development* do not delineate and describe only one part of human growth and development. Although it is useful to focus at times on different aspects of development—physical, emotional, and intellectual—there is also a need to integrate these aspects of development. Life career development is advocated as an organizing and integrating concept for understanding and facilitating human growth and development.

Wolfe and Kolb (1980) summed up the life view of career development as follows:

> Career development involves one's whole life, not just occupation. As such, it concerns the whole person, needs and wants, capacities and potentials, excitements and anxieties, insights and blindspots, warts and all. More than that, it concerns him/her in the ever-changing contexts of his/her life. The environmental pressures and constraints, the bonds that tie him/her to significant others, responsibilities to children and aging parents, the total structure of one's circumstances are also factors that must be understood and reckoned with. In these terms, career development and personal development converge. Self and circumstance—evolving, changing, unfolding in mutual interaction—constitute the focus and the drama of career development. (pp. 1–2)

Goals of a Program From a Life Career Development Perspective

One goal of a comprehensive school guidance and counseling program founded on the concept of life career development is to assist students to acquire competencies to handle the here-and-now issues that affect their growth and development. These issues may include changes in the family structure, expanded social relationships, substance abuse, sexual experimentation, changes in physical and emotional maturation, and peer pressure. Another goal is to create career consciousness in students to assist them to project themselves into possible future life roles, settings, and events; analyze them; relate their findings to their present identity and situations; and make informed personal, education, and career choices on the basis of their findings.

Learn About the Place of Comprehensive Guidance and Counseling Programs in the Educational Enterprise

Over the decades of the past century, discussions have centered on the proper place of guidance and counseling in education. Early on, writers stressed the point of view that guidance and counseling are an integral part of education, not something "being wished upon the schools by a group of enthusiasts because there was no other agency to handle it" (Myers, 1923, p. 139). Some writers, particularly Jones and Hand (1938), viewed guidance and counseling as an inseparable part of education. They emphasized that teaching involved both guidance and instruction.

What is the proper place of guidance and counseling? We support the position that guidance and counseling are an integral part of education. We envision education as having <u>two interrelated systems</u>, namely, the <u>instruction program</u> and the <u>guidance and counseling program</u>, as noted in Figure 3.1. The instruction program typically includes such disciplines as fine arts, career and technical education, science, physical education, mathematics, social studies, foreign language, and English (language arts). Each of these disciplines has standards that identify the knowledge and skills students are to learn as they progress throughout their school years. Similarly, comprehensive guidance and counseling programs have standards that identify the knowledge and skills students are to learn as they are involved in the activities and services of comprehensive programs. Typically, these knowledge and skills (standards) are grouped under titles such as academic, career, and personal–social development.

In a school setting, even though the instruction program is by far the largest in terms of numbers of student standards, it is not more important than the guidance and counseling program. That is why the circles in Figure 3.1, which depict the education systems, are equal

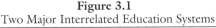

Figure 3.1
Two Major Interrelated Education Systems

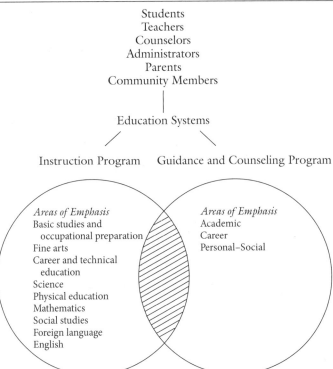

in size. Figure 3.1 also illustrates the fact that separate learnings in each system (unshaded areas) require specific attention. At the same time, these learnings overlap (shaded area), requiring that at times the instruction program supports the guidance and counseling program and that at other times the guidance and counseling program supports the instruction program. It is a case of not either–or but of both–and.

Learn About the Four Comprehensive Guidance and Counseling Program Elements That Constitute a Comprehensive Program

What is a comprehensive guidance and counseling program? We define a *program* as having a common language organizational framework with a specific configuration of planned, sequenced, and coordinated guidance and counseling activities and services based on student, school, and community needs and resources, designed to serve all students and their parents or guardians in a local school district. As the American School Counselor Association (ASCA; 2005) suggested, it is "comprehensive in scope, preventative in design, and developmental in nature" (p. 13).

The structure (see Figure 3.2) we recommend for a comprehensive guidance and counseling program has four elements: (a) program content; (b) organizational framework; (c) resources; and (d) development, management, and accountability. The content element identifies student competencies (cast as standards) considered important by a school district for students to master as a result of their participation in the district's comprehensive

Figure 3.2

Comprehensive Guidance and Counseling Program Elements

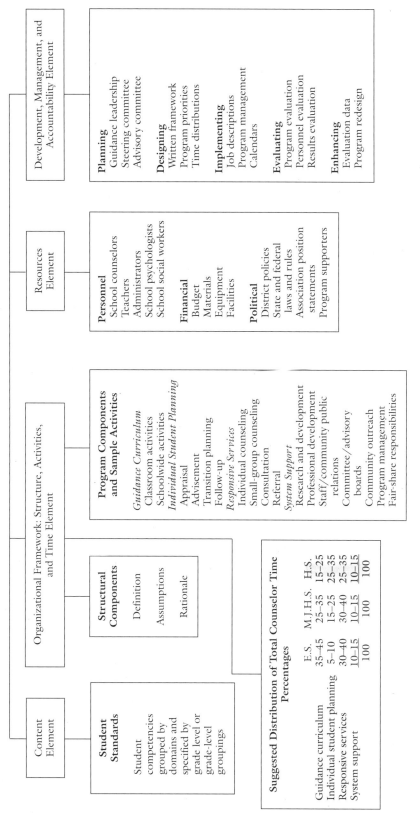

Content Element

Student Standards

Student competencies grouped by domains and specified by grade level or grade-level groupings

---

Organizational Framework: Structure, Activities, and Time Element

Structural Components

Definition

Assumptions

Rationale

Suggested Distribution of Total Counselor Time Percentages

	E.S.	M.J.H.S.	H.S.
Guidance curriculum	35–45	25–35	15–25
Individual student planning	5–10	15–25	25–35
Responsive services	30–40	30–40	25–35
System support	10–15	10–15	10–15
	100	100	100

Program Components and Sample Activities

Guidance Curriculum
Classroom activities
Schoolwide activities
Individual Student Planning
Appraisal
Advisement
Transition planning
Follow-up
Responsive Services
Individual counseling
Small-group counseling
Consultation
Referral
System Support
Research and development
Professional development
Staff/community public relations
Committee/advisory boards
Community outreach
Program management
Fair-share responsibilities

Resources Element

Personnel
School counselors
Teachers
Administrators
School psychologists
School social workers

Financial
Budget
Materials
Equipment
Facilities

Political
District policies
State and federal laws and rules
Association position statements
Program supporters

Development, Management, and Accountability Element

Planning
Guidance leadership
Steering committee
Advisory committee

Designing
Written framework
Program priorities
Time distributions

Implementing
Job descriptions
Program management
Calendars

Evaluating
Program evaluation
Personnel evaluation
Results evaluation

Enhancing
Evaluation data
Program redesign

Note. E.S. = elementary school; M.J.H.S. = middle–junior high school; H.S. = high school.

guidance and counseling program. The organizational framework element contains three structural components (definition, assumptions, rationale) and four program components (guidance curriculum, individual student planning, responsive services, system support), with examples of program activities and school counselor time distributions across the four program components. The resources element presents the human, financial, and policy resources required to fully implement the program. The fourth and final element contains the development, management, and accountability activities required to plan, design, implement, evaluate, and enhance the program.

These elements match the major systems of the *ASCA National Model: A Framework for School Counseling Programs* (2005):

ASCA's NATIONAL MODEL

Foundation
Content Standards
Beliefs, Philosophy, & Mission Statement

Delivery System
School Guidance Curriculum
Individual Student Planning
Responsive Services
System Support

Accountability
Results Reports
School Counselor Performance Standards
The Program Audit

Management System
Agreements
Advisory Council
Action Plans
Use of Time Calendars

COMPREHENSIVE GUIDANCE & COUNSELING PROGRAM MODEL

Content Element/Structural Component
Student Standards
Definition, Assumptions, & Rationale

Program Components
Guidance Curriculum
Individual Student Planning
Responsive Services
System Support

Development, Management, & Accountability Element
Planning
　Guidance Leadership
　Steering Committee
　Advisory Committee
Designing
　Written Framework
　Program Priorities
　Time Distributions
Implementing
　Job Descriptions
　Program Management
　Calendars
Evaluating
　Program Evaluation
　Personnel Evaluation
　Results Evaluation
Enhancing
　Evaluation Data
　Program Redesign

Resource Element
Personnel
Financial
Political

Element 1: Program Content

What knowledge should students acquire, what skills should students develop, and what attitudes should students form as a result of participating in the activities and services of a comprehensive guidance and counseling program? To answer this question for your school district, begin by reviewing the educational goals of your school district and your state. Such goals will often include guidance and counseling content focusing on such topics as academic achievement, career development, and personal–social development. Examine the professional literature and relevant professional association position statements. Make sure to review the multicultural and gender literature as well (Sink, 2002). Finally, review your state model or guide for comprehensive guidance and counseling programs as well as professional associations' lists of student standards such as those found in the ASCA National Model (ASCA, 2005) for ones that can be adopted or adapted for your local school district program. Many models or guides group standards under the domains of academic, career, and personal–social. These titles work well, but always consider state and local issues and circumstances when identifying the student standards that are right for your school district and the labels you will use to title the groupings of these standards.

In the following pages, you will find example lists of competencies or student standards, as they are often labeled, from ASCA, the State of Utah, and the State of Texas. Note the variation in how they are labeled and displayed. For the purposes of this chapter, we list only the broad student standards or competencies. In most guides, they are further sub divided by grade or grade-level groupings (sometimes labeled as grade-level expectations) so that a scope and sequence of expected student outcomes is provided. Remember, these are examples only. It is your job to select the program content for your local school guidance and counseling program that makes sense for your district.

Example: American School Counselor Association

ASCA (2005) recommended that guidance and counseling programs use three broad areas under which are student learnings stated as standards:

- *Academic Development Standards*
   1. Students will acquire the attitudes, knowledge, and skills that contribute to effective learning in school and across the life span.
   2. Students will complete school with the academic preparation essential to choose from a wide range of substantial postsecondary options, including college.
   3. Students will understand the relationship of academics to the world of work, and to life at home and in the community.
- *Career Development Standards*
   1. Students will acquire the skills to investigate the world of work in relation to knowledge of self and to make informed career decisions.
   2. Students will use strategies to achieve future career success and satisfaction.
   3. Students will understand the relationship between personal qualities, education and training, and the world of work.
- *Personal/Social Development Standards*
   1. Students will acquire the attitudes, knowledge, and interpersonal skills to help them understand and respect self and others.
   2. Students will make decisions, set goals, and take necessary action to achieve goals.
   3. Students will understand safety and survival skills. (pp. 102–107)

Example: State of Utah

The State of Utah's model for Comprehensive Counseling and Guidance: K–12 Programs (Utah State Office of Education, 2008) organizes program standards and competencies into four domains:

- *Academic/Learning Development*
  Standard A: Students will acquire the attitudes, knowledge, and skills that contribute to effective learning in school and across the lifespan.
  Standard B: Students will understand the relationship of school experiences and academic achievement to the world of work, home, and community.
  Standard C: Students will complete school with essential coursework that provides a wide range of substantial post-secondary options.
- *Life/Career Development*
  Standard A: Students will become aware of self in relation to the world of work.
  Standard B: Students will explore the world of work.
  Standard C: Students will use strategies to achieve future life/career goals.
- *Multicultural/Global Citizen Development*
  Standard A: Students will develop the ability to evaluate, and to approach life as a contributing citizen in our global community.
- *Personal/Social Development*
  Standard A: Students will develop the skills to understand and appreciate themselves and others.
  Standard B: Students will identify and utilize processes to set and achieve goals, make decisions, and solve problems.
  Standard C: Students will develop the resiliency skills necessary for safety and survival.
  (pp. 125–130)

Example: State of Texas

The State of Texas uses seven broad content domains, each having three skill levels and four human development dimensions, as shown in Figure 3.3. (Texas Education Agency, 2004, p. 53)

Element 2: Organizational Framework: Structural Components

Structural components are an important part of the organizational framework because they describe the nature of the program and provide a philosophical basis for it. The structural components define the program, state the rationale for the program, and list the assumptions on which the program is based. Examples of language for each of these components follow; remember they are examples only. It is your job to make sure that the contents of these components fit your school district.

Definition

A definition of the guidance and counseling program identifies the centrality of guidance and counseling within the educational process and delineates, in broad terms, the competencies students will possess as a result of their involvement in the program. Two examples of a definition of guidance and counseling follow. The first is the definition of guidance and counseling used by the state of Missouri, and the second is the definition from Northside Independent School District, San Antonio, Texas.

State of Missouri. The State of Missouri's definition of guidance and counseling is as follows:

Figure 3.3
Texas Skill Levels and Competency Domains

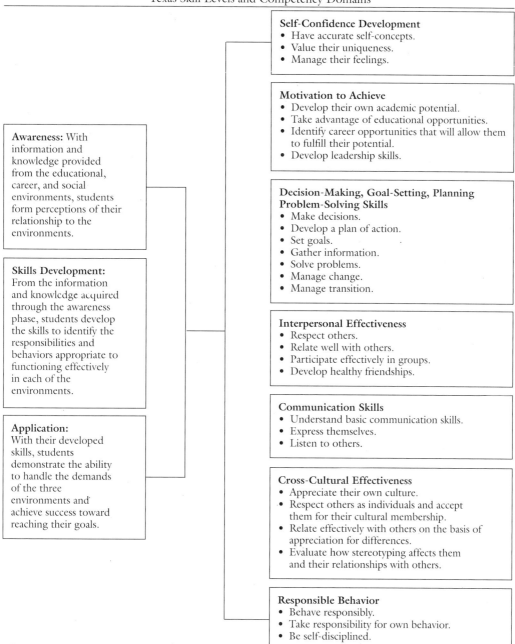

Awareness: With information and knowledge provided from the educational, career, and social environments, students form perceptions of their relationship to the environments.

Skills Development: From the information and knowledge acquired through the awareness phase, students develop the skills to identify the responsibilities and behaviors appropriate to functioning effectively in each of the environments.

Application: With their developed skills, students demonstrate the ability to handle the demands of the three environments and achieve success toward reaching their goals.

Self-Confidence Development
- Have accurate self-concepts.
- Value their uniqueness.
- Manage their feelings.

Motivation to Achieve
- Develop their own academic potential.
- Take advantage of educational opportunities.
- Identify career opportunities that will allow them to fulfill their potential.
- Develop leadership skills.

Decision-Making, Goal-Setting, Planning Problem-Solving Skills
- Make decisions.
- Develop a plan of action.
- Set goals.
- Gather information.
- Solve problems.
- Manage change.
- Manage transition.

Interpersonal Effectiveness
- Respect others.
- Relate well with others.
- Participate effectively in groups.
- Develop healthy friendships.

Communication Skills
- Understand basic communication skills.
- Express themselves.
- Listen to others.

Cross-Cultural Effectiveness
- Appreciate their own culture.
- Respect others as individuals and accept them for their cultural membership.
- Relate effectively with others on the basis of appreciation for differences.
- Evaluate how stereotyping affects them and their relationships with others.

Responsible Behavior
- Behave responsibly.
- Take responsibility for own behavior.
- Be self-disciplined.

Note. From *A Model for Comprehensive, Developmental Guidance and Counseling Programs for Texas Public Schools: A Guide for Program Development, Pre-K–12th Grade* (4th ed., p. 53) by Texas Education Agency, 2004, Austin, TX: Author. Adapted with permission.

The district's comprehensive guidance program is an integral part of the district's total educational program. It is developmental by design and includes sequential activities organized and implemented by professional school counselors with the active support of parents/guardians, teachers, administrators, and the community. As a developmental program, it addresses the needs of all students by facilitating their academic, personal/social, and career development as well as creating positive and safe learning climates in schools. At the same time, the program assists students as they face issues and resolve problems that prevent their healthy development. The program is delivered through the following four program components.

- Guidance Curriculum: structured group and classroom presentations
- Individual Planning: appraisal, educational and occupational planning, and placement
- Responsive Services: individual counseling, small-group counseling, consultation, and referral
- System Support: program management, fair-share responsibilities, professional development, staff and community relations, consultation, committee participation, community outreach, and evaluation. (Gysbers, Stanley, Kosteck-Bunch, Magnuson, & Starr, 2008, p. 29)

Northside Independent School District. Northside Independent School District's definition of guidance and counseling is as follows:

The Northside Independent School District Comprehensive Guidance Program is based on individual, school, and community needs and organized around skill development goals. The program is delivered through the direct service program components of guidance curriculum, individual planning system, and responsive services and is implemented by certified school counselors. Additionally, the program provides indirect services supporting the total educational program. The program is a developmental educational program responsible for assisting students to acquire knowledge and skills needed to develop and maintain their

- self-esteem
- motivation to achieve
- decision-making and problem-solving skills
- interpersonal effectiveness
- communication skills
- cross-cultural effectiveness
- responsible behavior

The developmental perspective recognizes that every student needs sound emotional and social skills to achieve optimum benefit from the educational program. The comprehensive guidance program is designed to assist all students in our schools systematically. It is implemented with the assistance of administrators, teachers, and paraprofessionals. The program also assists students as they face issues and resolve problems that prevent their healthy development. Although other topics arise from time to time, recurrent issues include academics, attendance, behaviors, being at risk of dropping out, career choices, child abuse, cross-cultural effectiveness, educational choices, family, loss, peer relationships, relationships with adults, self-esteem, sexuality, stress, substance abuse, and suicide. (Northside Independent School District, 2004, p. 6)

Rationale

A rationale presents the importance of the guidance and counseling program as an equal partner with other programs in education. It focuses on reasons why students need to acquire guidance and counseling competencies and have access to the assistance that school counselors, working in a comprehensive guidance and counseling program, provide. It should be based on the goals of the school, community, and state. Examples of areas and points you may wish to consider in writing the rationale for your comprehensive guidance and counseling program include student development, self-knowledge, decision making, changing environments, transition assistance, and relevant education.

Student Development. Students today face depersonalization in many facets of their lives because bureaucracies and impersonal relations are commonplace. Students often feel powerless in the face of masses of people, mass communication, and mass everything else, and they need help in dealing with these feelings, not at the expense of society but in the context of society. Their feelings of control over their environment and their own destiny, and their relations with others and with institutions, are of primary importance in guidance and counseling programs. Students must be viewed as totalities, as individuals. Their development can be facilitated by comprehensive guidance and counseling programs that begin in kindergarten and continue to be available on a systematic basis through Grade 12.

Self-Knowledge. Formerly, students were brought up in a fairly stable society in which their roles were defined and relationships with others were fairly constant. Now they face an increasingly mobile society in which relationships with both people and things are becoming less and less enduring. Society is characterized by transience and impermanence. Traditional beliefs and ways of doing things no longer seem sufficient for coping with the environmental demands. As a result, many students have problems defining their roles and thus seek answers to questions such as "Who am I?" and "Where do I fit in?" Guidance and counseling programs can help individuals respond to such questions through the development of self-appraisal and self-improvement competencies. Through these learnings, students can become more aware of personal characteristics such as aptitudes, interests, goals, abilities, values, and physical traits and the influence these characteristics may have on the people they are and can become. Being able to use self-knowledge in life career planning and interpersonal relationships and to assume responsibility for their own behavior are examples of needed competencies that students can acquire through participation in a comprehensive guidance and counseling program.

Decision Making. Students need help in decision making because planning for and making decisions are vital tasks in the lives of all individuals. Everyday decisions are made that influence each student's life career. Mastery of decision-making skills and the application of these skills to life career planning are central learnings in a guidance and counseling program. A preliminary task to effective decision making is the clarification of personal values. The degree of congruence between what individuals value and the outcomes of decisions individuals make contributes to personal satisfaction. Included in decision making are the skills for gathering and using relevant information. Understanding the influence of planning on the future and the responsibility each individual must take for planning are components of the life career planning process. Life career planning is ongoing. Change and time affect planning and decisions. A decision outcome that is satisfactory and appropriate for the present may become, with time or change, unsatisfactory or inappropriate. Thus, the ability to evaluate decisions in view of new information or circumstances is vital. Being able to clarify personal values, identify steps needed to make personal decisions, gather relevant information, and apply decision-making skills to life career plans are examples of desired and needed outcomes for a guidance and counseling program.

Changing Environments. Increasing societal complexity affects not only interpersonal relationships and feelings of individuality but also other life roles, settings, and events, specifically including those associated with the worlds of education, work, and leisure. Changes resulting from advances in technology are perhaps more apparent because they affect the world of work. No longer are students well acquainted with the occupations of family and community members or their contributive roles to the common good of society. Parents' occupations are removed from the home and often from the immediate neighborhood. In addition, because students over their lifetimes will be assuming a number of roles, functioning in a variety of settings, and experiencing many events, learning in this area emphasizes their understanding of the various roles, settings, and events that interrelate to form their life careers. The roles of family member, citizen, worker, and leisure participant; settings such as home, school, community, and work; and events such as birthdays, educational milestones, job entry, and job change are identified and examined in terms of their influence on lifestyles. Guidance and counseling programs can help students develop an understanding of the structure of the family and education, work, and leisure requirements and characteristics. The effect of change—natural as well as unexpected, social as well as technological, in self as well as in others—is a needed major lesson for students that a comprehensive guidance and counseling program can provide.

Transition Assistance. As students are and will be moving from one setting to another, they need specific knowledge and skills to make such moves as effectively as possible. They need help in making transitions. Although transitions are defined broadly, specific attention should be given to intra- and intereducational and occupational transitions and to the personal competencies needed to make such transitions. Personal competencies needed include knowledge of the spectrum of educational courses and programs, an understanding of the relationships they may have to personal and societal needs and goals, and skills in using a wide variety of information and resources. They also include an understanding of the pathways and linkages between those courses and programs and potential personal goals. Stress is placed on the need for employability skill development, including résumé writing, job searching, and job interviewing.

Relevant Education. Some of youths' dissatisfaction with education stems from the feeling that what they are doing in school is not relevant to their lives. A comprehensive guidance and counseling program is needed to create relevance in the schools and to show individuals how the knowledge, understanding, and skills they are obtaining and the courses they are taking will help them as they progress through their life careers.

Example Rationale: Northside Independent School District

An example rationale from the Northside Independent School District follows:

> The ever-increasing needs of children and the expectations of today's society impose growing demands on our educational system and its resources. Educators are challenged to educate students with diverse backgrounds at an ever higher level of literacy to meet the demands of an internationally competitive, technological marketplace. At the same time, societal and other factors cause some of our children to attend school ill equipped emotionally, physically, and/or socially to learn. Schools must respond by providing support for all students to learn effectively.
>
> Community influences and societal changes generate identifiable student needs that may not be met solely by classroom instructional programs. Meeting these needs is essential to individual growth, and can be accomplished through a planned educational program combining instruction and guidance. Northside Independent School District provides a comprehensive and balanced guidance program. The Framework describes the elements common to the program districtwide; however, each campus designs its program to meet the district minimum expectations and to meet the needs of the community it serves. As each school designs its guidance program, the rationale for the local design rests on an assessment of local student and community needs. Northside Independent School District educators identified student needs as follows:

- a sense of connection
- someone to listen
- support system
- advocacy
- personal management skills
- career skills, life skills
- goal-setting skills
- self-esteem
- valuing education as an investment in the future
- learning to give of oneself
- problem-solving skills. (Northside Independent School District, 2004, p. 2)

Assumptions

For the effective implementation of a comprehensive guidance and counseling program to occur, certain student, staff, and program conditions must exist. Assumptions are statements of these conditions. For example, the Northside Independent School District comprehensive guidance program is based on the following assumptions:

Students
- Every student in our schools has equal access to our guidance program.
- The services provided to all our students are equitable.

Staff
- Professional school counselors are essential in today's public schools.
- All school counselors adhere to the ethical standards of the profession.
- School counselors spend the majority of their time working directly with students.
- All school counselors are highly proficient in the seven school counselor roles.
- School administrators protect the professional integrity of the guidance program and the school counselors.

Program
- Guidance is a schoolwide responsibility.
- The essential goals of a school guidance program are to help students succeed academically.
- All students deserve assistance with their career development.
- The primary purposes of all guidance curriculum lessons and activities are directly related to or in direct support of one or more of the following three primary goals of the school:
  1. Academic success
  2. A safe, productive, and pleasant learning and working environment
  3. Helping each student develop and carry out an educational plan that matches with his or her abilities, interests, and future goals. (Northside Independent School District, 2000, pp. 3–4)

Element 2: Organizational Framework: Program Components

As more is learned about students' needs, the variety of new and traditional guidance and counseling methods, techniques, and the resources available, as well as the increased expectations of policymakers, consumers, and community members, it is clear that a comprehensive program is rapidly becoming the way to organize guidance and counseling activities and services in schools. The traditional formulation of guidance and counseling—a position with a number of services—once thought to be sufficient, is no longer adequate. When cast in the traditional way, guidance and counseling is often seen as ancillary and supportive, not as equal and complementary to the instruction program.

If the proposition that the traditional position-services formulation for guidance and counseling is no longer adequate is accepted, then the question is, "What is an appropriate formulation?" One way to answer this question is to ask what should be expected of a comprehensive guidance and counseling program:

1. Are there knowledge, skills, and attitudes (competencies) needed by all students that should be the instructional responsibility of guidance and counseling programs?
2. Do students and their parents or guardians have the right to have someone in the school system be sensitive to students' unique life career development needs, including their needs for planning, goal setting, making transitions, and follow-through?
3. Should school counselors be available and responsive to special or unexpected needs of students, staff, parents or guardians, and the community?
4. Does the guidance and counseling program, the educational programs of the district, and the staff of the school district require support that can be best supplied by school counselors?

The structure suggested by an affirmative answer to these four questions and by a review of the literature is a program of guidance and counseling techniques, methods, and resources containing four interactive components: guidance curriculum, individual student planning, responsive services, and system support (Gysbers & Henderson, 2006). The curriculum component was chosen because a curriculum provides a vehicle to impart guidance and counseling content to all students in a systematic way. The individual student planning component was included as a part of the program because of the need for all students, working closely with parents or guardians, to systematically plan, monitor, and manage their growth and development and to consider and take action on their next steps personally, educationally, and occupationally. The responsive services component was included because of the need in comprehensive guidance and counseling programs to respond to the direct, immediate concerns of students whether these concerns involve individual counseling, small-group counseling, referral, or consultation with parents, teachers, or other specialists. The system support component was included because it was recognized that, for the other guidance processes to be effective, a variety of guidance and counseling program support activities such as staff development, research and evaluation, and curriculum development are required. The system support component was also included because of the need for the guidance and counseling program to provide appropriate support to other programs in the school.

These components, then, serve as organizers for the many guidance and counseling methods, techniques, and resources required in a comprehensive guidance and counseling program. In addition, they also serve as a check on the comprehensiveness of the program. In our opinion, a program is not comprehensive unless it has activities in each of the components. We describe each of these components in detail in the following sections.

Guidance Curriculum

Purpose of the Guidance Curriculum. One of the assumptions on which our conception of a comprehensive program is based is that there is guidance and counseling content that all students need to learn in a systematic, sequential way. Before we present a description of the guidance curriculum of a comprehensive program, it is first necessary to define what a curriculum is and what a curriculum is based on. Squires (2005) defined curriculum as a document that "describes (in writing) the most important outcomes of the schooling process; thus, the curriculum is a document in which resides the district's 'collected wisdom' about what is most important to teach" (p. 3). It is also important to remember that a curriculum is discipline specific; hence, we have a guidance curriculum as part of a comprehensive guidance and counseling program.

What is the basis for a curriculum? According to Squires (2005), a "curriculum is based on standards" (p. 3). Standards usually describe appropriate content to be mastered by students over a range of grade levels. For guidance and counseling, standards are typically grouped under domain titles such as career, academic, and personal–social and identify the attitudes, beliefs, knowledge, and skills important for students to acquire as they progress through kindergarten to 12th grade. By implementing a guidance curriculum, professional school counselors are assisting all students to master local, state, or national content standards.

The idea of a curriculum for guidance and counseling is not new; it has deep, historical roots (Davis, 1914). What is new, however, is the array of guidance and counseling techniques, methods, and resources currently available that work best as a part of a curriculum. What is new, too, is the concept that a comprehensive guidance and counseling program has an organized and sequential curriculum (American School Counselor Association, 1984, 2005; Borders & Drury, 1992; Commission on Precollege Guidance and Counseling, 1986; ERIC Counseling and Personnel Services Clearinghouse, 1983).

Implementation Strategies. The guidance curriculum typically consists of student competencies chosen to fit the needs of students (organized by domains and specified by grade levels) and structured activities, presented systematically, chosen to fit the needs of students, schools, and community through such strategies as these:

- *Classroom activities:* School counselors teach, team teach, or support the teaching of guidance curriculum learning activities or units in classrooms. Teachers may also teach such units. The guidance curriculum is not limited to being taught in one or two subjects but should include as many subjects as possible in the total school curriculum. These activities may be conducted in the classroom, guidance center, or other school facilities.
- *Schoolwide activities:* School counselors organize and conduct large-group sessions such as career days and educational, college, and vocational days. Other members of the guidance and counseling team, including teachers and administrators, may also be involved in organizing and conducting such sessions.

Although school counselors' responsibilities include organizing and implementing the guidance curriculum, the cooperation and support of the entire faculty and staff are necessary for its successful implementation. Also critical is that parents or guardians be invited to provide input to the guidance curriculum that is taught in the school their children attend, that they be aware of what is taught, and that they be encouraged to reinforce learnings from the guidance curriculum at home.

Guidance Curriculum Scope and Sequence Design: A Learning Theory Perspective. As you select the domains you will use in the guidance curriculum and identify the competencies to be included in each domain, keep in mind the following assumptions about human growth and development:

1. Individual development is a process of continuous and sequential (but not necessarily uninterrupted or uniform) progress toward increased effectiveness in the management and mastery of the environment for the satisfaction of psychological and social needs.
2. The stage, or level, of individuals' development at any given point is related to the nature and accuracy of their perceptions, the level of complexity of their conceptualizations, and the subsequent development rate and direction. No individual in an educational setting is at a zero

point in development; hence, change must be measured from some relative point rather than from an absolute.

3. Positive developmental changes are potential steps toward the achievement of higher level purposive goals. This interlocking relationship dictates that achievement at a particular growth stage be viewed as a means to further development rather than as an end result.

4. Environmental or situational variables provide the external dimension of individual development. Knowledge, understanding, skills, attitudes, values, and aspirations are the product of the interaction of these external variables with the internal variables that characterize the individual.

5. The developmental learning process moves from a beginning level of awareness and differentiation (perceptualization), to the next level of conceptualizing relationships and meanings (conceptualization), to the highest level of behavioral consistency and effectiveness by both internal and external evaluation (generalization). (Wellman & Moore, 1975, pp. 55–56)

A major task in the development of the guidance curriculum is to organize and lay out student competencies so that they follow a theoretically sound scope and sequence. Note the concepts perceptualization, conceptualization, and generalization discussed in Assumption 5. These concepts can serve as guidelines for this very important task. What follows is a detailed discussion of these concepts and how they function in making decisions about the scope and sequence of student competencies from kindergarten through 12th grade (Wellman & Moore, 1975).

Perceptualization level. Competencies at this level emphasize the acquisition of knowledge and skills and focus attention on selected aspects of the environment and self. The most relevant knowledge and skills are those that individuals need in making appropriate life role decisions and in responding to the demands of the school and social environment. Attention is the first step toward the development and maturation of interests, attitudes, and values. Competencies at the perceptualization level reflect accuracy of perceptions, ability to differentiate, and elemental skills in performing functions appropriate to the individual's level of development. Competencies at this level are classified under two major categories: *environmental orientation* and *self-orientation.*

Environmental orientation competencies emphasize the individual's awareness and acquisition of knowledge and skills needed to make life role decisions and to master the demands of life career settings and events. The competencies at this level are essentially cognitive in nature and have not necessarily been internalized to the extent that the individual attaches personal meaning to the acquired knowledge and skills. For example, individuals may acquire appropriate study skills and knowledge, but it does not necessarily follow that they will use these skills and knowledge in their study behavior. However, such knowledge and skills are considered to be prerequisites to behavior requiring them. Thus, the acquisition of knowledge and skills required to make growth-oriented decisions and to cope with environmental expectations is viewed as the first step in individuals' development, regardless of whether subsequent implementation emerges. A primary and universally applicable goal of guidance is the development of knowledge and skills to enable individuals to understand and meet the expectations of their school and social environment and to recognize the values underlying social limits.

Self-orientation competencies focus on the development of accurate self-perceptions. One aspect of an accurate awareness of self is the knowledge of one's abilities, aptitudes, interests, and values. An integral part of identity is individuals' ability to understand and accept the ways that they are alike and different from other individuals. Attention to life career decisions and demands relevant to immediate adjustment and future development is considered a prerequisite to an understanding of the relationships between self and environment. An awareness, and perhaps an understanding, of feelings and motivations is closely associated with self-evaluation of behavior, with the formation of attitudes and values, and with voluntary, rationally based modification of behavior.

The goal of guidance at this level is to help individuals make accurate assessments of self so that they can relate realistically to their environment in their decisions and actions. Thus, the goal of guidance at this level is also individuals' development of self-awareness and differentiation so as to enable appropriate decision making and mastery of behavior in the roles, settings, and events of their lives.

Conceptualization level. Individual competencies at the conceptualization level emphasize action based on the relationships between perceptions of self and perceptions of environment. The types of action sought are categorized into personally meaningful growth decisions and adaptive and adjustive behavior. The general goal at this level of development is to help individuals (a) make appropriate choices, decisions, and plans that will move them toward personally satisfying and socially acceptable development; (b) take action necessary to progress within developmental plans; and (c) develop behavior to master their school and social environment as judged by peers, teachers, and parents. The two major classifications of conceptualization objectives are *directional tendencies* and *adaptive and adjustive behavior.*

Directional tendencies relate to individuals' movement toward socially desirable goals consistent with their potential for development. These competencies are indicators of directional tendencies as reflected in the choices, decisions, and plans that individuals are expected to make in ordering the course of their educational, occupational, and social growth. The acquisition of knowledge and skills covered by competencies at the perceptual level is a prerequisite to the pursuit of competencies in this category, although the need to make choices and decisions may provide the initial stimulus for considering perceptual competencies. For example, a ninth grader may be required to make curricular choices that have a bearing on post–high school education and occupational aspirations. The need to make an immediate choice at this point may stimulate an examination of both environmental perceptions and self-perceptions as well as a careful analysis of the relationships between the two. To this extent, then, the interrelationship and interdependence of perceptual and conceptual competencies preclude the establishment of mutually exclusive categories. Furthermore, the concept of a developmental sequence suggests this type of interrelationship. Any choice that may determine the direction of future development is considered to represent a directional tendency on the part of individuals, and competencies related to such choices are so classified.

The expected emergence of increasingly stable interests and the strengthening and clarification of value patterns constitute additional indicators of directional tendencies. Persistent attention to particular people, activities, or objects in the environment to the exclusion of others (selective attention) is an indication of the development of interests through an evaluation of the relationships of self to differentiated aspects of the environment. Objectives that relate to value conceptualization, or the internalization of social values, complement interest development. Here individuals are expected to show increased consistency in giving priority to particular behavior that is valued personally and socially. In a sense, the maturation of interests represents the development of educational and occupational individuality, whereas the formation of value patterns represents the recognition of social values and the normative tolerances of behavior.

Competencies in these subcategories include consistency in the expression of interests and values and the manifestation of behavior compatible with the emerging interests and value patterns. For example, high school students may be expected to manifest increasing and persistent interest (measured or expressed) in particular people, activities, and objects. They may be expected to develop a concept of self that is consistent with these interests and to place increasing importance, or value, on behaviors, such as educational achievement, that will lead to the development of related knowledge and skills and to the ultimate achievement of occupational aspirations. The directional tendency emphasis is on achieving increased consistency and strength of interests and values over a period of time. The incidental or occasional expression of an immediate interest or value with little or no long-range impact on the behavior of individuals should not be interpreted as an indication of a directional tendency.

Adaptive and adjustive behaviors at the conceptualization level include competencies related to the application of self-environment concepts in coping with environmental pressures and in solving problems arising from the interaction of individuals and their environment. *Adaptive behavior* refers to individuals' ability and skill to manage their school and social environment (with normative tolerances) to satisfy self-needs, to meet environmental demands, and to solve problems. There are two types of adaptive behavior. First, individuals may, within certain prescribed limits, control their environmental transactions by selection. For example, if they lack the appropriate social skills, they may avoid social transactions that demand dancing and choose those in which existing abilities will gain the acceptance of the social group. Second, individuals may be able to modify their environment to meet their needs and certain external demands. For example, students who find sharing a room with a younger brother or sister disruptive to studying may be able to modify this situation by arranging to study elsewhere.

Adjustive behavior refers to the ability and flexibility of individuals to modify their behavior to meet environmental demands and to solve problems. Such behavior modification may include the development of new abilities or skills, a change of attitudes, or a change in method of operation or approach to the demand situation. In the examples of adaptive behavior just mentioned, individuals might use adjustive behavior by learning to dance rather than avoiding dancing, and they might develop new study skills so they are able to study while sharing a room.

The basic competencies in this area involve an individual's ability to demonstrate adaptive and adjustive behavior in dealing with school and social demands and in solving problems that restrict the ability to meet such demands. The competencies may be achieved by applying existing abilities or by learning new ways of meeting demands.

Generalization level. Competencies at the generalization level imply a high level of functioning that enables individuals to (a) accommodate environmental and cultural demands, (b) achieve personal satisfaction from environmental transactions, and (c) demonstrate competence through mastery of specific tasks and through the generalization of learned behavior, attitudes, and values to new situations. Behavior that characterizes the achievement of generalization-level competencies may be described as purposeful and effective by one's own or intrinsic standards and by societal or extrinsic criteria. Individuals should be able to demonstrate behavioral consistency, commitment to purpose, and autonomy in meeting educational, occupational, and social demands. Individuals exhibiting such behavior are therefore relatively independent and predictable. Guidance competencies at this level are classified as *accommodation, satisfaction,* and *mastery.*

The concept of sequential and positive progress implies a continuous process of internalization, including applicational transfer of behavior and a dynamic, rather than a static, condition in the achievement of goals. The achievement of generalization competencies may be interpreted as positive movement (at each level of development) toward the ideal model of an effective person (self and socially derived) without assuming that individuals will ever fully achieve the ideal.

Accommodation competencies relate to the consistent and enduring ability to solve problems and to cope with environmental demands with minimum conflict. Accommodation of cultural and environmental demands requires that individuals make decisions and take action within established behavioral tolerances. The applicational transfer of adaptive and adjustive behavior, learned in other situations and under other circumstances, to new demand situations is inferred by the nature of the competencies classified in this category. The achievement of accommodation competencies can probably best be evaluated by the absence, or the reduction, of unsatisfactory coping behavior. The wide range of acceptable behavior in many situations suggests that individuals who perform within that range have achieved the accommodation competencies for a particular demand situation, whereas those outside that range have not achieved these competencies. For example, a student is expected to attend class, to turn in class assignments, and to respect the property rights of others. If there is no record of excessive absences, failure to meet teacher assignment schedules, or violation of property rights, it may be assumed that the student is accommodating these demands with normative tolerances. In a sense, the objectives in this category represent the goal that individual behavior conform to certain limits of societal expectancy, whereas the other categories of generalization competencies tend to be more self-oriented. The achievement of accommodation competencies may imply congruence of individual values with the values of one's culture. Caution should be exercised in drawing such inferences, however, because the individual may demonstrate relative harmony externally but have serious value conflicts that do not emerge in observable behavior.

Satisfaction competencies reflect the internal interpretation that individuals give to their environmental transactions. Individual interests and values serve as criteria for evaluating the decisions made and the actions taken within the guidance domains. Although the evaluations of parents, peers, and authority figures may influence individuals' interpretations (satisfactions), these competencies become genuine only as they are achieved in congruence with the motivations and feelings of individuals. The description of satisfaction competencies consistent with guidance programming should include individuals' evaluation of affiliations, transactions, and adjustments in terms of personal adequacy, expectations, and congruency with a perceived ideal lifestyle. Expressed satisfaction, as well as behavioral manifestations from which satisfaction may be inferred (such as persistence), seem to be appropriate criterion measures. Congruency between measured interests and voluntarily chosen career activities should also be considered.

Mastery competencies include the more global aspects of achievement and generalization of attitudinal and behavioral modes. Long-range goals, encompassing large areas of achievement, are emphasized here rather than the numerous short-range achievements that may be required to reach a larger goal. For example, a young child becomes aware of task demands and different ways to meet them (perceptualization). At the conceptualization level, task-oriented behaviors are developed and made meaningful. Generalization (mastery) competencies reflect the internalization of these behaviors so that tasks are approached and achieved to the satisfaction of self and social expectations.

In the social area, mastery competencies relate to social responsibility and individuals' contributions with respect to social affiliations and interactions appropriate to their developmental level. All of the competencies in this category are framed in the context of self- and social estimates of potential for achievement. Therefore, criteria for the estimation of achievement of mastery competencies should be in terms of congruency between independent behavioral action and expectations for action as derived from the self and social sources. For example, a mastery competency in the educational area might be achieved by high school graduation by one individual, whereas graduate work at the university level might be the expected achievement level for another individual.

Individual Student Planning

What Is Individual Student Planning? The individual student planning component of a comprehensive guidance and counseling program assists students, beginning in middle school, with developing and using individual learning plans (personal plans of study, career plans, student education, and occupational plans). What are student learning plans?

Student learning plans, often referred to as "roadmaps," assist students in creating courses of study that are aligned with high school graduation requirements, personal interests, and individually-defined career goals. Learning plans are dynamic documents that are updated regularly as students' educational and career goals change. They are developed collaboratively by students, parents, school staff, including teachers and guidance counselors. Students use learning plans to reflect upon and document their skills, hobbies, accomplishments, academic record, personal goals, career interests and other information relevant to them as individuals. Learning plans also include provisions for portfolio development and assessment of student progress toward defined objectives. (Rennie Center for Education Research and Policy, 2011, p. 3)

Importance of Individual Student Planning. Individual student planning is not a new idea either. A major goal of guidance and counseling over the years has been to assist students to think about and plan for their futures. However, no specific structure was provided that mandated individual student planning. That changed when Gysbers and Moore (1981) introduced the idea that individual student planning should be a major component of comprehensive guidance and counseling programs along with guidance curriculum, responsive services, and system support.

In the 1990s, the importance of individual student planning was demonstrated by a study of young people in Indiana titled *High Hopes Long Odds: Next Steps* (Orfield & Paul, 1994). The study found that

the difference in the high school experiences of students with plans for 4 years of high school courses and career plans versus students without such counselor-assisted plans was so great that providing help with these plans must be offered at every school. (Orfield & Paul, 1994, p. 11)

Is individual student planning still important today? Will it be important in the future? Pellitteri, Stern, Shelton, and Muller-Ackerman (2006) answered these questions by stating that

many students are unaware of how critical this skill, goal setting and planning, is to a full, rewarding, and successful life. . . . Goals give us our bearing and point us in a purposeful direction. (pp. 209–210)

To illustrate the importance of individual student planning, several states have passed legislation requiring or recommending that individual student planning activities take place in schools. For example, the State of Utah (Utah Administrative Code, 2011) translated the idea of individual plans for students into state law and state board of education policy requiring that all students develop and implement personalized student education–occupation plans (SEOPs).

The State of Washington passed a law similar to that passed by the State of Utah that encourages schools to help students develop and use plans of study (State of Washington, Session Laws, 2006). In addition, the State of Missouri required that an individual student planning system be in place in school no later than eighth grade and that it include the necessary planning forms and procedures (Missouri School Improvement Program, 2003).

At about the same time that Utah passed legislation to require individual student planning, the National Association of Secondary School Principals (1996) published a report titled *Breaking Ranks*. In it, they recommended that each high school student develop and use a personal plan for progress. The importance of individual student planning was emphasized again with the publication of *Breaking Ranks II* (National Association of Secondary School Principals, 2004). Recommendation 12 stated,

> Each student will have a Personal Plan for Progress that will be reviewed often to ensure that the high school takes individual needs into consideration and to allow students, within reasonable parameters, to design their own methods for learning in an effort to meet high standards. (National Association of Secondary School Principals, 2004, p. 84)

The idea behind personalized learning is that it "allows the student to understand who he or she is, what adult roles seem most desirable, and how to get from here to there in the most productive way" (p. 169).

In *Breaking Ranks in the Middle* (National Association of Secondary School Principals, 2006), individual student planning was also stressed. The report recommended that sixth or seventh graders and their parents be introduced to planning for their education and beyond. The report also emphasized the need for students to meet frequently and meaningfully with an adult to plan and review their development.

The American College Testing Program (2004) also stressed the importance of individual student planning in *Crisis at the Core: Preparing All Students for College and Work*. They recommended that career and educational planning services be provided to all students. In addition, they stated that parents must be involved in key educational and postsecondary planning.

In addition, Kalchik and Oertle (2011) stressed the importance of individual career plans for students. They examined the use of programs of study and career pathways as structures to guide students as they developed and used individual career plans. They also described a number of implementation issues, including the challenges involved in the implementation process.

The purpose of the individual student planning program component of the comprehensive guidance and counseling program is to provide all students with guidance and counseling activities to assist them to positively assess, plan for, and then monitor and manage their personal–social, academic, and career development (Cohen, 2001). The point of the activities is to have students focus on their current and future goals by developing life career plans (personal plans of study) drawing on the strengths-based career development content embedded in the guidance curriculum. As Pellitteri et al. (2006) suggested, "Goals give us our bearing and point us in a purposeful direction" (p. 25). The importance of goals was also emphasized in a publication titled *Addressing Barriers to Learning* (School Mental Health Project, 2011) that focused on school engagement, disengagement, learning supports, and school climate.

> Reviews of the literature on human motivation suggest that providing students with options and involving them in decision making are key facets of addressing the problem of engagement in the classroom and at school. For example, numerous studies have shown that opportunities to express preferences and make choices lead to greater motivation, academic gains, increases in productivity and on-task behavior, and decreases in aggressive behavior. Similarly, researchers report that student participation in goal setting leads to more positive outcomes (e.g., higher commitment to a goal and increased performance). (School Mental Health Project, 2011, p. 5)

Foundation for and Scope of Individual Student Planning. The foundation for individual student planning is established during the elementary school years through guidance curriculum activities. Self-concept development, the acquisition of learning-to-learn skills, interpersonal relationship skill development, decision-making skill building, and awareness and beginning exploration of educational and occupational possibilities are sample subjects that are covered during these years. Subjects such as these continue to be covered through the guidance curriculum during middle school and high school, providing new information and experiences to enable students to regularly update, monitor, and manage their plans effectively.

Building on the foundation provided in elementary school, beginning planning for the future is undertaken during the middle school years through the individual student planning component. During this period, students' plans focus on high school course selection, taking into account graduation requirements and the requirements of their postsecondary academic and career goals. Guidance curriculum activities continue to support and guide the planning process.

During the high school years, plans developed in the middle school are reviewed and updated periodically in accordance with students' postsecondary personal, academic, and career goals. The individual student planning component provides time for regular individual work with students as well as group sessions focusing on individual student planning. Guidance curriculum activities continue to support student planning by giving emphasis to the development and use of decision-making, goal-setting, and planning skills. The importance and relevance of basic academic and career and technical education preparation skills are stressed. The goal is for students' plans to become pathways or guides through which students can use the past and present to anticipate and prepare for the future.

Implementation Strategies. Individual student planning is implemented through the following strategies:

- *Individual appraisal:* School counselors assist students to assess and interpret their abilities, interests, skills, and achievement.
- *Individual advisement:* School counselors assist students to use self-appraisal information along with personal–social, academic, career, and labor market information to help them plan for and realize their personal, social, academic, and career goals.
- *Transition planning:* School counselors and other education personnel assist students to make the transition from school to work or to additional education and training.
- *Follow-up:* School counselors and other education personnel provide follow-up assistance to students as well as gather follow-up data for evaluation and program improvement.

Individual Student Planning in Action. What does individual student planning look like in action? Two examples are provided. The first example is from the Granite School District in Utah. The Granite district has implemented the Utah State requirement that every student in Grades 7 through 12 have a Student Education and Occupation Plan. The second example is from the Franklin Pierce School District in Washington State. The Franklin Pierce District developed an individual student planning system that has evolved into a statewide system titled "Navigation 101" (Severn, 2004).

Granite School District. In the Granite district, the SEOP is the form and the process through which individual student planning unfolds. The goal is to assist students in Grades 7 through 12 to plan, monitor, and manage their own learning as well as their personal and career development. Students can set, review, and evaluate their educational, personal, and career goals connecting them to activities that help them achieve their goals. The SEOP process is career guidance and counseling in action.

School counselors in the Granite School District have set a goal they call the 3×4 plan. The 3×4 plan means that in every middle and high school, school counselors or other educational personnel will have three individual SEOP planning meetings with each student (every school year) and at least one meeting with a parent or guardian in attendance. They will also conduct four classroom guidance activities, one activity each term for each grade level, 7 through 12 (Granite School District Comprehensive Counseling and Guidance Program, 2006).

The key to putting the 3×4 plan into full operation is calendaring. Calendaring individual student planning in the Granite district began with the decision of what percentage of time school counselors should devote to the planning process at the middle school and high school. Then, that percentage of school counselor time was translated into days of the school year and into the class periods available. Next, the ratio of school counselors to students was added to determine how much time each school counselor could spend with each student and in preparing for individual sessions. In the 2005 to 2006 school year, 95% of the students met at least once with their school counselor, and 52% of the parents involved met at least once with their students and a school counselor (Granite School District Comprehensive Counseling and Guidance Program, 2006, p. 2).

Franklin Pierce School District. According to Severn (2004), the foundation of individual student planning is the guidance curriculum. "Navigation 101," the title of the individual planning part of the curriculum, uses an advisor–advisee system in which teachers and school counselors meet twice a month with groups of 20 students. The Navigation 101 coursework includes

- discussion and analysis of student's test results,
- various assessments of personal interests and aptitudes,
- goal-setting skill development,
- planning for each year's high school course selection and personal goals,
- independent living skills lessons, such as how to budget and how to balance a checkbook,
- information about how the postsecondary education and training system works and how to access it, and
- development of a student portfolio and planning for annual, student-led planning conferences with their parents or guardians and the Navigation teacher. (Severn, 2004, p. 10)

The individual student planning part of Navigation 101 begins in sixth grade when students develop a portfolio. In the spring, conferences are held with students and parents or guardians to review student plans and progress. The interesting feature of these conferences is that students plan and lead them. They discuss what they have done and then describe their future plans. When the conferences end, all individuals involved sign the students' plans (Severn, 2004).

What are the results of this system? According to the Franklin Pierce School District ("Navigation 101," 2005), evaluation studies indicated

- A 10% increase in the number of students who progress from 9th to 10th grade on time.
- An 8% decline in students receiving an F in one or more classes.
- Dramatic increases in the number of students enrolling in rigorous, demanding classes: 28% increase in students requesting pre-calculus classes; 240% increase in students requesting physics classes, and 180% increase in students requesting chemistry classes.
- A school-wide transition to a more student-centered individualized way of thinking about education.

In addition, the system revealed a new way of creating school schedules in which students register first, and then school officials plan the class schedule to respond to students' preferences.

Responsive Services

Purpose of Responsive Services. The purpose of this component of the organizational framework is to work with students whose personal circumstances, concerns, or problems are threatening to interfere with or are interfering with their healthy personal, social, career, and academic development. Specific issues facing some students include academic success, career choice, child abuse, cross-cultural effectiveness, dropping out of school, educational choices, family loss, relationships, school attendance, stress, substance abuse, and suicide. As a result, there is a continuing need for individual counseling, small-group counseling, diagnostic and remediation activities, and consultation and referral to be an ongoing part of a comprehensive guidance and counseling program. In addition, there is a continuing need for the guidance and counseling program to respond to the immediate information-seeking needs of students, parents, and teachers. The responsive services component organizes guidance and counseling techniques and methods to respond to these concerns and needs as they occur. In addition, the responsive services component is supportive of the guidance curriculum and individual student planning components.

Responsive Services Activities. Responsive services consist of activities to meet the current needs and concerns of students whether these needs or concerns require counseling, consultation, referral, or information. Although counselors have special training and possess skills to respond to current needs and concerns, the cooperation and support of the entire faculty and staff are necessary for the component's successful implementation. Sink (2011) made this same point by suggesting that "school counselors become copilots with school administrators, staff, and faculty to effect positive student development" (p. iv). Parent or guardian involvement with and participation in activities of this component are critical in helping students overcome barriers to their educational progress and academic achievement. Parent involvement may include referring their children for assistance, working with school counselors and other school staff to identify issues of concern, giving permission for needed special services, and providing help in resolving the issues.

Implementation Strategies. Responsive services are implemented through

- *Individual counseling:* School counselors provide individual counseling for students who are experiencing educational difficulties, personal concerns, or normal developmental tasks. Individual counseling assists students in identifying problems, causes, alternatives, and possible consequences so that appropriate action can be taken.
- *Small-group counseling:* School counselors provide small-group counseling to students who need and will benefit from a small-group setting to address their current needs and concerns. Interventions may take the form of short-term issue groups or crisis intervention groups that deal with such topics as social skills, anger management, relationship issues, grief issues, and study skills.
- *Consultation:* Consultation is an interactive process that school counselors provide to help parents or guardians, teachers, and administrators address the academic, personal–social, and career needs of students.
- *Referral:* School counselors are familiar with school and community referral sources that deal with crises such as suicide, violence, abuse, and terminal illness. These referral sources may include mental health agencies, employment and training programs, vocational rehabilitation, juvenile services, and social services.

Adjunct guidance staff—peers, paraprofessionals, and volunteers—can aid school counselors in carrying out responsive services. Peers can be involved in tutorial programs, orientation activities, ombudsman functions, and—with special training—cross-age counseling and leadership in informal dialogue. Paraprofessionals and volunteers can provide assistance in such areas as placement, follow-up, and community–school–home liaison activities.

System Support

Purpose of System Support. The administration and management of a comprehensive guidance and counseling program require an ongoing support system. That is why system support is a major program component. Unfortunately, it is an aspect of a comprehensive program that is often overlooked or only minimally appreciated. And yet the system support component is as important as the other three components. Why? Because without continuing support, the other three components of the guidance and counseling program will be ineffective. Activities included in this program component are by definition those that support and enhance activities in the other three program components. That is not to say that these activities do not stand alone. They can and often do. But for the most part, they undergird activities in the other three components.

Implementation Strategies. The system support component consists of management activities that establish, maintain, and enhance the total guidance program. This component is implemented and carried out through activities in the following areas:

- *Research and development:* Guidance and counseling program evaluation, follow up studies, and the continued development and updating of guidance learning activities and the guidance and counseling program for enhancement purposes are examples of the research and development work of school counselors.
- *Professional development:* School counselors need to be involved in regularly updating their professional knowledge and skills. Examples are participating in regular school in-service training, attending professional meetings, completing postgraduate coursework, and contributing to the professional literature.
- *Staff and community public relations:* This area involves orienting staff and the community to the comprehensive guidance and counseling program through newsletters, local media, and school and community presentations.
- *Committee and advisory boards:* Serving on departmental curriculum committees and community committees or advisory boards is an example of activities in this area.
- *Community outreach:* Included in this area are activities designed to help school counselors become knowledgeable about community resources, employment opportunities, and the local labor market. These activities may involve school counselors visiting local businesses and industries and social services agencies on a periodic basis.
- *Program management:* This area includes the planning and management tasks needed to support the activities of a comprehensive guidance and counseling program. It also includes responsibilities that members of the school staff may need to fulfill.
- *Fair-share responsibilities:* These are the routine "running of the school" responsibilities that all members of the school staff take equal turns doing to ensure the school's smooth operation.

Also included in the system support component are those activities in the school that support programs other than guidance and counseling. These activities could include helping interpret test results to teachers, parents, and administrators; serving on departmental curriculum committees (helping to interpret student needs data for curriculum revision); and working with school administrators (helping to interpret student needs and behaviors).

Care must be taken, however, to watch the time given to system support duties because the prime focus for school counselors' time is the direct service components of the comprehensive guidance and counseling program. It is important to realize that if the guidance and counseling program is well run, it will provide substantial support for other programs and personnel in the school and community.

Element 2: Organizational Framework: Time Allocations

Figure 3.2 presents some suggested time allocations for school counselors by program component. These time allocations are not those for all school counselors at all levels in all school districts. They are not prescriptive. School counselors at each level in a school district must decide how to spend their time because the appropriate use of school counselors' professional time is crucial in developing and implementing a comprehensive guidance and counseling program. How should professionally certified school counselors allocate their time? What criteria should be used to guide the time allocation process? We recommend three criteria for your consideration: program balance, grade-level differentiation and need, and a 100% program.

Program Balance

The four program components provide the structure for making judgments about allocations of school counselors' time. One criterion to be used in making such judgments is program balance. The guidance curriculum, individual student planning, and responsive services program components represent the direct services school counselors and other guidance personnel provide to students, parents, teachers, and the community; the system support component organizes the indirect services of the program. The assumption is that counselors' time should be spread across all of the program components, but particularly the first three, perhaps in an 80:20 ratio, with 80% direct services to students, parents, teachers, and the community and 20% indirect services to these groups.

Grade-Level Differentiation and Need

Another criterion is that different grade levels require different allocations of school counselor time across the program components. For example, at the elementary level, more school counselor time may be spent working in the guidance curriculum with less time spent on individual student planning. In the high school, those time allocations will probably be reversed. How personnel in a school district or school building allocate their time depends on the needs of their students, parents or guardians, teachers, and their community as well as the resources that are available. Moreover, once chosen, the time allocations are not fixed forever. The purpose for making them is to provide direction to the program, to the administration, and to the school counselors involved.

A 100% Program

Because the program is a 100% program, 100% of school counselors' time must be spread across the four program components. Time allocations can be changed on the basis of newly arising needs, but nothing new can be added unless something is removed. The assumption is that school counselors should spend 100% of their time on task, on implementing the guidance and counseling program. Remember that this 100% includes the fair-share responsibilities found in the system support component.

The determination of school counselor time is a critical decision made in the designing phase (see Chapter 5). The time allocations presented in Figure 3.2 are those suggested by the State of Missouri as points of departure for local school district guidance and counseling program planning (Gysbers et al., 2008). These percentages were suggested by Missouri school counselors and administrators who had participated in the early field testing of the Missouri comprehensive guidance program model in the 1980s. Remember, the word is *suggested*, not *required* or *mandated*. School counselors working closely with administration establish their own time allocations according to grade level, building, need, and resources.

Element 3: Program Resources

Although local school district resources vary, sufficient resources are required to fully implement a district comprehensive guidance and counseling program. The resources that are required include personnel resources, financial resources, and political resources.

Personnel Resources

The personnel resources of a comprehensive guidance and counseling program—school counselors, guidance and counseling program staff leaders, teachers, other educational specialists, administrators, parents or guardians, students, community members, and business and labor personnel—all have roles to play in the guidance and counseling program. Although school counselors are the main providers of guidance and counseling services and coordinate the program, the involvement, cooperation, and support of teachers and administrators are necessary for a successful program that offers a full array of guidance and counseling activities. The involvement, cooperation, and support of parents or guardians, community members, and business and labor personnel are also critical for full student participation in the guidance and counseling program.

Financial Resources

Appropriate and adequate financial resources are crucial to the success of a comprehensive guidance and counseling program. The financial resource categories required for a program include budget, materials, equipment, and facilities. A budget for the guidance and counseling program is needed to fund and then allocate those funds across the district's buildings and grade levels. Materials and equipment are needed so that guidance and counseling activities across the four program components can be implemented fully. Well-designed facilities in each building, organized to meet the needs of the guidance and counseling program, are required.

Political Resources

The political resources of a comprehensive guidance and counseling program include district policy statements, pertinent state and federal laws, state and local board of education rules and regulations, and professional association statements and standards. Clear and concise board of education policies are mandatory for the successful operation of guidance and counseling programs in school districts. They represent statements of support and courses of action, or guiding principles designed to influence and determine decisions in school districts; those that pertain to guidance and counseling programs must take into account pertinent laws, rules and regulations, and standards as they are being written, adopted, and implemented.

Element 4: Development, Management, and Accountability

The development, management, and accountability element of a comprehensive guidance and counseling program (see Figure 3.2) describes the five transition phases required to fully operationalize such a program: planning, designing, implementing, evaluating, and enhancing. This element also includes the various management tasks that need to be completed in each transition phase to enable the change process to unfold smoothly and efficiently. Finally, this element describes how a comprehensive guidance and counseling program is accountable through program, personnel, and results evaluation, all leading to program enhancement to make a district's comprehensive guidance and counseling program even more effective.

Development Process

As noted in Chapter 2, the development of a fully functioning comprehensive guidance and counseling program proceeds through the five phases of planning, designing, implementing, evaluating, and enhancing. Chapter 2 includes an example timeline for these phases. Also, this book is organized around these five phases, enabling you to first grasp the overall change processes involved and then to see how these processes can be subdivided into a logical sequence of transition phases, one building on the other. Chapters 2 and 3 describe the first two points of the planning phases, and Chapter 4 completes the description of this phase. Chapters 5 and 6 focus on the design phase, and Chapters 7, 8, and 9 describe implementation issues. Finally, Chapter 10 looks at evaluation, and Chapter 11 describes the enhancement phase.

Management Tasks

Each phase of the change process contains a number of management tasks that must be addressed. These tasks are described in detail in each of the chapters of the book, beginning with Chapter 2. It is important that the guidance and counseling program leader and members of the steering committee know what the tasks are for each transition phase and have a plan to use work groups when appropriate to complete the tasks.

Accountability

A major set of management tasks focus on the need for accountability: on the impact of guidance and counseling program activities and services on students' academic, career, and personal–social development. Three types of evaluation lead to being accountable. The first type is program evaluation, the second type is personnel evaluation, and the final type is results evaluation. The details of each of these types of evaluation and their relationships are presented in Chapter 10. Chapter 11 focuses on how to use data from these types of evaluation to improve a district's comprehensive guidance and counseling program—the program enhancement phase.

Understand the Power of Common Language

To be effective, guidance and counseling programs require consistency, logical coherence, and functional continuity in their organizational frameworks. The program presented in this chapter was designed to meet these requirements. With this program, a common language for guidance and counseling is established. The language is marked by the orderly and logical relation of the four elements of a comprehensive guidance and counseling program and affords easy comprehension and recognition by laypeople and professionals alike (Heath & Heath, 2008).

Why is common language important for the framework of guidance and counseling programs? Common language enables school counselors, administrators, teachers, and parents or guardians to "coordinate their work and multiply the power of their intellects" (American College Testing Program, 1998, p. 9). Common language for the framework of guidance and counseling programs also allows these "individuals to communicate and replicate" guidance and counseling program activities (American College Testing Program, 1998, p. 9). In addition, common language for the framework of guidance and counseling programs provides the basis for program, personnel, and results evaluation across a school district, from kindergarten through 12th grade.

Understand the Importance of the Program Concept

Over the past 100-plus years, the field of guidance and counseling has evolved from having no organizational structure other than a person in a position with a list of duties, to a person with a set of services to provide, to a person who works within the structure of a comprehensive program. The position approach often consisted of lengthy uncoordinated lists of guidance and counseling activities mixed in with clerical and administrative tasks. No coherent overall organizational structure was provided, nor was professional time accounted for. The services model consisted of groupings of activities and interventions with titles such as assessment, information, and counseling. Again, no coherent overall organizational structure was provided, nor was professional time accounted for.

The introduction of the comprehensive program concept changed that because now guidance and counseling in the schools has an organizational structure to arrange guidance and counseling content and interventions coherently and systematically. School counselors' work tasks are derived directly from the program structure and 100% of their time is accounted for. Conceptually, guidance and counseling has become a program just like the other instructional programs in the school.

Appreciate the Flexibility and Adaptability of a Program

Does the use of common language for the framework of guidance and counseling programs restrict all school counselors in the district to carrying out the same tasks, in the same way, with the same timeline, for the entire school year? The answer is no. School buildings, grade levels, and students in districts differ in their needs. School counselors' expertise differ. School resources also differ. Although the common language of the framework of the guidance and counseling program is a constant and must remain so, school counselors' time allocations, the tasks they do, and the activities and interventions they use within the program structure to work with students, parents, and teachers will vary by school building and grade level and are often adjusted on the basis of evaluation data. Differentiated staffing using the professional expertise of the personnel involved is often a necessity (Henderson & Gysbers, 1998).

Learn About Six Program Imperatives

A comprehensive guidance and counseling program by definition leads to guidance and counseling activities for all students. It removes administrative and clerical tasks not related to the operation of the guidance and counseling program (remember that fair-share responsibilities of all staff members are part of the system support component), one-on-one counseling only, and limited accountability. It is proactive rather than reactive. School counselors are busy and unavailable for unrelated administrative and clerical duties because they have a planned comprehensive guidance and counseling program to implement. School counselors are expected to do individual and small-group counseling as well as provide structured developmental activities for all students.

To reach these outcomes, it is imperative to

Six Program Imperatives

1. understand that a comprehensive guidance and counseling program is student centered, not school management or school administration oriented;
2. operate a comprehensive guidance and counseling program as a 100% program in which the four program components constitute the total program with no add-ons;
3. begin the comprehensive guidance and counseling program the first day of school (not in the middle of October) and end it the last day of school (not at the end of April);
4. understand that a comprehensive guidance and counseling program is program focused, not position focused;
5. understand that a comprehensive guidance and counseling program is education based, not agency or clinic based;
6. understand that although a comprehensive guidance and counseling program uses a common organizational framework, the contents, activities, and school counselor time allocations are tailored to meet local student, school, and community needs and resources.

Your Progress Check

Chapter 3 is a foundation chapter in the planning process. It is designed to provide you with a theory base, the concepts, and vocabulary to design, implement, evaluate, and enhance a comprehensive guidance and counseling program for your school district. As a result of reading Chapter 3, you have learned about

- the theory base for comprehensive guidance and counseling programs;
- the place of comprehensive guidance and counseling programs in education;
- the vocabulary to describe the basic elements of a comprehensive guidance and counseling program;
- the importance of time on task and program balance;
- the importance of the program concept, its flexibility, and its adaptability;
- the six program imperatives.

Given what you have learned, you are now ready to move to the last phase of the planning process, conducting a thorough assessment of your current district guidance and counseling program.

References

American College Testing Program. (1998, Spring). The power of a common language in workplace development. *Work Keys, USA, 3,* 9.

American College Testing Program. (2004). *Crisis at the core: Preparing all students for college and work.* Iowa City, IA: Author.

American School Counselor Association. (1984). *The school counselor and developmental guidance: Position statement.* Alexandria, VA: Author.

American School Counselor Association. (2005). *The ASCA National Model: A framework for school counseling programs* (2nd ed.). Alexandria, VA: Author.

Borders, L. D., & Drury, S. M. (1992). Comprehensive school counseling programs: A review for policy makers and practitioners. *Journal of Counseling & Development, 70,* 487–498.

Cohen, M. (2001). *Transforming the American high school*. Washington, DC: Aspen Institute.

Commission on Precollege Guidance and Counseling. (1986). *Keeping the options open: Recommendations*. New York, NY: College Entrance Examination Board.

Davis, J. B. (1914). *Vocational and moral guidance*. Boston, MA: Ginn.

ERIC Counseling and Personnel Services Clearinghouse. (1983). *Comprehensive guidance program design* [Fact sheet]. Ann Arbor, MI: Author.

Granite School District Comprehensive Counseling and Guidance Program. (2006). *School counselor update*. Salt Lake City, UT: Author.

Gysbers, N. C., & Henderson, P. (2006). *Developing and managing your school guidance program* (4th ed.). Alexandria, VA: American Counseling Association.

Gysbers, N. C., Heppner, M. J., & Johnston, J. A. (2009). *Career counseling: Contexts, processes, and techniques* (3rd ed.). Alexandria, VA: American Counseling Association.

Gysbers, N. C., & Moore, E. J. (1975). Beyond career development—Life career development. *Personnel and Guidance Journal, 53*, 647–652.

Gysbers, N. C., & Moore, E. J. (1981). *Improving guidance programs*. Englewood Cliffs, NJ: Prentice-Hall.

Gysbers, N. C., Stanley, B. J., Kosteck-Bunch, L., Magnuson, C. S., & Starr, M. F. (2008). *Missouri comprehensive guidance program: A manual for program development, implementation, evaluation, and enhancement*. Jefferson City: Missouri Department of Elementary and Secondary Education.

Heath, C., & Heath, D. (2008). *Made to stick: Why some ideas survive and others die*. New York, NY: Random House.

Henderson, P. (2005). The theory behind the ASCA national model. In American School Counselor Association, *The ASCA National Model: A framework for school counseling programs* (2nd ed., pp. 79–101). Alexandria, VA: Author.

Henderson, P., & Gysbers, N. C. (1998). *Leading and managing your school guidance program staff*. Alexandria, VA: American Counseling Association.

Jones, A. J., & Hand, H. C. (1938). Guidance and purposive living. In G. M. Whipple & G. N. Kefauver (Ed.), *Yearbook of the National Society for the Study of Education: Volume 37, Issue 1. Guidance in educational institutions* (pp. 3–29). Bloomington, IL: Public School.

Kalchik, S., & Oertle, K. M. (2011, January). The relationship of individual career plans to programs of study and career pathways. *Transition Highlights, 3*. Retrieved from http://occrl.illinois.edu/files/Highlights/Highlight_01_2011.pdf.

Markus, H., & Nurius, P. (1986). Possible selves. *American Psychologist, 41*, 954–969.

McDaniels, C., & Gysbers, N. C. (1992). *Counseling for career development: Theories, resources, and practice*. San Francisco, CA: Jossey-Bass.

Missouri School Improvement Program. (2003). *Third-cycle procedures handbook: Revision 5*. Jefferson City: Missouri Department of Elementary and Secondary Education.

Myers, G. E. (1923). A critical review of present developments in vocational guidance with special reference to future prospects. *The Vocational Guidance Magazine, 3*, 139–140.

National Association of Secondary School Principals. (1996). *Breaking ranks: Changing an American institution*. Reston, VA: Author.

National Association of Secondary School Principals. (2004). *Breaking ranks II: Strategies for leading high school reform*. Reston, VA: Author.

National Association of Secondary School Principals. (2006). *Breaking ranks in the middle: Strategies for leading middle level reform*. Reston, VA: Author.

Navigation 101: The Franklin Pierce Model. (2005). Retrieved from http://www.k12 .wa.us/conferences/summerinstitute2005/materials/HOLTIMPLEMENTING.doc

Northside Independent School District. (2000). *Comprehensive guidance program framework.* San Antonio, TX: Author.

Orfield, G., & Paul, F. G. (1994). *High hopes long odds: Next steps.* Indianapolis: Indiana Youth Institute.

Pellitteri, J., Stern, R., Shelton, C., & Muller-Ackerman, B. (Eds.) (2006). *Emotionally intelligent school counseling.* Mahwah, NJ: Erlbaum.

Random House Webster's Unabridged Dictionary (2001). New York, NY: Random House.

Reich, C. A. (1971). *The greening of America.* New York, NY: Bantam Books.

Rennie Center for Education Research and Policy. (2011). *Student learning plans: Supporting every student's transition to college and career.* Cambridge, MA: Author.

School Mental Health Project/Center for Mental Health in Schools. (2011). *Addressing barriers to learning.* Los Angeles, CA: Author.

Severn, J. (2004). *Navigation 101: How a focus on planning skills leads to higher student performance.* Olympia, WA: Office of the Superintendent of Public Instruction.

Sink, C. (2002). Comprehensive guidance and counseling programs and the development of multicultural student-citizens. *Professional School Counseling, 6,* 130–137.

Sink, C. (2011). School-wide responsive services and the value of collaboration. *Professional School Counseling, 14,* ii–iv.

Squires, D. A. (2005). *Aligning and balancing the standards-based curriculum.* Thousand Oaks, CA: Corwin Press.

Texas Education Agency. (2004). *A model for comprehensive, developmental guidance and counseling programs for Texas public schools: A guide for program development, pre-K–12th grade* (4th ed.). Austin, TX: Author.

Utah Administrative Code, Rule R277-462, Comprehensive Counseling and Guidance Program (2011). http://www.rules.utah.gov/publicat/code/r277/r277-462.htm

Utah State Office of Education. (2008). *Utah model for comprehensive counseling and guidance: K-12 programs.* Salt Lake City, UT: Author.

State of Washington, Session Laws, 2006, 59th Legislature, Chapter 372, Bill Number ESSB, 6356, Fiscal Matters.

Wellman, F. E., & Moore, E. J. (1975). *Pupil personnel services: A handbook for program development and evaluation.* Washington, DC: U.S. Department of Health, Education, and Welfare.

Wolfe, D. M., & Kolb, D. A. (1980). Career development, personal growth, and experimental learning. In J. W. Springer (Ed.), *Issues in career and human resource development* (pp. 1–56). Madison, WI: American Society for Training and Development.

Chapter 4

Assessing Your Current Guidance and Counseling Program

Planning—Conducting a Thorough Assessment of the Current Program

- Gather student and community status information.
- Identify current resource availability and use.
- Study current guidance and counseling program delivery.
- Gather perceptions about the program.
- Present a report describing the current program.

☞ The next phase of the program improvement process involves assessing your current program. This assessment is a process of obtaining a concrete, detailed description of your school's or school district's guidance and counseling program as it currently exists. The program is viewed from as many angles as possible to discern its design. It is not an assessment of students' needs, but rather a way of determining what the current guidance and counseling program is.

The current program assessment tells you what resources are already available to the program and how those resources are being used for students and the school community. It is prerequisite to suggesting how to use the resources differently (Adelman & Taylor, 2003, p. 7). The assessment is done by describing the program using the framework of the four elements of the comprehensive guidance and counseling program model described in Chapter 3: (a) content; (b) organizational framework, structure, activities, and time; (c) resources; and (d) development, management, and accountability processes.

The assessment process reveals the current program's accomplishments, shape, and priorities. You are enabled to answer such questions as "What competencies do students acquire as a result of their involvement in the program's activities and, ultimately, in the program as a whole?" "What are the theoretical and policy supports for the program?" "What is the structure of the program?" "How are the competencies of the professional school counselor applied in the program?" "What are the other personnel and financial resources that are used?" and "How is the program developed, managed, and accountable?" The program assessment provides the basis for identifying what is good about the program that needs to be retained, for recognizing critical gaps in service delivery, and for planning needed program changes. The work accomplished during this phase of the program development process dispels the myth that the comprehensive guidance program will be a whole new program. It will be built on what is currently in place.

Knowing the design of the program means knowing its various parts and how they are arranged to form its shape. The design has two facets: qualitative and quantitative. The qualitative design describes the program's substance, the what and who of the program. Specifically, what activities are conducted within each component? What use is made of professional school counselors' specialized competence, their talents? Who is served through the program activities—students, parents, teachers, administrators, and other adults who work with the students? What are the results for students who experience these activities? The possibilities in the qualitative design are many, perhaps infinite, and so the qualitative design is shaped by priorities. Often, the current priorities of schools' guidance and counseling programs have not been consciously set, but that does not make them any less real.

The quantitative design describes the program's amounts, the measurable and countable parts, the "how much" of the program. Specifically, how much of the professional school counselors' time is spent in each component, that is, what is the balance of the program? How many students are served through each of the program components? How many students are served in each of the levels of need categories? How many students (what proportion) are served by population subgroup compared with the makeup of the total student population? The quantitative design is shaped by finite numbers that establish the parameters of its dimensions, and it consequently sets the parameters for the qualitative design.

In this chapter, we first discuss preparing for the current program assessment. Second, we suggest you study your students and school community to best understand the makeup of your program's client population. Different communities have different needs that have influenced and will continue to influence the guidance and counseling program. Third, we describe ways to assess what personnel, financial, and political resources are currently available to the program as well as how these resources are used. Fourth, we outline ways to study your current program delivery, the qualitative and quantitative facets of its design. Fifth, we suggest ways for you to gather perceptions about the program from students, teachers, administrators, parents, community members, and school counselors themselves. Sixth, we emphasize the importance of pulling together all of the data gathered in the assessment of your current program and preparing and presenting a report to the people concerned with improvement of the guidance and counseling program. Seventh, we encourage you to pay special attention to the realities of and issues posed by the diversity of today's school populations. The chapter concludes with an exploration of the leadership roles and responsibilities required to accomplish your current program assessment.

Getting Ready

Assessing the current program provides information that is the foundation of your future guidance and counseling program. It is important to take the time needed to ensure accurate data are gathered because these data help the guidance and counseling staff understand the current program design. They are also useful in helping others understand the current status of the program. They become the baseline from which your decisions for change are made and against which your changes will be evaluated. Having accomplished such a study, Taylor (2002) found

First, school counselors were able to document the amount of time they spent in guidance and non-guidance tasks and compare this with the state model. Second, school administrators and counselors obtained critical information regarding how others perceived guidance services and how they might be improved. Finally, administrators received information about state-of-the-art developmental guidance and counseling programs. . . . Until this time, the counselors' supervisor had been unaware of the developmental guidance model. (p. 26)

Assessing the current program takes time. You need to be realistic in establishing the anticipated time frame. Specific suggestions for accomplishing each of the tasks that will help save you some time are offered in the following sections, but completing a thorough assessment of all elements of the program could still take from 6 months to a year.

To accomplish the current program assessment, professional school counselors first and foremost need to take responsibility for their own program. They need to be advocates "in promoting and securing the appropriate delivery of services" (Shillingford & Lambie, 2010, p. 214). They provide leadership for the work that will lead to systemic change (American School Counselor Association [ASCA], 2005). However, they are not solely responsible for the program. School administrators, teachers, students, and parents also benefit from high-quality program delivery. The results of many studies have shown that developing supportive relationships, especially with school principals, leads to effective school guidance and counseling programs (Dollarhide, 2007). At the school district level, supportive relationships with superintendents are critical. It is the professional school counselors' responsibility to engage others in collaborative relationships to accomplish the developmental work (ASCA, 2005).

As described in Chapter 2, several work groups need to be formed. Identifying current program activities, school counselors' competence in their application, their clients, and their outcomes are interrelated tasks; thus, gathering this information should be the work either of one group or of groups working closely together. Concurrently, other work groups can begin identifying current program resource use and collecting perceptions about the current program. To make the data you gather useful in future planning, one basic rule must apply to all work groups and other data collection efforts: Always organize your current assessment according to the comprehensive program elements and delivery system components—guidance curriculum, individual student planning, responsive services, and system support.

Because assessing the current program is a substantial undertaking, guidance program leaders have important roles to play. If you are the leader of the guidance and counseling program, you have the primary responsibility for data collection and for ensuring the full and appropriate summary, analysis, and dissemination of the results. We recommend, however, that all school counselors in the building or district affected by the potential changes be involved in the assessment. Involvement in the assessment helps the staff become familiar with the program model selected and feel not only that most of what they are currently doing fits into the components of the model but also that the new program will not be completely different from the current program.

Involvement of administrators in work groups is also needed. In this way, administrators learn about the program model and are in a better position to support the changes called for in the future. Most administrators have strong experience-based opinions on how the program can and should be changed. Administrators help students, staff, and others understand where the guidance and counseling program is going. By helping craft the needed program changes, they provide support for the implementation of changes in their schools or districts. The work of some groups, however, is at times truly laborious. Staff who are not directly concerned with each minute detail may find it somewhat tedious, for example, to analyze the time study data for similarities and differences for each school or grade level. It is important to use administrators in areas in which they can make a solid contribution to the deliberations and not let them get bogged down in data that are in fact the internal concern of the guidance department staff.

We recommend that steering committee members chair the various work groups. Steering committee meetings can then provide opportunities to monitor and coordinate the work of the various groups. In any case, some vehicle for coordinating the work groups' efforts needs to be established; a committee of committee chairs also works.

In planning your current program assessment, you should use current program description materials. Many counseling departments in state education agencies have led schools and districts to develop program handbooks or plans. Much useful information can be extracted from these existing documents, such as listings of current program activities. A word of caution: Our experience has been that these plans are often outdated or include activities that are not actually performed.

Gather Student and Community Status Information

What Information Is Useful

Students

Gathering information about the current status of students informs the program decision makers about how well students are doing in school and suggests what they are getting that advances their healthy personal, social, career, and educational development.

Useful personal information includes demographic data (e.g., range and proportions of ethnicities and socioeconomic statuses). Useful social information includes identification of the youth subcultures present in the school (School Mental Health Project, 2010), rates of participation in extra- and cocurricular activities, conduct grades, discipline reports, and attendance and absence rates. Useful career development data include aggregated information on students' career interests and plans. Useful educational information includes patterns of students' grades, school attitude surveys, academic achievement tests; course failure, promotion and retention rates, and graduation rates.

The racial–ethnic balance of the student population in the nation's public schools continues to shift, as reflected in Table 4.1 (National Center for Education Statistics, 2009a).

The proportion of White students continues to decline and that of Hispanic, Black, and Asian students continues to increase. As Lee (2001) pointed out,

> In concrete terms, these demographic estimates mean that, as never before, U.S. schools are becoming a social arena where children who represent truly diverse behavioral styles, attitudinal orientations, and value systems have been brought together with one goal—to prepare them for academic, career, and social success in the 21st Century. (p. 257)

Table 4.1
Estimated Percentages of Public School Population by Race–Ethnicity in 1990, 2000, and 2009

Race–Ethnicity	1990	2000	2009
White	75.6	69.4	65.1
Black	11.8	12.2	12.2
Hispanic	9.0	12.6	15.8
Asian	2.8	3.7	4.4
Pacific Islander	—	0.1	0.1
American Indian/Alaskan Native	0.7	0.7	0.8
Two or more races–ethnicities	1.2	1.2	1.5

Note. From National Center for Education Statistics (2009a).

School Community Context

In addition to student information, other relevant data about the community context are useful in understanding students' worlds. This information also suggests values and priorities for the guidance and counseling program. Useful demographic-related data include languages spoken and preferred, economic base and labor market pool and placement, mobility rate, special program enrollments, parental levels of education, family configurations, neighborhood makeup and issues, political climate, immigration patterns, and homelessness numbers.

The context of the school and school district environment must also be considered. Relevant information about the school and district includes its size; the prevailing professional values, beliefs, mission, and goals; and the average cost of educating each student. It is also important to learn about the available special programs and technology. Because public schools are state governed, the political context includes the prevailing legislative climate and that of the local school board.

Ideas on How to Conduct an Assessment of Student and Community Status

Kaffenberger and Young (2007) described a four-step process, DATA, for gathering useful information:

1. Design: What is your question?
2. Ask: How will you answer your question?
3. Track: How will you make sense of the data?
4. Announce: How will you use your findings? (p. 2)

If this information has not already been gathered in developing the rationale for your program, a work group or groups should take on the task of identifying and collecting as much of these data as are readily available.

Initial collection of this information is not the responsibility of the guidance department and should probably not be taken on in this effort, but much is available through other sources. Schools' and districts' state education departments and local school districts' Web pages are rich sources of information. For example, on the Northside Independent School District Web site (http://www.nisd.net), a reader is able to learn about the numbers of various categories of staff members (professional, support, administrative, auxiliary), the range of teachers' salaries, administrative ratios, student–teacher ratios, and student–computer ratios. A reader can learn about the bus fleet, including the salient detail that 50% of all Northside students ride the bus (Northside Independent School District, 2009). Information is also provided about student ethnicity, academic achievements, enrollment numbers, dropout numbers, and numbers of students in special education and career and technology education, and number of those who are college bound. There is information about the community: the number of residents, households, and businesses.

In this era of accountability, many of these data are gathered and reported to the public. In Texas, for example, the Academic Excellence Indicator System pulls together a wide range of information on the performance of students in each school and district each year and includes academic information: state-administered assessment performance, attendance rates, dropout and completion rates, participation in advanced courses, college readiness, and participation in the SAT and ACT college entrance examinations (Texas Education

Agency, n.d.). Data on the number of students per grade level, their sex, and their ethnic distribution (African American, Hispanic, White, Asian/Pacific Islander, and Native American) are also provided. Mobility rates and percentages of students who are economically disadvantaged, have limited English proficiency, and experience disciplinary placements are given. Demographic information is reported about the professional and paraprofessional staff. Information is provided about student enrollment in special programs and about amounts and distribution of budget.

When compiled, this information provides insights into some of students' apparent needs. In light of the school's or district's mission, such information also suggests what student needs are for your program. (Conducting student needs assessments is discussed further in Chapter 5).

These data about students and their status provide a baseline against which to compare students in future years. They provide opportunities to look at trends concerning student growth and development and problem resolution.

Identify Current Resource Availability and Use

A myth that we hear quite frequently is that, to implement a comprehensive guidance and counseling program, a school or district has to have substantial resources. In reality, districts with both scant and substantial resources have successfully implemented comprehensive programs. The efficiency of a program is measured in terms of the ratio of resources applied to the benefits accrued. The goal of this phase of the process is to know what you have, and then in the next phase of the process you design how to best use your resources to address your students' identified high-priority needs. Gathering complete, concrete information about the resources currently available to the program is essential to making sound program improvement decisions (Adelman & Taylor, 2003). Most guidance and counseling program administrators and professional school counselors will be encouraged by the actual quantity of resources available. At this point, you are studying what is currently in place. It is premature to make recommendations about what you want to have. That comes later and is described in Chapter 5.

As described in Chapter 3, we categorize resources as personnel, financial, and political. Personnel resources include staff members' time and talents. Financial resources are those applied through the budget to provide materials, equipment, and facilities for the guidance and counseling program. Political resources are represented by policy statements and supporters of the current program and staff.

Because of the variety of resources used in a comprehensive guidance and counseling program, collecting this information is a giant step that requires time and staff commitment. Some of the ways in which districts have assessed the resources currently available are described by category in the following sections. How these resources are used is described in the Study Current Guidance and Counseling Program Delivery section.

Personnel Resources

Personnel resources include school counselors and guidance department paraprofessionals and other nondepartment personnel who contribute to the guidance and counseling program: teachers, administrators, other mental health professionals, and community-based volunteers. Of course, it is imperative that all personnel fulfill roles for which they have training and competence. Assessing these human resources involves identifying their talents and the time they spend on the program.

Professional School Counselors

Information is needed about the professional school counselors' training and experience, counselor–student ratio, counselor–student assignment patterns, and counselor time available.

School Counselors' Training and Experience. The school counseling staff is the basic resource of the guidance and counseling program. Clarification of school counselors' unique talents provides qualitative data about the contribution they are able to make to students' growth and development. The school counselors' unique training and experiences is what allows them to seek accountability for helping students learn to make decisions, solve problems, and perform other personal and social developmental tasks. Indeed, more often than not, when principals are asked to describe their guidance and counseling programs, they will say, "I have five counselors" or "I have six counselors and a registrar." As described in Chapter 1, they focus on their staffing units—the positions—rather than on program delivery or student results.

There is, however, a widespread lack of information as to what school counselors' unique talents are. As a result, it is useful to specify the requirements for school counselors' background and training. Ways to do this include ensuring that everyone concerned is aware of the certification requirements for professional school counselors, publicizing the training requirements for a master's degree in counseling, publicizing appropriately written job descriptions of school counselors, and disseminating ASCA's (2009a) role statement, *The Role of the Professional School Counselor.*

A review of the literature (ASCA, 2005; Council for Accreditation of Counseling and Related Programs, 2009; National Board for Professional Teaching Standards, 2002) describing the specialized training professional school counselors are expected to have in the 21st century suggested that they are equipped to counsel individuals and small groups; guide individuals and groups of students; teach students to guide their academic, career, and personal–social development; interpret assessment results to students to help them make educational and career plans; consult with other adults who work with students; manage individual student cases; coordinate resources for students; refer students and their families for special needs; advocate on behalf of individual students and groups of students; collaborate with colleagues; and manage and evaluate school guidance and counseling programs. They are expected to be multiculturally competent and fulfill leadership roles to enhance the school climate.

Traditionally, school counselors have read and talked much about the unique roles and functions they fulfill in schools. Thus, another way to make school counselors' skills known is to ask the school counselors themselves to identify their performance roles and relate them to the four program components. In Texas, professional school counselors have identified eight performance domains and their related standards to describe their competencies: guidance, counseling, consultation, coordination, student assessment, program management, and adhering to professional standards and professional behavioral expectations (Texas Counseling Association, 2004). Competencies are subsets of performance domains; for example, within the counseling performance domain, individual counseling is one area of competence and small-group counseling is another. Within the consultation domain, consulting with parents is one area of competence, consulting with teachers is another, and consulting with school administrators is a third.

Although all of these domains come into play in more than one of the program components, each component draws more heavily on some of the roles. Table 4.2 displays which domains encompass each of the comprehensive guidance and counseling program components. Relating the familiar performance roles to the program components also

Table 4.2
School Counselor's Performance Domains and Program
Components

Performance Domain	Primary Component Application
Guidance program managment	System support
	Guidance curriculum
	Individual student planning
Counseling	Responsive services
Consultation	Guidance curriculum
	Individual student planning
	Responsive services
	System support
Coordination	Guidance curriculum
	Individual student planning
	Responsive services
	System support
Student assessment	Individual student planning
	Responsive services
	System support
Professional standards	System support
Professional behavior	System support

helps school counselors distinguish between the components and build a common terminology base. If some of the professional school counselors are used in specialized roles, identifying the performance domains that are emphasized in their responsibilities allows for using common language to describe their expertise and at the same time for clarifying differences in their applications of it.

School Counselor–Student Ratio. An essential piece of quantitative data is the current school counselor–student ratio. During the discussions of the model program, everyone involved may be starry-eyed about the possibilities, but the realities of caseload are ever present. The range of school counselor–student ratios by state for 2007 to 2008 is from 1:203 in Wyoming to 1:1,076 in Illinois. The national average is 1:467 (ASCA, 2009b). Ultimately, your program design will have to acknowledge what each school counselor can be expected to do for his or her 200, 500, or 1,000 students (see Chapter 8). Moreover, knowing whether the ratio is the same from school level to school level allows you to tailor your expectations accordingly. For example, in some districts the recognition of disproportionately heavy loads at the elementary and middle school levels when contrasted with the high school level has led to immediate efforts to employ more elementary and middle school counselors.

School Counselor–Student Assignment Patterns. In addition to ratios, typical patterns of school counselor–student assignment need to be reviewed. Are school counselors assigned to a grade level or to an alphabetical group? How are specialized school counselors—career and technology, special education, substance abuse, multicultural—assigned their students? The rationale behind these assignments implies the philosophy of the guidance and counseling program. For example, caseload assignment by grade level reflects a developmental philosophy, whereas assignment by alphabet (i.e., surname) often reflects an emphasis on responding to students within their family context.

School Counselor Time. The primary resource of the guidance and counseling program is professional school counselors' time. How their time is used defines the program. At this point, it is important to identify how much time is available to the guidance and counseling program so that a realistic baseline can be established. It is also important to specify how much of students' time is available for guidance and counseling activities. Specific answers are needed to such questions as "How many hours constitute a school counselor's workday?" and "How many hours are in a student's school day?" For example, a counselor's workday may be 8 hours, whereas the student's school day is 7.5 hours. Students may be available for services before or after school; some of that availability depends on whether students walk to school, are bused, and so on.

How many days are in a student's school week? Some schools build schedules for specialists over 6- or 7-day spans. How many weeks or days are in a school counselor's school year? Length of school counselors' contracts varies from district to district and from level to level. A school counselor on a 202-day contract might accomplish a lot more program planning and staff development on nonstudent time than a school counselor on a 180-day contract. How many weeks or days are in a student's school year? Length of the school year varies from state to state—from 160 days in Colorado to 182 days in Ohio (National Center for Education Statistics, 2009b). Ultimately, the expectations for the program must fit within the parameters of actual time that school counselors work and that students are available for direct services.

Other Personnel. In addition to professional school counselors, guidance department paraprofessionals and secretaries fulfill essential support and service roles. Career center technicians, for example, provide many guidance activities for students.

Other school staff are important members of the guidance team, and as such their competencies and contributions to the program need to be identified. In some schools, school counselors share caseloads and collaborate with campus administrators. Teachers and administrators often conduct guidance activities, so they also need to be included. Teachers assist, particularly in the delivery of guidance curricula and in the referral of students for services.

Other related school specialists, such as school nurses, psychologists, and social workers, fulfill roles as referral sources. Other mental health professionals, such as school social workers and school psychologists, may participate in guidance program activities and collaborate with counselors in providing special services to some students.

Students are also important members of the guidance team when, for example, they work as peer counselors or aides in career centers or make alumni presentations to younger students. If your school or district uses community volunteers, such as business community representatives as career speakers or parent–teacher association volunteers as coleaders of parent involvement efforts or as clerical support, you will need to list them and clarify their contributions as well.

Financial Resources

Financial resources include all budget items that support the guidance and counseling program. In addition to salaries and other staff costs (typically 80% of the program budget), budget categories consist of appropriations for materials, equipment, and facilities.

Budget

The place to begin the assessment of financial resources is identifying the specific district or building budget line items that relate to the current guidance and counseling program. Even if there is no official budget labeled "guidance," as is often the case at both the district and the building level, funds are being spent for guidance, so begin there. Consider collecting data on such items as salaries for school counselors, secretaries, and aides; staff and program development appropriations; money spent for supplies such as paper, pencils, and record folders; money spent for guidance and counseling program materials such as books, videos, films, pamphlets, standardized tests, and scoring services; and capital outlay money available. All expenses for guidance activities in the district should be included as well as any special funding from federal, state, or private groups—such as the parent–teacher association (PTA)—or foundations. This information will give you a perspective on the guidance department's share of the total school district budget. It is often much larger than the guidance staff thinks.

Materials

If you do not already have one, it is important to take an inventory of the materials you have available. You will want to categorize your inventory by program components and by student outcomes as well as by grade level. The listing should include title, copyright date, a brief description of the content, and the use for which the resource was developed. Assuming that you will want to disseminate this list to the guidance staff, it is also helpful to include information about how to obtain the resource and about any restrictions on borrowing it.

Equipment

A study of your equipment inventory will reveal the quantity and kinds of audiovisual and computer equipment available as well as how the equipment is distributed. How accessible is it to all staff? You may want to consider an equipment use study to determine whether you are using the equipment to its maximum potential or to evaluate whether your current distribution system is the best for you. Depending on the size of your program and the quantity of audiovisual equipment, you need to consider whether the equipment is best used if housed centrally and shared on a checkout basis or permanently housed on each of the campuses. You need to carefully consider how the computer equipment is used and by whom and to what purposes, for example, legitimate guidance activities or nonguidance tasks.

Facilities

Baseline information as to the facilities available to the current guidance and counseling program is needed on a building-by-building basis. This, again, will show you the evenness of facility availability. As you begin to implement desired new program activities, your baseline data will provide realistic planning information about the space available. Any necessary remodeling takes time and planning. If additional space is needed, such as a classroom for developmental guidance or a guidance or career center, that information must be ready for submission to the district as the superintendent makes overall plans for the ensuing year.

Political Resources

Political here means the support that is rooted in district or building policies; in state and federal laws, rules, or regulations; or in the standards adopted by accreditation bodies or other professional associations to which your school or district subscribes. It also includes staff members' support for the guidance and counseling program and its improvement. A political reality to consider is the staff members who are not supportive of the change efforts.

Policy Statements

Relevant policy statements are made at the local, state, and national levels. Knowing the tenets that undergird your program provides you the context within which to operate.

Local Policies. To build the program from its current base, it is important to identify statements that indicate the rationale for, the underlying assumptions of, and the mission of the current guidance and counseling program—the structural components of the comprehensive guidance and counseling program model (Chapter 3). Some of these may be overtly stated; others may have to be inferred from what is written. Chapter 5 outlines more specifically the kinds of information that make up each of these components.

Adelman and Taylor (2003) noted,

> Of particular importance is awareness of prevailing and pending policies, institutional priorities and their current status. . . . This involves, for example, amassing information that clarifies the school and community vision, mission statements, current policies, and major agenda priorities. (p. 7)

It is useful to identify the school district's vision for its students. There may be a board policy about the guidance and counseling program, although it may be incomplete, focusing on the activities provided, the needs of students, or the staff members with responsibility (Gysbers, Lapan, & Jones, 2000). It would surely have a statement about the educational mission of the district, as do individual schools within districts. These have implications for the mission of your guidance and counseling program. In all likelihood, procedural expectations for school counselors are expressed in administrative handbooks. You need to review these official pronouncements and extract and synthesize from them the basic political platform supporting or detracting from the current guidance and counseling program.

If you have followed our suggestions so far, you have already begun to develop policy statements about the guidance and counseling program by adopting a program model and by developing the three structural components (Chapter 3). Writing your own program rationale, assumptions, and definition provides you with policy support that is most relevant to your efforts. Indeed, it is our opinion that unless you have these statements in hand, your reorganization effort may be ineffective because it will lack the needed focus that a theory-based belief system provides (ASCA, 2005).

Glaring gaps in policy statements were identified by MacDonald and Sink (1999). They studied state program models to identify the "developmental constructs in the models and their integration within each state's published guidelines and curricula" (p. 419). They found that most models lacked identification of a developmental theory base and also lacked attention to students' developmental needs and the developmental needs of specific groups of students (e.g., gifted students). "The most significant gap across the models [they found] is in attention to culture and ethnic developmental issues" (p. 424).

They also noted that the theoretical underpinnings for the programs were either not stated or not acknowledged or were only superficially apparent. This may also be true of your current guidance and counseling program. If so, identifying the underlying program assumptions will be an important exercise.

State and Federal Policies. Another useful survey is that of existing state and federal education laws, rules, and regulations that pertain to guidance. Federal education laws that allow money to be spent for guidance and counseling include those supporting bilingual, compensatory, migrant, special, and career and technology education and dropout prevention. This money is appropriated to the states, which in turn develop rules and regulations for its distribution within the state. Federal funding may also support grants to states and districts (e.g., the Elementary and Secondary School Counseling Programs, the American Recovery and Reinvestment Act of 2009; U.S. Department of Education, 2009a, 2009b).

In *A National Study of the Current Status of State School Counseling Models*, Martin, Carey, and DeCoster (2009) identified nine features at the state level that enhanced local-level program implementation:

1. written model
2. modern model features
3. model endorsement by the state department and counseling association
4. linked to career planning
5. identified school counseling leadership in state department
6. supportive legislation
7. supportive licensure and accreditation
8. provision of professional development
9. model evaluation

Because guidance is still a relatively new part of the total educational program, there may be no specific state guidance and counseling program legislation with related rules and regulations. Some states are including guidance curriculum as part of the regular instructional curriculum, and many state legislatures and boards of education are making guidance and counseling issues a high priority. In addition, many states have expressed concerns through policies or laws regarding lack of readiness for college, high dropout rates, school violence, adolescent suicide, substance abuse, teen parenting, and child abuse and neglect. With concern about these issues and awareness of the all-too-typical underuse of professional school counselors, some states have passed laws or established administrative regulations that would remedy the problem. For example, Texas passed a law that mandates an appropriate set of responsibilities for school counselors (i.e., counseling, comprehensive developmental guidance and counseling program development, consultation, coordination, standardized test interpretation to help students make educational and career plans, and classroom guidance) and delineates what the Texas developmental guidance and counseling program consists of (i.e., guidance curriculum, responsive services, individual planning, and system support; Texas Education Code, 2001).

Certification of educators is a state's right and responsibility. Thus, states have established certification laws and rules that stipulate the entry level and, often, the continuing education requirements prerequisite to earning and maintaining school counselor certification. A work-group visit with the state education department guidance staff may reveal much about state goals and the larger perspective. If you have not availed yourself of the statewide viewpoint, join the members of the work group on their visit to the state capitol. Much can also be learned by conducting online searches of your state's education codes and statutes, policies and rules.

Professional Standards

Standards relevant to guidance and counseling have been established by state departments of education guidance departments, regional accreditation bodies, and professional associations. Some of these standards include school counselor–student ratios; for example, ASCA (2009b) has identified 1:250 as an appropriate ratio. Standards for comprehensive guidance and counseling programs have been established by more than 40 states (Martin et al., 2009) and in the ASCA National Model and content standards for school guidance and counseling programs (ASCA, 2005). Several of the American Counseling Association divisions have published standards that also guide the professional practices of school counseling (e.g., National Career Development Association, Association for Specialists in Group Work). ASCA has published role descriptions for the three school levels: *Why Elementary School Counselors* (ASCA, 2004a), *Why Middle School Counselors* (ASCA, 2004b), and *Why Secondary School Counselors?* (ASCA, 2004c). These publications describe students' developmental needs at each level and how school counselors respond.

Staff Support or Nonsupport

Political also means the level of constituent support that is behind the momentum for change. Some school counselors are eager for changes and will accept them; others will resist. Guidance and counseling program leaders need to consider the feelings of the staff and make preparations for working with both supportive and nonsupportive individuals. Nurturing the positive attitudes of the school counselors who are supportive and building on their strengths allows the program to be improved.

As discussed in Chapter 2, perhaps the majority of school counselors are, at first, resistant. Change is frightening to many people. Assessing the causes of their resistance will help you and your leadership team to address those concerns as much as is feasible. Many of the resisters do not understand the program concept at first. Many are fearful that the new program will cause them to change their entire set of work-related behaviors. Many are fearful that they do not or will not have the competencies they will need in the new program. And some will resist until they retire or are moved to other positions. We advise you to keep focused on the positive, manage the negative as best you can, and wait out the rest.

The support of administrators and teachers—the representatives of the primary clients of the program, the students—is needed to make changes effectively. As with the school counselors, they, too, will fall onto a continuum of support and nonsupport. By and large, they want what is best for the students. They also, by and large, will look to the school counselors' expertise to tell them how professional school counselors can best help students.

As mentioned previously, the representation of administrators and teachers on the steering, advisory, and other working committees as appropriate is essential to hearing and responding to their perspectives and needs. Political support from the school board and senior administration also promotes support from other administrators and school staff members. Indeed, without board and senior administrative support, changes take longer or may not get done at all (Taylor, 2002).

At the local building level, the relationships between counselors and principals is especially critical to successful change and full implementation of the program (Lambie, 2004). It is best when the relationship is a true working alliance based on an understanding of each others' roles, trust, open communication, engagement, shared goals, and purposeful collaboration (Jansen, Millitello, & Kosine, 2008). Professional school counselors build this alliance by informing their principals about the program model, its design (e.g., recommended time allocations), appropriate and inappropriate (nonguidance) duties, and the known or foreseen benefits for students (Leuwerke, Walker, & Shi, 2009)

Study Current Guidance and Counseling Program Delivery

This step in assessing your current program entails gathering and analyzing data that will tell you the design of the program. By studying actual program implementation, you identify the existing priorities of the qualitative design and the parameters of the quantitative design.

Understanding the current qualitative design consists primarily of the study of the activities in place in the program. From studying the activities, you see how your current program aligns with the comprehensive guidance and counseling program components: guidance curriculum, individual student planning, responsive services, and system support. You learn that the comprehensive guidance and counseling program is not a new program but rather builds on what you already have in place.

From studying the activities, you can determine the priorities for the current use of the professional school counselors' competencies—the roles they perform in conducting the activities. You learn about the priorities of the clients within the program—by category, who is actually being helped. You identify the results for the program participants—the content addressed in the program. Thus, carefully and thoroughly identifying the program activities is essential to the overall program improvement process.

Understanding the quantitative design consists primarily of the study of how school counselors' time is currently allocated, again using the framework of the program delivery components. Through this information about the time spent on the components and from the analysis of what activities are done within that time, the numbers of students and other clients currently served can be inferred, as can the categories and subcategories of the current clients.

In the sections that follow, each part of the design is described, that is, what is to be assessed. Some example results are displayed. Finally, ideas about how you can gather the data you need are also provided. We firmly believe that the more thoroughly you gather these data, the more solid your foundation for program change will be. However, in some instances school counselors or their administrators are under pressure to get recommendations made. Thus, we first describe legitimate ways to gather the data, and then we offer some shortcuts that have been used with some degree of success in other schools or districts.

Qualitative Design

Identify Current Guidance and Counseling Activities

What Is Assessed. In this part of the study, you identify the specific activities that are conducted at each school level within each of the four comprehensive guidance and counseling program components. Identification of specific nonguidance tasks is also recommended. Studying the program activities provides information about many of the facets of the current program design. As described in Chapter 3, the program components are made up of activities that serve different purposes. You are identifying what activities make up your current program and how they fit within the program model. Additionally, an activity includes all aspects of the design: one or more school counselors' competencies being applied; one or more categories of students or other program clients being served; and an intentional activity that targets an objective for student competency development or learning—what the anticipated student results are. Quantitatively, you are able to identify how much time school counselors spend on the activity and how many students or other clients are actually served. When you aggregate this information by component, you learn a lot about your current program's priorities and shape (i.e., about which components are emphasized and which are not).

Identifying and recording the activities in which the guidance department and other staff members are involved yields worthwhile information about your program. It is a major task. There are several reasons for conducting it. One reason is that recording the actual activities accomplished ensures preciseness in program details. Another is that recording these activities renders them visible and thus more understandable to others. Traditionally, much of what school counselors do is invisible to others.

Visibility also helps school counselors see the commonalities among their programs. In some districts, it has provided a bridge between the elementary and secondary counselors and enabled them to focus on the similarities of rather than the differences between their programs. Yet another reason is that recording encourages school counselors as they learn more about the new program model and how what they are currently doing fits into it. In our experience, recording has helped the school counselors who are not in the mainstream of program remodeling and revitalization better understand the four program components by providing operational definitions for them.

In getting started, it is important that the school counselors involved in the data submission, collection, and recording understand the kinds of activities that make up each component. Table 4.3 provides some examples of activities (by program component). These are activities that groups of school counselors and school counselors-in-training (teachers) typically identify. They include guidance curriculum lessons that school counselors or their colleagues have taught to classrooms of students, traditional individual student planning activities such as test results interpretations and applications or helping students decide on their courses for the next year, counseling individuals with issues or problems, and consulting with parents and teachers. Nonguidance tasks vary from school to school or district to district, but some recurrent themes are evident in these assignments as well.

Ideas on How to Conduct the Assessment of Current Program Activities. We suggest that one or more work groups be used to develop and conduct the activity assessment survey. Groups can be organized by school level (elementary, middle or junior high, and high) or represent all school levels and be organized by the new program components. Every staff member should respond to the survey so that a complete picture is developed. However, if the staff is large, groups of staff members may complete the surveys together. Buildings with multiple staff members are an obvious grouping. Clusters of elementary counselors, or other clusters of single staff members, can be arranged.

The work groups—the group or groups processing this information—need to devise the forms they need to gather the information they want. It is important to anticipate that the data regarding the activities will be analyzed to learn how school counselors' competencies are used, what content is targeted, and what student results are anticipated. These analyses are often done by different groups, so the data collection forms need to be developed with the subsequent process plan in mind.

Each group should then distribute the forms to the staff for whom they are responsible and ask them to list the guidance and counseling activities by program components. The forms could contain a few examples by grade level to assist staff in knowing what to list; the work group members could generate their own examples (Gysbers, Stanley, Kosteck-Bunch, Magnuson, & Starr, 2008). Some districts have found it useful to use the activities described in their original district handbooks, ensuring that the activities listed are actual activities. The next step is to aggregate the data from individual staff members into a level-by-level, component-by-component composite.

Some shortcuts to substitute for the more thorough process just described include school counselors spontaneously generating lists of activities or using prepared models of

Table 4.3
Examples of Traditional Guidance Activities by Program Component

Guidance Curriculum	Individual Student Planning	Responsive Services	System Support	Nonguidance Tasks
Classroom guidance lessons re. program content	Career pathways	Individual counseling: school behavior, family problems, friendship problems	Faculty in-service training re: standardized testing	Lunch duty
	Assessment results interpretation			Writing schedule changes
Career Day	Progress on personal plans		Counselor staff development	Coordinating standardized testing programs
Character education	Course selection	Small-group counseling	Guidance program annual planning	
Red Ribbon Week	4-year high school plans			Tracking special education paperwork
College nights	Graduation plans	Child study teams	Parent–teacher association meetings	Acting as administrative designee
	College searches and visits	Crisis intervention	Counseling department meetings	
		Teacher consultation re. individual students		
		Parent consultation		

program activities, or the district or building guidance and counseling program leader gathering information and aligning the data according to a rubric.

All the school counselors in small districts or counselors representing each level in larger districts can, in the context of an all-day professional development meeting, generate lists of the activities that they can think of on the spot—or have thought about as homework for the meeting—using the program components as the organizer. These can be generated by each level group (elementary, middle, high school) separately and then brought to the whole group to review and supplement. Again, these need to be recorded for presentation and further use, but it is a way to begin.

Table 4.4 displays what we have learned are the hallmark activities of established, high-functioning comprehensive guidance and counseling programs. Assessing the status of your school or district in light of these gives you a general impression about what you currently have in place and what you are missing. Using this list as a basis provides a structure for counselors to generate their lists. We have used a blank copy of the four quadrants as a worksheet to be used by counselors to answer the question, "What activities are you currently doing that fit into each?" Another option is suggested in the ASCA National Model, which mentions using "the ASCA program audit to identify components and elements in place and to be developed" (ASCA, 2005, p. 69)

Another approach to this qualitative assessment of what actually occurs in the program has been used by district-level guidance and counseling program leaders as they meet with each building-level staff group. Building-level staff are interviewed regarding a predetermined set of criteria that allows leaders to gather the data to compare their programs with the program model adopted by the district. A similar approach can be used in a self-study format wherein leaders provide the questions to building staff, who then complete the responses in writing for the comparison process that ensues. Neither of these approaches, however, provides the specific information about the range of activities that is so useful in understanding the complete picture of the current program, and neither approach is useful in determining specific student results.

Table 4.4

Hallmark Activities of Comprehensive Guidance Programs

Guidance curriculum	Individual student planning
Regular pattern of guidance lessons provided to every student in each grade level	Individual-focused educational and career guidance activities provided as students anticipate and make transitions from one educational level to another
	Individual student advisement system supported by individual student portfolios
	Delineated, articulated career development program for all students
Responsive services	*System support*
Small-group counseling	Counselors manage, monitor, and evaluate program implementation
Systematic, planned individual counseling	Staff education provided re: guidance program priorities and activity plan
Regular and systematic consultations with teachers and administrators re: unsuccessful students	Guidance provided by teachers, administrators, and counselors is coordinated
Effective system for student referrals	Parents are partners in program design and delivery (as needed)
Regular parent consultation	Guidance advisory committee
Systematic procedure for helping students manage personal crises	Meaningful and fair evaluation of guidance program and counseling staff
Preplanned, team approach to crisis management	

Identify How Professional School Counselors' Competencies Are Used

What Is Assessed. Assessing how professional school counselor specialized competencies are used in your current guidance and counseling program requires, first, that you identify the competencies relevant to your state's certification requirements and district's expectations. If you are following our suggested process, you have already done this in assessing the human resources available to the program.

Ideas on How to Conduct the Assessment of Current School Counselor Competence Application. In analyzing the activities provided in your current program, you are able to identify which school counselor competencies are used and with what level of priority. For example, a counselor-led classroom guidance lesson applies the school counselor's teaching skills; a school counselor's developing a classroom guidance lesson with a teacher applies the school counselor's consultation skills. A school counselor's assisting students to set educational, career, or personal goals applies the school counselor's guidance skills. A school counselor's assisting parents to work with their students on their goals applies the school counselor's consultation skills. Individual and small-group counseling apply school counselor's counseling skills, and so on. The priority for each set of competencies (teaching, guiding, individual counseling, etc.) is inferred through the emphasis on the different kinds of activities—and is ultimately verified through the time study described later in this chapter.

Because by definition nonguidance tasks do not apply school counselors' specialized competencies that are the result of their advanced education and training, the competencies applied in those activities are not considered in this analysis. Some school counselor groups, however, have also considered what skills are used in nonguidance tasks. All too often, of course, nonguidance tasks apply quasi-administrative, instructional, or clerical skills.

Table 4.5 provides an example of data similar to that found in several districts with which we have worked. It displays the school counselor performance domains described in the *Texas Evaluation Model for Professional School Counselors* (2nd ed.; Texas Counseling Association, 2004) and records the priorities inferred by school counselors after having analyzed the legitimate guidance and counseling activities they were currently doing: 1 is the highest priority; 7 is the lowest. It is an example of a shortcut approach to this assessment because it relates priorities to performance domains, not to the longer list of school counselor competencies.

Identify Who Is Served by the Current Program: Groups and Subgroups

What Is Assessed. In assessing your current guidance and counseling program, it is important to identify who the program actually serves—who the clients are—and the balance of services or the level of service that each subset of clients receives. The assessment of your

Table 4.5

Current Priorities for Use of Counselor Competence and Performance Domain

Performance Domain	Elementary School	Middle School	High School
Program management	7	2	4
Guidance	6	6	6
Counseling	1	2	2
Consultation	2	5	1
Coordination	5	1	5
Student assessment	3	4	7
Professionalism	4	7	3

current program activities suggests who your student clients are and helps you be aware that there are many clients in addition to students, including teachers, students' parents, administrators, other specialists who work with the students, and the system itself.

According to the *Ethical Standards for School Counselors* (ASCA, 2010), included in Appendix A, "The professional school counselor has a primary obligation to the student who is to be treated with respect as a unique individual" (A.1.a.). The student population is made up of myriad subgroups that provide "the basis for promoting healthy development, preventing problems, intervening as soon as problems are identified, and providing effective ways to respond to pervasive, chronic, and serious problems" (School Mental Health Project, 2010, p. 4). We identify five groupings pertinent to comprehensive, developmental guidance and counseling programs: grade levels, developmental levels, service need levels, youth subculture groups, and cultural groups.

Grade levels. First, students are divided into grade levels that are essentially age groups. The National Board for Professional Teaching Standards (2002, p. viii) identified these age groups as 3–8 years, 7–12 years, 11–15 years, and 14–18 years.

Developmental levels. Second, students are at different developmental stages: early childhood, middle childhood, early adolescence, and adolescence and young adulthood (National Board for Professional Teaching Standards, 2002, p. viii). Although not all students experience these developmental stages at the same ages, each of these developmental stages brings with it developmental tasks for all students to accomplish. All students, then, can benefit from school counselors' interventions that facilitate their educational, career, personal, and social developmental progression (i.e., developmental guidance).

Students present a full range of developmental issues for which they are seeking help that school counselors can provide. Examples of educational developmental tasks with which students need help are those related to thinking and problem solving and those related to their future educational opportunities. Examples of career developmental tasks with which students need help are those related to their development as workers, decision making, and anticipating the future. Examples of social developmental tasks with which students need help are those related to their learning to behave according to the school's standards; their relationships with their parents, friends, teachers, and others; and their ethnic–cultural identity. Examples of personal developmental tasks with which students need help relate to their physical, self-concept, emotional, identity, personality, and moral development.

Service need levels. Third, students present different degrees of need for help from school counselors. In contrast to several related disciplines (e.g., mental illness, special education, medicine, substance abuse, social work, reading, professional learning communities) that use three-tier models, the school counseling profession has historically identified four levels of need that call for four types of interventions (Myrick, 1993).

As displayed in Figure 4.1, 100% of our students have developmental needs. An estimated 35% of students have preventive needs; they struggle more than others in trying to accomplish the developmental tasks for their stage or face problems, issues, or barriers that interrupt their attention to the accomplishment of these tasks. These students can benefit from responsive interventions that prevent them from getting farther off track (e.g., individual or small-group counseling). Fewer, approximately 15%, have already made choices or experienced situations that derail their healthy development. These students can benefit from responsive interventions that help them remedy their situation and get back on track. In addition to providing counseling, professional school counselors may refer them to relevant specialists or special programs. Relatively few students (1%–2%) face crisis situations, ones that are life threatening or are severely disruptive to their continued healthy development. These students require an immediate response from school counselors and, most typically, assessment, referral, and follow-up.

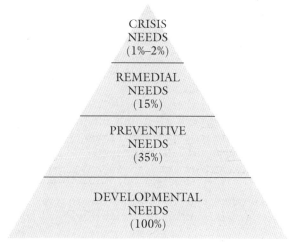

Figure 4.1
Levels and Percentages of Students' Intervention Needs

CRISIS
NEEDS
(1%–2%)

REMEDIAL
NEEDS
(15%)

PREVENTIVE
NEEDS
(35%)

DEVELOPMENTAL
NEEDS
(100%)

The four types of interventions and specific examples related to educational, career, social, or personal development follow.

1. *Preventive intervention needs:* One of the example educational development tasks suggested earlier is problem solving. Students who cannot identify solutions to problems they are having need preventive interventions. One career development task is anticipating the future. Students who cannot foresee a future for themselves need preventive interventions. One social development task is ethnic–cultural identity. Students who are insensitive to people who are ethnically or racially different from themselves need preventive interventions. One personal development task is moral development. Students who experiment with abandoning their personal behavioral standards in the face of peer pressure need preventive interventions.

2. *Remedial intervention needs:* Students who use inappropriate strategies for solving their problems need remedial interventions in their educational development. Students who believe they will not reach adulthood need remedial interventions in their career development. Students who are intolerant of people who are ethnically or racially different from themselves need remedial interventions in their social development. Students who consistently act contrary to their personal standards as a result of peer pressure need remedial interventions in their personal development.

3. *Crisis intervention needs:* Students who are truant because of being bullied need crisis interventions in their educational development. Students who attempt suicide to avoid their future need crisis interventions in their career development. Students who are involved in racial–ethnic conflicts need crisis interventions in their social development. Students who fear they are pregnant need crisis interventions in their personal development.

4. *Cultural needs:* Students come from different cultures. They are of different genders, sexual orientations, and preferences. They live with a variety of types of parents or guardians (e.g., biological, single, gay, adoptive, or foster parents; grandparent; residential facility) and related family configurations (e.g., two biological parents and siblings or none, extended, and blended). Their lifestyles vary (e.g., mobile, migrant,

homeless). They differ ethnically (e.g., African American, Hispanic, White, Asian/Pacific Islander, Native American). They come from a range of different socioeconomic circumstances (e.g., lower, middle, upper). Their family incomes may be steady or not, and they may come from public or private sector jobs, the military, welfare, or illegal work. They have parents with a range of educational levels. Their parents may be absent because of incarceration or abandonment. They come from homes and communities that speak a variety of languages other than English and affiliate with various religious beliefs.

Youth subculture groups. Youth culture groups and subgroups each have "distinct styles behaviors, and interests. The term *counterculture* is used to designate subgroups that manifest hostility to the dominant culture" (School Mental Health Project, 2010, p. 2). Typical groups seen today in schools include nerds, geeks, jocks, gangs, aggies, Goths, and many more.

The array of potential subgroups of students is daunting. In assessing whom your current program actually serves, it is imperative to identify which of these subgroups of students receive help. If your goal is to serve students as best as you can, then you must be clear about who the students you serve are to determine whom you can best help. This topic is discussed more fully in Chapter 5.

Adult clients. Students are the primary clients, but many states' laws and the ASCA (2010) *Ethical Standards* make it clear that school counselors also have responsibilities to the students' parents or guardians. School counselors also have responsibilities to colleagues and professional associates (*Ethical Standards*, Section C; see Appendix A), including teachers, administrators and staff, other mental health professionals, and other school specialists. They have responsibilities to the school, to the community, to themselves, and to the profession. These adult clients are also composed of subgroups, two of which are of particular importance: those who relate directly to the school counselors' student population and those who do not.

School system as client. The system as a client is also important to acknowledge because it is often the client served by nonguidance tasks. The system includes the school, the district, and the state or federal education systems.

Ideas on How to Conduct an Assessment of Students Served. The most complete means by which to learn who is currently being served in the guidance and counseling program is through a process of counselors keeping logs as to who is served and coding them according to their subgroups. This happens most readily through sign-in or counselor recording sheets maintained in guidance centers and in school counselors' offices. Data can also be accumulated by having students sign in at all activities. Coding the data usually requires computerizing the data collection so that students' subgroup codes may be entered and tallied as well. Given the large number of variables described previously, most districts with whom we have worked have undertaken this assessment and have at this point preselected the client variables they need to track—whether it is students' numbers by grade level, by intervention levels, or by demographics—as well as the categories of adults or other clients—teachers, parents, administrators, staff, other mental health professionals, other school specialists, the school system, community representatives or groups, themselves (e.g., pursuing professional development), or the profession (e.g., association work).

In the districts with which we have worked, the most accurate data about whom the served clients are and to what degree they are served come from counselors' logs recording the amount of time spent. By ensuring that the system-serving functions are distinct from the student-serving functions, the data may then be so analyzed. The results of one such log keeping for a group of high school counselors are presented in Table 4.6.

Table 4.6
Personnel Support Versus System Support (Baseline Data)

Personnel Support			vs.	System Support		
% of Time	Function	Rank		% of Time	Function	Rank
12.8	Individual counseling	2		19.9	Professional responsibilities	1
8.0	Individual guidance	4		8.3	Planning	3
6.3	Conferencing—staff	6		6.9	Record keeping	5
4.2	Enrollment–registration	8		5.2	Miscellaneous paperwork	7
3.5	Consulting staff	9		3.9	Special education	9
3.2	Conferencing—parent	12		3.8	Administrative assignments	11
2.5	Counseling parent	13				
2.3	Coordinate agencies	14				
2.0	Consulting other school specialists	15				
1.7	Guidance activities	16				
1.5	Consulting parents	17				
1.4	Career education	18				
1.3	Conferencing—student–parent	19				
0.6	Group guidance	20				
0.4	Small-group counseling	21				
0.2	Testing individuals	22				
0.1	Test district program	23				
52.0				48.0		

Another method for collecting this information relates to the current activities assessment discussed earlier in this section. By analyzing the activities accomplished, one can readily discern who the participants in the activities are—perhaps not by individual student but certainly by some of the categories. In general, guidance curriculum and individual student planning activities are interventions provided for students with developmental needs. Responsive services are interventions provided for students with preventive, remedial, and crisis needs. System support activities serve the legitimate nonstudent clients. These last two sets of activities, then, have to be analyzed in more depth for classification according to the three need levels. This method also lends itself to assessing the issues presented and responded to and the demographics of the students served.

Another shortcut to gathering information about the clients served is a survey. A survey is not as precise as the techniques just suggested but can yield useful information. For example, school counselors in one district were asked to guesstimate the percentage of their client-contact time spent with a listed set of clients. The original list was developed by a work group and distributed to all school counselors. The group collected and tallied the results and was encouraged by the consistency of the guesstimates. Although this is an imprecise way to get information, if enough individuals submit input, any real aberrations are modified by the uniformity of the majority. The results of one survey of this type are presented in Table 4.7.

An even quicker and less accurate but useful method is for school counselors as a group to guesstimate in a group setting the priorities for their client service. The method we use is to have individual school counselors guesstimate their own priorities and then compare them with those of others who work at the same school level. Sometimes these groups come to consensus about the districtwide priorities. This was the case of the group whose data are reflected in Table 4.8. This group decided that students who are truly in a crisis need immediate attention and are, therefore, at that time the Number 1 priority; hence the asterisks in that row. The primary criteria for the prioritization of the others, however, were based on a mixture of other variables, for example, the number of

Table 4.7
Guesstimates of Percentages of Time Spent With Clients (Baseline Data)

Clients	Average[a] Elementary	Average[a] Middle	Average[a] High
Student contacts			
Development guidance			
Group	23	13	10
Individual	11	12	25
Basic testing program	7	3	10
Preventive (counseling)	12	18	11
Remedial (counseling, referral)	4	8	3
Adult contacts			
District administration	5	8	3
School staff			
Principals	5	4	3
Teachers	9	9	7
Other counselors	3	3	5
Special education staff	8	6	5
Other specialists	3	3	3
Parents	7	10	8
Outside agency staff	2	2	1
Community representatives	1	1	2

Note. Data from Northside Independent School District, San Antonio, TX. Adapted with permission.
[a]Because of rounding, numbers do not add to 100%.

clients who presented themselves in each category, the amount of school counselors' time spent with each category of client, and the importance of the category as perceived by the school counselors and, in some cases, by the administrators. Sometimes it becomes clear that the variations from building to building are so wide that the only conclusion is that the clients served are those who are selected for service at the building level. Such was the case for the group in Table 4.8. The elementary school counselors determined that the priorities were very different in each building hence the tie for fourth place reflected in that column.

Table 4.8
Guesstimates of Current Client Priorities

Clients	Elementary School	Middle School	High School
Students with developmental needs	3	4	3
Students with preventive needs	2	5	1
Students with remedial needs	1	3	2
Students with crisis needs	*	*	*
Teachers	4 (varies)	6	5
Parents	4 (varies)	7	4
Administrators	4 (varies)	1	6
Others	7	2	7

Note. Asterisks indicate "not ranked" because when a student has a crisis, it always is the top priority, but over the course of the year crisis needs are not the top priority.

Identify the Current Results of the Program

What Is Assessed. Identifying the intended results students achieve by participating in each current program activity is the next task. If the activity results (objectives) were not identified in the activities study, identifying them entails taking one activity at a time and asking such questions as, "Why do we do this?" "How are students different as a result of this activity?" "What do students know, what attitudes do they form, or what can students do that they could not do before this activity?" For example,

If the activity is	*then the result is*
• assist students in planning their schedules	• all students can select classes consistent with their abilities and interests
• conduct a Career Day	• students who participate can identify an occupation consistent with their abilities and interests.

Although it is obvious that school counselors' major purpose is to serve students, not all school counselors have had experience in clearly stating the results of their work. For years, the profession subscribed to the notion that what school counselors did was not observable or measurable or that what school counselors did were processes and so the results were not visible.

Ideas on How to Conduct an Assessment of Current Program Results. If you have already defined the content domains and competencies that drive your guidance and counseling program, as suggested in Chapter 3, your task may be merely to synthesize available written statements. If in adopting the guidance and counseling program model, you adopted an outline of student competencies (e.g., those preexisting locally or those from your state or the national model), then your task is one of relating specific activities to student competencies. If neither of these options is available and your staff as a whole is not comfortable with the emphasis on results, you are advised to use your steering committee counselors, a group of other counselor leaders, or all the school counselors in small groups as a work group and guide them through the basic process of identifying student results for the activities they are currently doing. It is by demonstrating school counselors' contribution to students' growth and development that our position in the educational setting is assured. Thus, this exercise allows you to test the validity of program activities; if an activity has no visible outcome or if the identifiable outcome is of little relevance, then continuing it may be inadvisable.

After the guidance staff have identified the activities they perform and the intended results of each activity, the next question is, "Have all students for whom the activity was conducted reached these intended results?" Although the guidance staff may feel that the activities accomplished the desired results, there may be little evidence to prove it. (Suggestions for assessing student results are provided in Chapter 10.)

Having determined the intended or actual results of each activity and the clients served, you can generalize competencies developed through program participation. By grouping activities that are intended to deliver similar results under a program component, you can make general statements about the intended results of each component. For example, the results of the two activities just cited—schedule planning and Career Day—are related to students' development of educational and career plans. Aggregating the results from all such activities will describe the results of the individual student planning component. With all the results listed, you can draw larger generalizations about the intended results of your total current program. This list is then ready for use in comparing the program you currently have with the program your district or school desires.

As a shortcut, but on a much more global level, the steering committee or counseling staff can, again, spontaneously prioritize the domains, competencies, or both identified as those that define the program content. For example, in Texas seven major guidance content areas have been recommended for use by schools and districts (Texas Education Agency, 2005). An example of such a prioritizing that is somewhat typical of current programs is provided in Table 4.9.

Quantitative Design

Understanding the current quantitative design comes from studying how school counselors are actually spending their time in delivering the activities and figuring out how many students and other clients actually participate in them. Finally, if you already conduct results evaluation (as described in Chapter 10), data may be available about the numbers of students achieving the various results from participating in the program's activities.

Identify How School Counselors Currently Spend Their Time

What Is Assessed. How school counselors use their time in alignment with the comprehensive guidance and counseling program components provides the most concrete information about the actual design of your current program. Because school counselors are the basic program resource, records of their actual program-related behaviors are the most critical data you will gather. It is also important to collect data regarding the time spent on nonguidance tasks.

By specifying how school counselors allocate their time to each of the program components, you will be able to see what the program balance is. By aggregating the time of all the counselors at a school level, you will be able to see what the program balance is at each school level. Answer such questions as "Which of the components takes up most of the resources?" "Which the least?" "What proportion of school counselor time is spent on nonguidance tasks and is, therefore, depleted from the guidance and counseling program?"

As was true for qualitative design, these quantitative data also suggest information about the extent to which school counselors' competencies are used, how many students are served and from what subgroups of the total student population, and the number of results that might be achieved by the program's clients. In gathering the time information vis-à-vis the program components, you might also gather information regarding how the resource of school counselor time is appropriated to the school counselor performance domains.

Figure 4.2 shows a format that has been use by school counselors to document how their time is being spent in both the program components and the performance domains. For

Table 4.9
Current Program Content Priorities

Content Domain	Elementary School	Middle School	High School
Self-confidence development	6	5	2
Motivation to achieve	5	3	6
Decision making, goal setting, problem solving, planning	2	2	4
Interpersonal effectiveness	4	6	3
Communication skills	3	4	5
Cross-cultural effectiveness	7	7	7
Responsible behavior	1	1	1

Figure 4.2
Time Log: Components and Performance Domains

Date: _____

TIME	NOTE	PROGRAM COMPONENT[a]	PERFORMANCE DOMAIN[b]
7:00–7:15 a.m.			
7:15–7:30			
7:30–7:45			
7:45–8:00			
8:00–8:15			
8:15–8:30			
8:30–8:45			
8:45–9:00			

Total no. of minutes for the day	Guidance curriculum _____ Individual student planning _____ Responsive services _____ System support _____ Nonguidance _____	Program management _____ Guidance _____ Counseling _____ Consultation _____ Coordination _____ Student assessment _____ Professional behavior _____ Professional standards _____

[a]Program component legend: GC = guidance curriculum; ISP = individual student planning; RS = responsive services; SS = system support; NG = nonguidance tasks.
[b]Performance domain legend: PM = program management; G = guidance; Cou = counseling; Con = consultation; Cor = coordination; SA = student assessment; PB = professional behavior; PS = professional standards.

actual minutes or increments of time, school counselors record the component in which their activity fits and the performance domain they are applying.

A note of caution: A time study provides a golden opportunity to learn a great deal about what is actually happening in your program, but you need to resist the temptation to learn everything you always wanted to know but were afraid to ask. Studies need to be as simple as possible to implement, or your data will be meaningless. Because school counselors and other guidance staff are busy, consider carefully what you are asking them to record. Collect only data you know you will use. The simpler the time-recording system is, the more accurate your information will be.

Ideas on How to Conduct a School Counselor Time-Use Study. Planning your time use study carefully so that the data are meaningful and useful is also essential. Decisions need to be made about why you are conducting the study, whose time will be studied, and what you want to learn about their time as well as when, where, and how the study will be conducted. We recommend that you write out the purpose of the time study to ensure clarity among all school counselors and administrators; for example, "the purpose of this time study is to determine how the resource of school counselor time is appropriated to the four program components of the comprehensive guidance and counseling program model." Before school counselors begin to log their time, it is important to define the kinds of activities that make up each component. Align each currently identified guidance and counseling program activity with its proper component.

You will want to be able to identify the results for the counseling staff in broad categories; for example, distinguishing among elementary, middle or junior high, and high school counselors is useful because guidance and counseling programs at the different school levels are usually balanced differently. There may be concern that the data will be used for personnel evaluation rather than program description purposes. You need to decide whether you are willing to provide for anonymity or whether you need to establish an appropriate level of trust with the school counselors.

Because this is a time-use study, you need to decide when you will do the study and for how long: all year? a certain month? a scattering of days throughout the year? The study should cover enough time so that some activities that may occur only occasionally are not given undue attention. The most thorough study is one that is conducted for an entire school year. In this kind of study, school counselors log their time 1 day per week for a full school year, varying the day each week. They begin by recording time on Monday in the first week, Tuesday in the second week, Wednesday in the third week, and so on (Gysbers et al., 2008).

You must also determine the increments of time that school counselors will be recording: by minutes? by quarter hours? by half hours? by class periods? by the length of guidance activities? A rule of thumb is that the shorter the length of time the data are gathered, the smaller the logged time increments should be. If the study covers 1 month, school counselors' actual minutes should be used. If the study covers the entire year, 15- or 30-minute intervals are more feasible to work with. An advantage to recording actual minutes is that in a traditional program, many school counselor interventions are spontaneously conducted, brief interventions of inconsistent time increments. Using this more flexible approach may yield a more realistic picture. The advantage to recording a set block of time is consistency for each school counselor and across all school counselors.

Another decision to be made is when the school counselors should log their time: as they go? at the end of the morning and afternoon? at the end of the day? We recommend that they record only time spent during the 8-hour workday or the time spent during student access time. When school counselors who work extra hours log their time, the variances in the study's parameters become difficult to manage. The forms for data collection need to be as simple to use as possible, both for recording and for tallying. If it is readily available to all school counselors, a computer-based spreadsheet program used for ease of ongoing and cumulative tabulation can facilitate a time study. At a minimum, you will want to use a computer to aggregate the data and generate the reports you need. Be sure to consider the dictates of the computer before developing your forms.

Directions for implementing the study must be precise and clear. School counselors need to be schooled in the purpose of the study and in how to keep their records. The terminology used in the study categories needs to be thoroughly understood by everyone to ensure consistency of data. A system for fielding questions and for monitoring implementation of the study needs to be put in place. If you are running this study from a central office location, you must ensure that the campus guidance and counseling program leaders—the head or lead counselors—understand the study and its purpose and can monitor its implementation effectively. (See Appendix B for time and task analysis procedures and forms developed and used by school counselors in Missouri.)

School districts have conducted time studies for shorter periods of time that provide less data and lead to less valid generalizations but that are useful as long as the data users are aware of its limitations. Additionally, some provision must be made to ensure consideration of the special events that alter the balance of a program at different points in the year, for example, educational planning and student course selection that occur in the spring at the middle and high school levels.

When they are really in a time bind to respond to the opportunities to study their programs provided by school boards or school administrators, school counselors have guesstimated how they spend their time. This, of course, is vulnerable to the school counselors' perceptions, which may or may not be realistic. Our experience, however, supports the relative accuracy of this self-reporting technique. Again, aggregating the guesstimates of individual school counselors into one generalization for all school counselors for each level tempers the results. Table 4.10 displays an example of the accuracy of this method of data collection from a district that used two methods of data collection regarding school counselor time use: guesstimating and short-term logging. You can see that the results have some variance but in analysis might lead to similar conclusions. For example, nonguidance tasks take too much time away from the guidance and counseling program; the time spent in responsive services is more than that spent in the other program components; and the program is currently more responsive than developmental in nature.

Several examples of the results of school counselor time studies are provided in Tables 4.11 and 4.12. Table 4.11 presents data from a study of how school counselors spend their time conducted and reported by the Texas State Comptroller (Rylander, 2002, p. 18) in response to a legislative mandate. Table 4.12 presents data from a study conducted by the North Carolina Department of Public Instruction (n.d.), *How North Carolina School Counselors Spend Their Time,* in 2000–2001. This study is interesting because, in recognizing that not all school counselors at a specific school level spend the same percentage of time on a component's activities, the results generated are broken down by the percentages of school counselors spending a given percentage of time on each component. What is presented here are the data for all those surveyed (p. 6); the full report also presents the information by school level and by different categories of student services personnel. These ranges suggest the lack of uniformity for students across the state in guidance and counseling experiences. The data reveal that different school counselors work differently—they have different jobs—and that perhaps there is a lot of discretion being exercised by individual school counselors as to what they do. The report also presents information about the percentages of time that varying percentages of school counselors spent on nonguidance tasks.

Table 4.10

Current Program Design: Guesstimated and Logged Percentages of Counselor Time

Program Component	Guesstimated			Logged (Logs Kept April 2004)		
	Elementary School	Middle School	High School	Elementary School	Middle School	High School
Guidance curriculum	5	5	0	4	1	6
Individual student planning	0	10	5	0	3	14
Responsive services	50	50	40	40	21	28
System support	15	15	20	5	7	21
Nonguidance tasks	30	20	35	52	69	32

Table 4.11
Texas Comptroller School Counselor Survey
January/February 2002:
Counselor Timesheets Statewide by School Type

Category	Elementary %	Middle–Junior High %	High School %	Alternative %
Guidance curriculum	17.6	8.0	9.2	12.3
Individual planning	9.5	10.7	22.3	12.8
Responsive services	21.4	18.3	16.7	24.3
System support	16.0	11.6	11.6	12.0
Subtotal	64.5	48.6	59.8	61.4
Nonguidance activities	15.6	31.5	18.1	22.5
Staff development	3.3	2.3	2.9	1.9
Personal leave	3.8	3.5	3.7	3.5
Administration or clerical tasks	7.5	9.1	10.4	8.3
Other	5.2	5.1	5.1	2.4
Total	100	100	100	100

From these examples, you can see that useful information is generated that could lead to significant program improvement efforts, and that state-level policy makers are interested in the actual contributions that school counselors are making to students' development. The results they see includes similarities (e.g., significant portions of school counselors time is spent on nonguidance tasks) and differences (e.g., the portions of time spent on the other components). These data are used as the baseline from which progress is measured over time.

Some districts have conducted specific activity or task assessments on a particular part of the current program that is perceived to be out of balance. For example, to better understand the nature of its nonguidance activities, one district conducted a study of the quasi-administrative and clerical tasks school counselors perform. The process used was similar to that just described. A work group of school counselors identified the tasks they performed that did not require a master's degree in guidance and counseling to do. Individual staff members then estimated the number of hours or days a year they spent on each of these tasks. These specifics were then totaled, and their percentage of the total time was determined. Other districts have gathered this information in their original baseline study.

Table 4.12
How North Carolina Counselors Spend Their Time:
Percentages of Personnel/Percentages of Time Spent,
All Student Services Personnel

Activity	<10%	10%–20%	20%–30%	30%–40%	>40%
Guidance curriculum	37.8	29.0	13.5	8.2	6.8
Individual student planning	33.9	24	14.7	10.6	12.4
Responsive services	21.2	23.4	20.8	15.2	14.3
System support	32.2	29.0	13.5	8.2	6.8

Identify the Numbers of Students and Other Clients Currently Served

What Is Assessed. Assessing how many students and other clients are currently served by the program is also important baseline information. Traditionally, counseling services have targeted individual students and their related adults (teachers, parents, administrators). Today's programs emphasize a developmental basis and therefore target all students served in medium-sized groups to large groups. School counselors need to be accountable for the proportion of their caseload that benefits from the program, and students, teachers, administrators, and parents benefit from knowing how many students are actually served through each of the program components. It is important for all to understand that within the parameters of the school day, there are only so many minutes. Also, depending on the design of the program, there is a finite number of students who can be served during each day (see Chapter 8).

It also needs to be understood that the larger a school counselor's caseload, the less time each individual student can spend with his or her assigned school counselor either alone or in groups. By gathering the data regarding the numbers of students affected through each of the component's activities, school counselors and others will know what proportion of the student population currently benefits from the program activities (see Chapter 8). Similarly, it is useful to gather data about the number of student-related adults served through program activities. In analyzing their data, one district learned that the school counselors were spending more time with students' teachers than they were with the students. Another learned that 30% of their time was spent with parents in face-to-face conferences, on the phone, or through e-mail but that 30% of the parents represented fewer than 10% of their students.

Ideas on How to Conduct a Study of the Numbers of Clients Served. The primary way to collect the data is to record and tabulate them as the program is implemented, not unlike the time study. It may be done along with the time study but could prove to be a distraction. Many guidance and counseling departments already track the numbers of students who come into the counseling center by using sign-in sheets. Professional school counselors also keep notes about their clients for their personal, professional use. Reviewing these notes and tabulating the number of students and others served is also a legitimate method of gathering data. School counselors' systematic review of and tallying from their daily calendars also yields fairly accurate information. The report of these data may be as simple as "x number of students were served through current guidance curriculum activities; x number were served through individual students planning activities; x number were served through responsive services." For system support activities, the clients served directly—teachers, parents, administrators, school counselors in program management or professional development—are reported.

Through school counselors' individual calendars and through the annual calendar for the program (Chapter 8), an estimation of the number of clients served can be developed that, although not very precise, does provide substantiated data. These data could also be gleaned from the study of program activities described earlier in this chapter. This review of the planned activities entails calculating on the basis of the typical number of students involved in the various kinds of activities, for example, guidance lessons (average class size), small-group counseling (8–10 students), parent–teacher–student–school counselor conferences, teacher in-services (number of faculty), number of parents at parent education offerings, and so on. This, coupled with the records regarding individuals served, can provide descriptive numbers.

Identify the Number of Students and Other Clients Served by Subgroup

What Is Assessed. Another important means of information is to determine how many students from each subgroup are served and to determine whether the proportions of service reflect the school population as a whole. As described earlier, subgroups of students include those in different grade levels, those with varying levels of need (developmental, preventive, remedial, and crisis), and those in various cultural and social groupings. Many districts and schools have learned, to their chagrin, that their minority and low-income students are underserved.

Ideas on How to Conduct a Study of the Number of Clients Served by Subgroup. These data are subsets of the data gathered during the study of the number of clients served. The more global the subgroup, the easier it is to identify this information; for example, the number of students served by grade level should be evident. When done right, the various program activities and interventions are developed to meet different levels of student need. Numbers information can be divided on the basis of that premise; that is, classroom guidance serves those with developmental needs; small-group counseling typically serves those with prevention needs; individual counseling often serves those with remedial needs; and crisis counseling serves those groups or individuals in crisis. Assessing the number of clients served according to the demographic categories requires collecting data that includes students' names or other identifiers. This kind of assessment requires a separate study specifically designed to identify specific students.

Identify the Numbers of Students Currently Achieving the Anticipated Results of Program Activities

What Is Assessed. In addition to knowing how many clients participate in the guidance and counseling program, it is highly useful to know how many of them actually learn or are able to do what the program's activities were designed to help them with. This stage of the program improvement process is not the time to begin results evaluation, but if the information is readily available, it certainly informs the next decisions to be made.

Ideas on How to Conduct a Study of the Number of Clients Achieving Results. Indicate the number and percentage of students who achieved a particular outcome and how it was determined that this outcome was achieved. In this way, the guidance staff defines the results for specific subpopulations in the school. Follow this technique for each activity (or grouping of activities), and the result will be a listing of the results that the activity is achieving and its impact on students (see Table 4.13). It may be that only a small number of students attain many guidance objectives, or there may be little proof that any results are attained at all (achieving results is discussed more fully in Chapters 8 and 10).

Table 4.13
Activity, Results, and Impact

Activity	Result	Impact
Guide students in planning their schedules.	Students can select classes consistent with their abilities and interests.	1. Only 12% of the students change classes. 2. Follow-up study of graduates: 68% reported curriculum satisfaction
Conduct Career Day.	Students can identify an occupation consistent with their abilities and interests.	1. Participation and attendance records at the Career Day: low (only 30%) 2. Counselor contacts: high-quality response, but only 12% of the student body

Gather Perceptions About the Program

What Is Assessed

Gather perceptions about the current program from students, teachers, school counselors, administrators, parents, and community members. These assessments focus on what these groups think or feel about the current program. The focus is not necessarily on the realities of the current program or on the perceived needs of individuals, the school, or society. Needs assessment comes later in the program improvement process.

The data gathered may help you identify supportive people and groups who may be used as resources to inform you about what is right with the current program and about what might need to be changed. You can also use these data as baseline data in subsequent educational efforts.

Ideas on How to Conduct a Perception Survey

The most direct way to find out what people think about your current program is to ask them. However, as with any market research effort, selecting the population to be surveyed is very important. The sample must be representative of your program's consumers and reflective of the social and cultural demographics of your school community. Not all the perceptions will be flattering and not all will be negative; there may not be much uniformity between consumer groups. The more accurate your sample, the truer the picture of how people perceive your current program.

Gathering the perceptions of all your constituents at once is a one-time activity and should be done with proper care. If your system is small enough to tabulate by hand, or if you have access to a computer, it is best to survey random samples of students and parents. However, surveying total samples of school counselors and administrators is advised. Whether you poll all your teachers or a random sample depends on the size of your school system. If it is small, poll them all. If it is large, identify a statistically sound random sample. Computerized databases can generate such a sample. You need to ensure the sample appropriately reflects the demographics of the school community and the student population.

We suggest that you ask the members of your advisory and steering committees—who are representatives of their groups—to help you in this process of gathering perceptions. The parents as well as administrators and teachers on your school–community advisory committee, for example, can help you word the questions to parents, administrators, and teachers, respectively, by suggesting proper terminology and effective ways to encourage parents and others to respond to your questions.

Guesstimates and Brainstorming

Once steering committee members have agreed to help undertake responsibility for guiding the change process and are now faced with doing additional work, you can provide extra motivation by taking a quick assessment of their general perceptions of the program. One way to do this is to ask them to write their impressions of the design of the current guidance and counseling program. For example, they can guesstimate what percentage of school counselors' time they think is spent on each of the four components, what percentage is spent with each of the subcategories of clients, or what the top three or five priority results of the program are. A simple worksheet for gathering this information is displayed in Figure 4.3.

Another way to do a quick assessment is to have the steering committee members, representatives from other groups, or both identify, in brainstorming style, what activities they think of when they think of the guidance and counseling program. The guidance and

Figure 4.3
Current Program Design Worksheet

PRIORITY STUDENT/COMMUNITY GUIDANCE-RELATED NEEDS
1.
2.
3.
4.
5.

COUNSELOR PERFORMANCE DOMAINS (SKILLS/COMPETENCIES)	PRIORITIES (1–7)
Program management	
Guidance	
Counseling	
Consultation	
Coordination	
Assessment	
Professionalism	

CLIENTS	PRIORITIES (1–8)
STUDENTS	
Development needs	
Preventive needs	
Remedial needs	
Crisis needs	
TEACHERS	
PARENTS	
ADMINISTRATORS	
OTHERS	

STUDENT COMPETENCIES	PRIORITIES (1–7)
Self-confidence development	
Motivation to achieve	
Decision making, goal setting, problem solving	
Interpersonal effectiveness	
Communication skills	
Cross-cultural effectiveness	
Responsible behavior	

COUNSELOR TIME/PROGRAM COMPONENT	PRIORITIES # (1–5)	% (=100%)
Guidance curriculum		
Individual student planning		
Responsive services		
System support		
Nonguidance		

counseling program leader records these spontaneous inputs according to the program components, including a column for nonguidance tasks. If the program is in much need of improvement, the priorities evidenced by either of these exercises will help steering committee members anticipate the probable results of the current program assessment.

Interviews

Another way to find out what people think of your program is to interview a representative sample of individuals from the various groups involved using a structured approach. Separate work groups with advisory and steering committee members as leaders can help accomplish this task. Consider having your advisory and steering committee members interview leaders of their various subgroups. For example, the PTA representative to the advisory committee could interview the presidents of local PTA units. A caution here is that the leaders' opinions may not be representative of their groups' mainstream.

The guidance and counseling program leader has a specific role to play in this process. Especially if there is widespread and generalized criticism of the current guidance and counseling program, there is merit to the leader's asking key individuals such as superintendents, principals, teachers, and parent leaders direct questions such as "What do you like about the current guidance and counseling program?" "What do you dislike about it?" "What would you change about the program?" "What would you add to the program?"

Some example questions asked in interviews held to assess the current status of a districtwide program are listed here.

1. What do you like best about your guidance and counseling program?
2. What do you not like about your guidance and counseling program?
3a. What is the mission of your guidance and counseling program?
3b. How does the guidance and counseling program mission dovetail with your district or school mission?
4. Do you have a written description of your guidance and counseling program that you give to others? (May I have one?)
5. What student needs have you identified for which guidance and counseling program activities would be helpful?
6. What are the priorities for students who are served through the guidance and counseling program activities?
7. What knowledge or skills do students learn by participating in your guidance and counseling program?
8a. What is the size of your student caseload?
8b. Who else works in delivering the guidance and counseling program?
9a. How is your guidance and counseling program organized (services vs. program vs. spontaneous)?
9b. Please complete one Component Activities worksheet for your school.
10. Please complete the percentages and priorities worksheet with your estimated use of time.
11a. Have you completed a process for guidance program development (major)?
11b. Do you have a continuous process for ongoing program development and improvement (incremental)?
11c. What new activities have you or are you going to do this year? How or why did you decide to do this?
12. How do you evaluate the effectiveness of your
    a. students' achievement of results through your activities?
    b. professional performance?
    c. program as a whole?
13. What obstacles block your implementing a perfect program?
14. Other comments? Thoughts?

From the answers to those questions, the school district learned of the following weaknesses and strengths.

Weaknesses:
- underserving economically poor and minority students
- not having an articulated vision or mission for the program
- idiosyncratic decision making by individual counselors about what they do on the job (e.g., time and activities), leaving the counselors feeling insecure about their choices
- not having a clearly stated rationale for counselor staffing, yielding inequities in responsibilities
- underuse of professional school counselors
- lack of leadership for school counselors by professional school counselors
- not having a clearly defined program structure and design
- not having a clearly defined scope and sequence for guidance content
- program activities and services offered predominantly on a 1:1 basis, yielding inequities
- program services and activities were disjointed
- nonguidance activities were eating up an inordinate amount of counselor time (ranging from 20%–50%)
- not having systematic processes in place to design, monitor, evaluate, and improve the program
- no planned coordination of program delivery across school levels
- not having a professionally relevant school counselor performance evaluation process or form

Strengths:
- the community's and district's vision, mission, and goals, including healthy social, emotional, personal, and career development of students
- climates supporting collaboration and teamwork
- adequate counselor: students ratios (albeit unevenly divided)
- the published school counselor job description reflects that of the state model
- the program content at the elementary and middle school levels reflects that of the state model
- a large number of current program activities fitting into the model 4 delivery system components
- supportive relationships between counselors and principals
- counselors and principals desiring to further develop a systematic guidance and counseling program. (Henderson, 2010)

The advantages of using an interview approach are the direct contact with members of the various groups and the in-depth responses that can be gathered. The disadvantages include the time-consuming nature of the task, the small number of people who can be contacted, and the complexity of tabulating the results.

Questionnaires

Another way to ask people for their perceptions is to use a questionnaire or a series of questionnaires. Questionnaires can be prepared and distributed to large numbers of people. Tabulating results is easy, especially if you have access to a computer.

We suggest the same cautions in the development of questionnaires or questions as we did in the development of logs. Avoid the temptation to ask every question you ever wanted answered; keep the questions straightforward and simple. It is imperative that your questions be related to the components of your program model or to the results desired for students and other clients rather than to school counselors' functions. How you do your job is a professional decision.

The questionnaires should have wording suitable to the population being polled. Thus, the questionnaire for elementary children will be different from the questionnaire for adults, but for correlation, the substance must be the same. The questions and answers must correspond from one survey form to another so that you can aggregate the results and analyze them together. Comparisons of perceptions held by different groups are often useful.

Three questionnaires used successfully to assess high school students', teachers', and school counselors' perceptions about the services they received and the results students achieved from participating in guidance activities are provided in Appendix C. In the first questionnaire, high school students are asked to state the approximate number of times they met with school counselors in a range of configurations. From these numbers, data inferences can be made about which components students have participated in. The questionnaire then asks the students two sets of questions: "Was a topic discussed with them? (Did a service occur?)" and "Was it helpful? (Was it beneficial? Did results occur?)" The questions cover the content strands of the guidance curriculum, individual student planning, and responsive services components.

In the second questionnaire, school counselors are asked to provide similar information from their perspective. The questions again cover the content strands of the guidance curriculum, the major activities of individual student planning, and the primary responses in responsive services. In the third questionnaire, teachers are asked to provide their perceptions regarding school counselor activities for both students and teachers. The questions cover system support efforts in addition to guidance curriculum, individual student planning, and responsive services efforts. The response ranges in the questionnaires include a 3-point scale for identifying occurrence of a service (*yes, unsure, no*), a 5-point scale for classifying helpfulness (*very much, quite a bit, somewhat, very little, not really*) for students and teachers, and a 4-point scale for classifying helpfulness (*11, 1, 2, —*) for teachers. Six additional questionnaires (students', teachers', and school counselors' questionnaires for both elementary and middle school levels) have the same response ranges and address the same topics, but the wording is changed to suit the population. (These are not included in Appendix C.)

If the same forms are used at the start of the program improvement process and then used several years later as measures of program effectiveness, powerful sets of information can be gathered about the value of the program approach to guidance and counseling. We recommend that questionnaires such as these be prepared for the elementary, middle or junior, and senior high levels. Note that the range of responses concerning helpfulness could be modified to three (*agree, no opinion, disagree*) or even two (*yes* or *no*).

Present a Report Describing the Current Program

At the completion of your current guidance and counseling program assessment, you will have gathered an enormous quantity of information, all of which is needed as you proceed with the program improvement efforts. At this point, a report that presents the gathered data must be written and disseminated. Then, once the report is prepared, various decision-making groups can analyze the information and draw conclusions from it, which in turn inform the program-designing process (Chapter 5). Information about both the qualitative and the quantitative designs of the guidance and counseling program has been gathered. The data that we have found useful, the methods possible to use to collect them, and those data that represent parts of the qualitative design and of the quantitative design are summarized in Table 4.14.

Attend to Diversity

The demographics of the school community and, perhaps more important, the demographics of the student population as a whole set the standard for appropriate representation in the guidance and counseling program improvement process and for assessing the appropriateness of current guidance and counseling program participation. The makeup of the steering committee, advisory committee, and work groups that are leading, providing input, and analyzing the program data should reflect the diversity in the community and the school. Not only should the community representatives reflect the ethnic makeup of the community, but they should as much as possible also reflect the various family configurations, lifestyles, economic levels, and educational levels.

The demographics of the students and other clients who are served in the current program should reflect the demographics of the student body. If the makeup of the student body is 8% African American, 80% Hispanic, 11% White, and 1% Asian and Native American, then the makeup of the students participating in guidance and counseling activities should also be 8% African American, 80% Hispanic, 11% White, and 1% Asian and Native American. The current program assessment should include gathering data that describe the program's clientele.

Table 4.14
Reporting the Results of the Assessment of the Current Program:
Data, Methods, Element

Data	Collection Method	Element/Design
Community context	Demographic studies	Context
Student status	Risky behavior indicators	
	Discipline reports	
	Achievement indicators	
Counselor talent	Certification requirements	Personnel resources
Responsibilities of other personnel	Job descriptions	Personnel resources
Budget	Budget review	Financial resources
Materials and equipment	Inventory	Financial resources
Facilities	Inventory	
Laws, rules, regulations	Guidance office, state department of education	Political resources
Policies and procedures	Board and district publications	Political resources
Activities conducted according to program component	Activity survey	Qualitative
	Self-study	
	Program handbooks	
Counselor talent use	Job descriptions	Qualitative
	Calendars	
Clients served	Activity review	Qualitative
	Survey	
Results attained	Activity review	Qualitative
Counselor time use	Time/task study	Quantitative
	Calendars	
Numbers of clients served	Sign-in sheets	Quantitative
	Records review	
Perceptions	Surveys, questionnaires	Political resources
	Interviews	

In gathering perceptions of the current guidance and counseling program, schools and districts are well advised by Dellana and Snyder (2004) "to devote more research to the customer service perceptions of their distinct customer groups and to more fully consider the obstacles to trust that might be created by these perceptions" (p. 39). Identification of groups that are overserved or underserved suggests many possibilities to consider in the next phases of guidance and counseling program improvement. As Lee (2001) pointed out,

> School counselors are becoming increasingly aware that their practices are rooted firmly in the values of European-American middle class culture, whereas the cultural values of a significant portion of the students with whom they work represent worldviews whose origins are found in Africa, Asia, Mexico, Central America, the Caribbean, or the Middle East (Herring, 1997; Lee, 1995). (p. 258)

More diverse practices are needed to respond appropriately to students from non-European or non–middle-class cultures. Data as to whether the program currently responds to students with developmental, preventive, remedial, and crisis needs in proportion to their percentage of the population would shed light on whether the school counselors' practices are or are not being well received by some groups.

If the school or district in which you work serves a diverse community, program activities that address relevant cultural and social topics and issues should be evident in the program. Portman (2009) suggested 10 functions that professional school counselors as cultural mediators could do. These might be used as a rubric for assessing current program efforts:

(a) gather and examine demographic data on students enrolled in the schools in their community;
(b) develop an awareness of cultural backgrounds of all stakeholders in the school, including students, parents, teachers, staff administrators, and neighboring communities (e.g., rival athletic teams, cooperative education programs);
(c) communicate with families and community organizations regarding cultural diversity;
(d) seek further education in cultural competence and linguistic skills acquisition;
(e) work and think "outside of the box" or be culturally creative to affect ongoing social construction of themselves, students, parents, teachers, staff, and administrators;
(f) facilitate access to helping resources and social service agencies;
(g) help culturally diverse students gain intrapersonal skills to facilitate relationship building;
(h) help culturally diverse students develop social mediation skills to gain knowledge of cultural tools;
(i) create a supportive and encouraging culturally diverse school and community climate; and
(j) serve as an information hub for culturally diverse families. (p. 23)

A useful tool for assessing the cultural competence of a school's programs, policies, and practices has been developed by Nelson, Bustamante, Wilson, and Onwuegbuzie (2008). The makeup of the school counseling staff should reflect the makeup of the student and school communities. Minorities have historically been underrepresented as educators, including school counselors. Strides are being made in the recruitment and training of school counselors, but in practice balancing a school staff takes years. It often requires waiting for the retirement of currently in-place school counselors, expanding staff through student population growth, or decreasing the school's counselor-to-student ratio.

School counselors' multicultural competence or lack thereof has significant bearing on their ability to work with students from cultures different from their own. Multicultural counseling competence is referred to as counselors' attitudes or beliefs, knowledge, and skills in working with individuals representing various cultural groups (Arredondo et al., 1996; Sue, Arredondo, & McDavis, 1992).

One of Constantine and Gushue's (2003) findings was that multicultural training has an impact on school counselors' multicultural competence. Therefore, one can conclude that those who have not had such training—either in their preservice counselor education programs or in subsequent in-service training—are less competent in working across cultures than those that have.

In their study, Constantine and Gushue (2003) examined school counselors' case conceptualization competence. They found that

> school counselors who have higher ethnic tolerance attitudes may be better able to consider and integrate salient cultural information in the context of conceptualizing and addressing the presenting concerns of immigrant students . . . [and] that school counselors with higher levels of racism may be less aware of cultural issues in conceptualizing the mental health concerns of immigrant students, and these attitudes may ultimately compromise the emotional and developmental well-being of these students. (p. 189)

Bryan, Holcomb-McCoy, Moore-Thomas, and Day-Vines (2009) conducted a national study about who seeks college information from school counselors. They reported finding that "students in larger schools and in schools with higher levels of poverty were less likely to see the counselor about college" (p. 288). They also found that "public school students who perceived that the counselor expected them to pursue any option other than college were less likely to seek college information" (p. 288).

West-Olatunji et al. (2010) found that "school counselors who lack sufficient cultural competence may inadvertently assess culturally diverse students' behaviors from a deficit framework and fail to utilize their individual and cultural strengths" (p. 191). This may in turn contribute to the underrepresentation of minorities in math and science courses.

Leadership Roles and Responsibilities

If you are the guidance and counseling program leader—be you a district guidance and counseling program administrator or a school counselor in a building—you are responsible for accomplishing the current program assessment. First and foremost, you must acknowledge and make good use of your power (Henderson, 2009). Power here is defined as your ability to influence others to behave in desirable ways. Raven (2004) identified six bases of power available to you: expert, referent, information, legitimate, reward, and coercive. Hersey, Blanchard, and Johnson (2001) add a seventh: connection.

The scope of the undertaking will call on all of your leadership, supervision, management, and administration skills. In fulfilling your leadership role, you influence counseling and other staff members by your professional role modeling, and you rely on your referent power. In fulfilling your supervision role, you assist staff members to continuously seek feedback and improve their performance. Your expertise combined with your legitimate power support this role. In fulfilling your management role, you ensure efficient use of resources (e.g., time and budget) and apply your reward power. In fulfilling your administration role, you exercise authority over the program and the staff, relying on your legitimate power. In this role, you also evaluate staff members, which brings with it the potential to use your coercive power (Henderson & Gysbers, 1998).

Shillingford and Lambie (2010) found that school counselors who use the most effective leadership practices for improving their school guidance and counseling program do so by

(a) taking responsibility for the advancement of their program; (b) increasing their own visibility at their school; (c) communicating their vision of what an effective school counseling program represents; (d) collaboratively teaming to improve students' academic, personal/social, and career development; (e) clarifying their programmatic role as a unique professional. (p. 215)

Each of these practices calls for applying your advocacy competencies (Ratts, Toporek, & Lewis, 2010).

It is imperative that you take responsibility for ensuring that the results of the current program assessment are communicated to all interested parties. In fact, throughout the program improvement process, you should be communicating regularly and often with all administrative and counseling staff members, but at each milestone in the process, communication is imperative.

Analyzing your process as you go by using the four leadership frames for working effectively as a leader in the school setting described by Bolman and Deal (2002) could help you understand what is happening at different times in the group development process.

> The *political* frame points out the limits of authority and the inevitability that resources are almost always too scarce to fulfill all demands. . . . [The *human resource* frame] highlights the importance of individual needs and motives. . . . The *structural* frame emphasizes productivity and posits that classrooms and schools work best when goals and roles are clear and when efforts of individuals and groups are highly coordinated through authority, policies, and rules as well as through more informal strategies. . . . The *symbolic* frame centers attention on culture, meaning, belief, and faith through symbols, stories, rituals, and play. (Bolman & Deal, 2002, pp. 3–4)

As you read through the descriptions of the various tasks to be undertaken in this phase of program improvement, you will recognize that guidance and counseling expertise are essential to good leadership of the process. The summary that follows is provided to clarify your roles and responsibilities. Essentially, you have specific responsibilities for the initiation, implementation, and closure of this phase of the program improvement project.

Initiation

As the program leader, you need to keep the adopted program model in front of everyone involved in the project, including the decision makers and every member of the counseling staff. At this point, you may be the only person who truly understands the concept. You will find yourself continually clarifying and explaining the model.

Fullan, Bertani, and Quinn (2004) cautioned, "Think of the vision as an iceberg, the vast majority of which is underwater. Many leaders take shortcuts by slicing off the visible part of the iceberg and then assuming that they have captured its full power" (p. 43). They suggested 10 crucial components for effective leadership for systemic or incremental change: a compelling conceptualization, collective moral purpose, the right structure for getting the job done, individual capacity building, lateral capacity building, ongoing learning, productive conflict, a demanding culture, external partners, and focused financial investments.

Key external partners for improving your guidance and counseling program are your school administrators: the principals at the school level and the superintendent at the district level. Looking through the political frame, their support is essential for getting the program improvement planning work done and for bringing about future recommendations for change. Looking through the human resources frame, the more people who are engaged in the study and redesign of the guidance and counseling program, the more people who will be invested in the success of the group's efforts.

It is your responsibility to conceptualize the current program assessment process. As the guidance and counseling program leader, you identify the tasks to be performed and are able to explain them to the staff. We have described a multitude of tasks for accomplishing a complete assessment; you may not choose to do them all at this time or in the order we have set out. Ultimately, however, all the tasks need to be completed as the program improvement efforts continue. Once school administrators have a vision of what an improved program will look like, they are eager for changes to occur. As the guidance and counseling program leader, you respond to their needs, but you also need to ensure that the program change decisions are the right decisions. This is why a factual assessment of the current program is so essential: to ensure making the right changes, not just responding to some individuals' pet concerns. You need to determine how much time you have to complete your assessment and the data that are most critical to progress at a reasonable rate. Thorough planning is essential, and so is effective use of your time.

If you are in a multischool or multibuilding district, you share leadership of the program with the school-based counselor staff leaders. These school counselors can become the leaders of the subparts of the project and lead their colleagues by influence and delegated authority. You continue to lead by means of your personal traits and leadership skills (i.e., referent power) coupled with the authority of your position (i.e., legitimate power). You select as leaders school counselors who are ready to be effective leaders and work out mechanisms for continuing to provide leadership to them. The whole process becomes a matter of balance. In this case, you must strike a balance among knowing where you are going, what you need and want in results, and letting the staff of the work groups determine how they are going to provide the results.

Implementation

You are the overall leader of the data collection efforts. You must staff your work groups to get the tasks done, and you must delegate effectively. Effective delegation means being explicit and precise in the charges you give work groups and monitoring their progress as they proceed. We feel it is important for you to meet with each work group, if possible, and indeed to become a member of each group. Although you are the ultimate leader of these efforts, you do not have to have all the answers. We have found that thinking together with work group members is a useful strategy. Every district with which we have worked has implemented its current program assessment somewhat differently. The data needs are the same, but the process routes may be different.

In your district, you may need to engineer the development of the various assessment instruments and procedures. It is important that you ensure the adequacy of instrument development and then ensure that the instruments are relevant to the selected program model. Your perspective is broader than that of your staff, and you are more aware of the resources available to you from other district or campus departments; you will know about reports generated by district departments, and you will know about district computer capabilities. Your involvement will allow you to coordinate the work of the various work groups. It is imperative that you not bombard the staff with a variety of similar surveys. It is also appropriate for you, as the guidance and counseling program administrator, to collect and present some of the data on your own. For example, you probably already have much of the budget and facilities information. You are also in a better position to survey other administrators.

There are a variety of ways in which you will be able to help the committees implement their processes. Your authority will facilitate data collection. You can ensure the involvement, understanding, and responsiveness of every staff member. You will need to not only educate the counseling staff as to what they are doing and why but also understand and manage the resistance of some staff members.

Senge and Kaeufer (2000) identified three phases of the change process and the forces within each that impede change and suggested ways to deal with each. They described challenges in initiating change, challenges in sustaining change, and challenges in building a new design. Challenges in initiating change are time (as discussed in Chapter 2), needed help, perceived irrelevance, and leaders perceived as not walking the talk. The challenges in sustaining and spreading change are fear and anxiety, lack of immediate results, and conflicts between those who believe in the potential of the anticipated changes and those who do not. The challenges in building a new design are governance issues—of accountability and power, diffusion, and clarification of strategy and purpose.

Some example strategies Senge and Kaeufer (2000) offered to address the challenges associated with initiating the change—where we are at this point in our description of the change process—are to "enable people to regain control over their time," invest in help, "make information available to members," "build credibility by demonstration" (p. 4), and "develop patience under pressure" (p. 5).

If you have taken the steps in program improvement that we are suggesting, then you will be armed with the policy support you need to answer the concerns. It is also helpful to remind staff that the current assessment needs to be accomplished only once; after the program redesigning efforts are completed, you will evaluate what you have done, but your basic program description will be finished. You may find that you need to mandate some of the work, particularly the time-use study. The time-use study will involve more work on the part of each staff member than will other aspects of the assessment, and the importance of its results is such that completeness and accuracy are imperative. Moreover, there is a high correlation between the use of your supervisory skills in encouraging and praising staff and the success of this phase of the project. The more accessible you are to the counseling staff, both to the work groups and to the staff as a whole, the more comfortable everyone will be with the new model and its implementation.

Closure

Your final set of responsibilities in accomplishing the current program assessment will be to help the work groups summarize and disseminate the data they have collected and to help the steering committee and the staff analyze the results. Organizing the presentation of the data is not easy. You will probably want to present all of the data to the steering committee and to the counseling staff but only an executive summary to other interested staff such as building-based educators, campus administrators, and other guidance staff. It is useful to have leaders of the work groups present the information that their groups have gathered, but you must assume responsibility for ensuring that the information is understood. You will need to allow as much time to do this as is required. Some schools have used as much as an entire in-service education day for this purpose. This allows the staff time to process the information and to begin drawing their own conclusions. It also provides them the opportunity to raise questions and to learn more about the implied program changes. The data that have been gathered are tangible and impressive, and by presenting them all together, perspective is maintained. It will be rewarding to staff to see the fullness of their program. As already mentioned, this will probably be the first time that the entire program will seem visible, tangible, and concrete.

The data need to be analyzed by you, by the steering committee, and, either together or separately, by the school counselor leadership team or all of the school counselors if they are not all a part of the steering committee. You must be clear about what the data say to you. You must draw conclusions about what the current program is and what it is accomplishing. Then you are in a position to state what the design of the current program is and what the current priorities are.

By *design*, we mean the balance that has been struck between the program components and among the school counselor functions. You can state that as of this time, for example, the largest component of the current guidance and counseling program is system support, the second is individual student planning, the third responsive services, and the fourth guidance curriculum. You now know, for example, that the primary mode of operating for the counseling staff is individual counseling, the second is completing administrative assignments, the third is doing special education administrative work, and so on. An example of presenting that information from the Northside Independent School District's (1986) initial program improvement project is presented in Table 4.15.

Program component priorities clearly emerged in Northside Independent School District as a result of aggregating the information gleaned in the study of how school counselors applied their time:

- *First priority*
  Individual student planning
  Middle school: system support
  High school: system support
- *Fourth priority*
  Elementary school: guidance curriculum
  Middle school: guidance curriculum
  High school: guidance curriculum

After determining program component priorities, you can state the priority order of the student results addressed and of the clients served by the current program. For example, you may have learned that at the elementary level, 20% of your activities are aimed at helping students be safe at home and in the neighborhood. Those activities thus have a high priority. At the high school level, you may have learned that 60% of your activities relate to scheduling and schedule changes. You now also know the rank order that applies to the clients you serve. You may have learned that your first-priority clients are individual stu-

Table 4.15
Current Guidance Program Component Priorities (Baseline Data)

Component	School Level and Priority		
	Elementary	*Middle*	*High*
Guidance curriculum	4	4	4
Individual student planning	1	3	3
Responsive services	3	2	2
System support	2	1	1

Note. Data from Northside Independent School District (1986), San Antonio, TX. Adapted with permission.

dents who come to the counseling office, the second-priority clients are teachers, the third-priority clients are groups of students with remedial-level needs whom you call in for group counseling, and so on.

If you have not already done so, you need to write down these conclusions. Doing so will help you bring this phase of the project to closure and provide you with baseline information that will enable you to move on to subsequent steps without having to reanalyze the data every time you pick them up. The value of written statements, as mentioned earlier, is that they force you to be precise, provide a tangible focus for the steering committee and the school counselors to endorse, and provide a vehicle for communicating with others about the results of the work that has been accomplished.

Your Progress Check

At this point, the assessment of your current guidance and counseling program is finished. If you have followed our suggestions, you have involved many members of the school or district staff and learned much about your current program.

Staff Involvement

You have

- identified school counselor leaders and engaged them in the program improvement process;
- formed work groups of school counselors, other guidance and counseling program staff, and administrators;
- delegated leadership of the work groups to steering committee members;
- continued to use steering committee members in their advisory capacity on the committee, increasing their investment in the overall project;
- led counselors to understand that changes will come but that the decisions to change are not being made hastily;
- developed school counselors' knowledge about the adopted program model and the relationship between their current program and the new program model;
- described specifically your student population and your school community.

Current Program Learnings

You have

- determined how available personnel, financial, and political resources are used;
- identified the activities that compose the current program and sorted them by the model program components;
- clarified the program's priorities for (a) applications of school counselors' competencies, (b) client subgroups who benefit from program services and in what proportion, and (c) student learning;
- determined (a) how school counselors spend their time, (b) numbers of clients and subgroups of clients the program serves, and (c) numbers of students achieving anticipated results;
- surveyed the perceptions of your primary program users;
- presented a report describing your current program.

In short, you, the steering committee, the guidance and administrative staff, and the policy setters know the concrete details of the current guidance and counseling program.

The scope of the current program assessment is such that, once done, there is a tendency to think that the program improvement project is completed. It is not. Although you can now relate your current program data to the program model, making judgments at this time is premature. Your next questions are

- What do we want our guidance and counseling program to be (discussed in Chapter 5)?
- How does what we are doing now compare and contrast with what we want from our program (discussed in Chapter 6)?
- What will be the plan for making the transition from where you are to where you want to be (discussed in Chapter 6)?
- How will you implement the systemic and incremental changes needed (discussed in Chapter 7)?

References

Adelman, H. S., & Taylor, L. (2003). On sustainability of project innovations as systemic change. *Journal of Educational and Psychological Consultation, 14*(1), 1–25.

American School Counselor Association. (2004a). *Why elementary school counselors.* Retrieved from http://www.schoolcounselor.org/content.asp?contentid=230

American School Counselor Association. (2004b). *Why middle school counselors.* Retrieved from http://www.schoolcounselor.org/content.asp?contentid=231

American School Counselor Association. (2004c). *Why secondary school counselors?* Retrieved from http://www.schoolcounselor.org/content.asp?contentid=233

American School Counselor Association. (2005). *The ASCA National Model: A framework for school counseling programs* (2nd ed.). Alexandria, VA: Author.

American School Counselor Association. (2009a). *The role of the professional school counselor.* Retrieved from http://www.schoolcounselor.org/content.asp?pl=325&sl=133&contentid=240

American School Counselor Association. (2009b). *Student-to-counselor ratio by state 2007–2008.* Retrieved from http://asca2.timberlakepublishing.com//files/Ratios 2007-2008.pdf

American School Counselor Association. (2010). *Ethical standards for school counselors.* Retrieved from http://asca2.timberlakepublishing.com//files/EthicalStandards2010.pdf

Arredondo, P., Toporek, R., Brown, S., Jones, J., Locke, D. C., Sanchez, J., & Stadler, H. (1996). Operationalization of the multicultural counseling competencies. *Journal of Multicultural Counseling and Development, 24,* 42–78.

Bolman, L. G., & Deal, T. E. (2002). *Reframing the path to school leadership.* Thousand Oaks, CA: Corwin Press.

Bryan, J., Holcomb-McCoy, C., Moore-Thomas, C., & Day-Vines, N. (2009). Who sees the school counselor for college information? A national study. *Professional School Counseling, 12,* 280–291.

Constantine, M. G., & Gushue, G. V. (2003). School counselors' ethnic tolerance attitudes and racism attitudes as predictors of their multicultural case conceptualization of an immigrant student. *Journal of Counseling & Development, 81,* 185–190.

Council for Accreditation of Counseling and Related Programs. (2009). School counseling. In *2009 standards* (pp. 40–46). Retrieved from http://www.cacrep.org/doc/2009%20Standards%20with%20cover.pdf

Dellana, S. A., & Snyder, D. (2004). Student future outlook and counseling quality in a rural minority high school. *High School Journal, 88*(1), 27–42.

Dollarhide, C.T. (2007). Critical incidents in the development of supportive principals: Facilitating school counselor–principal relationships. *Professional School Counseling, 10,* 360–369.

Fullan, M., Bertani, A., & Quinn, J. (2004, April). New lessons for districtwide reform. *Educational Leadership,* 42–46.

Gysbers, N. C., Lapan, R. T., & Jones, B. A. (2000). School board policies for guidance and counseling: A call to action. *Professional School Counseling, 3,* 349–353.

Gysbers, N. C., Stanley, J. B., Kosteck-Bunch, L., Magnuson, C. S., & Starr, M. F. (2008). *Missouri comprehensive guidance program: A manual for program development, implementation, evaluation and enhancement.* Warrensburg: Missouri Center for Career Education, University of Central Missouri.

Henderson, P. G. (2009). *The new handbook of administrative supervision in counseling.* New York, NY: Routledge.

Henderson, P. (2010). Conclusions and recommendations. *Independent School District Guidance and Counseling Program evaluation.* Unpublished report, San Antonio, Texas.

Henderson, P., & Gysbers, N.C. (1998). *Leading and managing your school guidance program staff.* Alexandria, VA: American Counseling Association.

Hersey, P., Blanchard, K., & Johnson, D. E. (2001). *Management of organizational behavior: Leading human resources.* Upper Saddle River, NJ: Prentice Hall.

Jansen, C., Millitello, M., & Kosine, N. (2008). Four views of the professional school counselor–principal relationship: A Q methodology study. *Professional School Counseling, 11,* 353–359.

Kaffenberger, C., & Young, A. (2007). *Making DATA work.* Alexandria, VA: American School Counselor Association.

Lambie, G. W. (2004). The challenge to change from guidance counseling to professional school counseling: A historical perspective. *Professional School Counseling, 8,* 124–131.

Lee, C. L. (2001). Culturally responsive school counselors and programs: Addressing the needs of all students. *Professional School Counseling, 4,* 257–261.

Leuwerke, W. C., Walker, J., & Shi, Q. (2009). Informing principals: The impact of different types of information on principals' perceptions of professional school counselors. *Professional School Counseling, 12,* 263–271.

MacDonald, G., & Sink, C. A. (1999). A qualitative developmental analysis of comprehensive guidance programmes in schools in the United States. *British Journal of Guidance and Counselling, 27,* 415–430.

Martin, I., Carey, J., & DeCoster, K. (2009). A national study of the current status of state school counseling models. *Professional School Counseling, 12,* 378–386.

Myrick, R. D. (1993). *Developmental guidance and counseling: A practical approach* (2nd ed.). Minneapolis, MN: Educational Media Corporation.

National Board for Professional Teaching Standards. (2002). *School counseling standards.* Retrieved from http://www.nbpts.org/userfiles/File/ecya_sc_standards.pdf

National Center for Education Statistics. (2009a). Table 16. In *Digest of education statistics, 2009.* Retrieved from http://nces.ed.gov/programs/digest/d09/tables/dt09_016.asp?referrer=list

National Center for Education Statistics. (2009b). Table 167. In *Digest of Education Statistics, 2009.* Retrieved from http://nces.ed.gov/programs/digest/d09/tables/dt09_167.asp

Nelson, J. A., Bustamante, R. M., Wilson, E. D., & Onwuegbuzie, A. J. (2008). The school-wide cultural competence observation checklist for school counselors: An exploratory factor analysis. *Professional School Counseling, 11,* 207–217.

North Carolina Department of Public Instruction. (n.d.). *How North Carolina school counselors spend their time.* Retrieved from http://www.ncpublicschools.org/docs/curriculum/guidance/resources/programofstudy/schoolcounselor.pdf

Northside Independent School District. (1986). *Comprehensive guidance program framework.* San Antonio, TX: Author.

Northside Independent School District. (2009). Retrieved from http://www.nisd.net

Portman, T. A. A. (2009). Faces of the future: School counselors s cultural mediators. *Journal of Counseling & Development, 87,* 21–27.

Ratts, M. J., Toporek, R. L., & Lewis, J. A. (2010). *ACA advocacy competencies: A social justice framework for counselors.* Alexandria, VA: American Counseling Association.

Raven, B. H. (2004). *A glossary of terms related to interpersonal influence and social power.* Unpublished manuscript, University of California, Los Angeles.

Rylander, C. K. (2002). *Guiding our children toward success: How Texas school counselors spend their time.* Austin, TX: Office of the Comptroller.

School Mental Health Project. (2010). Youth subcultures: Understanding subgroups to better address barriers to learning and improve schools. *Addressing Barriers to Learning, 15*(2), 1–7.

Senge, P. M., & Kaeufer, D. H. (2000). Creating change. *Executive Excellence, 17*(10), 4–5.

Shillingford, M. A., & Lambie, G. W. (2010). Contributions of professional school counselors' values and leadership practices to their programmatic service delivery. *Professional School Counseling, 13,* 208–217.

Sue, D. W., Arredondo, P., & McDavis, R. J. (1992). Multicultural counseling competencies and standards: A call to the profession. *Journal of Counseling & Development, 70,* 477–486.

Taylor, E. R. (2002). Evaluation of counseling services in a rural school district: Assessing current program status. In P. Henderson & N. Gysbers (Eds.), *Implementing comprehensive school guidance programs: Critical leadership issues and successful responses* (pp. 23–30). Greensboro, NC: CAPS.

Texas Counseling Association. (2004). *Texas evaluation model for professional school counselors* (2nd ed.). Austin, TX: Author.

Texas Education Agency. (2005). *A model comprehensive, developmental guidance and counseling program for Texas public schools: A guide for program development pre-K–12th grade* (4th ed.). Austin, TX: Author.

Texas Education Agency. (n.d.). *Overview of the academic excellence indicator system.* Retrieved from http://www.tea.state.tx.us/perfreport/aeis/about.aeis.html

Texas Education Code. (2001). *Chapter 33, Service programs and extra-curricular activities; Subchapter A, School counselors and counseling programs.* Retrieved from http://www.statutes.legis.state.tx.us/Docs/ED/htm/ED.33.htm

U.S. Department of Education. (2009a). *American Recovery and Reinvestment Act of 2009.* Retrieved from http://www.ed.gov/recovery

U.S. Department of Education. (2009b). *Elementary and secondary school counseling programs.* Retrieved from http://www2.ed.gov/programs/elseccounseling/index.html

West-Olatunji, C., Shure, L., Pringle, R., Adams, T., Lewis, D., & Cholewa, B. (2010). Exploring how school counselors position low-income African American girls as mathematics and science learners. *Professional School Counseling, 13,* 184–195.

⌒ Part II ⌒

Designing

Chapter 5

Designing Your Comprehensive Guidance and Counseling Program

Designing—Adapting the Guidance and Counseling Program Model

- Define the basic structure of your program.
- Identify and list student competencies by content area and school level or grade grouping.
- Reaffirm policy support.
- Establish priorities for program delivery (qualitative design).
- Establish parameters for resource allocation (quantitative design).
- Write down and distribute the description of the desired program.

⌒ Once a comprehensive guidance and counseling program model has been selected and data have been gathered that describe the current guidance and counseling program in the light of the model, the next phase of the program improvement process is to design the specific program that will best meet the needs of your students and community and the goals of your school or district. The model provides a common language for the program elements but does not prescribe the details of the program design.

Conceptualizing your desired program in specific terms is essential because, as you will find, the program improvement process is somewhat analogous to remodeling your home while you are living in it. A specifically drawn blueprint of the renovations for your home is needed so that they can be made in an orderly sequence without totally disrupting your lifestyle. The more precise the blueprint, the more efficient the renovation, the more likely it is that the remodeled house will reflect what you want. The same is true for a comprehensive guidance and counseling program. Moreover, you may have a somewhat idealistic picture of the guidance and counseling program you think you want, but you need to temper this vision with reality.

Establishing the design of the program you want entails answering foundational questions in concrete and relevant terms:

- What content standards will provide its basis?
- What will its definition be?
- What is the rationale for it?
- What assumptions are being made about it?
- How is each delivery system component defined?

The next question is, How do you want to use the resources available to ensure having the right program for the students and the school or district? The hard decisions in this phase of the process require acknowledging the limitations of the program's resources and

- setting priorities for the (a) use of professional school counselors' competencies, (b) clients to be served, (c) competencies for students to develop, and (d) activities in each of the four program delivery system components;
- setting parameters for the (a) allocations of professional school counselors' time to be spent in each of the four program delivery system components and (b) allocations of professional school counselors' time to be spent serving each of the various categories of clients: students, adults, the system.

During the designing phase of the program improvement process, you will continue to use the steering and the school–community advisory committees already established. By this time, these committee members have become knowledgeable about the current program and have grasped the concept of the new program model. As representatives of the professionals who work in the program as well as the constituents who use the program, they help make the hard decisions to be faced. They help ensure that the changes you will be recommending are responsive to the needs of the school district and the community, and they may help in generating the new resources you will undoubtedly need.

If you are the guidance and counseling program leader, you have primary responsibility for the decisions and their implementation; however, we believe the broader your support base is, the sounder your decisions will be. You will need to continue to clarify information and the impending decisions. You will need to move the decision process along. In all likelihood, you will have the major responsibility for putting the vision of the model program in operation.

It is essential to establish the design that you want your program to have so that the implementation that follows can be realistic. If you are from a school district that has more than one building, clarifying the desired design at the district level will ensure consistency of the program from one building to another. The district design should be general enough, however, to allow buildings to tailor their programs to meet local needs and goals.

This chapter describes six major tasks that, when completed, will make up the established design for your program:

1. Define the basic structure that will be the organizer for your program, including crafting the structural components and defining the program components to suit your school or district program.
2. Identify and list student competencies by content area and school level or grade grouping.
3. Reaffirm the policy support for the emerging guidance and counseling program.
4. Establish priorities for program delivery, to complete the qualitative design.
5. Establish parameters for program resource allocations, to complete the quantitative design.
6. Put all of the decisions in writing and distribute the program description to all counselors and administrators. This task is typically done by the guidance and counseling program leader.

We then suggest ways to attend to diversity in designing your program. Finally, we describe the guidance and counseling program leader's roles and responsibilities in carrying out this phase of the program development process.

Define the Basic Structure of Your Program

With the assistance of your steering and school–community advisory committees and your district policy makers, decide what the organizational structure of your district or building guidance and counseling program will be. Currently, the structure may be organized according to the guidance services model (orientation, assessment, information, counseling, placement, and follow-up activities); it may be organized around the processes of counseling, consulting, and coordination; or it may be described by a list of duties. As described in Chapter 3, a comprehensive guidance and counseling program consists of four elements: content; organizational structure; resources; and development, management, and accountability. It is focused on students and their healthy development. The theoretical underpinnings of a comprehensive guidance and counseling program consist of the clarification of your program content areas and the structural components—definition, rationale, and assumptions. These are akin to Bolman and Deal's (2002) symbolic frame. The program components—guidance curriculum, individual student planning, responsive services, and system support—provide the organizational framework for your guidance and counseling program activities, prekindergarten through 12th grade. They comprise the delivery system and are akin to Bolman and Deal's structural frame. This section briefly summarizes what needs to be done to clarify the organizational structure for your program: its possible content areas and the structural and program components.

Content Areas

If you followed our previous advice, you selected content areas for the program that matched your beliefs about the dimensions of human development most appropriately addressed in your guidance and counseling program. Several examples were provided in Chapter 3. In general, five dimensions of child and adolescent development and their subtopics are listed in Table 5.1.

Table 5.1
Guidance and Counseling–Related Dimensions of Child and Adolescent Development

Physical Development
  Brain development
  Sexuality

Cognitive Development
  Thinking
  Problem solving
  Decision making
  Moral development

Personal Development
  Personal identity
  Personality
  Self-concept

Emotional Development
  Awareness
  Management

Social Development
  Relationship development
  Career development
  Cultural identity development

This is the first step in tailoring the program to meet your local community, district, and state needs and goals. The areas of human development you select as your focus dictate the content to be addressed through the delivery system—the program components. How to further specify the student learning goals and outcomes comes later in this chapter.

Structural Components

Definition

The program definition includes the mission statement of the program and its centrality in the school district's total educational program. To be complete, the definition statement should answer at least four questions:

1. Who delivers the program—professional certified school counselors, teachers, social workers, psychologists, administrators and other staff, parents, other community members?
2. What competencies will students or others possess as a result of their involvement in the program? Will they be responsible citizens, use problem-solving skills, and seek to achieve excellence, communicate effectively (from the district's mission)? Will they respect others and themselves (from the school's mission)? Will they maintain self-esteem or relate effectively across cultures?
3. Who are the clients of the program? Which students' development is assisted—all students; 12th-grade, eighth-grade, fifth-grade, or prekindergarten students; college-bound students; workbound students; disabled students; minority students; poor students; at-risk students; grieving students; or drug-abusing students? And what about parents and teachers?
4. How is the program organized—through the comprehensive guidance and counseling program components of guidance curriculum, individual student planning, responsive services, and system support? Or through some other organizational grouping?

Rationale

The rationale discusses the importance of guidance as an equal partner in the educational system and provides reasons why individuals in our society need to acquire the competencies as a result of their involvement in a comprehensive guidance and counseling program (as exemplified in Chapter 3). The rationale suggests that the guidance and counseling program is also engineered to help all students develop their potential through provision of developmental assistance and specialized assistance for individuals with unique personal, social, career, or educational needs. Although the purpose of the rationale is to express the needs for the program, it also guides program design decisions (e.g., subgroups of students to be served) and provides direction to program implementation. It includes the conclusions drawn from student and community needs assessments, as well as clarifications of goals of the local and state educational system and those of the nation as a whole. It references current professional theories, school or district mission and goals, and professional trends—both in education and in professional school counseling—that support the program and its design.

Student Needs and Realities. Specific student needs related to your selected guidance and counseling program content areas should be identified to help students in each of the grade levels accomplish developmental tasks. Schoolchildren fall into three levels of human development that roughly equate to their school levels. The developmental tasks of elementary school children, ages 5 to 12, are to build foundations. Those of middle or junior high school children, ages 10 to 14 ("tween-agers"), are to manage the turmoil of the myriad changes in their lives. Those of teenagers, ages 13 to 18, are to transition to being healthy, productive adults.

Needs may be assessed by means of surveys of the program's consumers or through the opinions of the school and community experts (e.g., counselors, teachers, principal, and other educators; community leaders). A currently popular, research-based approach to identifying students' developmental needs is assessing students' needs vis-à-vis the "40 Developmental Assets" described in the work of the Search Institute (n.d.). Stevens and Wilkerson (2010) provide a bridge between the Developmental Assets and the American School Counselors Association's (ASCA; 2005) National Model. Currently, "developmental research has been emerging that focuses on strengths as a means to promote positive student development" (Akos & Galassi, 2004, p. 196).

In addition to students' developmental needs, specific information should be identified regarding how many students have needs for preventative, remedial, and crisis interventions and the specific issues or situations that cause these needs. For example, the societal problems facing all of today's schools include underachievement, adolescent pregnancy, child and adolescent suicide, child abuse and neglect, substance abuse, racial tension and turmoil, bullying, violence, shifts in family structures (e.g., parental deployment), and fluctuations in the economy. The status of other student subgroups (i.e., cultural and youth subculture groups) should also be considered to identify their special needs for guidance and counseling. All of these issues differ from community to community and need to be assessed locally. (Chapter 6 includes more discussion of assessing student needs.)

Community Context. In assessing your current program (Chapter 4), you gathered community status information. Some of this information suggests some of the needs that students have in relation to their healthy development and to success in school and life. The specific needs of students for whom the school presents a second culture and who are striving to manage the acquisition of that culture successfully (Coleman, Casali, & Wampold, 2001), for example, should be specified. Students whose parents have not been fully educated by today's standards have different needs from those whose parents have benefited from college or some form of postsecondary education or training.

Professional Theories. A part of the reasoning behind the program—its rationale—is the belief system held by the guidance and counseling program leadership, including the steering and advisory committees and the professional counseling staff, about what is best for students.

Developmental guidance and counseling programs should be based on developmental theory and principles (MacDonald & Sink, 1999). The theories used to explain what having mental health entails and those that explain how to help students regain lost mental health should be clarified. Henderson (2005) reminded us that professional school counseling practice rests on psychological theories (ranging from Sigmund Freud to William Glasser) that seek to explain why people act, think, and feel the way that they do; what counselors can do to help them attain whatever goals they are striving for; and how they can best do that. Theories regarding the stages and facets of human growth and development (e.g., those described by John Dewey, Jean Piaget, Erik Erikson, and Lawrence Kohlberg) also support the work of professional school counselors and guidance and counseling programs. Geidner (2009) made a strong case for "a developmental systems approach to counseling" (p. 367).

Additionally, there are theories about how learning occurs and what promotes learning. In Chapter 3, we offered a learning theory for sequencing activities that lead to student competency development. The *ASCA National Model: A Framework for School*

Counseling Programs (ASCA, 2005) includes "The Theory Behind the ASCA National Model" (Henderson, 2005).

School Mission, Goals, and Educational Trends. In addition to the federal, state, and local policy statements identified in Chapter 4 as political supports for your improving guidance and counseling program, the current trends—the state of the art—of the education profession should also be considered. Although most educators agree that challenging all students, regardless of their background or circumstances, to strive for high levels of achievement is paramount, the education profession is at this time caught in a dilemma of wanting to respond to the continuing demands for accountability as set out in federal and state mandates and of increasing recognition that children are diverse individuals with multiple facets and needs that must be addressed for optimal learning to occur. Many of students' needs—feeling unsafe, unable to concentrate on schoolwork, and the like—cause barriers to student academic success.

Professional School Counseling Trends. As the state of the art of teaching and learning are important, so too are the current trends in professional school counseling. One can determine trends that suggest program priorities and some of its practices. The *ASCA National Model: A Framework for School Counseling Programs* (ASCA, 2005), which includes the ASCA National Standards for Students, provides standards to guide the rationale for establishing your basic program structure and the student competencies you aim to help students achieve. In its position statements *Why Elementary School Counselors* (ASCA, 2004a), *Why Middle School Counselors* (ASCA, 2004b), and *Why Secondary School Counselors?* (ASCA, 2004c), ASCA delineated some of the needs of students at each school level, what school counselors are qualified to do for the students, and how they implement the guidance and counseling program at that level. The statements close with an answer to their title questions. These succinct pieces are useful to support local rationale and to guide the development of local rationale statements.

Counseling journals, such as the American Counseling Association's *Journal of Counseling & Development*, and school counseling journals, such as ASCA's *Professional School Counseling*, consistently provide updated information about practices that have worked for counselors in addressing issues faced by students today. Noteworthy examples are the 2004 issue of the *Journal of Counseling & Development* that includes a special section on school violence (McGowan, 2004), and the 2008 special issue on multicultural counseling (D'Andrea & Heckman, 2008). Other current trends in topics school counselors address include college and career readiness, stress caused by academic rigor, and dating violence. These journals also provide special issues regarding trends in counseling and school counseling practice, such as strengths-based school counseling (Akos & Galassi, 2008).

These journals also present articles describing current research and evaluation. One of the major trends in the school counseling profession is the measurement of the effectiveness of school counselors, guidance and counseling programs, and specific practices. Although much of this research is documented elsewhere (e.g., National Center for School Counseling Outcome Research at the University of Massachusetts Amherst), ASCA summarizes a broad scope of research in its paper, "Effectiveness of School Counseling" (n.d.). One study of interest was conducted by the California Department of Education (2003). The study was mandated by the California Assembly and led to findings that suggested the need for more pupil support services—including counseling, particularly "school-wide prevention and intervention strategies and counseling services, psychological counseling for individuals, groups, and families, and targeted intervention strategies for children and families such as counseling, case management, and crisis intervention" (California Department of Education, 2003, p. 2).

Studies of the effectiveness of school guidance and counseling often focus on its primary outcomes—those related to students' personal–social, educational, and career development. Because the accountability measures currently applied to the educational system focus primarily on reading and math achievement and on school safety, an increasing number of studies have focused on school counselors' impact on these factors. For example, Brigman and Campbell (2003) conducted a research project that provides a good model for other researchers in this area: "The goal of the project was to examine the impact of school counselor–led interventions on student academic achievement and school success behavior" (p. 96). The interventions focused on specific skills related to cognitive, social, and self-management skill development, three areas directly connected to school success. "The results reveal that the combined school counselor interventions of group counseling and classroom guidance were associated with a positive impact on student achievement and behavior" (p. 97). They also concluded that "the facts that the interventions were targeted on specific skills associated with school success and that school counselors used research-based techniques to teach these critical skills were seen as central to the positive outcome of the study" (p. 97).

Assumptions

Assumptions are premises that shape and guide the program and its design. Many times assumptions are not expressed; they are things that individuals take for granted but that others may not have thought about or agree with. Assumptions are made about students and other clients, the program, and the program staff. In designing the program, it is very important for individuals' assumptions to be brought to the table and discussed. We next offer some examples to help trigger your thinking, but the assumptions on which your program is based must be your own.

Assumptions About Students and Other Clients. Some assumptions about students and other clients include these:

- All children and adolescents can and want to learn.
- Guidance and counseling programs assist students to develop their individuality, function effectively with others, and manage their own destiny (Borders & Drury, 1992).
- All students deserve assistance with their personal, social, educational, and career development.
- "Cultural differences are real and cannot be ignored" (Lee, 2001, p. 259).
- All students, parents, teachers, and other program users have equal access to the program regardless of their levels of need (developmental, preventive, remedial, or crisis) or of personal characteristics (e.g., gender, race, ethnicity, cultural background, sexual orientation, disability, socioeconomic status, learning ability level, or language; Texas Education Agency, 2004, p. 12).
- Parents are invited to be full partners with educators in the education of their children.

Assumptions About the Program. Some assumptions about the program include these:

- Accountable guidance and counseling programs provide an appropriate balance of activities and services, are an integral part and an independent component of the total educational program, and are systematically planned, designed, implemented, and evaluated.
- The minimum-level program provides for each of the four delivery system components.
- The conditions required for effective program implementation include being in a positive work environment: one with favorable interpersonal relations among the

school staff, one with administrative commitment to and support of the guidance and counseling program, and one that provides an adequate budget and guidance materials.

- For guidance and counseling programs to be effective, the educational system must be characterized by a healthy interpersonal climate and must be supportive of the program in terms of its policies and provision of resources.
- The services provided to all students are equitable.
- Guidance is a schoolwide responsibility.
- The essential goal of a school guidance and counseling program is to help students succeed academically.
- Time and opportunity are provided for guidance and counseling program planning, designing, and evaluation.
- The counselor-to-student ratio is adequate to implement the designed program, or the program is designed within the parameters of the ratio.
- Facilities are readily accessible to students, allow for implementation of the comprehensive developmental guidance and counseling program, and ensure privacy and confidentiality for the program's clients.

Assumptions About Program Staff. Some assumptions about the program staff include these:

- Professional school counselors are essential in today's public schools.
- School counselors spend the majority of their time working directly with students.
- Counselors are fully certified by their state's certification office and have the special training needed to carry out specialized job assignments.
- All school counselors are highly proficient in guidance and counseling competencies.
- School counselors adhere to the ethical standards of the profession.
- Time and opportunity are provided for in-service training for school counselors and other guidance and counseling program staff members.
- All staff members accept responsibility for guidance and counseling program goals and objectives.
- Staff members' roles and their organizational relations are clearly defined.
- Professional and interprofessional relationships are characterized by respect, collaboration, and cooperation.
- School administrators protect the professional integrity of the guidance and counseling program and the school counselors.
- The school or district employs professionally certified school counselors in sufficient ratio to carry out the intended design of the program.
- School administrators understand the program's priorities and demands and make decisions and establish procedures in light of this understanding.

Program Components

Guidance Curriculum

The guidance curriculum is the center of the developmental part of the comprehensive guidance and counseling program. Through the component's activities students learn knowledge, skills, and attitudes described by the goals for guidance instruction. The curriculum is organized by grade level; that is, a scope and sequence of learnings for prekindergarten through 12th grade is established. It is designed to serve all students and is often implemented through classroom, small-, or large-group guidance. Teachers and counselors collaborate to ensure delivery of the guidance curriculum.

Individual Student Planning

The activities of the individual student planning component are also developmental in nature. They are provided for all students and are intended to guide students in the development and implementation of their personal, social, educational, and career plans. They help students to understand and monitor their growth and development and to take action on their next steps educationally or vocationally. The activities in this component are delivered either on a group or an individual basis with students and parents. Teachers and administrators are often involved as advisers.

Responsive Services

The purpose of this component is to provide special help to students who are facing problems that interfere with their healthy personal, social, career, or educational development. As described in Chapter 4, activities in this component include preventive, remedial, and crisis responses as appropriate. This component includes such activities as individual and small-group counseling, consulting with staff and parents, and referring students and families to other specialists or programs. With the exception of a few crisis interventions, the majority of these activities are planned and intentionally delivered responses. Even most crisis responses, although reactive in timing, are anticipated and follow planned protocols.

System Support

In implementation, it helps to divide the system support component into two parts: (a) guidance and counseling program management and (b) school support services. Guidance and counseling program management includes the activities necessary to support the other three program components. It includes designated program and staff leadership; program and staff development; actions that result in budget, facilities, and appropriate policies, procedures, and guidelines; research; community relations; and resource development. It is our opinion that having a highly effective, efficient student-centered guidance and counseling program is the best system support professional school counselors can provide to students, their families, and the school.

School support services include the activities implemented by guidance staff that support schoolwide or other specific educational programs. These activities include consultation with teachers and principals about specific students, behavior management principles, school climate, and school improvement planning. Input to policymakers and curriculum developers on behalf of students also comes within this portion of the component, as do efforts to enhance parent involvement in school. Often, a goal within school support services activities is to ensure school counselors' contribution is their fair share, neither too much nor too little, of schoolwide responsibilities (i.e., similar to that of other school program staff).

Identify and List Student Competencies by Content Area and School Level or Grade Grouping

Once you have selected your program content areas and overall program structure, you next decide on the competencies that the guidance and counseling program will take responsibility for helping students acquire. You identify competencies that relate to the dimensions of child and adolescent development you have selected as your focus. What knowledge will students gain, what skills will students develop, and what attitudes will students form as a result of their participation in the guidance and counseling program?

For help in answering these questions, go to the results section of the current program assessment you have already completed. In that process, you identified the intended student outcomes resulting from guidance activities from prekindergarten through 12th grade in the current guidance and counseling program. As we suggested earlier, compare these outcomes with lists generated from the goals of your school district, your state department of education, or your local community. Some school districts and some state departments of education have developed competency lists. The Center for School Counseling Outcome Research "conducted a review and analysis of the educational, developmental and social psychology literature" (Carey, 2010, p. 60) and identified 13 characteristics that "reflect the desired outcomes of the [developmental and] preventative components of the school counseling program" (Carey, 2010, p. 60):

1. Students have optimism.
2. Students show self-efficacy in critical areas.
3. Students have a sense of agency.
4. Students have clear visions of their future possible selves.
5. Students show self-directed learning.
6. Students are competent in goal setting.
7. Students can identify subjects that are intrinsically motivating.
8. Students are actively engaged in school.
9. Students effectively use self-management strategies.
10. Students have strong relationship skills.
11. Students know how to seek help.
12. Students show self-knowledge related to key characteristics.
13. Students are comfortable with and competent in dealing with social differences. (Carey, 2010, pp. 60–61)

The available lists will give you a plethora of ideas, but we recommend that you build your own list, one that fits your school district's and community's stated mission, goals, and priorities. One of your ultimate goals is to ensure the centrality of the guidance and counseling program within the school district's total educational program. The more direct the link between the school district's goals and your program, the more clearly related the guidance and counseling program will be to the basic mission of the school district. For example, if the district's educational philosophy includes such items as helping students to become good citizens, be responsible for their actions, and make wise choices, then these words should be incorporated in the student competencies addressed by the guidance and counseling program.

You need to proceed through the list-building process in as systematic a way as possible. The process we recommend is to first identify the broad areas of human growth and development that you established as the scope of the guidance and counseling program (in Chapter 3, we called these *domains*). Second, specify goals and competencies for each domain and for each grade grouping or endpoint of a school level, such as at the end of the sixth grade for the elementary guidance and counseling program, at the end of the ninth grade for the middle or junior high school program, or at the end of the 12th grade for the high school program. Subsequently, as you plan and implement your program, you will develop anticipated student outcomes for competency development at each grade level. Each program activity will target objectives that help students make progress toward the desired outcomes.

The preliminary work of assembling your list can be done by a work group. Reviewing lists of competencies generated by others may be confusing at first, but once the work group gets involved it is an exciting task. It allows professional counselors to focus on the contributions they can make to students' growth and development. At each stage of the development of the list—after establishing the domains and stating the competencies—the list should be reviewed and approved by the total guidance staff as well as by other key members of the school staff, administration, students, and the community. Use your school–community advisory committee to assist you in the process.

Be parsimonious when it comes to the number of domains, goals, and competencies used as the basis for your improved program. The models presented in Chapter 3 exemplify how the content domains, goals, and competencies expand when the specifics are addressed. The life career development model identifies three domains and has five goals per domain, resulting in 15 goals for the overall program model. The ASCA (2005) model identifies three domains with three goals per domain, resulting in nine goals overall. The Texas model identifies seven domains that incorporate 28 skill goals. The Northside Independent School District (1994) model identifies seven domains and 24 skill goals for the overall program model. We suggest that you not exceed these numbers because longer lists become difficult to manage effectively, especially given the resources typically available to the guidance and counseling program. This list of competencies is the heart of the comprehensive guidance and counseling program. Remember, every activity conducted in each component of the program should aim toward mastery of one or more of these competencies.

Reaffirm Policy Support

If you have followed the process of program change outlined so far and are using a steering committee or a school–community advisory committee, you already have a group of guidance-educated and supportive others that includes administrators, parents, teachers, community representatives, and business and industry personnel. At this point in the process, however, it is a good idea to reaffirm the support of the school system's policymakers and administrators for the program's structural components, competencies, and delivery system model. Remember that they need to know what is envisioned for the guidance and counseling program and be willing to support the improvement efforts not only with the public but also with the guidance staff and other school staff members who may be anxious about the proposed changes.

To learn whether you have the support of the administrators in your school or district, begin with your immediate supervisor. If you are at the district level, this means your assistant or associate superintendent; if you are at the building level, it means your principal. Remember that to ensure that the changes you envision are consistent with the district's vision, you need at least one of the administrators to help you keep in touch with the district's basic mission. You also need the administrator to help you gain the support of the school district's board of education, and you need the administrator's assistance in enlisting the support of the other administrators, at the campus or district level, who supervise or have expectations for counselors. In addition, you need the reaffirmation of the upper-level administrators to convince counselors who resist the impending changes that the changes are, indeed, what the district wants and that they need to be responsive to those changes.

Because school districts operate within a delicate political balance, recognized leaders or a majority of constituents—including parents, principals, counselors, teachers, students, superintendents, other administrators, and board members—have to be willing to sign on to the new program vision. The more you prepare them at this stage of the process, the stronger your support will be in the challenging times of actual implementation.

Now that the program structure has been selected and student competencies have been listed, it is time to seek a guidance and counseling program policy statement. The fact that the advisory or steering committee has already endorsed the program helps because its members can take the program structure and student competency list to their constituent groups, educate them, and solicit feedback. However, it is also highly desirable to have your board of education adopt a guidance and counseling program policy that affirms the structure of the desired program. "Systemic change occurs when policies and procedures are examined and changed in light of new data" (ASCA, 2005, p. 25). Some districts adopt the program definition as the basic policy. Some policymakers state the priorities for the program, such as serving students who need developmental, preventive, remedial, or crisis help, and the relative priority of each of the four program components as well as the priorities for student skill development. You may find some of the data gathered in your study of the perceptions of the current guidance and counseling program useful in presenting the policy to the school board. You may also find useful the National School Boards Association's (2010) policy regarding counseling and guidance (cited in Chapter 2). An example of a local board of education policy is provided in Appendix D.

Establish Priorities for Program Delivery (Qualitative Design)

With your program broadly outlined, basic policy support established, and the rationale for the program in place, you are now ready to define in specific terms the desired design for the district's or building's comprehensive guidance and counseling program. Following are the basic questions that you are answering now:

- How do you want to use the resources available to the guidance and counseling program to ensure attainment of the program mission?
- What are the priorities within each component of the program?
- How much of the available resources should be expended within each component?

As described in Chapter 4, the priorities express the qualitative design of the program; the parameters for resource allocation express the quantitative design.

In developing the rationale, assumptions, and definition for the program, you began the values clarification exercise that must be completed now as you establish the qualitative and quantitative designs for program delivery. Once the program improvement leadership has completed assessment of the current program design, they will be able to see that choices are made, sometimes unconsciously, in program implementation. It is also no doubt clear that the students' needs for and within the program seem infinite, but the resources available to the program are quite finite. Purposeful development of the desired program design allows these choices to be made consciously and conscientiously. The design decisions provide the guidelines so that your guidance and counseling program can be organized for effective and efficient use of the resources currently and potentially available.

Designing the qualitative dimension of the program entails making decisions regarding the specific definitions of and priorities for program delivery. Priorities are established for the use of counselors' and others' competencies, for the clients to be served, for the student competencies to be targeted, and for the activities to be provided. Which student groups should have what priority? Which student competencies should be emphasized? What activities make up each of the comprehensive guidance and counseling program components and their priorities? Your answers should be based on the rationale that you have offered for the program, and they should suggest the priorities for staff roles, clients to be served, topics to be addressed, and activities to be undertaken within each component.

Priorities for School Counselors' Competencies

Before making specific recommendations concerning school counselors' role, it is important to remember the unique contributions that school counselors can and do make to students' growth and development. Although states vary in their requirements for certification of school counselors, some consensus is seen at the national level. The primary content suggested by national certification and accreditation agencies (e.g., Council for Accreditation of Counseling and Related Educational Programs, 2009; National Board for Certified Counselors, 2004; National Board for Professional Teaching Standards, 2002) include human growth and development, fundamentals of school counseling, student competency development, social and cultural contexts and multicultural competence, counseling theories and techniques, consultation and collaboration with other adults in students' lives, student assessment, program development, professional orientation, advocacy for clients, leadership, research and evaluation, information resources and technology, and practicum or internship.

Counselor role expectations and job descriptions need to be written. This process requires knowledge about what school counselors are educated to do and what competencies they have acquired in gaining certification. At this stage of the evolution of school counselor education, consensus on this set of competencies is being approached. For example, the *Texas Evaluation Model for Professional School Counselors* (Texas Counseling Association, 2004) delineated eight domains that describe school counselors' responsibilities: program management, guidance, counseling, consultation, coordination, student assessment, professional behavior, and professional standards. These are further described by 33 standards of competence and 230 descriptors.

The essential functions of all professional school counselors in the program should be identified and provide a generic job description for this classification of workers (Henderson, 2009). Subsequently, job descriptions that specify each individual counselor's responsibilities can be written (Henderson & Gysbers, 1998). An example of a generic high school counselor job description is included in Appendix E.

Having clearly defined what counselors are educated to do and what their generic responsibilities are within the program, priorities for the use of their competencies can now be established. Rank ordering by roles is one method, but establishing priorities by competency provides more direction. For example, should counselors spend more energy and time teaching the guidance curriculum or conducting small groups, counseling individuals or coordinating resources, serving students or being a social change agent, or all of these? What is being determined at this point is the relative value of each of the counselors' specialized skills in the context of the program. For example, "it is important that school counselors have a realistic sense of their strengths and limitations as social change agents" (Ratts, DeKruyf, & Chen-Hayes, 2007, p. 94). Table 5.2 displays the priorities for use of school counselors' competencies as determined by the Northside Guidance Steering Committee (Northside Independent School District, 1994). The highest priorities were given to skills that only the school counselors possessed: managing the guidance and counseling program and providing individual and group counseling services.

In the interests of time and simplicity, some districts have chosen to use broader categories to represent counselor competence than actual delineations of specific competencies (as seen in Table 5.2). Texas school districts have used the performance domains described in the *Texas Evaluation Model for Professional School Counselors* (Texas Counseling

Table 5.2

Priorities for Use of Counselor Competencies

Priority	Competency
1	Plan, implement, and evaluate a comprehensive program of guidance, including counseling services.
2	Counsel individual students with presenting needs or concerns.
3	Counsel small groups of students with presenting needs or concerns.
4	Consult with parents, teachers, administrators, and other relevant individuals to enhance their work with students.
5	Use accepted theories and techniques appropriate in school counseling.
6	Assist teachers in teaching guidance-related curriculum.
7	Guide individuals and groups of students through the development of education and career plans.
8	Coordinate with school and community personnel to bring together resources for students.
9	Teach the school developmental guidance curriculum.
10	Use an effective referral process for assisting students and others to use special programs and services.
11	Interpret test and other appraisal results appropriately.
12	Use other sources of student data appropriately for assessment purposes.
13	Participate in the planning and evaluation of the district or school group standardized testing program.
14	Supervise activities of guidance-program–related clerical, paraprofessional, and volunteer personnel.

Note. From *Comprehensive Guidance Program Framework*, by Northside Independent School District, 1994, San Antonio, TX: Author. Adapted with permission.

Association, 2004). As previously described, a performance domain includes multiple standards of competence; for example, the guidance performance domain includes seven standards, and the counseling domain contains three. Each standard is further described through multiple descriptors. An example of a district's priorities for the desired use of counselors' competence categorized by performance domain is provided in Table 5.3. As you can conclude from this, the district had already determined it wanted to have a developmental guidance and counseling program.

Priorities for Other Guidance and Counseling Program Staff

Now is also an appropriate time to consider the roles of other guidance department personnel such as registrars, career center technicians, counselors' secretaries, office aides, and peer facilitators. Ultimately, all personnel who work in the guidance and counseling program must have their roles defined, including teachers who act as advisers or who teach guidance or psychology classes and community volunteers who augment the guidance staff in specific guidance activities. The guidance and counseling program roles of related mental health specialists, such as licensed counselors, school social workers, and school psy-

Table 5.3

Desired Priorities for Use of Counselor Competence and Performance Domain

Performance Domain	Elementary School	Middle School	High School
Program management	6	5	1
Guidance	1	1	4
Counseling	2	2	3
Consultation	3	3	5
Coordination	5	4	6
Student assessment	7	6	7
Professionalism	4	7	2

chologists, should also be delineated. We recommend that you write the job descriptions for each of the positions so that differentiation of the various roles and multiple responsibilities is clear to all concerned. (Some example job descriptions for other guidance program staff are included in Appendix E.)

Because human resources are basic to the guidance and counseling program, you may find it useful to consider who else in addition to the school staff is available to help deliver the guidance and counseling program. Community members, for example, are some of education's chronically untapped resources. Thus, an inventory of community members who may be willing to serve is an important part of a community resource list. Historically, the most dramatic examples of community-assisted guidance and counseling programs have been provided in career education programs. Business, industry, and labor groups; service club members; and the like are often willing to speak on occupation-specific or employment realities. They may also become mentors to unmotivated students. Moreover, parent and grandparent groups have been used to provide role models of caring adults for schoolchildren. PTA leaders can be used to lead parent education groups, using the national PTA resources (http://www.pta.org).

Priorities for Parents

Ideally and importantly, school staff and parents are partners in providing guidance to students. The ASCA (2010) Ethical Standards state that professional school counselors "respect the rights and responsibilities of parents/guardians for their children and endeavor to establish as appropriate, a collaborative relationship with parents/guardians to facilitate students' maximum development" (B.1.a.). From the parents' perspective, what school guidance and counseling programs accomplish with their children is supplemental to their efforts. From the guidance and counseling program perspective, parents are extensions of the guidance and counseling program staff. Some parents at some times benefit from program activities or use program services and are therefore clients of the program. It is the responsibility of the school-based guidance and counseling program staff members and leaders to include parents in the delivery of the program as well as to provide them appropriate services as resources allow.

Parents as Program Staff

As partners with the school-based guidance and counseling program staff, parents assist in planning and designing the program by providing input as to students' needs and the desired outcomes. From the parents' perspective, they have ideas about what their children need and what they, as parents, would appreciate help with. They also have a voice in establishing program priorities. They provide data as to the apparent effectiveness of the activities of which they are a part. After data have been gathered as to the program's effectiveness and efficiency, parents assist in evaluation of the implemented program.

As extensions of the guidance and counseling program staff, parents are aware of what students are taught in guidance curriculum and reinforce the skills at home. Specific educational and career goal setting, planning, and decision making are the primary responsibilities of students and their parents. Parents fulfill these roles best when they participate fully in the activities of the individual student planning component. School guidance staff and the parents ensure that parents have the information they need to fulfill these roles and know when to participate.

In school counseling, the primary goal of responsive services is to help students overcome barriers to their successful educational progress. For students whose problems require nonschool-based resources and solutions, parents are the primary resource providers. They arrange for and pay for therapy, for example. For students whose parents do not fulfill this responsibility or who are part of the problem, school counselors may have to extend themselves further into identifying resources or advocating for students (Ratts, Toporek & Lewis, 2010), but they must be careful not to assume the parental role. (See Appendix F for an example of procedures for helping students manage personal crises.)

Parents who are partners with school counselors on behalf of their children refer their children to their counselors for help and allow counselors to apply their skills within the ethical standards of the profession. They work with counselors and other school staff members to clarify the issues affecting students' success in school and participate in implementing the solution plan.

Moreover, parent partners fulfill several roles in activities of the system support component. They assist in community relations, education, and outreach efforts of guidance and counseling program staff. They participate on guidance and counseling program steering and advisory committees. Some assist school counselors in providing education and training to other parents.

Parents as Clients

As benefactors or recipients of guidance and counseling program activities and services, parents are helped in implementing their home-based guidance and counseling by professional school counselors. Guidance curriculum activities assist parents to teach their children such basic life skills as self-acceptance, setting meaningful goals, making sound decisions, getting along well with others, and behaving responsibly.

Through school-based individual student planning activities, parents are provided with information that helps them help their children make and implement plans for their next steps in life. For example, as counselors help students anticipate what they will do after high school, they provide students and parents with information about and guide them in the use of information about careers as well as about colleges and other pathways to adult careers. Sheely-Moore and Bratton (2010) found that engaging the parents of low-income African American students is particularly critical to the students' continued pursuit of education after high school. Strategies for doing this effectively include contacting the parents directly, scheduling activities according to the parents' availability, providing child care, and providing materials for them to take home. Bryan, Holcomb-McCoy, Moore-Thomas, and Day-Vines (2009) offered related advice. It is "important that school counselors find creative ways to partner with parents of varying backgrounds in the college search and choice process (Bryan, 2005). This may involve using community venues (e.g., community centers, places of worship) to meet with parents" (p. 288).

As their children experience learning or social problems at school, parents benefit from consultations with school counselors. Counseling is most successful in schools when counselors create collaborative relationships with parents. This begins with helping them understand the role of the program and of counselors and the ethical standards (Huss, Bryant, & Mulet, 2008). School counselors are challenged to balance a child's right to privacy and parents' need to know. Through responsive services consultations, school counselors help parents to better understand their children, the typical learning and behavior patterns of children of that age, the operations of the school, and other special programs and services the school offers. When parents select additional program or service options for their children, it is often the school counselor who coordinates the transition with the parent and child.

It is not appropriate for school counselors to provide counseling services for parents. The students in their schools are school counselors' primary counseling clients (ASCA,

2010). The mission of most schools is to assist young people to learn; therefore, school counselors' counseling work (the application of counseling skills and techniques) targets the students and barriers to their learning. When parents' issues get in the way, school counselors consult with them about problems and solutions, advocate with them on behalf of their children, provide them with information, and refer them to appropriate sources for help.

In addition to consultations provided through responsive services, professional school counselors offer opportunities for parents to further develop their parenting skills. These parent education classes or workshops are offered under the umbrella of system support because they always have as one of their anticipated outcomes that parents will feel more closely connected to their children's school and to their children's learning.

Priorities for Clients to Be Served

During the assessment of your program, you identified the current program clients. Either by building on that list or by creating a new one, you need to consider all of the possible populations that could benefit from the comprehensive guidance and counseling program and to answer the question "What priority-for-service should be assigned to each of the various subsets of these populations?"

Globally, school counselors work with two basic populations: students and the adults who relate to the students. Within the student population, there are subgroups of students, as described in Chapter 4, with needs for developmental, preventive, remedial, or crisis interventions. In the building, each grade level represents a subpopulation developmentally and also includes students with needs for preventive, remedial, or crisis interventions. As previously described, subgroups (e.g., racial and ethnic groups) of students may include students from several grade levels. Subgroups of students may also fall in different places on the mental health–mental illness continuum.

Within the adult population, there are parents, school-related adults, and community-based adults who work with students. The parent population reflects the students' subsets. School staff include regular and special education teachers, other specialists, other counselors, and administrators. Community-based adults are those related to the direct delivery of the program, community-based specialists, and representatives from community resources—providers of mental health as well as of educational or career services.

Using a process similar to that described later in this chapter in the Establish Parameters for Resource Allocation (Quantitative Design) section, under the heading Set Priorities for Counselors' Time, the Northside Independent School District's steering committee established the client priorities presented in Table 5.4. The numbers suggest guidelines for percentages of time counselors should spend with the various population categories. Students clearly hold the highest priority, but other adults in students' lives are also important clients. There are differences in priorities for elementary, middle, and high school. Each campus and, indeed, each counselor specify even more discretely which subsets within those categories are served. For example, do all students in all grade levels benefit from equal developmental assistance, or do some grade levels of students benefit more? In assessing the students' needs, priorities for the more specialized responsive services are evidenced. For example, questions that are answered here include "Which subgroups of those students, as delineated in Chapter 4, should benefit from small-group counseling?" and thus "What topic-focused small groups should be offered or would process groups better serve them?"

Table 5.4
Desired Priorities for Clients Served (in Percentages)

Client Category	Elementary School	Middle School	High School
Students			
Developmental	29	24	17
Preventive	21	19	26
Remedial	15	15	23
Subtotal	65	58	66
Adults			
District administration	2.5	3.0	2.0
School staff	—	—	—
Principals	4.5	4.0	4.0
Regular ed. teachers	8.5	9.0	5.0
Counselors	3.5	5.0	6.0
Special ed. teachers	3.5	4.0	3.0
Other specialists	2.0	2.0	2.0
Parents	9.0	12.0	9.0
Community representatives	1.5	3.0	3.0
Subtotal	35.0	42.0	34.0

Priorities for Student Competencies

Basic Guidance Skills and Domains

It is important to have both the counselors and the consumers of the guidance and counseling program establish priorities for the competencies that students will acquire as a result of their participation in the guidance and counseling program. Helping all students in a school building or a system make progress toward acquiring competencies contained in the 15 goals—or 12 goals, or however many you have agreed on in your model—presents an overwhelming challenge if you are just beginning to implement a competency-based comprehensive guidance and counseling program. This challenge is compounded because you are also accepting accountability for helping students with developmental-, preventive-, remedial-, and crisis-level needs. Thus, priorities as to which competencies are to be included in the program at any given time need to be established.

The goals for student competency development can and should be ranked according to their overall importance for all students. You may also wish to suggest the importance of various goals (and the competencies involved) by different grade levels or grade groups. The sequence for helping students reach these goals needs to be agreed on as well. For example, many groups have agreed that helping students know and understand themselves is prerequisite to their learning to know and understand others.

This process of setting priorities becomes complicated, but the various approaches usually produce some consensus in terms of overall top priorities for attention, and as you move to more specific implementation plans, you will have a sense of where to begin and where to end. Figure 5.1 presents the goal priorities established in its initial qualitative program design by Northside Independent School District (1986). These skills are still stated in very broad terms; they are comparable with content element domains as defined in Chapter 3.

If you are in a smaller setting and can manage the attendant tasks, this is an appropriate time to conduct a student and community needs assessment to ascertain priorities for student competency development. In a larger district setting or a multibuilding setting, however, the competency statements are still too broad to be used as an assessment of students' needs. (Ideas on assessing needs are presented in Chapter 6.)

Figure 5.1
Priorities for Student Skill Development

Recommended Program Design

To have a comprehensive and appropriately balanced program, the following priorities for allocation of resources need to be considered as goals for campus programs.

Priority Rankings Assigned to Skills

Students will	Importance	Sequence	Level of Emphasis
1. understand and respect themselves.	1	1	E
2. understand and respect others.	2	2	E
3. behave responsibly in school.	3	3	E
4. behave responsibly in the family.	9	6	E
5. behave responsibly in the community.	9	10	M
6. make wise choices.	3	3	M
7. manage change successfully.	7	8	M
8. solve problems.	5	5	M
9. use educational opportunities well.	8	9	M
10. communicate effectively.	6	6	M
11. plan for personally satisfying and socially useful lives.	11	11	H
12. prepare for personally satisfying and socially useful lives.	12	12	H

Note. From *Comprehensive Guidance Program Framework*, by Northside Independent School District, 1986, San Antonio, TX: Author. Adapted with permission.
E = elementary; M = middle; H = high school.

Again, some Texas districts have set their desired program priorities using the more global student content domains (seven) rather than the related list of skill goals (28). This leaves more specific prioritization to be done by staff for the three school levels and ultimately for each grade level. Table 5.5 displays an example.

Anticipated Student Results

In previous work, you have established the domains, goals, and competencies for student development for which the guidance and counseling program and counseling staff are willing to be held accountable. And you have developed competency statements to describe the goals. At this point, you need to specify relevant results the program will aim for at each

Table 5.5
Desired Program Content Priorities

Content	Elementary School	Middle School	High School
Self-confidence development	2	6	2
Motivation to achieve	3	1	3
Decision making, goal setting, planning, problem solving	4	3	1
Interpersonal effectiveness	6	5	4
Communication skills	1	4	6
Cross-cultural effectiveness	7	7	7
Responsible behavior	5	2	5

grade level, grade grouping, or school level. This simply means breaking the competencies into their subparts and establishing results appropriate to the age levels of the students served by the program activities. The outcome lists for the life career development model presented in Chapter 3 (in Element 1: Program Content section) result in specific statements. These statements quickly expand from the basic list of 15 goals. For each grade level, there are 15 competencies, or 225 competencies total, for kindergarten through 12th grade.

Again, we stress the need to be parsimonious in identifying results for which you will be held accountable. Base the actual number you use on the assessment of your student needs and the priorities that are set. Seeking too many outcomes makes the program unworkable. The allocation of counselor time to the different program components has a direct bearing on what results you are able to assist students in reaching developmentally. As the program development efforts proceed, every one of these results can become an aim of some lesson, unit, or counseling session. In the comprehensive guidance and counseling program, every activity has a student objective, and every activity's objective must relate to a grade-level specific result that is on this list. An example of this conceptual flow is as follows:

Domain 1: Self-Knowledge and Interpersonal Skills
Goal A: Students will develop and incorporate an understanding of the unique personal characteristics and abilities of themselves and others.

- *Competency:* Students will specify those personal characteristics and abilities that they may value.
- *Student result:* Fifth-grade students will identify a variety of things about themselves that they value.
- *Activity objective:* Through this lesson, each student will identify six things he or she values about him- or herself.

The task of specifying competencies by grade level, grade grouping, or school level is one that counselors need to do. The work group that defined the broader list of goals and competencies should either continue with this task or provide leadership to an expanded group of counselors working on the results or outcomes list. It is instructive for all the counselors to have some experience in developing at least a portion of the list. It helps them think in terms of student outcomes so that when the shift is made to the activity development phase of the project, they are used to thinking in terms of specific student behaviors.

When it is near completion, the list of outcomes should be reviewed and ratified by the total counseling staff and by all others—the steering committee or the administrative staff—who are providing leadership to the program change efforts. The total list of outcomes will be a bit much for noncounselors to review, but the counselors need the opportunity to think through every piece of the outline. Moreover, the review by administrators and others allows people with different frames of reference to consider the specifics of the guidance and counseling program. In this way, outcomes that are potentially unpalatable to some community members or outcomes that have been overlooked and are seen as important can be identified and addressed from the beginning.

Priorities for Guidance Activities for Each Component

The program components now need to be defined in finer detail by describing the primary emphases and major activities included in each. Each component of the desired program should list activities that are performed effectively in the current program and identify and envision new activities that can better meet the program goals.

Guidance Curriculum

To further describe the guidance curriculum component, identify the curriculum strands, the basic student competencies that were established for the comprehensive program (see Figure 5.1). These competencies describe the scope of the guidance curriculum. Next, priorities for guidance instruction are established. This process serves to help counselors know the topics to be taught at particular school levels and, because there are time limitations for teaching students, the competencies that have the highest priorities. The sequence for assisting students to learn the competencies is also established. This learning may entail merely restating the student outcomes specified for each grade level in the previous effort. However, if in specifying student results you expressed outcomes by grade spans or school levels, you now need to clarify what is to be taught at each grade level. Again, an example from the life career development model helps portray this. The scope and a sequence for the kindergarten guidance curriculum in this model is depicted in Table 5.6.

Having done that, the next step is to group the outcomes into units for instruction. The domains have been the organizer for your development of student competencies so far. Now, as you identify specific outcomes for each grade level and sequence them, some natural groupings for learning from the different goal areas probably will emerge. For instructional purposes, you will probably want to teach these by logical units rather than in the order specified in your outline of competencies. The units that emerge from the kindergarten outcomes in our example might be as follows:

Unit	Competencies Addressed (from Table 5.6)
Self	1–4
Decision making	5 and 6
Others	7–9
School	10 and 11
Community and work	12–14
Future	15

Individual Student Planning

To further describe the individual student planning component, identify the major activities that assist students to make their personalized plans. For elementary, middle or junior

Table 5.6
Kindergarten Guidance Curriculum Scope and Sequence

Kindergarten students will
1. describe their appearance.
2. describe ways they care for themselves.
3. describe areas in which they are self-sufficient.
4. describe growing capabilities.
5. describe choices they make.
6. realize the difficulty of making choices between two desirable alternatives.
7. recognize that they listen to and speak with a variety of people.
8. describe people and activities they enjoy.
9. describe their work and play relationships with others and their favorite activities.
10. describe those things they learn at school.
11. describe their daily activities at school.
12. recognize the town, state, and country in which they reside.
13. describe the work activities of family members.
14. mentally project adults into work activities other than those they do presently.
15. describe situations that are going to happen in the future.

high, and high school, this component includes activities that help students orient themselves to new school settings; set goals, make plans, and take their next steps toward these goals; and factor in their own aptitudes and disabilities that are relevant to their planning. In the schools and districts with which we have worked, these activities focus on students' educational and career plans. If your program is so directed, you might also have activities that help students make plans that relate to their personal and social lives. These major activities must be related to the broad goals of the guidance and counseling program. An example of the activities and the skills they relate to as delineated by the Northside Independent School District is provided in Table 5.7.

As you can see, these are activities traditionally found in guidance and counseling programs. Decisions need to be made as to the priorities for the time spent in this component. Assisting students to complete their elementary and secondary education successfully is usually a priority for school counselors, with the transition grades receiving the highest priority. However, today heavy emphasis is placed on enhancing the college and career readiness of all students. Helping students develop their postsecondary educational and career plans falls in this component as well. At the elementary level, orienting primary-grade children to school and helping upper-grade children adjust to the increasing demands of the academic curriculum by developing effective, personalized approaches to studying and time management may have priority. Recently, the importance of postsecondary planning for middle school students has been recognized. Gibbons and Borders (2010) reported that "evaluators of effective college preparation have found that successful programs start in middle school, include counseling, involve parents and peers, and provide concrete information about college" (p. 234).

When counselor caseloads are larger than the 100:1 ratio suggested by those who would have school counselors work with individuals in one-on-one relationships, this component needs to be built around group activities. The group activities need to be designed to assist individuals to develop personally relevant plans and should provide for one-on-one assistance as a follow-up, if needed.

Responsive Services

To further describe the responsive services component, identify the topics that students, their teachers, and parents present most frequently, as well as those identified in any com-

Table 5.7
Individual Student Planning: Activities and Student Skills

Activity	Student Skills
Orientation	Use well their educational opportunities in school
Educational planning	Plan and prepare for personally satisfying lives
Preregistration[a]	Make wise choices
Registration[a]	Manage change successfully
Dissemination and interpretation of standardized test results	Understand and respect themselves
Career/vocational planning	Plan and prepare for personally satisfying and socially useful lives
Application of other skills taught in guidance curriculum	(As identified through local needs assessment)

Note. From *Comprehensive Guidance Program Framework*, by Northside Independent School District, 1986, San Antonio, TX: Author. Adapted with permission.
[a]Overlaps with system support.

pleted needs assessments. This will enable the establishment of a systematic means for attending to the high-priority topics or problems faced by the high-priority student clients and selection of the most efficient intervention activity. What problems interfere most often with students' personal, social, career, or educational development? How many students need counseling, consulting, or referral, and for what reason? What percentage need preventive help, small-group counseling, or brief family interventions? What percentage needs remedial help, one-on-one counseling, or referral? What percentage is apt to need crisis intervention? Which parents, teachers, and administrators need consulting help? The more specific you are, the more focused and accountable implementation can be.

If a topic, such as child and adolescent fears, affects a lot of students, you need to anticipate how to address it most effectively and efficiently. Although it might be ideal to work with children and adolescents on a one-on-one basis, that mode may not provide sufficient time to help all of the needy students. Coordinating activities from different components allows for better addressing students' needs. In the case of child or adolescent fears, resiliency can be taught through guidance curriculum interventions and then nurtured through group counseling that targets helping students cope or manage their fears (Burnham, 2009). More about using the right component activities to address optimum numbers of students' needs appropriately is discussed in Chapter 8.

Mellin (2009) made a compelling point about professional counselors' and professional school counselors' underdeveloped contributions to "the crisis in children's mental health" (p. 501). 70% of them are in schools" (p. 501). She cited several reports to underscore

the impact of poor mental health on academic outcomes, substance use, delinquent behavior, and child welfare. . . . Students with severe emotional and behavioral needs are 50% more likely than their peers without such needs to drop out of school (Wagner, 1995). Recent research has also suggested that up to 70% of children involved in the juvenile justice system have a diagnosable mental health disorder (Skowyra & Cocozza, 2006). Estimates have indicated that 39% to 80% of children in the child welfare system have mental health needs (Shin, 2005). Left untreated, some children are at risk for suicide (USPHS, 1999); in fact, suicide is the third leading cause of death among persons between the ages of 15 and 24 years (Centers for Disease Control and Prevention, 2007). (p. 502)

Professional school counselors are uniquely positioned and trained to provide appropriate services to this subgroup of children and adolescents in schools. They are one of the mental health specialists in the schools, along with school psychologists and school social workers. Because their caseloads encompass the total student body of their schools, they are the first line of defense in identifying, preliminarily assessing, counseling, and referring students with mental health issues. They are also positioned to consult with students' parents and other educators and to coordinate services with community-based service providers.

A challenge to professional school counselors is to understand what interventions to use with students depending on where a student falls on the mental health–mental illness continuum and what levels of interventions they need on the developmental–preventive–remedial–crisis response continuum (Chapter 4). Typically, the size of a professional school counselor's caseload is such that spending a large amount of time providing long-term, individual therapy for a few students is not the priority. Recognizing that they do have the training and professional responsibility to provide individual and group counseling for students, helping students whose mental health is temporarily or moderately impaired and collaborating with community-based mental health–mental illness workers in designing and implementing treatment plans relevant in the school setting are often allocated time in the design.

In the initial Northside Independent School District project, a subcommittee of the guidance steering committee asked the school counselors to list the topics they found themselves responding to over the course of the year. The steering committee established priorities for the counselors' attention to these topics from the school district's point of view. Again, each of these topics was related to the competencies the counselors strive to help students master. Clarifying this relationship from the outset assisted counselors in specifying appropriate student objectives for their counseling activities. The list of topics, the grade levels at which they were identified, and their priorities are presented in Table 5.8 (Henderson, 1987).

The information was surprising in two ways: First, there were not that many topics (12 in all), and second, there was much similarity between the lists submitted by the elementary and the secondary counselors. These two factors made the job of becoming better at helping students handle their problems more manageable. In-service training could focus on these issues. Exemplary practices could be developed and shared (e.g., protocols for providing services to grieving students). Northside Independent School District counselors felt that one side benefit of this massive redesigning effort was learning that there was not as much difference among the programs at the three levels (elementary, middle, and high school) as they had believed. The programs were shaped differently, but students' needs were similar, as were counselors' skills and interests.

Society changes, neighborhoods and schools change, and students change. Thus, the need for these specialized counselor services should be assessed each year and responded

Table 5.8
Responsive Services: Topics, Skills, and Priorities

Grade Level	Recurrent Topic	Skill
K–12	1. Academic failure	Use well their educational opportunities in school
K–12	2. Child abuse	Behave responsibly in the family
K–12	3. Divorced and single parents	Behave responsibly in the family
K–12	4. Grief–death and dying–loss	Manage change successfully
MS/HS	5. Suicide threats	Understand and respect themselves; solve problems
MS/HS	6. Sexuality issues such as appropriate dating behavior and wise date selection; pregnancy; sexually transmitted diseases	Understand and respect themselves; solve problems
K–12	7. Tardiness, absences, truancy, school phobia, dropping out	Use well their educational opportunities; plan and prepare for personally satisfying and socially useful lives
K–12	8. Discipline or behavior problems	School-related: behave responsibly in school
K–12	9. Peer problems	Understand and respect themselves and others
K–12	10. Alcohol, drug, inhalant abuse	Understand and respect themselves
K–12	11. Family situations	Behave responsibly in the family
K–12	12. Information seekers	(Varies with different information needs)
K–12	13. Application of other skills taught in guidance • academic problems • behavior problems • social problems	Solve problems

Note: From "A Comprehensive School Guidance Program at Work," by P. H. Henderson, 1987, *TACD Journal, 15,* 25–37. Adapted with permission. MS = middle school; HS = high school.

to accordingly. Although the major categories of problems are constant, the specific topics within these categories change. For example, counseling students with discipline or behavior problems are usually a high priority for school counselors, but unfortunately, such topics as bullying and gang involvement have surfaced as well.

If you are just beginning a program, we offer the following list of categories and some recurrent topics to spur your thinking:

- *Personal development issues:* cultural and ethnic identity; emotional disturbances; grief and loss; health (AIDS, serious or terminal illnesses, eating disorders); managing disabilities or disorders; misbehavior; self-esteem; sexuality, pregnancy, and gender identity; spirituality and morality; stress; substance use and abuse; suicide (prevention, intervention, postvention)
- *Social development issues:* adult relationships; athletic involvement; delinquency; family problems and divorce; bullying and violence; isolation; mobility; multicultural problems (ethnicity, racial tension, bigotry); physical and sexual abuse; peer relationships; sociopathology
- *Educational development issues:* attendance, school phobia, and dropping out; attention deficit disorders; attitudes; behavior or conduct problems or disorders; being gifted and talented; being new; lack of academic success; making educational choices (courses, high school, college); managing learning disabilities; study skills and habits; test anxiety
- *Career development issues:* applying interests and aptitudes; balancing dreams with reality; developmentally "stuck"; lack of goals; hopelessness; indecision.

The length of this list reinforces our point about the need to establish priorities relevant to the guidance and counseling program's mission, the goals of the school, and the needs of the students and community.

The responsive services component includes a continuum of school counselor activities from identification through appraisal, intervention, and follow-up. Counselors are competent to identify students with particular needs and school-related issues. These needs may be those of one individual student or groups of students. They may relate to school, home, or community situations. They may be affected by ethnic, racial, or other demographic variables. School counselors are competent to lead, coordinate, or participate in the specification of these students' problems through appraisal efforts. They gather and analyze personal and social data regarding the student and the situation. As summarized in Table 5.9, when students' issues are clarified, counselors are competent to intervene by providing individual, small-group, or crisis counseling; by consulting with parents, teachers, or others; and by coordinating or referring them to other service providers. School counselors are also trained to follow up with students in a planned, consistent, and evaluative manner and to determine whether the planned problem solution is in fact being carried out and effective.

The qualitative program design should provide guidelines for school counselors as to the priorities for the use of these competencies (identification, appraisal, intervention, and follow-up) within the school. Where others are also competent, their talents should be drawn on as well. Typically, teachers, relevant paraprofessionals, and administrators can identify and specify students with special needs. Teachers and school psychologists can appraise students. School counselors' unique competencies support counseling and consultation interventions. Follow-up may be divided among the adults on the campus involved with a student in the specific situation.

Table 5.9
Student Need Levels and Professional School Counselor Response Levels

Student Need Level (Percentage of Students in Subgroup)	Intervention Strategy	Professional School Counselor Competence
Developmental (100)	Education	Teaching, guiding, consulting, and collaborating
Preventive (35)	Individual counseling and small-group counseling	Counseling, consultation, and referral
Remedial (15)	Individual counseling and small-group counseling	Counseling, referral, consultation, and coordination
Personal crisis (1–2)	Individual counseling	Counseling, referral, consultation, and coordination

System Support

Guidance and Counseling Program Management. For the program to function optimally and accountably, designation of leaders and clarification of their responsibilities at the building and district levels are necessary. Generally, their responsibilities are to ensure accountable program delivery in accordance with established standards and to promote continuous improvement of the guidance and counseling program (Henderson & Gysbers, 1998). They lead the processes for program development, management and accountability.

Staff leadership responsibilities include holding school counselors and other guidance and counseling program staff members accountable for carrying out their professional responsibilities and providing support for their continuous professional development. They are also responsible for advocating for the guidance and counseling program and the staff and for students' personal, social, career, and educational needs. They act as liaisons between the guidance department and administration and other departments.

Recommendations should be made as to the appropriate placement for guidance within the organization. Should guidance be aligned with administration? With instruction? With student services? Or should it stand alone? These questions have been asked throughout guidance and counseling's history, and this model does not include a recommendation because in our experience the right placement varies from district to district depending on its size and philosophy. Program-based rationale needs to be established: for example, is it aligned with administration because it is a program that is central to the whole school; aligned with instruction because it is a developmental curriculum-based program; aligned with student services because it includes a special set of services; or stand alone because it is uniquely multifaceted?

The various activities counselors participate in require policies and administrative procedures, staff and program development opportunities, reasonable levels of budget provisions, adequate facilities and equipment, appropriate staff allocations to implement the desired program, relations support, and collaborating with guidance and counseling research. At this stage, these requirements may be more of a wish list than a statement of realistic choices, but addressing constraints can wait until later when specific implementation plans are made. These items are discussed more fully in Chapter 6 because many are key to the actual implementation of the newly conceptualized program.

Support Services. The first step in establishing the desired or needed support from the guidance and counseling program for schoolwide activities or to other specific programs is to develop the list of major activities in which the guidance staff is called on to participate, if this has not already been accomplished in the assessment of your current program.

Examples of participation in schoolwide activities are activities that address school climate enhancement (e.g., advocating and planning for a schoolwide approach for addressing sexual orientation in schools; DePaul, Walsh, & Dam, 2009), bullying, or harassment. Examples of services to other programs are coordinating referrals of students for special education or interpreting standardized achievement results to faculty and administration.

The second step is to prioritize the list and determine which of these tasks are appropriate for counselors to do and which are nonguidance tasks by asking the question "Is a master's degree in guidance and counseling needed to accomplish this task?" If the answer is no, then it becomes the responsibility of the counselors and the steering committee or the school–community advisory committee to make recommendations as to which other departments are served by—and thus responsible for—the tasks. Also, decisions are made about what the school counselors' fair share of schoolwide activities is in relationship to other programs; that is, how much of the guidance and counseling program resources should be spent on programs other than guidance? Do these apply school counselors' professional skills and knowledge? Considering these factors at this time will help later as you consider ways to handle activities that need to be displaced. This concept and the issues involved are discussed more fully in Chapter 8. Priorities for possible displacements, however, can be suggested at this point. Table 5.10 displays the order of priority established by the Northside Independent School District for counselor support to schoolwide efforts or to other programs. It is based on the lists originally generated in the assessment of the current program; that is, it ranks what the counselors were doing then and is not a statement of what they should do. In theory, displacements should start with the activities listed at the bottom and continue until the lowest priority tasks are displaced completely, shared equitably, or streamlined (see Chapter 8).

Qualitative Design Summary

Once the questions regarding what is most important in the delivery of the comprehensive guidance and counseling program have been answered, the answers should be sum-

Table 5.10
Order of Priority for Support Services

Elementary School	Middle School	High School
1. Consult with staff and parents	1. Consult with staff and parents	1. Consult with staff and parents
2. Student referrals	2. Preregistration	2. Preregistration
3. Test administration and interpretation to staff	3. Test interpretation to staff	3. Test interpretation to staff
4. School climate	4. Student referrals	4. Staff development
5. Staff development	5. School climate	5. School climate
6. Special education	6. New student registration	6. Curriculum planning
7. Gifted education	7. Record keeping	7. New student registration
8. Preregistration	8. Referrals to special education	8. Record keeping
9. Discipline management	9. Curriculum planning	9. Schedule changes
10. Curriculum planning	10. Schedule changes	10. Student referrals
11. Compensatory programs	11. Master schedule development	11. Admission, review, dismissal, committee meetings
12. Accreditation	12. Vocational education	12. Vocational education
	13. Attendance and discipline	13. Other special programs
	14. Other special programs	14. Test administration
	15. Test administration	15. Discipline management

Note. From *Comprehensive Guidance Program Framework*, by Northside Independent School District, 1986, San Antonio, TX: Author. Adapted with permission.

marized and presented to all the participants in the decision-making process: the steering committee, the advisory committee, relevant district and building administrators, and the school counselors. This review helps bring key players along and makes clear the decisions made to date. An example of such a summary is provided in Table 5.11.

Establish Parameters for Resource Allocation (Quantitative Design)

Having established the priorities for the substance of the program, the next set of decisions result in setting parameters for allocating the program resources, that is, in establishing the quantitative design for your program. The two factors that affect the quantitative program design are the program balance and the counselor–student ratio.

Deciding how much can be done by school counselors is expressed in the recommended balance among the program components—how counselors' time is best divided in providing the various kinds of program activities. Anticipating how many program clients will benefit from program activities is determined by the counselor–student ratio. Thus, a new recommendation emerges and is supported by program design rationale.

Table 5.11
Comprehensive Guidance Program Qualitative Design: Executive Summary

Qualitative Design Dimensions	Guidance Curriculum	Individual Student Planning	Responsive Services	System Support
Student clients	Developmental	Developmental	Preventive Remedial	Significant adults
Content priorities	Communicative skills Cross-cultural effectiveness Decision making and problem solving Interpersonal effectiveness Motivation to achieve Responsible behavior Self-esteem development	Educational and career goal setting and action planning	Academic success Career choice Child abuse Cross-cultural effectiveness Dropping out of school Educational choices Family issues Loss and grief Relationships with adults Relationships with peers Responsible behavior School attendance Self-esteem Sexuality Stress Substance abuse Suicide	Guidance program management Schoolwide activities Services to other programs
Priority activities	Lessons and units	Portfolio development Advisement Testing Transition Preregistration	Individual counseling Small-group counseling Referral Parent conferences Teacher conferences	Program development Staff development Resource development Public relations Other program support
Counselor role priorities	Guidance Consultation	Guidance Consultation Coordination Assessment	Counseling Consultation Coordination Assessment	Program management Professionalism

At this point, a "which came first, the chicken or the egg?" issue arises: Should the desired outcomes and program design dictate the allocation of resources, or should the allocation of resources dictate the shape of the program? In an ideal setting, the identified student and community needs will justify the allocation of sufficient resources to provide a complete, comprehensive program for meeting those needs. In a real setting, however, there are no doubt more needs and desired outcomes than the school or district is able to attend to, given feasible resource allocations. This is part of the challenge of "remodeling your house while you are living in it." You are probably not creating a program from scratch, nor are you creating one with the realistic potential for unlimited resources. In the last analysis, a guidance and counseling program must be designed to use resources that are available, or the campus or district must make available resources that are needed to implement the program as designed.

You must make recommendations on the basis of current resource allocations with some projections or requests for expanded resources. In our experience, school counseling staff first have to redirect their current resources and be prepared to use augmented resources appropriately. At this point, then, you need to make resource allocation decisions on the basis of the priorities and realities of your schools. For example, you have identified what a fully implemented guidance curriculum would contain; however, if there is time in the students' or counselors' schedules for only one guidance lesson per week (or month, or grading period), then the full guidance curriculum cannot be implemented at first.

In terms of both specialized skills and salary dollars, the most valuable resource applied to the guidance and counseling program is the time of the professional school counselor. Thus, priorities for the use of counselors' time must be decided to ensure that the program delivered makes the best use of these resources as defined by the steering committee and the counselor leadership. The two basic questions that are answered by the quantitative design are

- what constitutes a well-balanced program for your building or district?
- what counselor-to-student ratio is needed to best ensure attainment of the priorities established in the qualitative design?

Set Priorities for School Counselors' Time

Given that the counselors' talent as filtered through the realities of time is the primary resource of the guidance and counseling program, school counselors and counselor educators have long recognized that conscious decisions need to be made as to how counselors should spend their time. In 1955, Hoyt postulated an appropriate breakdown according to counselor functions:

Counseling	50%
Appraisal	10%
Working with Teachers	10%
Group Activities	5%
Environmental Information	10%
Administrative & Clerical Work	5%
Working with Parents & Community	5%
Local Research	5%

(p. 86)

In a comprehensive guidance program, an essential piece of the quantitative design is deciding the portions of professional school counselors' time to be spent implementing activities in each program component. This issue is critical because of the traditional add-on nature of guidance. In the past, as new issues or concerns were addressed in the school, tasks were added to school counselors' job responsibilities without much thought as to the time these tasks might take to complete. A comprehensive guidance and counseling program is not an add-on program. The program structure is established and the time available to staff is allocated so that, accounting for all school counselors, the time allocated to the program components equals 100%. Allocations of time within individual staff members' 100% may be different because of differences across grade or grade-grouping levels; and the allocation of time may vary from school building to building and district to district, depending on the needs of and priorities for the students and communities.

To help establish the desired time allocations for the program components, we have found that the steering committee and school–community advisory committee can provide direction. We have also worked with separate groups of counselors, principals and other administrators, and parents, but this is cumbersome. Consensus among the groups is hard to achieve when each group cannot hear the deliberations of the other groups.

As the preceding discussion implies, you need to implement a process that will lead the group or groups to consensus because you will most likely not find unanimity among the decision makers. The Northside Independent School District project used its steering committee and applied a modified Delphi process to reach a decision about the allocation of time across the program components. The committee was first asked to establish priorities for component resource allocation. Its decision is reflected in Table 5.12 (compare it with Table 4.15). Then committee members, who by this time had become educated about the program model, were asked to write down individually the percentage of counselor time that they thought ought to be appropriated for each of the four program components. Each member then posted his or her percentage allocations on blank sheets of easel paper that had been hung on the walls of the meeting room. These postings are displayed in Table 5.13. Note the ranges of time. The steering committee as a whole considered the ranges and apparent median ratings and deliberated and debated. Consensus on the percentages for each category was then reached. At a subsequent meeting—after some percolating time—the final balance in terms of percentages was considered and agreed on. The balance that was established as desired by the district is presented in Table 5.14 (Northside Independent School District, 1986). These figures were used to suggest allocations of staff time for Northside's desired program, and they became the template against which the current program assessment data were compared and contrasted. The St. Joseph School District (Hargens & Fuston, 1997) also established desired percentages, displayed in Table 5.15, for the allocation of time for the program components.

Table 5.12
Desired Guidance Program Priorities

Component	Priority and School Level		
	Elementary	Middle	High
Guidance curriculum	1	1	2
Individual student planning	2	1	1
Responsive services	2	3	1
System support	4	4	4

Note. Data from Northside Independent School District, San Antonio, TX. Adapted with permission.

Table 5.13
Individual Committee Members' Counselor Time Appropriations

| Component | % Counselor Time and School Level | | |
	Elementary	Middle	High
Guidance	40 40 40 35 40	40 35 30 30 30	25 10 20 15 35
curriculum	50 40 40 40 30	30 30 40 30 15	40 35 25 20 10
	60 45 65	30 50 50 50	30 20 30 40 50
Consensus	40	30	25
Individual student	20 25 35 30 30	20 25 30 25 30	30 35 40 40 25
planning	20 20 20 10 10	40 30 25 20 30	20 20 30 40 40
	20 10 10	15 25 15 15	30 35 30 20 20
Consensus	25	30	30
Responsive services	20 20 25 15 15	30 25 30 25 30	30 40 25 20 20
	20 20 20 40 40	15 25 25 30 40	20 30 30 20 40
	20 25 15	25 30 15 15	30 35 30 20 15
Consensus	25	25	30
System support	10 10 10 15 15	10 15 10 10 10	20 10 10 30 20
	10 10 10 20 30	15 15 30 20 15	20 20 15 10 10
	10 10 10	30 15 20 20	10 10 10 20 15
Consensus	10	15	15

Note. Data from Northside Independent School District, San Antonio, TX. Adapted with permission.

States using the comprehensive guidance and counseling program model, such as Missouri (Gysbers, Stanley, Kosteck-Bunch, Magnuson, & Starr, 2008) and Texas (Texas Education Agency, 2004), as well as some districts, suggest ranges of percentages of time to be spent in each component so that appropriate balances can be set for each district or building. This approach provides guidelines for program consistency and at the same time encourages local school staffs to make decisions appropriate for their students and school community. (An example of suggested ranges for an appropriately balanced guidance and counseling program is displayed in Chapter 3's Figure 3.2.)

Although each district or building within the district should decide on the program balance that best fits local needs and priorities, students' developmental ages permit some generalizations supporting different program balance recommendations for different school levels. The balance among the developmental guidance components shifts as students mature and accept more responsibility for their own growth and development. That is, the guidance curriculum component takes a larger share of the program pie at the elementary level than at the secondary level. In turn, the individual student planning component is larger at the secondary level than at the elementary level. Middle or junior high school stu-

Table 5.14
Desired Guidance Program Balance: Northside Independent School District

| Component | % Counselor Time and School Level | | |
	Elementary	Middle	High
Guidance curriculum	40	30	25
Individual student planning	25	30	30
Responsive services	25	25	30
System support	10	15	15

Note. Data from Northside Independent School, San Antonio, TX. Adapted with permission.

Table 5.15
Desired Guidance Program Balance: St. Joseph School District

| | % Counselor Time and School Level | | |
Component	Elementary	Middle	High
Guidance curriculum	25	20	15
Individual student planning	5	15	30
Responsive services	60	50	35
System support	10	15	20

Note. From "Comprehensive Guidance Program of the St. Joseph School District in Buchanan County, Missouri," by M. Hargens and J. K. Fuston, 1997, in N. C. Gysbers and P. Henderson, Eds., *Comprehensive Guidance Programs That Work—II* (pp. 61–74), Greensboro, NC: ERIC Counseling and Student Services Clearinghouse. Adapted with permission.

dents are developmentally ready to begin to formulate tentative career plans and make related educational decisions. It is developmentally necessary for high school students to make sound educational and other career-related choices to best ensure their readiness to enter postsecondary education or training and the work world.

The needs for responsive services and system support stay fairly constant, regardless of the students' ages; thus, these components maintain a similar share of the program throughout. The nature of responsive services may change from an emphasis on preventive counseling and consultation with parents and teachers at the elementary level to one of directly counseling students at the high school level.

The system support component, representing indirect services to students, is consistently the smallest of the four components. Note that in the models presented, the fifth component, nonguidance activities, is not included because that is the desired design. Because they are included as part of the data describing your current program design, however, you may want to include a zero percentage for this set of tasks. In so doing, you provide a vehicle for the steering and advisory committees to make the very important statement that extraneous tasks should not take up an undue amount of the guidance and counseling program's time.

Helping counselors and others envision what the program balance means for program implementation is better understood by translating the balance to number of hours per student school day, and the student school days per year, rather than by the percentages shown in Table 5.15. Table 5.16 displays these percentages for Northside Independent School District's desired program balance. The information regarding the days per year and

Table 5.16
Desired Percentages for Allocation of Counselors' Time During Student School Days

| | Elementary School | | | Middle School | | | High School | | |
Component	%	Hours/Day	Days/Year	%	Hours/Day	Days/Year	%	Hours/Day	Days/Year
Guidance curriculum	40	2.5	73	30	4	51	25	1.5	44
Individual student planning	25	1.5	44	30	4	51	30	1.75	51
Responsive services	25	1.5	44	25	1.5	44	30	1.75	51
System support	10	0.5	14	15	1	29	15	1	29

Note. Based on a 6-hour student day, 175-day student year. Figures are per counselor. Data from Northside Independent School District, San Antonio, TX. Adapted with permission.

hours per day per component has provided guidelines for counselors as they plan their weeks, months, and year and has helped program monitors understand in a tangible way what is desired for the program to be considered effective. Moreover, the statements of priorities are used heavily in the next stage of program improvement, planning the transition to the comprehensive guidance and counseling program, and subsequently to guide program scheduling to ensure appropriate balance in actual program implementation. (Scheduling is discussed in some detail in Chapter 8.)

Recommended Design-Related Counselor–Student Ratios

As Hoyt (1955) also suggested, with the program's basic structure and the desired levels of service to students and other clients outlined, it is now possible to use this information to determine the ratios needed to conduct the program as desired qualitatively and quantitatively. For example, using the Northside Independent School District's desired program figures, the mathematical process displayed in Figure 5.2 can be used to recommend appropriate ratios at the elementary, middle, and high school levels. (See Chapter 8 and Appendix G for examples of how different ratios affect the numbers of program clients that can be served in the various program activities.)

Other districts have relied on other methods of establishing a recommended counselor–student ratio. Many use the ASCA's (2009b) 1:250 recommendation or those of their state. The Texas Education Agency recommended a counselor–student ratio of 1:300 (Achieve Texas, n.d., p. 10). In the context of their published statewide ratio of 1:954, the California Department of Education (2003) study found that surveyed respondents wanted more school counselors. They perceived adequate ratios to be 1:834 for elementary schools, 1:461 for middle and junior high schools, and 1:364 for high schools.

Evidence is accumulating to support the notion that the lower a school counselor's caseload is, the more services students receive and the more positive outcomes are attained (Carrell & Carrell, 2006). It is also a reality that adding counselors in significant numbers is costly, albeit possibly cost-effective (Carrell & Carrell, 2006). Your desired program design needs to be tempered by the reality of the current resources available. As said previously, in moving to a comprehensive guidance and counseling program, you must first make the best use of the resources you currently have, and then you are in a better position to ask for additional ones. Fewer resources means fewer services, but the newly established priorities for using what you have do not change. Recommending ways to improve the program and the resources needed to fully achieve what you want comes in the next phase of the program improvement process (Chapter 6).

Determine Minimum Numbers of Students to Be Served

With the recommended program balance percentages determined, it is then possible to establish standards for minimum numbers of students and other clients to be served through each program component and ultimately for the program as a whole. The mathematical process for doing this is explained in detail in Chapter 8 in Enhance the Role of the Professional School Counselor section. In summary, determining the minimum number of students to be served entails determining the minimum number of students–clients served by a typical activity in the component and multiplying that number by the minimum number of that kind of activity that can be provided by counselors in the time appropriated through the program balance. For example, following Figure 8.2, it is determined that with the balance recommended for Henderson Public Schools' elementary counselors, 28

Figure 5.2
Counselor–Student Ratio Recommendations

Elementary School Ratio Recommendations

- Desired program design:

Curriculum	$40\% \times 70 = 28$ slots
Individual student planning	$25\% \times 70 = 17$ slots
Responsive services	$25\% \times 70 = 18$ slots
System support	$10\% \times 70 = 7$ slots

Program activity slots = 30 minutes each (average)
Student school day = 7 hours
7 hours yield 14 activities per day
14 activities $\times$ 5 days/week = 70 activity slots/week

- To implement *guidance curriculum* as desired:

$$\begin{array}{r} 28 \text{ slots} \\ -12 \text{ for planning}^a \\ \hline 16 \text{ classes}^b \\ \times\,25 \text{ (average number students per class)} \\ \hline 400 \end{array}$$

400 students per counselor is the ratio needed to implement the guidance curriculum.

- To implement *responsive services* as desired: 18 slots
  60% for preventive level, small group counseling
  40% for remedial level, individual counseling

$$\begin{array}{r} 18 \\ \times\,.6 \\ \hline 11 \text{ groups} \\ \times\,5 \text{ students} \\ \hline 55 \text{ students} \end{array} \qquad \begin{array}{r} 18 \\ \times\,.4 \\ \hline 7 \text{ students} \end{array}$$

55 students + 7 students = *62 students* in responsive services caseload
   Responsive services attends to 15% of population on the average
   62 is 15% of *413 students per counselor*

- *Thus, 400:1 is the recommended ratio for elementary counselors to implement the program as designed.*

Middle School Ratio Recommendations

- Desired program design:

Curriculum	$30\% \times 35 = 10.5 = 11$ slots
Individual student planning	$30\% \times 35 = 10.5 = 10$ slots
Responsive services	$25\% \times 35 = 8.75 = 9$ slots
System support	$15\% \times 35 = 5.25 = 5$ slots

Program activity slots = 1 hour each (average)
Student school day = 7 hours
7 hours yield 7 activities per day
7 activities $\times$ 5 days/week = 35 activity slots/week

- To implement *guidance curriculum* as desired:

$$\begin{array}{r} 11 \text{ slots} \\ -\,2 \text{ for planning}^c \\ \hline 9 \text{ classes per week per counselor}^d \\ 18 \text{ classes} = \text{curriculum caseload} \\ \times\,27 \text{ (average number students per class)} \\ \hline 486 \end{array}$$

486 students per counselor is the ratio needed to implement the guidance curriculum.

- To implement responsive services as desired: 9 slots
  50% for preventive level, small group counseling
  50% for remedial level, individual counseling

$$\begin{array}{r} 9 \\ \times\,.5 \\ \hline 4.5 \text{ groups} \\ \times\,9 \text{ students} \\ \hline 40.5 \text{ students} \end{array} \qquad \begin{array}{l} 9 \\ \times\,.5 \\ \hline 4.5 \text{ students} \\ (8\text{--}10 = \text{average size group}) \end{array}$$

40.5 students + 4.5 students = 45 students in responsive services caseload
   Responsive services attends to 15% of population on the average
   45 is 15% of 300 students per counselor

- *Thus, 393:1 is the recommended ratio for middle school counselors to implement the program as designed.*

(continued on next page)

Figure 5.2 (*Continued*)
Counselor–Student Ratio Recommendations

High School Ratio Recommendations

- Desired program design:

Curriculum	25% × 35 = 8.75 = 9 slots
Individual planning	30% × 35 = 10.5 = 10 slots
Responsive services	30% × 35 = 10.5 = 11 slots
System support	15% × 35 = 5.25 = 5 slots

Program activity slots = 1 hour each (average)
Student school day = 7 hours
7 hours yield 7 activities per day
7 activities × 5 days/week = 35 activity slots/week

- To implement guidance curriculum as desired:

$$\begin{array}{r} 9 \text{ slots} \\ -\ 2 \text{ for planning}^c \\ \hline 7 \text{ classes per week per counselor}^d \\ \\ 14 \text{ classes 5 curriculum caseload} \\ \times\ 27 \text{ (average number students per class)} \\ \hline 378 \end{array}$$

378 students per counselor is the ratio needed to implement the guidance curriculum.

- To implement responsive services as desired: 11 slots
    50% for preventive level, small group counseling
    50% for remedial level, individual counseling

$$\begin{array}{r} 11 \\ \times\ .5 \\ \hline 5.5 \text{ groups} \\ \times\ 9 \text{ students} \\ \hline 49.5 \text{ students} \end{array} \qquad \begin{array}{l} 11 \\ \times\ .5 \\ \hline 5.5 \text{ students} \\ (8\text{--}10 = \text{average size group}) \end{array}$$

49.5 students + 5.5 students = 55 students in responsive services caseload
    Responsive services attends to 15% of population on the average
    55 is 15% of 366 students per counselor

- *Thus, 375:1 is the recommended ratio for high school counselors to implement the program as designed.*

[a]Two slots per week at six grade levels. [b]Each class is to be guided one time per week.
[c]Planning: teachers, 1:6, counselors, 2:9. [d]Each class is to be guided every other week.

guidance curriculum activities should be provided per week. If the minimum number of students in a guidance classroom is 25, then in 1 week, multiplying 28 × 25, 700 students per week would benefit from guidance curriculum activities. This provides opportunities for professional school counselors to be accountable for the numbers of students they serve and to be able to publicize that number so that the program's consumers can know what level of service it is realistic to expect. The latter is particularly important with responsive services activities that are often a balance of individual and small-group work. Not nearly as many students can benefit from these 28 time slots, only 98 students a week (as displayed in Figure 8.2).

Attend to Diversity

Lee (2001) identified 12 characteristics of a culturally responsive school. The school

1. has adopted a "salad bowl" as opposed to a "melting pot" philosophy of education.
2. has forged a sense of community out of cultural diversity.
3. has the same high academic expectations for all students.

4. has a curriculum that fairly and accurately reflects the contributions of many cultures.

5. infuses multiculturalism and diversity in a nonstereotypical manner throughout the curriculum and the school year.

6. provides students with forums outside of the classroom to communicate with and learn about their peers from diverse cultural backgrounds.

7. has mechanisms in place to deal with racial/cultural tensions.

8. has committed educators who engage in ongoing staff development and are not afraid to take risks or improvise when necessary.

9. actively recruits a diverse staff of educators.

10. has educators who consider language and cultural customs in their interactions with parents.

11. has high levels of parental involvement representing the diverse cultures found in the school community.

12. defines cultural diversity to include people with disabilities, diverse sexual orientations, diverse religious traditions, and a range of ages—including older people. (Lee, 2001, p. 258)

To be culturally responsive, comprehensive guidance and counseling programs need to reflect the same characteristics. Much can be done during the designing phase of program development to attend to the diversity in the school or district. Principles regarding awareness, acceptance, and celebration of the diversity in the community and the school should be reflected in each of the structural components. The definition should ensure that all students have equal access to the program.

The rationale should include assessment of the special needs of diverse students. Schools, including guidance and counseling programs, must accept the reality that disparities exist between the dropout and graduation rates among different ethnic and racial groups. For example, according to the National Center for Education Statistics (2009), the 2007 status dropout rate of Whites was 5.3%; of Asians/Pacific Islanders, 6.1%; of Blacks, 8.4%; and of Hispanics, 21.4%. Stanard (2003) recognized that "school counselors are in a prime position to have a positive impact on the problem of high school dropouts" (p. 219). She cited the nonacademic problems that dropouts have and suggested systemic and programmatic interventions. Arredondo, Tovar-Blank, and Parham (2008) pointed out that working effectively with "multicultural-heritage populations, issues related to religion and spirituality, and global immigration are but a few of the opportunities and challenges that culturally competent counselors currently face" (p. 266).

The assumptions should include beliefs about diverse individuals and groups, about diversity itself, and about what contributions the guidance and counseling program makes in enriching the campus climate by valuing its diversity. The content competencies should address multicultural competence. The percentages of subgroups of students and other clients served in the program should reflect the percentages of the subgroups of the total school population.

The program itself should attend to topics that address differences among people. Cross-cultural effectiveness is a curriculum strand in the Texas program model (Texas Education Agency, 2004). Rayle and Myers (2004) reported a research study that indicated that "ethnic identity was a significant predictor of wellness for minority adolescents" (p. 87) but not for nonminority students, which perhaps indicates a need to address ethnic identity for part of the student population. Akos and Ellis (2008) found that middle school students, in the early stages of ethnic identity development, can especially benefit from proactive assistance with their development. If the program design did not include that as an important topic for all students, attention could be paid to it by providing differentiated guidance curriculum offerings or by providing it through a responsive service, such as small-group counseling (Malott, Paone, Humphreys, & Martinez, 2010).

Professional school counselors should continually develop their cultural competencies as described in the Association for Multicultural Counseling and Development's Multicultural Counseling Competencies, which are included in Appendix H. ASCA's (2009a) basic position statement on cultural diversity is that "professional school counselors promote academic, career, and personal/social success for all students. Professional school counselors collaborate with stakeholders to create a school and community climate that embraces cultural diversity and helps to remove barriers that impede student success" (p. 1). The ethical standards established by both ACA (2005) and ASCA (2010) make clear the expectation that professional counselors be multiculturally competent and advocates for embracing diversity. With the increase in the Hispanic–Latino student population, European American counselors who speak Spanish can be more effective with their clients than those who cannot (Ramos-Sanchez, 2009).

School (and other) counselors are advised to develop multicultural personalities, implying "more of an ability to function with sensitivity and competence in a variety of cultural settings" (Brummett, Wade, Ponterotto, Thombs, & Lewis, 2007, p. 73), one characteristic of which is having a universal–diverse orientation. Brummett et al. (2007) found that "people who have a universal-diverse orientation appear likely to have greater levels of psychological hardiness, psycho-social interpersonal functioning, and self esteem" (p. 80). Counselors can also help their colleagues and clients develop multicultural personalities and improve their psychological hardiness, psychosocial interpersonal functioning, and self-esteem.

School counselors are urged to chime in to the conversation about educating the poorest children. Amatea and West-Olatunji (2007) suggested that professional school counselors' education, training, and professional worldview support their ability to consult with others to effectively fulfill several appropriate indirect service roles:

(a) serving as a cultural bridge between teachers and students and blocking the blaming that often derails efforts to work with poor students and their families,
(b) functioning as a pedagogical partner with teachers by connecting the curriculum more directly to students' lives,
(c) teaming with teachers to create a more welcoming family-centric school climate. (p. 82)

To be cross-culturally effective, school counselors must confront their own personal and professional resistance to dealing with multicultural realities and issues. In turn, they help others—students, colleagues, parents and others—do the same. Arredondo et al. (2008) identified several common themes of resistance: xenophobia, unexamined privilege, and pseudointellectual resistance. Inadvertently displayed biases can be damaging to students and parents. Bryan et al. (2009) found that "public school students who perceived that the counselor expected them to pursue any option other than college were less likely to seek college information from the school counselor than those who perceived the counselor expected them to attend college" (pp. 288–289).

Bemak and Chung (2008) urged school counselors to move beyond the "Nice Counselor Syndrome" and become multicultural–social justice advocates to help bring about needed social changes. They offered 16 recommendations:

1. Align multicultural/social justice advocacy and organizational change services with school mission and goals.
2. Use strategies that are data driven.
3. Do not internalize victimization.
4. Remember that the work is toward a greater cause.

5. Be aware of [Nice Counselor Syndrome].
6. Remember that it is not personal.
7. Have the courage to speak up and speak out as a multicultural/social justice counselor.
8. Address environmental, cultural, social, historical, political, and organizational factors that affect students' personal, social, [career,] and academic development.
9. Take calculated risks.
10. Allow time for process when implementing multicultural/social justice advocacy and organizational change services.
11. Develop political and personal partners.
12. Remember that conflict is part of the package.
13. Be politically astute and knowledgeable.
14. Always maintain the high road.
15. Appreciate the necessity of dealing with uncertainty and ambiguity in the change process.
16. Have faith . . . in the evolutionary propensity of human development, social justice, and equality. (pp. 378–380)

Leadership Roles and Responsibilities

As the guidance and counseling program leader during the designing phase of the program development process, you must pay special attention to your responsibilities regarding the decision-making process used in determining the desired program design, in the writing of the agreed-on program description, and in continuing to empower the professional school counselors. In this phase of the program improvement process, the range of power bases available to you are not only your legitimate power (the power of your position), but also your expert (guidance and counseling knowledge and skills), referent (leadership charisma), information (school or district policies and procedures), and connection (with school or district decision makers and policy setters) powers (Henderson, 2009).

Throughout the process, you model advocating for the students' needs and rights to access quality services, for the appropriate standards for a comprehensive guidance and counseling program, and for the continued professionalization of school counseling and counselors. You also model respectful and honest collaboration with administrators, teachers, parents, and others involved in the process. As Stone and Zirkel (2010) advised,

> School counselors use their best political and collaborative skills to demonstrate respect for the position of authority that has been entrusted to school administrators, while carefully determining the most effective way to adhere to the school counseling profession's obligation to protect and advocate for students. (p. 247)

The steering committee might provide the right venue for opening the dialogue between counselors and administrators "regarding how using the advocacy competencies to address social justice issues benefits students" (Ratts et al., 2007, p. 93).

Decision-Making Process

As you have surmised in reading the sections on qualitative and quantitative designs and on establishing priorities and parameters for resource allocation, providing the detail to describe your desired program design is no small task. Again, the resources you use in this task will vary depending on the program redesign mechanism you are using. We recommend that you use the counselors from the steering committee to do or lead the bulk of this work. The same principle applies here as earlier: The more involved more counselors are, the smoother the needed transitions will be. In any case, counselor leaders need to ensure that the recommendations made are supported by the steering committee. The committee needs to assist in making the hard decisions, such as the priorities for displacing unwanted nonguidance tasks, but in many cases they need only to be educated as to the priorities that will become internal operating rules for the guidance department, such as determining who else on a campus can count the test booklets after administering standardized tests. The preliminary activities and design decisions to be made in establishing priorities and parameters are summarized in Table 5.17.

You need to be aware of topics that are of particular importance to the noncounselors on the steering committee and attend to these appropriately. For example, your high school principals might be attached to the traditional conferences held with individual 12th graders as to their post–high school plans. You need to make the effort to ensure that they understand the time these conferences take relative to the benefit in terms of student outcomes achieved. The committee needs to carefully consider any decision that will result in changing the shape of a major activity. A helpful rule of thumb is that if one committee member wants to discuss an issue, you had better give it fair hearing. Even if none of the other committee members are particularly interested in the discussion, there will be others outside the committee who hold that position as well, and ultimately that discussion will recur.

Table 5.17

Establishing Program Priorities and Parameters: Preliminary Activities and Design Decisions

Preliminary Activity	Design Decision
	Qualitative design
Student competency development	
List needed student competencies.	Establish priorities for content domains and student goals, competencies by grade span, results by grade level.
Clients to be served	
Define the student and adult populations served.	Establish priorities for subpopulations served through each component.
Program activities	Establish priorities within each component:
Specify minimum expectations for activities done within each component.	• Guidance curriculum: most needed outcomes by grade level
	• Individual student planning: most timely outcomes and activities at priority grade level
	• Responsive services: most relevant, recurrent topics
	• System support: most needed activities and programs making best use of counselors' time and professional skills
Counselors' roles	
Redefine and reaffirm counselor's job descriptions.	Establish priorities for use of the counselors' skills and service expectations.
	• Comprehensive counselors
	• Specialist counselors
Redefine and reaffirm job descriptions of other guidance program personnel.	Establish priorities for others' skills.
	Quantitative design
Program balance	
Define the priorities among program components.	Establish parameters for balanced program delivery in terms of percentages of resource allocation.
	Establish priorities for use of the counselors' time.
Number of clients served	Establish priorities for others' time.
Establish numbers of students to be served in program components.	Establish recommended counselor-to-student ratio.

In guiding the agenda of the decision-making process, remember that you need to discuss each topic—from defining the basic program structure to making recommendations regarding the levels of support needed by the guidance and counseling program—in separate meetings. The group will still be struggling to understand the basic concepts, so making the necessary decisions is not easy. Allowing them to focus on one topic at a time helps you in the long run, although it may extend the time you take on this step. It is your job, as the guidance and counseling program leader, to frame the questions for the group to answer. Just as it can take as much as a year to assess your current program, it can also take a year to select your desired program design. That design, however, as stated earlier, becomes the goal statement for everything that follows, so it must be done thoroughly and with sufficient deliberation (argument) to ensure support as you move into implementation.

Write Down and Distribute the Description of the Desired Program

With the design of the desired program established, your last task is to put in writing all of the decisions made. If you are the leader of the program improvement efforts, this task is yours alone. As with any written publication, the document must portray a cohesive whole, have a logical sequence, and be written in a consistent and concise style; thus, one writer is mandatory. As stated earlier, the written description depicts the basic structure that you have decided on and becomes the working document for you and your staff henceforth. It replaces the former guidance and counseling program handbook or plan. The Northside Independent School District (1986, 1994) called this document the *Comprehensive Guidance Program Framework*.

We recommend the write-up contain at least five sections: the structural components, the recommended design and resource allocations for the program, the generic job descriptions, the program components, and appendixes.

- *Structural components:* This first section should include the statements that express the philosophical basis of your program—the final versions of the rationale, the assumptions, and the program definition. In addition, the list of student competencies that are to be developed through the guidance and counseling program should be presented. Listing the specific grade-level outcomes is probably too lengthy for this section of the document, but they may be listed fully in an appendix (or in a separate document).
- *Recommended design and resource allocations:* The second section of the write-up should contain statements that describe the appropriate balance among the four components, the priorities for the clients to be served, the competencies to be sought, and the school counselors' skills to be used. This section presents what the program should look like numerically to be considered comprehensive and well balanced.
- *Generic job descriptions:* The third section should describe the various jobs guidance and counseling program staff perform. It should contain descriptions not only for the elementary, middle or junior, and senior high school counselors but also for any counselor specialists you have in your school or district, such as career and technology counselors, special or compensatory education–funded counselors, and head counselors. Job descriptions should also be included for other staff members who have been identified as having roles integral to the delivery of the guidance and counseling program, such as career center technicians, registrars, and related professionals (such as social workers, community-based licensed counselors, school psychologists). If you are using or planning to use community volunteers, their positions should also be described here.

- *Program components:* The fourth section should include more detailed descriptions of each component as tailored by your local decisions. Each component description should begin with the definition of the component and contain the design decisions made regarding each component. The priorities for students by subgroup, the priorities for other clients, and the minimum expectations for numbers of students to be served in component activities come next. The strands of the guidance curriculum, the major activities that make up the individual student planning component, the recurrent topics that are the focus of the responsive services, and the specific activities identified in system support should be listed. The content priorities and anticipated results within each component should be identified. The roles fulfilled by counselors, teachers, administrators, and parents in component implementation should be defined. The guidelines established for component activity implementation should be detailed and include the minimum number of component activities to be provided. The recommended mode of delivery for each component (i.e., small-group counseling as the preferred mode for responsive services, classroom-sized groups are the preferred mode for guidance curriculum, etc.) as well as the recommended allocation of resources to the component—especially that of the school counselors' time—should be written down. Each component description should end with a statement of expectations regarding evaluation of the overall impact on students of the component's activities, each activity's effectiveness, and the quality of the competencies used by the professional staff. All of the decisions made by the program developers that relate to a component should be reflected in the write-up so as not to be lost over time.

After you have written the program description and had it typed and printed, you need to have the steering committee and the school–community advisory committee, the upper echelon administrators, and the counselors review it in detail. We suggest that you view this as the last chance for input before complete, final adoption. For this final review, you need to use strategies that will assure you that everyone has read and considered the document. With the steering committee, this might mean one meeting spent discussing the overall product of its labors section by section. Framing basic questions for them to respond to may help focus their attention on the salient points.

Each counseling staff member must be held accountable for reading the document and must be provided an opportunity to discuss it. A strategy used successfully with counselors has been to schedule an in-service education day during which the counselors from the steering committee explain each of the sections, particularly those describing the four program components. If you then prepare an agenda for discussion and train the secondary and elementary counselor leaders in its use, you provide a means for counselors to consider the full scope and depth of the program design. With the discussion agenda in everyone's hands, small groups of counselors can be asked to consider the major tenets of each section of the document and to voice support or disagreement with each concept. Specific items of confusion or concern can be identified at this time.

The final revision of the document needs to be completed and presented to the school district board of education for adoption. In some districts, board members read these documents *in toto* and then ratify them. In others, members are presented an overview of the program and priorities and are then provided copies for review at their discretion. In yet other districts, board members are satisfied with a presentation and the knowledge that the documents are available should they choose to review them. The document becomes the basic administrative regulation supporting the guidance and counseling program.

Complete distribution to relevant parties then needs to be made. At a minimum, every counselor needs to have a copy of the document, as does every school principal. Other administrators need copies on a need-to-know basis. For example, if you are using career and technical education funds to support part of your guidance and counseling program, then your district's career and technical education director needs a copy. You may also wish to consider publishing sections of the document for those who need only portions of it. For example, the human resources department must have copies of the generic job descriptions; the instructional staff will want copies of the curriculum-related sections, and so forth.

Empowering School Counselors

Professional school counselors are empowered through the designing process if the guidance leadership communicates openly with them. They feel empowered when they have input into their own professional destiny and when their opinions, ideas, and concerns are heard and responded to (Henderson & Gysbers, 1998). Fulfilling meaningful roles in designing the program is in and of itself empowering. Designing a program that envisions making the best use of their talents for the students perceived as having the highest need for those talents is also empowering. Just as empowering is having their unique expertise appreciated not only by other counselors but also by the noncounselors involved in the process—the steering and advisory committees, the principals, and other school and district administrators. As their leader, you want to ensure that all the counselors are aware of the process that is occurring, have input into the decisions, and understand the results of the decision-making work. In his study, Wilkerson (2009) found that evaluating professional school counselors' workplaces, clarifying their roles, collaborating with others, understanding how their organizations work, and engaging in the school planning processes helps them feel empowered and mitigates potential burnout and impairment.

The new program design reflects a vision of how the program will better serve students. It is important that this vision be shared by all counselors—or as many as possible—and, as much as possible, by their principals. As Senge (2004) wrote, "New leadership roles require new leadership disciplines. Three of the most critical disciplines are building the shared vision, surfacing and challenging mental models, and engaging in systems thinking" (p. 16). As the leader, you must allow counselors to share their personal visions and help them blend them into a common vision for the program and for their work. You need to help them bring their personal models to the surface and challenge them to consider ways the emerging schoolwide or districtwide vision will help them accomplish their goals. Many counselors have, unfortunately, lost the idealism that they had when they first entered the profession. Helping them refind those ideals is a useful exercise.

Finally, the comprehensive guidance and counseling program requires a team approach to program implementation. Counselors may be used to operating independently, even in isolation, from other counselors and other school staff members. The team approach brings with it collegiality, cooperation, and collaboration. "A team is a group of people working together to achieve mutual goals" (Henderson & Gysbers, 1998, p. 62). But teams do not just result from bringing a group of people together. Leadership is required to help them work through the form, storm, norm, and perform process. Blanchard, Carew, and Parisi-Carew (2000) described the essentials of high-performing teams: shared purpose and values, empowerment, open relationships and communication, flexibility of members and the team itself, optimal performance as the goal, recognition and appreciation of the individuals, and high morale. Your responsibility is to lead them when leadership is required as well as to be a contributing member of the team.

Your Progress Check

At this point, you have designed the guidance and counseling program you want for your district or school. If you have followed our suggestions, you have defined the organizational structure; made hard, but important decisions about the substance and shape; and strengthened your support base for your desired program.

Definitions

You have

- selected the dimensions of human development that are the program's focus and broad content areas addressed through the program;
- stated the program's mission;
- established the rationale for the program, based on assessed student needs, recognition of the local context, knowledge of contemporary professional counseling theories and trends and your district or school's mission, goals, and educational trends;
- laid out your assumptions and beliefs about students and other clients, the program, and the program staff;
- described the purposes of and types of activities conducted in each of the delivery system components.

Design Decisions

You have

- established priorities to guide effective program implementation for
  a. use of professional school counselors' competencies, and for that of other program staff,
  b. student and adult subgroups benefitting from program activities and services,
  c. student learning,
  d. the appropriate balance for implementing the program components, and the activities within each component;
- set parameters for using program resources:
  a. counselors' time allocations to each program component,
  b. numbers of students to be served in each program component, based on the current counselor–student ratios;
- considered the implications of the diversity of your students and school community for your program design;
- written generic job descriptions for guidance and counseling program staff, including parents;
- written, distributed, and educated counselors and administrators of the desired program's framework.

Strengthened Support Base

You have

- involved the steering committee, the school community advisory committee, and counselor work groups in the decision-making process;

- developed a recommendation for counselor–student ratios that would allow for sufficient program implementation;
- reaffirmed support for the program design from district or school policymakers and administrators.

At this point, you, the guidance and administrative staff, and the policymakers know the concrete details that constitute the desired program. The blueprint for your improved program is completed. The steering committee members and the counselors are apt to think—again—that the work is done. However, in terms of the improvement process you have established only the objectives to be accomplished. The momentum that has been generated for change now must be channeled toward making plans and implementing changes systematically. Your next questions are

- how does what we are doing now compare and contrast with what is desired for our program (discussed in Chapter 6)?
- what will be the plan for making the transition from where we are now to where we want to be (discussed in Chapter 6)?
- how will we implement the systemic and incremental changes needed (discussed in Chapter 7)?
- how will we manage implementation of an ever-improving program (discussed in Chapter 8)?

References

Achieve Texas (n.d.) *Implementation guide*. Retrieved from http://content.yudu.com/A7zwt/AT-ImpGuide/resources/22.htm

Akos, P., & Ellis, C. M. (2008). Racial identity development in middle school: A case for school counselor individual and systemic intervention. *Journal of Counseling & Development, 86,* 26–33.

Akos, P., & Galassi, J. P. (2004). Training school counselors as developmental advocates. *Counselor Education and Supervision, 43,* 192–206.

Akos, P., & Galassi, J. P. (2008). Strengths-based school counseling: Introduction to the special issue. *Professional School Counseling, 12,* 66–67.

Amatea, E. S., & West-Olatunji, C. A. (2007). Joining the conversation about educating our poorest children: Emerging leadership roles for school counselors in high-poverty schools. *Professional School Counseling, 11,* 81–89.

American Counseling Association. (2005). *ACA code of ethics.* Alexandria, VA: Author.

American School Counselor Association. (2004a). *Why elementary school counselors.* Retrieved from http://www.schoolcounselor.org/content.asp?contentid=230

American School Counselor Association. (2004b). *Why middle school counselors.* Retrieved from http://www.schoolcounselor.org/content.asp?contentid=231

American School Counselor Association. (2004c). *Why secondary school counselors?* Retrieved from http://www.schoolcounselor.org/content.asp?contentid=233

American School Counselor Association. (2005). *The ASCA National Model: A framework for school counseling programs* (2nd ed.). Alexandria, VA: Author.

American School Counselor Association. (2009a). *The professional school counselor and cultural diversity.* Retrieved from http://asca2.timberlakepublishing.com/files/Cultural Diversity.pdf

American School Counselor Association. (2009b). *Student-to-counselor ratio by state 2007–2008*. Retrieved from http://asca2.timberlakepublishing.com//files/Ratios 2007-2008.pdf

American School Counselor Association. (2010). *Ethical standards for school counselors*. Retrieved from http://asca2.timberlakepublishing.com//files/EthicalStandards2010.pdf

American School Counselor Association. (n.d.) *Effectiveness of school counseling*. Retrieved from http://www.schoolcounselor.org/content.asp?pl=325&sl=133&contentid=241

Arredondo, P., Tovar-Blank, Z. G., & Parham, T. A. (2008). Challenges and promises of becoming a culturally competent counselor in a sociopolitical era of change and empowerment. *Journal of Counseling & Development, 86,* 261–268.

Bemak, F., & Chung, R. C.-Y. (2008). New professional roles and advocacy strategies for school counselors: A multicultural/social justice perspective to move beyond the nice counselor syndrome. *Journal of Counseling & Development, 86,* 372–381.

Blanchard, K., Carew, D., & Parisi-Carew, E. (2000). *The 1-minute manager builds high performing teams*. New York, NY: William Morrow.

Bolman, L. G., & Deal, T. E. (2002). *Reframing the path to school leadership*. Thousand Oaks, CA: Corwin Press.

Borders, L. D., & Drury, S. M. (1992). Comprehensive school counseling programs: A review for policy makers and practitioners. *Journal of Counseling & Development, 70,* 487–498.

Brigman, G., & Campbell, C. (2003). Helping students improve academic achievement and school success behavior. *Professional School Counseling, 7*(2), 91–98.

Brummett, B. R., Wade, J.C., Ponterotto, J. G., Thombs, B., & Lewis, C. (2007). Psychosocial well-being and a multicultural personality disposition. *Journal of Counseling & Development, 85,* 73–81.

Bryan, J., Holcomb-McCoy, C., Moore-Thomas, C., & Day-Vines, N. L. (2009). Who sees the school counselor for college information? *Professional School Counseling, 12,* 280–291.

Burnham, J. J. (2009). Contemporary fears of children and adolescents: Coping and resiliency in the 21st century. *Journal of Counseling & Development, 87,* 28–35.

California Department of Education, Counseling and Student Support Office. (2003). *Study of pupil personnel ratios, services, and programs* (School Counseling Research Brief 2.4). Amherst: University of Massachusetts, National Center for School Counseling Outcome Research. Retrieved from http://www.umass.edu/schoolcounseling/uploads/Research_Brief_2-4.pdf

Carey, J. C. (2010, January). Guidance in building the developmental curriculum. *Counseling Today,* pp. 60–61.

Carrell, S. E., & Carrell, S. A. (2006). Do lower student to counselor ratios reduce school disciplinary problems? *B. E. Journal of Economic Analysis and Policy, 5*(1), Article 11. Retrieved from http://www.bepress.com/bejeap/contributions/vol5/iss1/art11

Coleman, H. L. K., Casali, S. B., & Wampold, B. E. (2001). Adolescent strategies for coping with cultural diversity. *Journal of Counseling & Development, 79,* 356–364.

Council for Accreditation of Counseling and Related Educational Programs. (2009). *2009 standards*. Retrieved from http://www.cacrep.org/doc/2009%20Standards%20with%20cover.pdf

D'Andrea, M., & Heckman, E. F. (Eds.). (2008). Multicultural counseling [Special issue]. *Journal of Counseling & Development, 86*(3).

DePaul, J., Walsh, M. E., & Dam, U. C.(2009). The role of school counselors in addressing sexual orientation in schools. *Professional School Counseling, 12,* 300–308.

Geidner, J. M. (2009). Developmental science and counseling. *Journal of Counseling & Development, 87,* 364–372.

Gibbons, M. M., & Borders, L. D. (2010). A measure of college-going self-efficacy for middle school students. *Professional School Counseling, 13,* 234–243.

Gysbers, N. C., Stanley, J. B., Kosteck-Bunch, L., Magnuson, C. S., & Starr, M. F. (2008). *Missouri comprehensive guidance program: A manual for program development, implementation, evaluation and enhancement.* Warrensburg: Missouri Center for Career Education, University of Central Missouri.

Hargens, M., & Fuston, J. K. (1997). Comprehensive guidance program of the St. Joseph School District in Buchanan County, Missouri. In N. C. Gysbers & P. Henderson (Eds.), *Comprehensive guidance programs that work—II* (pp. 61–74). Greensboro, NC: ERIC Counseling and Student Services Clearinghouse.

Henderson, P. H. (1987). A comprehensive school guidance program at work. *TACD Journal, 15,* 25–37.

Henderson, P. (2005). The theory behind the ASCA National Model. In American School Counselor Association, *The ASCA National Model: A framework for school counseling programs* (2nd ed., pp. 79–101). Alexandria, VA: American School Counselor Association.

Henderson, P. G. (2009). *The new handbook of administrative supervision in counseling.* New York, NY: Routledge.

Henderson, P., & Gysbers, N. C. (1998). *Leading and managing your school guidance program staff.* Alexandria, VA: American Counseling Association.

Hoyt, K. B. (1955). What should be the pupil load for the school counselor? *Personnel and Guidance Journal, 34,* 86–88.

Huss, S. N., Bryant, A., & Mulet, S. (2008). Managing the quagmire of counseling in a school: Bringing the parents onboard. *Professional School Counseling, 11,* 362–367.

Lee, C. C. (2001). Culturally responsive school counselors and programs: Addressing the needs of all students. *Professional School Counseling, 4,* 257–261.

MacDonald, G., & Sink, C. A. (1999). A qualitative developmental analysis of comprehensive guidance programmes in schools in the United States. *British Journal of Guidance and Counselling, 27,* 415–430.

Malott, K. M., Paone, T. R., Humphreys, K., & Martinez, T. (2010). Use of group counseling to address ethnic identity development: Application with adolescents of Mexican descent. *Professional School Counseling, 13,* 257–267.

McGowan, A. S. (Ed.). (2004). School violence [Special section]. *Journal of Counseling & Development, 82,* 259–312.

Mellin, E. A. (2009). Responding to the crisis in children's mental health: Potential roles for the counseling profession. *Journal of Counseling & Development, 87,* 501–506.

National Board for Certified Counselors. (2004). *National Certified School Counselor.* Retrieved from http://www.nbcc.org/Specialties/NCSC

National Board for Professional Teaching Standards. (2002). *School counseling standards.* Retrieved from http://www.nbpts.org/userfiles/File/ecya_sc_standards.pdf

National Center for Education Statistics. (2009, September). *Dropout and completion rates in the United States: 2007.* Retrieved from http://nces.ed.gov/pubs2009/dropout07/findings3.asp

National School Boards Association. (2010). *Beliefs and policies of the National School Boards Association. Article IV, Section 4, Special Programs, 4.1 Counseling and Guidance.* Washington, DC: Author.

Northside Independent School District. (1986). *Comprehensive guidance program framework.* San Antonio, TX: Author.

Northside Independent School District. (1994). *Comprehensive guidance program framework*. San Antonio, TX: Author.

Ramos-Sanchez, L. (2009). Counselor bilingual ability, counselor ethnicity, acculturation, and Mexican American's perceived counselor credibility. *Journal of Counseling & Development, 87,* 311–318.

Ratts, M. J., DeKruyf, L., & Chen-Hayes, S. F. (2007). The ACA advocacy competencies: A social justice advocacy framework for professional school counselors. *Professional School Counseling, 11,* 90–97.

Ratts, M. J., Toporek, R. L., & Lewis, J. A. (2010). *ACA advocacy competencies: A social justice framework for counselors.* Alexandria, VA: American Counseling Association.

Rayle, A. D., & Myers, J. E. (2004). Counseling adolescents toward wellness: The roles of ethnic identity, acculturation, and mattering. *Professional School Counseling, 8,* 81–90.

Search Institute. (n.d.). *Introduction to assets.* Retrieved from http://www.search-institute.org/assets/

Senge, P. (2004). Building vision. *Executive Excellence, 21*(7), 16.

Sheely-Moore, A. I., & Bratton, S. C. (2010). A strengths-based parenting intervention with low-income African American families. *Professional School Counseling, 13,* 175–183.

Stanard, R. P. (2003). High school graduation rates in the United States: Implications for the counseling profession. *Journal of Counseling & Development, 81,* 217–221.

Stevens, H., & Wilkerson, K. (2010). The developmental assets and ASCA's national standards: A crosswalk review. *Professional School Counseling, 13,* 227–233.

Stone, C. B., & Zirkel, P. A. (2010). School counselor advocacy: When law and ethics may collide. *Professional School Counseling, 13,* 244–247.

Texas Counseling Association. (2004). *Texas evaluation model for professional school counselors* (2nd ed.). Austin, TX: Author.

Texas Education Agency. (1998). A model comprehensive guidance and counseling program for Texas public schools. A guide for program development pre-K–12th grade (3rd ed.). Austin, TX: Author.

Texas Education Agency. (2004). *A model comprehensive, developmental guidance and counseling program for Texas public schools: A guide for program development pre-K–12th grade* (4th ed.). Austin, TX: Author.

Wilkerson, K. (2009). An examination of burnout among school counselors guided by stress-strain-coping theory. *Journal of Counseling & Development, 87,* 428–437.

Chapter 6

Planning Your Transition to a Comprehensive Guidance and Counseling Program

Designing—Planning the Transition

- Specify changes needed to implement a comprehensive guidance and counseling program districtwide.
- Develop a plan for accomplishing districtwide program improvement.
- Begin building-level program improvement efforts.
- Expand the leadership base.

☞ Chapter 5 described the tasks and issues involved in delineating the design for a comprehensive guidance and counseling program. Delineating the design is an important phase of the change process because it describes and specifies the directions for change that will be required to install a comprehensive guidance and counseling program. Unfortunately, some administrators who want to make program changes stop after the designing phase. They conclude, wrongly, that if directions for the desired changes are clear, the desired changes will occur. However, some counselors and administrators believe that the total program must be implemented all at once or not at all. In reality, for the desired changes to be made successfully, the changes need to be planned. Remodeling the guidance and counseling program entails building on some of the original structure, removing some of the parts that do not belong in the new structure, and adding some new ones. Making such renovations takes time, energy, and other resources. Planning how you will make the transition to a comprehensive guidance and counseling program is a vital step.

Careful planning is also required because of the complexity of actually implementing the program. Implementation is accomplished in increments. Although some implementation tasks are completed at the district level, much of the actual program implementation occurs at the building level. Thus, two levels of planning are required: districtwide and buildingwide. Remember that these two levels of planning interact. Some building changes cannot be made without district changes occurring first, and some district changes cannot be made without building initiatives preceding them. The district initiates changes in policy, regulations, or support that facilitate building program implementation. Building trials of new activities and procedures are often needed before district changes can be made.

This chapter describes in detail the tasks involved in planning the transition to a comprehensive guidance and counseling program. First, changes that are indicated must be stated specifically. The desired program description (see Chapter 5) serves as a template to lay over your current program so that similarities and differences can be seen. What should be adopted directly from the comprehensive program model? What current activities should be maintained? What components of the program model not presently complete need to be created to fill gaps in the current program? Your answers to these questions will provide the information you need to establish goals for change and identify ways to effect change. Second, if you are working in a large school system, you need to make plans to accomplish program improvement at the building as well as the district level; thus, improved designs for the building programs and plans for implementing them must be developed. Third, you need to begin the building-level program improvement efforts. Fourth, as you move into implementation, multiple opportunities will become available to you to better attend to the diversity found in your students and in your communities. Fifth, if you are the program's director, we encourage you to expand your leadership base to include all the school counselors in a small school district or more of the school counselor leaders in a larger district. As you prepare for implementation, the more grassroots leaders you have available, the more effective your transition will be. You will also have the benefit of their advice and counsel in making the transition workable in this phase of remodeling and revitalizing your guidance and counseling program. To conclude the chapter, we summarize your roles and responsibilities as the guidance and counseling program leader during this transition period.

Specify Changes Needed to Implement a Comprehensive Guidance and Counseling Program Districtwide

Planning the transition to a comprehensive program entails specifying the needed changes. To do this, you will need to compare and contrast your current program with the program you desire, establish goals for change, and identify ways to bring the changes about. When you have completed this, you will have specified the changes that are wanted and be ready to begin the process of making or helping others to make the required changes.

Comparing and Contrasting Your Current Program With Your Desired Program

Having studied your current program and having established a design for the program you want, you now have the information you need to compare and contrast the two. The goal is to identify places where the programs overlap but, even more important, where there are gaps that may need to be filled. You will also identify some places where the design of the current program goes beyond the design that is desired. You will be asking and answering the question, "What are the discrepancies between what you want your guidance and counseling program to accomplish and what your guidance and counseling program is accomplishing currently?"

We advise you to conduct this discrepancy analysis from your data for both the current program and the desired program. If you have followed our suggestions in Chapter 4, you have information about student outcomes and results, the appropriation of school counselors' time and competence to the program components, the makeup of the program components, and the clients served. Careful analysis of this information provides you the data you need to specify needed changes.

Northside Independent School District studied the discrepancies in each of the aspects of the program design. The most useful data for redirecting the program were the data about the allocation of school counselor time to each program component and to nonguidance activities. As explained earlier, the program components consist of activities. An activity incorporates all the aspects of the design: Students or other clients participate in the activity; content objectives to yield specific student results are targeted; and school counselors' competence is used.

Some of the baseline data gathered by Northside Independent School District (1986) in assessing its then-current program design were displayed in Chapter 4 (see Table 4.15). Similar information was presented from the design for the desired program in Chapter 5 (see Table 5.13). When both sets of data were presented to the steering committee, the administrators, and the school counselors, they led to the obvious conclusion that change had to occur and sparked creative thinking as to how these changes could occur.

Others have found the data as to how school counselors allocate their time useful as well. In Table 6.1, the data generated in the Texas study *Guiding Our Children Toward Success: How Texas School Counselors Spend Their Time* (Rylander, 2002) are presented side by side with the percentages of how their time should be spent according to the Texas program model (Texas Education Agency, 2004). The information is presented in terms of percentages of school counselors' time that are and should be spent in delivery of the four program components and in nonguidance activities.

The discrepancy analysis of the quantitative design between what is and what should be yielded the following information concerning program components:

- Compares favorably (appropriate amount of time spent):
  a. Individual student planning: elementary, high school
  b. System support: elementary, middle or junior high, high school
- Gaps (too little time spent):
  a. Guidance curriculum: elementary, middle or junior high, high school
  b. Responsive services: elementary, middle or junior high, high school
  c. Individual student planning: middle or junior high school
- Spillovers (too much time spent):
  a. Nonguidance activities: elementary, middle or junior high, high school

In addition to analyzing the hard data collected in the current program assessment, analyzing more subjective data is also useful. Some themes have probably emerged as you gathered perceptions of the current program. Now that you have agreed on what is wanted from your desired program, other people's opinions about what has been good and what has been missing from the current program will give you more information on which to

Table 6.1
Texas School Counselors Actual Time Use and Texas Education Agency (TEA) Suggested Time Allocations (in Percentages)

Category	Elementary School		Middle School–Junior High		High School	
	Survey Results	*TEA Suggested*	*Survey Results*	*TEA Suggested*	*Survey Results*	*TEA Suggested*
Guidance curriculum	17.6	35–45	8.0	35–40	9.2	15–25
Responsive services	21.4	30–40	18.3	30–40	16.7	25–35
Individual student planning	9.5	5–10	10.7	15–25	22.3	25–35
System support	16.0	10–15	11.6	10–15	11.6	15–20
Subtotal	64.5	80–100	48.6	90–100	59.8	80–100
Nonguidance	35.5	0	51.4	0	40.2	0
Total	100	100	100	100	100	100

Note. Survey results are from Rylander (2002, p. 19); TEA suggested time allocations are from Texas Education Agency (1998).

base your decisions for change. The subjective information regarding results sought, clients served, school counselors' and other staff members' roles, and resources thus need to be analyzed as to how your current program compares and contrasts with the desired program. Categorize your analysis in the same manner as you did your analysis of hard data (compares favorably, gaps, and spillovers). For example, equal access by all subpopulations of students to the program is desired. The results of a survey might show that most people felt that the high school guidance and counseling program served the college-bound students adequately, did not serve the work-bound or minority students sufficiently, and invested too much time in serving individual students with difficult personal problems. The first is a subjectively stated favorable comparison, the second identifies a gap, and the third indicates a spillover from the desired design.

In analyzing the subjective data, you will also identify discrepancies between what counselors know or perceive and what others perceive about their work. For example, in studying the impact of the level of implementation of the Missouri Comprehensive Guidance Program on students' academic achievement, the data collected regarding nonguidance tasks done by high school counselors showed a difference between the tasks school counselors said they did and those that the principals identified. Large percentages of high school counselors said that they

1. coordinated the testing program;
2. balanced class loads;
3. handled transcripts;
4. calculated grade point averages, class ranks, and honor roll qualifications;
5. built master schedules;
6. managed schedule changes;
7. tested for special education and gifted programs;
8. coordinated or managed 504 files;
9. maintained permanent records;
10. developed and updated student handbooks and course guides; copied and mailed new student enrollment records.

High school principals identified smaller percentages of counselors doing Tasks 1–6, and they did not identify that counselors did Tasks 6–11 (Lapan, Gysbers, & Kayson, 2007). Addressing this perception gap would be important.

The degree of congruence between your objective and subjective data in relationship to the improved program you envision also needs to be studied. The ideal is for the hard data and subjective data to be as congruent as possible, and for your current and desired programs to match for each component of the program, the clients served, school counselors' functions, and so on. If your objective and subjective data are congruent but the two designs do not match, you have descriptive information from the subjective data on which to base your recommendations for change. For example, if your objective data tell you that school counselors spend too much time in system support or on nonguidance tasks, and the program's users feel that the school counselors function too much like clerks, you have a rationale to support the recommendation to decrease the time spent on the system support component or on nonguidance tasks. If your objective data and subjective data are not congruent, but the two program designs match, you have identified a need for public relations efforts. For example, if your school counselors are spending an appropriate amount of time responding to students with personal problems but your consumers do not perceive this, you know you need to educate all your consumers. At the same time, the subjective data might alert you to the reality that the school counselors are, for example, responding to students with personal problems on a one-to-one basis but that more group work is desirable so that more students with problems could be served.

If your objective data and subjective data are not congruent in an area in which the current and desired programs do not match, then the decisions you make depend on whether the subjective data represent a favorable or unfavorable opinion and on whether the mismatch in program design is a gap or a spillover. If the subjective data about the current program are favorable, our advice is to leave well enough alone until you have begun to implement your desired program. If the subjective data represent the opinion that you are not doing something that in fact takes a disproportionate amount of time, you need to educate the opinion holders before you can implement needed changes. For example, if high school principals think high school counselors are not spending enough time changing schedules and your current assessment data tell you they are, you need to help principals know about the disproportionate investment of valuable talent in an activity that does not use school counselors' education and talents to effect appropriate changes. That is, the principals need assistance to see the problem. School counselors should present these data to their principals because they have examples and anecdotes to share that will put life and meaning into the data.

Identifying, quantitatively or subjectively, the places in which your current program compares favorably with the desired program tells you and the staff what is right with the current program. That provides a morale booster for the staff, who by now are probably quite anxious about ongoing or proposed changes. It also provides you with a good foundation on which to build.

Identifying gaps in the design of your current program vis-à-vis the desired program points to two kinds of changes that may need to be made. The gaps mean either you are simply not doing enough of what is desired or you are not doing it at all. For example, in the Texas study (Rylander, 2002), the analysis of the discrepancies displayed in Table 6.1 (i.e., the difference between the Texas Education Agency's suggested time allocation and the actual time use) showed there was a 6%–16% gap in the use of the guidance curriculum component at the high school level, a 27%–32% gap at the middle school or junior high level, and a 17%–27% gap at the elementary school level. Thus, a change recommendation was to augment the current guidance curriculum efforts. In comparing and contrasting their current content emphasis with their desired content, through Northside's study of school counselors' use of their special knowledge and skills, it was learned that middle school counselors spent no time at most schools in career guidance activities. Thus, career guidance activities must be a new dimension to be added to the program at those middle schools.

Identifying where the design of your current program goes beyond that of the desired program also points to two kinds of potential change. You may be doing too much of what is desirable, or you may be doing something that is seen as inappropriate for the guidance and counseling program or as a waste of school counselors' time and talent. One conclusion drawn in the Texas study (Rylander, 2002) was that the data indicated

that counselor time in specific guidance areas during the survey period was far below the recommended level due to the impact of non-counseling duties. . . . In particular, the category "guidance curriculum," the area of guidance where counselors help students develop basic life skills such as problem-solving and goal-setting strategies, seemed especially low during the survey period among counselors in middle school/junior high and high schools. Guidance curriculum involves a significant amount of student contact, so the statistics seem to indicate that counselor time with students may be lost due to a counselor's need to perform other duties. (p. 19)

This echoes one of the conclusions from the Arizona study (Vandegrift, 1999)—that "time spent on non-guidance activities clearly is time *not* spent working with students, faculty and staff" (p. 5).

In the North Carolina Department of Public Instruction (n.d.) study of how North Carolina school counselors spend their time,

> the results revealed that school counselors in North Carolina are not dividing their time according to the suggested national standards and that a significant amount of time is spent on non-counseling activities, such as testing, covering classes, and registrar activities. (p. 17)

In the Arizona study (Vandegrift, 1999), it was learned that an average of 15% of Arizona school counselors' time was being spent on nonguidance activities. "Of course, using counselors in more proactive capacity suggests redirecting their time. The most obvious place to start is to *not* use counselors for 'non-guidance' activities" (p. 5). The report also identified that 40% of Arizona counselors' total time use was devoted to responsive–reactive services, raising the question, "Is it sound practice for counseling to be reactive or should it be more proactive?" (p. 5). The report concluded, "There will always be circumstances that warrant responsive[/reactive] services. However, the question is whether schools could, in fact, reduce the need for behavioral counseling by improving the quality and nature of educational services" (p. 5).

Scarborough and Culbreth (2008) examined why some school counselors spend more time on nonguidance duties than others. They identified several variables that "relate to the discrepancies found between the amount of time school counselors actually spend on school counselor activities and the amount of time they would prefer to spend on those activities" (p. 448): school level, years of experience, counselor self-efficacy, professional association membership, school staff support, and striving to implement the comprehensive, developmental guidance and counseling program model. Professional counselors who spend more time on guidance- and counseling–appropriate activities and who work at the elementary level have more years of counseling experience, have higher self-efficacy, belong to professional counseling associations, are supported by their school staff (teachers and administrators), and strive to implement the model. It is also interesting to note that in Scarborough and Culbreth's study, "the number of students in the school counselor's caseload was not found to be related to the discrepancy between actual amount of time and preferred amount of time spent in school counselor activities" (p. 456).

Establishing Goals for Change

Having clearly identified discrepancies between the current program and the desired program, you are ready to draw conclusions. This entails studying each set of discrepancy data and identifying the gaps and spillovers. As discussed earlier, the following conclusions from the Texas study (Rylander, 2002) were drawn from contrasting current and desired program designs:

- Too little time is spent in curriculum at all three levels.
- Too little time is spent in responsive services at all three levels.
- Too much time is spent in nonguidance activities.

The guidance and counseling program leader develops the list of conclusions. This list needs to be presented to the steering and the school–community advisory committees, the school counselors, and other administrators to enable them to see the specific problems that need to be addressed. It is from this list of conclusions that recommendations for change are drawn. Recommendations for change are restatements of the data-based conclusions into "should" statements. Recommendations for change from the Texas study (Rylander, 2002) in relation to the conclusions just listed are presented in Table 6.2.

Another step in the process is to assign priorities to the recommendations. For example, in the *Study of Pupil Personnel Ratios, Services, and Programs* conducted by the California Department of Education (as cited in Gray, Elsner, & Poynton, 2004), it was learned that

> the top priority identified by districts was the need for more school-wide prevention and intervention strategies. This calls for the development of a comprehensive pupil support program that serves all students proactively through prevention programs, and reactively through intervention strategies. (p. 4)

The chronological order of taking improvement steps may also need to be considered. An example relates to the national study of the levels of implementation of state counseling program models. Martin, Carey, and DeCoster (2009) identified features that, when present, influence the likelihood of statewide implementation: having a written model that addresses modern guidance and counseling program features and career planning; endorsement of the model by the state department of education, the state professional counseling association, and others; counseling leadership in the state department of education; state mandates and requirements; professional development; state certification and licensure regulations that relate to the model; and a system for evaluating the model. A state categorized as "beginning" or "progressing" that wants to make the changes needed for its model to qualify as established (p. 381) has to determine which feature or features are lacking and then work on improving them in the order that fits where they are and how the state operates. One logical order might be to (a) ensure counseling leadership in the state department of education and (b) seek state mandates and requirements; however, in some states, state department leadership in a discipline flows from mandates passed by the legislature. In some states, it might be best to have (a) a written model and (b) model endorsement.

Table 6.2
Guidance Program Change Goals

To attain the desired comprehensive, balanced guidance program for Texas Public Schools, it is recommended that counselors and administrators work together

At the elementary school level:
- To increase the time spent by counselors in guidance curriculum
- To increase the time spent by counselors in responsive services
- To decrease the time spent by counselors in nonguidance activities

At the middle school or junior high level:
- To increase the time spent by counselors in guidance curriculum
- To increase the time spent by counselors in responsive services
- To decrease the time spent by counselors in nonguidance activities

At the high school level:
- To increase the time spent by counselors in guidance curriculum
- To increase the time spent by counselors in responsive services
- To decrease the time spent by counselors in nonguidance activities

---

Some school districts with which we have worked have chosen to establish priorities by identifying changes that need to be made and those that they want to make. In a national survey of guidance program and staff leaders (Henderson & Gysbers, 2002), 10 recurrent issues were identified as critical—"recurrent" in that they occurred in multiple schools, districts, and states; "critical" in that their resolution makes for a strengthened guidance program, and if not resolved, the program is weakened. Priority was established on the basis of the issues' frequency of occurrence and rated importance; the 10 issues, listed in priority order, are

1. Displacement of non-guidance tasks, including school counselors' appropriate role in standardized testing programs
2. Program accountability
3. Accountability for the quality of school counselor performance
4. Program advocacy
5. Leader empowerment
6. Enhancement of an existing comprehensive guidance program
7. Appropriate use of technology
8. Parent involvement, including responding to parents who are critical of the program
9. Program development process
10. Enhancement of the cross-cultural competence of school counselors. (Henderson & Gysbers, 2002, p. 8)

Whether you choose to state the recommendations as needs and wants or to list all of them in order of priority is up to you. Because the process we have outlined generates rather lengthy lists of recommendations for change, listing changes in priority order and tempered by chronological feasibility makes accomplishing the changes more manageable.

Identifying Ways to Effect the Changes

Now that the issues have been identified through discrepancy analysis and explicit recommendations for changes have been made, all staff and others involved in the program development effort need to identify ways to attain the recommendations and to make the changes. Adelman and Taylor (2003) referred to this as "clarifying feasibility" (p. 8).

Most program improvement efforts entail making three kinds of changes in school guidance and counseling programs: systemic, incremental, and ongoing improvements. Systemic changes are major changes resulting in transformed programs. They affect not only the guidance and counseling department, but also other departments, and potentially a whole district or school. They address the whole program and take several years to take full effect. They entail collaborative work with individuals or their representatives who are likely to be affected by changes. Incremental changes are small steps in a sequence of changes. When successful, each results in a program shift. Most often, they are set in the context of systemic change goals. They usually address one or two separate elements of the program and may be accomplished in a year or two. They typically entail the collaborative work of one or more members of the guidance and counseling department. Ongoing improvements are most successful when they are part of an annual structured process. The improvements alter a program. They may be baby steps to achieving either systemic or incremental degrees of change, or they may be desirable changes addressing a newly identified student need or campus goal that calls for a new program element. As you prioritize the changes you envision as needed, it is important to clarify what kind of change is required. That, too, affects the priority assigned to it (Henderson, 2009).

We recommend that those involved—the steering committee, the school–community advisory committee, the school counselors, the administrators, and other staff—brainstorm ways to make the changes. It is best to involve everyone who will be affected by the changes; this process allows them to sense the feasibility of the changes and sets their thoughts in motion as to how recommendations might be carried out.

The steering committee should be the first to do this, preferably at the same meeting during which the recommendations for the changes are developed, as a reality check. The steering committee also ought to help design the process for presenting the change recommendations and soliciting from the appropriate staff ideas about how to make the changes. If your building or system is large enough, it is advisable to use the steering committee members to conduct the brainstorming meetings with the rest of the staff. These meetings ought to include enough people so that true brainstorming can occur, that is, so that many ideas can be thrown onto the table for further consideration.

In Northside Independent School District, the school counselors and principals from the steering committee conducted meetings with each of the three different principal groups: elementary, middle, and high school. The school counselors conducted the meetings with the other school counselors. Each group was presented with the discrepancy information relevant to its own level and was guided through the brainstorming process for each discrepancy and resultant recommendations. The groups responded to the question "How could this be done?"—for example, "How could school counselors spend more time in the guidance curriculum component?" "How could they spend less time on nonguidance tasks?" Many ideas were generated by the counselors and the principals. For example, high school counselors suggested such things as

- provide group guidance to teach all students decision-making skills;
- provide more in-service training with teachers to help them teach guidance concepts;
- increase time in ninth-grade advisories;
- provide orientations to the career center;
- hold brown-bag lunch sessions;
- make official time for counselors to go into classrooms (e.g., restructure the school day periodically);
- increase principals' and department heads' support.

High school principals suggested such things as

- use already available times (e.g., study halls, advisories, on-campus suspension classes);
- institute a "club" schedule (i.e., modified day);
- identify and work with classes that indicate needs for guidance (behavioral or academic);
- use different methods of assigning counselors to caseload responsibilities;
- provide in-service training for teachers;
- plan the calendar for a year.

The data from separate meetings such as these can then be aggregated and presented to the steering and school–community advisory committees to do the second half of the desired changes. The groups that brainstormed the suggestions need to see the notes from the various meetings so that they know their ideas were heard and are being considered. These lists are also useful in the future when specific changes are being implemented, both at the district and at the local levels.

Another approach to listing what needs to be done to implement changes is seen in the results of the Missouri study regarding the impact of more fully implemented comprehensive guidance programs on student achievement (Lapan et al., 2007):

> Given the major finding of this study that comprehensive guidance programs make significant contributions to student success (including academic achievement), Missouri school districts need to work at all levels to ensure that all students and their parents have access to and can participate in fully implemented comprehensive guidance programs staffed by professional school counselors. (p. 11)

Lapan et al. (2007) recommended action steps to "facilitate the adoption and implementation of districtwide comprehensive guidance programs" (p. 11). They identified actions that need to be taken by boards of education, administrators, teachers, parents, and school counselors.

You should now have a clear and concrete picture of what changes need to be made to your current program. You have formulated recommendations for the changes you are getting ready to implement, so that you will know you have achieved what you want when you get there, and you have begun to identify how to effect the desired changes. You are now ready to plan your program improvements.

Develop a Plan for Accomplishing Districtwide Program Improvement

At the district level, the steering committee and the school–community advisory committee and the guidance and counseling program leader should devise a master plan of action for accomplishing the districtwide tasks. A list of tasks to do can be developed from the suggestions resulting from the brainstorming sessions described in the preceding section. Then an action plan for accomplishing these recommendations needs to be written.

Listing What Needs to Be Done to Implement Changes

The to-do list should be an action-oriented list, not a list of vague wishes, and the actions should be feasible. The list may be rather long. Districts we have worked with have generated a range of 25 to 40 items that needed to be done before complete implementation could become a reality. This does not mean that all tasks have to be accomplished before some changes can be made, but it does mean that policymakers have to be realistic about their expectations for the new program implementation. To help you envision what it might take, we include in Table 6.3 a partial list of such actions from Northside Independent School District.

As you can see, these are major tasks to accomplish. By scanning the list, you can also see that there are categories of items, for example, those that relate to staff development, to budget development, and to product development. Other categories of recommendations might be those that relate to policy development and program development. As a result of her analysis of the Texas school counselor time study, Rylander (2002) made three recommendations: (a) that each district develop a local policy on the use of school counselors' time; (b) that the Texas Education Agency monitor local policies through the agency's compliance reviews; and (c) that the Texas Education Agency automate the information it collects from school counselors for better use in holding school districts accountable for their guidance programs. As a final example, as described in a model by the

Table 6.3

Recommended "To Do's" to Accomplish the Comprehensive Guidance Program

Develop guidance program component guides.
Develop a system for assisting local campuses to design their guidance programs.
Establish communication mechanisms.
Design a relevant counselor staff development program.
Design a relevant counselor evaluation system.
Provide program development time for counselors.
Establish campus departmental budgets for guidance department.
Assess costs associated with implementation of program and develop an appropriate
    budget (district).
Review and make recommendations to ensure adequacy of guidance facilities.
Modify counselor staffing formulas as recommended.
Hire technical assistants at secondary schools.
Review and recommend extended contracts for counselors.
Establish parameters for counselor access to students.
Develop a public relations plan.
Explore use of other-than-local funding sources.
Develop job descriptions for guidance department clerical staff.

Note. From *Comprehensive Guidance Program Framework*, by Northside Independent School District, 1986, San Antonio, TX: Author. Adapted with permission.

National Consortium for State Guidance Leadership, recommendations made to reduce the gaps between how the 2000 North Carolina school counselors were spending their time and how they should spend their time included the following:

- Staff development activities to help principals and school counselors schedule their time appropriately and to increase understanding of the major function areas.
- A study on how support personnel can be used to eliminate non-counseling duties.
- Resources to eliminate non-counseling functions are needed.
- A revised guidance curriculum for the school counseling program is needed. (North Carolina Department of Public Instruction, n.d., p. 12)

To ensure the completeness of your list, you may want to group the list by the categories of resources used in the original program assessment: personnel resources (talent, time, ratio, assignments), financial resources (budget, materials, equipment, facilities), and political resources (policy, identification of program supporters). Grouping by categories will help you and the committees make the next set of decisions: what to do first.

An example of recommendations for actions to be taken at the district level is excerpted from an evaluation of one school district's guidance and counseling program. The comprehensive guidance program elements were used as the organizer for the evaluation and subsequent recommendations.

PROGRAM FOUNDATION

- Use the impetus from the District's Strategic Plan to move the guidance program and professional school counselor performance forward.
- At each school, identify specific emotional and social needs of students related to the Strategic Plan objectives to define desirable goals and outcomes for students' personal, social, educational, and career development, and the program content.
- Develop a unified vision and mission program within the District's mission and within current legal, ethical, and professional school counseling standards.

COUNSELORS & OTHER STAFF MEMBERS IMPLEMENTING THE GUIDANCE PROGRAM

- Clearly define appropriate roles, responsibilities, and job descriptions for program-related staff members (e.g., professional school counselors, school social workers, campus administrators, behavior specialists, teachers). The current school counselor job descriptions published by the Personnel Office provides a good basis for addressing this recommendation.
- Encourage professionals to use current, appropriate labels for their professional identity.
- Make fuller use of professional school counselors' training and competencies (e.g., conducting small group counseling for students with developmental and preventive needs, and conducting individual student planning activities in small or classroom-sized groups with follow-up options for individuals with extra needs).

CONTENT DELIVERED TO STUDENTS IN THE PROGRAM

- Develop a Pre-K–12th grade guidance curriculum addressing the identified needs of students related to the District's Strategic Plan (i.e., character education, wellness/developmental assets enhancement, reducing risky behaviors, skills for studying, being organized, solving problems, making decisions, and leading.)

DELIVERY SYSTEM

- Provide in-service education and training for the professional school counselors in the [State] comprehensive, developmental guidance and counseling program model. This would be prerequisite to establishing expectations for program implementation.

PROGRAM DEVELOPMENT PROCESS

- Review existing guidance and counseling-related Board Policies, State statutes and rules, and professional standards to inform program development and design efforts.
- Implement a systematic process for Pre-K–12th program development, design, and improvement that leads to a clearly articulated guidance and counseling program mission compatible with that of the District, establishes program priorities for alignment of the unified program's resources and goals. The first step in this process entails aligning the current program activities that fit within the template of the model. After the design decisions are made, the process entails developing action plans for moving the program from its current status to the one deemed more desirable.
- Designate leadership and responsibilities for steering the program development process, monitoring program improvements, and supervising counselor performance quality. Assign the District counseling coordinator sufficient time to carry out these responsibilities.
- Strive systematically to reduce professional school counselors' time on non-guidance tasks. Use a "fair share" approach that broadens the number of school staff members who spend time on tasks that are not in their disciplines. Break the large tasks (e.g. testing, registration) into smaller tasks and assign the smaller tasks to the least costly human or computerized resource available.
- Encourage school counselors and their administrators to continue to seek creative ways to decrease counselor time in nonguidance tasks and with second priority clients (e.g., parents, teachers, administrators), and increase time in guidance curriculum, group counseling, and group guidance.
- Convene monthly meetings for all counselors for program and professional development.

EVALUATION AND ACCOUNTABILITY

- Once the program activities are based on guidance content addressing identified student needs, measures of student growth in these areas can be measured.
- Use a professionally relevant form and system for counselor performance evaluation (e.g., *The Texas Evaluation Model for Professional School Counselors*).
- Provide related training for the evaluators of counselors and social workers.
- Once standards are established for district program implementation aligned with the desired design, evaluate the program's developmental progress. (Henderson, 2010, pp. 1–2)

Outlining Your Master Plan for Resource Development

Needless to say, all of these tasks cannot begin at once. Adelman and Taylor (2003) described this in their clarifying feasibility stage as "formulating a longer range strategic plan for maintaining momentum, progress, quality improvement, and creative renewal" (p. 8). Some tasks to be done depend on the accomplishment of other tasks. Thus, the next step is to list the tasks to do in chronological order. Chronology is guided by consideration of whether certain tasks are prerequisite to the other tasks. Consider whether tasks are developmental or experimental and whether they are feasible to do at this time or if they might be difficult to accomplish. If they are tied to other, larger processes—such as district budget development—they must be done at times relevant to those processes.

A part of the Northside Independent School District master plan is displayed in Table 6.4. The first four items were related to the development of the district's budget for the next fiscal year and were also of top priority. The budget is submitted for consideration by the superintendent by May l; thus, the research work needed to be done in March and April. The written program description obviously needed to be finished before it could be presented to the board of education, and the board needed to approve the program description before it could be presented to the school counselors with authority.

The master plan specifies what needs to be done in what order and by whom. If you are the guidance and counseling program leader, the master plan gives you your job-related

Table 6.4

Master Plan for Implementation of a Comprehensive Guidance Program

Task	Deadline
Make recommendations regarding extended contracts.	2/25
Make recommendations regarding counselors' preference (lowered caseload vs. technical assistance).	3/28
Make recommendations regarding priorities for implementing lowered caseloads; elementary, middle, & high school.	3/28
Send memos to principals regarding campus guidance department budgets.	4/5
Develop counselors' job descriptions for inclusion in framework.	5/1
Complete framework; prepare for board presentation.	6/1
Plan guide development process.	5/1
Seek approval/funding.	5/15
Conduct leadership training.	6/30
Develop recommendations for minimum standards for facilities/equipment for principals.	8/1
Plan/implement in-service sessions for counselors on minimum expectations (framework).	8/30

Note. Data from Northside Independent School District, San Antonio, TX. Adapted with permission.

mandates for continuing the project you have been working on. You also have to identify the areas in which the members of the steering committee can help you and where you and the school counselors are on your own.

Begin Building-Level Program Improvement Efforts

At this point, the guidance and counseling program improvement project becomes two tiered. Up till now, we have been working primarily from the frame of reference of the school district. Building-level school counselors and administrators have been involved on a more or less voluntary basis, except for responding to the project's data-gathering needs. If you have followed our advice, many of the school counselors and some administrators have been involved in the work groups. Those school counselors who envision the new program as the wave of the future or the answer to their dreams have probably already experimented with new activities.

When the statement of the district's minimum expectations for the guidance and counseling program is adopted, responsibility shifts to the local school buildings in the district; their programs must be changed to meet these minimum expectations or go beyond them. They are now challenged to identify incremental and systemic changes that are needed in their building programs and to make those changes successfully. What you should have been saying to the building school counselors and administrators all along, as they raised the usual concerns regarding district mandates, is that there will be room to tailor the desired program to local community needs. It is at this time that the statement becomes the challenge. To make the right changes, school counselors and administrators in each building must redesign their programs to better align them with the district program and also to ensure they meet their students' and local communities' highest priority needs and goals. It must be remembered that school counselors and principals need to share a common vision of the guidance program.

> The mission of the school guidance program is a subset of the school's mission. The primary mission in any building is to help students learn. Thus, the guidance program supports the learning environment; at the same time, guidance programs make unique contributions in meeting students' needs and nurturing their progress. (Henderson & Gysbers, 1998, p. 58)

To ensure that program changes at the local level are made successfully, school counselors and administrators must use processes that support change and meaningful program planning.

Assisting Building-Level Staff to Prepare for Change

If you are the guidance and counseling program leader, you will need to assist the counseling staff as they face this challenge and empower them to make needed changes. Often-cited obstacles to change include school counselors' needing to change their philosophies about what they do and why they do it, to overcome their fears of failure in fulfilling new or different roles, to seek support from faculty and administration, and to learn to work together as a team (American School Counselor Association [ASCA], 2005). Guidance program leaders nurture school counselors' professional empowerment by establishing respectful interpersonal climates, by ensuring their understanding of the envisioned program and the expectations for their performance within it, by developing and maintaining a team approach to program development and implementation, and by holding school counselors accountable for their work in the program (Henderson & Gysbers, 1998).

Ultimately, the school counselors need help to internalize their understanding of the desired comprehensive guidance and counseling program as described. They need to be familiar with the program development model they will be asked to follow. They need to assess their current program in relation to the district model and to identify local needs and establish priorities for meeting those needs. Moreover, they need to design the desired program for the building on the basis of the desired district model. Sound familiar? It is the same process you have just been through at the district level. The basic difference is in the level of specificity and, of course, that difference depends on the size of the district. In the buildings, each school counselor needs to begin to think in personal terms, saying "I spend X hours a week in counseling," "I spend X hours a week in clerical tasks," and so on, as well as "At the building level, the 20 students who are contemplating suicide and need responsive services are somewhere in these hallways" and "At the building level, if a guidance activity is selected for third graders, I am the one who will or will not implement it." There is no longer room for "that's a good idea for someone else" kinds of thinking.

It is, in fact, quite the opposite. Each school counselor needs to become the leader in changing the guidance and counseling program at his or her school. Shillingford and Lambie (2010) found that school counselors who used the following practices were more apt to be successful school leaders:

(a) taking responsibility for the advancement of their program;
(b) increasing their own visibility at their school;
(c) communicating their vision of what an effective school counseling program represents;
(d) collaboratively teaming to improve students' academic, personal/social, and career development;
(e) clarifying their programmatic role as a unique professional with the knowledge and skills to collaboratively support students thereby improving student outcomes. (p. 215)

Understanding the Districtwide Desired Program Design and Description

It has probably taken you some time to reach this point—as much as a year or more—so the school counselors have had time to understand the concept of the comprehensive program and to know about the major impending changes, such as developmental guidance, small-group counseling, and more emphasis on career development. The proper balance for the district program has been decided. Now each school counselor needs to understand the new program structure fully.

We recommend that after a formal presentation and the distribution of the written comprehensive program description, small-group discussions be held with the school counselors to clarify any misconceptions, correct any misinformation, and ensure as much as possible not only that they have read it but also that they have understood it. The most logical small groups should be used—a building staff, a cluster of elementary school counselors, and so on. By small groups, we mean five to 10. Although the discussions are led by the school counselor leaders, the guidance and counseling program administrator needs to be present at as many of these discussions as feasible because the shifting of focus to the buildings in anticipation of moving from planning to implementation represents a milestone in the project.

The strategy mentioned in Chapter 5 and used in the Northside Independent School District involved the use of a discussion agenda. The director of guidance developed a form that identified key topics and issues addressed in the comprehensive guidance and counseling program guide. Building-level counselor leaders were assigned to discuss the agenda with their staffs. The director explained the issue points and the rationale behind the choices made. The school counselors were given 2 weeks to read the guide, write responses to the discussion agenda, and discuss these items in building staff meetings. Each counselor leader wrote a summary of the building discussion; when the director came to the next staff meeting, those items became the focal point of the discussion. The director also collected the completed forms because several topics surfaced that needed to be addressed further. The summary information was discussed with all the counselor leaders at one of their meetings. By the end of this process, the school counselors could legitimately be expected to know the district guidelines for the comprehensive guidance and counseling program.

As a final step, the school counselors were asked to conduct a meeting with their building administrators to summarize the program description and to suggest what it might mean to the building program. Because the principals had already been made aware of the document by the director, this was the opportunity to enlist the building administrators' support for the development of the building plan.

Understanding the Program Development Process

The responsibility for developing the building plan belongs to the building staff (Shillingford & Lambie, 2010). It is therefore important to ensure that building school counselors understand the program development process and establish mechanisms to facilitate it. At this point, we suggest that the school counselors be educated about the steps in the process that you want them to use. Following the process suggested in this book entails assessing their current program, assessing student and community needs, designing the desired program, establishing goals for change, and planning how those changes will be made. Again, depending on the size of the district, the process model may not need much elucidation if most school counselors have been involved in the development of the district program. However, if the district is large, at least one round of in-service education about the program development process may be required.

In addition to benefiting from the experiences of the district as a whole, the building staffs have the benefit of the district's theoretical base as written in the rationale, assumptions, and definition. The district program description also portrays the model for the program structure and lists student competencies to be addressed in the program. Thus, one challenge to the building staff is to study how their current program compares and contrasts with the district's desired program and make plans to improve. Another is to assess the needs of their students and the local community in terms of the broad parameters established for the district program and implement a program targeting these needs.

We also recommend that the building counseling staff lead the guidance and counseling program development effort but that they involve others as well. Janson (2010) identified two "preconditions to effective leadership" (p. 93) by school counselors: "having skillful performance of counseling activities and high-quality interactions with others in the school" (p. 93). Both of these develop over time and are built on now, at the time of change. High-quality interactions are essential to the level of collaboration and consultation with others needed in improving an existing or creating a new program.

Representatives from the faculty, the student body, parents, the administration, and any other group of significant others should be members of a committee charged with giving input into the guidance program improvement efforts. If a school has a building improvement committee or a community advisory committee, use it—or form one for the specific purpose of designing the local guidance and counseling program. We recommend that to provide you with continued advice and counsel, you continue to consult with the committee even after you have achieved the changes you are working for. In fact, the Texas statute directing school counselors and school counseling programs mandates that "a school counselor shall work with the school faculty and staff, students, parents, and the community to plan, implement, and evaluate a developmental guidance and counseling program" (Texas Education Code, 2001, §33.005). We, too, believe that a program always benefits from advice and counsel from its constituents or collaborators, but remember that the guidance staff and appropriate administrators need to remain the decision makers and leaders of the implementation and management of the guidance and counseling program.

Assessing Current Building-Level Program Status

The current-status study of the building program consists of the same steps needed in the district study. These steps were fully described in Chapter 4. Most likely, the building data are available from the original assessment, so at this time the task is not to collect the data but to study them in light of the now-established desired program design. Building guidance staff members should be cognizant of their currently available resources and how they are used. You will recall that we discussed three kinds of resources: human, financial, and political. Personnel resources include not only the guidance and counseling program staff but also the specialized talents of each and their caseloads, assignments, and time available as well as the appropriation of that time to the various functions and activities of the program. Financial resources include budget, materials, equipment, and facilities. Political resources include policy support as well as support by individuals within the building and the community.

At this point, the guidance activities conducted in the current building program need to be arranged according to the comprehensive guidance and counseling program components, and the competencies that they assist students to attain need to be specified. A listing of clients who the building program serves needs to be made, not by names of specific individuals but by categories and by numbers. For example, it is important to know how many or what percentage of students in the building receive preventive, remedial, or crisis assistance; how many or what percentage of faculty receive consultation services; how many parents have sought consultation or referral services; and so on. Other data that districts and schools have found enlightening are the data regarding the mix of students and other clients served. It is important to know whether the demographic mix of the clients actually served by the guidance and counseling program matches the school's mix of demographic and other social groups. If it does not, that generates another set of goals. In fact, every bit of concrete data that can be gathered regarding the current program needs to be assembled, so that as the building staff develops its plan for change, it is grounded solidly in reality. A premise here is that the design of the current guidance and counseling program has emerged in response to the most immediate and most visible student, teacher, administrator, and parent needs. Thus, the current program provides an informal assessment of these needs from these perspectives.

Assessing Building-Level Student and School Community Needs

Perceived Student Needs. Some program planners do this task before any other step in the planning process. The ASCA (2005) National Model stresses the value of gathering data and its use in focusing program planning, subsequent monitoring of student progress, and allowing for program accountability. A major reason we recommend waiting until this phase of the program improvement process to assess student needs is that it is not until now that you have identified the student competencies you are able to address through your program.

> A counseling needs assessment item which reveals a counseling need must be specific enough to indicate clearly that school counselor intervention is implicit and necessary for that particular student, even if that intervention is in terms of referral to a more appropriate source of assistance. The focus of a specific item, therefore, must be in an area in which [a school counselor] can take appropriate action on behalf of the child in question. (Thompson, Loesch, & Seraphine, 2003, p. 36)

In the type of assessment we are proposing, student competency statements become, in effect, the needs assessment items. In fact, this part of the designing process could just as well be called an inventory of student competencies—an inventory of where students are in competency development and where they should be in their competency acquisition. To illustrate how the competencies you have chosen can be converted to needs assessment items, we have provided examples in Table 6.5. From the competencies presented in Chapter 3, we have selected one competency from Grade 1, one from Grade 8, and one from Grade 11. To show you what a needs assessment questionnaire using converted competencies looks like, a section of a questionnaire on life career planning competencies used for Grades 10, 11, and 12 is presented in Figure 6.1.

Some needs are suggested through research. For example, Lee, Daniels, Puig, Newgent, and Nam (2008)'s study indicated that "patterns of educational attainment (and conversely of low performance) are determined as early as middle school for low-SES students" (p. 314). To attempt to prevent low performance later on, school counselors need to help these students to acquire academic skills during their elementary school years. Professional school counselors can support teachers' efforts to help children develop effective learning habits that match their learning styles.

Needs assessment is commonly described as a way of determining the discrepancy between what exists and what is desired. If this practice is observed rigidly, only contemporary needs will be recognized, and the needs of the past, or those that already have been met, may be overlooked. When asked to respond to a needs statement, individuals are justified in asking whether it makes a difference if the statement represents a need they feel is important but is being satisfied or if the statement represents an unmet need. For program planning, it is important to know the needs that are being met as well as the needs that deserve additional attention.

Table 6.5
Competencies as Needs Assessment Items

1st grade

Competency:	Students will describe how exercise and nutrition affect their mental health.
Needs assessment:	I can tell how exercise and eating habits make a difference in how I think, act, and feel.

8th grade

Competency:	Students will analyze effective family relations, their importance, and how they are formed.
Needs assessment:	I can tell why good family relations are important and how they are formed.

11th grade

Competency:	Students will evaluate the need for flexibility in their roles and in their choices.
Needs assessment:	I can explain the need for flexibility in my roles and in my choices.

Figure 6.1
Life Career Planning

To fill out this questionnaire, students are asked to complete the following steps.

Step 1:   *Read each sentence carefully.* Each one describes things students are able to do in order to demonstrate learning in that particular area.

Now make a decision. Are you able to do what the sentence describes? Are you not able to do what the sentence describes?

Fill in the circle that shows what you think.

If you think you are able to do what the sentence describes . . .
fill in circle A   (A)   (B) | (C)

If you think you are not able to do what the sentence describes . . .
fill in circle B   (A)   (B) | (C)

Step 2:   *Choose the five sentences on each page that describe what you would really be interested in learning to do.* Some of the statements will really interest you and some will not. *In the second column (circles are lettered C), fill in the circle for each of the five statements that you feel you need to learn how to accomplish.*

For example, if you feel you would really be interested in learning to analyze how characteristics and abilities develop, you would mark as follows:

I can

1. describe and analyze how an individual's characteristics
    and abilities develop.   (A)   (B) | (C)

The statements that follow are about things you can do to show you are preparing yourself for the future and are able to make decisions about what you want to do in your life. Review your instruction sheet carefully. Then fill in the circle that shows what you think about that statement.

I can

1. evaluate the importance of having laws and contracts to
    protect producers.   (A)   (B) | (C)

2. provide examples of decisions I have made based on my
    attitudes and values.   (A)   (B) | (C)

3. analyze the decision-making process used by others.   (A)   (B) | (C)

4. distinguish between alternatives that involve varying degrees
    of risk.   (A)   (B) | (C)

5. evaluate the importance of setting realistic goals and working
    toward them.   (A)   (B) | (C)

6. describe my rights and responsibilities as a producer.   (A)   (B) | (C)

7. explain and analyze how values affect my decisions, actions,
    and lifestyles.   (A)   (B) | (C)

8. identify decisions I have made and analyze how they will affect
    my future decisions.   (A)   (B) | (C)

9. analyze the consequences of decisions others make.   (A)   (B) | (C)

10. explain how my values, interests, and capabilities have
    changed and are changing.   (A)   (B) | (C)

11. speculate what my rights and obligations might be as a
    producer in the future.   (A)   (B) | (C)

12. summarize the importance of understanding my attitudes and
    values and how they affect my life.   (A)   (B) | (C)

13. use the decision-making process when making a decision.   (A)   (B) | (C)

14. provide examples and evaluate my current ability to generate
    alternatives, gather information, and assess the consequences
    in the decisions I make.   (A)   (B) | (C)

15. assess my ability to achieve past goals and integrate this
    knowledge for the future.   (A)   (B) | (C)

An additional means for considering met needs is to review the needs being met in the current program. It is likely that current program activities grew out of a prior informal or formal needs assessment. If students' evaluations of their activities indicate that they are valuable, then it is a good assumption that the activities are meeting a relatively important need. The opportunity to respond to a relevant sampling of needs is another important point. Simply stated, how can a need be identified if no one presents the statement? Limited coverage, insignificant choices, or redundancy may distort a needs survey. We recommend that you develop your own needs assessment survey from the list of competencies you have established as essential in your program.

Thompson et al. (2003) cautioned school counselors that "a results-based school counseling program necessitates the collection of data, but the data collected are meaningful and useful only to the extent that the means used to obtain them are psychometrically sound" (p. 38). If you are adapting competencies from the ASCA (2005) National Model, there are some needs assessment instruments that have been developed by others and could be adapted for your purposes. Thompson et al. developed a "a psychometrically sound needs assessment instrument appropriate for use with students in the upper three grades of an elementary school" (p. 36)—the *Intermediate Elementary School Students Counseling Needs Survey,* which is based on *The National Standards for School Counseling Programs* (Campbell & Dahir, 1997). Whiston and Aricak (2008) designed a similar instrument for use with high school students, the *School Counseling Program Evaluation Survey (SCoPES).*

If your district is similar to those with which we have worked, more needs (competencies) will be identified than the program resources can provide for; thus, one purpose of a needs assessment is to determine priorities for needs (competencies). Moreover, although there will be common needs (competencies) across a school district, there may also be differences as dictated by the needs of particular buildings in a district. If you are uneasy about or inexperienced in developing such surveys, you may find it advantageous to use an adopt–adapt strategy, that is, to select and modify needs statements from existing instruments rather than construct new ones. Be sure, however, to include a needs statement for each competency for which your program is accepting responsibility.

A final point to keep in mind is whose perceptions of students' needs should be assessed. The answer is those of anyone involved in the educational process, including those receiving education. This includes the following groups:

- *Students:* This group should receive top priority in any needs assessment. Who knows more about students than students? Students can tell you what they need as a group and as individuals. They will also let you know whether the current program is meeting their needs.
- *Educators:* Assessing members of this group will give you their perceptions of students' needs as well as of their own needs.
- *Parents:* Members of this group will help you identify what they feel their children should learn from school experiences. Including parents in the needs assessment process offers them an opportunity for involvement in planning the guidance and counseling program. As a result of their personal involvement, they may be more willing to offer their support.
- *Community members:* Included in this group are individuals who are not employers yet support the school financially. Information from this group may give a somewhat different perspective on the information gained from an assessment of parents.
- *Employers:* Those who are responsible for hiring graduates of your school system or for hiring students still in school have definite ideas about the outcomes of education they expect. Including employers in the needs assessment process will give the

school an opportunity to know what employers expect as well as to offer the employers a chance to know more about the guidance and counseling program.

- *Graduates:* An assessment of members of this group can provide information about the effectiveness of the guidance and counseling program for those who are applying their skills in post–high school pursuits. They can help identify areas that are of the most benefit as well as areas that need strengthening.

Because of time and resource limitations, you may not be able to assess all of these groups about student needs. If you must restrict the number of groups to be assessed, students and educators should receive attention first by virtue of being the most immediately involved. It may be that you could assess students and educators the first year and members of the other groups during following years, or it may be that you could use a formalized, paper-and-pencil assessment with students and educators and a less exacting strategy with parents and employers, such as a discussion format with a representative group. Each of these groups should, however, be assessed at some point in the periodic needs assessment process.

School Community Needs. Although students are the primary clients of the guidance and counseling program, it is important to remember that there are other clients whose actual and perceived needs must be surveyed and addressed as well. The school as a whole, individual teachers and administrators, other school specialists, and parents are all clients in one way or another. Some student needs are best identified by a thorough understanding of the community in which the students live. It is imperative that in helping students' personal, social, career, and educational development, you be knowledgeable about what those developmental areas and stages mean within the community and cultural contexts.

Currently, individual schools are challenged to assess and respond to the needs of their students in relation to specifically defined academic standards. Schools are encouraged to respond at each site as they determine the best uses of resources to achieve their goals for raising students' achievement levels. Progress toward these standards by individual students and by a school as a whole is often measured by standardized tests (criterion referenced to a state's standards).

This accountability and site-based decision-making system provides both challenges and opportunities for guidance and counseling program planners. School counselors are challenged to relate their programs and outcomes to the overall improvement and success of the school. In other words, they must be part of the site-based decision-making process and be clear as to which school goals their programs contribute most meaningfully. In most buildings, the students who are most challenging academically are those whose personal and social needs are greatest. School counselors' work with these students in helping them remove or overcome their barriers to successful learning is a key part of a building's school improvement plan. In some instances, teachers create, usually inadvertently, barriers to student learning. For example, some teachers are abusive to their students. They may be demeaning, prejudiced, authoritarian, and intimidating and use other negative strategies that hinder healthy student development (McEachern, Oyaziwo, & Kenny, 2008). School counselors and administrators can work collaboratively to address such issues. School counselors and their expertise are valuable assets to most of the school climate improvement efforts that we are aware of (e.g., goal setting, character development, social responsibility).

In addition, individual and specialized groups of teachers, parents, other school specialists, and administrators can identify ways in which the guidance and counseling program can assist them in addressing specific students' or sets of students' needs. A survey of these needs should be related to the student competencies you are seeking to develop or enhance.

For example, ask teachers to respond to items in terms of their needs for assisting students in attaining desired guidance competencies. Using the same examples as we did for the student needs assessment (see Table 6.5), we present a sample of teacher items in Table 6.6.

Assessing staff needs for system support activities is also important. This needs assessment can be focused in two ways. You can assess your clients' needs for system support activities performed in the current program, or you can assess their perceived needs for the proposed activities of the desired program. If the latter is your aim, this assessment cannot be done in a building until after the desired program has been established. At this time, however, it may be relevant to assess perceived needs for current activities or those you are thinking of doing, using the district's suggested activities. If conducted in the appropriate context—for example, in conjunction with the assessment of student needs—you will probably build a powerful case for reassigning some of the typical quasi-administrative and clerical tasks to other personnel. Staff assessment will identify their perceptions of the need for school counselors to do such tasks as senior credit checks or bus duty supervision. You will also identify tasks to be displaced or streamlined, such as recommending students for more or less rigorous course offerings or coordinating the testing program.

The context data gathered in clarifying the current program design suggest some needs inherent in the community served by the school. Different communities send their children to school with variations in such things as school readiness, parent involvement in and support of schooling, feelings of personal safety, optimism about the future, and cultural congruence with the culture of the school.

Such variations must be factored into program planning. In addition to addressing these needs with the students, you can identify topics that you need to address in faculty and parent workshops and consultation sessions.

Designing the Desired Building-Level Program

Armed with the district's model for a properly balanced and comprehensive guidance and counseling program, with data regarding their students' and other clients' needs, and with concrete information about the design of their current guidance and counseling program, the building guidance staff, with the assistance of the local school–community advisory committee, must now design their desired building guidance and counseling program. The vi-

Table 6.6
Teacher Needs Assessment

1st grade

Student competency: Students will describe how exercise and nutrition affect their mental health.

Teacher need: I need assistance in helping students learn to tell how exercise and eating habits make a difference in how they think, act, and feel.

8th grade

Student competency: Students will analyze effective family relations, their importance, and how they are formed.

Teacher need: I need assistance in helping students learn why good family relations are important and how they are formed.

11th grade

Student competency: Students will evaluate the need for flexibility in their roles and in their choices.

Teacher need: I need assistance in helping students learn to explain the need for flexibility in their roles and in their choices.

sion of the comprehensive guidance and counseling program is made realistic in the buildings through a clearly stated operational definition. The operational definition includes both the qualitative and the quantitative designs and must reflect what is desired tempered by the reality of available resources. It must be written rather than oral, for all the reasons explained heretofore.

The building description of its desired program should include the same parts as does the district program description. There should be a statement of the rationale for the building program, using local needs and demographic data, as described previously, that support its unique design. The assumptions should mirror the district's philosophical statement but, in addition, be localized to incorporate the philosophy of the building and its surrounding community. The program definition should likewise mirror the district's definition but provide specific detail for the desired structure and balance of the program. The competencies students are to attain as a result of participating in the school's guidance and counseling program need to be listed. Following the district-established minimum expectations, the building design needs to spell out the following for each component of the delivery system:

- *definition:* purpose and characteristics
- *clients served:* identified and prioritized
- *content:* topics and priorities, materials used
- *staff roles:* school counselors and other staff
- *modes of delivery:* basic activities and how they are done
- *scheduling:* such items as how often students benefit and when during the school day or year
- *resources available:* relevant building-established policies and procedures, budget, facilities, equipment; school counselors' time
- *evaluation strategies:* specific to the results students are expected to achieve, the activities of each component that are conducted, and the roles fulfilled by school counselors

As you can see, this basic design is quite lengthy, but its development forces the local planning and designing group to make the operational decisions essential to program implementation. Once this document is developed, it stays in place until a revision is needed. Although 8 to 10 years is the suggested length of time before complete redesign is undertaken, the actual length should be based on such factors as changes in the school's priorities, community, administration, or guidance staff. Annual program plans are also made to incorporate newly identified needs and goals, as discussed further in Chapter 8.

An important consideration in writing the description of the program that is desired for your building is the format you will use to present the program. As you no doubt have gleaned from the preceding discussion, the write-up must be as specific as you can make it, complete with the listing of materials and other resources you will use in program delivery. A committee of school counselors from the various school levels of your district needs to be formed to establish the format to be used by all buildings. Whatever format is chosen (and districts we have worked with have chosen different formats), the format must make sense to the school counselors and to others who will be reading and using the program design. Furthermore, the same format must be used by all buildings so that the quality of programs can be judged and consistency ensured across the district. A format that has been used to summarize program activities is presented in Figure 6.2. This format serves as a vehicle for identifying all activities provided for a certain competency (skill), a specific set of student clients (grade level; developmental, preventive, remedial), or a particular program component. The school counselors have found it a relatively easy and un-

Figure 6.2
Sample Format to Summarize Building-Level Program Activities

Building Name: _____

COMPREHENSIVE GUIDANCE PROGRAM
Identification of Activities

STUDENT SKILL: _____ GRADE LEVEL: _____

Student Need Level: (Circle One)	Developmental	Preventive	Remedial

Program Component: Guidance Curriculum   Individual Student Planning
(Circle One)
                           Responsive Service   System Support

INTENDED OUTCOMES: _____
_____
_____
_____

PROGRAM ACTIVITIES AND RESOURCES:

Activity Title	Resource Materials	Calendar Notations (Date/Length of Activity)

derstandable vehicle for displaying their repertoire of activities. These activities provide the detail behind the yearly program calendar.

Once the program for a building has been written, professional school counselors can work with their administration and faculty to show them what the guidance and counseling program for their building is. The appropriate roles for the school counselors can be clarified. Current activities can be judged as appropriate or inappropriate for the use of school counselors' time. The school counselor–student ratio can be evaluated, and if it is not appropriate, the principal, teachers, parents, and students can be enlisted in the struggle to improve it. Where better procedures are needed for delivering activities, a building team can be charged to develop them. Having established what is desirable, building staff can develop guidance and counseling program budget requests and renovate facilities. With a concretely drawn vision in hand, the building staff, in collaboration with the district staff, can work together to specify and implement the changes needed to attain the desired building program.

With development of the design for each building's desired program, the designing phase of the program development efforts is finished. You are ready to make the transition to program implementation. Before we move on to suggestions for making the transition to the new program, however, it is time to consider ensuring your attention to diversity and expanding the leadership base for the program implementation efforts.

Attend to Diversity

As it was in the previous phases of program development, attending to diversity is important in this phase in which you move from design to implementation. A plan for capitalizing on the rich diversity of a school and district should be a component of every plan for program improvement.

Many schools and districts with which we have worked have identified discrepancies in their levels of service to minority students or to students who were from cultural, ethnic, and economic backgrounds different from those of the school counselors. Gaps in school counselors' multicultural competence were discussed in Chapter 5. Although included in ASCA's (2005) National Standards for Students: Competencies and Indicators as "recognize, accept, and appreciate . . . [and] demonstrate a respect and appreciation for . . . individual differences, . . . ethnic and cultural diversity, . . . [and] recognize and respect differences in various family configurations" (p. 106), content targeted at helping students improve their cross-cultural effectiveness is often overlooked or avoided, no matter what the demographics of the school community are. In addition, we are increasingly aware of the importance of helping minority adolescents develop their ethnic identities (Cavazos-Rehg & DeLucia-Waack, 2009). Goals for filling in these program gaps must be included in the strategic plan for guidance and counseling program change. It has been, however, our experience that every community is culturally different from every other community; thus, at the district level diversity might be recognized globally, but each building and school community should be very specific about how its guidance and counseling program will be culturally responsive.

It is the guidance and counseling program district- and building-level counselor leaders' responsibility to scrutinize the district's guidance program framework and building guidance program designs as well as the program improvement plans to ensure attention to the challenges and opportunities afforded by the diversity present in the district's and school's populations. The counseling field may be ahead of other disciplines in recognizing the importance of attending to the diversity of students and helping them to capitalize on the riches that diversity brings, not to suffer from others' ignorance or prejudice—overt or covert.

Professional school counselors are ethically bound to advocate not only for their own programs, and for assisting students' educational, career, personal, and social development, but also for social justice and equity on their campuses (Curry & DeVoss, 2009). Seven strategies for advocating effectively for social justice change offered by Singh, Urbano, Haston, and McMahon (2010) are

1. political savvy;
2. consciousness raising;
3. initiating difficult dialogues;
4. building intentional relationships;
5. teaching students self-advocacy skills;
6. using data for marketing; and
7. educating others about school counselors' role as advocate. (pp. 135–140)

Leading colleagues to explore their own cultural biases and identities is a difficult but essential dialogue. Counselors benefit from its coverage in counseling literature (e.g., Watt et al., 2009). It is imperative that school counselors advocate for creating a climate that is culturally inclusive and socially just.

Expand the Leadership Base

If you are the district guidance and counseling program leader and are approaching implementation of a redesigned districtwide program, you will benefit from expanding your leadership base at this point. To date, leadership has been provided by the school counselors on the steering and school–community advisory committees. In addition, there are other designated leaders of school counselors—the building guidance and counseling program staff leaders (Henderson & Gysbers, 1998)—who have had some responsibility for the program improvement efforts and who will have much more responsibility as you move into program redesign and implementation at the local building level.

At this juncture, the leadership base should be expanded in two ways:

- Increase the number of school counselors developing appropriate program activities.
- Enhance the leadership role of the building-level guidance and counseling program and staff leaders.

By establishing two different categories of leaders, some options are provided in selecting leaders for program development. Thus, the program development leaders are those who assist in districtwide implementation of the new program and develop new program activities; they are the program innovators. The building guidance and counseling program and staff leaders are the managers of the program as implemented in the buildings; they are the program maintainers. They are accountable for program implementation.

The district-level guidance and counseling program and staff leader needs to be cognizant of the strengths and weaknesses of the designated, formal school counselor leaders in the buildings and needs to identify potentially successful program development peer leaders to build a strong leadership team for program implementation. In fact, one of the issues critical to effective comprehensive guidance program implementation identified in the national survey of school guidance and counseling program leaders and practitioners was that of empowering guidance leaders in schools and districts (Henderson & Gysbers, 2002). Clarifications of their roles and of their delegated authority are essential; that is, what are they supposed to do and how are they connected to the organizational structure of the building and of the district? With both sets of leaders in hand, the tasks each group will do then need to be specified, and the leaders have to be trained to do the tasks and must have opportunities to use their designated roles. The efforts they make need to be recognized and reinforced.

Building-Level Guidance and Counseling Program and Staff Leaders

For comprehensive guidance programs to be implemented successfully, leaders must be designated for each building (Henderson & Gysbers, 1998). In anticipation of the positive leadership that will be needed from them, they need to have their roles enhanced and supported. As just mentioned, the program and staff leaders in each building may already be in place, so identifying them is not a challenge, but becoming familiar with their operational style may be. Moreover, because the district guidance and counseling program and staff leader (Henderson & Gysbers, 1998) has the chance to participate in the selection of new building leaders, he or she needs to work diligently and skillfully with principals to ensure the selection of individuals who are aligned with the new program. In our experience, building principals want someone who will be loyal to them and to their school, but they will leave the assessment of the individual candidates' guidance and counseling expertise to the district guidance and counseling program and staff leader. Principals also want someone who will provide good leadership to the building program and who will work to make their building program the best in the district.

If you are the district guidance and counseling program and staff leader and you have not already begun to assist the building-level leaders to fulfill their roles more fully, you should begin at this time. Many districts with which we have worked have not spelled out their responsibilities. If your district does not have a specific job description for building guidance and counseling program and staff leaders, one needs to be developed. If you are starting from scratch, you may want to consider the job description developed in Northside Independent School District and provided in Figure 6.3. We suggest, however, that you begin the development of their job description with the building-level leaders themselves. By being asked what they do that is unique to their role, they not only develop an investment in the job description but also begin thinking of themselves as different from and leaders of the campus staff. They need to be identified as the on-campus program managers and supervisors of the guidance staff.

Once responsibilities are specified, you need to assist guidance and counseling program and staff leaders to develop the skills they need to carry them out. If they are not in-

Figure 6.3
Building Guidance Program Staff Leader Job Description

Title:	*Building Guidance Program and Staff Leader*
Primary Functions:	As a member of guidance department staff, fulfill the role of school counselor as described in the position guides; as the leader of the guidance department, effect the continuous improvement of the guidance program and personnel performance.
Major Job Responsibilities:	1. Implement the campus comprehensive guidance and counseling program and specifically provide services to meet the special needs of his/her caseload. 2. Administer the campus guidance program. 3. Lead the guidance department staff. 4. Contribute to the development of the district's guidance program, policies, and procedures. 5. Provide leadership to buildingwide goals and practices in cooperation with building administrators.
Key Duties:	1. *Implement the campus comprehensive guidance and counseling program and specifically provide services to meet the special needs of his/her caseload:* please refer to the appropriate level position guide. 2. *Administer the campus guidance program:* Lead the development and implementation of the campus guidance program consistent with the district and school goals and objectives; prepare request for and use allocation of department budget; conduct campus guidance department meetings; represent the guidance department to the administration and to other department coordinators; supervise the maintenance of student records and other guidance department procedures. 3. *Lead the guidance department staff:* Supervise the department staff; assist the principal and director of guidance in observations and evaluations of staff; assist the principal in selection of new counselors; assist the principal and director of guidance in providing staff development programs. 4. *Contribute to the development of the district guidance program, policies, and procedures:* Represent the campus staff at the district building guidance program and staff leader meetings; communicate and promote implementation of district policies and procedures. 5. *Provide leadership to buildingwide goals and practices in cooperation with building administrators:* Participate as a member of building leadership teams; assist in the development of schoolwide policies and workable procedures; provide input to and from the guidance department and the administration; cooperate with administration in mutually relevant program efforts and student cases.
Organizational Relationships:	Is supervised by the principal and the director of guidance; supervises and coordinates the work of department staff, professional and paraprofessional; collaborates with administration; cooperates with district and campus instructional staff leaders.
Performance Standards:	A building guidance program and staff leader's performance is considered satisfactory when 1. the principal and director of guidance concur and the building guidance program and staff leader's level of competence is reflected as such on the Northside Independent School District Building Guidance Program and Staff Leader Evaluation Form; and 2. evaluation of the Annual Guidance Program Plan indicates overall effectiveness of the program.

ternalizing the new program concept, you need to help them do that. You can help them through programmatic discussions in regularly scheduled meetings and by modeling for them during building-level school counselor staff meetings. They, too, want to do the best job they can, and they can benefit from a role model.

Because of the lack of specialized training for building guidance and counseling program and staff leaders and the dearth of literature on the subject, guidance and counseling program and staff leaders probably need in-service education and training on the staff leadership aspects of their jobs, including supervision, and the effective use of power. This is discussed in more depth in Chapter 9. Eleven essential leadership skills were identified in the examples of leaders who successfully resolved critical issues (Henderson & Gysbers, 2002):

1. Be sensitive and responsive to others' needs.
2. Accept reality.
3. Be open to and accepting of others.
4. Build rapport with others.
5. Communicate and collaborate with others.
6. Maintain the integrity of your professional value/belief system.
7. Accept responsibility for what is yours.
8. Accept the consequences of your actions.
9. Develop and make good use of support systems and the resources available to you.
10. Recognize that we are all works-in-progress.
11. Set improvement goals and plan how to achieve them. (p. 256)

Particularly critical to making optimum use of the program's resources is a team approach to program implementation. Teams do not just happen; they have to be created and nurtured. Guidance program staff leaders should be trained in this important leadership dimension. Regularly held staff meetings are essential, because they provide opportunities for empowering individuals and the group as a whole and for team maintenance as well as for accomplishing program-related tasks, communicating information, and carrying out departmental business. In addition, most building guidance and counseling program and staff leaders we have worked with have sought help in learning such basic skills as how to conduct effective meetings, provide constructive criticism, build a team, and help staff set appropriate goals.

If the district is large enough, or if there are neighboring districts or schools with which to cooperate, the building guidance and counseling program and staff leaders enjoy providing a support system for each other, that is, being a team of their own. This provides them with a support group that serves to enhance their growth as building leaders. They need to be supported as they try out new strategies and carry out leadership assignments. As discussed previously, they should be held accountable for the on-campus discussions of the district program framework and other topics related to the new program. As districtwide mandates are given for implementing new program activities, building-level guidance and counseling program and staff leaders should be held accountable for seeing that they are performed.

The building guidance and counseling program and staff leaders will need to have their authority supported in their newly defined roles. As they supervise and monitor their staff members, their leadership must be recognized, and the central office guidance and counseling program leader should model this recognition for the school counselors. Building-level leaders' effectiveness will mirror the amount of authority that is delegated to them.

In this area, the principal's role is also key. The principals want their department heads to be effective; it makes the principals' job easier. The more work that is done collaboratively between guidance and counseling leaders and their principals, the clearer the counselor leaders' responsibilities for campus program operation becomes.

It is the district-level counselor leader's responsibility to help building-level leaders acknowledge and use all seven of their power bases well: legitimate (delegated authority), information (information conduit between district and building and between school administration and counseling), expert (counseling experience), referent (relationship building experience), connection (with the broader school community), reward (recognition), and coercive (performance evaluator; Henderson, 2009).

Districtwide Program Development Leaders

Depending on the size of the district and the representation on the steering committee, it is probable that the number of program development leaders will need to be expanded by involving more school counselors as improved program implementation approaches. Program development leaders should be chosen from school counselors who are visibly supportive of the new program directions, have enough vision to be able to anticipate the benefits of the improved program, are either informal or formal leaders of other school counselors, and are creative innovators.

To identify these new innovative leaders, the steering committee school counselors should be consulted. They need to feel comfortable with the additions to their group because they have responsibility for bringing these new leaders on board and working with them. Their recommendations do not have to be binding, but their thoughts and concerns need to be attended to. Again, it depends on the size of the district, but even in reasonably small districts school counselors may not know each other from one building to the next. The people with primary responsibility for the program development efforts are the ones with the broader perspective.

After identifying the school counselors who are going to be brought onto the program development leadership team, you must take time to ensure that they feel comfortable in their understanding of the comprehensive program concept. That they were selected because of their initial understanding and support of the new concepts helps, and although initiation does not take a great amount of time, it does need to be done. At the same time, the expanded group needs to be built into a cohesive team of workers. This is accomplished by clarifying the roles and tasks that they need to carry out. The model that worked effectively in Northside Independent School District was to develop subgroups of experts for each component; that is, subcommittees were formed for each component—a guidance curriculum committee, an individual student planning committee, a responsive services committee, and a system support committee. Each committee had representation from each of the school levels—elementary, middle or junior, and high school. Thus, the total group could also be divided by level grouping, which was later useful for developing certain activities. A major responsibility of each committee was being the voice of its particular component to their colleagues.

A task for the committees to accomplish that is a good place to start is coordinating the collection of current practices that are examples of implementation of the various components. For instance, the curriculum committee collects sample guidance lessons and units that assist students at various grade levels to reach the priority competencies; the individual student planning committee collects samples of activities that help students develop personalized educational or career plans; and the responsive services committee collects samples of exemplary counseling, consulting, and referral practices. When compiled, these collections become resource guides for all school counselors to use as they refine their programs.

The program development leadership team then has the data it needs to become truly expert in the implementation of the components at their school levels. After being trained in the component definitions and after reviewing and selecting the multiple exemplary practices, the team is equipped to disseminate these ideas to colleagues. We have also found that they too benefit from training in leadership skills so that they can present themselves as peer leaders. The more the team members are used as leaders, the more depth their role takes on. If they are collecting materials for resource guides, let them plan the guide formats and their own processes for collecting the materials and for acknowledging other school counselors who are taking strides in the new direction. Provide them the opportunities they need to communicate with their colleagues; that is, call meetings as they need them, support their efforts with the rest of the school counselors, and so on. They operate from the power that is delegated to them; this delegation must be clear to the total group of school counselors. They, too, are well served by acknowledging using the various power bases they have (expert, referent, information, connection, reward).

Resource guide development is not the only task that a program leadership team can take on. As you approach implementation of the new program, many innovative or pilot efforts will need to be tried. Such efforts might be writing a curriculum, experimenting with new activities, or developing a recommended protocol for a campus response to a student suicide. Program leaders might take on the responsibility for designing the district's staff development plan. Whatever the project, the same principles apply. The team leaders' task needs to be given distinctly, their expertise developed carefully, and their authority recognized clearly.

If motivated and professionally committed individuals have been selected, and if they have been given meaningful tasks to do, they will be working hard at something that their colleagues may still be dubious about. It is imperative that their work and their worth be reinforced. Rewards for professionals, according to Hurst (1984, p. 84), may come from any of six motivators: "Achievement (what you believe you did), Recognition (what others think you did), Work itself (what you really do), Responsibility (what you help others do), Advancement (what you think you can do), Growth (what you believe you might do)." Program leaders feel a sense of achievement in completing each task that is part of their charge, for example, when the position statements or resource guides are published. They receive recognition by their very selection as a program leader, and this is maintained as they present new concepts and ideas to their peers. We have found that encouraging team leaders to make presentations at local, state, and national professional growth conferences not only is good for the emerging leaders but also helps others learn from what they are doing. If the new program leaders have been selected as we suggested from the ranks of those who believe in the new program concept, the work they do to better understand the new program and to help implement it is rewarding to them. If part of their charge is to help their colleagues learn about and implement new program strategies, the leaders are vitally responsible for the successful implementation of the program and for the effective performance of the rest of the counseling staff. Program leaders can be helped to feel like leaders and to envision themselves as the building-level guidance and counseling program and staff leaders and guidance supervisors and administrators of the future. Program innovators with whom we have worked consistently talk about how much they are learning from their experiences; they are eager to grow and find new opportunities, such as program improvement, as fuel for their own professional development.

District-Level Guidance and Counseling Program Leader Roles and Responsibilities

This phase of the guidance and counseling program improvement project results in a shift in overt leadership from the steering committee and the school–community advisory committee to the guidance and counseling program leaders. If you are the district-level guidance and counseling program leader, the district master plan for program improvement becomes the responsibility of your office. You are also responsible for helping building staff plan their improved programs. You have program management and administrative tasks as well as staff leadership and supervision tasks to accomplish. You also need to be clear about how much of the new design can be implemented with the currently available resources. Expectations for immediate change must be realistic.

As in the prior phases, you must, as the guidance and counseling leader, continue to be the prime mover. Although we describe the process as though tasks are done one at a time, in reality many activities go on simultaneously. For example, while you are developing the master plan, you will also be helping buildings assess their current program, and you will be training your new leaders and providing supervision training to building-level leaders. Again, it is up to you to keep each part of the project moving along a constructive course. You must use every opportunity to positively reinforce the individual change efforts professional school counselors make. You are probably the only individual in the district who sees the whole picture, although by this time the expanded program leadership team and the building-level leaders are beginning to see a lot of it, too, provided you keep them informed.

In all likelihood, there are some tasks in this project phase that only you can do. You need to compile and present the discrepancy data, that is, display the data and note the conclusions. You need to maintain an open discussion climate as staff members brainstorm ideas for discrepancy reduction. You need to write the district master plan and select and train the coleaders. You need to be prepared to use the expanded or redirected resources that begin to flow to the guidance department as soon as the steering committee makes its recommendations for changes. If ratios improve, you will be hiring more school counselors, and your selection criteria must be tailored to identify those who will fit into the new program. If your department receives a higher budget allocation, you need to be prepared to spend it. If you are allowed facility improvements, you need to have your blueprints ready. If school counselors' contracts are extended, you need to have your in-service training or program development activities ready to implement. This is the part of the project that is most fun, but it also presents challenges to you.

By now many of those with whom you work, including fellow administrators as well as school counselors, are beginning to get the program concept. This, too, is exciting, but you may find that some of the school counselors become frustrated because they have not yet been freed of all the undesirable nonguidance activities and the administrators become frustrated that school counselors are not yet seeing all of their students more often. Some counselors do not yet understand that the emerging program constitutes their whole job; it is not something that is added on to all of their previous duties. Some are concerned about change and are fearful about how the changed program will affect their day-to-day work (Poynton, Schumacher, & Wilczenski, 2008). You need to transform these frustrations into the energies that will cause the needed changes. The will to overcome the inertia simply to maintain the current program as it is comes from being dissatisfied with the current status, having a vision of how the situation could be better, and believing that the benefits you will reap when the vision becomes reality outweigh the anticipated costs of changing.

As they come to more fully understand and feel comfortable with the improved program model, the school counselors and principals feel empowered to make the needed changes. Empowerment comes from having knowledge and information, the support of others, and leadership. In the process we are recommending, the vision of the desired program and the data gathered in assessing your current program provide the knowledge and information. The support of other stakeholders in the school community comes through soliciting others' input and advice, such as surveys and advisory committees. The leadership is provided by the district model and by the committed leaders you are nurturing. Ultimately, all school counselors become leaders of change because they have the guidance expertise and they are the biggest stakeholders in the program. Helping them find the courage they need to use their assertiveness skills appropriately is your responsibility.

Your Progress Check

At this point, you have developed plans for and taken steps toward implementing an improving guidance and counseling program.

Program Development Process

You have learned in light of the comprehensive guidance program model

- what objective data clarifies is currently in place in your program that fits the model; does not fit; and what is missing, underdone, or overdone;
- what others perceive is good, missing, or underdone and what currently takes too many program resources.

You have continued the program development process by

- specifying goals and making recommendations for moving forward toward the desired program;
- assigning priorities for making needed systemic, incremental, and ongoing changes and improvements;
- clarifying action steps for accomplishing changes;
- developing a master plan for developing needed resources.

Expanded Focus

Building-level site teams have

- assessed their current program status in light of the district program model;
- assessed or perceived met and unmet student needs and school community goals;
- designed their desired programs;
- operationally defined the activity components for their programs;
- written and published their design and definitions.

You have expanded the leadership base for

- continuing to advance the districtwide program through innovative program development;

- developing and managing building-level guidance and counseling programs and staff members.

You probably will—and possibly should—feel at this point that you are constantly swimming upstream, explaining rationale, and defending recommendations, but each constructive change begets another. Ultimately, the momentum for change takes over. At this time, you are moving into the implementation phase of the program improvement project.

References

Adelman, H. S., & Taylor, L. (2003). On sustainability of project innovations as systemic change. *Journal of Educational and Psychological Consultations, 14*(1), 1–25.

American School Counselor Association. (2005). *The ASCA National Model: A framework for school counseling programs* (2nd ed.). Alexandria, VA: Author.

Campbell, C. A., & Dahir, C. A. (1997). *Sharing the vision: The national standards for school counseling programs.* Alexandria, VA: American School Counselor Association.

Cavazos-Rehg, P. A., & DeLucia-Waack, J. L. (2009). Education, ethnic identity, and acculturation as predictors of self-esteem in Latino adolescents. *Journal of Counseling & Development, 87,* 47–54.

Curry, J. R., & DeVoss, J. A. (2009). Introduction to special issue: The school counselor as leader. *Professional School Counseling, 13,* 64–67.

Gray, K., Elsner, D., & Poynton, T. (2004). *Study of pupil personnel ratios, services, and programs in California* (School Counseling Research Brief 2.4). Amherst: University of Massachusetts, Center for School Counseling Outcome Research. Retrieved from http://www.umass.edu/schoolcounseling/uploads/Research_Brief_2-4.pdf

Henderson, P. (2009). *The new handbook of administrative supervision in counseling.* New York, NY: Routledge.

Henderson, P. (2010). Recommendations. In *Evaluation of the _____ independent school district comprehensive, developmental guidance and counseling program.* Unpublished report, San Antonio, TX.

Henderson, P., & Gysbers, N. C. (1998). *Leading and managing your school guidance program staff.* Alexandria, VA: American Counseling Association.

Henderson, P., & Gysbers, N. (Eds.). (2002). *Implementing comprehensive school guidance programs: Critical leadership issues and successful responses.* Greensboro, NC: CAPS.

Hurst, D. K. (1984). Of boxes, bubbles, and effective management. *Harvard Business Review, 62,* 78–88.

Janson, C. (2010). High school counselors' views of their leadership behaviors: A Q methodology study. *Professional School Counseling, 13,* 86–97.

Lapan, R., Gysbers, N., & Kayson, M. (2007). *Missouri school counselors benefit all students: How implementing comprehensive guidance programs improves academic achievement for all Missouri students.* Jefferson City: Missouri Department of Elementary and Secondary Education, Division of Career Education.

Lee, S. M., Daniels, M. H., Puig, A., Newgent, R.A., & Nam, S.K. (2008). A data-based model to predict postsecondary educational attainment of low-socioeconomic status students. *Professional School Counseling, 11,* 306–316.

Martin, I., Carey, J., & DeCoster, K. (2009). A national study of the current status of state school counseling models. *Professional School Counseling, 12,* 378–386.

McEachern, A. G., Oyaziwo, A., & Kenny, M. C. (2008). Emotional abuse in the classroom: Implications and interventions for counselors. *Journal of Counseling & Development, 86,* 3–10.

North Carolina Department of Public Instruction. (n.d.). *How North Carolina school counselors spend their time*. Retrieved from http://www.ncpublicschools.org/docs/curriculum/guidance/resources/programofstudy/schoolcounselor.pdf

Northside Independent School District. (1986). *Comprehensive guidance program framework*. San Antonio, TX: Author.

Poynton, T. A., Schumacher, R. A., & Wilczenski, L. (2008). School counselors' attitudes regarding statewide comprehensive developmental guidance model implementation. *Professional School Counseling, 11*, 417–422.

Rylander, C. K. (2002). *Guiding our children toward success: How Texas school counselors spend their time*. Austin, TX: Office of the Comptroller.

Scarborough, J. L., & Culbreth, J. L. (2008). Examining discrepancies between actual and preferred practice of school counselors. *Journal of Counseling & Development, 86*, 446–459.

Shillingford, M. A., & Lambie, G. W. (2010). Contribution of professional school counselors' values and leadership practices to their programmatic service delivery. *Professional School Counseling, 13*, 201–217.

Singh, A. A., Urbano, A., Haston, M., & McMahon, E. (2010). School counselors' strategies for social justice change: A grounded theory of what works in the real world. *Professional School Counseling, 13*, 135–145.

Texas Education Agency. (2004). *A model comprehensive, developmental guidance and counseling program for Texas public schools: A guide for program development, pre-K–12th grade* (4th ed.). Austin, TX: Author.

Texas Education Code. (2001). *Chapter 33, service programs and extra-curricular activities; Subchapter A, school counselors and counseling programs*. Retrieved from http://www.statutes.legis.state.tx.us/Docs/ED/ED.33.htm

Thompson, D. W., Loesch, L. C., & Seraphine, A. E. (2003). Development of an instrument to assess the counseling needs of elementary school students. *Professional School Counseling, 7*(1), 35–39.

Vandegrift, J. A. (1999). *Are Arizona public schools making the best use of school counselors? Results of a 3-year study of counselors' time use* (Arizona School to Work Briefing Paper No. 16). Tempe: Arizona State University, Morrison Institute for Public Policy.

Watt, S. K., Curtis, G. C., Drummond, J., Kellogg, A. H., Lozano, A., Nicoli, G. T., & Rosas, M. (2009). Privileged identity exploration: Examining counselor trainees' reactions to difficult dialogues. *Counselor Education and Supervision, 49*, 86–105.

Whiston, S. C., & Aricak, O. T. (2008). Development and initial investigation of the School Counseling Program Evaluation Scale. *Professional School Counseling, 11*, 253–259.

❧ Part III ❧

Implementing

Chapter 7

Making Your Transition to a Comprehensive Guidance and Counseling Program

Implementing—Making the Transition

- Develop the personnel, financial, and political resources needed for full program implementation.
- Focus on special projects.
- Facilitate building-level changes.
- Implement public relations activities.

☞ Having organized for change, adopted a comprehensive guidance and counseling program model, assessed the current program, established the design for the desired program, and planned the transition, you, as the guidance and counseling program leader, are now ready to make the transition to an improved program. You are also ready to develop mechanisms to maintain the program once it is in operation. This phase is one of the most critical of the entire program improvement process. The questions to be answered include, "How is the transition to a comprehensive guidance and counseling program to be made?" "What new resources are needed to enhance the effectiveness and efficiency of the program?" "Are there special projects that will provide impetus to the needed changes in direction?" "How can district and building program leaders improve guidance and counseling programs in each building?"

In this chapter, we first discuss the tasks involved in implementing the master plan for change and present recommendations concerning the staffing patterns and financial and political resources required to operate a comprehensive guidance and counseling program. The change strategy of focusing on special projects is then introduced. Attaching the guidance and counseling program improvement process to federal, state, and local priorities can provide the energy, motivation, and support to carry the overall improvement process to completion. Next, we describe how to institute districtwide systems that facilitate building-level changes and how to collaborate with building-level leaders to support their program development efforts. We also present ideas about planning and implementing, with district leadership, public relations activities to make sure that students, teachers, parents, administrators, and the public at large are aware of the remodeled and revitalized comprehensive guidance and counseling program. Next, we focus on methods for attending to the diversity in the district and buildings. Finally, we delineate the roles and responsibilities of guidance and counseling program leaders in the transition process.

Make Efficient Use of Personnel, Financial, and Political Resources

In developing the master plan for system-level resource development, the guidance and counseling program leader, with the help of the guidance steering committee, identified the major tasks that needed to be done, developed an order for doing them, and identified people who would be involved in accomplishing them. Plans of action to accomplish the major tasks might also need to be developed to facilitate the efficiency of those responsible. A plan of action includes several parts: identification of the tasks to be done, the order in which they must be done, the person or people doing them, the time for accomplishing them, and a statement of how you will know they have been done, that is, identification of the end product or result. Table 7.1 presents a sample plan of action from the Northside Independent School District master plan.

The tasks that need to be done, their degree of feasibility, and the specific time frame for each building or district may be different. For example, if the school system is currently into curriculum writing, then resource or curriculum guide development fits right into already established district priorities. If the system's thrust is staff development, then the recommendations for in-service training, job description development or supervision, and performance evaluation improvement might be the most feasible to accomplish. Of course, any systemic improvement of resources requires the support and collaboration of the district and building administrations. The guidance and counseling program leader must continue to work closely with the superintendent and other senior-level administrators and with principals to effect needed changes.

However, some recurrent recommendations need attention for the program actually to change. Ideas that the guidance and counseling program leader might want to consider for the improved use of personnel, financial, and political guidance and counseling program resources as the master plan for change is implemented are included in the following list and explained in detail in this section.

Personnel Resources:

- implementing recommended counselor–student ratios
- developing school counselors' job descriptions
- establishing roles and responsibilities for building-level guidance and counseling program leaders
- developing job descriptions for other staff members working in the guidance and counseling program
- clarifying organizational relationships within the guidance and counseling program

Financial Resources:

- establishing budgets for guidance departments at the district and building levels
- exploring use of nonlocal funding sources
- developing guidance and counseling program component resource guides
- establishing guidance facilities standards and making recommendations for their application

Political Resources:

- updating policies and procedures
- engendering support from building-level counselors, administrators, and teachers
- working with resistant staff members
- working with critical constituents: concerned parents

Table 7.1
Plan of Action

Major Task	Enabling Tasks	Person Responsible	Date to Be Completed	Resources Needed	Comment
Make recommendations regarding extended contracts.	1. Develop questionnaire.	1. Director of guidance	1. March 1	None additional	
	2. Train steering committee counselors and principals to conduct survey with counselors/principals using questionnaire.	2. Director of guidance	2. March 5		
	3. Place on meeting agendas.	3. Steering committee, principals, and counselors	3. March 5		
	4. Make presentation; conduct surveys.	4. Steering committee, principals, and counselors	4. March 6–13		
	5. Tally results by school level (elementary, junior or middle school, high school).	5. Director of guidance	5. March 20		
	6. Prepare report and make recommendations.	6. Director of guidance	6. March 25		

Personnel Resources

As the preceding list indicates, to improve use of personnel resources, you need to consider implementing recommended counselor–student ratios, developing counselors' job descriptions, establishing roles and responsibilities for building-level guidance and counseling program leaders, developing job descriptions for other staff members working in the guidance and counseling program, and clarifying organizational relationships within the guidance and counseling program.

Implementing Recommended Counselor–Student Ratios

On the basis of the rationale of the design for the desired program, recommendations have been established for appropriate counselor–student ratios. Ratio improvement, however, is one of the more difficult resource improvements to make for two reasons: It is extremely costly, and there must be some evidence that the counselors already in the system are willing to extend their services to all students. Once that intent has been established and some effort has been applied in that direction, justification for improved ratios is more credible.

As districts with which we have worked have implemented the comprehensive guidance and counseling program more fully, lower ratios have been put in place. Often, the first goal has been to make the ratios more equal across the school levels (i.e., elementary, middle or junior high, and high school). Elementary counselors have been added in rather dramatic numbers in these program development projects. Moreover, many elementary guidance and counseling programs are developmentally based and thus are already closer to the desired program as defined by these districts than are secondary programs, which are still overwhelmed by reactive services—as contrasted with responsive services—and system support or quasi-administrative–clerical tasks (Peer, 1985). No district with which we have worked has stated that counselors as supporters of the system should have top priority in the program; all of the districts have assigned high priority for all school levels to the guidance curriculum and to individual student planning assistance for all students at the middle and high school levels.

It should be clear that the effectiveness of the program is tied directly to the ratio. The number of counselors needed to staff the program depends on the students' and school community's needs and the program goals and design. Thus, the ratio must be sufficient to implement the designed program, or conversely, the program has to be designed within the parameters of the ratio. The larger the counselor's caseload is, the less individual attention students receive; the smaller the load is, the more individual attention is allowed for. The larger the number of students in a caseload who have high-priority needs for responsive services is, the lower the ratios must be. A mechanism for ensuring a match between the design and the ratio and for communicating the impact of the ratio on the realities of service delivery is discussed in more detail in Chapter 8.

In school districts, salary costs often make up more than 80% of the budget. The salary costs associated with dramatic ratio improvements are high, tying this resource improvement to the district's overall financial situation and budget development procedures. The guidance and counseling program leader must present not only the rationale for the recommendations, but also the data that substantiate or project their value to students.

You also need to be prepared to implement the improvement incrementally. Stages of implementation might include extended counselor contracts so that there is more non-student time for them to accomplish some of the indirect services vital to success, such as planning and developing the program, benefiting from staff development activities, or accomplishing some of their system support responsibilities. Some districts have found it more feasible economically to raise existing counselors' salaries, because of increased recognition of their professionalism, than to lower their caseloads. Interim ratio improvements might occur. For example, instead of moving directly from a ratio of one elementary counselor per building to a ratio of 1:350, a 1:450 ratio might be affordable first. A lowered caseload is one of the primary goals of program improvement, but it is one of the most difficult to attain. Thus, we advise you to continue to implement other, more feasible changes while you are working toward that goal rather than waiting until ratios are improved to begin.

Developing School Counselors' Job Descriptions

Identifying the various personnel resources available to the guidance and counseling program brings with it the need to define the roles and functions of the various personnel to ensure appropriate use of their education and talents. The generic job description for all professional school counselors was discussed in Chapter 5 as a means for outlining their primary responsibilities and supporting equivalent job descriptions across the various school levels. In Chapter 8, we suggest a process for specifying each counselor's job description each year by detailing the specific ways each applies their competencies within the yearly program plan (Henderson & Gysbers, 1998). The professional school counselor is trained to fulfill the roles required to deliver the comprehensive guidance and counseling program. (For a summary of their application within the program components, see Chapter 4.)

Most school counselors fulfill comprehensive roles with their students; that is, they provide or are the links to the services needed by the students in their caseloads. Some school counselors may be assigned to carry out special program assignments or to serve special student groups. These special assignments often require additional training and may be tied to special funding sources, as described later in this chapter. Examples of special program assignments include guidance department leadership and crisis team membership. Examples of special student groups that may benefit from additional program services include students in compensatory education, special education, violence and substance abuse prevention programs, or career and technology education. It is essential to efficient implementation of the comprehensive guidance and counseling program that the services provided by such specialist counselors be integrated into the program delivery design. We recommend that job descriptions for these and other full-time, professional members of the guidance staff be developed and that they clearly delineate the organizational relationships among counseling professionals. These counseling positions are often funded or partially funded by the nonguidance programs, so there are specific expectations agreed to in appropriating the money. Thus, specially funded counselors have some prescribed responsibilities to the program that funds them. Their responsibilities to both programs and their placement in the organizational structure need to be clear: They are, first and foremost, school counselors and a part of the comprehensive guidance and counseling program. Their special assignments may also link them with other programs and departments, in which they must also continue to develop their specialty in the specific area; for example, counselors funded from special education funds provide guidance and counseling to students in special education; they need to continue to develop their competence in working with special needs students. Additionally, they need to understand the special education program rules and priorities and be able to interpret those rules to their counselor colleagues.

Establishing Roles and Responsibilities for Building-Level Guidance and Counseling Program Leaders

Key to implementing quality comprehensive guidance and counseling programs in the buildings is appropriate delegation of responsibility and authority to leaders of guidance departments throughout a district. Their authority can be delegated from both the building principal and the district guidance and counseling program leader. Such delegation must be clearly spelled out and be such that their responsibilities are clearly supported. On a day-today basis, they lead and manage the details of program planning and implementation as well as the quality of school counselors' use of their time and applications of their talent.

The roles that guidance and counseling program leaders fulfill are those of administration, management, supervision, and professional leadership (Henderson & Gysbers, 1998). In their administrative role, they apply their authority over and responsibility to the guidance and counseling program and its staff. They are ultimately accountable for the quality of program delivery and staff performance. In their management role, guidance and counseling program leaders acquire the personnel, material, and political resources needed to implement the program. In their supervisory role, they strive for efficient and effective use of these resources. In their professional leadership role, they assist school counselors to enhance their professionalism through adherence to the standards and the advancement of the school counseling profession.

The responsibilities of guidance and counseling program leaders include carrying out the tasks required in program planning, designing, implementation, and evaluation. Program planning includes projecting and managing such things as the department budget, acquiring and using appropriate program materials, and using the school's facilities. Designing the building guidance and counseling program includes developing the program calendar and assisting the school counselors in developing and adhering to regular schedules. Program implementation entails monitoring and participating in program delivery. Evaluation of the program, its results, and the performance of the school counselors and other program staff members requires their leadership. Building guidance and counseling program leaders also advocate for the guidance and counseling program, its clients, and staff with such groups as the building and district administrators, local site-based decision-making groups, teachers, parents, and other community representatives.

By far the largest resource provided to guidance and counseling programs in schools is that of the school counselor staff. Helping them to carry out their roles and responsibilities with the highest level of professionalism is critical to excellent program implementation (Gysbers & Henderson, 1997). Leadership of school counselors as staff members entails establishing and maintaining healthy and productive work climates. Leaders carry out the tasks required in implementation of the district's system for enhancing school counselors' performance. They help each school counselor define his or her job for the year, assess his or her levels of professionalism, and set goals and implement plans for enhancing his or her professional maturity. Building guidance and counseling program leaders provide professionally appropriate supervision to school counselors and evaluate their performance (Henderson & Gysbers, 1998).

Developing Job Descriptions for Other Staff Members Working in the Guidance and Counseling Program

More concise guidance and counseling program–related role statements and job descriptions need to be in place for others working in the guidance and counseling program. Some of these staff members might be full time, such as licensed professional counselors, social workers, parent involvement and education specialists, guidance department clerical help, or paraprofessionals. In many of the districts with which we have worked, insufficient use has been made of support staff, because of either understaffing or underuse of existing staff. Underuse is often the result of incomplete statements of job responsibilities. (Sample job descriptions for career center technicians and high school registrars are included in Appendix E.) Clear job descriptions allow others to recognize the importance or complexity of guidance department paraprofessionals' responsibilities, particularly as they assume the nonguidance tasks previously done by professional school counselors. Such descriptions have led to upgraded pay classifications and extended contracts.

Some staff members augment the guidance and counseling program as part of their responsibilities, such as teachers, administrators, and related specialists, including school psychologists or diagnosticians, community volunteers, and peer counselors. Although these job descriptions will not be as extensive as those for full-time staff members, they are just as important because they are the vehicle for ensuring that program delivery is coordinated and carried out by a cohesive staff team.

Not only do the roles and responsibilities of others need to be spelled out, but they also need to be appropriate to their training and competence. Personnel without school counselor certification should be trained to carry out their roles in the comprehensive guidance and counseling program. For example, teachers should be trained to be advisers; community representatives, to be mentors; and parent volunteers, to be parent liaisons. Individuals without school counselor certification should not be used in place of certified professional school counselors but rather should augment the services provided by school counselors (American School Counselor Association [ASCA], 2006). All staff members assisting in the delivery of the guidance and counseling program should adhere to the ethical and legal standards of the counseling profession. Key standards are those regarding students' and parents' rights and confidentiality.

Remember that job definition is prerequisite to any staff expansion, particularly if staff members with new job titles are to be added. It is through job task analysis and the development of related job descriptions that the functions of proposed new staff members can be delineated separately from those of existing staff. Such delineation supports the rationale for the new positions.

Clarifying Organizational Relationships Within the Guidance and Counseling Program

After clarifying the roles and expectations of each category of staff members in the delivery of the comprehensive guidance and counseling program, your next step is clarifying the organizational relationships between the counselors and the other professionals who augment the program or whose services dovetail with it and among the guidance department staff in a building.

Caseload Assignments: Team Approach. In implementing the guidance and counseling program, it is important to recognize that counselors are members of four teams. They are an integral part of the instructional team, along with teachers, administrators, and other education specialists, in implementing the developmental components of the program. They are an integral part of the school and district special services team, along with school psychologists, social workers, nurses, and administrators, in responding to the special needs of some students and parents. Counselors also form teams with community representatives who collaborate with the schools, specifically the business and the mental health communities, to augment the program. Perhaps most important, counselors from each school level and each building are part of the guidance team, working together to articulate and improve programs systemwide.

Clarifying who the team members are and respecting the roles that each member plays and the systems that each operates within are prerequisites to effective teamwork. Mutual design of the way teams operate contributes to efficient operation. For example, there is renewed interest in using the schools to integrate public health and human services provided to children, youth, and families. Coalitions of related professionals must meet and have open dialogue to determine how such integration will work. At the national level, the American Counseling Association (ACA) and ASCA represent school counselors in the National Alliance of Pupil Services Organizations. This coalition "promotes interdisciplinary practice and collaboration and advocates for ensuring access to quality pupil services for all students" (National Alliance of Pupil Services Organizations, 2007, para. 3). In addition to ACA and ASCA, National Alliance of Pupil Services Organizations members include organizations representing school nurses, teachers, occupational therapists, physical therapists, school psychologists, school social workers, special educators, speech–language pathologists, audiologists, and therapeutic recreation specialists as well as art, music, and dance therapists; administrators of pupil services programs; and parents. Although defining how collaboration occurs is a local challenge, a commitment to work together is a major step.

Implementation of the comprehensive guidance and counseling program as it is defined and designed is the guidance department's responsibility. Our opinion is that personnel without school counselor certification who are active participants in program delivery should do so under the supervision of professional school counselors.

Caseload Assignment: Staffing Patterns. Within a guidance department staff, the organizational patterns for operation need to be clearly established. "School counselor assignments seem to be a critical issue that can impact the effectiveness, efficiency, and equity of counseling service to students" (Akos, Schuldt, & Walendin, 2009, p. 27). Across the United States, there is wide variation in size of guidance department staffs. On the one hand, a large, urban high school might have 10 to 15 counselors, including comprehensive school counselors and specialist counselors, and six or more support staff, such as registrar, career center technician, counselors' secretary, data processing clerk, and a scheduling assistant. On the other hand, it is not unusual for one counselor to serve the elementary, middle or junior high, and high schools in a small, rural community. In this case, the definition of guidance staff must include the administrators, teachers, and support staff at each of the schools. Regardless of the number of staff involved, some organizational keys apply universally to enhancing healthy interprofessional and interpersonal relationships, which, in turn, affect program quality.

Caseload assignments for staff members need to be supported by a rationale relevant to the program design that is appropriate to each person's program responsibilities, training, and specialization. The question "What is the 'best' way for comprehensive school counselors to divvy up students into their caseloads?" still arises. Some of the options in use are dividing students by grade level, alphabetically by surname, by teacher, or, for specialists, by their participation in special programs. Although some research on this topic has begun to appear, more is needed to help school counselors answer this question. "It seems necessary for each school and school counselor to thoughtfully examine the school counselor assignment currently in use and determine what advantages and challenges exist" (Akos et al., 2009, p. 28). As discussed in Chapter 4, the decision about how to divide students among the comprehensive counselors should match the philosophy behind the guidance and counseling program.

1. *Caseload assignments by grade level.* Assigning caseloads by grade level is consistent with a developmental philosophy, thinking of the program in terms of how to best prepare to help students of different ages. This assignment pattern supports a counselor's guidance curriculum or individual student planning services and is often found at the elementary and middle school levels. It also effectively divides regular consultation with teaching and instructional staff among the counselors. This method also entails counselors' consulting with each other about children from the same homes and families who are in different grade levels. Consistency of services for students suggests that a student benefits most from having the same counselor during his or her tenure in the school, making it clear that counselors should move up a school's grade levels as his or her students move. Quality and amount of time available for services also suggest that each comprehensive counselor serve a similar number of students as other comprehensive counselors. One problem with this method of assignment is if the grade levels in a school vary widely in size; for example, in

many high schools there are many more ninth graders than 12th graders. Another issue is that if a district or school adds one additional counselor, how, then, do the grade levels of children become evenly divided; for example, if a middle school serves three grades of similar size (e.g., sixth, seventh, and eighth grade) and has four counselors, what is a logical caseload assignment for the fourth counselor? Typically, more than one of the grade levels is split up among the counselors. It can then be awkward for students, parents, and others to decipher who the counselor is for a particular student.

2. *Caseload assignments by surname.* Assigning students to counselors on the basis of the students' last name often reflects an emphasis on responding to students' needs and issues within knowledge of their family context. This often enhances the quality of a counselor's responsive services. Although not all children from the same home bear the same last names, many do. Working with siblings and parents over time provides counselors with increased information about the issues and assets of the child's home environment. It also supports the team approach to guidance and counseling program delivery, because developmental activities provided for each grade level are a shared responsibility among all counselors. It also dictates that all counselors consult consistently with all of the teachers and other instructional staff.

3. *Caseload assignments by teachers.* Caseload assignment for counselors according to groups of teachers focuses on the system support component. It emphasizes the counselors' role of helping teachers improve their work with individual students and groups of students and in their classrooms. It may facilitate implementation of counselors' classroom-based, developmental guidance activities. A large disadvantage is that students change counselors each year as their teachers change, minimizing consistency of counselors' services and demanding even more time in counselor-to-counselor consultation. It is also difficult for parents—and students, for that matter—to know who their children's counselors are each year.

4. *Special responsibilities.* Any special responsibilities need to be clearly stated and understood by other staff members. The department leader should be designated the authority to manage the program and staff (Henderson & Gysbers, 1998), including the capability to mediate between staff members when necessary. Intradepartmental rules need to be established to facilitate coordination and cooperation. For example, if two or more counselors provide services to the same student, the responsibilities, methods, and standards need to be spelled out to ensure that such services are conducted with the best interests of the student in mind. If teachers have the responsibility for contacting parents regarding their child's school-related problems and recommended solutions, the responsibilities and methods for ensuring that all staff members working with a student have the information they need must be spelled out. Staff meetings need to be held regularly to ensure open communication among staff members, coordinate program planning, and do the necessary problem solving (Henderson & Gysbers, 1998).

Although decisions about the best counselor staffing pattern are made at the local level, there are documented advantages to staying with students over time. For example, as cited in Akos et al. (2009), Hegde and Cassidy (2004) and Little and Dacus (1999) identified such advantages as "stability of care, increased understanding of children's needs, better relationships between [school staff] and parents, and easier transitions" (p. 27). In addition, Nichols and Nichols (1999, as cited in Akos et al., 2009) found that "both students and parents were more positive about their experience at school, had an increased sense of intimacy, and showed an increase in reported student motivation" (p. 27) as a result of such arrangements. Akos et al. studied counselors' perceptions of the advantages and disadvantages of counselor assignment patterns in use in middle and high schools: grade-level looping, grade-level static, and by surname.

Financial Resources

To improve use of financial resources, consider establishing budgets for guidance departments at the district and building levels, exploring use of nonlocal funding sources, developing guidance and counseling program component resource guides, and establishing guidance facility standards and making recommendations for their application.

Establishing Budgets for Guidance Departments at the District and Building Levels

In the assessment of the current program, one of the tasks was to review the financial resources available. In the review, you may have found that the financial resources were described in terms of a well-defined budget in which all of the money spent on guidance, including salaries, was part of the budget. Or you may have found that only money for such items as testing materials and a few other guidance resources was included. Or perhaps there was no budget at all. Within the budget policy guidelines for the school/district, the task is to establish a budget. To do that, consider such major categories as those displayed in Table 7.2.

Table 7.2
Budget Categories

I. *Personnel salaries and benefits*
   A. Counselors
   B. Secretarial and clerical
   C. Guidance administrators
II. *Program development*
   A. Curriculum development
   B. Local materials development
   C. Pilot projects
III. *Materials acquisition*
   A. Student materials
      1. Texts and workbooks
      2. Audiovisual materials
      3. Testing materials
      4. Reference materials
      5. Career and guidance center materials
      6. Assessment materials
   B. Professional resource materials
      1. Professional library books
      2. Journal subscriptions
      3. Training materials
   C. Supplies
      1. Office supplies
      2. Computer-assisted guidance equipment supplies
      3. Instructional supplies
IV. *Capital outlay*
   A. Furniture
   B. Equipment and maintenance
V. *Professional development*
   A. Meetings and conferences
      1. Registration
      2. Expenses
   B. Consultants
VI. *Office expenses*
   A. Telephone
   B. Postage
   C. Fax
VII. *Research and evaluation*

Prerequisite to any resource expansion is ascertaining the cost of implementing the recommendations. The guidance and counseling program leader needs to develop a cost analysis for each item for inclusion in the district department budget or in other budget categories if that is where an item fits. The total amount, presented all at once, could be overwhelming, so our advice is to prepare these cost analyses on an item-by-item basis. Thus, as each recommendation is brought forward for consideration, the guidance and counseling program leader can present the dollar figures associated with it. For example, if implementing the improved ratios recommended entails adding counselors to the staff, it is the guidance and counseling program leader's responsibility to know how much those additional staff positions will cost. Having specific cost information available allows the guidance and counseling program leader to anticipate others' concerns about the increased expenditures and to be prepared to defend the allocation of additional dollars.

Exploring Use of Nonlocal Funding Sources

A majority of the funds for the program probably comes from local and state regular education sources. There are, however, funds from other sources. Federal legislation is one source. Federal funds available to augment the comprehensive guidance and counseling program include those that support career and technology education, special education, compensatory education, bilingual and migrant education, and those that address special topics of national priority such as alcohol and drug abuse, safety, social skills development, college and career readiness, attendance, graduation rates, and obesity. Federal employment and training legislation may also have guidance funds available for schools.

Most federal funds are distributed by the state department of education. If the guidance and counseling program leader is not already familiar with these sources, a visit with the state's guidance consultants should be a rewarding experience. They will be able to tell you about federal and state monies that may be available for guidance and counseling programs. Although many states have still not solved the problem of adequate school financing, many states have established guidance-relevant priorities.

Keep in mind that most federal or state sources do not usually fund an entire program. Rather, they provide supplemental or additional support for target populations or facilitate achievement of their program objectives, such as counseling disadvantaged or substance-abusing students, augmenting a career center, or implementing a career assessment program. Most of the time, access to these funds is through a proposal or the development of a written plan. With the comprehensive program already designed, such a proposal or plan is readily developed because the program context and student needs have already been established. The proposal writer has to extract only the portions of the total program that are of interest to the funding source to present the plan.

Developing Guidance and Counseling Program Component Resource Guides

A major task in making the transition to a comprehensive guidance and counseling program is to choose the guidance activities and materials that will assist students to develop the competencies that have been decided on. Basing the work on sound ideas and research-based concepts and materials is one key to having good-quality activities through which the program is implemented and the identified desired results are achieved. Galassi and Akos (2004) identified examples of some bases on which to build your program's specifics, including strengths-based approaches that support resiliency and the development of competence in students.

Describing the specific activities that make up the program and having adequate program materials are prerequisite to successful implementation of the program. Counselors must have tools to assist them in their changed roles. Whether such guides are written for use in a building's program, for use in a small school district, or for use in an entire large district makes a difference in the approach to this task, but the end products will be similar. In the first two situations, the product may be one binder with four sections. In the case of a large district, the products are usually four binders, one for each component.

The resource guides describe activities used in the implementation of the comprehensive guidance and counseling program components. In developing the guides, new activities may be created or activities may be collected that have been used successfully in one or more buildings. In a medium-sized or large school district, the described activities provide illustrative examples for buildings to use as a foundation to build on. In a small district or single building, the descriptions are of actual activities conducted in the building.

No matter how large or how small the program is, however, the guidance and counseling program leader should attend to the details of the guide writing. In Northside Independent School District, the compilation of ideas into guides took 3 years to accomplish. Once guides are published, they have a permanency that provides part of the foundation on which the new program can rest. It is important that this foundation be solid.

Describing Exemplary Activities. On the basis of the recognition that the guidance and counseling program had content to deliver to students, in Northside, resource guide development was supported by district curriculum writing funds. The first approach to the task was to convene a group of 12 counselors—four counselors from each school level—who spent a week developing the units and lessons to teach decision making to Grades 4 through 12. Fifteen guidance curriculum strands had been identified. Neither the counselors nor the director wanted to wait 14 more years to have the curriculum guide completed, to say nothing of the guides for the other components. The second, more efficient approach was to collect exemplary practices that were currently performed in district buildings, write them up in a consistent format, and categorize them by program component.

The committee planned its work on the basis of the results of the current, already completed program assessment. Under the director's leadership, the 12 counselors developed the formats to be used to describe activities, for example, lesson plans, activity plans, counseling session outlines, and system support protocols. They then redivided themselves by program component, resulting in three counselors working on guidance curriculum, three on individual student planning, three on responsive services, and three on system support.

In turn, the work committee trained their peers on each component and the formats. Counselors were invited to submit the activities they had found to be most successful. The work committee sorted the submissions by component, screened them, and selected the best practices. They were in the prescribed format and were ready to be typed for inclusion in the guide. Finally, the leadership team developed session plans for glaring omissions in the collection, for example, interpreting standardized tests so students could understand what they meant and conducting small-group counseling for students whose social skills needed boosting.

Some benefits to this approach were that it was an excellent vehicle for cross-fertilization of ideas. Working with counselors from different school levels to pool ideas helped everyone learn about each other's programs and was a major step toward an articulated prekindergarten to 12th-grade program. Additionally, all participating counselors saw how what they were currently doing fit into the new program concept.

Guidance Curriculum Guide. A curriculum guide provides the description of curriculum units and specific lessons. We suggest that the guidance and counseling program leader use the curriculum-writing expertise that is available, such as instructional supervisors if the district has them, the administrator in charge of curriculum development or instruction, or regional consultants in curriculum writing. The leader must also keep in mind that there will probably not be a one-on-one match between a specific activity or resource and a specific competency. Often, a single guidance activity may result in the achievement of a number of student objectives.

To illustrate how an activity may be written and to show its relationship to the goals and competencies of the guidance curriculum suggested in previous chapters, an example is displayed in Figure 7.1. The example is from the self-knowledge and interpersonal skills domain of the life career development model and relates to Goal A for the fifth grade. You may wish to consider this format for your own activity descriptions. Note that the activity is described on one page and follows a straightforward outline that defines the basic activity. Counselors are encouraged to develop the lesson plan according to their teaching style.

Individual Student Planning Guide. An individual student planning guide describes in detail activities and procedures to help students apply information and develop their personalized plans. These write-ups exemplify the refocusing of some current activities from system support activities to student results-focused activities that help them make their educational plans. For example, the objective for preregistration of secondary-level students can be changed from "students will circle course numbers on course selection cards" to a student learning objective, such as "10th graders will select an 11th-grade course of study that is an appropriate next step toward their educational/career goals." The activities that might be envisioned as a unit include interpretation of career interest and aptitude assessments, information exploration in the guidance center, review of the high school graduation and college entrance requirements, revision of the students' high school 4-year plans, and, finally, preregistration for the 11th-grade year.

The objective for an elementary school Career Day can be changed from "the school staff will provide *x* number of career speakers" to "third-, fourth-, and fifth-grade students will list the educational requirements for five careers that relate to their identified career

Figure 7.1
Sample Activity and Format

Domain I
Goal A
Grade 5
Performance Indicator 2

COAT OF ARMS

Domain I:	Self-knowledge and interpersonal skills
Goal A:	Students will develop and incorporate an understanding of their and others' unique personal characteristics and abilities.
Competency:	Students will specify those personal characteristics and abilities that they value.
Performance Indicator 2:	Students will identify a variety of things that they value.

Activity Objective:

The student will identify six things he or she values.

Materials:	Coat of arms, pencil
Time:	One session of approximately 30 minutes
Directions:	Have each student fill in an outline of a shield with the following for a personal coat of arms:

Box 1: Draw a symbol to represent your greatest success.
Box 2: Draw a symbol to represent your family's greatest success.
Box 3: Draw a symbol to show a place you dream about.
Box 4: Draw symbols to show two things at which you are good.
Box 5: Draw a picture to show what you would do if you had 1 year to live and could be a success at anything you do.
Box 6: On one-half of the box, write two words you would like used to describe you; on the other half, write two words you would not like used to describe you.

---

interests." The guidance and counseling program activities provided to assist students attain their objective might include a career interest inventory, a guidance lesson on the relationship between levels of education and levels of occupations available in various job clusters, and Career Day speakers who describe their educational histories as they relate to their occupations. Parent involvement activities related to individual student planning should be described as well.

Responsive Services Guide. A responsive services guide can provide a description of the topics and modes—such as counseling, consultation, or referral—the counselor uses in response to student, student–parent, or student–teacher problems. Counseling session plans and the overview of a planned series of counseling activities can help other staff members as well as less experienced counselors benefit from the ideas used in activities. Many sound commercial materials are available to support this component. In addition to helping new counselors get started, identifying the materials used in the current program supports consistency in program delivery across schools and consultation among counselors. Including a list of the community referral sources counselors use in the building or across the district also enhances the implementation of this component. Developing this list not only provides the names of outside source people who have cooperated effectively with school counselors in the past but can also provide a vehicle for gathering consistent information about these sources' areas of expertise.

System Support Guide. The system support component guide needs to be written specifically to clarify what the guidance department staff does to support other programs and to itemize the support they need to ensure appropriate delivery of their own program. Support to other programs should be listed by program (state the activity and briefly describe the counselor role or roles and responsibilities). Support needed from the administration and staff should include such items as policy and procedural assistance; budget, equipment, and facilities needs; support for specific staff development opportunities; and public relations activities. Outlines of successful teacher in-service presentations should be included.

Establishing Guidance Facilities Standards and Making Recommendations for Their Application

Ensuring adequate guidance facilities and equipment may be difficult, considering the costs that may be involved. However, physical facilities are important because they often provide students with their first and sometimes permanent impression of the guidance and counseling program. Now that you have identified the desired program design and have chosen guidance activities for the program components, you are also aware of the facilities required. For example, if classroom guidance is to be an essential part of the developmental program, a guidance classroom may be deemed essential; if counselors are expected to conduct small-group counseling, an adequately sized room is needed; if a guidance center is to be the hub of the program, a large classroom and offices are needed; and so on. Space in growing districts may be at a premium, but in schools and districts where enrollment is declining, the facilities development challenge may not be as great.

Improving the facilities and equipment available to the guidance and counseling program, as with other program improvements, entails knowing what you want, being able to communicate that knowledge to others, and inserting guidance and counseling program needs into relevant district processes. In planning for building new facilities or remodeling existing ones and in upgrading the furniture and equipment, you will be communicating with architects, facilities planners, engineers, and purchasing agents. These professionals and technicians may or may not understand the guidance and counseling program, as you may or may not understand construction and purchasing. Your program is best served if you work with them to develop standards for the design of the guidance facilities and for provision of the basic equipment needed. You also need to work with them to incorporate into the overall system the plan to bring the guidance department's facilities up to the standards.

Facilities Standards. These standards detail the type of facilities needed, their size and most suitable location, and other basics that should be incorporated when schools are built or remodeled. Specific items often included in facilities standards are outlined in Table 7.3, with examples for a guidance and counseling program. When approved by the district administration and the school board, these standards become the specifications from which architects draw their plans and others contract to build or fulfill.

Furniture and Equipment. The guidance facilities should be furnished in as comfortable a way as possible for all users. Remember that students as well as staff and parents gain impressions about the program from your facilities.

A basic furniture and equipment list must also be developed. Such furniture items, and their types and sizes, might include a professional desk and chair, guest chairs, bookshelves, credenza, file cabinets, and student tables and chairs. Equipment might include such items as bulletin boards, CD and DVD players, TVs, and computers.

Equipment needs are identified through a process similar to that used for facilities. In the current program assessment, you surveyed the equipment available. Having identified the major material resources, you can now specify related equipment needs. Again, this information allows you to analyze the costs involved and to develop your budget request. The request is substantiated by the clearly stated relationship between equipment and facilities and the program design.

Guidance Center: A Way of Organizing Guidance Facilities. Traditionally, guidance facilities have consisted of an office or suite of offices designed primarily to provide one-

Table 7.3

Facilities Design Standards Categories and Examples

A. *Room type:* counselor's office; secretary and reception area; records, storage, and workroom area; group counseling room; conference room; registrar's office; data processing and scheduling assistant's area; career center area

B. *Location:* centered in the building; location of each of the offices and areas relative to one another

C. *Square footage:* in addition to activities done in the particular space, size depends on level (size of student body), size of school (typical number using facility at one time), furniture and equipment needed

D. *Functions performed in room type:* specific to each area and personnel working in the area

E. *Walls:* covering, tackable, soundproof, concrete blocks, fireproof

F. *Floor:* carpeting or vinyl

G. *Cabinets:* location, floor-to-ceiling, waist-high with countertop, depth, lockable, open

H. *Storage requirements:* specific equipment, types of materials, amount

I. *Lighting:* number, separate controls for fixtures

J. *Electrical outlets:* number and placement, computer hook-ups

K. *Plumbing:* not applicable

L. *Communications:* private telephone lines; intercoms with lights to ensure privacy; not hooked up to school public address system

M. *Unusual electrical requirements:* e.g., air conditioning separate from classrooms for counselors on contracts that extend into the summer; dedicated copier circuit

N. *Unusual equipment requirements:* marker boards, bulletin boards

O. *Other:* such as lockable doors, small windows; acoustic considerations (privacy in counseling offices and rooms); noise in the area that contains the audiovisual equipment used in the center.

on-one counseling. Such an arrangement has frequently included a reception or waiting area that serves as a browsing room where students have limited access to displays or files of educational and occupational information. This space has typically been placed in the administrative wing of the school so that the counseling staff can be close to the records and the administration. The need for individual offices is obvious because of the continuing need to carry on individual counseling sessions. However, there is also a need to open up guidance facilities, to make them more accessible to students, teachers, parents, and community representatives.

A comprehensive guidance center can bring together available guidance information and exploration resources and make them easily accessible to students. The center can be used for such activities as group sessions, self-exploration, and personalized research and planning. At the high school level, students can gain assistance in such areas as career planning, job entry and placement, financial aid information, and postsecondary educational opportunities. At the middle or junior high school level, students can gain assistance in such areas as career planning, high school educational opportunities, community involvement, and recreational opportunities. At the elementary school level, students and their parents can gain information about the school, the community, and parenting skills as well as read books about personal growth and development. An area for play therapy can be provided.

Although the center is available for use by school staff, parents, and community members, it should be student centered, and many of the center activities should be both student planned and student directed. At the same time, the center is a valuable resource for parents in guiding their children's development and for teachers in implementing their programs. College representatives and employers, too, find the center useful when seeking part- or full-time workers. Viewed in this way, the impact of the center on the school community can be substantial.

The guidance center should be furnished in as comfortable a way as possible for all users. Provision should be made for group and individual activities. Coordinating the operation of the guidance center should be the responsibility of the guidance staff. All school staff should be involved, however. We recommend that at least one paid paraprofessional be employed to ensure that clerical tasks are carried out in a consistent manner. Volunteers may also be used.

Political Resources

To improve use of political resources, consider updating policies and procedures, engendering support from building staff, and working with resistant staff members and critical constituents (e.g., concerned parents).

Updating Policies and Procedures

Another task to be completed to implement the new program is updating the policies and procedures that govern guidance as they appear in the district policy and procedural handbooks (those you identified in assessing the current program). If you have not already done so, you must—as a prerequisite to procedural changes—update the board policy that defines the purpose and design of the comprehensive guidance and counseling program. A model policy statement developed by the Missouri School Board Association (2010) is provided in Appendix D. Some of these procedural and regulatory changes may be merely editorial or cosmetic; others will be major changes in procedure and will not be easy to bring about. The former changes are those that merely translate board policy to administrators;

the latter are those that will need to be negotiated, particularly those that describe how the guidance department interacts with and supports schoolwide efforts and the programs of other departments. All of these statements should be built on the premise that the guidance and counseling program is an integral part of the total educational program and that it has integrity of its own.

In analyzing how the current program compares and contrasts with the desired program, you have documented something you already knew: A number of activities for which you are responsible are not guidance activities at all or are, at best, only tangentially related to guidance. They have become a part of the guidance and counseling program over the years, perhaps by design, but more likely by default. As you also know, no matter how these nonguidance activities became part of the program, once established, they are difficult to remove. What is worse, these responsibilities consume the valuable time and resources needed to conduct the actual guidance and counseling program for students.

> School counselors are encouraged to consider using various constructive confrontation interventions when dealing with school administrators who view counselors as being responsible for a broad range of quasi-administrative/clerical duties that ultimately detract from the counselor's ability to ameliorate the academic achievement gap. Passively accepting these administrative demands and unquestioningly fulfilling such organization duties represent characteristics of [Nice Counselor Syndrome]. (Bemak & Chung, 2008, p. 377)

Ways to manage the improvement of program activities, including displacing nonguidance activities, are discussed in Chapter 8.

Making optimum use of school counselors' professional skills is a goal of program remodeling. An issue related to recommending lower ratios, which increase students' access to their counselors, is ensuring opportunities for the counselors to access their students. Time for guidance and counseling must be seen as legitimate and valuable, and policies and procedures must be established to ensure that there is time to deliver the program appropriately.

Engendering Support From Building Staff

Recognizing that the new program design causes many operational-level changes in a building's guidance and counseling program, the district guidance and counseling program leader and all school counselors need to expend some energy reeducating the building staff members about the rationale and goals for the changes. Reeducation and engendering support call for communicating clearly what these changes are, providing guidelines for support from building administrators, and collaborating with building personnel to design and implement the local changes.

Armed with the district plan for guidance and counseling program improvement, you need to ensure that every staff member has the working knowledge he or she needs to respond to the changes. This entails formal presentations regarding the program conducted at the district level for the principals and at the building level for the faculty.

Because principals are accountable for the successful operation of every program in their building, they should have a copy of the program framework written at the end of the designing phase. It is also useful to provide a written set of guidelines that suggest to building administrators appropriate levels of support for their guidance and counseling programs and staff. These might entail statements about adequate facilities for counselors as well as adequate budget appropriations for guidance department supplies. Statements might also be made about work schedules for counselors concerning, for example, their expected work hours and including recognition of lunch hours and preparation periods. Some tasks identified for displacement may be handled in this manner, especially those that have become common practice at the building level but are not rooted in district policy. Examples include stating that elementary counselors should benefit from the secretarial services available at the school and should not be required to do their own typing; recommending that new middle school students begin the registration process in the administrative office and be referred to the guidance department after such items as verification of address and immunizations are taken care of; and recognizing that the standardized testing program provides useful information to faculty and administration as well as to counselors and thus test administration is a shared responsibility of all building staff members.

Another way to encourage building principals' support is for the senior district staff member who evaluates the principals to ask each one, "What have you done this year [evaluation period] to support improvement of the guidance and counseling program in your building?"

We believe that it is essential to involve the others who will be affected by changes in the guidance and counseling program in designing what those changes will be and how they will be made (Henderson, 1989, pp. 37–38). We recommend that you use the existing building program improvement committee to assist you in planning, designing, implementing, and evaluating the building guidance and counseling programs. A process for doing this is suggested later on in this chapter. Other formal mechanisms for collaborating with building staff colleagues are staff meetings. Counselors should meet periodically with the teachers with whom they work through grade-level, department, and faculty leadership meetings. Seeking their input, hearing and responding to their concerns, and informing them of your plans are essential to the success of the guidance and counseling program change process.

Working With Resistant Guidance and Counseling Staff Members

By now it will be clear that there are school counselors and other guidance staff who understand the new program and are eager for its implementation. And by now it will also be clear that there are school counselors and other staff members who resist the changes that are called for. The resisters probably fall into several categories: those who have not yet quite grasped the program concept; those who disagree with the educational–developmental basis of the program, preferring the psychological crisis–oriented services approach; those who are skeptical as to the validity of the changes; those who do not believe the changes will ever occur; those who are worried about their own competence for meeting the new mandates; and those who do not want change, period.

We recommend that the guidance and counseling program leader continue open dialogue with the counselors and other guidance staff about their concerns. As the change process continues to unfold, however, more and more of their concerns, anxieties, and fears will be addressed. Changes do not happen overnight, and the concept does become clearer with time. The superintendent is in support of the program; in-service training is provided. We also recommend that the district guidance and counseling program leader identify ways to acknowledge those who do support the changes and the efforts that lead in the right directions. We discuss this point more extensively in Chapter 8.

Working With Concerned Parents

Most parents want to know, understand, or have some input into what happens to their children at school. Some parents want to control what happens and are highly critical of things that happen to their children at school. These parents are often driven by anger or fear of what might happen to their children, making them emotional, irrational, or defensive and difficult to deal with. Many of these difficult and defensive parents are acting as individuals concerned about their own children. However, some of them come forward to try to censor the school guidance and counseling program. They may be members of local, state, or national groups that do not believe counseling belongs in the schools.

It is important for school counselors to respond to concerned parents appropriately (White, Mullis, Earley, & Brigman, 1995). These parents often initiate the dialogue with their children's school counselors unexpectedly, catching the counselor off guard and unprepared. However, with their program goals and priorities in mind, school counselors are prepared to advocate for—to share their perspectives about—their program and their students' needs (Henderson & Gysbers, 1998). One principle that school counselors endorse is that children's personal and educational well-being is best served when school counselors (and other educators) and parents are partners working together on behalf of the students. By responding to these difficult parents, school counselors strive to better align the parents' agendas with their own, to work together on behalf of children. Additionally, school counselors have skills that allow most of their parent contacts to be of the highest professional quality—that is, open, positive, and collaborative; based on professional analysis and reflection; and carried out with professional detachment.

Every parent who comes forward should be treated as an individual first. In some cases, after sufficient data have been gathered, there may be indications that a parent is a member of an anti–school counseling group. Most parents come forward on behalf of their own children and with concerns about one or two topics, and most of the time, the school counselor can address the parents' concerns for their children. As in effective counseling, the first step in working with concerned parents is to address their presenting concerns and to keep the discussion focused on resolution of their issues.

In striving to work successfully in interactions with such parents, school counselors must rise to two challenges: first, identifying the specific topics of concern to the parents and the motivation for their concern; second, selecting the response to parents that is appropriate to their topics and motives as well as to the counselors' goals.

As these relationships unfold, counselors assume management of the relationships, taking control once the objectives are clear or clearer and appropriate responses to the situation are planned and implemented. Although school counselors have no control over parents' responses, each parent response provides new data that augment the counselors' original assessment of the situation and inform the counselors' next set of choices.

When it appears that parents are not going to be easily pleased, when their concerns are emotionally driven, counselors strive to maintain their professional detachment and implement a systematic process, as outlined in Figure 7.2, for managing the interactions, the relationships, and the situation.

Assessing the Situation. Situation assessment entails identifying the parents' topics and motives. It also includes school counselors understanding their own topics and motives and clarifying the objectives of each party.

Parents' Topics and Motives. Guidance topics that parents may find objectionable include self-esteem, decision making, attending to children's feelings, affective education, or exploring family values and practices. Parents may want their religious beliefs to be taught and upheld in schools. They may believe firmly in parents' rights to complete authority over their offspring, including knowing and controlling what their children experience in school.

They may express concern about an array of guidance methods. Some of the parents are fearful of what counseling will do to the minds of their children. Others fear what counseling will reveal about the family dynamics, abuses, or other practices.

Figure 7.2
Strategy Selection Logic Flow Used by School Counselors in Response to Concerned Parents

	PARENT		SCHOOL COUNSELOR
1	Initiates conversation.		
		2	Determines who parent represents.
3	Expresses topic(s) of concern.	4	Specifies parent s topic; identifies own topic.
	Evidences motive for interaction.	5	Identifies parent's motive(s); clarifies own motive(s).
6	States objective(s).	7	Understands parent's objective; determines own objective.
		8	Chooses advocacy response: skills, resources, response level.
		9	Implements advocacy strategy through an activity.
10	Participates in counselor-selected activity and responds.		
		11 and 12 and 13 . . .	Implements response activities through to problem resolution.

They may be wary of psychological or career assessments, surveys that include any questions regarding the home and family, role playing, guided imagery, group counseling, and confidentiality. They may want their children to have fewer guidance services than are part of the comprehensive, developmental guidance and counseling program (e.g., no responsive services). Some guidance activities may be of specific concern, such as traditional values clarification activities (e.g., lifeboat exercises) or behavior modification practices.

Not all of these sometimes fearful or angry parents have the same motivation, however, although nearly all are motivated by concern for their children. In working effectively in the often difficult interactions with these parents, determining motivation is important. Motivations tend to fall into five categories: Some parents are misinformed, some are concerned about materials, some mistrust certain practices, some have experienced mistakes, and some are misusing an issue. Identifying which category describes a parent's motivation helps to suggest an appropriate response.

Professional School Counselors' Topics and Motives. To be effective, school counselors in these situations must be clear about their own topics and motivations. Their topics fit into three categories. Counselors want to (a) improve the services provided to the specific parents' individual children or to all students, (b) maintain the program benefits for individual or all students, and (c) allow the program to continue for students other than those of the critical parent or parents. While keeping the conversation focused on manageable problems, school counselors usually identify which of these topics represents the best-case scenario for the outcomes of these interactions.

School counselors, too, have a wide range of motivations, from altruistic to self-serving. On the altruistic end of the continuum, school counselors are motivated to maintain the integrity of the program for all students. School counselors are best served in the face of adversaries when they are secure in the basis of their program, when they know what the content and rationale are. They are secure when the basic mission of the program is tied to the mission of the school and school district. They are secure when they are well grounded in their own professional integrity, in their competent work with and on behalf of children.

Most districts have policies and procedures regarding censorship and the curriculum. If you or the counselors are not aware of these policies, they should be included in the department's operational handbook. Especially when districts have designed their guidance and counseling programs as carefully as we are suggesting and have clearly defined the integral nature of their program, defense of program participation is soundly supported. Program modifications must not be made without due consideration of whether the modification violates access to services needed by children or the integrity of the program.

Sometimes school counselors become fearful or angry and are motivated not on behalf of children but on their own behalf. There are times when groups of parents threaten the very existence of the program, and school counselors fear that their jobs are not secure. Such times, however, are not that frequent. Not all parents who disagree with the program want it and the counselor eliminated from the school.

Some concerned parents want to change the shape of the program—by, for example, eliminating group counseling—which, in turn, changes the school counselors' job description. That is not a parent's prerogative. Some school counselors get angry and defensive about being told what to do or what not do. Guarding against overreacting in these circumstances is essential for school counselors. Fear for job security or anger at differences of opinion are not strong positions, and they may add grounds for other confrontations.

School counselors may also be fearful of parents' concerns because they do not fully understand them and may be threatened by the lack of clarity of the parents' goals. They may resent having others suggest that what they do is inappropriate when they believe it is appropriate and the right thing to do. They may be hurt by the appearance of someone not liking them. If they are insecure in their role or unsure about the value of their programs, this insecurity may undermine their professional demeanor.

Clarifying Differences. When the topics of concern and motives are clarified, professional school counselors state for themselves and for the parents what each side presents as objectives for the interactions and relationships. One hopes that these are in the best interests of the children in question. Parents' objectives relate to their topics of concern and their motivations. Counselors' objectives are specific to each child–parent situation and to their motivations on behalf of the specific children involved or all children whose access to services may be threatened. For example,

- Misinformed parents may ask to have their children removed from classroom guidance because of fear of the humanistic nature of the content. A counselor's objective would be to allow the child to reap the benefits of the guidance curriculum.
- Parents who have heard negative things about particular material may want that material's use censored from the program (Brigman & Moore, 1994). A counselor's objective would be to maintain its use in relevant aspects of the program.
- Mistrusting parents may not want their children to participate in small-group counseling. A counselor's objective would be for the students to participate in groups that address their needs.
- Parents who have experienced a mistake made by counselors may want to have different counselors assigned to their students. A counselor's objective would be for parents to recognize the counselor's awareness of the error and assurance that it was a momentary lapse, not a permanent condition of incompetence.
- Parents who want visibility in the community and misuse the issue may want the guidance and counseling program eliminated from the school. A counselor's objec-

tive would be to provide a means for those parents' children to opt out of the program or some of the activities, leaving the rest intact for the children of parents who want the program to continue.

Finding Common Ground. In managing possibly contentious relationships, school counselors intentionally select responses and strategies that incorporate their and the parents' objectives, allow them to apply their skills and resources effectively, and are within the identified level of advocacy response they have decided is most efficient. They select strategies and related activities that appear to have the best chance of responding to the parents' agenda and to best move their own agenda on behalf of students forward. The goal is, of course, resolution of the issues to the satisfaction of both sides of the dialogue.

Selecting Appropriate Responses. Professional school counselors choose from one of nine advocacy responses and implement strategically relevant activities. The responses fall on a continuum of involvement by school counselors (e.g., degree of participation, energy expended, level of commitment, expenditure of resources such as time). The responses range from being physically present to acting assertively on someone's behalf, from giving time to giving time plus ideas, initiative, power, professionalism, and so on. Counselors' response choices are whether they will simply represent the program or profession, inform the parents, welcome them, reach out to them, support their objectives, cooperate or collaborate with them as they work toward their objectives, or consult or advocate with them on behalf of their children.

Examples of activities that school counselors do at each advocacy response level include

- representing their program at parent functions;
- informing parents about their program in conferences;
- welcoming parents who come into the guidance center and reaching out to those who seem reluctant;
- supporting parents who have concerns about the school and are seeking ways to communicate these to the right people;
- cooperating with parents, even those who are critical of the program, and seeking collaborative opportunities to work with parents on mutual agendas;
- consulting with parents about ways they can help their children be successful in school;
- advocating for parents with other school staff members, when the parents are fearful or for some reason cannot find their own voices.

Conducting Strategically Appropriate Activities. Professional school counselors intentionally select activities that have the best chance for bringing the dialogue to a successful end. With parents who are misinformed, some proactive efforts that school counselors can undertake are to present overviews of their programs at open houses, parent–teacher association meetings, and parent workshops and to publish newsletters or articles regarding the topics addressed in the program's curriculum.

With those who complain about specific materials used in the program, it is important that people be allowed to study them to become familiar with their actual content. Encouraging parents to preview materials before they become concerned is proactive, and with a planned program this is feasible. To help keep confrontations from escalating, it may be useful to have procedures for opting out of nonmandatory aspects of the program or for benefiting from alternative assignments. For example, Northside Independent School District developed a procedure for parents to follow that requires their learning the information they need to make good decisions about their children's participation in the developmental guidance and counseling program, and that requires them to be very specific about what content they do not want their child exposed to (see Appendix I). Counseling is provided only with parental permission. These procedures help counteract parents' feelings of having no control over what happens to their children at school.

The mistrust of the parents who question the purposes of the guidance and counseling program usually goes beyond mistrust of the program and the individual counselor. Their concerns should be attended to by a building administrator. Schools cannot and probably should not change to attend to the concerns of these parents, and administrators are best able to express what is legally required and done in the best professional judgment of those responsible for the school program.

For the parents who have experienced mistakes or bad practice by school counselors, the first step is to hear and investigate the parents' complaints. These, too, are best handled by administrators. They, in turn, need to follow due process as spelled out in policy or regulations to determine the facts and consequences.

Those parents who misuse the guidance and counseling program by making it an issue for their own purposes are also best handled by administrators or other authorities. Politically motivated parents may be listened to and then referred to administrators to handle. Entrepreneurs are best exposed for what they are. Those involved in illegal activities, including child neglect, need to be reported to the proper authorities.

Clarifying the Conclusion. As with any counselor–client problem-solving interaction, the counselor ends the conference or meeting by summarizing the original problem, the status of that problem at the time, and the plan for the future regarding resolution of the problem and any related issues. The summary statement may include such items as restating the original problem, how the differences have been resolved so far, and what measures are planned to continue resolution of the problem. One resolution of the problem is to agree to disagree. Hopefully, next steps will have been planned that relate to working together for mutual goals regarding the children involved in the situation. Such summarizing provides clarity for the counselors and for the parents.

Being confronted or challenged by individuals presents an uncomfortable situation. For their own peace of mind, professional school counselors consult with mentors and colleagues and continue to keep in touch with parents who are supporters of their work. They develop strategies for adding to or using their support base. They do this formally through the school–community advisory committee and informally by being in contact with the multitude of appreciative clients who have been well served by the program. In times of conflict, many supporters are willing and eager to present their side of the story. Do not be shy about using them.

Provide Impetus for Making Desired Changes

Focus on Special Projects

Once the design for the guidance and counseling program has been established, program leaders are encouraged to focus on special projects that help incorporate current trends in education to keep pace with their educator colleagues. The energy provided by an educational reform or other professionwide movements can facilitate some of the changes that need to be accomplished. New directions from the federal, state, local community, district, and building level could be mirrored by special emphases within the guidance department. Such changes keep counselors abreast of changes in the total educational system and help maintain their position on the educational team. That is, other staff who have to change see that counselors also have to change.

Such changes also have the side benefit of helping counselors avoid having change forced on them that may be inappropriate to the directions of the new program. For example, many of the current reforms have increased the paperwork and accountability burden of school staff, such as noting students' mastery of required instructional outcomes. If the counselors have to attend to changes of their own, they can better avoid being assigned to some of the paperwork tasks that belong to teachers or administrators; if the counselors are visibly augmenting the guidance curriculum component, for example, fellow staff members will see more readily that the counselors do not have time to make such notations and instead make them themselves.

Recurrent issues that were deemed to be critical to successful development and implementation of comprehensive school guidance and counseling programs were identified in a national survey (Henderson & Gysbers, 2002). These issues, in priority order, are

1. Displacement of non-guidance tasks, including school counselors' appropriate role in standardized testing programs
2. Program accountability
3. Accountability for the quality of school counselor performance
4. Program advocacy
5. Leader empowerment
6. Enhancement of an existing comprehensive guidance program
7. Appropriate use of technology
8. Parent involvement, including responding to parents who are critical of the program
9. Program development process
10. Enhancement of the cross-cultural competence of school counselors. (Henderson & Gysbers, 2002, p. 8)

Examples of leadership responses that led to successful resolution of these issues are also provided.

Federal and State Priorities

The review of the history of guidance and counseling provided in Chapter 1 demonstrates the impact of federal priorities on the development of the profession. In addition, contemporary guidance and counseling program changes can and should relate to the current federal emphasis on at-risk populations. Surely, children and youth who are at risk because of violence, drug and other substance abuse, lack of academic success, disabilities (hidden or otherwise) that interfere with their learning, premature sexual activity, or adolescent depression are priority clients for school counselors implementing the responsive services component of a comprehensive guidance and counseling program. That these clients have federal priority (ACA, n.d.-b) provides a rationale for their needing counseling services. That the effectiveness of counseling has been established (ACA, 2008a, 2008b; ASCA, n.d.) provides a rationale for the guidance department to receive some of the funds appropriated for the special programs designed to meet these needs. In addition, some priority has been given for character education at the federal level. Fittingly, ASCA (2011, para. 1) has taken a position that "endorses and supports character education in the schools."

Current state-level reforms emphasize excellence in education as defined in tighter standards for instructional methodology, improved curriculum, improved student achievement, and improved student discipline. These emphases have caused the development of new teacher appraisal/evaluation systems, new requirements for lesson planning, efforts to better facilitate the achievement of academic excellence, and increased emphasis on college and career readiness. There continues to be an emphasis on accountability as demonstrated through achievement of minimum competencies on tests and other standardized achievement measures. Mandates for improved student discipline include systems that provide consistent and logical consequences for student misbehavior and require more parental involvement for students who act out.

Reforms have focused on the science of education and on the human dimensions of education. Politicians and businesspeople have had a big say in educational reforms. Legislators and businesspeople have stated what they think students should know and be able to do as a result of schooling (Secretary's Commission on Achieving Necessary Skills, 1991). This list of skills is still promoted by the U.S. Department of Labor's Employment and Training Administration (2009). The National Governor's Association and the State Education Chiefs have developed *Common Core State Standards* that define the knowledge and skills students should have within their kindergarten through 12th-grade education careers so that they will graduate from high school fully prepared for college and careers. The standards are

- Aligned with college and work expectations;
- Clear, understandable and consistent;
- Include rigorous content *and* application of knowledge through high-order skills;
- Build upon strengths and lessons of current state standards;
- Informed by top-performing countries, so that all students are prepared to succeed in our global economy and society; and,
- Evidence and/or research-based. (Common Core State Standards Initiative, 2010, p. 1)

In addition, the National Center for Educational Achievement (http://www.nc4ea.org/index.cfm) and various states have promulgated college and career readiness standards.

These suggested results describe to educators what our product should be. Standards are high, accountability is measured by such hard data as test results, but increasing autonomy is given to local districts and schools to plan their own methods for achieving the standards. The focus is on excellence in the education system and on recognition of the diversity of students served, and it is balanced with calls for equity and for attending to the unique needs and plans of individual students. The continued fiscal conservatism of state governments has helped public servants recognize that getting more money for services is very difficult. Thus, efforts to integrate educational, health, and human services as well as to coordinate provision of vocational education and training continue.

Each of these efforts can be used to enhance and support needed changes in the guidance and counseling program. The actual specifics of reforms vary from state to state and according to local priorities and needs; nonetheless, some common themes point to directions for counselors. New systems for assisting teachers to use current teaching methodology include clinical supervision strategies of observation and feedback, refined appraisal–evaluation models, and professional development plans. The same strategies can be used for counselors and are discussed more extensively in Chapters 9 and 10 and more fully in *The New Handbook of Administrative Supervision in Counseling* (Henderson, 2009). Asking counselors to write their plans for counseling sessions and guidance lessons is a companion piece to asking teachers to develop better lesson plans. Districts across the United States are using school improvement planning techniques and developing multi-year strategic plans. Counselors and guidance departments, too, should be asked to clarify their plans for the year by submitting calendars and using a goal-based improvement approach. This fits nicely into the comprehensive program concept and aligns with *The ASCA National Model: A Framework for School Counseling Programs* (ASCA, 2005).

Curriculum development in other disciplines provides counselors with the opportunity to write the guidance curriculum and to provide for the infusion of guidance curriculum into the academic curricula. For example, in addition to the guidance dimension within the mental health curriculum strand of the health and science curricula, the social skills outcomes that are part of the guidance curriculum can easily be infused into the social studies curriculum; communication skills can be infused into language arts; and problem solving can be infused into science and math. Because the concept of a guidance curriculum has grown, much of what we see as students' needs already has been stated in outcome terms, making us prepared to work within the outcomes-based approach. Another relevant aspect of this approach, and one that is already a part of the guidance curriculum, is the emphasis on helping students learn processes—such as decision making, planning, and relating to others—including those from cultures different from their own.

The continued emphasis on testing calls for counselors to help students with their test-taking skills and to help teachers use test results responsibly. This provides counselors the opportunity to shift their role from being test administrators to being consultants on appropriate test use. Adding the dimension of attending to each individual student's needs renews the interest in one of counselors' basic services: identification of individual students' strengths, weaknesses, and needs. Although counselors are already recognized for this expertise, the magnitude of the challenge of providing such insights for every student means ensuring that counselors' own methods are up to date (e.g., recognizing the limits of tests and being comfortable with using multiple sources of data) and entrusting some of this responsibility to other educators, under the counselors' supervision.

Similarly, improved discipline-management programs rest heavily on guidance content—the content of psychology. Counselors can seize this area of high priority to administrators and work collaboratively with them in helping students learn new ways to behave responsibly and to make decisions through guidance curriculum and individual student planning activities. Both of these emphases give counselors clear priorities for providing students with special services; students who fail to meet minimum academic standards and students who consistently misbehave can often benefit from effective small-group or individual counseling.

Moreover, the effort to bring community services into the schools draws on counselors' expertise in coordination and augments the mental health services provided to children, youth, and families. How this is accomplished will be different in each locale, but school counselors must be in on the planning of integrated delivery systems to ensure that students' needs are well articulated and to ensure that the role envisioned for them is professionally appropriate. The emphasis on coordinating the resources for helping children, youth, and adults enter and succeed in the workforce also provides opportunities for school counselors to enhance the career development dimension of their programs, providing that they (and you) are involved in the development of the new systems.

District Priorities

With or without impetus from federal or state sources, school districts typically have priorities of high interest to their school boards or to their superintendents. School board members are often interested in academic excellence reflected in the number of scholarship winners or in the "back to the basics" of the school's mission that can include the basic of responsible behavior. District administrators are challenged by declining or expanding enrollment; both have implications for teachers' morale. Counselors can be visible in their role of helping others as well as themselves cope with change in a healthy manner. Wellness programs bring with them a potential interest in mental health. These activities that apply the expertise of the guidance and counseling field are system support of the best kind. For example, districts around the country are responding to the challenge to help students connect with the adults in the schools, minimizing alienation and making the interpersonal climate more inviting. One mechanism for doing this is having effective classroom meetings at all school levels (Edwards & Mullis, 2003). Several roles for professional school counselors in instituting successful classroom meetings are to advocate for the practice, explaining the benefits for students; to train teachers in how to conduct effective meetings; and to consult with teachers as they implement them.

Community Priorities

Influential community groups, such as the parent–teacher association (PTA), chamber of commerce, and service clubs (e.g., Lions and Kiwanis), have priority projects that can bring positive visibility to improving the guidance and counseling program. The PTA is interested in youth problem topics such as suicide prevention. Lions Clubs are actively working to combat drug abuse and to help children care for their personal safety. In some areas, locally elected public officials are concerned about violence and gangs. Economic development groups are interested in career development programs. As education opens up to the communities it serves, guidance and counseling program reformers are advised to listen to the priorities of these groups; areas in which their interests dovetail with guidance goals suggest priority areas for guidance efforts as well.

Building Priorities

If you are the guidance and counseling program leader in your building, you are able to make use of districtwide improvements and resources and tailor them to your school community. You and your colleagues identify local priorities and establish related initiatives through your school improvement planning. By merging the district and local priorities, you build support for your efforts and can carry them out with integrity.

In addition, major events in school buildings can highlight the need for specific changes in the guidance and counseling program. Accreditation self-studies and visits provide opportunities to make recommendations for improving the guidance and counseling program. Visible student problems—teen suicides, drug busts, gang-related uprisings—demand counselors' attention. Principals have goals for their schools.

Counselors should collaborate with their administrators by showing them how the comprehensive guidance and counseling program supports the development of strategies to help attain school goals. Principals' goals quite often include such items as holding high expectations for students, working to enhance the self-esteem of students, and improving interpersonal relationships among the staff. Counselors can and should share parts of these goals. Needless to say, the more counselors' and principals' goals have in common, the more support counselors will have from key decision makers. The more school counselors are viable members of schoolwide teams, the more support they have in their buildings.

Moreover, individual counselors or counseling staffs have special talents, interests, and areas of expertise. Some high school counselors are expert in helping teenagers deal with grief and loss; some elementary counselors are creative in using popular toys as materials in developmental guidance and counseling programs. By capitalizing on these, the guidance and counseling program leader not only can give appropriate recognition to those counselors but also can provide for the development of special projects that, when successful, can be shared with other buildings.

Facilitate Building-Level Changes

The district-level guidance and counseling program leader assists the building-level leaders and counselors by establishing systems that help make the operational-level changes needed to effect implementation of the comprehensive guidance and counseling program. This entails, as Adelman and Taylor (2003) phrased it, "establishing an infrastructure and action plan[s] for carrying out the changes" (p. 9). Two such mechanisms are as follows:

- Have building staff commit to goals for guidance program improvement and develop the plans for achieving those goals. This is a way to repair discrepancies identified between the current and the desired program designs and a means for changing the activities done within the program.
- Have building staff develop transition and implementation plans similar to those developed at the district level. This is a way to change the resources appropriated to the guidance and counseling program at the building level.

At the building level, school counselors, their department heads, and principals use the strategies described next: a goal-based program improvement system, a master plan for change, and action plans for implementation.

Using a Goal-Based Program Improvement System

Goals are tools for turning visions into realities. They help individuals focus their energies on changes counselors and others perceive as important, and they make change manageable. In the circumstance we are describing—remodeling and revitalizing your program while you are living in it—the thought of striving to implement all the changes at once can be overwhelming. Focusing on a handful of goals is conceivable to most people; being allowed to develop their own strategies for attaining those goals allows counselors a sense of autonomy and comfort in making the needed changes. In the Northside Independent School District, the goal areas are established at the district level. The district initiates the goal-setting and action-planning processes, but each building has latitude in choosing specific implementation strategies that fit its needs or specialties. Establishing the goals for high-priority skill development, clients, or activities and the process of goal setting, action planning, monitoring, and evaluating progress toward these goals provide a consistency of focus across the district. These efforts serve to affect the continuity of newly implemented programs, allow for the continuation of dialogue between counselors from different buildings about change efforts, and give direction for in-service training and staff development activities.

Goal Setting

In reviewing the current and desired guidance and counseling programs, you discovered some discrepancies, as we discussed in Chapter 6. These discrepancies are the targets for program improvements districtwide. Likewise, each building's guidance and counseling program design team should compare and contrast its existing program with its articulated desired program. These identified discrepancies become additional targets for building-level program improvement goals.

The number of goals people are asked to consider depends on the number of discrepancies found, the size of the discrepancies, and the priorities the district or building has set. Goals should be delineated for program improvements and for performance improvements. A sample memo developed to assist counselors to attend to meaningful goals is presented in Figure 7.3. The goals are presented to individual staff members as challenges to each to do something to help repair the identified discrepancies.

These goals are broad and leave each counselor or building staff with choices. What they do to improve the quality of time spent in responsive services and how they do it are left to them. For example, counselors may strive to decrease reactive individual counseling time by initiating small-group counseling or systematically consulting with teachers. A sample of more specific goal targets is presented in Figure 7.4. These goals establish more specific activities for counselors to implement at the building level but leave the implementation plan to them. For example, they are asked to conduct group counseling for targeted populations, but the actual design of the counseling series is left to them. In both cases, the counselors specify the student outcomes and objectives for their new activities; they plan their own strategies and methods of evaluation on the basis of local needs and their own resources.

Counselors are asked to set their own goals to be reviewed by their immediate supervisor. When there is more than one counselor in a building, the guidance department as a whole should also have goals, such as "The department will develop an annual plan for expanded implementation of the guidance curriculum."

Within the department, individuals' goals should be related to each other's, and all counselors on the staff should be cognizant of their colleagues' goals. This helps to develop a support system that is useful in assisting the counselors meet success in striving for their goals. We also recommend that building principals sign off on the goals to indicate not only their awareness of the counselors' endeavors but also their approval. The head counselor or, in buildings where there is no such designated department leader, all of the counselors should meet and discuss their goals with the principal. This approach ensures that the guidance goals are consistent with the general building goals and provides a vehicle for enlisting the principal's support in goal attainment. The goals should ultimately be submitted to the district office for review by the administrator responsible for guidance.

Figure 7.3
Goals Memo

To:	Counselors
From:	Director of Guidance
Re:	Program and Performance Goals

Below are listed general goals that have been identified for *program* and *performance* improvements. Please pick two from each category to focus on for this school year, and specify the improvement you envision on the action planning form that is attached.

Program Goals
- to increase time spent in *curriculum*/developmental guidance
- to decrease time spent in *responsive services*/to improve quality of time spent in responsive services
- to decrease time spent in *system support*
- to decrease time/to improve quality of time spent with school *staff*
- to increase time spent with *parents*.

Performance Goals
- to improve group guidance skills
- to improve counseling skills
- to improve consulting skills
- to improve program planning/evaluation skills
- to improve referral skills.

Note. Data from Northside Independent School District, San Antonio, TX. Adapted with permission.

Figure 7.4
Counselors' Goals Memo

To: Elementary School Counselors

From: Director of Guidance

Re: Counselors' Goals

The goal-setting process implemented for the past several years worked well to help focus the guidance program improvement efforts. The districtwide goals are listed below. Please discuss these goals with your principals and add others who respond to the needs of your campus community.

1. To continue to contribute to students' education by effectively teaching guidance curricula outlined in the *Comprehensive Guidance Program Framework*.

2. To respond to campus-identified high-priority student-clients through effective group counseling. "High-priority student-clients" may include students who are underachieving or who are behaving irresponsibly.

3. To respond to campus-identified high-priority parent-clients through systematically implemented parent consultation or parent education.

4. To decrease student-contact time spent in clerical or quasi-administrative tasks by identifying personal "time-eaters" and minimizing the time spent on these.

5. To provide a better balanced guidance program by systematically planning the year's activities to adhere as much as feasible to the district-outlined and campus-specified comprehensive program design. (Planning assistance will be provided by the Director of Guidance.)

6. To increase the effectiveness of counseling and guidance activities by clear articulation of the counselor's theoretical base.

As in previous years, we will be discussing the strategies you identify as appropriate for striving to attain your goals. A copy of the revised Planning Form is attached. Please submit a copy of your "Guidance Program Improvement Planning" forms to me by September 15.

Approved: _____
             Associate Superintendent

cc: Elementary School Principals

Note. Data from Northside Independent School District, San Antonio, TX. Adapted with permission.

Guidance and Counseling Program Improvement Planning

Once specific goals have been established, each counselor and each department should develop plans for meeting these goals. As mentioned previously, such planning encourages forward and realistic thinking. It sets in motion a series of decisions and actions that actually help implement the strategies. A sample planning form is provided in Figure 7.5.

Once counselors' goals have been identified and counselors have committed themselves to implementation strategies, the guidance and counseling program leader has a means of monitoring counselors' progress toward these goals. This process is discussed in more depth in Chapter 8.

Developing and Implementing the Building Master Plan for Change

As at the district level, a master plan for change should guide the transition efforts at the building level. In addition to making changes in the activities done in the guidance and counseling program through the previously described goal-setting process, the building staff needs to consider the need for improvement in the resources that support the program at their level. The counselor or counselors, principal, guidance and counseling program development team, school–community advisory committee—all of the players with an interest in the program—should consider the status of the personnel, financial, and political resources available to the program. At this point in the improvement process, there are probably systemwide standards or guidelines established for resource allocation in the

Figure 7.5

Guidance Program Improvement Planning Form

GUIDANCE PROGRAM IMPROVEMENT PLANNING

School: _____

Name: _____

Principal/Head Counselor Signature: _____

Date: _____

USE A SEPARATE FORM FOR EACH GOAL

PLANNING			EVALUATION	
(To Be Completed by September 1)			(To Be Completed by Contract End-June)	

Goal: _____

Program Objective/Strategy	Tasks to Accomplish	Time Frame	Level of (1–5) Accomplishment	Students'/Others' Outcomes

Overall Assessment of Level of Accomplishment:

1	2	3	4	5
(Not Achieved)			(Fully Achieved)	

Counselor's Signature: _____

Principal/Head Counselor: _____

Date: _____

buildings; however, if there are not, then the local team can develop its own realistic ideals to shoot for by asking the questions outlined here and others that come to mind as they consider these questions.

- *Personnel resources:* Have all school staff members accepted responsibility for the guidance program? Are the guidance program–related jobs being done in accord with the system's job descriptions? Are the organizational relationships among the guidance and counseling program staff clear and working well? Are the organizational relationships between the guidance staff and the administrative staff, the instructional staff, and the other subsets of campus staff members working well? Do counselors have access to students to provide the program fully? Are time and money allocated to support program and professional development activities by the counselors and other guidance staff?
- *Financial resources:* Is there a guidance department budget for supplies and materials? Is it adequate? Are there other funding sources that could augment the budget, for example, the PTA for parent workshops; federal, state, district, or other grants for pilot projects; or local businesses for career development or mentoring programs? Are adequate materials available to support the program? Is time available to the staff to develop needed materials? Do the facilities meet established standards? Are the facilities welcoming and attractive? Is the necessary equipment available and working?
- *Political resources:* Are campus policies and procedures supportive of implementation of the desired guidance and counseling program design; for example, are counselors' nonguidance tasks decreasing and student-centered activities increasing? Is the principal supportive of the newly defined and designed program and the staff? Are the teachers? How are resisters being handled? Is the guidance and counseling program an integral part of schoolwide programs? Are school counselors active members of schoolwide planning teams? Are there guidance and counseling program objectives in the school improvement plan? Are there systematic mechanisms such as weekly or monthly meetings that facilitate communication between counselors and administrators and between counselors and teachers? Are the relationships between the guidance and counseling program staff and the community good? Is there an effective advisory committee? Are the guidance and counseling program public relations objectives a part of the school's public relations efforts? Is there an active or almost active group of critical constituents who need to be or are being worked with in a concerted manner?

After asking and answering these and other questions, the next step is to identify the goals or targets and relative priorities for change and then to lay out the master plan, listing what needs to be done, in what order, within what time frame, and who the person with primary responsibility is (see Table 6.4).

Developing the Building Action Plans for Implementation

As the time approaches to accomplish each of the goals or targets, a relevant plan of action should be developed (see Table 7.1). For example, if guidance curriculum time must be negotiated with the academic teachers to access students in a junior high or middle school, several tasks need to be accomplished before the counselor can infuse the guidance learning activities into the various curricula: (a) The counselor must have lesson objectives planned, (b) the principal's support must be enlisted, (c) a meeting with the academic department chairs needs to be established, and so on. Plans must be made to accomplish each of these tasks successfully.

A point needs to be made here: The changes must begin with reallocation of the resources currently available and in anticipation of new resources that probably will be allocated. Counselors must resist the mentality of waiting until everything at the system level has been done. This is where the top-down–bottom-up dynamic (Fullen, 2001) is most evident. Only so much change can occur at the building level within the current resource allocation, but those changes need to be made. For example, if a principal wants counselors teaching or developing guidance lessons for use in a homeroom-type situation and perceives counselors as sitting in their offices spending undue amounts of time with individual students, the counselors should devise ways to attend to the principal's goal. It is conceivable that if they manage their time taking into consideration that the principal has an important priority for them, the lessons could be developed. The principal will then be more likely to believe that the counselors use their time efficiently when they ask for other considerations.

Often, the success of district resource expansion depends on the evidence of maximum resource use at the school level. Spending all the money appropriated for buying program materials is an obvious example. Furthermore, once buildings have established their local plans, the district can identify and target problems and solutions identified in several buildings. For example, if several building guidance and counseling program plans seek to augment the guidance curriculum through use of homeroom periods, a districtwide group might be formed to work together to develop appropriate guidance learning activities.

Advocate for Your Changing Program: Implement Public Relations Activities

The best generator of good public relations is a good program. Now that you have designed your new program and have clarified the language used to describe it, you are ready to inform your program's clients and supporters about its improvements and what they can expect. Counselors, too, need to feel they are conducting the best program feasible and feel secure in the priorities that have been set. They are the program's primary communicators with students, teachers, administrators, parents, and local community members. In addition, they need to make every consumer contact a high-quality, customer-friendly experience (even at those impossibly busy times of the year).

Communicating with your clients, colleagues, and the public is "a form of advocacy—helping clients find and use the services they need" (Henderson, 2009, p. 256). Thus, the primary purpose of public relations work is for people to know enough about the program so they can access and make appropriate use of its services. As defined by the National School Public Relations Association (NSPRA; n.d.-b, para. 2),

> Educational public relations is a planned and systematic management function to help improve the programs and services of an educational organization. It relies on a comprehensive two-way communications process involving both internal and external publics, with a goal of stimulating a better understanding of the role, objectives, accomplishments and needs of the organization. Educational public relations programs assist in interpreting public attitudes, identify and help shape policies and procedures in the public interest, and carry on involvement and information activities which earn public understanding and support.

Planning public relations begins with study of the data that were gathered in the assessment of the current program regarding how others perceive the guidance and counseling program. The goal at this time is to help people move from what they thought the program was to what the new program structure is. To accomplish this task, we recommend that a work group be formed to assist in planning and implementing the public relations program. The work group should include not only counselors but also representatives—preferably leaders—of the publics with whom you plan to relate. The work group could be ad hoc, and it could include representatives from the steering or school–community advisory committees. Ultimately, the group that will continue public relations activities, once they are undertaken, is the school–community advisory committee.

Planning Your Public Relations Program

Planning a public relations program is not different from the planning used in the rest of the guidance and counseling program improvement process. You need to know where you are by performing a current assessment—in this case, the perception survey. You need to know where you want to go, the desired end—in this case, the established goals for the public relations program. And you need to know how you are going to get there. Establish a plan of action that includes the public relations objectives and strategies to be accomplished and the time frame involved.

Public relations should be systematically installed as an ongoing part of the program's overall improvement and management procedures. Public relations activities that are not related in this integrated fashion to the total program may be superficial and, as a result, may not have sufficient impact. Thus, careful attention to the planning is important. To develop your plan for public relations, consider these steps:

1. Establish goals for your public relations efforts. Examples include program consumers being informed about, understanding, and being supportive of and able to use the comprehensive guidance and counseling program.
2. Identify the target populations for your public relations efforts. Examples include students, teachers, parents, administrators, school board members, referral agency personnel, and community representatives and leaders.
3. Find out what these publics think about what you are doing and what they think you should be doing. The specific data gathered in the current program perception survey should tell you this.
4. Establish specific objectives for each subgroup. Examples include informing all parents about the program and gaining support from some parents for the program.
5. Identify the resources available to assist in your efforts. Examples include campus and district Web pages, Meet Your Counselor pamphlets, PTA newsletters and programs, official school communiqués, and public media.
6. Consider the relative impact each resource may have on the target population. Examples include inviting PTA leaders to serve on the advisory committee to provide them an opportunity to fulfill their leadership–representative role and, if advice is taken, to enlist their support for the program.
7. Translate these resources into strategies to be used. Where possible, use the already existing resources that have demonstrated effectiveness for reaching the target population, such as the administrator's association newsletter to communicate with administrators. Where none exists, consider creating unique resources such as guidance department newsletters or Counselor Corner columns in the local newspaper.
8. Outline the steps that will be taken in the development of these strategies and relate them to the overall plan.

9. Assign a person to be responsible for the activities.
10. Establish your time frame.

Well-planned public relations activities are an integral part of the guidance and counseling program improvement process. Remember that an effective public relations program is done in the public interest (NSPRA, n.d.-b). A premise of NSPRA is that

> schools have a Public Responsibility to tell parents and taxpayers how schools are spending their money, seeking their insight on helping the school district deliver high quality and an efficient educational program. The public has a right to know and be engaged in their schools. (NSPRA, n.d.-b, para. 3)

Remember that an effective public relations program is sincere in purpose and execution in keeping with the total guidance and counseling program's purpose and characteristics, positive in approach and appeal, continuous in application, comprehensive in scope, clear and with simple messages, and beneficial to both sender and receiver.

Public relations activities have two purposes: (a) to let consumers know how good the program is and how to access it and (b) to change any negative perceptions they may have to more positive ones. To do this, it is important to listen for and understand the negative perceptions that some consumers may have. For example, some teachers do not know about the program and are often dissatisfied that they do not get instant service when they think they need it. They are not aware that guidance counselors, too, take work home at night. They do not think that counselors, too, are tied to a set schedule that someone else has determined. Many are not familiar with counselors' role as student advocates; they see them in problem situations as adversaries. For another example, administrators may think that counselors do not work very hard. Administrators work evenings supervising activities, and they do not think that counselors do, too. Moreover, some counselors are perceived as not being loyal to the school because they do not attend extracurricular activities. In yet another example, some parents do not feel that they get the response they want, or perceive counselors as having made recommendations about their children that have damaged their educational careers. Many are not aware of counselors' specialized training.

Some in the population at large still—unfortunately—have negative biases against people with psychological problems and are skeptical about the value of mental health services. In addition, some students do not recognize or acknowledge the help they receive from counselors. They perceive them as paper pushers who were not helpful when they perceived they were having a problem. In general, because counseling programs have not been well defined, people have had unrealistic expectations about counselors and the services counselors can and should provide.

We might consider some food for thought gleaned from the corporate reputation literature. Corporations and companies have learned that their reputations are important in achieving not only employee satisfaction but also customer satisfaction. One delineation of the dimensions that make up a corporation's image identifies them as agreeableness, competence, enterprise, ruthlessness, and chic (Davies, Chun, Da Silva, & Roper, 2004). Davies et al. (2004) found positive customer satisfaction to be most highly correlated with agreeableness. The second highest correlation is with competence. A reputation for enterprise and chic correlated with customer satisfaction, but not as highly as with the first two. Agreeableness, as defined by Davies et al., entails honesty and social responsibility and not being aggressive or arrogant. *Competence* is defined as being reliable and ambitious. *Enterprise* is defined as being innovative, exciting, and daring and is likened to extraversion in human personalities. *Chic* is defined as stylish and prestigious. The one dimension that correlates negatively with customer satisfaction is *ruthlessness,* defined as arrogant and controlling. Professional school counselors can learn from these corporate reputation makers and consider ways to project their program (the corporation) and themselves (the employees) positively to their customers. NSPRA's (n.d.-a) *Code of Ethics* clarifies basic standards to adhere to in carrying out activities in a public relations program.

Implementing Your Public Relations Program

There are two essential factors to consider in implementing your public relations program: timing and quality. Public relations activities should be planned to capitalize on times when you have your audience's attention. The quality of any activity ought to be high; you need to put your best foot forward. Having handout materials prepared in advance helps you be ready at a moment's notice. An example is a flier developed and used by Missouri school counselors to explain their programs and services, provided in Appendix J.

We suggest that you consider conducting your public relations activities with your various target populations at those times when you are changing or working on improved activities that affect particular consumer groups. When you are asking teachers for classroom time to conduct the guidance curriculum activities, some may be reluctant to cooperate. This can be balanced by conducting effective lessons when an opportunity is provided. Teachers may be upset when they look for a counselor to assist them with a problem and learn that the counselor is scheduled into classrooms for guidance for a certain amount of time. This can be the ideal time to explain to them the benefits gained from developmental guidance. Administrators may also be resistant when counselors try to divest themselves of the quasi-administrative or clerical tasks that take up so much time and talent. They get weary of counselors saying, "That's not my job." If, however, they become convinced that the time saved is focused directly on helping students through the guidance curriculum, individual student planning, or responsive services, this negative feeling may be dissipated. Parents who are used to the notion that counselors work one-on-one with students may be put off by group guidance activities. If group guidance is unexplained, it may further parents' feelings of not getting adequate service from this specialist for their own child. At such times, careful explanation of how many more students and parents are receiving service offsets this concern.

Shepherd (2000) offered 29 proven strategies for informing and engaging the multiple publics of professional school counselors: students, parents, teachers, administrators, community, and school board members. She indicated that implementing them is the third phase of a process. After setting goals and developing options, her strategies include a variety of ideas about making presentations; participating in site-based teams; publishing newsletters and columns, brochures, calendars, and annual reports; attending school functions; sharing resources with staff members; and having ongoing communications within the building.

Attend to Diversity

In making the transition to a comprehensive guidance program, professional school counselors and guidance and counseling program leaders need to keep their eyes open for opportunities to attend to diversity realities and issues. As human, material, facilities, and political resources are developed; special projects are implemented; goals are set; and public relations efforts are designed and made, many opportunities arise to enhance the multicultural dimensions of the guidance and counseling program. Some of them are mentioned in this section. As discussed in previous chapters, schools tend to uphold middle class values and mores, and professional school staff members are members of the middle socio-economic class. Therefore, gaps occur between the values and experiences held by the school and those held by individual students, families, and non–middle-class communities.

In developing human resources, attention can be paid to ensuring the cultural and ethnic representativeness of the counseling and guidance program staff. Every staff member must acknowledge the cultural backgrounds of the individuals with whom they come in contact. They need to develop respect for and their capacity to work with people from the diverse cultures in their community. Virtually every school and school counselor we have worked with can grow in this area. Some recent research has begun to suggest that as a result of cultural insensitivity, school counselors inadvertently contribute to the underrepresentation of minorities in math and science courses and, ultimately, careers (West-Olatunji et al., 2010).

In the first place, multicultural competence development is a lifelong process. We are just now coming out of a long period of denial about differences among people—color blindness that focused only on similarities. Similarities are good; but so are differences. The ACA's (n.d.-a) Multicultural Counseling Competencies (see Appendix H) provide guidelines for counselors targeting this area of their professional development. Some counseling staffs have designated one of the counselors to be the multicultural competence specialist, whose responsibilities are to have internalized the competencies and objectives and to help the entire staff keep their work and the program cognizant of the impact that diversity might be having.

Increasingly, professional school counselors are being called on to promote the rights of all students to equal educational opportunities. We are asked to advocate for social justice for underrepresented students. Recommendations are made for school counselors to lobby "for policies, opportunities, and activities that promote" (Akos & Gelassi, 2004, p. 200) attention to student development for all students and for promoting strengths-based approaches. They are urged to confront unintentional and intentional discrimination "against students in marginalized and de-valued groups" (Bemak & Chung, 2008, p. 375). "Specific practices [are suggested] for school counselors as they work to improve the cultural proficiency of their school settings" (Nelson, Bustamante, Wilson, & Onwuegbuzie, 2008, p. 215). Nelson et al. (2008) offered a checklist for assessing a school's cultural competence. School counselors participating in a qualitative study identifying advocacy strategies identified the importance of "raising concerns with teachers about how students were being treated; this included addressing teachers' assumptions about and stereotyping of students' cultures" (Singh, Urbano, Haston, & McMahon, 2010, p. 139). They also expressed how difficult it is to initiate such dialogues. Collins and Pieterse (2007) described the goal as "replacing the natural avoidance or denial of racial reality with an active understanding and acceptance of one's participation in creating racial reality" (p. 16).

Bemak and Chung (2008) offered 16 recommendations for school counselors in moving beyond the "Nice Counselor Syndrome" to become effective multicultural–social justice advocates and organizational change agents. Their recommendations address the ASCA National Model (ASCA, 2005), for example, aligning the advocacy work with the school mission, using local data. They caution professional school counselors about adopting inhibiting personal attitudes, for example, "3. Do not internalize victimization. . . . 6. Remember that it is not personal" (Bemak & Chung, 2008, pp. 378–379). They remind counselors of the importance of altruism, courage, risk taking, and more.

All guidance and counseling program staff members need to work constantly to establish a welcoming and respectful climate in the guidance office and the school. The office receptionist staff is particularly critical in this endeavor. The attitudes, thoughts, words, and deeds of professionals and paraprofessionals must be respectful and inclusive. Many school paraprofessionals come from the local school community. It is wise, however, to remember that the local community is probably not all of one mind, even though they may primarily be of one ethnic or racial group. Many school paraprofessional staff, although local, have worked hard to raise their standards of living and are relatively new arrivals in the middle class. Some are not as tolerant as they should be of those who are more content with their economic status or who are struggling to maintain their current living conditions.

Developing the component resource guides provides many opportunities to enhance the multicultural nature of the guidance and counseling program. Each guide can include examples of techniques that are effective across various cultures and include information for counselor-users about keeping students' cultural identities in mind and being responsive to them. The guidance curriculum guide should include lessons aimed at enhancing students' multicultural competence. Also, lessons should be included that address intercultural issues in the buildings. The individual student planning guide should include activities based on the same expectations, hopes, and dreams as for all students and not be ratcheted up for some groups of students and dumbed down for others on the basis of stereotypes. Indeed, Unwah, McMahon, and Furlow (2008) found that

> the simple act of inviting students to play a more active part in the school community—and the students' perception that they are welcomed and appreciated—may play a crucial role in helping underserved populations believe that they can succeed in a school environment. (p. 302)

Inviting students to participate in their own academic and career development through participation in academic and career guidance activities "can help [them]shape realistic educational aspirations" (Unwah et al., 2008, p. 302). Test results interpretation activities that help students establish educational and career plans must be done with awareness of biases found in most standardized assessments. The responsive services guide should include activities that portray a range of counseling and consultation modalities, helping counselors be ever mindful that the development of our profession is deeply rooted in European American, middle-class culture (Lee, 2001). The highest level of multicultural competence development is that counselors use "culturally appropriate intervention strategies" (ACA, n.d.-a). Advocacy is defined in the ASCA National Model as

> actively supporting causes, ideas or policies that promote and assist student academic, career, personal/social needs. One form of advocacy is the process of actively identifying underrepresented students and supporting them in their efforts to perform at their highest level of academic achievement. (ASCA, 2005, p. 129)

Responsive services need to be implemented that help students whose culture is different from that of the school or the dominant society as they wrestle with their racial or cultural identity development and with finding their place in the larger society. The system support guide should provide strategies that demonstrate how school counselors can help their schools become culturally responsive (Lee, 2001), including but not limited to reaching out to their communities and inviting the community in—to lower the protective walls, both literal and figurative, that are effectively keeping out the community.

In re-creating the facilities of the guidance program—the guidance center, offices, reception area, career center, and conference room—counselors should ensure that the presentation of information reflects diversity, from the reading materials available for center users to the posters on the walls. (A picture is worth a thousand words!)

In developing and using the political resources, inclusion—the conscious engagement of all of your constituent groups—is a rule. Take comfort in the fact that "school counselors who develop goals, prepare programs and are proactive about serving their community seem to . . . have more successful outcomes" (Bodenhorn, Wolfe, & Airen, 2010, p. 171). In working with the program's critics, in particular seemingly hostile parents, counselors learn much by being sensitive to their personal histories with school: Many non–middle-class, minority, and poor people have had school experiences that have led to mistrust of school systems. Listen carefully and probe sensitively and without prejudice.

In considering special projects, there are also multiple opportunities for attending to the diversity of students and of the school community. One expressed intent of the current accountability movement is to strive to ensure that schools hold all students to the same standards—the standards for achievement being academic tests. The requirements to disaggregate the data generated regarding test scores force schools and local, state, and federal policymakers to recognize those who are not being well served by the current system. Federal funds are targeted toward helping underachievers, unsuccessful learners, and dropouts; those who are neglected, latchkey, delinquent, or at risk; racial and ethnic minorities; children from lower socioeconomic classes; children who are or have been violent; children who use or abuse drugs; children who are truant, suspended, or expelled; and children in correctional facilities or who are homeless.

These groups of students have needs that counselors can and should be responding to. Many of them come to school from cultures that are very different from that represented in the school. Counselors can be the bridge. Portman (2009) made a strong case for school counselors being cultural mediators, applying

> an intentional process through which a school counselor . . . engages in prevention, interventions and/or remediation activities that facilitate communication and understanding between culturally diverse human systems (e.g., school, family community, and federal and state agencies) that aid the educational progress of all students. (p. 23)

Specifically, school counselors are urged to develop and apply cultural mediation skills "to advocate and serve (a) linguistic diverse students and families, (b) culturally competent family partners, and (c) community consultants and social advocates" (p. 24).

Finally, schools across the United States are experiencing racial and ethnic tension among faculty or between faculty and students. In a national survey of critical issues facing comprehensive guidance programs (Henderson & Gysbers, 2002), the example successful responses to the issue of enhancing school counselors' multicultural competence were by counselors who facilitated strategies for enhancing that competence in all staff members in a school (Locke, 2002) and in a school district (Zambrano, 2002). They provide excellent models of counselors advocating for improved situations for students.

The goals set for guidance program improvement in a school building must relate to the realities of the school's demographics, not be based on the population the school used to have or that people perceive is there but on the population that the data tell you is there. Goals should target discrepancies in services to various groups of students or issues with the faculty projecting stereotypes. On the positive side, goals can be established that celebrate diversity—that help counselors, students, faculty, and parents acknowledge, learn to work with, respect, and value all of the differences that individuals and groups bring to the community.

Any public relations or communications program or plan should consider the strategies that are most apt to reach all of the publics of the service provider. Therefore, nontraditional means of communication and working with the public must be considered. For example, in communities in which parents are intimidated or otherwise made uncomfortable by the school and school staff, providing services on their turf can be effective. Our ethical standards suggest we communicate with our clients in language that they understand; so too should we communicate in situations in which the clients are comfortable and, thereby, more apt to understand our messages.

Guidance and Counseling Program Leaders' Roles and Responsibilities

The role of the district and building program leaders shifts during this phase to that of staff leader and program manager for ongoing successful program implementation and to that of advocate for the changing program and the guidance program staff. Although the transition to the new program is being made, the roles that the leaders will play in continuing leadership and supervision of the improved program begin.

The program leaders keep the momentum for change focused and alive during the transition and, in implementation, maintain the focus on continuing improvement and fine tuning of the improved program (Henderson & Gysbers, 1998). A qualitative research study by Scarborough and Luke (2008) suggested that successful implementation of a comprehensive, developmental guidance and counseling program entails school counselors being motivated to help children and adolescents; having essential personal abilities and characteristics, appropriate training, school counseling models, professional role models, and experience as school counselors. They need to feel a sense of self-efficacy and have an awareness of the system in which they work and be integrated into it.

The district program leader steers the district changes and is the chief implementer of the district master plan for change. The leader brings in appropriate consultants to assist with the implementation of special projects. The central office guidance staff members are in a position to know what is going on at the district, state, and federal levels and have the responsibility to communicate and interpret that information to the rest of the guidance staff. The guidance and counseling program leaders manage the ongoing public relations efforts.

The district program leader develops planning and improvement systems to be used by building leaders and staff when the program has settled into ongoing planning, evaluating, and adjusting. The ultimate accountability for program success and for performance improvement is up to the designated program leaders. They work not only to ensure that guidance department staff members continue to strive for program improvements but also to encourage and reinforce their efforts. One of the methods for empowering staff is allowing them to select and plan their own improvements (Henderson & Gysbers, 1998). At the same time, it is conventional wisdom among personnel specialists that employees do what is "inspected" not what is "expected"; thus, inspectors are needed.

Some of this authority is delegated by the district leader to the building guidance and counseling leaders. The latter need assistance in carrying out their roles effectively. As is discussed more fully in Chapter 9 and in *Leading and Managing Your School Guidance Program Staff* (Henderson & Gysbers, 1998), this will probably entail the district leader directly modeling appropriate conduct as administrator, supervisor, manager, and professional leader. It will also entail encouraging these leaders as they try leadership strategies. A study by Dollarhide, Gibson, and Saginak (2008) suggested that essential leadership activities include

designing and implementing a viable school counseling program; believing in and empowering students, colleagues, and parents; negotiating the formal and informal power structures within a school or district; and developing and communicating a vision of healthy students and healthy schools, inspiring others, and leading by example. (p. 263)

To ensure full implementation, we encourage the continued use of other staff leaders—informal or otherwise—to ensure healthy communication between the district guidance and counseling program leader and the entire guidance staff. Informal leaders are often the best vehicles for honest feedback.

Senge and Kaeufer (2000) delineated several forces that might impede change during this developmental phase, which they labeled "Challenges of Initiating" (p. 4). These challenges occur "often after groups have achieved certain goals, only to encounter new problems, [and] as the project draws in more people" (p. 5). One is based on the fear and anxiety of the staff. They are anxious because they are afraid to make mistakes, show ignorance, or hurt others. Such anxiety needs to be acknowledged or individuals withdraw and become defensive. A second challenge that often arises at this phase is captured in the sentiment, "'This stuff is not working'" (p. 5). This is a result of expecting immediate results from implemented changes. Senge and Kaeufer offered two suggestions to leaders of change: "to appreciate the time delays involved in profound change" (p. 5) and develop clear mechanisms for assessing progress toward the desired goals. The third challenge they discussed is the tendency for staff members to "split into believers and non-believers" (p. 5). They explained,

> Because innovative groups create sub-cultures, a clash between insiders and outsiders is inevitable, but it need not escalate if leaders: 1) operate effectively within new sub-cultures and the mainstream culture; 2) seek mentoring from other leaders with high credibility in the mainstream culture; 3) build the group's ability to engage the larger system; 4) cultivate openness; 5) respect people's inhibitions about change; and 6) develop common language and values. (p. 5)

District guidance and counseling program leaders need to establish their roles with the principals and other administrators. Because administrative responsibilities are probably shared with them, they must be educated as to the guidance department's goals and priorities, and their support must be enlisted for the changes and the ongoing efforts as well. Their concerns and goals need to be attended to and supported by the counselors.

An essential goal is that of striving for open and clear communication between the building counselors and their administrators; this is sometimes problematic and deserves conscious attention. For guidance and counseling program change efforts to be successful, collaboration must occur between the counselors and the administrators (ASCA, 2005). This often puts counselors in the role of advocating for their program. The interactive nature of educational program decision making presents challenges to both building and district administrators; successful program implementation depends on taking correlated steps toward program improvement. The more these actions are orchestrated, the more effective the guidance and counseling program will be in achieving its goals of helping more students learn what the program teaches. The better training support building-level counselors have for their advocacy role, the better implementation will be.

During implementation of the newly conceived guidance and counseling program, it is time to focus on efforts to ensure that the guidance department staff members—professional and paraprofessional, leaders and followers—have the competencies they need to conduct the well-balanced and comprehensive program that is envisioned. Chapter 9 discusses in more detail how the staff leader can work to ensure that each staff member is striving to reach full professional potential, that each staff member is operating competently.

Your Progress Check

At this point in the program development process, you have made the initial transition to full implementation of your comprehensive guidance and counseling program. If you have followed our suggestions, you have begun making efficient use of the resources available to your program, seized opportunities to carry out special projects that align with others' priorities, developed plans and systems to facilitate building-level changes, and developed a public relations program and activities.

Efficient Use of Resources

For personnel resources, you have

- begun to improve counselor–student ratios;
- developed job descriptions for school counselors and other program-related staff members;
- established responsibilities for the building program leaders;
- clarified relationships among program staff members.

For financial resources, you have

- established district and building department budgets;
- developed resource materials to support ongoing implementation;
- established standards for facilities development and for provision of equipment.

For political resources, you have

- updated school board policies and administrative procedures;
- built support for the program among building-level staff members;
- worked with resistant staff members and constituents.

Provide Impetus for Making Needed Changes

You have begun

- focusing on special projects that address federal, state, district, community, or building priorities;
- facilitating building-level changes through use of concrete plans for change and goal-based systems for improvement;
- implementing public relations activities to communicate your new program design to the program's constituents.

References

Adelman, H. S., & Taylor, L. (2003). On sustainability of project innovations as systemic change. *Journal of Educational and Psychological Consultation, 14*(1), 1–25.

Akos, P., & Gelassi, J. (2004). Training school counselors as developmental advocates. *Counselor Education and Supervision, 43,* 192–206.

Akos, P., Schuldt, H., & Walendin, M. (2009). School counselor assignment in secondary schools. *Professional School Counseling, 13,* 23–29.

American Counseling Association. (2008a). *The effectiveness of and need for professional counseling services.* Retrieved from http://www.counseling.org/PublicPolicy/Washington.aspx

American Counseling Association. (2008b). *Effectiveness of school counseling.* Retrieved from http://www.counseling.org/Files/FD.ashx?guid=c051cc74-f3cc-4a59-9d81-770b5a4ab073

American Counseling Association. (n.d.-a). *Cross-cultural competencies and objectives.* Retrieved from http://www.counseling.org/Resources/Competencies/Cross-Cultural_Competencies_and_Objectives.pdf

American Counseling Association. (n.d.-b). *Resources for school counselors.* Retrieved from http://www.counseling.org/PublicPolicy/TP/ResourcesForSchoolCounselors/CT2.aspx

American School Counselor Association. (2005). *The ASCA National Model: A framework for school counseling programs* (2nd ed.). Alexandria, VA: Author.

American School Counselor Association. (2006). The professional school counselor and the use of non-school-counseling-credentialed personnel. In *ASCA position statements* (p. 52). Alexandria, VA: Author. Retrieved from http://www.schoolcounselor.org/files/PositionStatements.pdf

American School Counselor Association. (2011). The professional school counselor and character education. In *ASCA position statements* (pp. 4–5). Alexandria, VA: Author. Retrieved from http://www.schoolcounselor.org/files/PositionStatements.pdf

American School Counselor Association. (n.d.). *Effectiveness of school counseling.* Retrieved from http://www.schoolcounselor.org/content.asp?pl=133&sl=241&contentid=241

Bemak, F., & Chung, R. C. (2008). New professional roles and advocacy strategies for school counselors: A multicultural/social justice perspective to move beyond the nice counselor syndrome. *Journal of Counseling & Development, 86,* 372–381.

Bodenhorn, N., Wolfe, E. W., & Airen, O. E. (2010). School counselor program choice and self-efficacy: Relationship to achievement gap and equity. *Professional School Counseling, 13,* 165–174.

Brigman, G., & Moore, P. (1994). *School counselors and censorship: Facing the challenge.* Alexandria, VA: American School Counselor Association.

Collins, N. M., & Pieterse, A. L. (2007). Critical incident analysis based training: An approach for developing active racial/cultural awareness. *Journal of Counseling & Development, 85,* 14–23.

Common Core State Standards Initiative. (2010). *Introduction to the common core standards.* Retrieved from http://www.corestandards.org/assets/ccssi-introduction.pdf

Davies, G., Chun, R., Da Silva, R. V., & Roper, S. (2004). A corporate character scale to assess employee and customer views of organization reputation. *Corporate Reputation Review, 7,* 125–147.

Dollarhide, C. T., Gibson, D. M., & Saginak, K. A. (2008). New counselors' leadership efforts in school counseling: Themes from a yearlong study. *Professional School Counseling, 11,* 262–271.

Edwards, D., & Mullis, F. (2003). Classroom meetings: Encouraging a climate of cooperation. *Professional School Counseling, 7*(1), 20–28.

Employment and Training Administration. (2009). *Secretary's Commission on Achieving Necessary Skills.* Retrieved from http://wdr.doleta.gov/SCANS/

Fullen, M. (2001). *Leading in a culture of change.* San Francisco, CA: Jossey-Bass.

Galassi, J. P., & Akos, P. (2004). Developmental advocacy: Twenty-first century school counseling. *Journal of Counseling & Development, 82,* 146–157.

Gysbers, N., & Henderson, P. (1997). *Comprehensive guidance and counseling programs that work—II.* Greensboro, NC: ERIC Counseling and Student Services Clearinghouse.

Henderson, P. (1989). How one district changed its guidance and counseling program. *The School Counselor, 37,* 31–40.

Henderson, P. (2009). *The new handbook of administrative supervision in counseling.* New York, NY: Routledge.

Henderson, P., & Gysbers, N. C. (1998). *Leading and managing your school guidance program staff.* Alexandria, VA: American Counseling Association.

Henderson, P., & Gysbers, N. (Eds.). (2002). *Implementing comprehensive school guidance programs: Critical leadership issues and successful responses.* Greensboro, NC: CAPS.

Lee, C. C. (2001). Culturally responsive school counselors and programs: Addressing the needs of all students. *Professional School Counseling, 4,* 257–261.

Locke, D. (2002). Applying multiculturalism in a problem(matic) situation. In P. Henderson & N. Gysbers (Eds.), *Implementing comprehensive school guidance programs: Critical leadership issues and successful responses* (pp. 233–240). Greensboro, NC: CAPS.

Missouri School Board Association. (2010). *Sample policy: Student guidance and counseling program.* Columbia, MO: Author.

National Alliance of Pupil Services Organizations. (2007). *NAPSO.* Retrieved from http://www.napso.org

National School Public Relations Association. (n.d.-a). *Code of ethics.* Retrieved from http://www.nspra.org/code-ethics

National School Public Relations Association. (n.d.-b). *Getting started.* Retrieved from http://www.nspra.org/getting_started

Nelson, J. A., Bustamante, R. M., Wilson, E. D., & Onwuegbuzie, A. J. (2008). The school-wide cultural competence observation checklist for school counselors: An exploratory factor analysis. *Professional School Counseling, 11,* 207–217.

Peer, G. G. (1985). The status of secondary school guidance: A national survey. *The School Counselor, 32,* 181–189.

Portman, T. A. A. (2009). Faces of the futures: School counselors as cultural mediators. *Journal of Counseling & Development, 87,* 21–27.

Scarborough, J. L., & Luke, M. (2008). School counselors walking the walk and talking the talk: A grounded theory of effective program implementation. *Professional School Counseling, 11,* 404–416.

Secretary's Commission on Achieving Necessary Skills. (1991). *Report.* Washington, DC: U.S. Department of Labor.

Senge, P. M., & Kaeufer, D. H. (2000). Creating change. *Executive Excellence, 17*(10), 4–5.

Shepherd, L. J. (2000). Promoting professional identity in an era of educational reform. *Professional School Counseling, 4,* 31–41.

Singh, A. A., Urbano, A., Haston, M., & McMahon, E. (2010). School counselors' strategies for social justice change: A grounded theory of what works in the real world. *Professional School Counseling, 13,* 135–145.

Unwah, C. J., McMahon, H. G., & Furlow, C. F. (2008). School belonging, educational aspirations, and academic self-efficacy among African American male high school students: Implications for school counselors. *Professional School Counseling, 11,* 296–305.

West-Olatunji, C., Shure, L., Pringle, R., Adams, T., Lewis, D., & Cholewa, B. (2010). Exploring how school counselors position low-income African American girls as mathematics and science learners. *Professional School Counseling, 13,* 184–195.

White, J., Mullis, F., Earley, B., & Brigman, G. (1995). *Consultation in schools: The counselor's role.* Portland, ME: J. Weston Walch.

Zambrano, E. (2002). Opening the dialogue. In P. Henderson & N. Gysbers (Eds.), *Implementing comprehensive school guidance programs: Critical leadership issues and successful responses* (pp. 241–249). Greensboro, NC: CAPS.

☞ Chapter 8 ☜

Managing Your New Program

Implementing—Managing the New Program

- Improve program activities.
- Enhance the role of the professional school counselor.
- Develop the building program plan.
- Monitor program implementation.

☞ At this point in the program improvement process, you are ready to focus on implementation. You know what changes your students need and what the professional and parent communities want from your program. The plans and systems are in place to facilitate ongoing improvement as well as implementation. Challenges continue in the buildings and the district, however. In this chapter, we discuss some concrete ways to help make program changes in the buildings successful and suggest ideas for maintaining the momentum for change in the years to come. Questions answered in this chapter include the following: How can the counselors do new student-centered activities when they are still faced with so many nonguidance tasks? What is different about the school counselor's role? What does the revamped program look like in a building? What is the role of the guidance and counseling program leader in ongoing implementation?

First, ideas for improving program activities are discussed. These ideas include displacing some activities from the guidance and counseling program and streamlining the involvement of the school counselors in others as well as adding activities to the program and augmenting existing activities. Next, we present ideas for enhancing the role of the school counselors through a job description process, through explicit program planning and accountability, and through time management skills. Ways for you to monitor and encourage continuous program improvement and ways to attend to diversity are then discussed. Finally, guidance and counseling program leader roles and responsibilities in this phase are summarized.

Improve Program Activities

In comparing and contrasting their current programs with those desired, building personnel have identified where the designs match and where there are discrepancies. In a building, these point to specific program activities. As we discussed in Chapter 5, when the qualitative and quantitative designs match—that is, when the activities are effective in helping the right number of students achieve important outcomes and do not take an undue amount of school counselors' time—changes are not called for. It is our recommendation that in your program improvement process you take time to consider what you are doing that is right. Be careful not to throw the baby out with the bathwater. In addition, identifying effective, efficient, high-quality activities in the program is good for the staff's morale; it assures them that a lot of what they have been doing is worthwhile.

When there are discrepancies between the designs—either spillovers or gaps—changes in program activities need to be made. Spillovers in design include activities that take more program resources (e.g., more school counselors' time) than is desirable. Gaps indicate that too few resources are appropriated (e.g., not enough school counselors' time). To eliminate the design spillovers, activities need to be eliminated—or displaced—from the program or the appropriation of resources needs to be streamlined. To fill in the design gaps, desirable activities need to be added or existing activities need to be augmented to allow more fully for program goal achievement. Using the goal-based program improvement system described in Chapter 7, school staffs systematically set about repairing the discrepancies by developing specific program improvement plans for ways to displace, streamline, add, or augment activities.

As goals are set and changes made, guidance and counseling program leaders in the buildings need to ensure that the right changes are made. *Right changes* are those that have been identified by the guidance and counseling program improvement planning team, advisory committee, or both as having high priority for the students and being the best use of the professional school counselor's time and competency. For example, if adding parent education activities is the first priority and adding an afterschool small group for latchkey children is the second priority, those should be the first and second activities added to the newly arranged program. If removing the clerical work associated with referrals for special education is the first priority for displacement and shifting the counseling of students who are returning from school suspension back to the administrators is the third priority, these need to be accomplished in the order set. This order may differ from the counselor's preferences, but such is the collaborative process.

In addition to ensuring that only important changes are made, the counseling staff should strive to make the changes successful, to do them well, or to help others do them well. In general, this means having the skills needed to do the activity, planning the activity carefully, and including those affected by the change in the planning process.

Designing Program Activities

Intentionally designing or redesigning effective and efficient program activities requires making a series of decisions, as displayed in Figure 8.1. The steps are interrelated, and you can enter the process at any point, but most often identifying the student need level, number of students to be served, and desired student learning outcomes should precede the intervention selection. Table 8.1 displays options to consider as you work through the process.

Student Need Levels and Number of Students

As discussed in Chapter 5, students evidence varying degrees of need for counselor interventions. They present developmental needs common to most students in an age group (100%). Some, approximately 35%, present preventive-level needs. Fewer, approximately 15%, present remedial level needs. One to two percent present crisis-level needs.

Figure 8.1
Designing the Right Activity: Thought Process

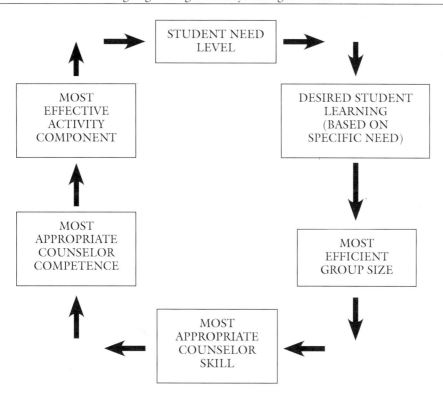

Desired Student Learning

Having identified what student needs you want to address, the next step is specifying what you want the students to learn or be able to do as a result of your activity. As described in Chapter 3, identifying your basic guidance program content goals (e.g., related to academic, career, or personal or social standards or related to self-confidence development and motivation to achieve; decision making, goal setting, planning, and problem solving; interpersonal effectiveness, communication skills, cross-cultural effectiveness, and responsible behavior) is fundamental to the design of your overall program. The specific outcomes of every guidance program activity should help students take incremental steps toward achieving one or more of those goals. Because it is situation specific, it is blank on Table 8.1. Example activity learning objectives are provided later in this chapter in the Adding New Activities section.

Most Efficient Group Size

Knowing the need level and the number of students you want to help suggests the group size that would allow the largest number of students to achieve the outcome. Generally, developmental needs can be met through large, class-sized, or small groups. Preventive needs can be met through small groups or individual sessions. Remedial and crisis needs are most often best met through individual sessions. Addressing developmental needs

Table 8.1
Designing the Right Activities: Options

Student Need Level/ Percentage Age Group	Desired Student Learning[a]	Most Efficient Group Size	Most Appropriate Counselor Skill	Most Appropriate Counselor Competence	Most Effective Activity Component[b]
Developmental (100%)		Large	Telling		Guidance curriculum
Developmental (100%)		Class	Teaching	Guidance	Guidance curriculum
Developmental (100%)		Class	Advising	Guidance	Individual student planning
				Student assessment interpretation	
Preventive (35%)		Small group Individual			
Developmental (100%)		Small group	Guiding	Guidance	Individual student planning
Preventive (35%)		Individual		Counseling	Responsive individual student planning
Preventive (35%)		Small group	Counseling	Counseling	Responsive services
Remedial (15%)		Individual	Counseling	Counseling	Responsive services
Personal crisis (1–2%)		Individual	Counseling	Counseling, assessment, referral, consultation, and coordination	Responsive services

[a]Based on specific need and appropriate guidance content. [b]Program model.

through activities designed to address crises (e.g., individual counseling) is inefficient. Addressing preventive or remedial needs through activities designed to address developmental needs (e.g., group lessons) is ineffective.

Most Appropriate Counselor Skill

Professional school counselors use a continuum of skills to help students (and others) learn. From most directive to nondirective, counselors tell, teach, advise, guide, or counsel students. The choice of counselor skill to be applied depends on the desired outcome. *Telling* is one-way communication from counselor to students. *Teaching* is an instructor-directed and learner-centered function designed to impart knowledge and to assist students to apply their learning. *Advising* is an advisor-directed, student-centered function that assists students with acquiring and evaluating objective and subjective information and offering illustrations of possible student decisions based on this information. *Guiding* is a student-centered and counselor-directed function that assists students with acquiring objective and subjective information and applying that information as they progress through decision making, goal setting, action planning, or problem solving. *Counseling* is a student-centered and counselor-facilitated process that entails applying appropriate theories and techniques to assist students to specify and resolve personal issues, problems, concerns, or dilemmas.

Most Appropriate Professional School Counselor Competence

Competencies consist of knowledge, skills, attitudes, and behaviors. The previously listed skills are at the core of various counselor competencies. Figure 8.2 identifies the relevant competency domains from the *Texas Evaluation Model for Professional School Counselors* (Texas Counseling Association, 2004).

Figure 8.2
Desired Program Balance—Henderson Public Schools:
Activity Slots/Program Component/Week

Elementary School	
Activity slot = 30 minutes	
School day = 7 hours	
Activity slots/day = 14	
Activity slots/week = 70	
Guidance curriculum	40% (70) = 28
Individual student planning	10% (70) = 7
Responsive services	40% (70) = 28
System support	10% (70) = 7
Middle School	
Activity slot = 45 minutes	
School day = 7 hours	
Activity slots/day = 9	
Activity slots/week = 45	
Guidance curriculum	35% (45) = 16
Individual student planning	20% (45) = 9
Responsive services	35% (45) = 16
System support	10% (45) = 4
High School	
Activity slot = 55 minutes	
School day = 7 hours	
Activity slots/day = 7	
Activity slots/week = 35	
Guidance curriculum	20% (35) = 7
Individual student planning	30% (35) = 11
Responsive services	35% (35) = 12
System support	15% (35) = 5

Most Effective Program Activity Component

Telling and teaching are skills applied in guidance curriculum component activities. Advising and guiding are applied in individual student planning activities. Counseling is applied in responsive services component activities. Table 8.1 displays the options for counselors in designing effective and efficient activities.

Displacing Nonguidance Activities

Activities from the current program that do not fit into the desired program become targets for displacement. The displacement strategy entails replacing undesired or inappropriate activities or duties with desired guidance and counseling program activities. Even more than the other strategies, displacing extraneous tasks from the guidance department is accomplished in increments. It typically requires consistent advocacy for doing what is right for the students.

In describing the current program (see Chapter 4), you identified ways in which the guidance department provides support to the overall educational program. Many activities to be displaced are those performed in support of other programs; others are administratively based activities.

> Counselors manifesting [Nice Counselor Syndrome] frequently agree to undertake any task that they are asked to do by administrators and teachers . . . even if assisting these persons compromises the professional services they have been trained to implement. (Bemak & Chung, 2008, p. 374)

Two acid tests to identify whether an activity is a nonguidance task are (a) Does this task make use of my specialized counseling skills? and (b) Does the activity objective lead to accomplishment of a guidance program content outcome? If you have followed our suggestions, you have identified these inappropriate activities by specific program.

Guidance departments often provide support for regular education programs by, for example, referring students to special programs, implementing orientation and articulation activities, participating in curriculum planning, assisting in the development of accreditation reports, preregistering students for next year's courses, consulting in the development of the master schedule, and making student schedule changes. Guidance departments also sometimes provide support for other programs such as testing, discipline management, gifted education, special education, and career and technology education. In the Northside Independent School District (1986) study, the activities performed in support of these various programs were time consuming. They absorbed 30% to 40% of the school counselors' time districtwide and left far less than 100% for the delivery of the guidance and counseling program. Similar results were found in the statewide time studies discussed in Chapter 4. In the study conducted by the North Carolina Department of Public Instruction (n.d.), specific noncounseling activities were identified, and counselors recorded the range of the percentages of their time spent on those five tasks and on "other." Table 8.2 displays the percentage of counselors who spent more than 10% of their time on each task. A study was conducted in Missouri (Gysbers, Lapan, & Roof, 2004) to determine what nonguidance tasks were being done by their school counselors. Table 8.3 displays the percentage of counselors in Missouri at each level who reported spending more than their fair share of time (i.e., more than 10%) on the identified nonguidance activities. It is clear that in neither case are students benefiting from a "100% guidance and counseling program." In both cases, the differences and similarities across the school levels are interesting.

Nonguidance tasks performed by counselors fit into four categories: student supervision, instruction, clerical, and administrative. Supervisory duties include developing and monitoring assemblies and hall, cafeteria, bus, or restroom duty. Instructional duties include tutoring or substitute teaching. Clerical duties include selling lunch or bus tickets, collecting and mailing progress reports, maintaining permanent records and handling transcripts, counting the credits that high school students accumulate toward graduation, monitoring attendance, calculating grade point averages, developing student handbooks and course guides, and scheduling admission, review, and dismissal committee meetings. Administrative duties include coordinating a schoolwide testing program, developing the master schedule, covering for the absent principal, assigning disciplinary consequences, writing principals' annual reports, making schedule changes, or even supervising teachers. Such tasks are targets for displacement.

Solid data provide strong rationale for displacements. They suggest which activities, that when removed, would return the most to the guidance program. Additional data that

Table 8.2
Percentage of North Carolina School Counselors
Spending More Than 10% of Time in Specific
Noncounseling Activities, by School Level

Noncounseling Activity	Elementary School	Middle School	High School
Duty (e.g., bus, lunch)	13.1	16.9	8.5
Registrar responsibilities	17.0	47.9	54.5
Schedule changes	2.0	24.6	53.6
Test coordination	48.9	51.8	50.0
Substitute teaching (covering class)	2.2	1.8	2.6
Other noncounseling	11.3	11.7	10.8

Table 8.3
Percentage of Missouri School Counselors Performing Nonguidance Duties, by School Level

Task	Elementary School	Middle School	High School	K–12 Schools
Coordinating testing program	71	83	64	81
Individual testing for special/ gifted education	67	65	37	56
Coordinator/manager 504 files	45	58	36	10
Supervision: cafeteria	42	37	15	37
Supervision: bus loading/unloading	40	26	9	10
Coordinating/monitoring school assemblies	33	28	20	32
Supervision: hallway	32	35	26	24
Principal of the day	32	9	7	22
Maintaining permanent records	31	51	46	66
Coordinating/managing Individualized Education Program process	29	33	12	
Administering discipline	24	17	6	10
Handling transcripts	22	41	65	73
Copy/mailing new student enrollment records	21	40	31	46
Monitoring attendance	21	27	27	27
Substitute teaching	18	23	19	32
Balancing class loads	17	69	70	56
Calculating GPAs, class ranks, honor rolls	6	36	46	56
Developing/updating student handbook/course guides	6	25	57	34
Building the master schedule	4	51	44	54
Supervision: restroom	3	9	4	0
Collecting/mailing progress reports	3	30	29	24
Managing schedule changes	3	74	86	71
Selling lunch tickets	1	2	0	0

Note. From "Non-Guidance Duties Performed by School Counselors," by N. C. Gysbers, R. T. Lapan, and C. Roof, 2004, *The Counseling Interviewer, 36,* Tables 1–4, pp. 28–31. Copyright 2004 by the Missouri School Counselor Association. Adapted with permission.

help support displacements include identification of the number of tasks involved, the amount of time spent, and the dollar cost of having counselors or others do them. But time is the essential quantity. Others often do not understand how much time is consumed by the activities that inhibit counselors and students working together for legitimate guidance purposes. Sometimes school counselors' perceptions as to how much time different nonguidance tasks take are colored by their feelings about having to do them. The data help counselors as well as the other decision makers in the process (Madden, 2002).

In addition, negotiating to displace activities requires solidarity among counselors. That is, they all must agree that the tasks are not appropriate guidance tasks and should be given up. As Anderson (2002) put it,

> I may be extreme, but I believe counselors must realize their role in the school building is as important as any other professional. Counselors are not in the building to "serve" others; they are in the school to implement a program and apply the distinct skills and knowledge that only they possess. . . . It requires a belief that what counselors and counseling programs do in the school is so important that, without them, the school could not meet its mission and the needs of all students. (p. 320)

Displacement entails a process of specifying the tasks that are done and either eliminating them or shifting the responsibility for doing them to someone else. It is easiest to manage if the big nonguidance responsibilities are broken down into a collection of small tasks. Then decisions can be made regarding each task rather than the whole project.

A special time study was conducted in Northside Independent School District whereby counselors identified the amount of time they spent in specific school management tasks, that is, quasi-administrative and clerical tasks that did not require a master's degree in guidance and counseling to accomplish. The first step in conducting the survey was to develop the list of tasks. Of such tasks, 41 were identified by the elementary counselors, 47 by the middle school counselors, and 34 by the high school counselors. The counselors then determined how much time each of these tasks took in an average year. If part of the task required counselors' expertise, it was recommended for streamlining—for keeping the subtasks that made good use of counselors' professional skills and displacing the others. The next steps were to identify the nature of each task (was it clerical or professional?) and answer the question, "Who else could do this task?" Table 8.4 presents data excerpted from the Northside study and displays the level of specificity that was found to be useful.

Table 8.4
Quasi-Administrative and Clerical Tasks Study
(School Management Tasks)

Program and Tasks	Average Time/ Counselor/Year	Recommen- dation	Nature of Task	Who Else?
Elementary School				
Special education				
Initial referral paperwork collection	7 days	D	Clerical	Principal's secretary
Test individuals	4 days	S	Prof	Teachers
Attend admission, review, dismissal conferences	5 days	S	Prof	Teachers
Total of all	39 days (21%)			
Middle School				
Regular education				
Register new student	8 days	S	Clerical	Administrative secretary
Change schedules	9 days	D/S	Clerical	Scheduling secretary
Special education				
Initial referral paperwork collection	4–5 days	D	Clerical	Secretary
Attend admission review, dismissal conferences	5 days	S	Prof	Teachers
Total of all	54 days (29%)			
High School				
Regular education				
Check numbers of courses chosen	6 days	D	Clerical	Secretaries
Change schedules	11 days	D/S	Clerical	Scheduling secretary
Check graduation status	7 days	D	Clerical	Registrar
Total of all	66 days (34%)			

Note. Data from Northside Independent School District, San Antonio, TX. Adapted with permission. D = displace; S = streamline; Prof = professional.

Although none of the tasks took an overwhelming amount of time, the total of all of the "nickel and dimed" time was 39 days per counselor per year at the elementary level, 54 days at the middle school level, and 66 days at the high school level. If all of the desired displacements were accomplished, 27 days of elementary counselor time, 35 days of middle school counselor time, and 45 days of high school counselor time could be recaptured. Having the data regarding the specific tasks and the amount of time they took made it possible to set priorities for displacing or eliminating the worst time eaters, and knowing the nature of the task suggested which other staff members could accomplish the task most efficiently.

Identification of the tasks leads to another question to be answered before displacement is considered: Does this task need to be done at all? The Northside study, which involved several buildings, found that counselors were doing tasks on some campuses that were not done at all on other campuses. Different buildings have different procedures and habits in place that need to be scrutinized.

If you decide that the task does need to be done, then the question is, How can it be done most efficiently? *Efficiently* means least expensively in labor costs or in time. Identifying who should spend time on these activities or how else the activity might be accomplished is the responsibility of the counselors seeking to divest themselves of the tasks. If the counselors suggest a reasonable plan, their chances of effecting the displacements are increased substantially. They need to answer such questions as who is the primary beneficiary of the activity? Who has the knowledge or skills to conduct the activity? How can the task be delegated to as many people as possible so as to take as little time as possible from each individual's time?

At the district level, agreements can be made between the guidance and counseling program leader and the leaders of other programs to facilitate the shift in responsibility for these activities to the related department staff. If you have other department administrators on the steering committee, you will benefit from their understanding of the comprehensive guidance and counseling program's primary mission and the new expectations for counselors. It is not easy to figure out who else will add these usually tedious or burdensome tasks to their calendars because other staff will not volunteer for them eagerly. If, however, the administrators know that counselors are not saying "It's not my job" but rather "But my job is to guide and counsel students," these transitions can be supported. Again, these changes are not made overnight or magically. Some fit into the hard-to-do category and require clarity of direction and joint planning by those involved (Petersen, 2002). The guidance and counseling program leaders and counselors must work with others to develop the new procedures for implementing the changes. An example of such a plan is included in Appendix K.

The additions to the guidance and counseling program that result from the additional time recaptured from displaced tasks should be made highly visible. An example of what we often hear principals say is, "If I assign the testing administration to the academic dean, what will I get from the counselors?" In addition to being prepared for such negotiation, counselors are advised to follow up by presenting the information about the additional student activities they are now able to do. To illustrate, consider another example from the Northside Independent School District project. Middle school counselors were spending 7.1% of their time on special education–related administrative tasks and 2.15% in group guidance. Further data showed that counselors were attending the annual review meetings during which the individualized educational programs (IEPs) were developed for students already enrolled in special education. Because special education staff members were already familiar with the students, the primary purpose for counselors' attendance was to ensure that the proposed schedule could be accommodated rather than to provide professional input regarding the students' needs. It was agreed that in lieu of counselors attending these meetings, special education staff would consult with them before and after the meetings. The counselors translated the hours of meeting time saved directly into a schedule for conducting classroom guidance, which benefited all of the students.

As counselors must plan with others how the nonguidance tasks will be displaced from the guidance and counseling program, so must they train those newly assigned to these responsibilities. Training people to do new assignments helps ensure that they will be done correctly. If you truly want to be free of these assignments, the first few experiments in accomplishment by others must be successful. This is easy to see if new personnel are hired, but not as clear if the task is given to someone who has worked in the district or building for a while. If, for example, you are asking teachers to make the schedule changes associated with their decisions to change individual students or groups of students to better match individual teachers' curriculum, training the teachers in the steps involved in making the changes is essential. Unless the teachers are naturally gifted at jigsaw puzzles, they will need to be taught about the delicate balances reflected in the school master schedule, about checking the impact that their change will have on the students' other subjects and other teachers, about completing the necessary forms precisely to communicate clearly with the data-processing system, and so on. In other words, moving students from one class to another is not as easy as it sounds.

Some displacements will entail hiring additional staff. Often, the case can be made for hiring less-expensive staff to free the counselors for activities that their guidance and counseling education has prepared them to do. For example, counselors are often asked to maintain cumulative student records, to become the school registrar. Those of you who have this responsibility know that it is time consuming. The answer to this problem is to work toward hiring a registrar or at least sufficient clerical personnel to do the job. A secretary or paraprofessional can handle the clerical aspects of scheduling. The sample nonguidance activities reassignment plan in Appendix K also identifies costs associated with needed new personnel.

Streamlining Counselor Involvement in Nonguidance Activities

The displacement strategy for reducing what we have labeled *design spillover* is to give up the task altogether. The second strategy is to reduce the amount of time that professional school counselors spend on an activity, that is, to streamline their involvement. In the activities targeted for streamlining, there is often an appropriate role for counselors to play, but over time counselors' involvement has become counselors' overinvolvement. Useful resources in streamlining efforts are the position statements adopted by the American School Counselor Association (ASCA; 2011) that articulate the appropriate role for school counselors in relation to a variety of issues.

Which activities are targeted is, again, a decision best made by the committee recommending ways to improve the guidance and counseling program on the basis of the time study data. The hard questions are, again, if this task needs to be done, who can best do it? How can it be done more efficiently? Taking time to answer these questions is worth your while. The Northside Independent School District, for example, learned from its time study that by spending half as much time on the tasks recommended for streamlining, an elementary counselor could on average spend 6 more days a year on guidance and counseling activities; a middle school counselor, 7.5 more days; and a high school counselor, 11 more days.

Streamlining the counselors' involvement in an activity, like displacing, often means increasing someone else's. By carefully analyzing the tasks that make up an activity, we can answer the questions, Who else can do it? Who best can do it? We have learned that there are others in a building who are better equipped or who want to do some of the tasks. In some cases, clear procedures or definitions need to be established and committed to paper to help someone else accept his or her responsibilities. In other cases, technology can help, or spreading the responsibility across a larger number of staff members. In still other cases, counselors can handle activities that do belong in the guidance department more efficiently than they are currently.

Some of the tasks that counselors do in support of other programs are, in fact, tasks that others are better equipped to do, but because of their systemic link to counselor-appropriate tasks, they have become the counselors' responsibilities. For example, assisting students to make and implement their educational plans, including selection of their courses for the following year, is an appropriate counselor responsibility. However, linked to that are activities such as making recommendations regarding the next math class for which the student might be best suited or developing course description catalogues. But the math teacher who has the students in class has more complete information on which to base recommendations: He or she knows the student's math skills and apparent abilities and knows the math curriculum more fully than the counselor. And the staff members who are closest to the information describing every course available in a comprehensive high school or middle or junior high are the teachers who teach those courses; thus, the instructional leaders of a district or building are the best producers of course guides.

Other tasks that counselors do are those that rightfully belong to someone else but that have been delegated inappropriately to the guidance department. Examples include developing the master schedule, the vehicle for putting students and teachers together. (The curriculum guide example may fit here as well.) Building the master schedule reflects the educational philosophy and priorities of the school, and it is the principal's responsibility. The graduate school program in which master schedule building is taught is educational administration, not counselor education. Delegation skills are critical for counselors to develop as they implement an improved program; delegating up is a particularly sensitive but viable undertaking. Petersen (2002) described an example of a school district that completed a process that ended with building administrators being in charge of the standardized testing program and with all school staff being part of its coordination and implementation. If the school is large, remember that a vice principal or assistant principal could develop the master schedule. These individuals often want to become principals and are eager to have the experience of doing the task.

Hidden resources for streamlining counselors' involvement in tasks are often the individuals on campus, such as the administrators just mentioned, who want to do the identified tasks because they are related to their program responsibilities or professional goals. In the Northside Independent School District, for example, classroom teachers, who feel great responsibility for helping each student in their classroom to learn the subject matter, wanted to be involved more intimately in the process of identifying their students' special needs. They wanted to learn from being part of the process that occurs before and when referring a student for special education services; thus, they were willing to coordinate the initial referral paperwork and have a voice in the admission, review, and dismissal committee meetings. Subsequently, the federal regulations guiding special education have clarified that the representative of the school on the IEP team must be someone who

1. Is qualified to provide, or supervise the provision of, specially designed instruction to meet the unique needs of children with disabilities
2. Is knowledgeable about the general curriculum
3. Is knowledgeable about the availability of resources of the public agency
4. Has the authority to commit agency resources and be able to ensure that whatever services are set out in the IEP will actually be provided (Rehabilitative Services Rule, 2008)

Related to counselors fulfilling more appropriate roles in this committee that is charged with developing an IEP for a child with a disability, the regulation states, "(6) At the discretion of the parent or the agency, other individuals who have knowledge or special expertise regarding the child, including related services personnel as appropriate" (Rehabilitative Services Rule, 2008). School counselors are considered related services personnel.

Other examples of who else can and may want to have responsibilities currently assigned to school counselors include program specialists, such as reading teachers and teachers of gifted and talented students, whom we have found often want to do the individual assessments needed for students to benefit from their programs. Yet other examples are staff members who are willing to carry out tasks because they consider the experience to be beneficial, such as teachers who benefit from covering the office in the absence of the principal because they want to be administrators and teachers who enjoy helping to plan and implement such activities as assemblies and student recognition programs because they believe that education is larger than what goes on in classrooms.

To make some larger activities more efficient, clear procedures often help streamline the work involved. As operational policies are set, procedural guidelines for conducting a series of activities or activities that involve many staff members need to be written. Such guidelines ensure that each staff member involved has the needed information and that there is consistency of implementation. In the Northside Independent School District effort, guidelines for making schedule changes brought order to what was formerly beginning of-the-semester chaos in the middle and high schools. Guidelines for times when testing individuals was encouraged—which implied when it was discouraged—helped save large amounts of elementary counselor time.

The secretarial and paraprofessional staff may also be used more effectively to streamline the amount of counselor time spent on nonguidance tasks. Tasks that are primarily clerical should be assigned to appropriate personnel; for example, routine dissemination of information and paperwork associated with such activities as registration for school and applying for scholarships can be distributed by clerks.

In many instances, modern technology can be more guidance-department friendly. We often hear the complaint that the computer runs the staff rather than vice versa. Thus, each computer-related decision and deadline should be analyzed with the same detail that other tasks are by asking such questions as does this need to be done? Is this the best time to do this task? Is there a simpler way to handle this? If there is a computer-assisted system for storing and processing student information, routine tasks related to this information, such as compiling lists of retainees or potential graduates, monitoring student attendance, and computing grade point averages, should be done by computer rather than by hand by a staff member.

As discussed, in considering the design of the desired program, some activities are necessary for its operation and benefit all or large numbers of students. These can be massive, labor-intensive jobs. Most often these tasks could be done with less cost borne by any one program by spreading the responsibilities to all or a large number of staff members and by allowing students to take some of the burden. Examples of these schoolwide labor-intensive tasks include supervision of students during their nonclass time on campus, providing extracurricular activities for students, preregistering students for classes, and assisting students to monitor their educational progress. Helping the entire staff to understand that the activities benefit them and are thus their responsibilities, and designing systems for accomplishing them efficiently, are ways to effect these shifts.

In a teacher–student advisory system, such tasks as checking students' progress toward successful completion of the school year or high school graduation become staffwide responsibilities rather than time-consuming tasks for one relatively small group of staff members. Moreover, by giving some of the responsibility to the students, counselors enable them to monitor their own progress toward graduation and thus be more in control of their own status. Advanced technology can assist this greatly, as exemplified in Provo, Utah, and described by Evans and Ward (2002). In addition, scheduling does not have to be done one student at a time by guidance staff over a period of 3 to 4 months—and then, in our experience, done again in the next school semester because of massive numbers of schedule changes. If the entire staff and the various departments work together, a university-type scheduling or Internet–telephone registration system can allow the vast majority of scheduling to be accomplished in 1 day.

Some streamlining can be done within the guidance department itself. As schools have grown and times have changed, many activities have "grown like Topsy," with innovations— and time—added on to the activities already in place. An example of an activity that needs streamlining is beginning the preregistration process in high schools in December, continuing it throughout the spring, and giving students a week to consider their course selections. An example of streamlining is using the information stored in permanent record files rather than regathering similar information, such as using group-standardized test results generated in another district in lieu of conducting new individual assessments. Another example of streamlining is using a subgroup of two or three to develop the details of an activity and present them to the staff instead of having the larger counseling staff plan every activity as a whole group. Another example of an activity that needs streamlining is maintaining systems of checking and double-checking work in reaction to previous errors, even though such systems take even more time and provide additional opportunities to make mistakes. We are aware of one high school in which each counselor checked the senior students' credit accrual three times. Streamlining in this case could be establishing a system in which the registrar maintains the report of each student's progress and counselors review the exceptions or complicated cases.

More about helping counselors manage their time is discussed later in this chapter, but at this point it is important to recognize that individual counselors fall into habits that eat up valuable student-contact time. Some counselors keep copious notes regarding their sessions with students, teachers, or parents; keeping records is important, but the systems used should be efficient. Some counselors take extended coffee or lunch breaks, often without realizing it, because student-centered conversations occur with other staff members who are also in the staff lounge; the relative priority of these conversations needs to be considered—to say nothing about the possible ethical breaches. Some counselors do their paperwork on student time, whereas teachers do much of their paperwork outside of the school day.

As guidance staff members strive to streamline the amount of time spent in nonguidance tasks, communicating and collaborating with those affected by the changes are critical to the successful implementation of changes. Through communication, others can be helped to understand the original problem, the rationale for the change that is to be made, and the ideas behind the change. As activities are eliminated or moved from the guidance and counseling program to others' programs, counselors must collaborate with the others to ensure that the plans are complete and that those responsible have the knowledge and skills they need to accomplish them.

Adding New Activities

The third strategy to improve program activities is adding new activities. As mentioned earlier, new activities must be developed to address high-priority but underaccomplished guidance and counseling program outcomes and objectives. It is imperative that the new activities be recognized as important and that they be done well so that their success is reasonably assured. In adding new activities, you have most likely displaced some traditional ones; thus, others will be observing the merit of the new activities very closely. Counselors who conduct the new activities, therefore, must have the skills needed to ensure that the activities are of high quality. As with everything else, careful planning ensures more successful implementation.

One set of new activities that is consistently identified as needed is small-group counseling in high schools. Ripley and Goodnough (2001) "offer[ed] strategies [they] found to be successful in planning and implementing group counseling" (p. 62) when they were high school counselors. They learned that successfully "implementing group counseling in a high school was contingent upon supportive school policies and personnel, thorough planning, and advocating for programmatic initiatives" (p. 65). It did not just happen because they wanted it to. They implemented a plan for improvement, gathered the necessary support, and added a set of new activities that benefited students highly.

A growing body of research has provided evidence that school counselors' small-group counseling interventions are effective in helping students with problems (Whiston & Quinby, 2009). In their review of school counseling outcome research, Whiston and Quinby (2009) also found evidence that school counseling interventions are effective with discipline issues, problem solving, and helping students improve their academic achievement. The Center for School Counseling Outcome Research and Evaluation's Research Brief 8.2 (Carey & Harrington, 2010) reported that in high schools in two states,

> school counseling was shown to be related to a range of important student outcomes including increased Math proficiency levels, increased Reading proficiency levels, lower suspension rates, lower disciplinary rates, increased attendance rates, greater percentages of students taking the ACT and higher average ACT scores. (p. 3)

The brief also supported other research that "indicate[d] that career development-focused interventions seem to be particularly important in producing positive academic outcomes" (p. 3). The current emphasis on helping students be more ready for college and careers is a nationwide priority. The counseling literature has supported the effectiveness of school counseling interventions related to other nationwide priorities, such as dating and sexual violence (Hillenbrand-Gunn, Heppner, Mauch, & Park, 2010), dropout prevention (White & Kelly, 2010), and adolescent depression (Dixon, Scheidegger, & McWhirter, 2009).

Just as counselors help others who pick up new responsibilities to develop the competencies they need to accomplish them successfully, so too do counselors need to strive to be highly competent as they undertake new challenges. If middle and high school counselors are just beginning to conduct classroom guidance sessions, for example, they should update their instructional skills. In the Northside Independent School District program, high school students benefit from an average of only six counselor-led guidance lessons a year and middle school students from an average of eight. Even in the elementary schools, for which there is a regulation that every classroom of children receives a guidance lesson once a week, there are only 36 weeks in the school year. It is clear that those few lessons need to be delivered skillfully not only to best ensure achieving the objectives for the students' sake but also to model student-centered instruction (guidance) for the teachers. Ways to assist school counselors to develop the competencies they need to implement the comprehensive guidance and counseling program are discussed in Chapter 9. Also, when school counselors are adding small-group counseling to their repertoire of interventions, professionally established standards are available to help them update their competence, for example, the *Best Practice Guidelines* developed by the Association for Specialists in Group Work (Thomas & Pender, 2008).

New activities need to be planned thoroughly so that students accomplish the desired objectives and outcomes. Thorough planning entails stating the objectives clearly, designing an effective and efficient procedure for helping students achieve the objectives, using relevant materials to support the procedure, collaborating with others involved, and managing the logistics of implementing the activity.

In Chapter 5, we described the conceptual flow for defining the domains, goals, competencies, outcomes, and objectives of guidance and counseling program activities. In designing your program, you have identified the outcomes appropriate for each grade level. In planning each activity, you need to specify the objectives that students will attain as a result of the session. Here is an example:

Domain: Make Wise Choices
Goal: Students will use a systematic decision-making process.
Competency: Sixth graders will apply the eight-step decision-making process with emphasis on generating alternatives and understanding decision strategies.
Student Outcome: Sixth graders will describe the advantages and disadvantages of using the three decision strategies they use most often.
Activity Objective: At the end of the guidance lesson introducing decision-making strategies, each student in the class will describe accurately 10 of the 13 decision strategies. (Gelatt, 1972)

At each level of increased specificity, more potential subitems exist. For example, in the Make Wise Choices domain, more goals are possible than the one cited, such as "Students will use an emotionally based decision-making process." Within the goal "Students will use a systematic decision-making process," there are more competencies than the one given, such as "Sixth graders will apply the eight-step decision-making process with an emphasis on the role their values play in making a decision" or "Seventh graders will apply the eight-step decision-making process with an emphasis on gathering facts." Within the one competency cited, there are more outcomes for sixth graders, such as "Sixth graders will generate at least three alternatives in a variety of decision-making situations" or "Sixth graders will apply the eight-step decision-making process to the selection of their eighth-grade elective." Furthermore, within the outcome given, there are more objectives than "Sixth graders will describe accurately 10 of 13 strategies," such as "identify the three strategies they use most often" or "describe the advantages and disadvantages of using the 'wish' strategy." The objectives for a whole content unit of activities should be outlined from the beginning.

As described in Chapter 3, activities within the different delivery system components of the guidance and counseling program typically have different kinds of objectives. In the guidance curriculum component, groups of students make developmentally appropriate cognitive progress. In the individual student planning component, individual students make implementation plans to progress toward identified goals. Through responsive services, students with problems or special needs strive to work out those problems or meet those needs. Activities in the system support component are focused on helping the students indirectly by consulting with others regarding them. An example of a series of activity objectives related to the same outcome is as follows.

Outcome: Seventh graders will manage their moods to be optimally receptive to learning.

Sample activity objectives:
- *Guidance curriculum.* All seventh graders will compare and contrast the appearance of different moods in seventh graders.
- *Individual student planning.* Each seventh grader will analyze the causes of his or her most prevalent, negative mood or moods and plan ways to cope with those causes.
- *Responsive services.* Eight to 10 seventh-grade boys identified as being emotionally withdrawn by their teachers will express their feelings in the counseling group.
- *System support.* All seventh-grade teachers will evaluate the moods displayed by their students for the purpose of identifying those students who are unable to manage their moods to be optimally receptive to learning.

In addition to demonstrating the interrelationship between the four program components, the differently stated objectives clearly lead to different kinds of activities.

An activity may also help students or others achieve more than one objective. For example, in the group counseling session implied in the responsive services activity objective just given for seventh-grade boys, a companion objective might be that the boys will identify words to label their feelings.

After stating your objectives and identifying the appropriate activity type (component), it helps to ensure connection with the school's mission and goals if you are able to connect your guidance and counseling objective to the district, state, or local established instructional learning standards (e.g., college and career readiness standards, state or locally adopted curriculum standards).

The next step in planning a new activity is to determine the best procedure for attaining the objectives, including identifying useful and relevant materials. The selected procedure needs to be written down, again not only to ensure precision in planning but also to allow all counselors involved with the activity to be operating somewhat literally from the same page. With the procedure written down, reusing or revising the activity is easier.

If you are operating on a multischool basis, using the same format systemwide facilitates sharing of successful ideas and strategies. It is our opinion that all proactive guidance and counseling program activities—that is, guidance lessons, individual student planning sessions, counseling, and consultation sessions—can and should be planned. Activity plans are different from the guidance and counseling program improvement plans described in Chapter 7. The improvement plans outline how the counselors will accomplish changing their activities. The activity plans discussed here describe what counselors (or others carrying out the activity) will do in implementing an activity. Items to be included in the written plan are as follows:

- program component
- title (which relates it to other program activities, e.g., the unit title and session number)
- grade level or levels
- group size (e.g., individual, small, class-size, or large group)
- time (of year, in which activity takes place)
- domain, goal, competency, and outcome or outcomes
- relevant academic learning standards
- activity objectives
- key concepts
- procedures outlined

- suggested methods
- resources needed and available
- evaluation strategy

Some schools and districts have found different formats useful for the different program components; others use similar ones. Example formats are provided in Appendix L. In addition to the plans for specific sessions, the Northside Independent School District counselors found it useful to have an overview sheet to summarize the lessons in a unit, the sessions in an individual student planning series, the various strategies for responding to recurrent student issues, and the various activities or tasks done by other personnel and counselors in the major system support activities.

Who develops new activities depends on whether you are changing a district program or the program of one school. In the Northside Independent School District project, activities to be implemented districtwide were developed by the program development leaders and reviewed by all of the counselors who were to be conducting the activities. Flexibility in methodology can be left up to individuals, but suggestions as to what works are helpful. Some activities were developed on individual campuses and shared with staff in other buildings. Activities that involve other staff members, such as teachers or administrators, should be developed collaboratively.

Relevant materials should be selected after the objectives have been determined: The program should dictate the materials; the materials should not dictate the program. Quality materials, however, not only assist the students but also can augment counselors' understanding of the topics. At the elementary level, various commercial materials are available to support the guidance curriculum and even, to some extent, the individual student planning and responsive services components. At the secondary level, not as many commercial materials are available, although the supply is increasing. It may be that materials will need to be developed locally to implement the activities properly for your community context. In any case, the guidance and counseling program leader and the counselors need to be realistic about how far the budget resources will go and should plan their expenditures in accordance with the program priorities. The new materials need to be ordered in ample time.

Whether a districtwide or single-building effort, new activities are best designed before the beginning of school (as much as possible). Once the school year has begun, it is difficult to take the necessary time to plan a new activity thoroughly to ensure it is being done with quality. However, finishing touches to the activity itself and the logistics plan may have to be accomplished after the realities of the school year are known. Logistics to be determined include what facilities will be used, how the students will be accessed, and the time frame for the activity and securing the necessary equipment as well as the materials. Again, the decisions that affect other staff members, such as how to access the students and the best time frame, should be made jointly with those staff members or their representatives. Your steering, planning, and advisory committees can be helpful here.

Augmenting Existing Activities

Many activities currently being done are consistent with your program goals and fit in the desired design. The fourth strategy to improve the program is augmenting or adding to these activities. In addition to extending the resources appropriated to existing practices, activities can be augmented by improving their quality, by adding objectives, and by linking related activities.

With a clearly stated developmental emphasis to the comprehensive guidance and counseling program, many schools have extended the amount of time counselors at all levels spend in classroom guidance activities. In elementary school programs, the small-group counseling service has been extended, in contrast to the secondary school programs, where this service has been added. Extending activities may be easier to accomplish than adding activities because the rest of the staff and the students are already familiar with the counselors' fulfilling this role.

In this context, enhancing the quality of existing activities means ensuring that the activity objectives are student focused, not system focused. An example is shifting the emphasis in preregistration from submitting the information to helping students make their choices. Enhancements might also be related to activities being displaced or streamlined. For example, if counselor involvement in test administration is being streamlined, it might be politically astute for counselors to expand their efforts in assisting others to use the test results appropriately. If counselors are displacing the task of developing the lists of students who might be retained, they could in its place provide specialized counseling for students who have been held back or left behind. If counselors are being taken out of the role of disciplining students, they could substitute parenting skills workshops for those students' parents.

Another way to expand on existing activities is by adding objectives to a set of activities, for example, making an activity more efficient by having it help students take several steps at one time. When guidance and counseling learning standards are aligned with academic learning standards, activities are enriched. Examples of academic standards include local, state, and nationally adopted curriculum standards (e.g., Common Core State Standards Initiative, 2010), college readiness standards (e.g., American College Testing, 2006), and state-adopted college and career readiness standards (e.g., Texas Higher Education Coordinating Board, 2009). We offer examples of enriching an activity by enriching its objectives using the Texas Guidance Program Content (Texas Education Agency, 2004), Texas Essential Knowledge and Skills (Texas Education Agency, n.d.), and *Texas College and Career Readiness Standards* (Texas Higher Education Coordinating Board, 2009).

> Guidance Content:
> Expected Result: Students in grade 10 will accept responsibility for decisions they have made. (Texas Education Agency, 2004)
> Algebra 1: Interpret and make decision, predications, and critical judgments from functional relationships. (Texas Education Agency, n.d.)
> College & Career Readiness Standard: Understand and adhere to ethical codes of conduct. (Texas Higher Education Coordinating Board, 2009)
> Objective: Each student will list five decisions they made during the previous 24 hours that were good and five decisions they made during the same time period that were bad.

A guidance lesson that would aim to assist students to attain the objective might include their

- identifying personal choices made and the consequences of each;
- considering their personal ethical codes as to what constitutes a "good" or "bad" choice;
- making judgments about the goodness or badness of their choices on the basis of their personal ethical standards.

In addition, counselors need to examine what they do to ensure that the level of difficulty of their activities is developmentally appropriate and sufficiently challenging. If your program has not been well articulated from one school level to the next, there may be overlap (or gaps) in what counselors have as objectives for students. We have seen instances in which counselors from all levels of a system have attended an impressive workshop and returned to incorporate the ideas or materials into their programs. The net result of this was—and could be—for students to be exposed to the same material in elementary, middle, and high school. This exposure to the same material may be all right, but only as long as the applications increase in difficulty to match the students' developmental levels.

Another way to add program objectives is to add to the number of staff members who help students attain outcomes. For example, if the teachers at a grade level help by doing preliminary activities before or follow-up activities after a counselor-led session, the students' progress will be enriched. For another example, teachers can infuse guidance content into their regular curriculum. Initiating this augmentation of the teachers' role in implementing the guidance and counseling program often entails the counselor assisting in the development of activities with the teachers.

Many guidance and counseling programs have grown like untended gardens. One result of this is that some activities have a relationship but that relationship is not formally established. The students will be better helped by connecting these activities. For example, activities that assist students' career development were developed more recently than the more traditional activities that assist students' educational development. We have seen guidance and counseling programs in which these activities were not viewed by the counselors, and thus not by the students, as related; yet it is clear that the more a person's career and educational development are intertwined, the richer that development. Linking career interest and aptitude assessments or visits to the career center with educational planning helps students learn the connection between education and work. Helping students as ninth graders redevelop the 4-year high school plan they did as eighth graders takes coordination by the middle or junior high and high school counselors. By planning the sequence of the two activities jointly and overcoming the logistics hurdle of passing the tentatively completed 4-year plan forms on from one school to the next, the impact of the activities is enhanced.

Enhance the Role of the Professional School Counselor

Implicit in changing the activities done by counselors in the newly designed program is changing the role of those counselors. The first explicit way to ensure that counselors are used in ways appropriate to their training and expertise is to establish appropriate job descriptions for counselors within each building. A second is to help counselors recognize the potential number of students who will benefit from their activities. A third is to use methods for helping counselors manage their time. A fourth is to help counselors manage their caseloads.

Clarifying Job Descriptions

Earlier in the program improvement process, we recommended that you develop generic job descriptions to outline appropriate professional school counselors' roles and responsibilities (Chapter 5). It is now advisable to specify each counselor's job description within the program. The job description, rooted in the generic job description based on the roles fulfilled by all school counselors carrying the same job title, clarifies the expectations for individual counselors, given their caseloads, work setting, special assignments, specific goals for the year, and any other relevant specifics (Henderson & Gysbers, 1998). For example, the sixth-grade counselors' job descriptions might have them be accountable for weekly guidance curriculum lessons during the first grading period to facilitate the students' transition into middle school; the eighth-grade counselor's curriculum responsibility may be heaviest in the spring in anticipation of the transition to high school. The seventh-grade counselor's annual job description might include the expectation of more small-group counseling because it is not a transition year.

We recommend that each counselor's job description be defined collaboratively at the beginning of each year by the counselor and his or her evaluator. This process provides a way to use the different skills that individual staff members bring to the comprehensive program and helps them to know what each is accountable for. It allows the school administrator and the counseling department head to ensure that all the desired facets of the comprehensive guidance and counseling program are assigned to someone to carry out and that those responsibilities will be integrated through the program implementation process (Henderson & Gysbers, 1998).

Recognizing Potential

Role statements and job descriptions clarify what counselors do on their jobs. It is also important for counselors and their supervisors to be cognizant of how much they can do for how many of their clients (including students, teachers, parents). The quantity of services provided is a function of the quantitative design of the program, that is, the parameters set for the program by the desired program balance and the counselor–student ratio.

The desired program balance establishes the amount of counselor time available for the various kinds of program activities in a month or a week. The desired percentages of time to be spent in the four program components suggested in the Missouri Comprehensive Guidance and Counseling Program (Gysbers, Stanley, Kosteck-Bunch, Magnuson, & Starr, 2008, pp. 94–96) are displayed in Table 8.5.

We suggest that each local system (district or building) adopt its own desired percentage within the given range. Within the suggested ranges, a school might, for example, choose the balance displayed in Table 8.5. This is the range we use in the rest of our examples.

To translate these percentages into actual times available for guidance and counseling program activities, determine the average time allotted for an activity and divide the school day by that number to determine the number of activity slots per day, using 100% of the student school day. (It is realistic to deduct one or one-half activity slot per day for the counselors' lunch.) Multiply that number by 5 to determine the number of activity slots per 5-day week. To determine the number of activity slots per week that, according to the desired design balance, ought to be allotted to a component, multiply the total number of activ-

Table 8.5
Desired Program Balance—Missouri Comprehensive
Guidance Program

Component	Elementary School	Middle School	High School
Guidance curriculum	35–40	35–40	15–25
Individual student planning	5–10	15–25	25–35
Responsive services	30–40	30–40	25–35
System support	10–15	10–15	15–20
Nonguidance	0	0	0

Note. From *Missouri Comprehensive Guidance Program: A Manual for Program Development, Implementation, Evaluation, and Enhancement* (pp. 94–96), by N. C. Gysbers, J. B. Stanley, L. Kosteck-Bunch, C. S. Magnuson, & M. F. Starr, 2008, Warrensburg, MO: Missouri Center for Career Education, University of Central Missouri.

ity slots by the component percentage. Figure 8.2 displays an example and includes some rounding for practicality.

Your translation computations tell you, from a counselor's frame of reference, how many of what kinds of activities a counselor can provide in 5 school days (100% of student access time) if all the assumptions are true. Not all of the activities take one class period or activity slot. If a counselor serves more than one building, the design desired for each building needs to be applied to the time (number of days per week) assigned to that building. Doing this somewhat oversimplifies the real complexities of a guidance and counseling program but nevertheless gives you a sense of what the balanced program would be like if all of the variables were in your control. Remember also that any change in the recommended program balance changes the projected time available for any kind of activity. Within a program, different counselors' job descriptions might call for their parts of the program to have different designs. For example, crisis counselors might spend a larger percentage of their time in responsive services than comprehensive program counselors. (The impact of a different program balance is included in Appendix G.)

To find out how many students can benefit from the activities, apply the counselor–student ratio. To determine the number of students affected, several assumptions again need to be established, such as the average number of students in a class for guidance activities and the average teacher–student ratio for teacher consultations. Some assumptions regarding the configurations of students in the activities also need to be applied. In the examples in Figures 8.3, 8.4, and 8.5, it is assumed that guidance curriculum is conducted with class-size groups, that individual student planning activities are done one-on-one, that responsive services are equally balanced between one-on-one and small groups, and that system support is spent primarily in counselor–teacher consultation. The impact of the component balance and the ratio on the level of services that elementary students can receive is displayed in Figure 8.3; that middle school students receive, in Figure 8.4; and that high school students receive, in Figure 8.5. The ratio used is a not-atypical 1:300. To demonstrate the impact of different ratios on the potential levels of service, examples of the

Figure 8.3
Elementary School Service Levels: Impact of Program Balance and
Counselor–Student Ratio of 1:300

Average class size: 1:25   *Average teacher–student ratio:* 1:20
36 weeks 1 school year

Guidance curriculum   40% (70) = 28 activity slots/week
  300 counselees/25 students per class = 12 classes
  28 activity slots/12 classes = 2.3+ activities/class/week
  83+ guidance lessons/year/class

Individual student planning   10% (70) = 7 activity slots/week
  7 activity slots × 36 weeks = 252 slots/year
  252 slots × 30 minutes/slot = 7,560 minutes/year
  7,560 minutes/300 counselees = 25+ minutes/student/year

Responsive services   40% (70) = 28 activity slots/week
  14 slots for groups (average 6)   = 84 students
  14 slots for individuals   = <u>14</u> students
  Total students served at one time   = 98
                                              (98 is 32+% of the caseload)

System support   10% (70) = 7 activity slots/week
  300 students/20 students per teacher = 15 teachers
  7 slots/15 teachers = 0.5 slot/week/teacher
  7 slots/week × 30 minutes/slot = 210 minutes/week
  210 minutes/5 days = 42 minutes/day

Figure 8.4
Middle School Service Levels: Impact of Program Balance and Counselor–Student Ratio of 1:300

Average class size: 1:25   *Average teacher–student ratio*: 1:20
36 weeks/school year

Guidance curriculum   35% (45) = 16 activity slots/week
   300 counselees/25 students per class = 12 classes
   16 activity slots/12 classes = 1.3+ activities/class/week
   42+ guidance lessons/year/class

Individual student planning   20% (45) = 9 activity slots/week
   9 activity slots × 36 weeks = 324 slots/year
   324 slots × 45 minutes/slot = 14,580 minutes/year
   14,580 minutes/300 counselees = 48+ minutes/student/year

Responsive services   35% (45) = 16 activity slots/week
   8 slots for groups (average 9)   = 72 students
   8 slots for individuals   = _8 students
   Total students served at one time   = 80
                                         (80 is 27% of the caseload)

System support   10% (45) = 4 activity slots/week
   300 students/20 students per teacher = 15 teachers
   4 slots/15 teachers = 0.25+ slot/week/teacher
   4 slots/week × 45 minutes/slot = 180 minutes/week
   180 minutes/5 days = 36 minutes/day

minimum recommendation (1:100) and an unfortunately typical ratio (1:500) are used in Appendix G. A blank worksheet is also provided in Appendix G for you to calculate your own potential. Although the math is somewhat arduous, we strongly recommend that you do this exercise because it is essential to understanding the finite realities of your program. It helps you and others have realistic expectations for your work.

Potential for the Elementary School Program

In the Henderson Public School example, each elementary school class will benefit from at least two guidance lessons per week (see Figure 8.3). If seen individually, each child

Figure 8.5
High School Service Levels: Impact of Program Balance and Counselor–Student Ratio of 1:300

Average class size: 1:25   *Average teacher–student ratio:* 1:20
36 weeks/school year

Guidance curriculum   20% (35) = 7 activity slots/week
   300 counselees/25 students per class = 12 classes
   7 activity slots/12 classes = 58 activities/class/week
   20+ guidance lessons/year/class

Individual student planning   30% (35) = 11 activity slots/week
   11 activity slots × 36 weeks = 396 slots/year
   396 slots × 55 minutes/slot = 21,780 minutes/year
   21,780 minutes/300 counselees = 72+ minutes/student/year

Responsive services   35% (35) = 12 activity slots/week
   6 slots for groups (average 10)   = 60 students
   6 slots for individuals   = _6 students
   Total students served at one time   = 66
                                         (66 is 22% of the caseload)

System support   15% (35) = 5 activity slots/week
   300 students/20 students per teacher = 15 teachers
   5 slots/15 teachers = 0.33 slot/week/teacher
   5 slots/week × 55 minutes/slot = 275 minutes/week
   275 minutes/5 days = 55 minutes/day

could receive individual student planning assistance from a counselor for 25 minutes a year. Of course, if children were grouped for guidance, each child would benefit from more time. At any one time, 32% of the children would benefit from responsive services, if the assumption that half the slots are spent on group counseling and half on individual counseling, parent consultation, or referral is accurate. An additional assumption about how many slots the average case or group uses could give an estimate of the total percentage of students in the caseload who could be served in this component in a year. A counselor could spend, on average, 15 minutes consulting with each teacher individually each week or could take a little more than 2 weeks to consult with each teacher for a full 30 minutes. Looked at another way, 42 minutes a day are available for other indirect services to students, such as program planning, public relations work, or professional development activities.

Potential for the Middle School Program

Each class of middle school students in a counselor's caseload could experience one guidance lesson a week (see Figure 8.4). The students could be seen one-on-one for individual student planning for 48 minutes each year, but again, if grouped for these guidance activities, each child could have more counselor contact time. With the assumptions stated earlier, 27% of the counselees could receive responsive services at one time. It is not atypical for middle school small-group counseling offerings to last a grading period (6 weeks in Henderson Public Schools). Thus, in our example, 432 students (72 six-week grading periods) could benefit from small groups over the course of a year. In other words, all children could be in at least one group and 132 could be in two groups. Each teacher served by a counselor could consult for 11 minutes a week, or it could take nearly 3 weeks to consult with all of them for a full 45-minute period. Because the system support component entails activities in addition to teacher consultation, a different way to consider how to use this time is to recognize that 36 minutes a day are available.

Potential for the High School Program

Given the length of the high school class periods (activity slots) and the shifted balance of the program, the students benefit from fewer guidance lessons: less than 1 per week or only 20 in a year (see Figure 8.5). High school counselors could take approximately 2 weeks to conduct an activity with each class in their caseload. However, 72 minutes per student per year are available to conduct individual student planning activities. Ideally, these activities are a mix of one-on-one and group guidance. At any one time, 22% of the students are receiving counseling, based on the assumption that half the slots are spent in group counseling and half in individual counseling or other responsive services work. As in the middle school program, small-group counseling series for high school students are usually planned for 6 weeks. Thus, over the course of the year, 360 students could have this experience. Eighteen minutes are available to consult with each assigned teacher, or to consult with each for a full period could consume nearly 3 weeks of system support time. Grouping teachers by department or by shared students makes use of this time more efficient. From the other perspective, 55 minutes a day are available for other indirect services to students.

Managing Time

Because the counselors' time is the most valuable resource in the guidance and counseling program, it is imperative that counselors and everyone else interested in the guidance and counseling program understand the possibilities and limitations of time. Developing the quantitative design (Chapter 5) was the first step in striving to ensure that the program that is delivered is the one that is wanted. Through combining that design in terms of real time with the realistic parameters placed on counselors by their student ratios, we are able to recognize what levels of services to students are possible. A primary way to realize that potential is through time management. Indeed, time management strategies must be used to ensure optimum use of the counselor's resources. As we believe that if something—especially something new—is not planned, it does not get done, so too do we believe that if an activity is not specifically scheduled, it does not get implemented.

Having established priorities for who is to be served, the content areas, and the types of activities, and having committed to goals for program improvement, counselors have the basis on which to plan how to use their time most efficiently. This planning is reflected on a series of calendars: yearly, quarterly or monthly, weekly, and daily.

The yearly calendar is developed before school starts and is guidance staff members' means for projecting how the program will unfold over the months available. It requires discipline to be realistic about how much time the major activities identified in the building program plan (discussed in the next section of this chapter) will take. A format for a calendar portraying the yearly program plan is displayed in Figure 8.6. The format obviously provides only an overview of the activities and the time, both of which need to be spelled out in more detail in other formats. However, in addition to being an effective time management tool, the calendar is a simple and graphic way to make the guidance and counseling program visible to others. It allows others to see the totality of the program at a glance, including the time required to carry out the activities. Traditionally, others are only able to see the small pieces of the program that they experience.

Things never go quite as planned in the school business. Activities take more or less time than anticipated; other priorities surface. The calendar should be restudied, adjusted, and

Figure 8.6
Yearly Calendar: Program Activities/Component/Month

Guidance Department CALENDAR for _____ Campus: _____				
	Guidance Curriculum	Individual Student Planning	Responsive Services	System Support
Aug.				
Sept.				
Oct.				
Nov.				
Dec.				
Jan.				
Feb.				
Mar.				
Apr.				
May				
June				
July				

filled out as needed regularly during the school year. *Regularly* might mean monthly, quarterly, or at the beginning of each grading period, whatever best fits your situation. At these intervals, measures of the progress being made are taken, and complete plans for activities for the upcoming time period are made.

To manage their own time and to ensure that they are adhering to the guidelines of the comprehensive guidance and counseling program and their individual job descriptions, counselors also establish a weekly schedule that details the major activities for the week and leaves sufficient space for responding to the unexpected. Depending on the consistency of the program and the students served, a weekly schedule may be set and used for a longer block of time. Elementary school counselors are often able to establish patterns, which (barring unforeseen events) are maintained for a year. Middle and high school counselors are often able to establish patterns for a month or for a grading period. To work compatibly with teachers, or in a school with a guidance schedule, a classroom guidance schedule is usually set and provides the basis for the weekly schedule. Small groups meet at set times, whether fixed or rotating, and are plotted on the schedule. Appointments for individual students who are regular clients for a time period are also set. Staffings and other regular or major activities are noted. Weekly schedule formats for elementary, middle, and high school are displayed in Figures 8.7, 8.8, and 8.9, respectively.

To ensure achieving the desired program balance, the weekly schedule is developed to reflect that balance. In the Henderson Public Schools example (see Figure 8.2), the desired program balance yielded a specific number of activity slots per week for each component for each school level, as follows:

Elementary School

Guidance curriculum	28	30-minute slots
Individual student planning	7	30-minute slots
Responsive services	28	30-minute slots
System support	7	30-minute slots

Middle School

Guidance curriculum	16	45-minute slots
Individual student planning	9	45-minute slots
Responsive services	16	45-minute slots
System support	4	45-minute slots

High School

Guidance curriculum	7	55-minute slots
Individual student planning	11	55-minute slots
Responsive services	12	55-minute slots
System support	5	55-minute slots

Figures 8.7, 8.8, and 8.9 contain weekly schedules for each school level developed to reflect these balances. The projected program balance and thus the weekly schedule project the use of school counselors' time during the student school day. Schedules may be set for activities that are planned for before and after school hours as well; however, a majority of counselors leave those times unscheduled so as to be available for spontaneous responsive services ("reactive services") or for unanticipated system support activities such as teacher conferences.

Weekly schedules are built on the basis of experience of such things as when responsive services typically occur in a week (Monday mornings, Friday afternoons) and when it is "quiet" enough to have a staff meeting (Thursday afternoons). Guidance curriculum

Figure 8.7
Elementary School Counselor Weekly Schedule Format

MONDAY

7:00 am	_____	11:20 am	Individual Student Planning–3
7:15 am	_____	11:50 am	Guidance Curriculum–3
7:30 am	_____	12:20 pm	Guidance Curriculum–4
7:50 am	Responsive Services–1	12:50 pm	Guidance Curriculum–5
8:20 am	Responsive Services–2	1:20 pm	Responsive Services–4
8:50 am	Responsive Services–3	1:50 pm	Responsive Services–5
9:20 am	Guidance Curriculum–1	2:20 pm	Responsive Services–6
9:50 am	Guidance Curriculum–2	2:50 pm	_____
10:20 am	Individual Student Planning–1		
10:50 am	Individual Student Planning–2		

TUESDAY

7:00 am	_____	11:20 am	Guidance Curriculum–8
7:15 am	_____	11:50 am	System Support–2
7:30 am	_____	12:20 pm	Responsive Services–10
7:50 am	Responsive Services–7	12:50 pm	Guidance Curriculum–9
8:20 am	System Support–1	1:20 pm	Guidance Curriculum–10
8:50 am	Individual Student Planning–4	1:50 pm	Guidance Curriculum–11
9:20 am	Responsive Services–8	2:20 pm	Responsive Services–11
9:50 am	Responsive Services–9	2:50 pm	_____
10:20 am	Guidance Curriculum–6		
10:50 am	Guidance Curriculum–7		

WEDNESDAY

7:00 am	_____	11:20 am	Responsive Services–15
7:15 am	_____	11:50 am	Individual Student Planning–5
7:30 am	_____	12:20 pm	System Support–4
7:50 am	Responsive Services–12	12:50 pm	Guidance Curriculum–15
8:20 am	Guidance Curriculum–12	1:20 pm	Guidance Curriculum–16
8:50 am	Guidance Curriculum–13	1:50 pm	Guidance Curriculum–17
9:20 am	Guidance Curriculum–14	2:20 pm	Responsive Services–16
9:50 am	System Support–3	2:50 pm	_____
10:20 am	Responsive Services–13		
10:50 am	Responsive Services–14		

THURSDAY

7:00 am	_____	11:20 am	Guidance Curriculum–20
7:15 am	_____	11:50 am	Responsive Services–19
7:30 am	_____	12:20 pm	Responsive Services–20
7:50 am	Responsive Services–17	12:50 pm	Guidance Curriculum–21
8:20 am	Guidance Curriculum–18	1:20 pm	Guidance Curriculum–22
8:50 am	System Support–5	1:50 pm	Guidance Curriculum–23
9:20 am	System Support–6	2:20 pm	Responsive Services–21
9:50 am	Responsive Services–18	2:50 pm	_____
10:20 am	Individual Student Planning–6		
10:50 am	Guidance Curriculum–19		

FRIDAY

7:00 am	_____	11:20 am	Responsive Services–25
7:15 am	_____	11:50 am	Guidance Curriculum–26
7:30 am	_____	12:20 pm	Guidance Curriculum–27
7:50 am	Responsive Services–22	12:50 pm	Guidance Curriculum–28
8:20 am	Responsive Services–23	1:20 pm	Responsive Services–26
8:50 am	Responsive Services–24	1:50 pm	Responsive Services–27
9:20 am	Guidance Curriculum–24	2:20 pm	Responsive Services–28
9:50 am	Guidance Curriculum–25	2:50 pm	_____
10:20 am	System Support–7		
10:50 am	Individual Student Planning–7		

Note: Guidance curriculum = 40%; individual student planning = 10%; responsive services = 40%; system support = 10%.

Figure 8.8
Middle School Counselor Weekly Schedule Format

MONDAY	
8:00 am _____	2:20 pm Guidance Curriculum–3
8:15 am _____	2:45 pm System Support–1
8:30 am _____	3:30 pm _____
8:45 am Responsive Services–1	3:45 pm _____
9:30 am Responsive Services–2	4:00 pm _____
10:15 am Guidance Curriculum–1	4:15 pm _____
11:00 am Guidance Curriculum–2	
11:45 am Individual Student Planning–1	
12:30 pm Responsive Services–3	
1:15 pm Individual Student Planning–2	

TUESDAY	
8:00 am _____	2:20 pm Individual Student Planning–4
8:15 am _____	2:45 pm Guidance Curriculum–6
8:30 am _____	3:30 pm _____
8:45 am Responsive Services–4	3:45 pm _____
9:30 am Guidance Curriculum–4	4:00 pm _____
10:15 am Individual Student Planning–3	4:15 pm _____
11:00 am Responsive Services–5	
11:45 am Guidance Curriculum–5	
12:30 pm System Support–2	
1:15 pm Responsive Services–6	

WEDNESDAY	
8:00 am _____	2:20 pm Responsive Services–8
8:15 am _____	2:45 pm Responsive Services–9
8:30 am _____	3:30 pm _____
8:45 am Guidance Curriculum–7	3:45 pm _____
9:30 am Responsive Services–7	4:00 pm _____
10:15 am Guidance Curriculum–8	4:15 pm _____
11:00 am System Support–3	
11:45 am System Support–4	
12:30 pm Guidance Curriculum–9	
1:15 pm Guidance Curriculum–10	

THURSDAY	
8:00 am _____	2:20 pm Individual Student Planning–7
8:15 am _____	2:45 pm Guidance Curriculum–13
8:30 am _____	3:30 pm _____
8:45 am Responsive Services–10	3:45 pm _____
9:30 am Guidance Curriculum–11	4:00 pm _____
10:15 am Individual Student Planning–5	4:15 pm _____
11:00 am Guidance Curriculum–12	
11:45 am Responsive Services–11	
12:30 pm Responsive Services–12	
1:15 pm Individual Student Planning–6	

FRIDAY	
8:00 am _____	2:20 pm Guidance Curriculum–16
8:15 am _____	2:45 pm Responsive Services–16
8:30 am _____	3:30 pm _____
8:45 am Guidance Curriculum–14	3:45 pm _____
9:30 am Responsive Services–13	4:00 pm _____
10:15 am Individual Student Planning–8	4:15 pm _____
11:00 am Responsive Services–14	
11:45 am Guidance Curriculum–15	
12:30 pm Individual Student Planning–9	
1:15 pm Responsive Services–15	

Note: Guidance curriculum = 35%; individual student planning = 20%; responsive services = 35%; system support = 15%.

Figure 8.9
High School Counselor Weekly Schedule Format

MONDAY	
8:00 am _____	3:45 pm _____
8:15 am _____	4:00 pm _____
8:30 am _____	4:15 pm _____
8:45 am Responsive Services–1	
9:45 am Responsive Services–2	
10:45 am Guidance Curriculum–1	
11:45 am Individual Student Planning–1	
12:45 am Responsive Services–3	
1:45 pm Individual Student Planning–2	
2:45 pm Individual Student Planning–3	

TUESDAY	
8:00 am _____	3:45 pm _____
8:15 am _____	4:00 pm _____
8:30 am _____	4:15 pm _____
8:45 am Responsive Services–4	
9:45 am Individual Student Planning–4	
10:45 am System Support–1	
11:45 am Guidance Curriculum–2	
12:45 am Individual Student Planning–5	
1:45 pm System Support–2	
2:45 pm Responsive Services–5	

WEDNESDAY	
8:00 am _____	3:45 pm _____
8:15 am _____	4:00 pm _____
8:30 am _____	4:15 pm _____
8:45 am Individual Student Planning–6	
9:45 am Guidance Curriculum–3	
10:45 am Responsive Services–6	
11:45 am Responsive Services–7	
12:45 am Guidance Curriculum–4	
1:45 pm Individual Student Planning–7	
2:45 pm System Support–3	

THURSDAY	
8:00 am _____	3:45 pm _____
8:15 am _____	4:00 pm _____
8:30 am _____	4:15 pm _____
8:45 am Guidance Curriculum–5	
9:45 am Individual Student Planning–8	
10:45 am Individual Student Planning–9	
11:45 am Responsive Services–8	
12:45 am System Support–4	
1:45 pm System Support–5	
2:45 pm Guidance Curriculum–6	

FRIDAY	
8:00 am _____	3:45 pm _____
8:15 am _____	4:00 pm _____
8:30 am _____	4:15 pm _____
8:45 am Individual Student Planning–10	
9:45 am Individual Student Planning–11	
10:45 am Responsive Services–9	
11:45 am Responsive Services–10	
12:45 am Responsive Services–11	
1:45 pm Guidance Curriculum–7	
2:45 pm Responsive Services–12	

Note: Guidance curriculum = 20%; individual student planning = 30%; responsive services = 35%; system support = 15%.

schedules are worked out in collaboration with the teachers whose classes will be taught by the counselor and are typically arranged first, before the schedule can truly be set. Although the schedule is planned using the class-period increments of a school, those time increments may be divided differently by counselors in their actual work. For example, high school counselors may not use a full hour for one responsive services activity but rather conduct two 30-minute activities or three 20-minute activities in the time available. Because the weekly schedule reflects the desired program balance, that balance must be maintained to end the year with a balanced program. If something occurs that interrupts the weekly schedule, counselors know that subsequently—and, ideally, very soon—they need to make up the time lost. For example, if a true crisis comes up with a student and the counselor cancels a classroom guidance appointment that day, the class that was missed should be made up the following week. It is through planning and calendaring that school counselors and their administrators are accountable for the use of the resource of school counselors' talent.

Each day should begin and end with the counselor planning and reviewing the details of the day and anticipating what comes next. Specific appointments are noted. Many counselors list the topic of the guidance lessons or group counseling sessions on their schedules and calendars for planning and for record-keeping purposes. The daily schedule should end up reflecting what really happened during the day, so that both counselors and their guidance and counseling program staff leaders, if need be, can analyze where their time is going. The schedules and calendars are tools used for both planning and tracking or monitoring the use of time. This not only helps counselors evaluate what they are doing now and this year but also allows for realistic planning in the future.

By definition, counseling is a responsive service, so unplanned-for events do occur. Some of these unexpected events affect counselors' daily plans, such as when the parent of a troubled student chooses to visit. The effects of major crises, like students' or staff members' deaths or school fires, can last weeks or even months. The traditional response to a crisis has been to drop everything and respond to it until some resolution has been reached. Depending on the nature of the crisis and its school relevance, this may still need to happen; however, through intensive program planning, it is clear that other priorities are important as well. The definition of a crisis needs to be clear; strategies for handling the drop-in visitor need to be developed; a balance needs to be struck. At the same time, schedules must be flexible enough to be adjusted while maintaining focus on the basic program.

An unfortunate by-product of the traditional, crisis-oriented, reactive approach to guidance and counseling is the perception that counselors and guidance and counseling programs are not accountable for what they do or do not do. Counselors may feel frustrated and are easily burned out when they feel impotent, when they feel that they do not manage their own professional destiny. Planning allows individuals to manage their own jobs and fulfill their promises to students, to the school system, and to themselves. Planning helps counselors know that the decisions they make about how they spend their time are in concert with those of other decision makers. Counselors can be and are accountable.

Managing Student Caseloads

In the local design of the comprehensive guidance and counseling program, priorities and parameters have been established for providing services to students. Not only are these priorities set for the provision of program activities and what students will achieve through participation in them, but they also distinguish among the categories of students for the various levels of service provided. Thus, counselors are accountable not only for their time and for students' achievement of specified results but also for the provision of services to high-priority student clients. Managing their caseloads means that counselors intentionally provide for students according to these established priorities. It also means that counselors operate in compliance with professional, legal, and ethical standards.

Professional school counselors' caseloads consist of the students assigned to them within the system. According to the *Ethical Standards for School Counselors* (ASCA, 2010), "Professional school counselors have a primary obligation to the student" (Standard A.1.a.). As described in earlier chapters, other clients with whom school counselors work include students' parents, teachers, administrators, other specialists, and community representatives. This ethical standard guides school counselors to know that the students have the highest priority. Within the student population, there are a range of subgroups, and it is within this range of subgroups that the next level of priorities to which counselors adhere are set. In a developmental guidance and counseling program, the first priority for student clients is to address all of the students and focus on their developmental needs. By definition, this means counselors help 100% of the students in their caseloads to achieve their developmental tasks and to progress to their next developmental level.

In the designing phase of program improvement, priorities were set to guide counselors in responding to students with needs for preventive, remedial, or crisis interventions. Each counselor is responsible for knowing the priorities and allocating his or her resources (competence and time) accordingly. In managing their caseloads, counselors need to spend what has been designated as the right proportion of their time with students according to their priority for service. Typically, students with needs for preventive interventions are school counselors' second highest priority; they benefit well from school-based counseling. Typically, the service provided to students with needs for remedial or crisis interventions is consultation with parents for the purposes of referral to community-based services or other specialists.

In addition to adhering to the standards established for the program, caseload management entails adhering to relevant legal standards on behalf of the students. Legal standards are set for school counselors' competence in certification standards, job responsibilities in state statutes or in district policy, and record keeping and maintenance of personal notes in federal law (Family Educational Rights and Privacy Act, 1997). Other legal standards that must be adhered to have to do with such topics as parents' rights, the limited rights of minors, child abuse reporting, duty to warn, and the rights of clients who are HIV positive. Although minors' rights may be limited, the exceptions are important to know. For example, in Texas it is legal for minors to consent to counseling without parental permission for suicide prevention; sexual, physical, or emotional abuse; or chemical dependency or addiction.

To manage their caseloads properly, the ethical standards of both ASCA (2010) and the American Counseling Association (2005) provide guidelines. Both sets of standards address clients, relationships, services, and professional competence. They address issues related to working with other professionals, conducting group counseling, and developing and following treatment plans, as well as records and notes.

Professional school counselors must manage their student caseloads to provide the right services to the right number of students with the designated needs. They must also manage adherence to the professional, legal, and ethical standards related to the students and to the services school counselors provide.

Develop the Building Program Plan

If you have been following the process we are recommending, at this point each building in the system has studied its current program design and established the design desired for the building program. The available and needed human, financial, and political resources have been identified. A plan for the transition from the traditional program to a comprehensive one has been developed and implementation is under way. Program improvement goals for changing the program activities have been set; that is, new activities are envisioned, ways to augment previously done activities are being worked on, and there is a plan for displacing nonguidance tasks and for streamlining the counselors' involvement in marginal activities. Job descriptions are written to ensure that appropriate roles are played by guidance and counseling program staff members, including the counselors and others such as clerks, aides, teachers, and principals.

Some counselors and administrators fear that the comprehensive, developmental guidance program is too complicated and time consuming to operate. However, it is our experience that once the program is designed, it provides an efficient and effective framework for organizing each school counselor's work. Counselors' multiple and varied responsibilities are clarified and prioritized. They can be understood by providers and clients alike. Counselors find they have more autonomy over the work and work days. They are also better able to be accountable for what is implemented. Also, evidence is mounting that suggests "that the more strongly organized programs are better able to produce positive outcomes for students" (Carey & Harrington, 2010, p. 3). Building program plans reflect realistic application of the existing program resources to the new design for the program. Decisions are made about which student competencies have priority for achievement, the activities that will be done through each program component, and how the program resources will be applied. The plan includes the annual job descriptions for guidance staff members. The activities are spelled out in enough detail so that it is clear what the program is accomplishing and how—that is, who does what, how long they take, what materials are used, which rooms activities are held in, and so on. Somewhere one or several large notebooks or file drawers contain plans for each activity session, so that a new counselor can walk into the program and carry it on without missing a beat.

Thus, the building program plan is a very specific description of what is planned to happen in a school's comprehensive guidance and counseling program: how many guidance lessons are taught at each grade level, by whom, and what the topics are; what individual student planning activities are done for each grade level, how they are organized, what the outcomes are, and how they relate to the past and future planning activities; and what the small-group counseling service offers, to how many children at which grade levels, and on what topics. Parent education and staff consultation plans are included. Moreover, the time frames for conducting the planned activities are established and laid out for the upcoming school year. The summary of this plan is displayed on the yearly calendar (see Figure 8.6).

The plan also contains relevant district and building definitions, rules, and regulations. Such clarifications as what constitutes a crisis and how counselors and other staff members should respond to a crisis are helpful. The principal's rules related to guidance and counseling are made visible and state, for example, that all advisories must meet for a minimum of 45 minutes a week, that procedures for consulting about students having difficulty should be laid out, and so on.

Monitor Program Implementation

By now, all involved are well into the implementation of a comprehensive guidance and counseling program. As difficult as planning and designing the program was, it is even more difficult to maintain the momentum for change and the improvements so that the program does not revert to its original traditional form. Systems for monitoring progress toward the established goals and for monitoring overall improved program implementation are developed and used. Staff continue to be encouraged to try the new activities and are reinforced in their efforts. Finally, program adjustments are made as a result of monitoring the changes.

Monitoring Improvement Plans

If you have used the guidance and counseling program improvement planning process and the format we have recommended, the guidance and counseling program leader, building principals, and counselors have vehicles for monitoring progress toward the goals that have been set. In planning the process to attain their goals, counselors have listed the activities they need to do and established a time frame for doing them. Depending on the size of the district, the guidance and counseling program leader can monitor counselors' efforts according to their time frames—a "tickler file" system will help—or reports of counselors' progress can be elicited on an announced schedule: monthly, quarterly, or once per semester. If there are head counselors, it is appropriate for them to monitor the progress of the counselors and for the district program leader to monitor their progress.

Monitoring does not need to be heavy handed; most staff will have worked hard to succeed and will be proud of their accomplishments. Indeed, monitoring provides guidance and counseling program leaders with the opportunity to support and reinforce their work. Moreover, if staff need resources that the program leader can provide, the leader will be aware of their needs. If for some reason insurmountable obstacles get in the staff's way or a well-planned activity does not yield the anticipated results, the program leader will be aware of their hurt and will be able to encourage them to continue to strive for improvement. Changing involves risk taking.

Monitoring Overall Program Implementation

The district has established guidelines or rules for the desired program and ways to accomplish it. Methods for monitoring the content and shape of the buildings' changing programs (and of the district's) must be used. These methods provide the program leader with information about who is and is not working toward the desired improvements and about what is and is not possible in the given circumstances—that is, about what else outside the guidance department needs to change for the program to be as comprehensive, balanced, and student directed as the newly established policy states.

To monitor the changing content of the program, the guidance and counseling program leader can use some of the methods described in Chapter 10, such as aggregating student outcome data or using unobtrusive measures such as cataloging the new program materials that counselors order for their programs. To monitor the changing shape of the program, the guidance and counseling program leaders can continue to ask the counselors to account for their use of time through calendars or logs. We recommend that the guidance and counseling program leader use the same time accounting measures because over time they will provide graphic evidence of the shift in the program. This evidence proves to be a reward in itself for the counselors. Remember that success breeds success!

Providing Encouragement and Reinforcement

Part of the difficulty of maintaining a program stems from problems associated with trying to change staff work behavior patterns. It is relatively easy to do something new once, particularly if it is highly visible. Some staff members may sabotage the improvement process by going along with a new activity once but withdrawing their support when it is over. As a result, it is important to build into the program ways of assessing the need for reinforcement and ways to provide such reinforcement.

Because the need for reinforcement occurs over time, at least part of the staff development program should be designed to provide it. Skill-building and discussion sessions that take place on a regular basis are vital. Skill-building opportunities can be provided by encouraging counselors in the system to share their successful new activities with others in a mini-conference format, if the system is large enough to do this, or at local, state, or national professional development conferences.

Staff meetings provide the vehicle for ensuring that the school counselors in a building provide a unified guidance and counseling program (Henderson & Gysbers, 1998). Through regular weekly meetings, counselors discuss the activities they have just completed and suggest any improvements that seem feasible for the next year. They finalize plans for the activities coming up in the next week and begin or continue planning for large events that are in the near future. They monitor the implementation of the program in line with the plans they have for the year, ensuring progress toward their improvement goals as well.

Staff meetings also provide the vehicle for school counselors to build a department team, and working as a team not only enhances integration of the program activities but also empowers counselors by providing them opportunities for professional "reassurance and collegiality" (Henderson & Gysbers, 1998, p. 74). Staff meetings also provide counselors opportunities to talk with their colleagues about guidance and counseling issues. Professional dialogues, noted Glickman and Jones (1986), are one of the critical factors in creating a successful school, and "essentially a dialogue occurs when supervisors provide the elements of time, focus, and structure for individuals to meet and talk" (p. 90). Thus, counselors' staff meetings are an essential vehicle for continuing to encourage needed changes as well as for ensuring basic communication of information.

More informally, birthday parties, potluck dinners, and other socials are helpful ways to provide reinforcement and form interbuilding teams. When such events are planned, consider the downtime that occurs in any academic year. For example, the last part of January and the first part of February often need special events to brighten the season. Midyear conferences can be held on a regional basis and are usually well attended.

Making Program Adjustments

As the program unfolds, there will be times when it is necessary to make program adjustments. Keep in mind that such adjustments are fine-tuning adjustments; they are not major adjustments made as part of the initial program improvement. Those come after more thorough evaluation, as discussed in Chapter 11. Any changes made in the program now should be made only after careful thought. Some needed changes will be obvious, as with activities that simply do not work. Others will not be obvious on the surface but will become visible after systematic evaluation. As a rule, count to 10 before making any substantial changes. Some activities need time to take hold and as a result may not show up well at first. For example, a shift from individual guidance to group guidance may not be appreciated at first by students who are used to individual attention, but as more students receive more guidance through groups, the positive effects will influence the evaluation.

Monitoring and adjusting the program are the results of formative evaluation. For now, the kinds of changes you can expect to be making most often as you fine-tune the program may include modification of timetables, modification of activity schedules, substitution or modification of activities, substitution of resources, and changes in priorities for student competency development at various grade levels. Major adjustments are the result of summative evaluation and lead to program revision. The example of Northside Independent School District's revision process and product is discussed in Chapter 11.

Attend to Diversity

This phase of the program development process—implementing the desired program design—presents opportunities to attend to the needs and wants as well as the topics and issues presented by the diversity found in the district's and buildings' students and communities. The recaptured time from displacing and streamlining counselor involvement in nonguidance activities can be directed toward adding or augmenting activities that fill in gaps in services that target students' cross-cultural competence, cultural identity development, and the like. Currently, professional journals and publications describe activities that help students become more multiculturally competent (e.g., Orbé-Austin, 2010; Roaten & Schmidt, 2009). Continuing research is clarifying similarities and differences between students from different cultural backgrounds (e.g., Burnham & Lomax, 2009).

As resources expand, professional school counselors who are hired can help balance the staff to reflect the demographics of the student population. Program improvements can be designed that target enhancement of the buildings' cultural responsiveness. Within the goal-setting process, each building's guidance program staff can be encouraged to advocate for strategies that attend to the unique culture of its community. As each building identifies its demographics and related issues, each staff can better strive for equity of and equal access to services for all their students. Specific targets can be set for better serving underserved student clients, often the school's minority students.

Guidance and Counseling Program Leader's Roles and Responsibilities

During the program implementation phase, the guidance and counseling program leader's responsibility shifts to helping counselors achieve the right program balance and manage their time for efficiency and accountability. Monitoring their programs and performance is accomplished through ongoing use of goal-setting and planning processes. It is imperative that someone review the plans and encourage their implementation and that someone assist the counselors in assessing their level of goal attainment. Accountability is a key to successful ongoing implementation. Hersey, Blanchard, and Johnson (2001) echoed, "Two basic tenets of management—measure and monitor your expectations. . . . Briefly, inspect what you expect" (p. 411).

Accomplishing the desired changes in a district takes continuing work also, both programmatically and in resource development. Hersey et al. (2001) made some relevant points about helping people change their work behaviors. One is to identify "areas where immediate successes can be achieved as a means of reinforcing implementation" (p. 408). Another "is to find a change that is not only easy to implement in terms of necessary skills, but that also will only minimally disrupt the usual roles in the organization" (p. 408). And then, "A related idea is to find a change that will have a high probability of acceptance" (p. 409) among leaders, counselors, and clients.

It may be helpful to have a new emphasis each year to help counselors focus on the program design discrepancies. As mentioned earlier, you work through the addition and subtraction of activities in priority order. The guidance and counseling program leader keeps track of that order. As activities are displaced, it is helpful for the district to issue some mandates for new or improved guidance and counseling activities. These mandates help make it clear that counselors are not just giving up some tasks but that they are being held accountable for other, more appropriate guidance activities. In several districts with which we have worked, the counselors had given up on parent education efforts, often because parents did not readily come to school functions. Guidance and counseling program leaders have restated counselors' responsibility to help parents learn parenting skills and have encouraged the elementary, middle, and high school counselors in their community to work together to meet that responsibility in light of the community's needs. This has improved the parenting efforts as well as the collegiality within local communities.

Items in the district master plan for change that require money (such as ratio improvements) take time to accomplish. Not only does the program leader continue to seek these resource improvements, but the designers and decision makers also often have to be reminded that they cannot have more than the resources will cover. Remember: The counselor-to-student ratio has to be adequate to implement the designed program, or the program has to be designed within the parameters of the ratio; until the desired ratio is established, the desired program cannot be implemented fully.

New and improved activities often call for new operational policies or administrative regulations. Broadly shared activities may need written definitions for tasks, responsibilities, and timelines that were formerly handled by one department. For example, with the entire school staff involved in preregistration tasks because of streamlining, the series of events needs to be planned carefully. However, an additional benefit has been that the overall job can be done in a shorter time frame because the labor is shared more broadly.

Clarifying responsibilities for the entire caseload and providing special services for identified high-priority caseload members dictate that leaders provide training and develop systems to help school counselors manage their caseload-related responsibilities. Renewed sensitivity to student issues and problems results in counselors (and other specialists) managing more complicated cases. It is important to define rather specifically what constitutes a student crisis that is worthy of interrupting a counselor's planned schedule. Procedures for intervening appropriately should also be spelled out. Included in Appendix F is a regulation developed in Northside Independent School District to clarify the district's position about what various staff members should do to help students manage personal crises. The procedure outlined provides guidelines for balancing the responsibilities to the student and the parent with those of various staff members and suggests a procedure for collaboration. In Texas and other states, school districts and buildings are required to have crisis management plans that spell out what is to be done in case of a student suicide or other major catastrophe that affects the total—or a large portion of the total—school population.

An additional challenge for the guidance and counseling program leader in implementation is to continually build support for the program and the agreed-on design. There will always be a minority of staff members—counselors, administrators, teachers, and others—who do not understand or appreciate the changed program. In many districts, there are new principals, counselors, and other key staff members who need to be educated about the program and its priorities. At the district level, this demands direct work by the district guidance and counseling program leader; at the building level, by the building program leaders and counselors, with support from the district. Finally, the staff leadership continues to help all staff members be aware of and responsive to the full range of diversity presented by individual students and families and to the issues posed and opportunities provided by the diversity in the United States and locally.

Keys to Success

After nearly 40 years of experience with developing and managing comprehensive guidance programs, we have identified several keys to successful implementation of a program. Having systems in place to support these strategies facilitates continuing improvement and maintenance of ground already gained in the program. Many of these have been described in this chapter; others are described in subsequent chapters. They are

1. developing a yearly program plan each year;
2. developing weekly schedules;
3. planning, implementing, and assessing guidance program improvement goals;
4. providing leadership and supervision for the guidance program and its staff;
5. defining each individual professional school counselor's job for the year;
6. helping school counselors plan, implement, and assess professional development goals for each year;
7. holding weekly building guidance program staff meetings;
8. holding regular district guidance program staff meetings;
9. holding professional school counselors and their administrators accountable for achieving student results through the guidance program, adhering to guidance program implementation standards, evaluating the quality of school counselor performance, and striving to implement program improvements.

Your Progress Check

At this point, you are implementing an ever-improving program, moving toward the program you want. If you are following our suggestions, you are improving your program activities and supporting professional school counselors' systematic work.

Improving Program Activities

You have

- aligned your current program activities with each of the four program components;
- begun displacing or streamlining identified nonguidance tasks that take more than a fair share of professional school counselors' time;
- begun making needed changes in program activities to make use of school counselors' specialized competencies by (a) adding new, high-priority ones (e.g., small-group counseling, enhancing students' cross-cultural competence) and (b) augmenting existing activities;
- calculated the potential numbers of activities to be done in each component and the number of students who could benefit from the various component activities and services.

Working Systematically

You are

- planning, designing, implementing, evaluating, and enhancing activities;
- intentionally designing or redesigning activities;
- managing professional school counselors' time by using calendars and schedules;
- managing student caseloads according to established priorities and standards;
- monitoring program improvements and implementation;
- making program adjustments on the basis of formative evaluations;
- developing resources for further program improvement;
- conducting program-relevant staff development for professional school counselors;
- convening guidance department staff meetings and social events.

After 5 years or so of program implementation, the program design and framework ought to be reconsidered and revised as necessary. As discussed in Chapters 10 and 11, evaluation results will have much to tell the redesigners. Experience with the program balance will have told you whether it is appropriate. Ongoing assessments of students', parents', and school staff members' needs will better guide prioritizing delivery of the program components. An enhanced role for school counselors allows for a focused staff development program, but priorities will change over time. As mentioned throughout this book, helping counselors have the competencies they need is essential to successful implementation of the comprehensive guidance and counseling program; ways to do this are discussed in the next chapter.

References

American College Testing. (2006). *College readiness standards for EXPLORE, PLAN and the ACT.* Iowa City, IA: Author.

American Counseling Association. (2005). *ACA code of ethics.* Alexandria, VA: Author. Retrieved from http://www.counseling.org/resources/CodeOfEthics/TP/Home/CT2.aspx

American School Counselor Association. (2010). *Ethical standards for school counselors.* Retrieved from http://asca2.timberlakepublishing.com//files/EthicalStandards2010.pdf

American School Counselor Association. (2011). *ASCA position statements.* Alexandria, VA: Author. Retrieved from http://www.schoolcounselor.org/files/PositionStatements.pdf

Anderson, K. (2002). A response to common themes in school counseling. *Professional School Counseling, 5,* 315–321.

Bemak, F., & Chung, R. C. (2008). New professional roles and advocacy strategies for school counselors: A multicultural/social justice perspective to move beyond the nice counselor syndrome. *Journal of Counseling & Development, 86,* 372–381.

Burnham, J. J., & Lomax, R. G. (2009). Examining race/ethnicity and fears of children and adolescents in the United States: Differences between White, African American, and Hispanic populations. *Journal of Counseling & Development, 87,* 387–393.

Carey, J. C., & Harrington, K. M. (2010). *The impact of school counseling on student educational outcomes in high schools: What can we learn about effectiveness from statewide evaluations of school counseling practice in Nebraska and Utah?* (Research Brief 8.2). Amherst, MA: Center for School Counseling Outcome Research and Evaluation.

Common Core State Standards Initiative. (2010). *Introduction to the common core standards.* Retrieved from http://www.corestandards.org/assets/ccssi-introduction.pdf

Dixon, A. L., Scheidegger, C., & McWhirter, J. J. (2009). The adolescent mattering experience: Gender variations in perceived mattering, anxiety, and depression. *Journal of Counseling & Development, 87,* 302–310.

Evans, B., & Ward, S. (2002). Solving the "time and information" dilemma through technology. In P. Henderson & N. Gysbers (Eds.), *Implementing comprehensive guidance programs: Critical leadership issues and successful responses* (pp. 55–64). Greensboro, NC: CAPS.

Family Educational Rights and Privacy Act, 34 C.F.R. § 99 (1997).

Gelatt, H. B. (1972). *Deciding.* New York, NY: College Entrance Examination Board.

Glickman, C. D., & Jones, J. W. (1986). Supervision: Creating the dialogue. *Educational Leadership, 44,* 90–91.

Gysbers, N. C., Lapan, R. T., & Roof, C. (2004). Nonguidance duties performed by school counselors: What are they? Why are they a problem? What can be done about them? *The Counseling Interviewer, 36,* 23–32.

Gysbers, N. C., Stanley, J. B., Kosteck-Bunch, L., Magnuson, C. S., & Starr, M. F. (2008). *Missouri comprehensive guidance program: A manual for program development, implementation, evaluation and enhancement.* Warrensburg: Missouri Center for Career Education, University of Central Missouri.

Henderson, P., & Gysbers, N. C. (1998). *Leading and managing your school guidance and counseling program staff.* Alexandria, VA: American Counseling Association.

Hersey, P., Blanchard, K. H., & Johnson, D. E. (2001). *Management of organizational behavior: Leading human resources* (8th ed.). Upper Saddle River, NJ: Prentice-Hall.

Hillenbrand-Gunn, T. L., Heppner, M. J., Mauch, P. A., & Park, H.-J. (2010). The efficacy of a high school rape prevention intervention. *Journal of Counseling & Development, 88,* 43–51.

Madden, J. (2002). Displacing nonguidance tasks and initiating program improvement. In P. Henderson & N. Gysbers (Eds.), *Implementing comprehensive guidance programs: Critical leadership issues and successful responses* (pp. 55–64). Greensboro, NC: CAPS.

North Carolina Department of Public Instruction. (n.d.). *How North Carolina school counselors spend their time.* Retrieved from http://www.ncpublicschools.org/docs/curriculum/guidance/resources/programofstudy/schoolcounselor.pdf

Northside Independent School District. (1986). *Comprehensive guidance program framework.* San Antonio, TX: Author.

Orbé-Austin, R. (2010, April 1). Multicultural career counseling competence: 5 key tips for improving practice. *Career Convergence.* Retrieved from http://associationdatabase.com/aws/NCDA/pt/sd/news_article/28865/_PARENT/layout_details_cc/false

Petersen, J. (2002). Sharing responsibility for schoolwide testing programs. In P. Henderson & N. Gysbers (Eds.), *Implementing comprehensive guidance programs: Critical leadership issues and successful responses* (pp. 65–74). Greensboro, NC: CAPS.

Rehabilitative Services Rule, 34 C.F.R. § 300.344 (2008).

Ripley, V. V., & Goodnough, G. E. (2001). Planning and implementing group counseling in a high school. *Professional School Counseling, 5,* 62–65.

Roaten, G. K., & Schmidt, E. A. (2009). Using experiential activities with adolescents to promote respect for diversity. *Professional School Counseling, 12,* 309–314.

Texas Counseling Association. (2004). *The Texas evaluation model for professional school counselors* (2nd ed.). Austin, TX: Author.

Texas Education Agency. (2004). *A model comprehensive, developmental guidance and counseling program for Texas public schools: A guide for program development pre-K–12th grade.* Austin, TX: Author.

Texas Education Agency. (n.d.). *Texas essential knowledge and skills* (TEKS). Austin, TX: Author.

Texas Higher Education Coordinating Board. (2009). *Texas college readiness standards.* Austin: University of Texas at Austin. Retrieved from http://www.thecb.state.tx.us/index.cfm?objectid=EADF962E-0E3E-DA80-BAAD2496062F3CD8

Thomas, R. V., & Pender, D. A. (2008). *Association for Specialists in Group Work: Best practice guidelines 2007 revisions. Journal for Specialists in Group Work, 33,* 111–117. Retrieved from http://www.asgw.org/PDF/Best_Practices.pdf

Whiston, S. C., & Quinby, R. F. (2009). Review of school counseling outcome research. *Psychology in the Schools, 46,* 267–272.

White, S. W., & Kelly, F. D. (2010). The school counselor's role in school dropout prevention. *Journal of Counseling & Development, 88,* 227–235.

Chapter 9

Ensuring School Counselor Competency

Implementing—Ensuring School Counselor Competency

- Implement a counselor performance management system.
- Support professional development.
- Address incompetence.
- Bring new counselors into the program and to the proper roles.
- Clarify roles of building-level guidance and counseling program staff leaders.

≈ In the past, the school counseling profession has emphasized the process (skills and techniques) of guidance, such as counseling, consultation, and coordination. Emphasis on the content of guidance, such as decision making, problem solving, and communicating, has been of secondary importance until recently. Currently, the American School Counselor Association's (ASCA's; 2005) *ASCA National Model: A Framework for School Counseling Programs* recommends content related to students' academic, career, and personal–social development. In addition, the comprehensive, developmental approach is relatively new to guidance and counseling program conceptualization and implementation. School counselors have been defining roles for themselves and have had their roles defined for them since the birth of the profession. Mirroring both history and the marketplace, school counselor training has been (and may continue to be) inconsistent across the United States. Essential, then, to successful improvement of today's guidance and counseling programs is ensuring not only that counselors' roles and responsibilities are defined clearly (as discussed in earlier chapters) but also that a system is in place for ensuring that school counselors have the competencies they need to carry out these expected roles.

In this chapter, we discuss the facets of a performance management system. To achieve their optimum competence, professional school counselors should benefit from appropriate supervision and should be evaluated meaningfully. Their professional growth and development should be encouraged. The contextual resources supporting staff development are discussed, including consideration of counselors' preservice education experiences, the definition of the guidance and counseling program, and the availability of resources to support education and training. Although it is not pleasant to think about, guidance staff leaders must be prepared to address incompetent performance. Inducting new counselors into the field offers critical opportunities to start them off on the right foot. The Attend to Diversity section highlights ways to ensure continuously improving multicultural competence of school counselors. This chapter includes discussions about the changing role of building and district guidance and counseling program and staff leaders.

Implement a Counselor Performance Management System

School districts historically, and by law in many states, require job descriptions associated with credentialing requirements for professional staff. School districts assign someone to provide administration, supervision, and other leadership functions to school counselors and others. They provide a means to evaluate their performance and provide for staff development activities. When these activities are connected or brought together in one system, they become more meaningful to school counselors than if they are isolated events (Somody, Henderson, Cook, & Zambrano, 2008). As described in some detail in *The New Handbook of Administrative Supervision in Counseling* (Henderson, 2009), a complete performance management system is based on professionally appropriate standards for performance and has four groups of activities that assist counselors' focus on meeting these standards. Table 9.1 provides a graphic overview of the grouped activities of a school counselor performance management system (Henderson & Gysbers, 1998). It is important to be clear that responsibility for the quality and quantity of work an individual does belongs to the individual. The designated administrators and supervisors, whom we have elected to call *guidance and counseling program staff leaders* (Henderson & Gysbers), assist by providing objectively collected data-based feedback to their subordinates, comparing and contrasting an individual's performance with the performance standards. They also nurture the professionalism of their supervisees through feedback provision and assistance in goal attainment.

These groups of activities are tied together not only because they rely on the same set of performance standards but also because each group has evolved from previous group activities. The job definition establishes the expectations for application of the standards by individual school counselors. Supervision is provided to assist school counselors with continuously improving their performance. Performance evaluation is tied directly to individuals' job descriptions, and evaluative judgments are based on data gathered in supervision

Table 9.1
Counselor Performance Management System

Job Definition	Supervision	Performance Evaluation	Professional Development
Components			
Position assignment	Clinical	Self-evaluation	Professionalism assessment
Job description	Developmental	Administrative evaluation	Goal setting and action planning
	Administrative	Assessment of goal attainment	In-service education and training
Forms			
Individual job descriptions	Observation	Self-evaluation	Professional development plan
Preevaluation conference worksheet	Action plans	Performance evaluation	Goal statement and action plans
	Office management (e.g., calendars, sign-in sheets, phone logs)	Program and performance goals	Counselor staff development plan

activities. Professional development goals are established as a result of feedback received by school counselors in supervision and evaluation activities. Each of the four groups of activities is described briefly in this section.

Standards

Accepted professional standards provide the basis for a counselor performance management system. They provide the specifics that clarify the expectations for and guide school counselors' work. We identify four categories of professional standards: performance, ethical, legal, and other professional. Legal standards must be adhered to. Ethical standards are expectations to which school counselors' clients, administrators, and colleagues have rights. Other professional standards inform school counselors of guidelines to follow in working in special areas of their practice.

Performance Standards

Performance standards describe the domains in which school counselors perform. As explained in Chapter 5, domains are clarified by competency statements and further specified through performance indicators or descriptors. These indicators are expressly stated by school districts in the criteria for evaluation that are adopted for school counselors by the local or state school board. The application of performance standards in performance evaluation is discussed later on in this chapter.

In the ASCA (2005) National Model, 13 performance standards for school counselors are delineated:

Standard 1: Program organization
Standard 2: School guidance curriculum delivered to all students
Standard 3: Individual student planning
Standard 4: Responsive services
Standard 5: Systems support
Standard 6: School counselor and administrator agreement
Standard 7: Advisory council
Standard 8: Use of data
Standard 9: Student monitoring
Standard 10: Use of time and calendar
Standard 11: Results evaluation
Standard 12: Program audit
Standard 13: Infusing themes (i.e., leadership, advocacy, collaboration and teaming, systemic change)
 (p. 63)

More recently ASCA (n.d.) has published *School Counselor Competencies* that detail the "skills, knowledge and attitudes necessary for meritoriously performing the range of school counselor responsibilities" (Development of the Competencies, para. 3).

The National Board for Professional Teaching Standards (2004) identified the following performance standards for school counselors. In their work, *teachers* includes all educators. They identified five core propositions that apply to all educators and 11 areas of standards for school counselors. The five core propositions are

1. Teachers are committed to students and their learning.
2. Teachers know the subjects they teach and how to teach those subjects to students.
3. Teachers are responsible for managing and monitoring student learning.

4. Teachers think systematically about their practice and learn from experience.
5. Teachers are members of learning communities. (pp. vi–vii)

The 11 areas of standards for accomplished school counselors include

1. School counseling program
2. School counseling and student competencies
3. Human growth and development
4. Counseling theories and techniques
5. Equity, fairness, and diversity
6. School climate
7. Collaboration with family and community
8. Informational resources and technology
9. Student assessment
10. Leadership, advocacy, and professional identity
11. Reflective practice (pp. 5–6)

Ethical Standards

Ethical standards are developed by professional associations and provide professional value statements and offer guidelines for professionals' actions. School counselors follow the *Ethical Standards for School Counselors* published by ASCA (2010a) and the *ACA Code of Ethics* published by the American Counseling Association (ACA; 2005). The former is provided in Appendix A. Additionally, the National Education Association (n.d.) published the *Code of Ethics of the Education Profession*, which describes standards for all educators, including school counselors.

As the counseling profession and professionals continue to mature, ethical discussions become more textured. Ponton and Duba (2009) explained that codes of ethics "reflect the counseling profession's understanding of the responsibilities inherent in the covenantal relationship with society" (p. 119) and that changes in the code "reflect the profession's understanding of changes in the role of the professional or changes in the society counselors serve" (p. 119). In addition to the codes themselves, increasing emphasis is put on the basic principles that guide practitioners when facing dilemmas, and the importance of using a sound ethical decision-making process is recommended.

Legal Standards

Legal standards are expressed in the laws passed by federal, state, and local governing bodies with legal jurisdiction over the school district and related regulations developed by administrative bodies to implement those laws. Examples of legal standards that are relevant to school counselors include those regarding school counselor certification and certification renewal, job roles and responsibilities, parental rights, when minors may consent to counseling regardless of parent rights, child abuse and neglect responses, referrals to community-based services, rules regarding records and notes, and special considerations for special student populations (e.g., those affected by substance abuse, special education students, students from migrant families, and at-risk students).

Other Professional Standards

Other professional standards are statements published by professional organizations; for example, counseling associations that consist of specialists offer standards for others who practice within that specialty. School counselors need to know and apply the professional standards published by specialty groups that are relevant to their job assignments. Some particularly relevant standards are those related to group work, career development, on-line communications, and assessment. Also essential in the 21st century are the standards for working across cultures.

The latter are discussed in the Attend to Diversity section of this chapter. The Association for Specialists in Group Work (ASGW) has established *Professional Standards for the Training of Group Workers* (ASGW, 2000) and *Best Practice Guidelines* (ASGW, 2007) to guide effective implementation of counseling groups. In addition, the National Board for Certified Counselors (2001) has published guidelines on *Ethics: The Practice of Internet Counseling.*

The Association for Assessment in Counseling (1998) and ASCA collaborated on a statement of *Competencies in Assessment and Evaluation for School Counselors.* It describes nine competencies that, in this era of high-stakes testing, all school counselors should possess. School counselors

1. are skilled in choosing assessment strategies;
2. can identify, access, and evaluate the most commonly used assessment instruments;
3. are skilled in the techniques of administration and methods of scoring assessment instruments;
4. are skilled in interpreting and reporting assessment results;
5. are skilled in using assessment results in decision making;
6. are skilled in producing, interpreting, and presenting statistical information about assessment results;
7. are skilled in conducting and interpreting evaluations of school counseling programs and counseling-related interventions;
8. are skilled in adapting and using questionnaires, surveys, and other assessments to meet local needs;
9. know how to engage in professionally responsive assessment and evaluation practices.

The Association for Assessment in Counseling (2003) also has an informative policy statement on the *Responsibilities of Users of Standardized Tests.*

The American Psychological Association (2005) published the *Code of Fair Testing Practices in Education,* a guide for professionals for providing and using "tests that are fair to all test takers regardless of age, gender, disability, race, ethnicity, national origin, religious, sexual orientation, linguistic background or other personal characteristics" (p. 2). The guide described "four critical areas: Developing and Selecting Appropriate Tests, Administering and Scoring Tests, Reporting and Interpreting Test Results, Informing Test Takers" (p. 3). The National Council on Measurement in Education (1995) also has a *Code of Professional Responsibilities in Educational Measurement* that

> applies to any type of assessment that occurs as part of the educational process, including formal and informal, traditional and alternative techniques for gathering information used in making educational decisions at all levels. These techniques include, but are not limited to, large-scale assessments at the school, district, state, national, and international levels; standardized tests; observational measures; teacher conducted assessments; assessment support materials; and other achievement, aptitude, interest, and personality measures used in and for education. (para. 3)

Defining School Counselors' Jobs

In Chapter 5, we described the value of generic job descriptions outlining the roles fulfilled and competencies demonstrated by school counselors as they carry out their jobs. These guide all individuals holding positions with the same title. In Chapter 8, we described individual job descriptions as statements that distinguish each counselor's specific job responsibilities from every other school counselor's. Each individual's job description is unique within the context of the comprehensive guidance and counseling program and within the context of the individual schools in which he or she works.

The job definition is the basic statement of the expectations for counselors' performance for the year and becomes the basis for the rest of the performance management system activities. It clarifies how much is expected of the counselors in implementing each dimension (each role) of their job through the weighting process (Henderson & Gysbers, 1998). It describes how they will apply their competencies during the year. On the basis of their job definition, their guidance and counseling program staff leader reminds them of the relevant performance standards—the descriptions of the quality expectations.

The data gathered in preparing for an individual's performance evaluation are done in relationship to his or her job description. The staff leader's supervision activities are done to highlight the job priorities. At the beginning of the year, a conference is held between each school counselor and his or her evaluator. During this conference, they agree on the specifics of each counselor's job description, agree on the weights assigned to each role, discuss how the evaluator will know what quality of performance is provided, discuss what constraints may get in school counselors' or their staff leaders' way of doing their jobs as defined, and reaffirm the school counselor's program improvement and professional development goals for the year.

Providing Appropriate Supervision

Professional supervision is the most effective means of assisting another's growth and development. Another goal of supervision is to enhance counselors' thoughts and commitment to their professional responsibilities by creating meaningful dialogue between supervisors and counselors (Glickman, Gordon, & Ross-Gordon, 1995) and to influence the work of the supervisees (Bernard & Goodyear, 1992). In addressing challenges and opportunities for school counselors in the 21st century, Paisley and McMahon (2001) stated that school counselors will need to continue to update and upgrade their professional competence. They also noted, "Skill building alone will be inadequate, however. School counselors must also participate in continued . . . supervision in order to enhance their professional development" (p. 111). Indeed, without it, there is some evidence that the skill level of counselors decreases (Wiley & Ray, 1986, as cited in Borders, 1989).

"The existing literature on supervision of practicing school counselors reveals a wealth of information regarding the lack of, and the need for, more supervision" (Somody et al., 2008, p. 22). There is, however, a growing body of research that describes the benefits of supervision to professional school counselors. Leach and Stoltenberg (1997) found that meaningful supervision enhanced counselors' self-efficacy. Rutter (2006) reported that group supervision contributed to counselors' feelings of "trust and safety, learning from others, self-awareness, social support, and professional identity" (p. 164). Lambie (2007) learned that "clinical supervisors can help promote ego development in their . . . supervisees, thereby improving their cognitive and socioemotional coping abilities and better equipping them with the necessary qualities to cope with occupational stress" (p. 82). Lambie estimated that 39% of counselors are burned out. Recognizing that burnout "leads to deterioration in the quality of service provided" (p. 82), Lambie also stated that "professional school counselor supervision may serve as an effective form of occupational support to combat burnout" (p. 86). In his study of school counselors receiving supervision, he found that "as the level of occupational support increased, emotional exhaustion and depersonalization decreased while feelings of personal accomplishment increased, thereby reducing the degree of burnout" (p. 86).

A process that supports effective supervision entails (a) observing a counselor's behavior (e.g., conducting an activity, an isolated work behavior); (b) comparing and contrasting the behavior with established performance, ethical, or professional standards; (c) assessing how the behavior matches the standards; (d) establishing objectives for providing relevant feedback; (e) delivering the feedback in a style that is most apt to lead the counselor to growth; and (f) setting goals for performance improvement (Henderson, 2009; Somody et al., 2008). Through this process, both supervisor and counselor are forced to be concrete about strengths and deficiencies. In our experience, when professional counselors have been assisted to see specifically what they can do to improve, they are eager to improve.

As suggested by Barret and Schmidt (1986), we have found it useful in schools to use three types of supervision: clinical, developmental, and administrative. Each type targets different dimensions of a school counselor's professionalism and uses different strategies in its implementation. These have been fully detailed in *Leading and Managing Your School Guidance and Counseling Program Staff* (Henderson & Gysbers, 1998) and are outlined only briefly here.

Clinical Supervision

Clinical supervision focuses on counselors' direct service delivery and on counselors' unique professional skills such as guidance, counseling, consultation, and referral. Observing counselors' use of their skills and providing specific feedback regarding what was observed is the essence of clinical supervision. A five-step process model is suggested:

1. Preobservation conference
2. Observation
3. Analysis of data
4. Postobservation conference
5. Postconference analysis

Aubrey (as cited in Boyd, 1978, p. 306) defined skills as "behaviors that are operational, ratable, and predictable within a delimited range of effects." The counselors' professional skills (we use the word *competencies*) can be delineated so as to lend themselves to this form of observation. Many counselor education programs and school districts have listed the competencies that they expect of school counselors they educate and employ. Competency lists provide the basis for observation. To illustrate, the descriptors used for this purpose by Northside Independent School District are provided in Appendix M. Supervisors certified as school counselors (such as head counselors, central office guidance administrators or supervisors, or counselors assigned supervisory responsibility of their peers) should perform clinical supervision if it is to be effective. "Observation is actually the act of (1) noting and then (2) judging" (Glickman et al., 1995, p. 237). Forms can assist the supervisor to note the presence or absence of specific, important behaviors. They also provide vehicles for communication between the observer and the person being observed. Sample forms from Northside Independent School District are provided in Appendix N.

No matter how minutely competencies are described or how refined the observation forms are, training is required to provide supervisors with the background they need to make professionally appropriate judgments of the quality of an individual's performance and to provide meaningful feedback to the practitioners. The postobservation conference has two parts: "first describing what has been seen and then interpreting what it means"

(Glickman et al., 1995, p. 238). This feedback should be given within 48 hours after an observation occurs so that both parties have a fairly accurate recollection of the events.

It is difficult to recommend an ideal number of contacts that the clinical supervisor and counselor should have. If counselors are not unduly threatened by such observations and the related feedback conferences, then the more the merrier, because professionals do value feedback to help them improve their competencies. Clinical supervision is akin to tutorial assistance; it is one-on-one, direct, and competency focused. Counselors can benefit from clinical supervision in each of the functions required in their work: instruction, guidance, counseling, consultation, and referral. We recommend that observations occur at least twice a year. Remember that observation and feedback about counseling competencies will not necessarily provide counselors with ideas about how to improve their consultation competencies.

Developmental Supervision

Developmental supervision focuses on school counselors' knowledge base, including their theoretical and client understandings, their program and caseload management capabilities, and their commitment to their jobs, school, district, and profession. Its purpose is to direct counselors' professional cognitive and affective growth and development.

The traditional professional development activities of participating in in-service education, attending conferences, and professional association involvement support developmental supervision. Another strategy used in developmental supervision is assisting school counselors to implement their goal-related plans and to measure their levels of goal attainment. Monitoring their progress toward goals can be accomplished through individual conferences and sharing among the counselor team. Some goals lend themselves to written reports.

A third developmental supervision strategy is formal, planned case consultation. This strategy assists counselors to grow in their conceptualization of their clients (Biggs, 1988) and helps them learn not only to look objectively at their own experiences but also to learn from others' cases. The larger the supply of case examples a counselor has, the better he or she is able to recognize patterns in clients' behaviors and respond appropriately (Etringer, Hillerbrand, & Claiborn, 1995).

A fourth developmental supervision strategy is providing mentors to inexperienced or weak school counselors. Mentors share their experience and expertise with other counselors by, for example, teaching them, encouraging them, and befriending them (Tentoni, 1995). Being a mentor is also a developmental supervision strategy. Mentors learn as they articulate their learnings (VanZandt & Perry, 1992). The counseling literature also describes mentors' need for training to fulfill that role most effectively (Peace, 1995).

Administrative Supervision

As we have defined it here, administrative supervision targets the traditional areas of the soundness of counselors' professional judgments, their mental health, their fidelity to their job descriptions and program, their work habits, their adherence to rules and standards, and the effectiveness of their relationships with colleagues and clients (Henderson, 2009; Henderson & Gysbers, 1998). Observing and assessing the adequacy of school counselors' professional judgments, their mental health, and their relationships with others require careful and complete data gathering and often ambiguous applications of standards. Observing and assessing work habits and compliance with professional, ethical, and legal standards are more concrete. A bulk of administrative supervision work occurs in daily, spontaneous supervision, based on incidental observations made during a workday (Henderson, 2009).

Administrative supervision relies on several strategies to address a wide range of topics. Administrative supervisors hold individual conferences with their supervisees; sometimes these conferences involve confrontation or counseling. They also consult with supervisees spontaneously as difficult cases present themselves. Conducting staff meetings with the entire department team is another widely used administrative supervision strategy (Henderson, 2009).

Assessing Professionalism and Responding Appropriately

All of the efforts to assist school counselors in continuously improving their performance are based on assessments of their levels of professionalism, a challenge mutually undertaken by school counselors and their staff leaders. These assessments are made by both parties. Counselors have subjective perspectives and large quantities of data. The latter have objective perspectives and selective data. Assessments are ever evolving: Every work-related performance experienced by counselors, observed by supervisors, and received in feedback by school counselors contributes, in turn, to their professionalism assessments (Henderson, 2009; Henderson & Gysbers, 1998).

The purpose of professionalism assessments are to pinpoint areas in which professional development may not be needed by a counselor and areas that when addressed would contribute to a counselor's effectiveness with his or her clients. Assessing professionalism levels supports intentional supervision. The assessment of a counselor's professionalism level suggests the supervisor's response style that is most apt to spur development of the supervisee (Somody et al., 2008).

Having a working definition of professionalism that is understood by both parties is a prerequisite to effective professional development efforts. We have found it useful to define professionalism as a combination of school counselors' competence to carry out the roles required in the fulfillment of their jobs and their levels of professional identity and commitment. As defined in the model in this book, the roles and competencies are guidance, counseling, consultation, coordination, assessment, and program management. They also include school counselors' commitment to their clients and their jobs, that is, their specific assignments within the program as well as their commitment to their places of employment (school and district) and to their profession. Each of these dimensions includes many facets. Individuals' professionalism levels vary from situation to situation; thus, aggregating situational examples into patterns is one of the challenges for both school counselors and their evaluators.

In selecting the most appropriate response style, supervisors strive for allowing their supervisees to maintain their own autonomy (ACA, 2005, D.2.C). They select responses that apply an appropriate degree of directiveness (from nondirective to controlling) and rely on the power base (expert, information, referent, reward, legitimate, connection, coercion) most meaningful to the supervisee. They also identify an empowerment strategy and the supervisor function (mentoring, consulting, coaching, teaching, counseling, judging) most apt to help the supervisee maintain motivation and seek growth (Henderson, 2009).

Evaluating Staff Fairly

Counselor evaluation is done most fairly when it is conducted as part of the total performance management system. The multiple activities of the system provide meaningful data on which to base the judgments relative to clearly stated performance standards. An approach to counselor evaluation is discussed extensively in Chapter 10; we include a brief discussion here to allow you to see how it relates to the other parts of the system.

As with the other parts of an overall performance management system—job definition, supervision, and professional development—performance evaluation rests on the expectations held for school counselors as clarified in their job definition and specific job descriptions and on standards established for performance quality. Remember, the job description is based on the desired comprehensive guidance and counseling program. There must, then, be congruence among the program, the job description, and the procedures used in performance evaluation.

The purposes of the three groups of activities that build on the job definition are related, but each has a separate goal. The goal of supervision is to use the resources (i.e., the supervisors) of the system to assist school counselors to reach their professional potential within the district. The goal of professional development is to encourage school counselors to continue to grow in their professional competency and identity, using both school district and personal resources. The goal of evaluation is to rate the competency and commitment levels of school counselors from the school district's perspective, to judge how professionally they are performing the job to which they are assigned.

In theory, supervision and professional development are conducted in a nonjudgmental manner, but in reality they also provide some of the data that support the judgments made in evaluation. If, for example, counselors are observed by their clinical supervisor as consistently giving misinformation to students or as consistently projecting their own values onto students' decisions, the clinical supervisor is responsible for providing that information to the evaluator. The relationship can work the other way as well. If the evaluator perceives counselors as not being authoritative enough with students, the clinical supervisor can explain to the evaluator the professional rationale for being nonjudgmental.

Supervision and professional growth also provide strategies for assisting counselors to repair deficiencies identified through evaluation. If the evaluator perceives that a counselor is not effective with groups of children, the clinical supervisor can observe the counselor in action with groups and provide technical assistance. In developmental supervision, the counselor and supervisor might agree that a professional development goal for the counselor is to improve the use of instructional methodology. Through strategies provided for professional development, the counselor might attend workshops on effective teaching techniques. Thus, evaluation is the central part of an overall performance management system.

Support Professional Development

Although professional development is primarily the responsibility of the individual school counselor, district and building guidance and counseling program staff leaders also have some accountability for the quality of individuals' performance. In addition to helping clarify job and performance expectations and providing data-based feedback, they nurture individuals' professional identity development and motivation and strive to empower them to attain optimum professional maturity (Henderson, 2009; Henderson & Gysbers, 1998).

A school district can and should provide many resources, but the needs and wants of the district must be balanced with the needs and wants of the individuals on the staff. From the district's perspective, the purpose of providing professional development opportunities is to provide cost-effective in-service education and training that meets the needs of the largest number of counselors in relation to priority needs of the district and building guidance and counseling programs. From the school counselors' perspective, the purpose of participating in professional development opportunities is to improve their professional and personal competencies in areas that they perceive as important. As stated earlier, the goal of professional development is to encourage staff members to continue to grow in their professional identity and competency, using both district and personal resources.

The challenge is to provide mechanisms that help both the district and the district counselors target specific competencies—knowledge, skills, and attitudes—that need enhancement. We recommend developing a process for encouraging professional development that begins by having counselors, assisted by their guidance and counseling program staff leaders, identify their own competencies and compare them with the competencies required to implement the desired district comprehensive guidance and counseling program. From these two data sources, a master plan for counselor staff development for the district is developed that identifies the competencies to be addressed for the various subpopulations of school counselors and describes how these will be addressed.

Individual Responsibilities

Strengthening Professional Identity Development

The first principle of ACA's vision for the future is that "sharing a common professional identity is critical for counselors" (ACA, 2009, para. 3). For individual counselors, the foundation of their professionalism is the strength and depth of a counselors' professional identity. "Achieving a professional identity is usually thought to be a vital part of becoming a mature professional" (Hansen, 2010, p. 102). Your professional identity is about who you are and what you are about in your professional work. It is your property, and you are responsible for its continuing development. It develops across your professional life span, beginning with your preservice counselor training. It continues to develop as long as you continue to strengthen and deepen it. A mature professional identity is the result of spiral learning, based on new knowledge, experiences, and reflection.

Your professional identity also rests on others' perceptions of who you are and what you are about in your professional work. Ponton and Duba (2009) suggested, "For counselors to collectively and individually answer the question, 'Who am I as a counselor?' counselors must first ask, 'Who are we called to be by the society that has created the profession?'" (p. 118). They concluded that "in whatever specialty counselors practice, they are asked to provide expertise to the problem of balancing an individual's needs, strengths, and identity with the group or society within which that individual functions" (Ponton & Duba, 2009, p. 118).

Current research has suggested some ingredients of professional identity. Gibson, Dollarhide, and Moss (2010) concluded that a counselor-in-training's "transformational tasks" toward having a professional counselor identity are having a definition of counseling, taking responsibility for professional growth, and having an identity related to the professional counseling community. In considering the spectrum of apparent professional identities of school counselors in the work setting, Henderson, Cook, Libby, and Zambrano (2006) learned that the core of school counselors' professional identities is defined by how committed they are to their work and their students, fulfilling appropriate roles, pursuing increased competence, and affiliating with other counselors. At a minimum, then, four factors of professional identity that continue to develop in counselors who maintain strong professional identities are putting their clients first, knowing and carrying out appropriate roles, continuously striving to provide optimal services, and affiliating with the professional community.

Putting the Client First. ASCA's (2010a) *Ethical Standards for School Counselors* and the *ACA Code of Ethics* (ACA, 2005) are clear that professional school counselors are obligated to hold their student clients as their primary focus (Henderson, 2009). This is often challenging when working in a system (the school) that has many other people and procedures that pressure counselors for their time or talent. When faced with conflicting demands, ethical school counselors focus their attention on their students. The overriding goal of counseling is to empower your clients as they find their own paths and move forward along them. It is also essential to be mindful that, for counseling to work, the client must actively participate, even lead, the counseling process.

Professional school counselors respect their students' needs, social and environmental contexts, worldviews, and goals. When working with students, they are nonjudgmental about who the students are as individuals and about their situations. Professional school counselors do not make assumptions about what is right for their students, nor do they inject their needs into or impose their values on the counseling relationship.

Knowing and Carrying Out Appropriate Roles. A strong professional school counselor identity is rooted in an individual's being clear about the right role he or she is to fulfill. Only recently has the counseling profession defined counseling, the hallmark competency of counselors regardless of specialty: "Counseling is a professional relationship that empowers diverse individuals, families, and groups to accomplish mental health, wellness, education, and career goals" (ACA, 2010, consensus definition).

School counselors build those relationships and apply the skills needed to help students maintain or regain their mental health and wellness and to set and make progress toward their educational and career goals. Professional counseling is different from other skill sets used by school counselors, for example, guiding, advising, teaching, and telling. At all times, regardless of the skill set being used, professional school counselors align their work with established professional ethical and performance standards.

School counselors are sometimes challenged to avoid role confusion. Professional school counselors are mindful of what their specialty is—school counseling—and how their role is similar to and different from those of other educational specialists in the schools, for example, teachers and administrators. They also are clear about how school counseling is similar to and different from counseling in agency or private practice settings. They are able to articulate their appropriate roles. School counselors with strong professional identities feel called to work with children and adolescents and are courageous in advocating for doing right by their clients. In fact, Ponton and Duba (2009) "suggest that the question of professional identity cannot be adequately addressed in the absence of the notion of vocation" (p. 118).

Continuously Striving to Provide Optimal Services. Professional school counselors pursue ever-higher competence in providing services to students and the adults related to those students. They seek out opportunities for continuing education and development. They reflect on their work with their clients, consult with other counselors, and welcome feedback from supervisors and peers as to the quality of their work. They continue to struggle to provide a well-planned, -designed, -implemented, -evaluated, and -enhanced program that serves all students developmentally and provides responsive services, as feasible, to students whose issues or situations interrupt their healthy progress. They provide services in a balanced and intentional manner.

Affiliating With the Professional Counseling Community. Recognizing that the profession continues to advance, professional school counselors maintain a strong and developing professional identity by keeping pace with its changes. They also contribute to the advancement of the counseling profession and the school counseling specialty. Excellent vehicles for affiliating with the local, state, national, and international professional counseling communities are the professional groups affiliated with ACA and ASCA. Unfortunately, in 2005 only 11% of employed school counselors were members of ASCA (Bauman, 2008). Consulting with counselor mentors and leaders in one's professional environment also helps you hone your professional identity. Mutual dialogue helps all involved professionals clarify who they are and what they believe in. Professional school counselors understand that a strong professional identity supports their motivation to continually advance their level of professional development and that their professional development supports their increasing levels of professionalism.

Developing Individual Professional Development Plans

Paisley and McMahon (2001) identified ongoing professional development as essential to vital programs and professionalism in school counseling. As a result of clinical, developmental, and administrative supervision and of data-based performance evaluation, counselors and their staff leaders will have identified specific competencies that need to be targeted for improvement. Counselors' professional development plans are developed in the context of their long-range professional and personal goals as well as in the context of the comprehensive guidance and counseling program.

Some targets for professional development relate to the currently defined *Role of the Professional School Counselor* (ASCA, 2009b). School counselors are expected to be competent to provide structured lessons, coordinated systemic activities, individual and group counseling, consultation with teachers and other educators, referrals to other school support services or community resources, peer helping, information dissemination, confidential relationships, program management and operations, professional development, use of data, planning, calendaring, and time management. Additionally, in the Education Trust's (2003) Transforming School Counseling initiative and as reflected in ASCA's (2005) National Model, skills are called for in advocacy, leadership, teaming, collaboration, counseling, consultation, and use of data—all to serve the purpose of removing barriers to successful achievement by students.

Modern technology is also affecting school counseling. Kenny and McEachern (2004, p. 200) stated, "The field of counseling is certainly being affected by current technological advances. The use of the telephone and other telecommunications devices (i.e., faxes, electronic mail, Internet, cellular phones) are increasingly popular methods of providing counseling." These communications methods call for different competencies or different applications of traditional competencies. They also pose some new ethical dilemmas.

Bowers (2002), B. Evans and Ward (2002), and Van Horn and Myrick (2001) identified different ways school counselors can use computer technology to work more efficiently and help students succeed. They mentioned retrieving and disseminating information through such tools as e-mail, Web sites, electronic newsletters, and online journals; distance learning through video conferencing and online schools; helping students develop individual plans through computerized data storage and electronic (phone and Internet) registration; exploring colleges and careers through Web sites and guidance information systems; using the computer as a counseling tool; networking; and training and supervision.

In developing their professional development plans, counselors should be explicit about their long-range plans and encouraged by their staff leaders to identify the intermediate and immediate goals that will help them reach their larger goals. Both sets of data—the specific job performance improvement targets and the professional–personal goals—provide information to counselors as they develop professional development plans. Counselors should be encouraged to develop such plans for a 5-, 2-, or even 1-year period. As a district, however, you will have more than enough data to work with if you know the counselors' immediate needs and wants for competency acquisition or improvement.

In a formally defined performance management system, school counselors write professional development plans in collaboration with their staff leaders and submit them to the guidance administrator. Methods and procedures for accomplishing this are described elsewhere (Henderson, 2009; Henderson & Gysbers, 1998). A form used for this purpose is displayed in Figure 9.1. With a form such as this, counselors and their building-level staff leaders agree on a targeted competency area, such as the implementation of effective group counseling. They also discuss appropriate objectives that, if met, will increase counselors' effectiveness, such as the ability to (a) articulate a theoretical base for counselor behaviors, (b) use a variety of response techniques, and (c) facilitate students' development of behavioral plans. Counselors then identify tasks or activities that they plan to perform to meet the objectives. The plan includes a time frame and a statement to the guidance and counseling program staff leader about potential evidence of achievement. (The second half of the form relates to the evaluation of the counselors' accomplishment of the plan—when the tasks were completed, what documentation of accomplishment is available, and to what degree tasks were accomplished. These are reviewed at the end of the year by the counselors and their staff leaders as part of the evaluation system described in Chapter 10.) Having received the counselors' plans, staff leaders and administrators know what their staff members want. They are then in a position to encourage counselors to seek educational opportunities.

Assessing Needs for Counselor Competency Development

Knowing what the counselors want is only one part of the needs assessment in a plan for staff development. Also necessary is assessing counselors' needs for performance improvement in terms of the competencies and commitments needed to implement the comprehensive program desired by the building or district. It is important to assess counselors' competencies to find out those they have as well as those they need to work on.

The same methodology that was used to assess the perceived needs of students can be used to assess counselor competencies; only the items are changed. The items to be used are generated from the standards for performance that have been identified as necessary to organize and implement the comprehensive guidance and counseling program. The competencies and their indicators and descriptors that you have identified to support the supervision and evaluation components of the performance management system provide these specifics. By using aggregated data from counselors' performance evaluations, questionnaires, or other assessment technique, data are gathered and tabulated. Many such assessments ask counselors not only how much they need to acquire the competency but also how important they feel acquiring the competency is.

From the system's perspective, the guidance and counseling program staff leader also has a viewpoint as to the importance of each competency that should be considered as the plans for staff development are made. If in comparing and contrasting the current and the desired programs, discrepancies have been identified that seem to be related to competencies not used in the current program but wanted in the desired program, the district guidance and counseling program leader will know the importance of staff development in those competencies, whereas the counselors might not yet be aware. For example, if the desired program calls for more group counseling than is currently done, competency improvement in those skills will receive a high priority from the district's perspective.

Within the counseling staff, not only will different groups of counselors want to acquire different professional competencies, but different groups of counselors will also need to acquire different competencies. New counselors have different needs than do experienced counselors. Some experienced counselors are more competent than others and may need advanced training, whereas others may need remedial training. The program improvement process itself will dictate some staff development needs. The priority needs for training guidance and counseling program staff leaders may be different from those for staff counselors. If you have a cadre of peer leaders, they may have different professional development needs.

Figure 9.1
Counselor Professional Growth Plan Form

COUNSELOR PROFESSIONAL GROWTH PLAN

School: _____

Name: _____

Principal/Head Counselor Signature: _____

Date: _____

USE A SEPARATE FORM FOR EACH COMPETENCY AREA

PLANNING
(To Be Completed by _____)

EVALUATION
(To Be Completed by _____)

Targeted Competency Area:
Objective(s):

Description of Tasks/ Activities	Time Frame	Evidence of Achievement	Actual Completion Date	Verification of Achievement	Level of (1–5) Accomplishment

Overall Assessment of Achievement:

1	2	3	4	5
(Not Achieved)			(Fully Achieved)	

Counselor s Signature: _____

Principal/Head Counselor: _____

Date: _____

Relating Staff Development to the Program Improvement Process

As they proceed through the program improvement process, school counselors learn a variety of new concepts. They learn about the comprehensive guidance and counseling program, about their roles in it, and about some of the processes to implement it. The presentation of the information gathered in assessing the design of the current guidance and counseling program provides insights into the program and its facets, as does the recasting of the program that is presented in the expression of the district's basic structure. Whether you have chosen to select current examples of effective practices or ventured into innovative activities that fit the desired program, counselors learn about operational details of a comprehensive guidance and counseling program.

If, as a first step in assessing the design of their building programs, counselors kept logs of their activities, they learned about their own piece of the program and watched as their data were aggregated with those of others. This helped them further internalize the program concept and provided them with insights into their own work habits. Such information, when compared with the expectations for their roles as stated in their job descriptions, provides counselors with ideas as to how they can add to their professional competencies. At the same time, study of the job descriptions of other staff in the guidance department helps all staff members understand the chain of command as well as the responsibilities of the guidance and counseling program staff leader and those of the various paraprofessionals.

One of the opportunities identified by Paisley and McMahon (2001) for school counselors is "determining appropriate roles and areas of program focus" (p. 110). Counselors need to learn processes related to planning such as goal setting, ranking for priority, and action planning. They also need to learn about program planning and personal planning. By being involved in the program improvement process, they learn about program planning through such activities as conducting needs assessments, assessing the current program, and establishing the desired program structure. They learn about collaborating with other stakeholders to shape their programs appropriately and about setting appropriate boundaries to focus their roles to best assist students' development. By setting goals and developing action plans for attaining those goals, counselors learn personal planning.

One of the major benefits of establishing a comprehensive guidance and counseling program with clear-cut priorities is that the program becomes manageable to the counselors. Instead of a series of days that just happen, the counselors' work year becomes a planned year. Not every minute of every day can be planned—that will never happen as long as the important responsibility of responding to students and others in crisis is present. The major events of the program can be planned, however, enabling counselors to feel a sense of accomplishment. Having control of the major parts of the program and their job empowers counselors, contributes to their professional pride, and consequently helps revitalize their commitment to their profession.

Of interest here is a study that underscores the importance of program management: Fitch and Marshall (2004) found that "the area of program management, evaluation, and research showed the largest discrepancy" (p. 175) in how school counselors allocated their time between high- and low-achieving schools in Kentucky. Counselors in high-achieving schools also "spent more time on tasks relating to professional standards" (p. 176), and "coordination activities of school counselors were more prevalent in high-achieving schools" (p. 176). Their conclusions suggested that program management and evaluation leads to more systematic and continuously improving programs. Relating programs to professional standards helps programs to be focused on meaningful outcomes, and through coordinating schoolwide activities and programs, counselors influence the total school.

Counselors, especially those who are not used to thinking of the program as having any resources, need to learn the processes for effective use of resources, such as budgeting, careful selection of materials, and time management. During the program improvement process, counselors need to learn to use assertion and political skills; they need to feel empowered.

Once the desired comprehensive program design has been established for the building and district and the discrepancies between what should be and what is are clear, generating as many ideas as possible for repairing these discrepancies not only provides a plethora of ideas but also gets the counselors' creative juices flowing. Brainstorming sets in motion "How can I change?" thought processes.

If in the program improvement process special projects are used to enhance the program change process, some counselors may need competency development related to those special efforts. They need to learn to take risks comfortably, and they also need to learn the competencies associated with the specific projects they are participating in. If you are experimenting with curriculum writing, for example, in-service training in curriculum development is important, as is training in the specific content area to be developed. If some buildings are trying out large-group guidance activities, then competency in working with large groups is required. If you purchase materials for possible districtwide use, counselors need training in the effective use of these materials.

Once the analyses of the disparities between the current and the desired programs have been completed and the basic directions for program change have been established, the training needs of counselors in the district can be anticipated. Lately, much has been learned about the teaching–learning process, motivation, and student engagement (Mental Health in Schools, 2011). Counselors need updating on these topics if they are to deliver the guidance curriculum effectively and maintain their credibility as consultants to teachers. They can also benefit from staff development activities that focus on instructional methodology such as task analysis, lesson design, and effective teaching practices. In addition, the new program design requires that counselors update their competencies in working competently across cultures; in guidance and counseling group work; in effective methods of parent and teacher consultation; in brief family intervention techniques; in incorporating career development activities into the program such as decision making, planning, and problem solving; and in addressing the needs of at-risk students (such as dropouts and potential dropouts, substance abusers and children of substance abusers, unmotivated learners and those who continually fail to succeed academically, and depressed adolescents and those who threaten or attempt suicide). Schoolwide efforts to enhance the school climate are also getting renewed attention (Center for Social and Emotional Education, n.d.; National School Climate Center, n.d.). A consistent need of school counselors, and one of which administrators are aware, is that of acquiring time management skills. Moreover, counselors need to fine tune their advocacy and public communication skills.

As the guidance and counseling program shifts to require better use of counselors' education and training, their sense of professionalism should be enhanced. Workshops or study sessions on ethical standards (ACA, 2005; ASCA, 2010a; National Education Association, n.d.) and issues could be held to further this feeling. Counselors should also be encouraged to belong to professional counseling associations and to become involved in association work. When available, attainment of licensure or registry should be encouraged, with such accomplishments being publicly acknowledged.

From the outset, guidance and counseling program staff leaders and other peer leaders can benefit from learning about leadership characteristics and leadership styles. A personal benefit from participating in the program as a leader is increased self-knowledge and actualization. Benefits also arise for leaders from learning about situational leadership, team building, the use of power, the needed balance of both task and relationship orientation, and the roles they play in groups and leader–follower situations (Hersey, Blanchard, & Johnson, 2001). As their program and staff leadership roles evolve, they acquire many new competencies (Henderson, 2009; Henderson & Gysbers, 1998). If you are the guidance and counseling program leader, or if your role as program administrator does not require special administrative or supervisory certification, you too will benefit because most of this material is not included in guidance preservice education.

Staff Development Resources

Systematic efforts to ensure the competency of school counselors rest on knowledge and appropriate use of available resources. Relevant resources include preservice training experienced by certified school counselors, clear definition of the guidance and counseling program with specific expectations for school counselor positions, and the personnel, financial, and political support resources available to assist in professional development efforts.

Preservice Counselor Education

Certification of individuals' preparedness to counsel in the schools is a function of state departments of education. Requirements for certification vary from state to state, and within a state, institutions of higher education differ in how they prepare their students to meet requirements. National standards for school counselor preparation have been set by the Council for Accreditation of Counseling and Related Educational Programs (CACREP, 2009). These standards state that all counselors, regardless of specialty, should experience curriculum in areas of professional orientation and ethical practice, social and cultural diversity, human growth and development, career development, helping relationships, group work, assessment, and research and program evaluation orientation (pp. 10–14). In addition, students preparing to practice school counseling should experience curriculum in foundations of school counseling; counseling, prevention, and intervention; diversity and advocacy; assessment; research and evaluation; academic development; collaboration and consultation; and leadership (pp. 40–46).

Knowing the competencies acquired through the counselor training programs in your area provides you with baseline information about the skills and knowledge competencies graduates of those programs bring to counseling jobs. Being familiar with the professors in the programs also gives you some idea about the attitudes and beliefs to which their students have been exposed. The program for ensuring counselor competency builds from this baseline.

Guidance and Counseling Program Definition

In designing your comprehensive guidance and counseling program, you have written generic job descriptions that state the basic expectations of staff members in implementing the program. The example we used from Northside Independent School District (1997) delineates the expectations that school counselors should

- teach the guidance curriculum;
- guide groups and individual students through the development of their educational and career plans;
- counsel small groups and individual students with problems or concerns;
- consult with teachers and parents;
- refer students or their parents to other specialists or special programs;

- coordinate the work of others (e.g., faculty doing tasks previously done by school counselors and community volunteers participating in comprehensive guidance and counseling program activities);
- collaborate with school faculty and staff to design and implement the guidance and counseling program;
- plan, manage, and evaluate the school's guidance and counseling program;
- pursue continuous professional development.

Thus, counselors in a system that uses this generic job description are expected to have the competencies needed to teach, guide, counsel, consult, refer, coordinate, and collaborate effectively. Further delineation of these competencies—the related skills, knowledge, attitudes, and beliefs—is not the subject of this book. What is important for our purposes here, however, is that you be aware that ensuring counselor competency can occur only if you and your district have identified the counselor competencies required to deliver a comprehensive guidance and counseling program successfully.

Identify Available Resources

As you work to ensure school counselor competency, you need to consider the resources available. Buildings, districts, and communities have human, financial, and political resources available to use in ensuring counselor competency. The question is, how can these resources be used most efficiently and effectively?

Personnel Resources. Effective performance in a position is a shared responsibility of the position holder and the school district. Counselor applicants have a responsibility to define themselves adequately so that prospective employers can evaluate whether they are right for the jobs available. Employers have a responsibility to clearly and specifically define the positions available. Counselors have a professional responsibility to be competent in what the district has the right to expect, that is, the educational areas defined as minimum standards for certification by the state and the ethical and other relevant standards defined by the profession.

Every school and district employs administrators who are responsible for the performance of the guidance department staff. The titles of such administrators vary, as do levels of authority and responsibility. Administrators may have such titles as principal, superintendent, head counselor, guidance and counseling director, coordinator, or supervisor. The roles that each fulfills on behalf of ensuring school counselor competency need to be specifically defined. The number of these administrators who may be involved and the degree of their competency in guidance and counseling will vary by the size of the school district as well as by its commitment to the comprehensive guidance and counseling program concept. Chance may also enter the picture in terms of the career paths of the administrators involved. For example, a principal who was formerly an effective school counselor may provide a different type of administrative direction and supervision from one who has no counseling experience, and the quality of such direction and supervision may vary depending on the principal's experiences as a school counselor.

Certain communities and geographical regions have resources that counselors may be able to use. For example, CACREP has accredited more than 600 counselor training institutions. Many school districts are sufficiently close to these institutions to have access to counselor educators. Other school counselors, professional counseling association leaders, mental health counselors, counseling psychologists, psychiatrists, training consultants, business and industry human resources specialists, and other specialists may also be available. To make optimum use of these specialists for professional development, however, their expertise needs to be surveyed and cataloged. We suggest that you compile a list of such individuals and identify their areas of expertise, the topics on which they present workshops, their professional licenses and certificates, and their fees.

Other resources include the professional counseling associations available at the local, state, national, and international levels. Schools and districts play a key role in "encouraging and supporting a workplace culture that values professional organizations" (Bauman, 2008, p. 173). There is some evidence that association membership results in "higher levels of education, more hours worked, higher income levels . . . [and] higher levels of job satisfaction" (Bauman, 2008, p. 165).

Financial Resources. The financial resources available to the guidance and counseling program should make provision for the professional development of the counseling staff. Districts provide money and opportunities for in-service training and attendance at professional conferences and conventions. Regional offices and state departments of education also provide education and training opportunities for school counselors. Larger school systems and intermediate school districts often provide professional journal subscriptions, books, and training tapes through professional libraries.

Political Resources. In this era of educational reform, there is increased support to enhance professional educators' competency and accountability. Many states' reform efforts include renewed emphasis on professional growth in the form of mandatory in-service education, professional renewal requirements for recertification, and career ladders. Even if counselors are not mentioned directly in these efforts, the movement to improve overall staff competency can be used specifically to assist counselors. For example, in 1995 Texas mandated a Professional Development and Appraisal System (Texas Education Code, 2011) that provided the training of the trainers, the training materials, and the hourly requirements for teachers and administrators to be trained in the supervision and evaluation model. Counselors and counseling supervisors were not included in the mandate; however, counseling administrators were. It then became the counseling administrators' responsibility to see that counselors were also provided opportunities to learn about effective teaching, counseling, and supervision.

Developing a District Master Plan for Staff Development

Knowing what the staff's wants and needs are for competency development is a first step. The next step is to develop a plan to meet these needs efficiently and effectively. The plan includes identifying the strategies and resources available for staff development, developing a time frame for the staff development activities that the building or district will provide, and considering how to evaluate the effectiveness of the strategies used. Figure 9.2 displays a format that could be used for writing a building or district staff development plan.

Strategies

A variety of delivery methods are available for staff development, including lectures, reading materials, audiovisual materials, demonstrations, programmed learning, discussions, simulations, and direct experience. Each method has costs and benefits. Making decisions about which methods to use depends on the outcome intended for the staff. Lectures typically help listeners to become aware of ideas or practices, whereas direct experiences such as internships or shadowing help participants internalize the content.

The lecture or activity-based learning formats are effective for in-service education. The lectures can be motivational or instructive. Consultants can be brought into the district, or staff can be encouraged to attend professional growth conferences held at the local, regional, state, and national levels. Skilled counselors should be encouraged to present at

Figure 9.2
Format for Staff Development Plan

Staff Category	Staff Outcome	Strategy	Time Frame	Resources			Evaluation Method
				Expertise	Facilities/Equipment	Cost	

such conferences because organizing and presenting can help them refine their practices and ideas.

Reading materials include professional texts and journals. Individuals seeking growth in specific areas can use bibliographies. Some recent highly useful resources include the article "Web-Based Resources for Legal and Ethical Issues in School Counseling," by Guillot-Miller and Partin (2003) and a special issue of *Professional School Counseling*, "Professional School Counseling in Urban Settings," edited by Holcomb-McCoy and Lee (2005), that is a must-read for every school counselor in an urban setting.

If the goal is for a number of people to consider certain topics (as in the case of the special issue just mentioned), readings can be assigned and groups can be formed to discuss the content of the readings. The discussion can be focused by means of a discussion agenda such as that displayed in Figure 9.3 and used in the Northside Independent School District. Professional journal reading is a cost-effective, readily accessible, and professionally sound staff development vehicle that staff development planners typically underuse. Where such reading is encouraged, follow-up discussions to assist the readers to process the ideas they have read are not often held, but they should be.

Other vehicles for professional discussions include staff meetings and retreats. Case consultations, particularly those led by an expert consultant, provide meaningful learning opportunities as well. Feedback conferences held as a part of clinical supervision can also provide learning experiences for counselors. New counselors can learn much by observing master counselors as they demonstrate their skills in actual work settings.

Resources Available

Having identified the resources potentially available to help in staff development, it is important to be specific as to the expertise of the people available. Then the expertise available can be matched with the priority needs of the staff. Some consultants are available within the school system; others will cost money. Thus, the guidance department budget must be considered. Once the priority needs of staff have been identified and the means by which they can pursue professional development have been decided, it is possible to project how much money is required to make optimum use of the resources. Ideally, every staff member has the opportunity to grow professionally in the course of a year. Thus, the resources available should be distributed with this principle in mind. At the same time, having a means for individuals to share ideas and information they have gained is a way to

Figure 9.3
Group Counseling Project Discussion Agenda

High School Counselor Staff Meetings
Group Counseling Project Discussion Agenda

1. *Uses/values/limits of groups*
2. What *counseling* is/is not
3. Individual's *theoretical models*
4. Professional *processes and techniques* used in group counseling
5. *"Climate"* needed for group to succeed
6. Forming your groups
7. *Group process*
    Norms:
    Organization:
    Structure:
8. *Leader's role(s)/responsibilities*

Note. From Northside Independent School District, San Antonio, TX. Reprinted with permission.

spread the wealth. For example, if only one counselor from a district can attend a state or national professional conference, that counselor could give a report at the staff meeting.

A further important consideration in implementing the staff development plan is planning the use of the facilities and equipment available. Be sure to consider where the various activities will be held, what the seating capacity is, and whether the atmosphere is conducive to discussions. If plans include the use of equipment, make sure that the necessary equipment is present and that it is in working order. This may seem obvious, but all too often the excitement of the topic causes lapses in memory about meeting logistics.

Time Frame

Careful consideration should be given to when staff development activities will take place. Some writers have suggested, with good reason, that late afternoon or evening sessions are to be avoided if possible. Sessions during school hours are recommended but are costly because they use staff student-contact time. Saturday and holiday sessions may work out well, particularly if you are in a state in which certification or licensure requirements include accumulating continuing education hours.

We recommend that staff development activities be interspersed over the length of the program improvement process. Such activities are often enjoyable and serve as a means to increase morale. Staff development activities need to be planned well in advance so that all involved can participate. Furthermore, staff development should not stop once the major program development efforts have ceased. Professional growth should continue as a means of maintaining continuous individual professional development and program improvement.

Evaluation

Each staff development activity should be evaluated so that its effectiveness can be judged. Ways to evaluate the impact of activities include questionnaires, achievement-type tests, observations, and demonstrations. Whatever approach is used, it should be appropriate to the outcomes sought for the staff development activity. For example, observation of new behaviors is a more appropriate evaluation device for experiential staff development activities than it might be for lectures.

The effectiveness of the overall staff development program also needs to be evaluated. Reassessment of the staff's competencies through use of the original needs assessment instrument provides information as to the staff's growth. Continued monitoring of the staff's expressed needs through their professional development plans also provides evaluative data regarding the effectiveness of the professional growth activities provided.

Address Incompetence

As in all professions, some individuals in the counseling profession have either made the wrong career choice or have not developed their professional promise sufficiently. In short, there are those who are working as school counselors, as guidance and counseling program staff leaders, or as guidance administrators who are not competent to meet the position or job requirements. With performance standards outlined as concretely as we have recommended and with a system in place to help staff improve their professional competence, it is possible to terminate those whose performance is detrimental to students' growth and development. Due process rules are in place in most states to protect individuals from arbitrary terminations or reassignments, yet most systems have procedures outlined for helping those who are not in the right career to move. It is important not only for the students we serve but also for the profession as a whole to help incompetent counselors find other jobs (Henderson, 2009).

Termination involves legal procedures with important roles for administrators, personnel departments, and school system lawyers. Reassignment to different buildings sometimes helps employees regain their professional commitment. In many instances, the clarification of expectations associated with the program and performance improvement processes causes individuals to see that they are in the wrong position. Such self-determination is—obviously—preferable, but it also entails work for the administrators.

In any of these circumstances, the guidance and counseling program staff leader's role is to base evaluative judgments on the concrete, behavioral criteria established in the comprehensive guidance and counseling program, the job descriptions, and the related performance standards. If the impaired workers (Henderson, 2009) have been informed about the criteria and have been offered the staff development opportunities to acquire the competencies they need, it is professionally appropriate for them to be encouraged to leave the profession.

Bring New Counselors Into the Program and to the Proper Roles

Once job descriptions are written and available resources are identified, a systematic approach to staff development may begin. The primary task for ensuring competency of school counselors is to have the right people in the right roles. Finding the right people to hire requires the guidance and counseling program leader to collaborate with the colleges and universities at which most counselors are trained, to recruit the most highly skilled graduates to apply for available positions, and to select the most talented and skilled applicants to fill those positions. Helping school counselors fulfill the right roles requires the program leader to place them properly and to orient them to their new assignments.

Collaboration

Most college and university counselor education departments seek to develop collaborative relationships with the school districts in their areas that are most apt to hire their graduates. Such relationships are built by the professors seeking advice about various aspects of their training program. Many counselor education departments have formed formal advisory committees consisting of counselors and guidance and counseling program leaders from their neighboring districts. In addition, counselor educators seek advice through professional discussions and involvement in local or state professional associations for counselors. Often, practitioners are invited to make presentations to counselor education classes, whereby both the students in preservice training and the professors themselves gain insight into the actual work of school counselors.

Field experiences provide a primary opportunity for meaningful collaboration between counselor educators and local school districts. Field experiences for counselors-in-training are an important aspect of their preservice education. In fact, the 2009 CACREP accreditation standards for counselor education programs require 100 hours of supervised practicum experiences and an additional 600 hours of supervised internship experiences. Supervision is to be provided by a certified school counselor with a minimum of a master's degree. Making these experiences effective is a shared responsibility of the college or university staff and the building or district staff. To ensure successful completion of coursework that includes fieldwork, professors need to be explicit about the experiences that counselors-in-training should have. Requiring them to counsel individuals and write up case studies, to conduct group counseling sessions with students with problems, and to teach developmental guidance lessons guarantees that counselors-in-training will have these experiences. At the same time, school counselors responsible for supervising counselors-in-training need to be explicit about the experiences they know to be valuable in relation to the design of their school guidance and counseling program. Figure 9.4 provides an example of guidelines for practicum students and interns used by Northside Independent School District to help counselors-in-training consider from what experiences they would benefit to learn to be effective school counselors within that district. Guidelines such as these and students' related experiences help the counselors-in-training to conceptualize the program and to understand the relationship between the skills and techniques they are learning and the program in which they will use these skills. For most counselors-in-training, it becomes their first opportunity to explore this relationship.

Recruitment

Interacting with counselors-in-training is one way to recruit applicants. The purpose of recruitment is to develop a quality pool of applicants. The better the applicant pool, the more potential there is for those selected to become outstanding counselors. The basis for recruitment is to have a quality program and to let people know about it. Explaining the guidance and counseling program clearly to district faculty provides teachers who are certified as counselors or those who are planning to seek advanced training with an opportunity to consider the merits of being part of the school counseling staff. Providing teachers with quality feedback about students they refer and consulting effectively with them as they face problems with students or parents are often recruitment vehicles. If your school or district hires experienced counselors, presenting quality programs at professional conferences

Figure 9.4
Guidelines for Practicum Students and Interns

To ensure that you have experience in each of the components that constitute the District's Comprehensive Guidance Program, please consider the following as activities to be included in your field experience.

Guidance Curriculum Component
- Developmental group guidance (guiding–teaching of guidance content using guidance techniques)

Individual Student Planning Component
- Helping groups of students apply
  1. skills learned through curriculum component
  2. test results information
  3. career information and experiences
- Helping groups or individuals develop educational plans

Responsive Services Component
- Individual counseling
- Small-group counseling
- Consultation with parents regarding students with issues
- Consultation with teachers regarding students with issues
- Referral of students for special services or programs

System Support Component
- Guidance program planning
- Interpreting group standardized test results
- Providing teacher in-service
- Participate in the CHILD process (interpreting information participating in solution-focused staffings regarding students' individual learning and behavioral needs)

Please read the Texas Education Agency (2004) publication *The Comprehensive, Developmental Guidance Program for Texas Public Schools* (4th ed.); the Northside Independent School District (2002a) publication *Comprehensive Guidance Program Framework;* the Texas Counseling Association (2004) publication *Texas Evaluation Model for Professional School Counselors* (2nd ed.); and the Northside Independent School District (2002b) publication *Guide to Counselor Performance Improvement.*

and workshops is also a useful recruitment activity. Furthermore, the more active the school counselors in a district are in local, state, and national professional organizations, the more visible the program will be; if the quality of the school counselors' leadership and sense of responsibility is impressive, others will want to be part of the district's comprehensive guidance and counseling program.

Selection

After attracting quality applicants, the next challenge is selecting the best as candidates for school counseling positions. As we have said before, school counselor positions must be defined explicitly to match the applicants' qualifications with the expectations of the positions. The competencies required for the counselor positions have already been defined for the district, but each building may have specific demands that must be made explicit as well. These demands may include needing individuals with certain personality characteristics as well as certain preferences for various guidance and counseling program functions. The goal is to assemble a balance of characteristics and competencies across a building or district staff. For example, balanced staffs may have conceptualizers and logistics specialists, leaders and followers, those who enjoy group work and those who enjoy consultation, and so on. They may also include an ethnic and racial balance parallel to that of the student body, as well as a balance of men and women.

The process for staff selection includes interviewing applicants, considering the recommendations of people familiar with their work, and reviewing their experiences and achievements. Interviews of prospective counselors should be conducted not only by the personnel department staff but also by the supervisor or administrator who will oversee the work of the staff member. In the case of the school counselor, this means the building principal as well as the district guidance and counseling program leadership. Some systems have also effectively involved the current counseling staff in the interview process. Although effective interviewing by a large group is difficult to orchestrate, some schools have all the counselors participate in a group discussion with applicants. Others have had individual counselors conduct different parts of the interview with, for example, one counselor taking the applicant on a tour of the school and another explaining the guidance center. The size of the current staff and the number of candidates to be interviewed directly influence the interview format to be used.

The interview should provide an atmosphere conducive to self-expression. Interview questions should lead the applicants to report as much about themselves in relation to the position as possible in a reasonable length of time. There should be a direct relationship between the questions asked in an interview and the job requirements. Much has been written about the value—or lack of value—of the interview as a selection tool, but it is one way of allowing candidates the opportunity to provide a self-report of their experiences and abilities to fill the position competently. It also allows the employer the opportunity to gain insight into the candidate's personality and professionalism.

In soliciting recommendations from other professionals who have worked with a candidate, the administrator or supervisor should ask specific questions about the quality of the applicant's experiences in relationship to the role of the school counselor in the district, such as how effective a teacher has the applicant been? What has been the quality of the applicant's relationships with parents? People who give recommendations should be encouraged to provide concrete examples to support their opinions. In addition, a review of the applicants' strengths and weaknesses as noted in their past performance evaluations provides insight as to their probable success or failure as school counselors. We believe that it is imperative for a counselor to have been an effective teacher to begin to be an effective school counselor. School counselors should come from the ranks of the best teachers if they are to deliver a quality developmental guidance and counseling program that includes classroom guidance. Because the ability to be part of a team is also essential to delivering a comprehensive guidance and counseling program, indicators of individuals' past relationships in this regard are important. The guidance and counseling program and staff are at center stage in a school, thus potential counselors must have demonstrated that they are first and foremost good employees. Evidence of such traits as these is usually found in past performance ratings.

Proper Placement

A well-developed selection process provides needed information about candidates selected to fill available school counselor positions. It is imperative that staff members be placed in positions that will make maximum use of their strengths and in which their weaknesses will be minimized by the strengths of others. As already indicated, strengths and weaknesses in terms of competencies and personal characteristics need to be considered in placing individuals in specific assignments. The chemistry of a staff, although difficult to define, is as important to consider as are the competencies available and those required. For example, if a staff already has several highly assertive individuals, the addition of a follower will probably do more for staff balance than the addition of a person seeking a leadership position. With a clear definition in mind of the program that is desired for your building, you are better able to make judgments about who will best fit the job available.

Within a school system, it is often possible to redistribute staff members to make optimum use of their talents. The same clarity regarding the competencies and personality characteristics needed in a particular work setting is required if you have the opportunity to transfer individual staff members from one work setting to another. Transfer opportunities can occur naturally in districts in which growth provides new positions, or when counselors retire or move on.

Orientation

To help new counselors fulfill their roles properly and continue to embrace their new professional identity, orientation to the requirements of the job itself and the context of the work setting is necessary. By orientation, we mean providing new counselors with as much information about the comprehensive guidance and counseling program policy and operations as possible. New counselors receive information about the counselor role in their training programs and about the work setting in the job application and selection process. Once placed, however, they need more specific information about their role and the appropriate use of their competencies in the program. If the new counselor was previously a teacher, it is important to remember that counselors' roles and identities and teachers' roles and identities are different; the transition from one to the other is not automatic. New counselors need to know how the guidance and counseling program, perhaps only globally defined to them up till now, actually operates in the building to which they are assigned. The specific activities that define the four comprehensive program components need to be conveyed. New counselors also need to be informed about the structure of the building in which they will work, the principal's priorities, and the organizational relationships.

A member of the existing staff should be designated to help newcomers learn the facts they need and to ease their evolution into the new role and identity. Helping new counselors use their unique competencies is a role for the building guidance department head.

This role may include helping new counselors to broaden their perspective from a class-room perspective to the school perspective, to act as a consultant to other staff members and as an advocate for students, to put the concept of the guidance and counseling pro-gram in operation, and to learn the informal power structure of a school.

Orientation should begin with formal meetings conducted by supervisors and admin-istrators. Other topics are best handled through ongoing dialogue with the new counselor and a counselor colleague, who may or may not be the building supervisor. In some pro-grams, a designated mentor system has been used effectively. In any case, there is a lot of information for new counselors to learn, and the more systematic their induction into their new position is, the smoother the transition will be.

Attend to Diversity

The pluralism of our society, the students who come to our schools, and school coun-selors' professional and ethical standards dictate that school counselors be cross-culturally competent. Unique among the various counseling settings, school counselors work with all students and strive to do it without discrimination based on something other than the priorities established for the guidance program by the representative groups involved in the program design process. It is not sufficient in this era to be nonjudgmental. Key to a school counselor's meeting the challenges of the 21st century is "becoming a culturally respon-sive counselor" (Paisley & McMahon, 2001, p. 112).

Working with all students poses some daunting challenges because the counselors them-selves are probably not representative of or even knowledgeable about every facet of di-versity present in their schools. School counselors must learn to respond in responsible and sensitive ways to individuals who present a wide range of differences. In addition, it is well recognized that "integrating multicultural factors into the counseling process is an ex-tremely complex challenge" (Coleman, 2004, p. 62). But these are challenges school coun-selors must respond to. At the base of it is the

> *multicultural self-efficacy* of school counselors[,] . . . defined as [their] perceived abilities (i.e., be-
> liefs) to carry out and perform tasks that are relevant and specific to equity among students in
> [Pre-]K-12 schools, and the ethnically and culturally diverse needs of [Pre-] K-12 students. *Equity*
> . . . refers to fairness and justice for all students, taking into account their unique situations and
> experiences. (Holcomb-McCoy, Harris, Hines, & Johnston, 2008, p. 167)

Holcomb-McCoy et al. (2008) suggested that "if school counselors believe that they are capable of working for equity and with diverse populations of students, then they will act accordingly" (p. 172). Higher levels of multicultural self-efficacy means they are better able "to perform tasks . . . related to increasing minority student achievement, increasing . . . involvement of minority parents, and advocating for students from culturally and racially diverse backgrounds" (Holcomb-McCoy et al., 2008, p. 176). The researchers identified six factors of multicultural self-efficacy:

- Knowledge of multicultural concepts
- Using data and understanding system change
- Developing cross-cultural relationships
- Multicultural counseling awareness
- Multicultural assessment
- Application of racial and cultural knowledge to practice. (Holcomb-McCoy et al., 2008)

Standards and Definitions

In their efforts to further develop their cultural responsiveness, school counselors must be guided by the ethical standards and by established multicultural competencies. The structured ways to help school counselors continue to develop their professional competency are described in this chapter. In each of the ways described—job responsibilities, supervision, professional development, performance evaluation—both the counselors' and their leaders' awareness of and commitment to a counselor's enhanced cross-cultural effectiveness facilitate counselors' development in this critical area.

Ethical Standards

The ethical standards guiding professional school counselors' practice that are relevant to this discussion are clear in their mandates. ASCA's (2010a) *Ethical Standards for School Counselors* state in the Preamble:

> Each person has the right to be respected, be treated with dignity, and have access to a comprehensive school counseling program that advocates for and affirms all students from diverse populations including: ethnic/racial identity, age, economic status, abilities/disabilities, language, immigration status, sexual orientation, gender, gender identity/expression, family type, religious/spiritual identity and appearance.

In the section on "Responsibilities to Students" (A.1.), it is stated that

> professional school counselors:
> a. Have a primary obligation to the students, who are to be treated with dignity and respect as unique individuals.
> c. Respect students' values, beliefs and cultural background and do not impose the counselor's personal values on students or their families.

The ACA's (2005) *Code of Ethics* states in the Preamble that counselors "recognize diversity and embrace a cross-cultural approach in support of the worth, dignity, potential, and uniqueness of people within their social and cultural contexts." In the introduction to Section A: The Counseling Relationship, it states, "Counselors actively attempt to understand the diverse cultural backgrounds of the clients they serve. Counselors also explore their own cultural identities and how these affect their values and beliefs about the counseling process."

In Section A.4.b., Personal Needs and Values, it is stated:

> b. *Personal Values*. Counselors are aware of their own values, attitudes, beliefs, and behaviors . . . and respect the diversity of clients, trainees, and research participants.

In Section C: Professional Responsibility. C.5. Nondiscrimination, it is stated,

> a. Counselors do not condone or engage in discrimination based on age, culture, disability, ethnicity, race, religion/spirituality, gender identity, sexual orientation, marital status/partnership, language preference, socioeconomic status, or any basis proscribed by law.

Multicultural Counseling Standards

The profession's standards for multicultural counseling competence were presented first in 1992 by Sue, Arredondo, and McDavis as the Multicultural Counseling Competencies and Standards and are now identified as the Multicultural Counseling Competencies (Arredondo et al., 1996; see Appendix H). These standards outline the attitudes and beliefs, knowledge, and skills needed by multiculturally competent counselors:

1. Counselor awareness of their own cultural values and biases;
2. Counselor awareness of the client's worldview;
3. Culturally appropriate intervention strategies.

The Association for Multicultural Counseling and Development has continued to refine the multicultural counseling competencies by supporting development of "explanatory statements" that are now published in the *Operationalization of the Multicultural Counseling Competencies* (Arredondo et al., 1996; Sue et al., 1992). The explanatory statements offer criteria for counselors to meet in achieving each competence. These standards are increasingly well recognized in the counseling field and are being adapted by groups to fit their counseling specialty and membership; for example, the ASGW (1998) has adapted them to guide group workers. The National Career Development Association (2009) has promulgated "Minimum Competencies for Multicultural Career Counseling and Development."

ASCA has published position statements regarding diversity issues that suggest standards as well, such as *The Professional School Counselor and Cultural Diversity* (ASCA, 2009a); *The Professional School Counselor and Students with Special Needs* (ASCA, 2010b); *The Professional School Counselor and Gender Equity* (ASCA, 2008); and *The Professional School Counselor and LGBTQ Youth* (ASCA, 2007).

Definitions

The use of several labels—*diversity, multicultural,* and *cross-cultural*—describing similar or related concepts is confusing for some and calls for some clarification. Dialogue about these definitions is ongoing in our society. The terms *multiculturalism* and *diversity* are often used interchangeably, blurring the distinctions. Vontress and Jackson (2004) agreed that the concepts are used imprecisely:

> In the literature and society at large, these terms often convey the same meaning. We have resisted using them when we wish to refer to therapeutic encounters. Instead, we use cross-cultural counseling to communicate the idea of a helping dyad or group consisting of at least one person who perceives him- or herself to be culturally different. (p. 76)

Coleman (2004) pointed out that the purpose of the multicultural competencies is "to focus on those competencies that need to be integrated into a mental health professional's practice when working with racial, ethnic, or cultural minorities" (p. 58). Sue et al. (1992) clearly stated that the competencies are aimed at assisting counselors working with clients from "four [racial/ethnic minority] groups in our society: African Americans, American Indians, Asian Americans, and Hispanics and Latinos." (p. 477)

Some distinctions have been made between considering "multicultural factors (e.g., race, ethnicity, or culture) [and] diversity factors (e.g., physical or intellectual ability, sexual orientation, or age)" (Coleman, 2004, p. 57). By dictionary definition, *diverse* means "different" and has come to imply consideration of all of the variables that describe potential differences between individuals. The Association for Multicultural Counseling and Development, having defined its meaning of *multicultural*, suggested that the dimensions of personal identity (Arredondo & Glauner, 1992) describe facets of individuals that contribute to their uniqueness—to their similarities to and differences from each other. The following variables are cited: age, culture, ethnicity, gender, language, physical and mental well-being, race, sexual orientation, social class, educational background, geographic location, hobbies or recreational activities, health care practices and beliefs, religion and spirituality, military experience, relationship status, work experience, and historical context. These kinds of lists are ever growing. It is safe to say that each individual consists of myriad ingredients, and in working with children, school counselors not only work with all of the facets presented by an individual child but also work with these facets in consulting with their parents and teachers.

We use the term *cross-cultural* to mean when one person from his or her personal cultural base (Arredondo et al., 1996) reaches across to another's cultural base to collaborate on the work at hand. In this sense, *cultural* includes all of the variables cited. *Cross-cultural effectiveness,* then, is when that effort to reach across cultures results in successful work. The work for school counselors and their students includes all of the elements of school guidance and counseling work (e.g., relationship building, problem solving, continuing positive growth and development).

Although the cross-cultural competencies may have been developed with the intent of guiding counselors' work with members of racial, ethnic, and cultural groups, they are also useful for work with students with other diversity factors. As mentioned earlier, the competencies themselves are about beliefs and attitudes, knowledge, and skills in working with people who are culturally different from the counselor. They guide a counselor to be self-aware, to be aware of the other member of the relationship, and to use intervention strategies and techniques that are appropriate to the client (Appendix H).

Similarities and Differences Between Counselors and Clients

Counselors' finding commonalities with their clients to build counseling relationships is basic to successful counseling. Awareness of differences is equally as important and, again, is done for the purpose of being as effective a counselor as possible with each client. Building on commonalities and minimizing the impact of differences is most likely to lead to successful guidance and counseling interventions.

Similarities

Conventional wisdom based on experience and some research tells us that clients prefer counselors who they perceive have something in common with them. According to Vontress and Jackson (2004, p. 76), "Perception is a significant relationship factor. Individuals generally establish better rapport with those they perceive to be like themselves than they do with those whom they perceive to be unlike themselves." Esters and Ledoux (2001) summarized,

> The extant literature indicates that, if given the choice, most people prefer to enter into counseling with a counselor similar to them. It would appear that issues of similarity and difference are integral to understanding the nature of counseling relationships. (p. 168)

Today's research has suggested that those preferences may go beyond "readily discernible physical characteristics" (Esters & Ledoux, 2001, p. 169). Esters and Ledoux (2001) summarized previous studies of clients' preferences among counselor characteristics, and "the general conclusions derived from these studies support the hypothesis that participants of various races and ethnicities prefer counselors possessing characteristics similar to themselves, but that similarity is not necessarily defined by race or ethnicity alone" (p. 166). Their study was with at-risk high school students who were asked to rank order the importance of eight counselor characteristics. The rank-ordered preferences for counselor characteristics from highest to lowest were as follows: "same attitudes and values, same background and socioeconomic status, same sex, same race, opposite sex, different background and socioeconomic status, different race, different attitude and values" (p. 168). "The characteristics ranked highest were those indicating similarity and those ranked lowest were those indicating difference" (p. 169). Esters and Ledoux commented,

> After all, a school counselor who shares a student's attitudes and values and a similar background and socioeconomic status will, by most definitions of culture, share more of the culture and will thus be more similar than a school counselor who is simply a member of the same race. This finding should be encouraging to school counselors who find themselves attempting to build a counseling relationship with a student or a group of students with whom they differ in either race, sex, or both. (p. 169)

Differences

According to Constantine et al. (2001),

> Effective multicultural counseling is rooted in the premise that although people share common or universal experiences (e.g., basic biological functions or life processes), they also have important differences based on cultural group memberships such as race or sex. (pp. 13–14)

One premise is that

> counselors' ability to effectively communicate and interact with clients in therapeutic relationships involves the counselors' competence in focusing on both similarities and differences (Miville et al., 1999). Thus, school counselors' awareness of how culturally diverse students may be alike and different from them may be vital to building successful alliances with these students (Fuertes et al., 2000). (Constantine et al., 2001, p. 14)

Some recurrent examples that school counselors come in contact with on a regular basis have been studied and have led to important clues about effective cross-cultural work for school counselors. The first example is from a study by Constantine and Yeh (2001) that addressed the differences between Eastern and Western cultures and the degree to which individuals are encouraged to define themselves as independent individuals, as in Western culture, or as interdependent on others, as in East Asian and African societies. Their results led them to caution:

> It is important to note that some behaviors of school counselors (e.g., offering specific opinions and advice, providing direction and structure, and being interpersonally assertive) are associated with having more independent self-construals (Lee, 1996; Leon, Wagner, & Tata, 1995). Thus, when such behaviors or values are displayed in counseling practice, they could be detrimental to the social, emotional, and academic development of culturally diverse, school-aged children with more interdependent self-construals. Consequently, school counselors with higher independent self-construals may incorrectly encourage interdependent students' (a) separation and individuation from the family, (b) emotional expressiveness without regard to important others' feelings, and (c) assertiveness in interpersonal relationships. (pp. 205–206)

Regarding cultural differences in expressing emotions, Constantine and Gainor (2001) reminded school counselors that it is crucial that [they] are cognizant of possible culturally based differences in students' expressions of emotional states. School counselors who are unaware of differences in how feelings may be expressed or regulated across cultures may erroneously interpret or even pathologize such behaviors in some students of color. As a result, these students may feel that their mental health issues are not being understood or addressed in culturally sensitive ways. (p. 135)

Professional Development Goals

Professional school counselors also recognize that, like every other aspect of counseling, growth in their multicultural competence is ongoing, and counselors working in a pluralistic society with an increasingly diverse population are always works in progress. Professional school counselors use many strategies to continuously develop their competency. In our opinion, these strategies are most productively used when they are driven by professional development goals established by counselors, as described in this chapter. Potential goals for school counselors to enhance their multicultural competence relate to all 31 of the Association for Multicultural Counseling and Development Multicultural Counseling Competencies (Arredondo et al., 1996; Sue et al., 1992). Given the myriad goals potentially related to ensuring that they are works in progress in their effectiveness with the diverse populations they serve, professional school counselors probably ought to have a multicultural competence development goal every year of their professional lives.

It begins with self-awareness. Constantine et al. (2001) noted,

> The development of multicultural knowledge and awareness, particularly school counselors' own self-awareness in relation to various cultural issues, seems critical to their ability to (a) consider the potential salience of cultural variables in working with students, and (b) effectively meet the mental health needs of culturally diverse students. (p. 17)

Constantine et al. concluded, "It is feasible to consider that school counselors could have an interest in and appreciation for cultural diversity without necessarily experiencing comfort in interpersonal situations involving culturally diverse students" (p. 17). Constantine and Gainor (2001) conducted a study "to better understand the relationships among school counselors' emotional intelligence, empathy, and self-reported multicultural counseling awareness" (p. 132). They found that "school counselors with higher levels of emotional intelligence reported higher levels of multicultural counseling knowledge" (p. 135) and concluded that "emotionally intelligent school counselors appear to possess interpersonal strengths that may enable them to better comprehend or be attuned to the experiences of issues of culturally diverse others" (p. 135). They also made an interesting point about overempathizing. They found that school counselors who had higher personal distress scores (anxiety and discomfort) perceived themselves as having less multicultural counseling knowledge. They concluded,

> It is possible that school counselors who become unduly anxious or unsettled when empathizing with the difficulties of culturally diverse students may be somewhat less proficient in counseling situations because their anxiety may impede them from effectively applying their multicultural counseling knowledge. (p. 135)

Constantine and Gainor also wrote,

> A possible implication of these findings is that school counselors may wish to identify ways to increase their multicultural counseling awareness so that they may understand better how their own and others' cultural group memberships could affect counseling relationships. (p. 136)

There are also school counselors who resist all or some aspects of enhancing their multicultural competence. Awareness of one's cultural values and biases is an important place to start, but awareness is just the beginning. It should lead to "constructive confrontation with oneself" (Arredondo, Tovar-Blank, & Parham, 2008, p. 265). In addition to some school counselors being close minded or fearful of addressing multicultural issues, Arredondo et al. (2008) explored other dimensions of counselor resistance: "xenophobia, unexamined privilege, and pseudointellectual[ism] . . . (dependency on scientific explanations)" (p. 265). In addition to self-confrontation, Watt et al. (2009) described deepening multicultural competence (e.g., exploring privileged identity) through counselors-in-training and practicing counselors engaging in "difficult dialogues" (p. 86).

Goals for developing appropriate cross-cultural interventions may cause changes in school counselors' techniques. Holcomb-McCoy (2004) noted,

> As school counselors work with larger numbers of ethnic minority students, they may need to alter their perceptions, learn to effectively counsel and consult with diverse populations, become knowledgeable of other cultures and the manifestations of racism, and assume the role of social change agent. (p. 182)

Holcomb-McCoy (2004) identified areas of multicultural competence that she "believes are essential for the practice of school counseling" and offered a Multicultural Competence Checklist to "guide professional school counselors' multicultural development and training" (p. 178). The checklist identified nine categories of multicultural competence:

1. multicultural counseling;
2. multicultural consultation;
3. understanding racism and student resistance;
4. understanding racial identity development;
5. multicultural assessment;
6. multicultural family counseling;
7. social advocacy;
8. developing school–family–community partnerships;
9. understanding interpersonal interactions.

In addition to using the checklist "as a guide for professional development [goal-setting and] activities" (p. 181), Holcomb-McCoy suggested that "school counselors can enhance their multicultural counseling competence by soliciting feedback on their practice and understanding of multicultural issues from others who are culturally different" (p. 181).

Related to Esters and Ledoux's (2001) findings, one goal that when reached would help counselors be received more favorably by students would be to "present themselves as dispositionally more similar to the students, so long as the similarities are genuine" (p. 169). This is not to say that school counselors should falsely represent their attitudes and values or mislead students to believe that the counselor is of a similar background and socioeconomic status.

> On the other hand, counselors who find themselves attempting to build a relationship with students who are different from them regarding attitudes and values and background and socioeconomic status should be aware that by consciously disclosing this difference, they might be alienating the student and endangering the formation of a solid, trusting counseling relationship. It would seem that school counselors who present themselves as dispositionally more similar to the student, so long as the similarities are genuine, may be received more favorably by that student. (Esters & Ledoux, 2001, p. 169)

Green and Keys (2001) challenged professional school counselors and comprehensive, developmental guidance programs to consider basing their programs on "development-in-context" (p. 86) models. Such models demand consideration of the contexts in which students live. They stated, "Developing an awareness of self-in-context is both an important program focus and program outcome for all students" (p. 93). Certainly, deeper understanding of the contexts in which students live, the impact that their community context has on their development, and its probable divergence from the school context are all areas for growth for school counselors.

Increasingly, there are calls for professional school counselors to combine their deepening multicultural competence with their advocacy skills to help schools be more effective with students from cultures that are different from the traditional school culture. Portman (2009) suggested that school counselors be cultural mediators and identified 10 functions to carry out this role, such as gathering and examining demographic data on students enrolled in their schools; becoming aware of the cultural backgrounds of their schools' stakeholders; communicating with others about cultural diversity; seeking further cultural competence; helping culturally diverse students advance their skills to facilitate relationship building; and creating a supportive culturally diverse school and community climate.

Several authors have addressed the needs of school counselors to advance their advocacy skills through professional development. Holcomb-McCoy et al. (2008) suggested "using data and . . . understanding systemic change" (p. 176). Toporek, Lewis, and Crethar (2009) described ways to promote systemic change through applying the ACA Advocacy Competencies (Ratts, Toporek, & Lewis, 2010). M. P. Evans, Zambrano, Cook, Moyer, and Duffey (2011) suggested strategies for enhancing school counselors' leadership in multicultural advocacy.

Clarify Roles of Building-Level Guidance and Counseling Program Staff Leaders

Strengthening the means by which we help counselors improve their job performance, as well as more clearly defining expectations for the guidance and counseling program, calls for recasting the role of the building guidance department head. Various titles are used to label this position, such as head counselor, guidance department chair, guidance coordinator, and director of guidance. We use *guidance and counseling program staff leader* to underscore and differentiate their two distinct areas of responsibility (Henderson & Gysbers, 1998). Traditionally, building guidance and counseling program staff leaders have served as liaisons between the guidance staff and the administration and between the guidance department and the instructional departments. In some instances, they have been expected to do the quasi-administrative tasks assigned to the guidance department, such as building the testing schedule or the master schedule.

In a building that is changing its guidance and counseling program to the comprehensive one that we are proposing and that is striving to use all its available resources to enhance the effectiveness of the counselors, the guidance and counseling program staff leader's job description must change. First, it is imperative that some member of the staff be designated as the leader of the building guidance and counseling program. Second, a job description appropriately tailored to address the additional responsibilities of that person must be written. A sample program staff leader job description is provided in Figure 6.3 (Chapter 6). It states the expectations that they are to provide leadership to the program development efforts in their buildings and that they will supervise the counseling staff, in addition to the more traditional responsibilities of serving their own caseload and representing the department to others. It also clarifies that building guidance and counseling program staff leaders' authority to fill these expectations is delegated to them by the principal and the district guidance and counseling program leader (those designated as their leaders in the building and in the central office).

The principals and the central office guidance and counseling program staff leaders must work with and for the building leaders to help them carry out their responsibilities. Lieberman (2004) systematically studied counseling literature and administration literature. He made the point "that effective schools are characterized by high agreement among staff as to the guidance goals and purposes" (p. 554) of the school and of their specific role in it. He described the concept of leadership density: "overall leadership available from different staff possessing various expertise and perspectives within their own areas, all on behalf of the school's work" (p. 554). In his research, he found "statistically significant divergence in how principals and counselors each view the role of the counselor" (p. 556). Effective school leaders are "proactive in learning the appropriate roles and functions for school personnel so that they may direct and encourage more appropriate and productive functioning of each individual towards the overriding and shared school goals" (p. 555). He concluded that it is up to school leaders to learn the appropriate roles of their staff members. It is also a responsibility of the leaders of a staff group to educate the school leader about the expertise and perspectives their staff members bring to the school mission.

The newest challenge for building guidance and counseling program staff leaders is the responsibility of providing regular and intentional supervision of the counseling staff in their buildings. The regular staff members need to be informed as to the authority of the building guidance and counseling program staff leader. The guidance and counseling program staff leaders should be provided the skill development they need to conduct their clinical, developmental, and administrative supervisory roles appropriately.

The performance management system model proposed in this chapter and the system for clearly defining individual guidance staff members' roles and responsibilities discussed in Chapter 7 demand a partnership between professional school counselors and their guidance and counseling program staff leaders. The latter's staff management responsibilities include negotiating the annual job description specification; team building to implement a coordinated, comprehensive program; orienting new counselors to the field of counseling as well as to the established guidance and counseling program; providing supervision; and performance evaluation. When these activities are to be accomplished should be spelled out; an example is provided in Figure 9.5.

Guidance and counseling program staff leaders benefit from specialized training that helps them to better implement their newly clarified roles. Where you begin their in-service training depends on the individuals involved and the roles identified for them. We recommend beginning with action planning because that is basic to their work with counselors and to their responsibilities for leading the building guidance and counseling program redesign and implementation. Guidance and counseling program staff leaders and peer leaders may also have needs for competencies in motivating staff members, conducting observations, providing constructive criticism, risk taking, delegating, asserting, and managing stress. They may need help in developing the skills and attitudes needed for effectively encouraging others. They may need to learn the leadership roles associated with mutual goal setting as well as those associated with effective monitoring of plan implementation. They undoubtedly need education and training to support their using their power bases appropriately. Seven power bases have been identified: legitimate, information, coercive, expert, referent, reward, and connection (Henderson, 2009). If your district organizational structure involves a team approach with the principals sharing the guidance and counseling program staff leader responsibility for the counselors, principals need to be

Figure 9.5
Guidance Program Staff Leadership Activities: Suggested Time Frame

August
In-service training
Job description development
Yearly guidance program calendar development
Program and performance improvement goal setting and action planning
Administrative supervision

September
Clinical supervision
Administrative supervision

October
Clinical supervision
Administrative supervision

November
Clinical supervision
Administrative supervision

December
Formative performance evaluation
Clinical supervision
Administrative supervision

January
Goal accomplishment progress checks
Clinical supervision
Administrative supervision

February
Clinical supervision
Administrative supervision

March
Clinical supervision
Administrative supervision

April
Clinical supervision
Administrative supervision

May
Summative performance evaluation
Assessment of program and performance improvement goal attainment
Administrative supervision

June
Professional development goal setting and action planning
Administrative supervision
In-service training

informed to ensure their understanding of the newly designed comprehensive guidance and counseling program. Thus, the district staff development plan ought to include principals.

Not many universities offer training in school counselor supervision; thus, the district or school system guidance and counseling program leaders may need to provide the skill development experiences needed by the building department heads. The Association for Counselor Education and Supervision (1989) has adopted standards for counseling supervisors. These standards describe "eleven core areas of personal traits, knowledge and competencies that are characteristic of effective supervisors" (p. 8). These encompass

1. effective counselors;
2. personal traits and characteristics;
3. ethical, legal, and regulatory aspects;
4. supervisory relationship;

5. supervision methods and techniques;
6. counselor development process;
7. case conceptualization and management;
8. assessment and evaluation;
9. oral and written reporting and recording;
10. evaluation of counseling performance;
11. research in counseling and counselor supervision.

A companion piece to these standards is the *Ethical Guidelines for Counseling Supervisors* (Association for Counselor Education and Supervision, 1993). These guidelines address

1. client welfare and rights;
2. supervisory role;
3. program administration role.

In addition to establishing these standards for counseling supervisors (Dye & Borders, 1990), the Association for Counselor Education and Supervision has supported the development of a curriculum guide for training counselor supervisors (Borders et al., 1991). An outline used to assist new Northside Independent School District guidance and counseling program staff leaders is available in *Leading and Managing Your School Guidance and Counseling Program Staff* (Henderson & Gysbers, 1998). Other resources to support such training include two handbooks developed through the Association for Counselor Education and Supervision, one on counseling supervision (Borders & Brown, 2005) and one on administrative supervision (Henderson, 2009).

Guidance and counseling program staff leaders in turn need to be supervised. Administrative supervision of the building-level guidance and counseling program staff leaders is done by the building principal. Clinical and developmental supervision should be done by the central office guidance and counseling program leaders. Clinical supervision could entail observing a guidance and counseling program staff leader conducting a post-observation conference with a counselor and providing and modeling techniques for providing feedback. Developmental supervision could entail setting goals that are specific to guidance and counseling program staff leaders' program leadership responsibilities (e.g., instituting group guidance activities for 12th graders in which they learn their status relative to high school graduation, and initiating a post–high school plan) and to staff supervision responsibilities (e.g., implementing a specific teambuilding strategy).

District Guidance and Counseling Program Staff Leaders' Roles and Responsibilities

Ensuring the competency of the school counselors is a primary responsibility of all of the guidance and counseling program staff leaders. The best-designed program is meaningless in the hands of insufficiently competent staff. We have said that an effective guidance and counseling program staff leader plays a range of roles to ensure against this. The leader collaborates with the preservice training institution staff as counselor educators develop their programs. Recruitment of qualified applicants provides a pool of talent available for filling jobs that become available. In addition to helping select the best people for the jobs, the program leader has a responsibility to strive to match new counselors' talent with the positions that will use their capabilities to the maximum advantage of the students and the program.

Once school counselors are selected, the leader orients them to the comprehensive guidance and counseling program design and goals and ensures their orientation to the buildings they will serve. The roles of the guidance and counseling program leaders and the campus administrators must be carefully outlined, and an efficient and effective performance management system should be designed. The district guidance and counseling program leader's role mirrors that of the building leaders and supports the systemwide program and performance improvement efforts. A primary role of the system leader is to train and supervise the building staff leaders. As we have said, the resources of supervision, evaluation, and professional development should be focused to assist the school counselors to attain their optimum level of professional competency and commitment. In the few cases of incompetence, the guidance administrator must be able to articulate the professional and program standards clearly so that such individuals can seek better use of their particular skills. Clarity of role expectations is critical to ensure the competency of school counselors.

A successful guidance and counseling program leader must maintain the vision needed to help the program succeed at its mission, must uphold the basic principles of the profession at large, must keep in touch with the staff and those whom the program serves, must be able to manage change, and must select good people as subordinates, trust them to carry out their roles appropriately, and help them when they do not. The program leader must develop appropriate and adequate performance indicators so that problems may be addressed in a timely fashion and opportunities for improvement are allowed to emerge. Furthermore, with the program and performance standards in place, a district is ready to evaluate its guidance and counseling program and the school counseling staff. This is covered in detail in Chapter 10.

Often, it is not until the implementation phase of the program development process that school districts identify the need for expanded guidance program leadership at the district level. By this time, the need for a leader who has guidance expertise becomes quite apparent. Being a new district guidance program staff leader has its challenges (Krueger, 2002; Larivee, 2002). Learning new roles and responsibilities, meeting and engaging a larger staff more often than you are used to, developing your own leadership style, and implementing changes are only some of the challenges involved in these new positions. Larivee (2002) summarized some of her learnings in making the transition:

> My enthusiasm is not necessarily contagious. I have learned that no matter what kind of credentials I have, I still have to earn my stripes. I have been reminded that change is a slow . . . process. . . . I must be very passionate about my cause. . . . Making administrative decisions sometimes takes me out of my comfort zone. Professional peer groups are not as available in this position as in most others. (p. 40)

Concluding Thoughts

Ensuring that school counselors have the competencies and levels of commitment they need to fulfill their roles requires continuous attention. Not only can each individual continue to develop as a professional, but also the context in which he or she works is ever changing. Counselors mature professionally with each new client and with each new activity. Helping individuals to process these new experiences and blend them into their existing competency system enhances their development and lessens the chances of burnout. The profession advances; resources change; new modalities for effective staff development are discovered. The program priorities shift as students present new challenges and as evaluation clarifies weaknesses and strengths of the program. Continuous program improvement depends on continued improvement of staff members' competency.

Your Progress Check

Your efforts to ensure the competency of the school counselors in your school or district began when you started the program improvement process. They continue for the life of the program. If you have followed our recommendations, you have defined appropriate roles for professional school counselors to fulfill, established standards for their performance, and developed systems that support meaningful, continuous professional growth and development.

Defined Roles

You have

- described an appropriate professional identity for school counselors;
- specified the competencies that produce meaningful and effective guidance, counseling, consultation, coordination, assessment, and program management; and
- clarified the roles of and trained building-level guidance and counseling program staff leaders.

Established Standards

You have

- adopted standards for competent, ethical, legal, and professional performance;
- clarified that each individual's job description establishes the expectations for that individual;
- supported the continuous improvement of school counselors' cross-cultural competence.

Developed Systems

You have

- implemented a systematic approach to managing the performance of the school counselors, linking the job description, supervision, performance evaluation, and goal-setting for professional development;
- clarified responsibilities of individuals and the school or district;
- trained school guidance and counseling program staff leaders to provide clinical, developmental, and administrative supervision for school counselors;
- defined an effective supervision process, including methods for assessing levels of professionalism and selecting a counselor-relevant supervisory response style;
- installed a system for school counselors that supports individuals' professional development and targets specific standards based on the needs of individuals and the needs of the school or district guidance and counseling program;
- developed a master plan for ongoing staff development and identified resources for implementing it;
- implemented a systematic and legally appropriate approach for recruitment, selection, placement, and orientation of school counselors;
- defined a process for addressing incompetence in school counselors.

References

American Counseling Association. (2005). *ACA code of ethics.* Alexandria, VA: Author.

American Counseling Association. (2009). *20/20 statement of principles advances the profession* [Press release] Retrieved from http://www.counseling.org/PressRoom/PressReleases.aspx?AGuid=4d87a0ce-65c0-4074-89dc-2761cfbbe2ec

American Counseling Association. (2010). *ACA milestones.* Retrieved from http://www.counseling.org/AboutUs/OurHistory/TP/Milestones/CT2.aspx

American Psychological Association. (2005). *Code of fair testing practices in education.* Washington, DC: Author.

American School Counselor Association. (2005). *The ASCA National Model: A framework for school counseling programs* (2nd ed.). Alexandria, VA: Author.

American School Counselor Association. (2007). *The professional school counselor and LGBTQ youth.* Retrieved from http://asca2.timberlakepublishing.com//files/PS_LGBTQ.pdf

American School Counselor Association. (2008). *The professional school counselor and gender equity.* Retrieved from http://asca2.timberlakepublishing.com//files/PS_Gender%20Equity.pdf

American School Counselor Association. (2009a). *The professional school counselor and cultural diversity.* Retrieved from http://asca2.timberlakepublishing.com//files/CulturalDiversity.pdf

American School Counselor Association. (2009b). *The role of the professional school counselor.* Retrieved from http://www.schoolcounselor.org/content.asp?pl=325&sl=133&contentid=240

American School Counselor Association. (2010a). *Ethical standards for school counselors.* Retrieved from http://www.schoolcounselor.org/files/EthicalStandards2010.pdf

American School Counselor Association. (2010b). *The professional school counselor and students with special needs.* Retrieved from http://asca2.timberlakepublishing.com//files/SpecialNeeds.pdf

American School Counselor Association (n.d.). *School counselor competencies.* Retrieved from http://www.schoolcounselor.org/files/SCCompetencies.pdf

Arredondo, P., & Glauner, T. (1992). *Personal dimensions of identity model.* Boston, MA: Empowerment Workshops. Retrieved from http://counseling.org/Files/FD.ashx?guid=8a0eb81f-6139-4f38-a139-a8152c9dde3a

Arredondo, P., Toporek, R., Brown, S., Jones, J., Locke, D. C., Sanchez, J., & Stadler, H. (1996). Operationalization of the Multicultural Counseling Competencies. *Journal of Multicultural Counseling and Development, 24,* 42–78.

Arredondo, P., Tovar-Blank, Z. G., & Parham, T. A. (2008). Challenges and promises of becoming a culturally competent counselor in a sociopolitical era of change and empowerment. *Journal of Counseling & Development, 86,* 261–268.

Association for Assessment in Counseling. (1998). *Competencies in assessment and evaluation for school counselors.* Retrieved from http://www.theaaceonline.com/competency.pdf

Association for Assessment in Counseling. (2003). *Responsibilities of users of standardized tests* (3rd ed.). Retrieved from http://www.theaaceonline.com/rust.pdf

Association for Counselor Education and Supervision. (1989, Spring). ACES adopts standards for counseling supervisors. *ACES Spectrum,* 7–10.

Association for Counselor Education and Supervision. (1995). Ethical guidelines for counseling supervisors. *Counselor Education and Supervision, 34*(3), 270–278.

Association for Specialists in Group Work. (1998). *Principles for diversity-competent group workers.* Retrieved from http://www.asgw.org/diversity.htm

Association for Specialists in Group Work. (2000). *Professional standards for the training of group workers*. Retrieved from http://www.asgw.org/training_standards.htm

Association for Specialists in Group Work. (2007). *Best practice guidelines 2007 revision*. Retrieved from http://www.asgw.org/pdf/Best_Practices.pdf

Barret, R. L., & Schmidt, J. (1986). School counselor certification and supervision: Overlooked professional issues. *Counselor Education and Supervision, 26*, 50–55.

Bauman, S. (2008). To join or not to join: School counselors as a case study in professional membership. *Journal of Counseling & Development, 86*, 164–177.

Bernard, J. M., & Goodyear, R. K. (1992). *Fundamentals of clinical supervision*. Boston: Allyn & Bacon.

Biggs, D. A. (1988). The case presentation approach in clinical supervision. *Counselor Education and Supervision, 27*, 240–248.

Borders, L. D. (1989). A pragmatic agenda for developmental supervision research. *Counselor Education and Supervision, 29*, 16–24.

Borders, L. D., Bernard, J. M., Dye, H. A., Fong, M. L., Henderson, P., & Nance, D. W. (1991). Curriculum guide for training counseling supervisors: Rationale, development, and implementation. *Counselor Education and Supervision, 31*, 58–80.

Borders, L. D., & Brown, L. (2005). *The new handbook of counseling supervision*. Alexandria, VA: American Counseling Association.

Bowers, J. (2002). Using technology to support comprehensive guidance program operations. In P. Henderson & N. Gysbers (Eds.), *Implementing comprehensive school guidance programs: Critical leadership issues and successful responses* (pp. 115–120). Greensboro, NC: CAPS.

Boyd, J. (Ed.). (1978). *Counselor supervision: Approaches, preparation, and practices*. Muncie, IN: Accelerated Development.

Center for Social and Emotional Education. (n.d.). *School Climate Research Summary*. Retrieved from http://nscc.csee.net/effective/school_climate_research_summary.pdf

Coleman, H. L. K. (2004). Multicultural counseling competencies in a pluralistic society. *Journal of Mental Health Counseling, 26*, 56–66.

Constantine, M. G., Arorash, T. J., Barakett, M. D., Blackmon, S. M., Donnelly, P. C., & Edles, P. A. (2001). School counselors' universal-diverse orientation and aspects of their multicultural counseling competence. *Professional School Counseling, 5*, 13–18.

Constantine, M. G., & Gainor, K. A. (2001). Emotional intelligence and empathy: Their relation to multicultural counseling knowledge and awareness. *Professional School Counseling, 5*, 131–137.

Constantine, M. G., & Yeh, C. J. (2001). Multicultural training, self-construals, and multicultural competence of school counselors. *Professional School Counseling, 4*, 202–207.

Council for Accreditation of Counseling and Related Educational Programs. (2009). *2009 standards*. Retrieved from http://www.cacrep.org/doc/2009%20Standards%20with%20cover.pdf

Dye, H. A., & Borders, L. D. (1990). Counseling supervisors: Standards for preparation and practice. *Journal of Counseling & Development, 69*, 27–32.

Education Trust. (2003). *Transforming school counselor preparation*. Retrieved from http://www.edtrust.org/dc/tsc

Esters, I., & Ledoux, C. (2001). At-risk high school students' preferences for counselor characteristics. *Professional School Counseling, 4*, 165–170.

Etringer, B. D., Hillerbrand, E., & Claiborn, C. D. (1995). The transition from novice to expert school counselor. *Counselor Education and Supervision, 35*, 4–17.

Evans, B., & Ward, S. (2002). Solving the "time and information" dilemma through technology. In P. Henderson & N. Gysbers (Eds.), *Implementing comprehensive school guid-*

ance programs: Critical leadership issues and successful responses (pp. 121–135). Greensboro, NC: CAPS.

Evans, M. P., Zambrano, E., Cook, K., Moyer, M., & Duffey, T. (2011). Enhancing school counselor leadership in multicultural advocacy. *Journal of Professional Counseling: Practice, Theory, and Research, 38,* 52–67.

Fitch, T. J., & Marshall, J. L. (2004). What counselors do in high-achieving schools: A study on the role of the school counselor. *Professional School Counseling, 7,* 172–177.

Gibson, D. M., Dollarhide, C. T., & Moss, J. M. (2010). Professional identity development: A grounded theory of transformational tasks of new counselors. *Counselor Education and Supervision, 50,* 21–37.

Glickman, C. D., Gordon, S. P., & Ross-Gordon, J. M. (1995). *Supervision of instruction: A developmental approach* (3rd ed.). Boston: Allyn & Bacon.

Green, A., & Keys, S. G. (2001). Expanding the developmental school counseling paradigm: Meeting the needs of the 21st century student. *Professional School Counseling, 5,* 84–95.

Guillot-Miller, L., & Partin, P. W. (2003). Web-based resources for legal and ethical issues in school counseling. *Professional School Counseling, 7,* 52–57.

Hansen, J. T. (2010). Consequences of the postmodernist vision: Diversity as the guidance value for the counseling profession. *Journal of Counseling & Development, 88,* 101–107.

Henderson, P. (2009). *The new handbook of administrative supervision in counseling.* Alexandria, VA: Association for Counselor Education and Supervision.

Henderson, P., Cook, K., Libby, M., & Zambrano, E. (2006). "Today I feel like a professional school counsellor!": Developing a strong professional school counsellor identity through career experiences. *Guidance & Counselling, 21,* 128–142.

Henderson, P., & Gysbers, N. C. (1998). *Leading and managing your school guidance and counseling program staff.* Alexandria, VA: American Counseling Association.

Hersey, P., Blanchard, K. L., & Johnson, D. E. (2001). *Management of organizational behavior: Leading human resources* (8th ed.). Upper Saddle River, NJ: Prentice-Hall.

Holcomb-McCoy, C. (2004). Assessing the multicultural competence of school counselors: A checklist. *Professional School Counseling, 7,* 178–186.

Holcomb-McCoy, C., Harris, P., Hines, E. M., & Johnston, G. (2008). School counselors' multicultural self-efficacy: A preliminary investigation. *Professional School Counseling, 11,* 166–178.

Holcomb-McCoy, C., & Lee, C. C. (Eds.). (2005). Professional school counseling in urban settings [Special issue]. *Professional School Counseling, 8*(3).

Kenny, M. C., & McEachern, A. G. (2004). Telephone counseling: Are offices becoming obsolete? *Journal of Counseling & Development, 82,* 199–202.

Krueger, D. (2002). A leader's 3 r's: Reading, reflecting, and relationships. In P. Henderson & N. Gysbers (Eds.), *Implementing comprehensive school guidance programs: Critical leadership issues and successful responses* (pp. 43–49). Greensboro, NC: CAPS.

Lambie, G. W. (2007). The contribution of development level to burnout in school counselors: Implications for professional school counseling. *Journal of Counseling & Development, 85,* 82–88.

Larivee, G. (2002). Establishing a new position: District director of guidance. In P. Henderson & N. Gysbers (Eds.), *Implementing comprehensive school guidance programs: Critical leadership issues and successful responses* (pp. 35–41). Greensboro, NC: CAPS.

Leach, M. M., & Stoltenberg, C. D. (1997). Self-efficacy and counselor development: Testing the integrated developmental model. *Counselor Education and Supervision, 37,* 115–125.

Lieberman, A. (2004). Confusion regarding school counselor functions: School leadership impacts role clarity. *Education, 124,* 552–557.

Mental Health in Schools Program and Policy Analysis. (2011). School engagement, disengagement, learning supports, & school climate [Special issue]. *Addressing Barriers to Learning, 16*(1).

National Board for Certified Counselors. (2001). *The practice of Internet counseling.* Retrieved from http://www.nbcc.org/assets/ethics/internetcounseling.pdf

National Board for Professional Teaching Standards. (2004). *School counseling standards.* Retrieved from http://www.nbpts.org/pdf/userfiles/File/ecya_sc_standards.pdf

National Career Development Association. (2009). *Minimum competencies for multicultural career counseling and development.* Retrieved from http://associationdatabase.com/aws/NCDA/asset_manager/get_file/26627

National Council on Measurement in Education. (1995). *Code of professional responsibilities in educational measurement.* Retrieved from http://www.natd.org/Code_of_Professional_Responsibilities.html

National Education Association. (n.d.). *Code of ethics of the education profession.* Retrieved from http://www.nea.org/home/30442.htm

National School Climate Center. (n.d.). *National school climate standards.* Retrieved from http://www.schoolclimate.org/climate/standards.php

Northside Independent School District. (1997). *Guide to counselor performance improvement through job definition, professionalism assessment, supervision, performance evaluation, and professional development goal-setting.* San Antonio, TX: Author.

Northside Independent School District. (2002). *Comprehensive guidance program framework.* San Antonio, TX: Author.

Paisley, P. O., & McMahon, G. (2001). School counseling for the 21st century: Challenges and opportunities. *Professional School Counseling, 5,* 106–115.

Peace, S. D. (1995). Addressing school counselor induction issues: A developmental counselor mentor model. *Elementary School Guidance and Counseling, 29,* 177–190.

Ponton, R. F., & Duba, J. D. (2009). The *ACA Code of Ethics:* Articulating counseling's professional covenant. *Journal of Counseling & Development, 87,* 117–121.

Portman, T. A. A. (2009). Faces of the future: School counselors as cultural mediators. *Journal of Counseling & Development, 87,* 21–27.

Ratts, M. J., Toporek, R. L., & Lewis, J. A. (2010). *ACA Advocacy Competencies: A social justice framework.* Alexandra, VA: American Counseling Association.

Rutter, M. E. (2006). Group supervision with practising school counsellors. *Guidance and Counselling, 21,* 160–167.

Somody, C., Henderson, P., Cook, K., & Zambrano, E. (2008). A working system of school counselor supervision. *Professional School Counseling, 12,* 22–33.

Sue, D. W., Arredondo, P., & McDavis, R. J. (1992). Multicultural counseling competencies and standards: A call to the profession. *Journal of Counseling & Development, 70,* 477–486.

Tentoni, S. C. (1995). The mentoring of counseling students: A concept in search of a paradigm. *Counselor Education and Supervision, 35,* 32–42.

Texas Education Code. (2011). *Recommended appraisal process and performance criteria* (§§21.351, 21.356). Retrieved from http://www.statutes.legis.state.tx.us/Docs/ED/htm/ED.21.htm#21.351

Toporek, R. L., Lewis, J. A., & Crethar, H. C. (2009). Promoting systemic change through the ACA Advocacy Competencies. *Journal of Counseling & Development, 87,* 260–268.

Van Horn, S. M., & Myrick, R. D. (2001). Computer technology and the 21st century school counselor. *Professional School Counseling, 5,* 124–130.

VanZandt, C. E., & Perry, N. S. (1992). Helping the rookie school counselor: A mentoring project. *The School Counselor, 39,* 158–163.

Vontress, C. E., & Jackson, M. L. (2004). Reactions to the Multicultural Counseling Competencies debate. *Journal of Mental Health Counseling, 26,* 74–80.

Watt, S. K., Curtis, G. C., Drummond, J., Kellogg, A. H., Lozano, A., Nicoli, G. T., & Rosas, M. (2009). Privileged identity exploration: Examining counselor trainees' reactions to difficult dialogues. *Counselor Education and Supervision, 49,* 86–105.

~ Part IV ~

Evaluating

Evaluating Your Comprehensive Guidance and Counseling Program, Its Personnel, and Its Results

Evaluating—Evaluating the Program, Its Personnel, and Its Results

- Evaluate school counselor performance.
- Conduct program evaluation.
- Conduct results evaluation.
- Evaluate guidance and counseling interventions.

☞ Now that the planning and designing phases of the program improvement process have been completed and the implementation phase is under way, we are ready to discuss the next phase of the process: evaluation. Before we discuss the process of evaluation, however, it is first necessary to define it. According to Dimmitt (2010),

> Evaluation is gathering and analyzing information about a program or intervention in an orderly and planful way to make decisions . . . . The usual end goal of evaluation is information that can be used to make better judgments and consequent decisions about what is being done and whether or not it is working. (p. 45)

Three kinds of evaluation are required to achieve accountability for your guidance and counseling program. *Personnel evaluation,* the first kind, describes the procedures used by your district to evaluate school counselors and other personnel who may be assisting school counselors in implementing the district's guidance and counseling program. *Program evaluation* (often called a *program audit*), the second kind, reviews the status of your district's guidance and counseling program against a set of established program standards. *Results evaluation,* the third kind, consists of two types. The first type deals with the impact that the overall guidance and counseling program has on critical markers of student success. The second type looks at whether specific guidance and counseling interventions have had the desired impact on targeted student behaviors.

Unfortunately, many school districts, driven by federal legislation, have interpreted the phrases *student success* and *targeted student behaviors* narrowly as student academic achievement, usually measured by achievement test scores. Although achievement test scores are useful indicators, more than a narrow-band approach to accountability is required. What is needed are broad-band indicators that focus on "a whole person approach to student outcomes" (Center for Mental Health in Schools at UCLA, 2011, p. 15).

It is also important to remember that although overall program evaluation is important and must be done, it is often beyond what can be done internally by local school counselors. Dimmitt (2010) stated that

> Often full program evaluations are done by outside evaluators hired by administrators or school boards to provide information about educational programs and outcomes in a school (Curcio, Mathai, & Roberts, 2003; Schmidt, 2003) because a full program evaluation can be time-consuming to do internally. (p. 50)

Each kind of evaluation is important. Equally as important, however, is how they relate to and interact with each other. To express this relationship, we use the formula Personnel + Program = Results. The personnel of a program need to be doing the work of the program, and the program elements need to be fully in place and functioning the way they should to achieve the desired results.

In this chapter, we present a detailed discussion of each of these kinds of evaluation. The chapter opens with a focus on personnel evaluation. It highlights self-evaluation, administrative evaluation, and the assessment of goal attainment. We follow with program evaluation, with attention being given to the instrumentation used as well as to the procedures that guide the program evaluation process. Next, in the Conduct Results Evaluation section we present ways to evaluate guidance and counseling interventions as well as discuss important issues surrounding intervention evaluation.

Evaluate School Counselor Performance

As discussed in Chapter 9, a key part of comprehensive guidance and counseling program implementation and management is a counselor performance management system. The basic purpose of such a system is to assist school counselors to reach and maintain their professional potential. Such a system includes helping individuals define their jobs, providing professional supervision, conducting fair performance evaluations, and setting goals for professional development (Henderson & Gysbers, 1998). This section is focused on school counselor performance evaluation.

The purposes of evaluating school counselors' performance are to improve the delivery to and impact of the program on the students it serves and to provide for communication among school counselors, guidance program staff leaders, and school administrators. For school counselors, evaluation specifies contract status recommendations and provides summative evaluation as to their effectiveness. For the school district, evaluation defines expectations for counselors' performance and provides a systematic means of measuring counselors' performance in relation to these expectations. Fair performance evaluations effectively done aim for continuous improvement of professional school counselors' performance (Bunch, 2002).

The three facets of the performance evaluation component of a counselor performance management system are (a) self-evaluation, (b) administrative evaluation, and (c) assessment of goal attainment (Northside Independent School District, 1997). The self-evaluation and administrative evaluation focus on job performance competencies and represent data-supported professional judgments as to individuals' proficiency in using the skills and commitment levels required in their jobs. The assessment of goal attainment focuses on individuals' program and professionalism improvement efforts.

For performance evaluation to be done fairly, many data sources are used as each component of a performance management system is implemented. Specific examples of typical behaviors of individual school counselors are gathered throughout the year and documented. These patterns of behavior are then compared and contrasted with clearly, overtly stated professionalism standards. Standards are expressed professionwide for school counselors' performance and program delivery and regarding ethical judgments. Standards are expressed for educators in general through relevant laws and through district policies and procedures.

Self-Evaluation and Administrative Evaluation

We recommend that all counselors be evaluated annually. Often, counselors on probationary status, in the final year of their contract term, or whose term contracts have not been extended for performance reasons are evaluated more frequently. Appropriate dates are usually expressed in state law.

To carry out their evaluation responsibilities fairly, evaluators of school counselors' performance should be trained to understand school counselors' jobs and professional roles and in appropriate methods for gathering data to support evaluation (Synatschk, 2002). For elementary school counselors, the administrative evaluator is often the school principal. For counselors who serve more than one building, central-office–based guidance administrators may conduct the evaluations or designate one individual as the primary evaluator, with the other administrators providing relevant data to the primary evaluator. A primary evaluator conducts the evaluation conference or may coordinate a joint evaluation conference. A director of guidance is often a reviewing officer and, in this capacity, discusses the evaluation results with the primary evaluator before the results are presented to the staff member.

Central-office–based guidance administrators are also available to provide data or assist primary evaluators in making their evaluative judgments. District guidance program staff leaders are usually required to be involved in an individual counselor's evaluation when (a) the contract status recommendation will mean a decrease in contract status, (b) the overall rating of the counselor will be either *unsatisfactory* or *clearly outstanding*, or (c) there is disagreement among the evaluators, including the counselor, after his or her self-evaluation. District guidance leaders may also be involved at the request of any of the parties involved in the evaluation process—the counselor, the building guidance program staff leader, or principal—as a second evaluator.

The self- and performance evaluation process consists of six steps: data collection, data analysis, evaluation write-up or draft evaluation form completion, evaluation conference, postevaluation conference analysis, and evaluation form completion. In this process, the school counselor and the evaluator complete the first three steps separately. In the evaluation conference, the fourth step, they discuss their evaluations of the counselor's performance. The evaluator then effects the fifth and sixth steps, obtains the necessary signatures, and distributes the copies of the form as prescribed.

The forms used in the performance evaluation process must support appropriate and fair performance evaluation of school counselors and be relevant to the expressed expectations for their performance within the context of the established guidance program as well as relevant to each school counselor's specific job description. Having a team of counselors or counselors and administrators develop the instrument and related process helps create a relevant and well-understood performance evaluation system (Henderson, 2009). A system for weighting a school counselor's various roles as well as rating them has been suggested by Northside Independent School District (2002) and the Texas Counseling Association (2004). In any case, appropriate performance evaluation forms must be designed to provide meaningful presentation of evaluative judgments. Figure 10.1 provides a form that has been used successfully in this process (Northside Independent School District, 1987). The Missouri Department of Elementary and Secondary Education (2000) has a similar model. Details of how the self- and performance evaluation process works are as follows:

1. *Data collection*. Although the nature of evaluation is judgmental, fair and effective judgments concerning professional performance must be data supported. In drawing conclusions about performance, performance evaluators are asked to rely on data that have been gathered through the supervision system. In clinical supervision, observations and feedback conferences generate relevant data. In developmental supervision, program and performance improvement accomplishments generate data. In administrative supervision, data are gathered regarding daily adherence to standards for program implementation and professional standards, interprofessional relationships, work habits, commitment to the job and the profession, and sound professional judgment. Guidance program staff leaders keep notes and records of their supervisory and other leadership contacts with school counselors. Performance deficiencies are addressed in other leadership activities aimed at performance improvement before they are recorded in a formal, summative evaluation.

2. *Data analysis*. The school counselor and the administrative evaluator consider how the example data compare and contrast with the professionalism standards (Henderson, 2009; Henderson & Gysbers, 1998). Where and how these data are to be collected are established at the beginning of the year in the job-defining conference.

3. *Completion of draft evaluation forms*. Draft evaluations are completed by both the school counselor, as a self-evaluation, and the evaluator. In completing the forms, the evaluators are drawing their preliminary conclusions—making their preliminary judgments—regarding the overall quality of a school counselor's professionalism. Primary evaluators are encouraged to consult with designated reviewing officers before completing the draft. The page that represents the summative judgment and overall rating of school counselors' performance is completed last.

On the sample form (Figure 10.1), the six areas for evaluation (instructional skills; guidance skills; counseling, consultation, and referral skills; system support implementation; establishment of professional relationships; and fulfillment of professional responsibilities) are considered separately. Performance strengths and weaknesses are identified and are supported by specific, behavioral examples. (Example descriptors as well as example observation forms are provided in Appendixes M and N.) Suggestions for improvement are made for incorporation in the counselor's professional development plan.

We recommend holistic scoring. That is, the rating for an area reflects a summative judgment of the school counselor's performance of the various tasks that contribute to the delivery of the skills identified and produces a comment such as, "In most instances, the counselor performs most of these subskills in a (an) _____ manner." To be judged as *clearly outstanding*, performance of the listed indicators as well as many of the discretionary items is consistently outstanding, exemplary, or excellent. To be judged as *exceeding expectations*, performance of the listed indicators as well as discretionary items is at an observably high level. In rating a counselor's performance as *clearly outstanding* or *exceeding expectations*, the evaluator considers how the school counselor handles not only required duties but also discretionary tasks.

Standards for professional school counselors should be high. To be judged *satisfactory*, performance of at least the listed indicators is judged as meeting standard expectations, that is, as being good most of the time. *Satisfactory* is the rating earned by counselors who

Figure 10.1
Counselor Performance Evaluation Form

NAME _____

SCHOOL _____

REVIEW PERIOD: FROM _____ TO _____ DATE EVALUATION COMPLETED: _____

RATINGS SUMMARY:	POINTS	RATING
1. Guidance curriculum implementation:	____	____
2. Individual student planning system implementation:	____	____
3. Responsive services implementation:	____	____
4. System support implementation:	____	____
5. Effectiveness of professional relationships:	____	____
6. Fulfillment of professional responsibilities:	____	____
Total Points	____	

CRITERIA FOR OVERALL
PERFORMANCE RATING
SCORING RULES: The highest applicable rating applies.

OVERALL
PERFORMANCE

RATING

Clearly Outstanding is earned with at least 27 points and no rating less than Satisfactory (3).

Clearly
Outstanding ☐

Exceeding Expectations is earned with at least 21 points and no rating less than Satisfactory (3).

Exceeding
Expectations ☐

Satisfactory is earned with at least 16 points, no more than two scores less than Satisfactory (3), and no rating less than Below Expectations (2).

Satisfactory ☐

Below Expectations is earned with at least 14 points and no more than one rating less than Below Expectations (2).

Below
Expectations ☐

Unsatisfactory is earned in all other cases.

Unsatisfactory ☐

EVALUATION: FALL _____ SPRING _____
CONTRACT STATUS RECOMMENDATION: (Spring Only)
_____1-yr. term contract: Second
_____3-yr. term contract: First year of 3
_____Nonextension 3-yr. term contract: Second year of 3 years
_____Nonextension 3-yr. term contract: Third year of 3 years
_____Nonrenewal (term contract)

Signature of Evaluator: _____ Title of Evaluator: _____
Signature of Reviewing Officer: _____
Title of Reviewing Officer: _____
Signature of Employee: _____ Conference Date: _____

Original: Personnel
Copies: Yellow — Counselor   Pink — Principal   Gold — Director of Guidance

COUNSELOR PERFORMANCE EVALUATION FORM
1. Implement GUIDANCE CURRICULUM through the use of effective INSTRUCTIONAL SKILLS, including
   a. appropriate task analysis
   b. effective use of lesson design
   c. active involvement of students in learning
   d. selection of topics consistent with identified, high-priority student needs and district goals

Clearly Outstanding	Exceeding Expectations	Satisfactory	Below Expectations	Unsatisfactory
☐ (5)	☐ (4)	☐ (3)	☐ (2)	☐ (1)

COMMENTS: _____
_____
_____

(*continued on next page*)

Figure 10.1 *(Continued)*
Counselor Performance Evaluation Form

2. Implements the INDIVIDUAL STUDENT PLANNING SYSTEM through the effective use of GUIDANCE SKILLS, including
   a. careful planning of sessions
   b. presentation of accurate, unbiased information
   c. involvement of students in personalized educational and career planning
   d. accurate and appropriate test results interpretation
   e. selection of individual planning activities consistent with identified, high-priority student needs and district goals

Clearly Outstanding	Exceeding Expectations	Satisfactory	Below Expectations	Unsatisfactory
☐ (5)	☐ (4)	☐ (3)	☐ (2)	☐ (1)

COMMENTS: _____

3. Implements RESPONSIVE SERVICES through effective use of COUNSELING, CONSULTATION, and REFERRAL SKILLS, including
   a. proper identification of problems/issues to be resolved
   b. selection of counseling, consulting, and/or referral interventions appropriate to students problems and circumstances
   c. use of counseling, consulting, and/or referral skills appropriate to students' problems and circumstances
   d. conducting well-planned, goal-oriented sessions
   e. use of group and individual techniques that are appropriate to the topic and to students' needs and abilities
   f. active involvement of clients in the counseling, consulting, and/or referral process
   g. timely follow-up
   h. provision of services consistent with high-priority, identified student needs and district goals

Clearly Outstanding	Exceeding Expectations	Satisfactory	Below Expectations	Unsatisfactory
☐ (5)	☐ (4)	☐ (3)	☐ (2)	☐ (1)

COMMENTS: _____

4. Implements SYSTEM SUPPORT through PROVIDING effective SUPPORT for other programs and by effectively ENLISTING SUPPORT for the guidance program, such as
   a. providing a comprehensive and balanced guidance program
   b. selecting program activities that meet identified, high-priority student needs and are consistent with campus and district goals
   c. collecting evidence that students achieve meaningful outcomes from program activities
   d. operating within established procedures, policies, and priorities
   e. contributing to organizational solutions outside of assigned responsibilities
   f. working cooperatively with school administrators to garner support for the guidance program
   g. implementing programs that explain the school guidance program
   h. attending to ideas/concerns expressed regarding the guidance program
   i. supporting campus administration policies and goals
   j. supporting district policies and goals

Clearly Outstanding	Exceeding Expectations	Satisfactory	Below Expectations	Unsatisfactory
☐ (5)	☐ (4)	☐ (3)	☐ (2)	☐ (1)

COMMENTS: _____

5. Establishes effective PROFESSIONAL RELATIONSHIPS by building rapport with
   a. students
   b. staff
   c. parents
   d. other counselors
   e. administrators
   f. other in-school/district specialists
   g. community representatives

Clearly Outstanding	Exceeding Expectations	Satisfactory	Below Expectations	Unsatisfactory
☐ (5)	☐ (4)	☐ (3)	☐ (2)	☐ (1)

COMMENTS: _____

(continued on next page)

Figure 10.1 *(Continued)*
Counselor Performance Evaluation Form

6. Fulfills PROFESSIONAL RESPONSIBILITIES by
   a. seeking professional development
   b. keeping records consistent with ethical and legal guidelines
   c. maintaining professional work habits
   d. practicing according to the profession's ethical standards
   e. demonstrating appropriate personal characteristics
   f. demonstrating effective use of basic skills (e.g., communication, decision making, problem solving, educational)

Clearly Outstanding	Exceeding Expectations	Satisfactory	Below Expectations	Unsatisfactory
☐ (5)	☐ (4)	☐ (3)	☐ (2)	☐ (1)

COMMENTS: _____
_____
_____

7. Additional Comments:
_____
_____
_____
_____
_____

Note. From *Guide to Counselor Performance Improvement Through Supervision, Evaluation, and Professional Development,* by Northside Independent School District, 1987, San Antonio, TX: Author. Reprinted with permission.

perform their job skills with proficiency. To be judged *below expectations,* performance on the listed indicators is in need of specifically identifiable improvement and judged as consistently poor most of the time. To be judged *unsatisfactory*, performance on the listed indicators is either not done or is done in a clearly unacceptable manner. Performance that is rated below or above *satisfactory* should be supported by documentation. Currently, state departments of education, school counseling associations, and others are striving to develop rubrics that specify the tasks counselors do or do not do that distinguish between the five levels of performance ratings.

An overall performance rating is a reflection of the summary of ratings for each of the six skill areas plus consideration of the rating levels. To arrive at the overall performance rating, the ratings for each area and the related points are transferred to the cover page, and the points are totaled. The criteria for overall performance rating are studied, and the appropriate overall rating is applied and recorded.

The contract status recommendation is made in the summative evaluation, although an indication of probable or possible contract status recommendation may be discussed in the formative evaluation, especially for those counselors for whom a decrease in contract status is envisioned. State laws usually apply here.

4. *Evaluation conference.* The school counselor and the evaluator bring their drafts of the evaluation form to the conference to facilitate mutual discussion. The evaluation conferences are scheduled by the primary evaluator with sufficient advance notice provided so that the drafts and related data are available at the time of the conference. The school counselor's strengths and weaknesses are discussed. Discrepancies between the two evaluation drafts are also discussed. Because the purpose of evaluation is to help each counselor attain his or her professional potential, suggestions for performance improvement are offered for all counselors. The more collaborative this process is, the fairer the evaluation will be (Bunch, 2002).

5. *Postevaluation conference analysis.* The primary evaluator is responsible for developing the formal evaluation. The evaluator is encouraged to consider the school counselor's

input in arriving at his or her final performance evaluation and may seek the advice of the director of guidance and other campus administrators or gather additional relevant data in resolving discrepancies between the two opinions.

6. *Evaluation form completion.* The primary evaluator completes the district-approved Counselor Performance Evaluation Form. It is typed by someone other than the counselor's secretary. The signature of the reviewing officer, indicating prior review, is obtained before obtaining the counselor's signature. The counselor's signature verifies that the evaluation has been discussed but does not necessarily indicate agreement with the information. In most states, the school counselor and the primary evaluator have the right to attach additional statements to the formal evaluation form, provided the statements are signed and dated by both parties and the reviewing officer; again, the signatures verify discussion, not agreement.

Assessment of Goal Attainment

The program improvement and professional development plans are a means to continuously improve the comprehensive guidance program as defined by the district. The purpose of this evaluation is to assess the level of the counselors' contribution to the improvement of the guidance program on the campus and in the district, as well as the level of their efforts to upgrade their professional skills knowledge and levels of commitment. The judgment assesses the counselors' efforts to reach goals they have set for themselves under the leadership of their guidance program staff leaders, directors of guidance, and principals. It also reflects, where appropriate, the effectiveness of an individual counselor's efforts as reflected in the guidance program evaluation.

The data for this evaluation grow out of the developmental supervision component. It is a summative judgment as to the counselors' level of effort in implementing the action plan directed toward the goal and in attaining the goals established at the beginning of the school year. Both are recorded on the Guidance Program Improvement Planning Form (see Figure 7.5) and on the Counselor Professional Growth Plan Form (see Figure 9.1). A performance report is submitted to the director of guidance at the end of the school year, recording the primary evaluator's assessment of the levels of plan accomplishment and goal attainment (Henderson & Gysbers, 1998). Documentation includes student outcome data gathered in activity and program evaluation and skill improvement data gathered in clinical supervision.

Conduct Program Evaluation

As guidance and counseling emerged in the schools in the early 1900s, leaders were faced with the task of deciding what activities and services constituted a complete program. Proctor (1930) noted this when he stated,

> One of the great needs in the field of guidance is some fairly objective means of comparing the guidance activities of one secondary school system with that of another. It is only in this manner that we shall ever arrive at an estimate of what constitutes a standard set-up for the carrying out of a guidance program. (p. 58)

Today we know "what constitutes a standard set-up for the carrying out of a guidance program" (Proctor, 1930, p. 58). Owing to the work of Gysbers and Henderson (2006), Myrick (2003), Johnson, Johnson, and Downs (2006), and the American School Counselor Association (ASCA; 2005), we know what the guidance and counseling activities and services are that, when brought together, constitute a complete guidance and counseling program. This knowledge allows us to develop the program evaluation instrumentation and procedures necessary to conduct program evaluation. Examples of program evaluation instruments and procedures, as well as the types of data used in program evaluation, are discussed next.

Program Evaluation Instrumentation

Most program evaluation instruments consist of a number of standards that are derived from a model of a comprehensive guidance and counseling program. These standards are acknowledged measures of comparison used to make judgments about the size, nature, and structure of a program. How many program standards are required to establish whether a comprehensive guidance and counseling program is in place and functioning? The answer is enough standards to ensure that judgments can be made as to whether a complete comprehensive guidance and counseling program is actually in place and functioning to a high degree to fully benefit all students, parents, teachers, and the community. Once a sufficient number of program standards are written to represent a comprehensive guidance and counseling program, the next step is to write criteria for each standard. Criteria are defined as statements that specify important aspects of the standards; thus, enough criteria need to be written for each standard to provide evaluators with the confidence that each standard is in place and functioning. Then a 5- or 6-point scale is usually created for each criterion, allowing for the quantification of data.

Adopt, Adapt, or Create an Instrument

Given the variety of program evaluation instruments available today, you can adopt an instrument as is from those available in your state comprehensive guidance and counseling program model or the ASCA (2005) National Model. If adopting one does not work, then you can adapt an available instrument, tailoring it to fit your local circumstances. Finally, if none of the available instruments will work, you have the option of creating one specifically designed for your local situation. To help you in your search for a program evaluation instrument, several examples follow.

American School Counselor Association. The first example of a program evaluation instrument was developed by ASCA (2005) and is called the Program Audit. It contains 17 standards under which criteria are listed that specify important aspects of the standards. It uses a 4-point scale to identify the degree to which a specific criterion is being met (*none, in progress, completed, implemented*). There is also a *not applicable* category available. The Program Audit is designed to be used primarily in a self-study of a program for program improvement purposes. See Figure 10.2 for a list of the standards and the criteria for one of the standards used in the ASCA Program Audit.

State of Utah. The state of Utah developed a program evaluation instrument that contains 12 standards derived from their state model (see Figure 10.3). The rating of each standard is done on a 5-point scale ranging from 0 to 4. A scoring guide is provided for each point on the scale describing what an evaluator would look for, from 0 (*no evidence of development or implementation*) to 4 (*exemplary level of development and implementation*).

State of Missouri. In Missouri, school counselors can use the Internal Improvement Review (IIR) instrument to determine the degree of implementation of the Missouri Comprehensive Guidance Program in their buildings and districts. The IIR uses the five program standards as the basic elements to be assessed, describes those standards in detail, and provides a scoring rubric of 1 (*minimal/no implementation*) to 4 (*full implementation*). It is recommended that the IIR be filled out by school counselors and administrators work-

Figure 10.2
American School Counselor Association Program Audit:
Standards and Example Criteria for One Standard

Foundation

1. Beliefs and Philosophy
2. Mission of School Counseling Programs

Example Criteria

2.1 A mission statement has been written for the school counseling program.
2.2 Written with the student as the primary client.
2.3 Written for every student.
2.4 Indicates the content or competencies to be learned.
2.5 Links with the vision, purpose, and mission of the state, district, and school.
2.6 Indicates the long-range results desired for all students.
2.7 The mission statement has been presented to and accepted by administration, counselors, advisory council, and school board.

3. Domains and Goals
4. ASCA National Standards/Competencies

Delivery System

5. Guidance Curriculum
6. Individual Student Planning
7. Responsive Services
8. System Support

Management System

9. School Counselor/Administrator Agreements
10. Advisory Council
11. Use of Data and Student Monitoring
12. Use of Data and Closing the Gap
13. Action Plans
14. Use of Time/Calendar
15. Results Report
16. Counselor Performance Standards
17. Program Audit

Note: From *The ASCA National Model: A Framework for School Counseling Programs* (2nd ed. pp. 131–141), by the American School Counselor Association, 2005, Alexandria, VA: Author. Adapted with permission.

ing together. To obtain a copy of the IIR, go to http://www.mcce.org and click on eLearning Center. Finally, click on Evaluation: Program + Personnel = Results.

Standards for a Guidance Program Audit. Appendix O contains eight standards against which a guidance and counseling program can be audited (reviewed). In this example, the standard is stated, followed by a description telling how a district would meet the standard. Next, the evidence an auditor would expect to find is presented, along with the documentation required to show that the standard has been met.

Program Evaluation Procedure

Self-Study Review

How frequently a district conducts program evaluation depends on the purposes to be achieved. If it is being done for self-study, ASCA (2005) recommends that program evaluation be conducted when a program is being designed and then yearly thereafter. Whether it is done once a year, every other year, or periodically, the self-study process provides school counselors with the opportunity to determine whether the written district program is the actual district program implemented. The results of program evaluation can reveal where progress has been made or where progress is lacking in program implementation,

Figure 10.3
Utah Comprehensive Counseling and Guidance Performance Review Standards

STANDARD I: *Board Adoption and Approval* of the CCGP by the local board of education/ governing board and ongoing communication with the local board regarding program goals and outcomes supported by data.

STANDARD II: *Comprehensive Counseling and Guidance Training.* Regular participation of Guidance Team members in USOE-sponsored Comprehensive Counseling and Guidance Training.

STANDARD III: *Structural Components.* Structural components and policies support the Comprehensive Counseling and Guidance Program. This includes adequate resources and support for guidance facilities, materials, equipment, clerical staff, and school improvement processes.

STANDARD IV: *Time Allocation.* Evidence is provided that EIGHTY PERCENT of aggregate counselors time is devoted to DIRECT services to students through a balanced program of individual planning, guidance curriculum, and responsive services consistent with the results of school needs data.

STANDARD V: *Interschool Communication.* This includes communication, collaboration, and co-ordination with the feeder system regarding the CCGP. The Comprehensive Counseling and Guidance Program is discussed and coordinated as a K–12 concept.

STANDARD VI: *Program Leadership and Management.* Structures and processes are in place to ensure effective program management, including an advisory and steering committee. Evidence is present that counselors are working as program leaders and the CCGP is an integral part of the school improvement team.

STANDARD VII: *Data and Program Effectiveness.* The program uses current school data including a formal student/parent/teacher needs assessment, which is completed and analyzed every three (3) years, and annual data projects as defined by USOE.

STANDARD VIII: *Responsive Services.* These services are available to address the immediate concerns and identified needs of all students through an education-oriented and programmatic approach, and in collaboration with existing school programs and coordination with family, school, and community resources.

STANDARD IX: *School Guidance Curriculum.* The program delivers a developmental and sequential guidance curriculum in harmony with content standards identified in the Utah Model for CCGP. The guidance curriculum is prioritized according to the results of the school needs assessment process.

STANDARD X: *Career Exploration and Development.* The program provides assistance for students in career development, including awareness and exploration, job seeking and finding skills, and post-high-school placement.

STANDARD XI: *SEOP Process.* Programs shall establish Student Education Occupation Planning (SEP/SEOP) for every student, both as a process and a product, consistent with local Board policy and the goals of the CCGP, Secondary School Accreditation (R277-413) and Applied Technology Education (R277-911).

STANDARD XII: *Every Student.* All program elements are designed to recognize and address the diverse needs of every student.
(This standard provides the platform for a guidance program that reaches 100 percent of students. All other standards should have provided evidence that the program meets this standard.)

Note. From *Comprehensive Counseling and Guidance Program Performance Review*, by the Utah State Office of Education, 2008, Salt Lake City, UT. Reprinted with permission.

which allows school counselors, working closely with administration, to establish goals to ensure that the written district guidance and counseling program actually becomes the district's fully implemented program.

External Review

Sometimes program evaluation is conducted using personnel external to the school district. The board of education or the administration may want the program reviewed because of dissatisfaction with the program and they employ external evaluators. Or the program may be seeking funding or accreditation, and external evaluators are often used for this purpose.

Curcio, Mathai, and Roberts (2003) reported on a situation in which a superintendent, prompted by the board of education because of criticism from parents, hired outside evaluators to review the district's guidance and counseling program. The evaluators developed surveys and interview protocols for school counselors, administrators, parents, leaders, and students. On the basis of their work, they identified 27 findings, each of which was followed by a recommendation for program improvement.

In the State of Utah, program evaluation is conducted for the purposes of funding. The review process begins when district counselors use the Comprehensive Counseling and Guidance Program Performance Review (Utah State Office of Education, 2008) to do a self-study of their program. The results of this review, along with other relevant information, are then presented to a review team composed of school counselors and administrators from other districts. To become an approved comprehensive guidance and counseling program and receive state funding, all standards in the performance review must be met. If all standards are not met, the school may be held harmless for 6 months without losing funding, provided the program passes a reevaluation within that 6-month period.

Types of Data Used in Program Evaluation

One type of data used in program evaluation is the data generated from a program evaluation instrument. Using 4-, 5- or 6-point scales for the criteria under each standard, data can be quantified, yielding means and standard deviations that can be used for yearly comparisons. Trends over time can be ascertained using these data. For example, the IIR instrument contains a summary page on which the scores for all of the criteria under the five standards can be entered, allowing for various types of analyses.

Another type of data is called process data. Process data describe what guidance and counseling activities and services took place and for whom. For example, all 150 tenth graders were seen individually to review their individual plans. Process data provide an evaluator with documentation that guidance and counseling activities and services were actually provided to groups or individuals as specified in the program.

Still another type of data that can be useful in program evaluation is perception data. Perception data tell us what students, parents, teachers, and administrators think about or feel about guidance and counseling activities and services in the program and the work of school counselors. Surveys and interviews are typically used to collect perception data.

When combined, these three types of data can provide an overall picture of a district's existing guidance and counseling program. Areas of strengths as well as areas that need improvement become visible from three perspectives, allowing for the development of program improvement goals.

Conduct Results Evaluation

Evolution of Results Evaluation in the Schools

Today, results evaluation is at the forefront of professional dialogue (Dimmitt, 2010; Gysbers & Henderson, 2006; Gysbers & Lapan, 2009; Johnson et al., 2006; Stone & Dahir, 2007; Whiston & Quinby, 2009). School counselors, working within the framework of comprehensive guidance and counseling programs, are increasingly being asked to demonstrate that their work contributes to student success, particularly student academic achievement. Not only are school counselors being asked to tell what they do, but they are also being asked to demonstrate how what they do makes a difference in the lives of students.

Why is results evaluation important? Dimmitt (2010) stated its importance as follows: "Counseling gains value and legitimacy when we evaluate our programs and interventions, discover how our work benefits students, seek greater effectiveness and efficiency, and share the results with our colleagues and community" (p. 44).

Is the focus on results evaluation a new phenomenon, or has our profession always been concerned about assessing the effects of the work of school counselors? The answer is no, it is not a new phenomenon. Concern has been expressed about the need for results evaluation almost from the beginning of guidance and counseling in the schools in the early 1900s.[1] For example, before the 1920s, the work of professionals focused on establishing guidance and counseling in the schools. However, by the 1920s, concern about the results of guidance and counseling was beginning to be expressed in the literature, as indicated by this statement by Payne (1924):

> What method do we have of checking the results of our guidance? For particular groups was it guidance, misguidance, or merely a contributing experience? We simply must work out some definite method of testing and checking the results of our work. If we do not, some other group will, with possibly disastrous results for our work. (p. 63)

Over the decades that followed, numerous statements were made in the literature about the need to focus on results evaluation. By 1930, desirable student outcomes of guidance and counseling programs were already being identified. For example, Christy, Stewart, and Rosecrance (1930), Hinderman (1930), and Rosecrance (1930) identified the following student outcomes:

- Fewer pupils dropping out of school
- Increase in the standard of scholarship
- Better morale in the student body
- Better all-round school life
- Fewer student failures and subject withdrawals
- Young people better informed about the future
- Satisfactory adjustment of graduates to community life and vocation and to a college or university
- Fewer disciplinary cases
- Fewer absences
- More intelligent selection of subjects
- Better study habits

At the same time that student outcomes were being identified, discussion was also taking place about design issues. In a landmark document on evaluation that appeared in the 1940s, Froehlich (1949, p. 2) reviewed and classified 173 studies according to the following evaluation designs:

1. External criteria, the do-you-do-this? method.
2. Follow-up, the what-happened-then? method.
3. Client opinion, the what-do-you-think? method.

---

[1]For individuals interested in a detailed presentation of the evolution of accountability in school counseling since the early 1900s, see Chapter 8 in Gysbers (2010).

4. Expert opinion, the "Information Please" method.
5. Specific techniques, the little-little method.
6. Within-group changes, the before-and-after method.
7. Between-group changes, the what's-the-difference? method.

Thus, discussion concerning the need to use scientifically based research designs for results evaluation (Froehlich, 1949; Neidt, 1965; Travers, 1949) has appeared in the literature for many years. Not only did such discussion occur, but a number of studies were also actually conducted on the impact of guidance and counseling programs on student development using experimental and control group methodology. Kefauver and Hand (1941), Rothney and Roens (1950), Rothney (1958), and Wellman and Moore (1975) conducted such studies beginning in the 1930s and into the 1960s.

What Results Do We Have So Far?

Beginning in the 1930s and onward, Kefauver and Hand (1941), Rothney and Roens (1950), Rothney (1958), and Wellman and Moore (1975) all described experimental control group studies that demonstrated that guidance and counseling programs positively affected the academic, career, and personal–social development of children and adolescents. More recently, in a major review of the literature in school counseling, Borders and Drury (1992) found that guidance program interventions have a substantial impact on students' educational and personal development and contribute to students' success in the classroom. Gerler (1985) analyzed a decade of research on the results of elementary school counseling and found that guidance program interventions in the affective, behavioral, and interpersonal domains of students' lives affected students' academic achievement positively. The results of a study by Lee (1993) showed that classroom guidance lessons in elementary school led by school counselors positively influenced students' academic achievement in mathematics. Similar results were found by St. Clair (1989) in her review of the impact of guidance program interventions at the middle school level. Furthermore, Evans and Burck (1992) conducted a meta-analysis of 67 studies concerning the impact of career education interventions (career guidance) on students' academic achievement. The results supported the value of these interventions as contributors to the academic achievement of students.

In a study conducted in high schools in Missouri, Lapan, Gysbers, and Sun (1997) found that students in high schools with more fully implemented guidance programs were more likely to report that they had earned higher grades, their education was better preparing them for their future, their school made more career and college information available to them, and their school had a more positive climate. In Utah, Nelson and Gardner (1998) found that students in schools with more fully implemented guidance programs rated their overall education as better, took more advanced mathematics and science courses, and had higher scores on every scale of the ACT. In their review of outcome research in school counseling, Sexton, Whiston, Bleuer, and Walz (1997, p. 125) made the following points:

- Reviews of outcome research in school counseling are generally positive about the effects of school counseling.
- Research results do indicate that individual planning interventions can have a positive impact on the development of students' career plans. There is some support for responsive services activities such as social skills training, family support programs, and peer counseling.
- Consultation activities are also found to be an effective school counseling activity.

In the first decade of the 21st century, student academic achievement became a major concern in the schools with the passage of the No Child Left Behind Act of 2001 (McGannon, Carey, & Dimmitt, 2005). Studies conducted in this time period demonstrated outcomes similar to studies conducted in the 1980s and 1990s. For example, Lapan, Gysbers, and Petroski (2001) found that when 4,868 middle school classroom teachers in Missouri in 184 small-, medium-, and large-sized middle schools rated guidance programs in their schools as more fully implemented, 22,601 seventh graders in these schools reported that they earned higher grades, school was more relevant for them, they had positive relationships with teachers, they were more satisfied with their education, and they felt safer in school. Sink and Stroh (2003), in a comparison of elementary students (Grades 3 and 4) enrolled for several years in schools with well-established comprehensive school counseling programs with students enrolled in schools without such programs, found that students enrolled in schools with well-established programs had significantly higher academic achievement test scores on the Iowa Tests of Basic Skills–Form M and the Washington Assessment of Student Learning. Brigman and Campbell (2003) tested a guidance curriculum titled *Student Success Skills* that focuses on student cognitive, social, and self-management skills using a quasi-experimental, pretest–posttest design. School counselors conducted group sessions for students in Grades 5, 6, 8, and 9. The treatment group scored significantly higher than the control group on the reading and math scales of the Florida Comprehensive Assessment Test.

Statewide studies of the impact of comprehensive guidance and counseling programs continued to be conducted in the last half of the first decade of the 21st century. Three studies in particular are presented. One study was conducted in Missouri, one in Utah, and one in Washington.

Lapan, Gysbers, and Kayson (2006) found that when school counselors in Missouri work in schools with more fully implemented programs, they make contributions to overall student success, including student academic achievement. More specifically, they found that students in schools with more fully implemented programs had higher 10th-grade Missouri Assessment Program mathematics scores and higher 11th-grade Missouri Assessment Program communication arts scores. They also found that more students in these schools were likely to attend school, fewer had discipline problems, and fewer received out-of-school suspensions.

Nelson, Fox, Haslam, and Gardner (2007) conducted the fourth major study of Utah's comprehensive counseling and guidance program. They had four major findings:

- Comprehensive counseling and guidance has fostered more targeted course selection for students and has resulted in more students taking a greater number of higher-level English, science, math and technology-oriented courses.
- The percentage of students who describe their own program of study as "general" has fallen precipitously in the nine years between evaluations.
- Students in high-implementing comprehensive counseling and guidance schools achieve higher levels of academic achievement and make better decisions about education and career planning than do students in matched lower-implementing schools. The importance of this finding cannot be overstressed. Even more powerful is the fact that this same pattern of results was evident in both the 1997 Utah evaluation and the most recent study reported here.
- These studies show that the comprehensive counseling and guidance program is more effectively implemented with adequate counselor-to-student ratios in Utah's schools, whether urban, suburban or rural. (p. 2)

In a study in Washington State, Sink, Akos, Turnbull, and Mvududu (2008) compared middle school students' academic achievement in schools with at least 5 years of comprehensive school counseling program (CSCP) implementation versus students in nonprogram schools and found,

> When CSCP versus non-CSCP schools were compared, there were largely nonsignificant mean differences on Grade 6 ITBS [Iowa Test of Basic Skills] and Grade 7 WASL [Washington Assessment of Student Learning] scores. Only grade 7 WASL math scores showed significant group differences, favoring the non-CSCP students. However, high-CSCP-implementation schools significantly outperformed non-CSCP schools on Grade 6 ITBS language, math and core total scores and on Grade 7 reading and math WASL scores. Additionally, students in the high-CSCP-implementation schools tended to perform better than their peers in the low-CSCP-implementation group. (pp. 49–50)

They ended their article by stating that the empirical results from their study provided "provisional evidence for the linkage between long-term CSCPs and the educational development of middle school students" (p. 51).

A research brief published by the Center for School Counseling Outcome Research and Evaluation concerning the impact of school counseling on student educational outcomes in high schools in Nebraska and Utah (Carey & Harrington, 2010a, 2010b), highlighted the following findings:

- School counseling in high schools contributes to important academic outcomes including increased math proficiency levels, increased reading proficiency levels, lower suspension and disciplinary rates, increased attendance rates, and higher graduation rates.
- Organizing the school counseling program according to the ASCA National Model had positive effects on student outcomes.
- In Nebraska, more favorable counselor-to-student ratios were related to improved attendance rates. In Utah, more favorable ratios were related to increased attendance rates and decreased discipline incident rates.
- Both Nebraska and Utah results indicated that career development–focused outcomes were particularly important in producing positive academic outcomes.

On the basis of these studies, Carey and Harrington (2010a, 2010b) concluded

> that if a high school wants to improve its educational outcomes, school leaders should hire enough counselors to satisfy the needs of students and parents, support the counselors as they establish a well-organized program that serves all students, and focus on implementing more effective interventions and discontinuing ineffective interventions. (p. 4)

Whiston, Tai, Rahardja, and Eder (2011) conducted a study of school counseling outcomes using a meta-analytic examination of various interventions. In reviewing the findings, they concluded that more research is necessary. At the same time, however, Whiston et al. stated that there is some empirical support for school counseling:

> This call for additional research, however, should not be interpreted as indicating there is no empirical support for school counseling interventions. In general, school counseling interventions have a positive effect on students. Furthermore, we found significant effect sizes for interventions at the elementary, middle, and high school levels. School counselors' influence on increasing students' abilities to solve problems and decrease discipline problems is noteworthy; however, we were unable to identify specific programs or approaches that produced these positive outcomes. Therefore, as a way to develop empirically supported interventions for school

counseling, there needs to be additional research that addresses what works, with what students, and under what circumstances. (p. 48)

What results do we have so far concerning the effectiveness of comprehensive guidance and counseling programs and the work of school counselors? As you have seen, the evidence that these programs are effective is substantial and continues to increase. The results so far indicate that having a fully implemented comprehensive guidance and counseling program makes strong contributions to students' academic achievement as well as to their personal–social and career development.

Evaluate Guidance and Counseling Interventions

The focus of this section of the chapter is on how to evaluate the guidance and counseling interventions that you use to effect change in student behavior. It opens with discussion of developing an intervention evaluation plan. Next, several ways to conduct the evaluation of interventions are presented, followed by a discussion of important points to consider in developing your intervention evaluation plan. Included in this discussion is a presentation of the Outcome Research Coding Protocol created by the National Panel for School Counseling Evidence-Based Practice (Carey, Dimmitt, Hatch, Lapan, & Whiston, 2008). The final section describes the status of intervention evaluation today and closes with some concluding thoughts.

Develop an Intervention Evaluation Plan

Do guidance and counseling interventions produce measurable results? Because the answer is yes, does this mean that no further evaluation work is necessary because such evidence already exists in the literature? The answer is no, because as Gerler (1992) pointed out a number of years ago, "Although the cumulative evidence is clear, school superintendents and principals [and boards of education] will probably be convinced more by local data than by evidence gathered elsewhere" (p. 500). Following Gerler's admonition, our job is to establish a plan to conduct intervention evaluation at the local level. What are the tasks involved in developing and carrying out an evaluation plan? The following sections describe those tasks.

Identify Student Outcomes

As you begin to develop an intervention results evaluation plan, review your school district's mission and your district's comprehensive school improvement plan. Both of these documents, but particularly the comprehensive school improvement plan, will help you identify student outcomes that are priorities for the district. To illustrate, these documents often focus on such goals as improving student academic achievement, creating safe building environments free from disruptive behavior, and ensuring that students are well prepared to go to work or on to further education upon graduation. Because comprehensive guidance and counseling interventions have substantial contributions to make to the achievement of goals such as these, specific student outcomes within these goals can be identified that are believed to result from student participation in guidance and counseling interventions. They become the outcomes you will focus on in your evaluation plan.

Consider the Use of Different Types of Data

Three types of data need to be considered in developing your evaluation plan: process data, perception data, and results data (ASCA, 2005).

Process Data. Process data are used in overall program evaluation but can also be used in intervention evaluation. Remember, process data describe what guidance and counseling interventions took place and for whom. They provide evidence that they actually were provided.

Perception Data. Perception data can be used in program evaluation, as we described earlier, but they also have a role to play in intervention evaluation as well. Perception data tell us what students, parents, teachers, administrators, or others think about or feel about guidance and counseling interventions and the work of school counselors.

Results Data. What impact did guidance and counseling interventions have on students? Results data consist of scores on knowledge tests or improvement on such variables as attendance rates, discipline referral rates, grade point averages, and achievement test scores. Something has changed in outcomes such as these as a result of students' participation in the guidance and counseling interventions. Such data are already being collected in schools and are available to be used as outcome measures to establish the effectiveness of guidance and counseling interventions.

Select a Way to Conduct Evaluations of Interventions

This section provides two examples of ways to conduct results evaluations of guidance and counseling interventions. The first example is called IDEAS! It was developed by Lapan (2005) and is described in Gysbers and Lapan (2009). The second example is MEASURE, developed by Stone and Dahir (2007).

IDEAS! IDEAS! is a way for school counselors and other professionals to conduct evaluations of interventions. This evaluation process unfolds by first identifying (I) a problem. Then the problem is described (D) and existing (E) school data are used to provide information to answer questions posed by the problem. The data are analyzed (A) using basic statistics, qualitative data analysis skills, and various software packages. Then the data are summarized (S), and the results are used to improve work with students and inform various stakeholders about the impact and importance of comprehensive guidance and counseling interventions.

The first step in IDEAS! according to Lapan (2005), is to identify a critical problem. The Comprehensive School Improvement Plan is one place to look because it contains critical problems and anticipated outcomes that the school district or building leadership have identified as being important. In addition, in your work with students and teachers you know about specific problems that individual students or groups of students are facing and student problems with which teachers are dealing in the classroom.

The second step Lapan (2005) recommended is to describe the problem thoroughly. He suggested that the problem needs to be described in terms of four things, namely, students, interventions, measurements, and settings. Who are the students involved in the problem to be investigated? Are the interventions we are evaluating directly tied to the constructs we are implementing? Are the measurements directly connected to these constructs? What is the setting in which the intervention takes place?

Next, Lapan (2005) urged the use of existing school data. He pointed out that today, most school districts and buildings have data available on student achievement, performance, and behavior. Some schools also regularly collect data on student behavior in classrooms. Excel spreadsheets can be used to collect and organize this information.

Once data are available on Excel spreadsheets, it is time to analyze the data. Lapan (2005) recommended mastering and using five basic statistical concepts for this purpose—means, standard deviations, percentages, correlations, and t tests. The next steps he recommended were to convert the results of the analyses into PowerPoint presentations and to conduct qualitative evaluation interviews with some of the students involved in the intervention. He stated that the use of interview data adds personal dimensions to the results that the quantitative data do not show.

The next step Lapan suggested was to summarize the findings. When preparing the PowerPoint presentations you need to include the following:

1. Provide your audience a clear statement of the critical problem that your activity focused on.
2. Briefly describe, in highlights, what you did in response to this problem.
3. In two or three graphs or tables, clearly communicate what you found out.
4. And finally, conclude your PowerPoint by pointing out what you plan in the future to do about this critical problem based on the information you have to help all students and improve your comprehensive program. (Gysbers & Lapan, 2009, p. 176)

The final step recommended by Lapan (2005) is to use the results data to help students by advocating with stakeholders and policymakers to support the work of school counselors working within the framework of comprehensive guidance and counseling programs. The goal is to make presentations to stakeholder and policymaker groups when and wherever possible. Lapan underscored the importance of presentations by stating, "Risk using your evaluation results to educate significant others about your role in helping all students succeed. It will benefit your students and help to improve your comprehensive program" (Gysbers & Lapan, 2009, p. 177).

MEASURE. According to Stone and Dahir (2007), "MEASURE is a six-step accountability process that helps school counselors demonstrate how their interventions impact critical data, those components of a school report card that are the backbone of the accountability movement" (p. 23). MEASURE is an acronym formed from the initial letters of its six steps: mission, elements, analyze, stakeholders, unite, results, and educate.

The first step in MEASURE is *mission*. The goal is to connect the comprehensive guidance and counseling program to the mission of the school and the outcomes specified in the school's comprehensive school improvement plan. The second step, *element*, involves identifying and examining the data critical to the comprehensive school improvement plan. Data disaggregation is an important part of the element step.

The next step in MEASURE is *analyze*. This step involves determining barriers that may have an impact on student achievement. It involves analyzing school and district data by separating the data (disaggregating) by such factors as gender, race, ethnicity, socioeconomic status, and teacher or counselor assignment.

Steps 3 and 4 are called *stakeholders–unite*. The goal in these steps is to involve individuals from inside and outside the school in interventions that will address the barriers that affect student achievement. The use of disaggregated data provides stakeholders with insight into where to focus interventions, develop timelines, and identify responsibilities.

Step five is called *results*. "Did the results of everyone's efforts show that the interventions and strategies successfully moved the critical data elements in a positive direction?" (Stone & Dahir, 2007, p. 27). If not, then the task is to determine why the chosen interventions did not achieve the desired results. *Reanalyze* and *refocus* are the terms used by Stone and Dahir (2007) to describe this process.

Educate is Step 6. This is the time to publicize the results of your interventions. Stone and Dahir (2007) recommended the development of report cards to show how what has been done connects with the mission of the school, with the comprehensive school improvement plan, and to student success.

Important Points to Consider

"School counselors do not have to be skilled statisticians to meaningfully analyze data" (ASCA, 2005, p. 51). This statement is true, but school counselors do need to master some basic statistical concepts to successfully analyze and interpret results data. In addition, school counselors need to know how to disaggregate data appropriately, enter data on spreadsheets such as Excel, do appropriate analyses, and develop graphs and charts displaying the data in understandable ways.

Basic Statistics. Recall that Lapan (2005) recommended that school counselors master at least five basic statistical concepts, means, standard deviations, percentages, correlations, and t tests. When equipped with these five concepts, you will be able to analyze the data collected from your evaluations of the interventions that you have chosen to use.

Disaggregate Data. Data disaggregation is an important step in data analysis because it allows one to see whether there are any students who are not doing as well as others. ASCA (2005, p. 50) suggested that the common fields for disaggregation are

- Gender
- Ethnicity
- Socioeconomic status (free and reduced lunch)
- Vocational (multiperiod vocational program trades)
- Language spoken at home
- Special education
- Grade level
- Teacher(s)

Use Spreadsheets. An important tool for results data analysis is a spreadsheet software such as Excel. Spreadsheets allow one to enter results data and conduct various statistical procedures as appropriate. In addition, various charts and graphs can be created to show relationships of results data to possible outcomes such as state achievement test scores and external tests such as the SAT or ACT.

Some types of evaluation information are not easily adaptable to spreadsheet analyses, however, and may in fact be more meaningful when analyzed by you and your staff. For example, subjective counselor reports of guidance and counseling activities or of certain types of student behavior may lose meaning if quantified. These subjective analyses may be critical in the interpretation of other outcome data. In addition, small samples of activities or students may not warrant the use of computer analysis and will thus need to be handled manually. In such cases, precautions should be taken to reduce human error to a minimum by establishing checks and rechecks.

PowerPoint Presentations. PowerPoint presentations are effective in presenting in straightforward language data concerning what happened to students who participated in specific guidance and counseling interventions. Bar graphs and pie charts are effective ways to present results. As the old adage states, "A picture is worth a thousand words."

B. Stanley, M. Maras, and M. Dowdy (personal communication, May 3, 2010) suggested that a PowerPoint presentation might contain the following points:

- Title of project with contact information
- A bulleted outline of the problem
- A bulleted outline of the response (the intervention)
- A graph of the results

- A bulleted outline of the implications
- A bulleted outline of recommendations

Report Cards. An example of a report card is the Support Personnel Accountability Report Card. It was developed by personnel from the California Department of Education and the Los Angeles County Office of Education (2010). The Support Personnel Accountability Report Card "is a continuous improvement document that provides a school's counseling program and student support team an opportunity to demonstrate effective communication and a commitment to getting results" (p. 1). It is a one-page (front and back) document that provides space for six categories of information: principal's message, student support personnel team, school climate and safety, student results, community partnerships and resources, and content. As stated on the Support Personnel Accountability Report Card Web site (http://www.lacoe.edu/sparc/), the report card can be thought of as a résumé of the program, providing the opportunity to show case-relevant data to a wide range of audiences, all on one page. Results data are featured.

Possible Unanticipated Side Effects

As the results evaluation unfolds, be alert to possible unanticipated side effects (Johnson, 1991). Sometimes guidance and counseling interventions will create effects that were unforeseen when they were initially conducted. The results evaluation process used should be sensitive enough to pick up these effects so that they can be handled immediately or can be explained when they appear in later evaluation results.

Unanticipated outcomes may be positive or negative. On the one hand, student results may be achieved through the guidance curriculum but at an unusually high expense of students' time. The same may be true for the time of some teachers. On the other hand, some of the most valued outcomes of a guidance and counseling program may not have been stated in the original design. For example, attendance may have improved or the dropout rate may have declined.

Outcome Research Coding Protocol. Whether you are using IDEAS!, MEASURE, or some other way to evaluate the impact of the interventions you are using, it is important for you to be aware of the Outcome Research Coding Protocol developed by the National Panel. Carey et al. (2008) stated that the panel "was established to improve the practice of school counseling by helping to develop the research base that is necessary for responsible and effective practice" (p. 197). To accomplish this mission, the panel developed an outcome research coding protocol that consisted of the following seven domains: measurement, comparison groups, statistical analysis of outcome variables, implementation fidelity, replication, ecological validity, and persistence of effect. "Within each domain, research studies can be categorized as presenting strong evidence, promising evidence or weak evidence that an intervention causes a change in an important student outcome" (p. 198). Because of its importance the full protocol appears in Figure 10.4.

Status of Intervention Evaluation

Two major developments over the past several decades have facilitated school counselors' direct involvement in intervention evaluation. The first is the development of the comprehensive program approach to school counseling. The second involves the widespread use of personal computers and the availability of software that provides school counselors with all of the tools they need to evaluate the results of the interventions they use.

Figure 10.4
Outcome Research Coding Protocol

Domain 1: Measurement
> *Principle:* Important academic, career and/or personal/social outcomes are measured using reliable and valid instruments.

Domain 2: Comparison Groups
> *Principle:* Comparison groups with adequate controls are included so that resulting group differences can be attributed to the intervention.

Domain 3: Statistical Analyses of Outcome Variables
> *Principle:* Statistical analysis documents low probability of type 1 error and potency of intervention.

Domain 4: Implementation Fidelity
> *Principle:* Intervention can be delivered with fidelity across contexts and is not contaminated by implementer.

Domain 5: Replication
> *Principle:* The same intervention independently implemented with an equivalent population results in equivalent outcomes.

Domain 6: Ecological Validity
> *Principle:* The intervention can be implemented effectively in a public school with consistent effects across all student subgroups or with known differences between student subgroups. Limitations of the generalizability of results are clearly explicated.

Domain 7: Persistence of Effect
> *Principle:* The intervention results in a lasting effect on an important outcome measure.

Note. From "Report of the National Panel for Evidence-Based School Counseling: Outcome Research Coding Protocol and Evaluation of Student Success Skills and Second Step," by J. C. Carey, C. Dimmitt, T. A. Hatch, R. T. Lapan, and S. C. Whitson, 2008, *Professional School Counseling, 11*, pp. 205–206. Copyright 2008 by the American School Counselor Association. Reprinted with permission.

Why is a program approach for school counseling important for evaluation? We believe that the common language structure of a program, with its planned, coordinated, and sequenced approach, centers the school counseling program firmly in education, providing school counselors with stability and focus for their work. With a program approach, evaluation is not an added duty; it is an expected part of all school counselors' work.

Although it is now possible for all school counselors to evaluate the impact of their work with students, it is not yet a reality. Why? First, some school counselors still fear evaluation and will do anything they can to avoid it. Fear of evaluation is a powerful force. It often arises because school counselors do not feel competent to do evaluation, and yet they are being asked to be accountable for their work. They carry a script in their heads that says, "I can't do evaluation because I don't know how, and besides, I'm too busy anyway."

Most states, through the leadership of state supervisors of guidance and counseling and state school counselor associations, are providing school counselors with the training to conduct intervention evaluation. For example, the State of Missouri, working closely with the Missouri School Counselor Association, and counselor educators developed a train-the-trainer intervention evaluation model called Program Results-Based Evaluation. Workshops using this model are ongoing across the state. In addition, it is being used in the mentoring program for all new school counselors in Missouri (Gysbers, Lapan, & Stanley, 2006).

Concluding Thoughts

Remember, a comprehensive guidance and counseling program is a student-centered program guided by the effective use of data, which means that the program improvement process is based on evaluation data. Thus, as the planning, designing, and implementing phases get under way, and during the time they are taking place, the interventions involved and the guidance and counseling program frameworks and content that evolve need to be constructed and implemented on the basis of sound evaluation principles and procedures so that they can be evaluated. Thus, the work completed in the first three phases of the improvement process must be done well so that the work involved in the evaluation phase can be completed in a similar manner. Demonstrating accountability through the measured effectiveness of the delivery of evidence-based guidance and counseling interventions and the performance of the guidance and counseling staff helps ensure that students, parents, teachers, administrators, and the general public will continue to benefit from quality comprehensive guidance and counseling programs.

Remember, too, that a major goal of intervention evaluation and overall program evaluation is to improve the specific interventions and overall program provided to students, parents, teachers, the school, and the community. The data collected during evaluation provide feedback for improving the interventions of a district's guidance and counseling program as well as the program. How evaluation data are used to ensure quality comprehensive guidance and counseling interventions and overall programs is the subject of the next phase of the program change process—the enhancement phase, discussed in Chapter 11.

Your Progress Check

You now know how to approach evaluating your district's comprehensive guidance and counseling program, its personnel, and its results. As a result, you have learned how to evaluate the performance of school counselors, including

- school counselor self-evaluation and administrative evaluation;
- the assessment of school counselor goals.

You have learned how to conduct program evaluation, including

- how to develop and use program evaluation instruments;
- how to conduct program evaluation.

You have learned how to conduct the evaluation of guidance and counseling interventions, including

- how to develop an intervention evaluation plan;
- how to identify student outcomes;
- how to use different types of data, including process, perception, and results data;
- how to conduct evaluations of interventions, using approaches such as IDEAS! and MEASURE;
- how to use basic statistics, disaggregate data, use spreadsheets, and use PowerPoint presentations;
- being aware of possible unanticipated side effects;
- being aware of the outcome research coding protocol.

References

American School Counselor Association. (2005). *The ASCA National Model: A framework for school counseling programs* (2nd ed.). Alexandria, VA: Author.

Borders, L. D., & Drury, S. M. (1992). Comprehensive school counseling programs: A review for policy makers and practitioners. *Journal of Counseling & Development, 70,* 487–498.

Brigman, G., & Campbell, C. (2003). Helping students improve academic achievement and school success behavior. *Professional School Counseling, 7,* 91–98.

Bunch, L. K. (2002). Ensuring professionally relevant supervision and professional development: A state-level experience. In P. Henderson & N. Gysbers (Eds.), *Implementing comprehensive guidance programs: Critical leadership issues and successful responses* (pp. 193–198). Greensboro, NC: CAPS.

Carey, J. C., Dimmitt, C., Hatch, T. A., Lapan, R. T., & Whiston, S. C. (2008). Report of the National Panel for Evidence-Based School Counseling: Outcome research coding protocol and evaluation of student success skills and second step. *Professional School Counseling, 11,* 197–206.

Carey, J. C., & Harrington, K. M. (2010a). *Nebraska school counseling evaluation report.* Amherst, MA: Center for School Counseling Outcome Research and Evaluation.

Carey, J. C., & Harrington, K. M. (2010b). *Utah school counseling evaluation report.* Amherst, MA: Center for School Counseling Outcome Research and Evaluation.

Center for Mental Health in Schools at UCLA. (2011). *A Center Policy Brief: About short-term outcome indicators for school use and the need for an expanded policy framework.* Los Angeles, CA: Author.

Christy, E. B., Stewart, F. J., & Rosecrance, F. C. (1930). Guidance in the senior high school. *The Vocational Guidance Magazine, 9,* 51–57.

Curcio, C. C., Mathai, C., & Roberts, J. (2003). Evaluation of a school district's secondary counseling program. *Professional School Counseling, 6,* 296–303.

Dimmitt, C. (2010). Evaluation in school counseling: Current practices and future possibilities. *Counseling Outcome Research and Evaluation, 1,* 44–56.

Evans, J. H., & Burck, H. D. (1992). The effects of career education interventions on academic achievement: A meta-analysis. *Journal of Counseling & Development, 71,* 63–68.

Froehlich, C. D. (1949). *Evaluating guidance procedures: A review of the literature.* Washington, DC: Federal Security Agency, Office of Education.

Gerler, E. R. (1985). Elementary school counseling research and the classroom learning environment. *Elementary School Guidance and Counseling, 20,* 39–48.

Gerler, E. R. (1992). What we know about school counseling: A reaction to Borders and Drury. *Journal of Counseling & Development, 70,* 499–501.

Gysbers, N. C., & Henderson, P. (2006). *Developing & managing your school guidance and counseling program* (4th ed.). Alexandria, VA: American Counseling Association.

Gysbers, N. C., & Lapan, R. T. (2009). *Strengths-based career development for school guidance and counseling programs.* Ann Arbor, MI: Counseling Outfitters.

Gysbers, N. C. (2010). *Remembering the past, shaping the future: A history of school counseling.* Alexandria, VA: American School Counseling Association.

Gysbers, N. C., Lapan, R. T., & Stanley, B. (2006). No fear results evaluation: The Missouri story. *ASCA School Counselor, 43,* 35–37.

Henderson, P. (2009). *The new handbook of administrative supervision in counseling.* New York, NY: Routledge.

Henderson, P., & Gysbers, N. C. (1998). *Leading and managing your school guidance program staff.* Alexandria, VA: American Counseling Association.

Hinderman, R. A. (1930). Evaluating and improving guidance services. *Nations' Schools, 5,* 47–52.

Johnson, C. D. (1991). Assessing results. In S. K. Johnson & E. A. Whitfield (Eds.), *Evaluating guidance programs: A practitioner's guide* (pp. 43–55). Iowa City, IA: American College Testing Program.

Johnson, S., Johnson, C., & Downs, L. (2006). *Building a results-based student support program*. Boston, MA: Lahaska Press.

Kefauver, G. N., & Hand, H. C. (1941). *Appraising guidance in secondary schools*. New York, NY: Macmillan.

Lapan, R. T. (2005, December). *Training school counselors to do results-based evaluation*. Presented at a pre-conference workshop for the Association for Career and Technical Education, Kansas City, Missouri.

Lapan, R. T., Gysbers, N. C., & Kayson, M. (2006). *How implementing comprehensive guidance programs improves academic achievement for all Missouri students*. Jefferson City: Missouri Department of Elementary and Secondary Education.

Lapan, R. T., Gysbers, N. C., & Petroski, G. (2001). Helping 7th graders be safe and academically successful: A statewide study of the impact of comprehensive guidance programs. *Journal of Counseling & Development, 75*, 292–302.

Lapan, R. T., Gysbers, N. C., & Sun, Y. (1997). The impact of more fully implemented guidance programs on the school experiences of high school students: A statewide evaluation study. *Journal of Counseling & Development, 75*, 292–302.

Lee, R. S. (1993). Effects of classroom guidance on student achievement. *Elementary Guidance and Counseling, 27*, 163–171.

Los Angeles County Office of Education. (2010). *SPARC 2010 rationale, requirements, rubric and application*. Los Angeles, CA: Author.

McGannon, W., Carey, J., & Dimmitt, C. (2005). *The current status of school counseling outcome research* (Research Monograph No. 2). Amherst: University of Massachusetts, School of Education, Center for School Counseling Outcome Research.

Missouri Department of Elementary and Secondary Education. (2000). *Guidelines for performance-based professional school counselor evaluation*. Jefferson City, MO: Author.

Myrick, R. D. (2003). *Developmental guidance and counseling: A practical approach* (4th ed.). Minneapolis, MN: Educational Media Corporation.

Neidt, C. O. (1965). *Relation of guidance practices to student behavioral outcomes* (OE-5-99-222). Washington, DC: U.S. Department of Health, Education, and Welfare.

Nelson, D. E., Fox, D. G., Haslam, M., & Gardner, J. (2007). *An evaluation of Utah's comprehensive counseling and guidance program: The fourth major study of Utah's statewide program*. Salt Lake City, UT: Institute for Behavioral Research in Creativity

Nelson, D. E., & Gardner, J. L. (1998). *An evaluation of the comprehensive guidance program in Utah public schools*. Salt Lake City: Utah State Office of Education.

No Child Left Behind Act of 2001, Pub. L. No. 107–110, 115 Stat. 1434 (2002).

Northside Independent School District. (1987). *Guide to counselor performance improvement through supervision, evaluation, and professional development*. San Antonio, TX: Author.

Northside Independent School District. (1997). *Guide to counselor performance improvement through supervision, evaluation, and professional development*. San Antonio, TX: Author.

Northside Independent School District. (2002). *Guide to counselor performance improvement through job definition, professionalism assessment, supervision, performance evaluation, and goal setting for professional development*. San Antonio, TX: Author.

Payne, A. F. (1924). Problems in vocational guidance. *National Vocational Guidance Association Bulletin, 2*, 61–63.

Proctor, W. M. (1930). Evaluating guidance activities in high schools. *The Vocational Guidance Magazine, 9*, 58–66.

Rosecrance, F. C. (1930). Organizing guidance for the larger school system. *The Vocational Guidance Magazine, 9*, 243–249.

Rothney, J. W. M. (1958). *Guidance practices and results.* New York, NY: Harper.

Rothney, J. W. M., & Roens, B. A. (1950). *Guidance of American youth: An experimental study.* Cambridge, MA: Harvard University Press.

Sink, C. A., Akos, P., Turnbull, R. J., Mvududu, N. (2008). An investigation of comprehensive school counseling programs and academic achievement in Washington State Middle Schools. *Professional School Counseling, 12,* 43–53.

Sink, C. A., & Stroh, H. R. (2003). Raising achievement test scores of early elementary school students through comprehensive school counseling programs. *Professional School Counseling, 6,* 350–364.

Sexton, T. L., Whiston, S. C., Bleuer, J. C., & Walz, G. R. (1997). *Integrating outcome research into counseling practice and training.* Alexandria, VA: American Counseling Association.

St. Clair, K. L. (1989). Middle school counseling research: A resource for school counselors. *Elementary School Guidance Counseling, 23,* 219–226.

Stone, C. B., & Dahir, C. A. (2007). *School counselor accountability: A MEASURE of student success* (2nd ed.). Upper Saddle River, NJ: Pearson Education.

Synatschk, K. O. (2002). Ensuring professionally relevant supervision and professional development: A district-level experience. In P. Henderson & N. Gysbers (Eds.), *Implementing comprehensive guidance programs: Critical leadership issues and successful responses* (pp. 199–206). Greensboro, NC: CAPS.

Texas Counseling Association. (2004). *Texas evaluation model for professional school counselors* (2nd ed.). Austin, TX: Author.

Travers, R. M. W. (1949). A critical review of techniques for evaluating guidance. *Educational and Psychological Measurement, 9,* 211–225.

Utah State Office of Education. (2008). *Comprehensive counseling and guidance program performance review: Connecting program improvement and student learning.* Salt Lake City, UT: Author.

Wellman, F. E., & Moore, E. J. (1975). *Pupil personnel services: A handbook for program development and evaluation.* Washington, DC: U.S. Department of Health, Education, and Welfare.

Whiston, S. C., & Quinby, R. F. (2009). Review of school counseling outcome research. *Psychology in the Schools, 46,* 267–272.

Whiston, S. C., Tai, W. L., Rahardja, D., & Eder, K. (2011). School counseling outcomes: A meta-analytic examination of interventions. *Journal of Counseling & Development, 89,* 37–55.

❧ Part V ❧

Enhancing

☞ Chapter 11 ☜

Enhancing Your Comprehensive Guidance and Counseling Program on the Basis of Needs and Evaluation Data

Enhancing—Redesigning Your Comprehensive Guidance and Counseling Program

- Commit to the redesign process.
- Begin the redesign process by gathering needs and evaluation data.
- Make redesign decisions on the basis of needs and evaluation data.
- Implement the new design.
- Understand that revitalization follows redesign.

☞ In Chapter 2, the sample timetable of tasks suggests that after gathering program, personnel, and results evaluation data for several years, it is necessary to step back and rethink your entire program. It is time to consider redesigning it to incorporate any smaller revisions you have been making on a regular basis over time. Also, enough time has probably elapsed from the time you gathered student, school, and community data to use in designing your original program that student needs and school and community circumstances may have changed. We call this redesign process *program enhancement*.

Redesigning is based not only on data from your ongoing evaluation work but also on your observations and those of students, parents, and administrators about how well the program has been functioning over time. In addition, it is based on any new realities that are currently present in your district. Redesigning the program periodically is how you ensure its relevancy for your students and for your schools and communities. Redesigning may lead to new or shifted priorities for the program's content, clients, and interventions. It may also lead to new or shifted priorities for the use of school counselors' time and talent.

It is important to remember that the redesign process does not change the basic framework of the program described in Chapter 3. The language used to describe the basic framework remains the same. What may change, however, will occur inside the framework of the program: the content (student standards), the descriptions and assumptions, the interventions, and the use of school counselor time and talent. Program and personnel priorities may also change.

In this chapter, we first highlight the need to commit to the redesign process. We discuss how often the program should be redesigned, who should be involved, and what steps should be taken. Then we focus on what is involved in beginning the redesign process. Attention is given to gathering the necessary data to use to begin the redesign process. Next, we give attention to making redesign decisions on the basis of the data that were collected. Finally, we describe what is involved in implementing the new design and stress the fact that program and personnel revitalization follows the redesign process. You will note that the redesign process follows the same process that you used originally to design your comprehensive guidance and counseling program. Redesign examples from Northside Independent School District in San Antonio, Texas, are used throughout the chapter to illustrate what happens when a school district goes through the redesign–enhancement process.

Commit to the Redesign Process

In thinking about redesigning a comprehensive guidance and counseling program, you need to answer three questions: How often should a program be redesigned? Who should be involved? What steps should be taken in the redesign process?

How Often Should a Program Be Redesigned?

You will recall that Chapter 2 provided a 10-year timetable that begins with Year 1 planning and ends with Years 9 and 10 enhancing. You will also recall that Years 4 to 8 focused on personnel, program, and results evaluation so that once the program is up and running, evaluation is ongoing. Finally, recall that the 10-year cycle was chosen for purposes of illustration. Your district may be on a shorter timetable.

So, how often should a program be redesigned? We use the term *periodic* to designate an interval of time long enough for the ongoing evaluation process (personnel, program, and results) to begin to indicate that major changes are needed. Remember, changes should always be made on an ongoing basis as needed, but the program redesign (enhancement) phase should begin when enough evaluation data have accumulated to warrant major changes, which could be 9 to 10 years or shorter depending on your district's timetable for program reviews. Schools and school districts change their priorities as new educational reforms come to their attention, as new academic or behavioral goals for students surface, and for a myriad other reasons. As integral parts of school districts, guidance and counseling programs need to have their priorities assessed on a timely basis to ensure alignment with the bigger systems in which they operate and with the district's comprehensive school improvement plan.

Who Should Be Involved?

Redesigning to enhance your guidance and counseling program requires the same attention and thoroughness as was required in creating the initial design. Major changes require major efforts. Quick fixes and simple solutions disrupt program designs. They often add interventions or consume time without consideration being given as what interventions will be replaced or streamlined to make room in the design for them. Redesigning a program is best done using the same program development steps that were taken the first time.

As in creating the initial design for a comprehensive guidance and counseling program, three different groups are involved in the redesign process: the steering committee, the school–community advisory committee, and work groups. The steering committee consists of individuals who support and implement the program. It includes school counselors who make up or represent the guidance leadership team and district-level administrators who manage programs that use the guidance program and staff and that provide resources to the program. Building-level representatives include principals and teachers. The steering committee guides the process and makes recommendations about the program, its structure, and priorities. Their recommendations are forwarded to district policy and administrative decision makers.

The school–community advisory committee, as you will remember from Chapter 2, consists of program consumers: students, parents, teachers, and community members. Committee members may be representatives from student councils, from parent–teacher associations, from building site-based management committees, and from the business and mental health communities. They make suggestions from the perspectives of the groups they represent regarding the rationale for the program, possible priorities to be addressed in the program, and new directions they see the schools of the district and the community at large moving in.

The work groups involve as many school counselors as possible. (Remember our adage: Never use one when two will do!) These groups assist in analyzing the evaluation data that describe the status of the current program, show the results of the program, and point out trends in the larger context of the school and community. They identify new and continuing needs of groups of students. They do much of the legwork in presenting data and information to the steering committee.

What Steps Should be Taken?

The redesign-to-enhance process is a major undertaking, and its steps mirror those used in the initial development of your program: getting organized, planning, designing, planning the transition, and implementing the new program design. Table 11.1 provides an overview of this redesign process.

As the steering committee proceeds through the phases of the program redesign process, its members consider evaluation data in the context of the initial program design, current realities, and new design possibilities. These considerations lead to new design decisions, such as new program priorities and new parameters for resource allocations. Evaluation data are provided to the steering committee regarding the use of counselors' talent and time, the program balance and interventions conducted, the students served (by subpopulations), and the content outcomes addressed and achieved. Information is also provided regarding the other elements of your comprehensive guidance and counseling program: the structural components (Chapter 3) and the resources appropriated, including the funding sources for the various aspects of the program.

Current realities are identified by data from the three kinds of evaluation (program, personnel, and results) and from new school and community information as well. Given that school counselors are making every effort to adhere to the originally established program priorities and parameters, areas in which evaluation data suggest good and bad matches with the desired design indicate a force that we call reality. Good matches indicate that the original design fits the realities (needs, goals, time parameters) of the school. Bad matches indicate that the original design may not be feasible. The steering committee, for example, may have set priorities for the topics or areas to be addressed through planned interventions in the responsive services component, but program evaluation data may indicate that in the past several years school counselors spent a portion of their time working in an area

Table 11.1
Program Redesign Process

Getting Organized
- Review external sources regarding status of guidance and counseling and in district or school personnel, results, and program evaluation data
- Secure commitment to redesign
- Convene guidance and counseling leadership team
- Identify need for redesign
- Develop redesign plan
- Form guidance and counseling steering committee, school–community advisory committee
- Develop student needs assessment strategy
- Gather input re: program improvement needs

Planning
- Review recent history of program development and implementation
- Reconfirm commitment to program model
- Assess students and other clients' needs
- Discuss new contextual information
- Revise structural components: rationale, assumptions, definition
- Analyze evaluation data as current status assessment

Redesigning
- Revise qualitative design: priorities for student results, balance for client services, operational standards for components (program delivery), priorities for counselor competency use
- Revise quantitative design: program balance, ratio

Planning Transition
- Gather input to final draft of the redesigned program
- Gather additional data regarding redesigned program dimensions
- Rewrite comprehensive guidance and counseling program framework
- List final recommendations for program improvement
- Recommend district or campus program development process

Implementing the Redesigned Program
- Return to the Designing—Planning the Transition (Chapter 6) and Implementing—Making the Transition (Chapter 7) sets of tasks and subsequent tasks in the initial installation plan

---

that was not even on the list. In Northside Independent School District in San Antonio, Texas, for example, evaluation data uncovered such an area in problems stemming from racial and ethnic tension and from the lack of student and staff effectiveness in cross-cultural situations.

Begin the Redesign Process by Gathering Data From Various Sources

Now that a commitment has been made to redesign your comprehensive guidance and counseling program and you know who should be involved and the necessary steps to take, the next task is to begin the redesign process. One task in this process is to gather and analyze internal and external data, including student needs data, school goals, community context data, and professional school counseling trends. Another task is to gather and analyze personnel, program, and program intervention data. You will also need to gather and analyze qualitative design data concerning school counselor performance, clients served, program component standards, and new knowledge and skills students need. Finally, you will need to gather and analyze quantitative design needs information concerning program balance, counselor–student ratios, and number of students served.

Internal and External Data

Student Needs Data

Reassessments of students' needs for assistance from comprehensive guidance and counseling programs are done periodically to identify new needs and to suggest new priorities among previously identified needs. In some school districts, reassessments of students' needs have found that more attention should be given to multiculturalism. Other districts have found that their students needed more help in coping with the violence around them and in developing better anger and conflict management skills. Other student needs identified have included increased numbers of students who felt alienated from school and school staff and increased numbers of students who needed more assistance as they made educational and career development plans. Also, students in some districts needed help in setting challenging goals for themselves.

School Goals

As school boards, superintendents, principals, and other senior-level school administrators change, philosophies and policies may also change. As the community and school customers change, the priorities for education may change as well. Even the mission of the school district may be altered by the political bent of the community. States' attempts to equalize funding have brought more money into some schools. Insufficient funds plague other school districts. District education goals and initiatives vary from year to year as legislatures change and as educators identify ideas for improvement. The standards movement brought increased emphasis on academic achievement. Districts' strategic-planning efforts such as their school improvement plans have enabled them to better understand their communities and to design their school system—building to building—to respond to the needs and goals of their communities.

The processes by which decisions are made in schools change, changing not only the climates of schools, but also their priorities. Site-based decision making, whereby more people have input into the choices of what is most important for their schools and communities, is an example. Also, districts and states are increasingly demanding that local decisions be based on hard data that present needs and solutions that are supported by research. These same data can support the priorities established for the guidance and counseling program because they include such things as clarity about what students know, learn, and need to learn. Schools are being held accountable for their retention and promotion rates. Students' adherence to conduct codes is reflected in discipline reports and in attendance and absence rates. Rates of participation in school activities indicate how affiliated or how alienated students are from school.

Curriculum realignment has accompanied standards development and implementation. Ways to assist individual students succeed academically are being sought. The focus on individual students suggests they also need to become more responsible for their learning, which in turn emphasizes programs and processes that support student goal setting, self-evaluation, and self-tracking through such strategies as portfolios. As the society continues to become more pluralistic, conflict management, character development, and self-responsibility are being emphasized. Another trend that is currently seen is the increased involvement of parents and businesses in the schools. It is hoped that their involvement will help students learn the content they need to be successful in their adult lives and at the same time bring more support for the education enterprise.

Community Context Data

Communities change over time. They grow larger or smaller. The average age of the population may shift, or the types of individuals who live there may change. People move in and out. Industries and businesses begin, grow, and decline. The labor market may change. Houses gain and lose their value. All of these changes may have an impact on the school district that serves that community. Guidance and counseling programs serve all the students in a school district and provide special services to many students with personal, social, educational, and career needs.

At the time of redesigning a district's guidance and counseling program, you need to survey all of the relevant community variables to identify significant changes in demographics, socioeconomics, mobility rates, average level of parents' education, family configurations, immigration patterns, and so on. Growth and decline in the student population, changing ages of the faculty, and school openings and closings are also environmental events that have implications for the guidance and counseling program. As with the rest of these efforts, data are studied that, in turn, support conclusions about what these changes mean for the program currently and in the near future (i.e., for 10 years, if an original design can stay valid that long).

Professional School Counseling Trends

Trends in professional school counseling today include better understanding of new or additional groups of clients, different content and techniques addressing students' and society's needs, ways to organize and manage guidance and counseling programs to better serve students, and methods for assisting school counselors' professional development. New groups of clients include subgroups of students. Increasingly, it is finally being recognized that elementary-school-age children benefit from guidance and counseling. In our increasingly pluralistic society, school counselors are working more often with adolescents who are facing more openness regarding sexual preferences. The expansion of special education services has helped schools develop sensitivity to a diversity of disabilities that students manage and that affect their lives. Efforts are being made to help parents to be better partners with the schools and involved in their children's learning. Although school counselors have always provided bridges for parents to be part of the schools, recent parents' rights policies have opened the schoolhouse doors even wider.

As delineated in the American School Counselor Association (ASCA, 2005) National Model, new guidance and counseling content includes helping students develop and maintain high expectations for their academic achievement. There is renewed interest in facilitating students' career development. Our diverse society has led us to understand more fully what cross-cultural effectiveness entails. Helping students set goals, develop plans for achieving them, and monitor progress toward goal accomplishment requires culturally responsive approaches as well as a system for providing such assistance.

Organized guidance and counseling programs represent successes for the school counseling profession, even though many schools are still striving to implement comprehensive guidance and counseling programs. The ASCA (2005) National Model offers a professional consensus that comprehensive guidance and counseling programs are the most effective means for organizing the work of school counselors and assisting students to reach personal–social, educational, and career development results. The emphasis in schools on helping individual students achieve success requires more individualized guidance and counseling services. Systems are being set in place for schoolwide guidance and counseling approaches that involve teachers and volunteer community members. Site-based decision making is allowing for flexibility within buildings and for greater responsiveness to local needs.

Within the guidance and counseling field, professional supervision continues to develop as the standards for professionalism become clearer. Leadership for school counselors' professional development is emerging as a specialty of its own, as are specialties within school counseling (Henderson, 2009). External funds are supporting such specialists as substance abuse prevention counselors, special education counselors, and bilingual counselors. The use of paraprofessional guidance staff in appropriate roles, such as parent education coordinators, testing program specialists, data-processing clerks, registrars, and career center technicians, is helping guidance and counseling program delivery become systematic and efficient. Professionals from related specialties, such as school social work and school psychology, are increasingly being hired in schools and augment professional school counselors' work in the responsive services (Fuston & Hargens, 2002).

Redesign possibilities are also suggested by various external sources. These sources describe trends in and outside of education that may have an impact on the redesign process. Examples of these sources at the national level include the National Association of Secondary School Principals' (2004, 2006) two reports *Breaking Ranks II: Strategies for Leading High School Reform* and *Breaking Ranks in the Middle: Strategies for Leading Middle Level Reform*. Other reports that describe national trends are *A Developmental Perspective on College and Workplace Readiness* (Lippman, Atienza, Rivers, & Keith, 2008) and *Promotion and Prevention in Mental Health* published by the Substance Abuse and Mental Health Services Administration's Center for Mental Health Services (2007). Many states have also revised their state models of comprehensive guidance and counseling manuals and are excellent sources of state trends and issues.

Personnel, Program, and Intervention Data

In addition to gathering needs data and identifying local, state, and national trends, it is also important to gather personnel, program, and intervention data. Together with needs data and trend information, these types of data add vital information concerning the direction the program redesign process should take.

Personnel Data

The strengths and weaknesses of the school guidance and counseling staff as a whole may be learned from aggregating the relative strengths and weaknesses of individual school counselors as reflected in the evaluations of their performance. The more closely aligned the school counselor performance evaluation form is with the program, the more relevant the conclusions will be. As discussed in Chapter 10, analysis of performance evaluation data from a form that records evaluations according to program component tells you whether school counselors perform competently in the activities provided in guidance curriculum, individual student planning, responsive services, and system support. It tells you in which components the performance of school counselors is strongest or weakest. For example, school counselors may be most competent in providing responsive services and least competent in providing guidance curriculum. This tells you and your program decision makers that their performance is best when they are providing counseling and consultation services but not as effective when they are providing guidance instruction.

If the school guidance and counseling staff is large, performance across the school levels will probably vary greatly. Elementary counselors may be evaluated as better at guidance curriculum work and high school counselors as better at individual student planning work. There may also be variances within levels. For example, some middle school counselors may be evaluated as better at small-group counseling than other middle school counselors.

Program Data

As discussed in Chapter 10, there are multiple ways to evaluate to what degree the implemented comprehensive guidance and counseling program meets the standards set out in the qualitative design for each program component. The design standards for each component state the priorities for guidance content addressed through program interventions, the roles carried out by school counselors within component interventions, and how the interventions are conducted. School counselors should evaluate their entire program against the full set of standards on a regular basis. The aggregation of these data informs the redesign process.

Annual studies that ask school counselors to compare and contrast their yearly plan for interventions with the interventions actually conducted also keep everyone aware of emerging needs and new trends. Assessment of the attainment of program improvement goals provides two sets of information considered by the steering committee and other groups assisting in the redesign process. First, the choices for improvement themselves, when grouped, suggest improvement needs across school levels or within school buildings. Second, their aggregated levels of accomplishment can suggest the feasibility of adding, augmenting, streamlining, or displacing interventions districtwide. For example, expanding small-group counseling within responsive services is often a high priority in districts adapting a comprehensive guidance and counseling program. Annual reports that tell the number of small-group programs provided in each building, the topics they addressed, the numbers of students served through them, and the apparent quantity and level of attainment of the goals and objectives for the groups are useful pieces of information—especially when the groups are offered on the basis of assessments of students' and staff members' current needs.

When the district has set content priorities for the program, reports of interventions completed to address these can (and should) be submitted and totaled. For example, in Northside Independent School District, the districtwide strategic-plan–related guidance and counseling program content priorities were goal setting, conflict management, and substance abuse education and prevention. Annual reports by school counselors by building inform the district about such things as the number of school staff members who participated in goal setting training and used goal-setting processes in their teaching and for themselves. The growth or decline in participation levels informs your district-level decision makers about adherence to their standards for student participation on the one hand and the value placed on these priorities at the local level on the other hand. One way to assess to what degree school counselors are fulfilling their assigned roles appropriately, as conceived by your original program designers, is to study the proportion of time they spend conducting interventions in various configurations of meeting clients.

Program Intervention Data

Maintaining the quality of a program requires ongoing evaluation of program interventions and their results. Every guidance and counseling program intervention ends with a measure of its effectiveness in helping students learn or apply the guidance and counseling content that was the focus of the intervention. Additionally, after every guidance and counseling curriculum lesson or unit, every guidance and counseling session aimed at assisting students' individual planning, and every counseling or consulting session held in response to a student's needs or parent's concerns, school counselors need to evaluate the intervention's impact on students and parents and the quality and efficiency of the intervention itself. In other words, each intervention is evaluated as it is implemented, as described in Chapter 10.

Continuous evaluation of program interventions allows for ongoing monitoring and adjustment of the interventions as the program is being implemented. If a guidance and counseling intervention was not as effective as was hoped, then additional interventions may be needed to ensure students' achievement of the desired outcomes. If, during a guidance and counseling session, for example, students were unable to complete action plans related to their personal goals, additional time and assistance may need to be provided (i.e., another intervention in the near future). Many guidance and counseling program interventions are annual events—done once a year. Thus, if the implementation of an intervention was not as streamlined or as crisp as it might have been, determining how it could be done more efficiently next year is best done immediately after its conclusion this year. (Many details are forgotten over a year!)

Qualitative Design Needs Data

Needs information relating to the guidance and counseling program's qualitative design emerges from analyzing data regarding the quality of school counselors' performance, identifying new subsets of clients needing services, examining the standards for the program components, and identifying new knowledge and skills that are needed by students.

School Counselor Performance

Even with a program that is being well implemented, new or different needs for the application of school counselors' talents may be identified. In many districts, school counselors feel overwhelmed with the quantity of students who need their help, and at the same time, they still have too many nonguidance tasks and paperwork. Advisory committees suggest that more counselors are needed to serve fewer children. Fuller use of support staff—educational and clerical assistants, other paraprofessionals—and expanded use of volunteers to help students within carefully defined roles (e.g., as mentors) seems desirable.

School counselors themselves identify performance improvement needs. If you have followed our advice in Chapter 9 and have school counselors set annual performance improvement goals, their needs are monitored regularly and, at this point, may be summarized for your program redesigners. Three kinds of decisions will be made by your program redesigners regarding school counselors' needs for professional development assistance:

1. areas related to the ongoing expectations for their performance, as indicated by their performance evaluations;
2. areas in which other staff members may be as competent or more competent to carry out responsibilities;
3. new dimensions of the comprehensive guidance and counseling program design.

For example, aggregated school counselor performance evaluation data can tell you and your program planners that school counselors' current needs for continued improvement may include enhanced group counseling competence, in both group process skills and specific information regarding recurrent topics addressed through small groups. Newer counselors may continue to need information and to hone their skills in working with referral sources. High school counselors may need more training in modern instructional technology, such as use of cooperative learning strategies in instruction. Although many school counselors perform well in teacher consultation, some do not. Many school counselors are still uncomfortable in advocating with and for parents.

You and your comprehensive guidance and counseling program redesigners need to discuss whether students are best served when teachers, who are competent in modern instructional methods, provide much of the guidance curriculum, with counselors helping teachers learn guidance content. Remember to consider identifying, as part of the transition process discussed at the end of this chapter, the in-service training needs of staff members whose roles will change as a result of the program redesign. Moreover, you may learn that the school counselor performance evaluation process itself needs improvement to better assist school counselors' efforts to improve their performance. Northside Independent School District, for example, found that the more specific standards for counselor performance were, the more distinct definitions among the basic performance roles of counselor were, and the more clarity was needed regarding each individual's job description (Henderson & Gysbers, 1998). The district also identified shortcomings in the performance evaluation form. Without a form that supports clarity and accuracy in drawing evaluative conclusions, aggregating data for improvement decisions is difficult.

Clients Served

Educators and concerned community members increasingly recognize the special needs of the majority of students who fall, educationally, in the center section of the bell curve. These students do not give evidence of needing highly specialized educational services nor intensified mental health treatment, but they nevertheless are students who may not feel self-worth, connected to school, or cared for at school, and they may not be getting help with the typical challenges of growing up. They may be inattentive in classes or have problems (as they define them) that make them unable to concentrate on academic learning. Many are stressed, and some (more than we admit) are abused. These students want and need to have opportunities to discuss their problems and to be taken seriously. At the same time, schools are formally identifying more special needs students, including those who are at risk, persistent misbehavers, homeless, or involved in gangs.

Teachers are seeking more help with specific classroom problems. They want even more consultation regarding individual students who are having problems. They want more consultation for themselves about student, school, and personal problems. They want a fuller understanding of the guidance and counseling program—its practices, operations, and ethical standards. They want more help with understanding standardized testing and its appropriate uses. At the same time, parents seem to need and want more parenting skills, but new ways of providing them with these skills need to be developed. Their lack of involvement in schools may be indicative of their being busy or of their discomfort with school. The latter tells us we need to find more effective ways to reach out to them.

Program Component Standards

With the comprehensive guidance and counseling program in place, one of the side benefits is that school counselors not only are able to educate students, teachers, and parents regarding how they deliver the program, but they also have a common language to describe the program. The four program components are few enough and distinct enough in purpose and practice to be readily understood. Thus, asking their opinions about the value of the activities in each of the components provides useful information to add to your redesign efforts.

Knowing the relative value assigned to each set of activities by your customers helps you establish priorities among the components. If, for example, program consumers value responsive services assistance significantly more than they value classroom guidance, that could support a significant rise in the priority of responsive services over the guidance curriculum, or vice versa. If individual student planning activities are perceived as more valuable than responsive services, that could contribute to the priority setting.

If you have followed the model presented in this book for ongoing program improvement, you will have noted that guidance and counseling program improvement goals are set each year, based on the program's annual evaluation, across the buildings and districts. Aggregations of these building-specific goals also provide trend data regarding possible new program priorities. Annual program improvement goals, of course, reflect the improvements recommended in the initial program design process, but they also reflect new priorities at the district (all levels or across a specific level) and building levels. For example, in Northside Independent School District new district priorities were established within the strategic plan: goal setting, conflict management, career development, character development, and cross-cultural effectiveness. Traditionally, needed improvements that arise frequently from building needs include small-group counseling, parent involvement and education, and staff consultation. New topics arising from the buildings that need to be considered in program redesign include assisting teachers to teach guidance curriculum, behavior management, educational motivation, making the best out of standardized testing, and responding to special needs students.

The school–community advisory committee or other parent and student advisory committees identify changes in the program they might like to see. These inputs provide ideas for the steering committee to consider. Advisory committee members often want more guidance curriculum, both more content and more frequent lessons. Sometimes they see the need for better presentation methodology. Advisory committee members also often want more individual student educational and career planning assistance than is currently done. Because a number of these activities are annual events, it is often hard for students, parents, and community people to identify what activities are provided in the individual student planning component. It is important to help students and parents make connections between elementary career days and middle school instruction regarding job families and clusters and high school career center–based activities, between eighth- and 10th-grade career assessments and 11th- and 12th-grade college entrance examinations, and between middle school career-related goal setting and 4-year high school planning and high school career and educational planning.

Guidance and counseling program customers consistently want more counseling made available to students, both individual and group. Parents want more consultation opportunities and help with difficult moments with or for their children. Increasingly, crisis intervention is called for in our schools. Rethinking the priorities for the responsive services component and explaining them to students, parents, teachers, and others are essential. Finding ways to expand responsive services through referrals, collaborative relationships among service providers, and more efficient and effective strategies by school counselors is called for.

As education itself continues its efforts for reform, and as increasingly diverse students come to school, teachers' needs for training and support shift. In turn, school counselors are required to refresh their competence continuously in such topics as learning styles and motivation, classroom management and organization, teaching the hard-to-teach or hard-to-reach students, and helping students develop social skills. Because standardized testing is a popular vehicle for holding school systems accountable, and because it is an area traditionally connected to guidance and counseling (albeit unfortunately so), school counselors continue to be challenged to help colleague educators maintain a balanced approach regarding the administration and use of test results. Balance in test administration means all staff members must fulfill their fair share of the responsibilities for this massive program. Balance in use of test results means helping staff members know the limitations of individual test results and the value of using multiple sources of information to make judgments about students.

New Knowledge and Skills

Student needs assessment data provide important information regarding new or different needs that students have that should be considered by the steering committee as it approaches program redesign. As with the initial program design (Chapter 6), identifying what students need is best accomplished by asking the students themselves as well as school counselors, teachers, parents, and others. Repetition suggests priorities. Student skill development needs identified in Northside Independent School District included the following:

- personal management skills,
- career skills,
- life skills,
- goal-setting skills,
- self-confidence development,
- learning to give of oneself,
- problem-solving skills, and
- valuing education as an investment in the future.

In addition, teachers, parents, and administrators in Northside recognized that students in schools needed resources to help them as they faced the challenges of growing up and of being in school. Cited were needs for

- a sense of connection,
- a sense of belonging in the school community,
- someone to listen to them,
- support systems, and
- advocacy.

Each of these had implications for the redesign of the guidance and counseling program in Northside Independent School District.

Quantitative Design Needs Data

The needs data regarding each of the three dimensions of the quantitative design—program balance, counselor–student ratio, and number of students needing and receiving services—result from your consideration of the qualitative needs as well as analysis of the reasons for lack of adherence to your previously set standards. For example, if for most of the years since the initial design, and in many of the buildings in which the program was implemented, actual program delivery has been out of balance, perhaps a new balance standard is called for. If the counselor–student ratio is such that the counselors and their clients are consistently frustrated because of insufficient time to connect, the ratio is probably not adequate for the needs. If the number and percentage of students who actually benefit from guidance services are unacceptably low in relation to their needs, then the quantitative design will need to be altered.

Three sets of data are required to complete the collection of data needed to redesign the program: the actual balance of the programs, the actual counselor–student ratio, and the actual number of students and other clients served through the program. How closely the building programs are aligned with the originally established design can be determined separately. If the alignments are fairly close, some inferences may be drawn about the overall impact of the balance of interventions and the ratio on the numbers of clients served by interrelating the data.

Program Balance

Data had been gathered annually from the school counselors in each of Northside Independent School District's buildings regarding the percentage of time they spent in interventions associated with the four program components. These data were used to compare and contrast the quality of program implementation across the various buildings of the district and, if there was consistency, to compare and contrast the districtwide aggregated data with the original design of the district's comprehensive guidance and counseling program goal.

If most of the buildings at a school level implement balanced programs but a few do not, the few that do not should be studied more closely to determine the reasons for their being out of alignment. If the differences are the result of student needs, some consideration of these causes is in order. If the differences are the result of a lack of understanding of or adherence to the district program, attention should be given to the program leadership.

If most of the buildings at a school level are out of alignment with the originally established design, then the design should be reexamined. The original design may be flawed. If the design is not flawed, then the obstacles to implementing the design need to be identified and considered as problems to be solved.

For example, after analyzing the data and drawing conclusions, the steering committee at Northside made recommendations for what members should consider when they approached program redesign. These recommendations are summarized as follows.

- Considerations for elementary schools
  Guidance curriculum: Lower ratios to entail fewer classes resulting in reduced percentages.
  Individual student planning: Lower the desired percentage.
  Responsive services: Increase the desired percentage.
  System support: Assign other personnel some of the major activities that indirectly serve students.
- Considerations for middle schools
  Guidance curriculum: Lower the desired percentage (two lessons per grading period is 16%).
  Individual student planning: [None]
  Responsive services: Increase the desired percentage.
  System support: Realign the assignment of indirect services to other departments.
- Considerations for high schools
  Guidance curriculum: Lower the desired percentage.
  Individual student planning: [None]
  Responsive services: Increase the desired percentage.
  System support: Realign administrative tasks to administration or other departments.
- General consideration: Suggest a range of percentages for buildings to work within.

Counselor–Student Ratio

To evaluate the adequacy of the counselor–student ratios in effect at the time of your program's redesign, you may want to conduct comparison studies of the results and levels of service in buildings with significantly different ratios. Using the mathematical model described in Chapter 8 (see Recognizing Potential section) and applying the actual ratio information within the program balance actually implemented, you can estimate the differences in services resulting from different-sized student caseloads.

Number of Students Served

A basic decision to wrestle with in the redesign process is the choice between a developmental guidance and counseling program and a program that is responsive to students' problems and concerns. Making this choice requires having a sense of what students need to make the best of their educational opportunities and knowing how school counselors can best be used to help them. In Northside Independent School District's original comprehensive guidance program design, the developmental guidance program components were assigned top priority at all three levels (guidance curriculum at the elementary level and individual student planning at the middle and high school levels).

Make Redesign Decisions on the Basis of Needs and Evaluation Data

At this point in the redesign process (program enhancement), evaluation data have been collected and updated needs data are also available. The task now is to make the needed redesign decisions that will lead to a redesigned and enhanced program. As we stated in the Preface, the program enhancement process follows evaluation and connects back to the beginning as program redesign unfolds, but at a higher level. Thus, the process is spiral, not circular. Each time the redesign process unfolds, a new and more effective guidance and counseling program emerges.

For the program redesign process to move forward, you will need to consider the conclusions drawn from the evaluation data about what and how well the program is doing and combine them with the information about new needs and trends. By combining the two, you can make decisions about the current program design (comparable with those described in Chapter 5). You can decide whether the program is working as previously designed, whether it is still important, and whether it should be maintained. You can also decide where the design is not working; whether the priorities are still the same and, therefore, should be targeted for improvement; or whether the priorities should be replaced by something more needed or feasible. These decisions lead to new standards for your redesigned guidance and counseling program.

Each of the comprehensive guidance and counseling program elements (as outlined in Chapter 3) are considered in this task. New decisions are made or previous decisions are reaffirmed regarding the student standards and competencies developed through the program, the structural components (rationale, assumptions, definition, policy), the program delivery components (qualitative design), and the resource allocations (quantitative design).

Student Standards and Competencies Redesign Decisions

New ways of defining the basic content of the comprehensive guidance and counseling program have probably emerged since the initial program adoption. Thus, the first set of recommendations for a redesigned program should be reaffirmation or readjustment of the basic student learning standards for the program. Changes may be made at the domain and competency levels.

Structural Components Redesign Decisions

After redesigning the basic content (student learning standards) of the program, the next step involves revision of the structural components of the program: the statements of rationale for the program, the assumptions that undergird the program, and the definition of the program as well as the school district policy for guidance and counseling.

Rationale

Data from the evaluation and from the updated needs information provide you with ideas on how to revise the rationale for your program. New information may, on the one hand, reveal seemingly larger numbers of students who are alienated from school: Increases in student violence and continued widespread substance abuse, the diversity of family configurations, and unstable economies result in students who come to school from situations that make it difficult for them to attend to their schoolwork. New information may, on the other hand, also make it clear that in the 21st century, schools will continue to be challenged to hold increasingly higher academic standards for and expectations of students. Schools are charged to help every student, regardless of circumstances, to succeed in school. These somewhat conflicting aims for schools underscore the value of guidance and counseling for helping students manage their own destinies and solve their problems.

The new information may indicate that teachers, facing increasingly diverse student populations, need meaningful consultation to enhance their work with parents. The parents' rights movement has brought increasing numbers of parents to school in efforts to assist with or intervene in their children's education. The continuing shift of educational decision making to the building level requires school counselors to have the knowledge, skills, and professional values to manage locally appropriate programs, with sufficient leadership available to nurture professional growth. Recognizing such community, school, and student needs is critical in redesigning your program in general and in reviewing and revising the rationale for the program in particular.

Assumptions

You will probably find that you are more aware of the assumptions that undergird your program operation than you were during the original designing of your program. As mentioned earlier, because of their very nature, assumptions are somewhat hard to recognize until they are challenged. They also help staff members remember the basic values of the program. For example, Northside Independent School District's redesign work included reaffirming the following assumptions:

- Students are the primary clients of the program.
- All counselors are held to the profession's ethical standards.
- No matter what the presenting problem or issue, each student merits the same nonjudgmental reception and assistance.
- The best program is one in which the resources are consciously allocated to the established priorities of the program.
- Differently credentialed staff members are used in job assignments that appropriately apply their training and competence.
- As much as possible, school counselors enlist parents as partners in assisting students' personal, social, educational, and career development.

Definition

Because by now you have had extensive experience with guidance and counseling program implementation, you may be more willing to debate and decide on the essential mission of the program than you were when everything was new. Members of the school–community advisory and steering committees have opinions based on their experiences as to who fulfills structured roles in the program, who in addition to the students the program's clients legitimately are, and the true meaning of the comprehensive guidance and counseling program's organizational structure. Furthermore, because of the accountable nature of comprehensive guidance and counseling programs, you will probably be quite clear as to what the resources of the program will support. If all students in schools are to receive more in-depth guidance and counseling assistance, more staff members will have to be involved. If additional individualized assistance is desired, then more individual advisers will have to be provided. If a broader range of troubled students are to have their specialized needs attended to, additional service providers will have to be identified. With changes such as these envisioned, the staff implementing the program might expand to include all teachers providing guidance curriculum, all professional staff providing individual student planning system assistance, and community-based mental health professionals and in-school related professionals providing responsive services. As a result, the definition of the program will need to be revised.

School District Guidance and Counseling Policy

If you followed our recommendations in the initial program development, your school district developed a policy that supports the guidance and counseling program. The initial policy statement was based on your previous identification of the content of the program and its rationale, assumptions, and definition. When the steering committee reaches consensus regarding these basic statements (remember that unanimity is often difficult to achieve if your committee is truly reflective of the diversity of your school community), the new or newly reaffirmed content domains, rationale, assumptions, and definition of the program should be ratified by your school district's top-level administration and school board.

When that approval has been achieved, the new policy statement is distributed to the district's principals and school counselors and to anyone else who is interested at this stage of the game. This is the perfect opportunity to help others begin to internalize the changes that may follow after the next step—program redesign. It also provides a vehicle for eliciting even more people's input into the all-important priority setting that ensues.

Qualitative Redesign Decisions

Qualitative redesign decisions are those regarding priorities for the use of school counselors' competencies, for clients to be served, for program interventions to be delivered, and for student results to be achieved. We suggest that you ask the qualitative design questions first. It is important for you to know what you want before you deal with the reality of how much of it you can have, given the resources available. Final recommendations nearly always include suggestions for additional resources.

School Counselors' Competencies

On the basis of the experience of working in a program for a number of years, the school–community advisory and steering committees need to establish at least two kinds of priorities regarding school counselors' skills. These priorities are for the skills to be used within the program and for the skills that need strengthening through professional development. In Northside Independent School District, it was clear that the steering committee members wanted school counselors to manage their own program. They also valued both the individual and the small-group counseling expertise that the school counselors brought to their buildings. Consulting with other adults on behalf of their students was the fourth priority. These priorities fit what the school counselors had envisioned as their appropriate roles.

Professional development needs are identified through a discrepancy analysis of priorities and evaluation data. Target areas are the high-priority competencies or commitments that school counselors are not performing well. Some school counselors may need further refinement of their program (including time) management skills. Some may need to attend to their small-group counseling skills, and so on.

With discussion focused on applications of school counselors' competence, new or refined ideas about ways to help school counselors improve their performance also come up. For example, the tool for evaluating the quality of school counselors' performance (the performance evaluation form) may need fine-tuning to provide better feedback to individuals. The activities that address job focus and improvement (job descriptions, professional supervision) may need clarification, strengthening, or more resources. In many districts, the professional leadership for school counselors is unclear or is provided by individuals without school counseling expertise, such as principals. Because of this, school counselors' leadership systems need substantial improvement nationwide (Henderson & Gysbers, 1998).

Clients Served

Evaluation data provide insights into who is actually being served in the current guidance and counseling program by revealing the balance among services provided to students, services provided to adults, and system support tasks. The percentage of students served at each grade level and the percentage of students served through developmental, preventive, or remedial interventions as well as data regarding services provided to various subgroups of students, such as those experiencing divorce or grief, are also available. New information regarding students' needs and the needs suggested by the issues apparent in the school community may suggest different priorities for the clients to be served. Changed or refocused school and district goals may suggest different priorities.

In Northside Independent School District's redesign, the desired balance between serving elementary students and serving adults stayed the same: 65% of counselors' time was spent with students, 35% with adults. Differences were seen, however, in the recommendations for the breakdown of times within these large categories. The time recommended to be spent providing students with developmental assistance was reduced by about 10%, with that time reallocated to the students with needs for prevention or remediation. This recommendation was one of several that indicated an increased understanding of and respect for school counselors' specialized skills in working with students facing issues and problems.

Program Interventions to Be Delivered

The centerpieces of qualitative redesign are the minimum standards and operational definitions for each program component. The language used in defining the program components does not change. What is subject to change are the interventions and the priorities for these interventions within each component. For example, you may need to rearrange the priorities for each of the curriculum strands because of increased learning about what is most needed and appropriate at each grade level or because of the changing needs of the population served by the school. Increasingly, the emphasis on career development as the purpose for educational planning may cause refinement of these interventions within the individual student planning system. New needs identified for counseling services should be responded to. Specification of the school counselors' roles in relation to academic standards may be needed to enhance school counselors' support for the total educational system.

A needed addition to many guidance and counseling program descriptions is clarification of parents' roles in each program component (see Chapter 3). The reason for this is the increasing recognition of parents' rights with regard to their children's schooling and of the need for their involvement to enable their children's success in school. Spelling out parents' responsibilities and opportunities within guidance curriculum and individual student planning interventions causes schools and school counselors to better ensure that parents have the information they need to be active participants in the developmental guidance provided their children. Clarifying how parents' permission for counseling occurs in responsive services and how parents can access the services on behalf of their students is important, especially in light of those parents who do not want their children to benefit from these services at school. Expanding parent involvement within the system support component, such as in advocacy activities and parent advisory roles, provides parents with vehicles for input into program development and delivery.

A change that had widespread impact in the Northside Independent School District's program was the expanded definition of teachers' roles in the delivery of developmental guidance and counseling interventions. The expanded definition was based on the recognition that if we were truly going to help all students acquire all of the basic competencies in the major life skills represented by the guidance curriculum, every educator needed to contribute to these ends. If we were truly going to help each individual student establish educational and career goals and plans, as well as provide means for monitoring their progress, every educator had to assist in providing accurate and unbiased information and meaningful advice to students in the individual student planning component.

Student Results

In assessing the needs of students, new priorities may emerge for the content (student standards) of the guidance and counseling program. Evaluation data may clarify what students and others think is beneficial for the guidance and counseling program to address. Therefore, new strands, such as cross-cultural effectiveness, may be added to the content of the program and to the priority-setting process. Evaluation data on effectiveness of the in-place content may also raise or lower a strand's importance. For example, self-esteem development in children is increasingly recognized as not sufficient as an end in itself and is instead seen as a part of students' feelings of competence in other dimensions, such as making friends, acting responsibly, and being able to express themselves so others understand their thoughts and feelings.

Quantitative Redesign Decisions

On the basis of qualitative design decisions, decisions on allocation of the program's resources need to be adjusted to match those revisions. The quantitative design is most influenced by the recommendations regarding the balance of resource allocation among the four program components, that is, by the guidelines regarding how school counselors spend their time. As described in Chapter 8, the counselor–student ratio affects how many students can be served through the actual program balance.

Program Balance

Evaluation data concerning the initial program implementation provide a reality check for you. New priorities within the qualitative design also contribute to the deliberations regarding the new program balance. In the Northside Independent School District redesign process, the specialized skills of school counselors were better appreciated than they were during the initial program design efforts. Therefore, ensuring effective use of these skills for as many students as possible became an overriding priority for the redesign decision makers.

For example, in comparing the redesign with the original Northside Independent School District's design, shifts in priorities can easily be seen. The amount of time projected for school counselors to spend in guidance curriculum was decreased at all three levels, most significantly at the high school level (by 15%–20%) and was cut by half (from 30% to 15%–20%) for the middle school level. The amount of time allocated to individual student planning activities decreased significantly at the elementary level (from 25% to 5%–10%), decreased somewhat at the middle school level, and stayed about the same at the high school level. Responsive services time was increased at all three levels (from 25% to 40%–45%). System support time stayed fairly consistent. In addition, in the redesigned program, the steering committee chose to clearly express its opinion that school counselors' time should not be spent in nonguidance activities. They did this by appropriating zero time to these school management and clerical tasks.

Counselor–Student Ratio

Since the initial design of the comprehensive guidance and counseling program, the counselor–student ratio in the Northside Independent School District had been reduced significantly, from 1:550 to an average of 1:400. The positive results of an evaluation study reinforced the value of lower ratios, and the lower ratios made some of the shifts in program balance possible. The district still wanted (and has) a developmentally based guidance and counseling program, but with each school counselor responsible for fewer students, all of a school counselor's caseload could be serviced in less time.

At Northside, the steering committee adopted a goal of one counselor for every 350 students (1:350). Recommended ratios were altered for the school counselor specialists as follows:

- guidance department heads: 1:250 in middle and magnet high schools
- high school head counselors: no assigned student caseload, considering the expanded expectations for their leadership roles (Henderson & Gysbers, 1998)
- substance abuse counselors: 1:100 in their active caseload
- Special education counselors: 1:250

Number of Students Served

With a new program balance and with lowered caseloads, coupled with a better understanding of what each component included, the potential number of students served at Northside Independent School District in the various component activities was projected. This projection allowed the steering committee to establish minimum standards for the provision of activities for students. For example, the steering committee in Northside determined that it was feasible, within the balance and with the caseload, for elementary school students to benefit from 12 counselor-led guidance lessons per semester, for middle school students to benefit from eight counselor-led guidance lessons per year, and for high school students to benefit from six counselor-led guidance lessons per year. A legitimate expectation was that at any given time, approximately 25% of the students in a school counselor's caseload would benefit from responsive services.

Implement the New Design

Implementing a redesigned program entails specifying new directions for the redesigned program and planning for and making the improvements that are called for. These steps are identical to those described in Chapters 6 and 7 for implementing the initial comprehensive guidance and counseling program. The newly redesigned program must be approved by your district's policymakers, the senior administrators, and the school board. A new program handbook must be written and distributed to school counselors, building principals, and other program administrators. In-service education for these key players must be provided regarding the redesigned program and its implications.

Now that you have identified the discrepancies between the original design of your program and your redesigned program, you need to specify the changes required to implement the new design and to develop a plan for accomplishing the program improvements. You will most likely need new resources. Additional school counselors may be needed. New program improvement goals need to be set at the district and the building levels. Using new staff members, such as teachers, in the program requires education and training for carefully defined roles. Targeted training and other professional development activities are needed by school counselors to assist them to make the needed changes in their job descriptions as well as to ensure their competence in their changed roles. If new content areas are added, new materials must be developed or acquired. New advocacy efforts must be undertaken to inform staff members, parents, and other community members of the new priorities and resulting changes—especially the changes that will affect them. During the redesign process, your school district's steering and school–community advisory committees may also have recommended some changes in the ongoing processes used to plan, implement, monitor, and evaluate the program, its staff, and its results. These changes need to be attended to.

Understand That Revitalization Follows Redesign

Armed with data from the three types of evaluation described in Chapter 10 and with the new information you gathered regarding changes in students and in the school and community, you have fuel to spark the redesign of your program. Redesigning results in new standards for the program, new priorities, and new parameters. The memo summarizing the changes made in Northside Independent School District's program is provided in Appendix P. As can be seen, changes were made in every element of the program: content, use of counselors' skills, definition of the providers of the program, program shape and activities, and standards for accountability. In addition, the entire system for helping school counselors perform at their best was changed and is described in detail in *Leading and Managing Your School Guidance Program Staff* (Henderson & Gysbers, 1998).

An additional direct benefit in Northside Independent School District was that the evaluation and redesign sparked a revitalization of the program. The rethinking, replanning, and repreparing for implementation caused individual school counselors to recommit themselves as they pursue the growth it requires of them. Every building in the district took the opportunity to address the implications of the new design for their programs. At the district level, several initiatives were put in place to extend guidance program responsibilities across more staff members to provide more assistance for student development. The guidance curriculum component was extended by the addition of schoolwide character development programs. The individual student planning component was extended by implementing a student advisory program that focuses on helping students set and accomplish educational and career goals. The responsive services component was extended by more systematically coordinating the resources used to make schools safe and drug free with the guidance program and by establishing protocols for and clarifying staff roles in managing schoolwide crises.

In redesigning their programs after implementing them for some time, other school districts have enhanced their programs in other ways. In the School District of St. Joseph in St. Joseph, Missouri, they found a number of "ways to stretch the school day through collaborative strategies" (Fuston & Hargens, 2002, p. 211) that allow school counselors to do their work. They use retired counselors to substitute for absent counselors so that the work does not get omitted or backlogged. They have improved the ways that computers assist in guidance program implementation. Career education is done in collaboration with teachers and community members. The district hired social workers to respond to the social work–type needs of students and families and collaborate with community agencies that provide group counseling. In Davis School District in Farmington, Utah, the relationship between the guidance program mission and that of the school district was firmed up. Successful comprehensive guidance and counseling program implementation at the secondary level led to initiation of one at the elementary level and the hiring of elementary counselors (Davis, 2002).

In summary, redesigning your comprehensive guidance and counseling program after years of implementation leads to continued program enhancement and revitalization of the program, the school counseling staff, and the staff of the school as a whole. Revitalized commitment yields expanded services to students.

Your Progress Check

The program enhancement process or the redesign of your program follow the same process you used to develop and implement your program originally. As a result of reading this chapter, you know

- how often the program should be redesigned;
- who should be involved; and
- what steps should be taken.

You know how to begin the redesign process by gathering needs and evaluation data.
You can make redesign decisions on the basis of needs and evaluation data.
You know how to implement the enhanced or redesigned program.
You understand that revitalization follows redesign.

References

American School Counselor Association. (2005). *The ASCA National Model: A framework for school counseling programs* (2nd ed.). Alexandria, VA: Author.

Davis, D. (2002). Revising and enhancing Davis School District's comprehensive guidance program: Working together works. In P. Henderson & N. Gysbers (Eds.), *Implementing comprehensive school guidance programs: Critical leadership issues and successful responses* (pp. 219–228). Greensboro, NC: CAPS.

Fuston, J., & Hargens, M. (2002). Extending the program's resources. In P. Henderson & N. Gysbers (Eds.), *Implementing comprehensive school guidance programs: Critical leadership issues and successful responses* (pp. 211–217). Greensboro, NC: CAPS.

Henderson, P. G. (2009). *The new handbook of administrative supervision in counseling.* New York, NY: Routledge.

Henderson, P., & Gysbers, N. C. (1998). *Leading and managing your school guidance program staff.* Alexandria, VA: American Counseling Association.

Lippman, L., Atienza, A., Rivers, A., & Keith, J. (2008). *A developmental perspective on college and workplace readiness.* Washington, DC: Child Trends.

National Association of Secondary School Principals. (2004). *Breaking ranks II: Strategies for leading high school reform.* Reston, VA: Author.

National Association of Secondary School Principals. (2006). *Breaking ranks in the middle: Strategies for leading middle level reform.* Reston, VA: Author.

Substance Abuse and Mental Health Services Administration, Center for Mental Health Services. (2007). *Promotion and prevention in mental health: Strengthening parenting and enhancing child resilience* (DHHS Publication No. CMHS-SVP-0175). Rockville, MD: Author.

Appendixes

American School Counselor Association Ethical Standards for School Counselors

(Adopted 1984; revised 1992, 1998, 2004 and 2010)

Preamble

The American School Counselor Association (ASCA) is a professional organization whose members are school counselors certified/ licensed in school counseling with unique qualifications and skills to address all students' academic, personal/social and career development needs. Members are also school counseling program directors/supervisors and counselor educators. These ethical standards are the ethical responsibility of school counselors. School counseling program directors/supervisors should know them and provide support for practitioners to uphold them. School counselor educators should know them, teach them to their students and provide support for school counseling candidates to uphold them.

Professional school counselors are advocates, leaders, collaborators and consultants who create opportunities for equity in access and success in educational opportunities by connecting their programs to the mission of schools and subscribing to the following tenets of professional responsibility:

- Each person has the right to be respected, be treated with dignity and have access to a comprehensive school counseling program that advocates for and affirms all students from diverse populations including: ethnic/racial identity, age, economic status, abilities/disabilities, language, immigration status, sexual orientation, gender, gender identity/expression, family type, religious/spiritual identity and appearance.
- Each person has the right to receive the information and support needed to move toward self-direction and self-development and affirmation within one's group identities, with special care being given to students who have historically not received adequate educational services, e.g., students of color, students living at a low socio-economic status, students with disabilities and students from non-dominant language backgrounds.
- Each person has the right to understand the full magnitude and meaning of his/her educational choices and how those choices will affect future opportunities.
- Each person has the right to privacy and thereby the right to expect the school-counselor/student relationship to comply with all laws, policies and ethical standards pertaining to confidentiality in the school setting.
- Each person has the right to feel safe in school environments that school counselors help create, free from abuse, bullying, neglect, harassment or other forms of violence.

In this document, ASCA specifies the principles of ethical behavior necessary to maintain the high standards of integrity, leadership and professionalism among its members. The Ethical Standards for School Counselors were developed to clarify the nature of ethical responsibilities held in common by school counselors, supervisors/directors of school counseling programs and school counselor educators. The purposes of this document are to:

- Serve as a guide for the ethical practices of all professional school counselors, supervisors/directors of school counseling programs and school counselor educators regardless of level, area, population served or membership in this professional association;
- Provide self-appraisal and peer evaluations regarding school counselors' responsibilities to students, parents/guardians, colleagues and professional associates, schools, communities and the counseling profession; and
- Inform all stakeholders, including students, parents and guardians teachers, administrators, community members and courts of justice, of best ethical practices, values and expected behaviors of the school counseling professional.

A.1. Responsibilities to Students

Professional school counselors:

a. Have a primary obligation to the students, who are to be treated with dignity and respect as unique individuals.
b. Are concerned with the educational, academic, career, personal and social needs and encourage the maximum development of every student.
c. Respect students' values, beliefs and cultural background and do not impose the school counselor's personal values on students or their families.
d. Are knowledgeable of laws, regulations and policies relating to students and strive to protect and inform students regarding their rights.
e. Promote the welfare of individual students and collaborate with them to develop an action plan for success.
f. Consider the involvement of support networks valued by the individual students.
g. Understand that professional distance with students is appropriate, and any sexual or romantic relationship with students whether illegal in the state of practice is considered a grievous breach of ethics and is prohibited regardless of a student's age.
h. Consider the potential for harm before entering into a relationship with former students or one of their family members.

A.2. Confidentiality

Professional school counselors:

a. Inform individual students of the purposes, goals, techniques and rules of procedure under which they may receive counseling. Disclosure includes the limits of confidentiality in a developmentally appropriate manner. Informed consent requires competence on the part of students to understand the limits of confidentiality and therefore, can be difficult to obtain from students of a certain developmental level. Professionals are aware that even though every attempt is made to obtain informed consent it is not always possible and when needed will make counseling decisions on students' behalf.
b. Explain the limits of confidentiality in appropriate ways such as classroom guidance lessons, the student handbook, school counseling brochures, school Web site, ver-

bal notice or other methods of student, school and community communication in addition to oral notification to individual students.

c. Recognize the complicated nature of confidentiality in schools and consider each case in context. Keep information confidential unless legal requirements demand that confidential information be revealed or a breach is required to prevent serious and foreseeable harm to the student. Serious and foreseeable harm is different for each minor in schools and is defined by students' developmental and chronological age, the setting, parental rights and the nature of the harm. School counselors consult with appropriate professionals when in doubt as to the validity of an exception.

d. Recognize their primary obligation for confidentiality is to the students but balance that obligation with an understanding of parents'/guardians' legal and inherent rights to be the guiding voice in their children's lives, especially in value-laden issues. Understand the need to balance students' ethical rights to make choices, their capacity to give consent or assent and parental or familial legal rights and responsibilities to protect these students and make decisions on their behalf.

e. Promote the autonomy and independence of students to the extent possible and use the most appropriate and least intrusive method of breach. The developmental age and the circumstances requiring the breach are considered and as appropriate students are engaged in a discussion about the method and timing of the breach.

f. In absence of state legislation expressly forbidding disclosure, consider the ethical responsibility to provide information to an identified third party who, by his/her relationship with the student, is at a high risk of contracting a disease that is commonly known to be communicable and fatal. Disclosure requires satisfaction of all of the following conditions:

- Student identifies partner or the partner is highly identifiable
- School counselor recommends the student notify partner and refrain from further high-risk behavior
- Student refuses
- School counselor informs the student of the intent to notify the partner
- School counselor seeks legal consultation from the school district's legal representative in writing as to the legalities of informing the partner

g. Request of the court that disclosure not be required when the release of confidential information may potentially harm a student or the counseling relationship.

h. Protect the confidentiality of students' records and release personal data in accordance with prescribed federal and state laws and school policies including the laws within the Family Education Rights and Privacy Act (FERPA). Student information stored and transmitted electronically is treated with the same care as traditional student records. Recognize the vulnerability of confidentiality in electronic communications and only transmit sensitive information electronically in a way that is untraceable to students' identity. Critical information such as a student who has a history of suicidal ideation must be conveyed to the receiving school in a personal contact such as a phone call.

A.3. Academic, Career/College/Post-Secondary Access and Personal/Social Counseling Plans

Professional school counselors:

a. Provide students with a comprehensive school counseling program that parallels the ASCA National Model with emphasis on working jointly with all students to develop personal/social, academic and career goals.

b. Ensure equitable academic, career, post-secondary access and personal/social opportunities for all students through the use of data to help close achievement gaps and opportunity gaps.

c. Provide and advocate for individual students' career awareness, exploration and post-secondary plans supporting the students' right to choose from the wide array of options when they leave secondary education.

A.4. Dual Relationships

Professional school counselors:

a. Avoid dual relationships that might impair their objectivity and increase the risk of harm to students (*e.g.*, counseling one's family members or the children of close friends or associates). If a dual relationship is unavoidable, the school counselor is responsible for taking action to eliminate or reduce the potential for harm to the student through use of safeguards, which might include informed consent, consultation, supervision and documentation.

b. Maintain appropriate professional distance with students at all times.

c. Avoid dual relationships with students through communication mediums such as social networking sites.

d. Avoid dual relationships with school personnel that might infringe on the integrity of the school counselor/student relationship.

A.5. Appropriate Referrals

Professional school counselors:

a. Make referrals when necessary or appropriate to outside resources for student and/or family support. Appropriate referrals may necessitate informing both parents/guardians and students of applicable resources and making proper plans for transitions with minimal interruption of services. Students retain the right to discontinue the counseling relationship at any time.

b. Help educate about and prevent personal and social concerns for all students within the school counselor's scope of education and competence and make necessary referrals when the counseling needs are beyond the individual school counselor's education and training. Every attempt is made to find appropriate specialized resources for clinical therapeutic topics that are difficult or inappropriate to address in a school setting such as eating disorders, sexual trauma, chemical dependency and other addictions needing sustained clinical duration or assistance.

c. Request a release of information signed by the student and/or parents/guardians when attempting to develop a collaborative relationship with other service providers assigned to the student.

d. Develop a reasonable method of termination of counseling when it becomes apparent that counseling assistance is no longer needed or a referral is necessary to better meet the student's needs.

A.6. Group Work

Professional school counselors:

a. Screen prospective group members and maintain an awareness of participants' needs, appropriate fit and personal goals in relation to the group's intention and focus.

The school counselor takes reasonable precautions to protect members from physical and psychological harm resulting from interaction within the group.

b. Recognize that best practice is to notify the parents/guardians of children participating in small groups.

c. Establish clear expectations in the group setting, and clearly state that confidentiality in group counseling cannot be guaranteed. Given the developmental and chronological ages of minors in schools, recognize the tenuous nature of confidentiality for minors renders some topics inappropriate for group work in a school setting.

d. Provide necessary follow up with group members, and document proceedings as appropriate.

e. Develop professional competencies, and maintain appropriate education, training and supervision in group facilitation and any topics specific to the group.

f. Facilitate group work that is brief and solution-focused, working with a variety of academic, career, college and personal/social issues.

A.7. Danger to Self or Others

Professional school counselors:

a. Inform parents/guardians and/or appropriate authorities when a student poses a danger to self or others. This is to be done after careful deliberation and consultation with other counseling professionals.

b. Report risk assessments to parents when they underscore the need to act on behalf of a child at risk; never negate a risk of harm as students sometimes deceive in order to avoid further scrutiny and/or parental notification.

c. Understand the legal and ethical liability for releasing a student who is in danger to self or others without proper and necessary support for that student.

A.8. Student Records

Professional school counselors:

a. Maintain and secure records necessary for rendering professional services to the student as required by laws, regulations, institutional procedures and confidentiality guidelines.

b. Keep sole-possession records or individual student case notes separate from students' educational records in keeping with state laws.

c. Recognize the limits of sole-possession records and understand these records are a memory aid for the creator and in absence of privileged communication may be subpoenaed and may become educational records when they are shared or are accessible to others in either verbal or written form or when they include information other than professional opinion or personal observations.

d. Establish a reasonable timeline for purging sole-possession records or case notes. Suggested guidelines include shredding sole possession records when the student transitions to the next level, transfers to another school or graduates. Apply careful discretion and deliberation before destroying sole-possession records that may be needed by a court of law such as notes on child abuse, suicide, sexual harassment or violence.

e. Understand and abide by the Family Education Rights and Privacy Act (FERPA, 1974), which safeguards student's records and allows parents to have a voice in what and how information is shared with others regarding their child's educational records.

A.9. Evaluation, Assessment and Interpretation

Professional school counselors:

a. Adhere to all professional standards regarding selecting, administering and interpreting assessment measures and only utilize assessment measures that are within the scope of practice for school counselors and for which they are trained and competent.

b. Consider confidentiality issues when utilizing evaluative or assessment instruments and electronically based programs.

c. Consider the developmental age, language skills and level of competence of the student taking the assessments before assessments are given.

d. Provide interpretation of the nature, purposes, results and potential impact of assessment/evaluation measures in language the students can understand.

e. Monitor the use of assessment results and interpretations, and take reasonable steps to prevent others from misusing the information.

f. Use caution when utilizing assessment techniques, making evaluations and interpreting the performance of populations not represented in the norm group on which an instrument is standardized.

g. Assess the effectiveness of their program in having an impact on students' academic, career and personal/social development through accountability measures especially examining efforts to close achievement, opportunity and attainment gaps.

A.10. Technology

Professional school counselors:

a. Promote the benefits of and clarify the limitations of various appropriate technological applications. Professional school counselors promote technological applications (1) that are appropriate for students' individual needs, (2) that students understand how to use and (3) for which follow-up counseling assistance is provided.

b. Advocate for equal access to technology for all students, especially those historically underserved.

c. Take appropriate and reasonable measures for maintaining confidentiality of student information and educational records stored or transmitted through the use of computers, facsimile machines, telephones, voicemail, answering machines and other electronic or computer technology.

d. Understand the intent of FERPA and its impact on sharing electronic student records.

e. Consider the extent to which cyberbullying is interfering with students' educational process and base guidance curriculum and intervention programming for this pervasive and potentially dangerous problem on research-based and best practices.

A.11. Student Peer Support Program

Professional school counselors:

a. Have unique responsibilities when working with peer-helper or student-assistance programs and safeguard the welfare of students participating in peer-to-peer programs under their direction.

b. Are ultimately responsible for appropriate training and supervision for students serving as peer-support individuals in their school counseling programs.

B. Responsibilities to Parents/Guardians

B.1. Parent Rights and Responsibilities

Professional school counselors:

a. Respect the rights and responsibilities of parents/guardians for their children and endeavor to establish, as appropriate, a collaborative relationship with parents/guardians to facilitate students' maximum development.
b. Adhere to laws, local guidelines and ethical standards of practice when assisting parents/guardians experiencing family difficulties interfering with the student's effectiveness and welfare.
c. Are sensitive to diversity among families and recognize that all parents/guardians, custodial and noncustodial, are vested with certain rights and responsibilities for their children's welfare by virtue of their role and according to law.
d. Inform parents of the nature of counseling services provided in the school setting.
e. Adhere to the FERPA act regarding disclosure of student information.
f. Work to establish, as appropriate, collaborative relationships with parents/guardians to best serve student.

B.2. Parents/Guardians and Confidentiality

Professional school counselors:

a. Inform parents/guardians of the school counselor's role to include the confidential nature of the counseling relationship between the counselor and student.
b. Recognize that working with minors in a school setting requires school counselors to collaborate with students' parents/guardians to the extent possible.
c. Respect the confidentiality of parents/guardians to the extent that is reasonable to protect the best interest of the student being counseled.
d. Provide parents/guardians with accurate, comprehensive and relevant information in an objective and caring manner, as is appropriate and consistent with ethical responsibilities to the student.
e. Make reasonable efforts to honor the wishes of parents/guardians concerning information regarding the student unless a court order expressly forbids the involvement of a parent(s). In cases of divorce or separation, school counselors exercise a good-faith effort to keep both parents informed, maintaining focus on the student and avoiding supporting one parent over another in divorce proceedings.

C. Responsibilities to Colleagues and Professional Associates

C.1. Professional Relationships

*Professional school counselors, the school counseling program director/
site supervisor and the school counselor educator:*

a. Establish and maintain professional relationships with faculty, staff and administration to facilitate an optimum counseling program.
b. Treat colleagues with professional respect, courtesy and fairness.
c. Recognize that teachers, staff and administrators who are high-functioning in the personal and social development skills can be powerful allies in supporting student success. School counselors work to develop relationships with all faculty and staff in order to advantage students.

d. Are aware of and utilize related professionals, organizations and other resources to whom the student may be referred.

C.2. Sharing Information with Other Professionals

Professional school counselors:

a. Promote awareness and adherence to appropriate guidelines regarding confidentiality, the distinction between public and private information and staff consultation.
b. Provide professional personnel with accurate, objective, concise and meaningful data necessary to adequately evaluate, counsel and assist the student.
c. Secure parental consent and develop clear agreements with other mental health professionals when a student is receiving services from another counselor or other mental health professional in order to avoid confusion and conflict for the student and parents/guardians.
d. Understand about the "release of information" process and parental rights in sharing information and attempt to establish a cooperative and collaborative relationship with other professionals to benefit students.
e. Recognize the powerful role of ally that faculty and administration who function high in personal/social development skills can play in supporting students in stress, and carefully filter confidential information to give these allies what they "need to know" in order to advantage the student. Consultation with other members of the school counseling profession is helpful in determining need-to-know information. The primary focus and obligation is always on the student when it comes to sharing confidential information.
f. Keep appropriate records regarding individual students, and develop a plan for transferring those records to another professional school counselor should the need occur. This documentation transfer will protect the confidentiality and benefit the needs of the student for whom the records are written.

C.3. Collaborating and Educating Around the Role of the School Counselor

The school counselor, school counseling program supervisor/director and school counselor educator:

a. Share the role of the school counseling program in ensuring data driven academic, career/college and personal/social success competencies for every student, resulting in specific outcomes/indicators with all stakeholders.
b. Broker services internal and external to the schools to help ensure every student receives the benefits of a school counseling program and specific academic, career/college and personal/social competencies.

D. Responsibilities to School, Communities and Families

D.1. Responsibilities to the School

Professional school counselors:

a. Support and protect students' best interest against any infringement of their educational program.
b. Inform appropriate officials, in accordance with school policy, of conditions that may be potentially disruptive or damaging to the school's mission, personnel and property while honoring the confidentiality between the student and the school counselor.

c. Are knowledgeable and supportive of their school's mission, and connect their program to the school's mission.

d. Delineate and promote the school counselor's role, and function as a student advocate in meeting the needs of those served. School counselors will notify appropriate officials of systemic conditions that may limit or curtail their effectiveness in providing programs and services.

e. Accept employment only for positions for which they are qualified by education, training, supervised experience, state and national professional credentials and appropriate professional experience.

f. Advocate that administrators hire only qualified, appropriately trained and competent individuals for professional school counseling positions.

g. Assist in developing: (1) curricular and environmental conditions appropriate for the school and community; (2) educational procedures and programs to meet students' developmental needs; (3) a systematic evaluation process for comprehensive, developmental, standards-based school counseling programs, services and personnel; and (4) a data-driven evaluation process guiding the comprehensive, developmental school counseling program and service delivery.

D.2. Responsibility to the Community

Professional school counselors:

a. Collaborate with community agencies, organizations and individuals in students' best interest and without regard to personal reward or remuneration.

b. Extend their influence and opportunity to deliver a comprehensive school counseling program to all students by collaborating with community resources for student success.

c. Promote equity for all students through community resources.

d. Are careful not to use their professional role as a school counselor to benefit any type of private therapeutic or consultative practice in which they might be involved outside of the school setting.

E. Responsibilities to Self

E.1. Professional Competence

Professional school counselors:

a. Function within the boundaries of individual professional competence and accept responsibility for the consequences of their actions.

b. Monitor emotional and physical health and practice wellness to ensure optimal effectiveness. Seek physical or mental health referrals when needed to ensure competence at all times.

c. Monitor personal responsibility and recognize the high standard of care a professional in this critical position of trust must maintain on and off the job and are cognizant of and refrain from activity that may lead to inadequate professional services or diminish their effectiveness with school community members. Professional and personal growth are ongoing throughout the counselor's career.

d. Strive through personal initiative to stay abreast of current research and to maintain professional competence in advocacy, teaming and collaboration, culturally competent counseling and school counseling program coordination, knowledge and use of technology, leadership, and equity assessment using data.

e. Ensure a variety of regular opportunities for participating in and facilitating professional development for self and other educators and school counselors through continuing education opportunities annually including: attendance at professional school counseling conferences; reading *Professional School Counseling* journal articles; facilitating workshops for education staff on issues school counselors are uniquely positioned to provide.

f. Enhance personal self-awareness, professional effectiveness and ethical practice by regularly attending presentations on ethical decision-making. Effective school counselors will seek supervision when ethical or professional questions arise in their practice.

g. Maintain current membership in professional associations to ensure ethical and best practices.

E.2. Multicultural and Social Justice Advocacy and Leadership

Professional school counselors:

a. Monitor and expand personal multicultural and social justice advocacy awareness, knowledge and skills. School counselors strive for exemplary cultural competence by ensuring personal beliefs or values are not imposed on students or other stakeholders.

b. Develop competencies in how prejudice, power and various forms of oppression, such as ableism, ageism, classism, familyism, genderism, heterosexism, immigrationism, linguicism, racism, religionism and sexism, affect self, students and all stakeholders.

c. Acquire educational, consultation and training experiences to improve awareness, knowledge, skills and effectiveness in working with diverse populations: ethnic/racial status, age, economic status, special needs, ESL or ELL, immigration status, sexual orientation, gender, gender identity/expression, family type, religious/spiritual identity and appearance.

d. Affirm the multiple cultural and linguistic identities of every student and all stakeholders. Advocate for equitable school and school counseling program policies and practices for every student and all stakeholders including use of translators and bilingual/multilingual school counseling program materials that represent all languages used by families in the school community, and advocate for appropriate accommodations and accessibility for students with disabilities.

e. Use inclusive and culturally responsible language in all forms of communication.

f. Provide regular workshops and written/digital information to families to increase understanding, collaborative two-way communication and a welcoming school climate between families and the school to promote increased student achievement.

g. Work as advocates and leaders in the school to create equity-based school counseling programs that help close any achievement, opportunity and attainment gaps that deny all students the chance to pursue their educational goals.

F. Responsibilities to the Profession

F.1. Professionalism

Professional school counselors:

a. Accept the policies and procedures for handling ethical violations as a result of maintaining membership in the American School Counselor Association.

b. Conduct themselves in such a manner as to advance individual ethical practice and the profession.

c. Conduct appropriate research, and report findings in a manner consistent with acceptable educational and psychological research practices. School counselors advocate for the protection of individual students' identities when using data for research or program planning.

d. Seek institutional and parent/guardian consent before administering any research, and maintain security of research records.

e. Adhere to ethical standards of the profession, other official policy statements, such as ASCA's position statements, role statement and the ASCA National Model and relevant statutes established by federal, state and local governments, and when these are in conflict work responsibly for change.

f. Clearly distinguish between statements and actions made as a private individual and those made as a representative of the school counseling profession.

g. Do not use their professional position to recruit or gain clients, consultees for their private practice or to seek and receive unjustified personal gains, unfair advantage, inappropriate relationships or unearned goods or services.

F.2. Contribution to the Profession

Professional school counselors:

a. Actively participate in professional associations and share results and best practices in assessing, implementing and annually evaluating the outcomes of data-driven school counseling programs with measurable academic, career/college and personal/social competencies for every student.

b. Provide support, consultation and mentoring to novice professionals.

c. Have a responsibility to read and abide by the ASCA Ethical Standards and adhere to the applicable laws and regulations.

F.3. Supervision of School Counselor Candidates Pursuing Practicum and Internship Experiences:

Professional school counselors:

a. Provide support for appropriate experiences in academic, career, college access and personal/social counseling for school counseling interns.

b. Ensure school counselor candidates have experience in developing, implementing and evaluating a data-driven school counseling program model, such as the ASCA National Model.

c. Ensure the school counseling practicum and internship have specific, measurable service delivery, foundation, management and accountability systems.

d. Ensure school counselor candidates maintain appropriate liability insurance for the duration of the school counseling practicum and internship experiences.

e. Ensure a site visit is completed by a school counselor education faculty member for each practicum or internship student, preferably when both the school counselor trainee and site supervisor are present.

F.4. Collaboration and Education about School Counselors and School Counseling Programs with other Professionals

School counselors and school counseling program directors/supervisors collaborate with special educators, school nurses, school social workers, school psychologists, college counselors/

admissions officers, physical therapists, occupational therapists and speech pathologists to advocate for optimal services for students and all other stakeholders.

G. *Maintenance of Standards*

Professional school counselors are expected to maintain ethical behavior at all times.

> **G.1. When there exists serious doubt as to the ethical behavior of a colleague(s) the following procedure may serve as a guide:**

1. The school counselor should consult confidentially with a professional colleague to discuss the nature of a complaint to see if the professional colleague views the situation as an ethical violation.
2. When feasible, the school counselor should directly approach the colleague whose behavior is in question to discuss the complaint and seek resolution.
3. The school counselor should keep documentation of all the steps taken.
4. If resolution is not forthcoming at the personal level, the school counselor shall utilize the channels established within the school, school district, the state school counseling association and ASCA's Ethics Committee.
5. If the matter still remains unresolved, referral for review and appropriate action should be made to the Ethics Committees in the following sequence:
   • State school counselor association
   • American School Counselor Association
6. The ASCA Ethics Committee is responsible for:
   • Educating and consulting with the membership regarding ethical standards
   • Periodically reviewing and recommending changes in code
   • Receiving and processing questions to clarify the application of such standards.

Questions must be submitted in writing to the ASCA Ethics Committee chair.

• Handling complaints of alleged violations of the ASCA Ethical Standards for School Counselors. At the national level, complaints should be submitted in writing to the ASCA Ethics Committee, c/o the Executive Director, American School Counselor Association, 1101 King St., Suite 625, Alexandria, VA 22314.

> **G.2. When school counselors are forced to work in situations or abide by policies that do not reflect the ethics of the profession, the school counselor works responsibly through the correct channels to try and remedy the condition.**

> **G.3. When faced with any ethical dilemma school counselors, school counseling program directors/supervisors and school counselor educators use an ethical decision-making model such as Solutions to Ethical Problems in Schools (STEPS) (Stone, 2001):**

1. Define the problem emotionally and intellectually
2. Apply the ASCA Ethical Standards and the law
3. Consider the students' chronological and developmental levels
4. Consider the setting, parental rights and minors' rights

5. Apply the moral principles
6. Determine Your potential courses of action and their consequences
7. Evaluate the selected action
8. Consult
9. Implement the course of action

Note. From *Ethical Standards for School Counselors.* Copyright 2010 by the American School Counselor Association, Alexandria, VA. Reprinted with permission.

Guidelines and Template for Conducting an Annual Time–Task Analysis

The goal of the time–task analysis is to obtain a representative sample of counselor time spent in carrying out the comprehensive guidance and counseling program. The data are then used to determine the extent to which time is appropriately divided between the components of the school's comprehensive guidance and counseling program. Used in conjunction with the Internal Improvement Review, the data can provide information about how fully the comprehensive guidance and counseling program is being implemented. The time–task analysis is to be conducted periodically throughout the school year. An electronic format for conducting the time–task analysis was developed by the statewide Time/Task Committee and is available online at http://www.mcce.org.

The state committee established the following guidelines for conducting the annual time–task analysis:

I. *Categorizing Time and Task by Program Components*

A. **Guidance and Counseling Curriculum:** The guidance and counseling curriculum provides guidance and counseling content based on the guidance and counseling standards to all students and their parents through classroom presentations and large-group activities such as career days, college fairs, and parent workshops. Remember that the guidance and counseling curriculum provides direct services to all students and their parents. Therefore, time spent in conducting classroom and parent presentations, other large-group activities, and curriculum planning is to be documented as guidance and counseling curriculum.

B. **Individual Student Planning:** The focus of individual student planning is to assist all students to develop Personal Plans of Study, enabling them to plan, monitor, and manage their academic, career, and personal–social development. Work on individual student planning can be done with individual students, with small groups of students, in student–parent conferences, and workshops. Remember that individual student planning provides direct services to all students. Therefore, time spent in preparation and working directly with students and their parents using Personal Plans of Study is to be documented as individual student planning. The following are examples of individual student planning activities:

1. Individual and small group meetings with students to develop Personal Plans of Study using appropriate student data, including test data (i.e., Explore, Plan, PSAT, ACT), and career and educational information
   a. Enrollment of new students;

2. Reviewing and revising Personal Plans of Study with students individually or in small groups
   a. Course advisement and selection
   b. Schedule revision, based on identified need;
3. Personal Plans of Study conferences with students and parents
   a. Post–high school planning
   b. Retention conferences;
4. Preparing for individual student planning activities.

C. **Responsive Services:** Responsive services include preparation for and delivery of individual counseling, small-group counseling, consultation, and workshops about specific student behaviors with teachers, administrators, parents, and other professional school staff and referral. Remember, responsive services are available to all students, but all students may not require these services. The following are examples of responsive service activities:

1. Individual counseling: Regularly scheduled individual counseling sessions with students.
2. Small-group counseling: Regularly scheduled small-group counseling sessions. The focus is on small-group counseling and not on the guidance and counseling curriculum or individual student planning activities.
3. Consultation: Conferences and workshops with teachers, administrators, parents, other professional school staff, or community agency personnel about individual student behaviors.
4. Referral: The referral process includes such activities as
   a. referral paperwork;
   b. initial and ongoing consultation with parents and other professional staff;
   c. initial and ongoing contact with referral agencies;
   d. activities relating to the reentry process;
   e. ongoing monitoring of student readjustment;
   f. preparation for responsive services activities.

D. **System Support:** System support includes those activities that support the implementation and delivery of the comprehensive guidance and counseling program as well as other educational programs in the school, district, or both. System support includes such activities as

1. guidance and counseling program evaluation activities;
2. school and community committees;
3. program advocacy activities, including presentations to staff, parents, and community;
4. professional development activities;
5. fair-share responsibilities—those activities that are the responsibility of all school faculty, including school counselors, and that may include such things as schoolwide testing, master schedule consultation, bus and playground duty, class or club sponsorship, ticket selling or taking, etc.

E. **Non–Guidance and Counseling:** The Missouri Comprehensive Guidance and Counseling Program cannot be fully implemented if school counselors are involved in non–guidance and counseling duties. Non–guidance and counseling duties are duties other than fair share that counselors may currently be performing but that are not part of the district's comprehensive guidance and counseling program. These activities take time away from school counselors' ability to fully implement the program. As such, the Missouri Comprehensive Guidance and Counseling Program does not support the inclusion of non–guidance and counseling activities as school counselor responsibilities. These activities are grouped as follows:

1. Supervisory duties:
   a. coordinating and monitoring school assemblies;
   b. hall duty, cafeteria and playground supervision, bus loading and unloading supervision, and restroom supervision;
   c. chaperoning school functions and athletic event supervision;
   d. substitute teaching;
2. Clerical duties:
   a. selling lunch tickets;
   b. collecting and mailing out progress reports and deficiency notices;
   c. paperwork involved in 504 plans, student assistance teams, and other special programs that could be performed by clerical staff;
   d. maintaining permanent records and handling transcripts;
   e. monitoring attendance;
   f. calculating grade point averages, class ranks, and honor rolls or gathering data for special programs such as Missouri Scholars Academy, Joseph Baldwin Academy, Talent Identification Program, etc.;
   g. completing the paperwork related to changing students' schedules;
3. Administrative duties:
   a. developing and updating the student handbook;
   b. developing and updating course guides;
   c. developing the master schedule;
   d. acting as the principal of the day;
   e. administering discipline;
4. Coordination of the schoolwide testing program: The overall coordination and administration of the schoolwide testing program is the responsibility of the administration. If everyone else in the building is involved in the administration or proctoring of schoolwide testing, then school counselors should also be involved on a fair-share basis. The following steps will assist school counselors in determining how to categorize time spent in the testing process:
   a. Figure out how much time, on average, a teacher spends involved in the testing process.
   b. Calculate how much time you spend involved in the same testing process.
   c. Any amount of time that a counselor spends that is equal to the teacher's average involvement should be categorized as system support. Any amount of time that a counselor spends over and above the teacher's average time involvement is considered non–guidance and counseling.

II. *Conducting the Time–Task Analysis*

A. All school counselors in the district will select the same 5 days spread throughout each semester to conduct the time–task survey. These 5 days should reflect typical days within the month that contain a variety of guidance and counseling program activities within the four components as well as any non–guidance and counseling activities that may be present.

B. Because school days in every building consist of a minimum number of minutes, the time–task analysis survey results will be recorded in minutes. The sample survey form included in this appendix uses 15-minute intervals for the recording of time spent in activities. Note that the survey form includes opportunities to record time spent in guidance and counseling program activities conducted before and after school. An electronic version of this form can be found at http://www.mcce.org.

C. **Special Considerations:** The following are not counted in the time–/task analysis:
1. duty free lunch;
2. personal breaks;
3. doctors' appointments.

Counselor Time & Task Analysis Form: 15 Minute

Time	Guidance and Counseling Curriculum	Individual Planning	Responsive Services	System Support	Non–guidance and Counseling Activities
7:00–7:15 a.m.					
7:15–7:30 a.m.					
7:30–7:45 a.m.					
7:45–8:00 a.m.					
8:00–8:15 a.m.					
8:15–8:30 a.m.					
8:30–8:45 a.m.					
8:45–9:00 a.m.					
9:00–9:15 a.m.					
9:15–9:30 a.m.					
9:30–9:45 a.m.					
9:45–10:00 a.m.					
10:00–10:15 a.m.					
10:15–10:30 a.m.					
10:30–10:45 a.m.					
10:45–11:00 a.m.					
11:00–11:15 a.m.					
11:15–11:30 a.m.					
11:30–11:45 a.m.					
11:45–12:00 p.m.					
12:00–12:15 p.m.					
12:15–12:30 p.m.					
12:30–12:45 p.m.					
12:45–1:00 p.m.					
1:00–1:15 p.m.					
1:15–1:30 p.m.					
1:30–1:45 p.m.					
1:45–2:00 p.m.					
2:00–2:15 p.m.					
2:15–2:30 p.m.					
2:30–2:45 p.m.					
2:45–3:00 p.m.					
3:00–3:15 p.m.					
3:15–3:30 p.m.					
3:30–3:45 p.m.					
3:45–4:00 p.m.					

Time	Guidance and Counseling Curriculum	Individual Planning	Responsive Services	System Support	Non–guidance and Counseling Activities
Number of blocks:	0	0	0	0	0
Daily percentage:					
Total number of blocks:		0	Total percentages = 100%		
Counselor:				Date:	

Counselor Time & Task Analysis Form 15 Minute

Time	Guidance and Counseling Curriculum	Individual Planning	Responsive Services	System Support	Non–guidance and Counseling Activities
7:00–7:15 a.m.					
7:15–7:30 a.m.					
7:30–7:45 a.m.					
7:45–8:00 a.m.					
8:00–8:15 a.m.	15				
8:15–8:30 a.m.	15				
8:30–8:45 a.m.	15				
8:45–9:00 a.m.	15				
9:00–9:15 a.m.					
9:15–9:30 a.m.		15			
9:30–9:45 a.m.		15			
9:45–10:00 a.m.		15			
10:00–10:15 a.m.		15			
10:15–10:30 a.m.		15			
10:30–10:45 a.m.		15			
10:45–11:00 a.m.		15			
11:00–11:15 a.m.		15			
11:15–11:30 a.m.					
11:30–11:45 a.m.			15		
11:45–12:00 p.m.			15		
12:00–12:15 p.m.			15		
12:15–12:30 p.m.	15				
12:30–12:45 p.m.	15				
12:45–1:00 p.m.	15				
1:00–1:15 p.m.		15			
1:15–1:30 p.m.		15			
1:30–1:45 p.m.		15			
1:45–2:00 p.m.				15	
2:00–2:15 p.m.				15	
2:15–2:30 p.m.				15	
2:30–2:45 p.m.					15
2:45–3:00 p.m.					15
3:00–3:15 p.m.				15	
3:15–3:30 p.m.				15	
3:30–3:45 p.m.				15	
3:45–4:00 p.m.				15	

Time	Guidance and Counseling Curriculum	Individual Planning	Responsive Services	System Support	Non–guidance and Counseling Activities
Number of blocks:	7	11	3	7	2
Daily percentage:	23.33%	36.67%	10.00%	23.33%	6.67%
Total number of blocks:		30	Total percentages = 100%		
Counselor:				Date:	

Time Distribution Form
Elementary Level

Current District Program Percentages

Current District
Program Percentages:

____ guidance curriculum
____ individual planning
____ responsive services
____ system support
____ nonguidance

State-Suggested
Percentages:

35%–45% guidance curriculum
5%–10% individual planning
30%–40% responsive services
10%–15% system support
0% nonguidance

State Suggested Percentages

Desired District Program Percentages

Desired District
Program Percentages:

____ guidance curriculum
____ individual planning
____ responsive services
____ system support
____ nonguidance

Time Distribution Form
Middle School/Junior High Level

Current District Program Percentages

Current District Program Percentages:

_____ guidance curriculum
_____ individual planning
_____ responsive services
_____ system support
_____ nonguidance

State-Suggested Percentages:

25%–35% guidance curriculum
15%–25% individual planning
30%–40% responsive services
10%–15% system support
0% nonguidance

State Suggested Percentages

Desired District Program Percentages

Desired District Program Percentages:

_____ guidance curriculum
_____ individual planning
_____ responsive services
_____ system support
_____ nonguidance

Time Distribution Form
High School Level

Current District Program Percentages

Current District Program Percentages:

____ guidance curriculum
____ individual planning
____ responsive services
____ system support
____ nonguidance

State-Suggested Percentages:

15%–25%	guidance curriculum
25%–35%	individual planning
25%–35%	responsive services
15%–20%	system support
0%	nonguidance

State Suggested Percentages

Desired District Program Percentages

Desired District Program Percentages:

____ guidance curriculum
____ individual planning
____ responsive services
____ system support
____ nonguidance

Note. From *Missouri Comprehensive Guidance Program: A Manual for Program Development, Implementation, Evaluation, and Enhancement,* by N. C. Gysbers, L. Kosteck-Bunch, C. S. Magnuson, & M. Starr, 2012. Copyright by the Department of Elementary and Secondary Education, Jefferson City, MO. Reprinted with permission.

Appendix C

Guidance Program Evaluation Surveys

1. A LOOK AT THE COUNSELORS—FROM THE HIGH SCHOOL STUDENT'S POINT OF VIEW

INSTRUCTIONS: Circle one category in each of the three demographic areas in the box below.

GRADE: 9 10 11 12 **GENDER:** Female Male **ETHNICITY:** Native American Asian Black Hispanic White

WAYS IN WHICH YOU MET WITH A COUNSELOR: About how many times has a counselor met with you in each of the following ways?

	Since Winter Vacation	For the Entire School Year
Classroom presentation by a counselor	_____	_____
Small-group meetings with a counselor	_____	_____
One-on-one meetings with a counselor	_____	_____
Student–parent–counselor conferences	_____	_____
Student–teacher–counselor conferences	_____	_____
Meetings with a counselor and someone from outside the school	_____	_____

SERVICES PROVIDED OR TOPICS DISCUSSED BY A COUNSELOR

	HAS A COUNSELOR MET WITH YOU TO . . .			IF IT HAPPENED, WAS IT HELPFUL?			
	Yes	Unsure	No	Very Much	Quite a Bit	Some-what	Very Little	Not Really
. . . help manage your feelings?							
. . . provide guidance so you can make good decisions?							
. . . guide you in taking responsibility for your educational planning?							
. . . assist in setting goals and making plans?							
. . . help you in accepting the consequences of your decisions?							
. . . help you manage changes?							
. . . aid in understanding others' behaviors?							
. . . help you take responsibility for your behavior?							
. . . help you cope with peer relationships?							
. . . set challenging educational goals?							

432

SERVICES PROVIDED OR TOPICS DISCUSSED BY A COUNSELOR (*Continued*)

	HAS A COUNSELOR MET WITH YOU TO . . .			IF IT HAPPENED, WAS IT HELPFUL?				
	Yes	Unsure	No	Very Much	Quite a Bit	Some-what	Very Little	Not Really
. . . help establish personal goals?								
. . . make available information on educational opportunities?								
. . . help you select specific high school courses reflecting your educational goals?								
. . . assist in making plans for achieving short-, intermediate, and long-term goals?								
. . . relate jobs to interests, skills, values, and education?								
. . . assist in career and/or vocational planning?								
. . . discuss the importance of time management?								
. . . talk about peer pressure?								
. . . address health-related problems?								
. . . help with behavior problems?								
. . . aid in explaining test results?								
. . . help you to deal with feelings of grief and/or loss?								
. . . give you information on community agencies and/or resources?								
. . . provide help when you were experiencing academic difficulty?								
. . . just listen?								
. . . help you deal with stress?								
. . . coordinate conferences between your parents and school staff?								
. . . help you deal with a drug and/or alcohol problem?								
. . . offer guidance on a personal, private issue?								

YOUR CLOSING THOUGHTS: What was the one service or topic of discussion that was *most beneficial* or *helpful* to you?

_____

_____

YOUR CLOSING THOUGHTS: Overall, is the high school guidance program meeting your needs?   YES   UNSURE   NO   Why?

_____

_____

2. A LOOK AT THE COUNSELORS—FROM THE HIGH SCHOOL COUNSELOR'S POINT OF VIEW

STUDENT CONTACT: Over the course of the school year, of the total student body, about what percentage did you meet with in each of the following ways (to the nearest 5%)? To the nearest 10th (X.X times) about how many times did you meet with the average student in each of the following ways?

	Percentage of Student Body	Number of Times per Student
Classroom presentations	_____	_____
Small-group meetings	_____	_____
One-on-one meetings	_____	_____
Student–parent–counselor conferences	_____	_____
Student–teacher–counselor conferences	_____	_____
Meetings with a student and someone from outside the school	_____	_____

SERVICES PROVIDED OR TOPICS DISCUSSED

	FOR THE STUDENTS FOR WHOM YOU WERE ASSIGNED, HOW MANY DID YOU MEET TO...							WAS IT HELPFUL TO THE STUDENTS?				
(see scale below)	6	5	4	3	2	1		Very Much	Quite a Bit	Some-what	Very Little	Not Really
. . . help manage their feelings?												
. . . provide guidance to help them make good decisions?												
. . . guide them in taking responsibility for their educational planning?												
. . . assist in setting goals and making plans?												
. . . help in accepting the consequences of their decisions?												
. . . help manage changes?												
. . . aid in understanding others' behaviors?												
. . . help take responsibility for their behavior?												
. . . help cope with peer relationships?												
. . . help set challenging educational goals?												
. . . help establish personal goals?												

6 = All, virtually all   5 = Most   4 = Quite a few   3 = Some; more than just a few   2 = Only a handful, or so   1 = None, virtually none

SERVICES PROVIDED OR TOPICS DISCUSSED
(Continued)

SERVICES PROVIDED OR TOPICS DISCUSSED (see scale below)	FOR THE STUDENTS FOR WHOM YOU WERE ASSIGNED, HOW MANY DID YOU MEET TO...						WAS IT HELPFUL TO THE STUDENTS?				
	6	5	4	3	2	1	Very Much	Quite a Bit	Some-what	Very Little	Not Really
...make available information on educational opportunities?											
...help select specific high school courses reflecting their educational goals?											
...assist in making plans for achieving short-, intermediate, and long-term goals?											
...relate jobs to interests, skills, values and education?											
...assist in career and/or vocational planning?											
...discuss the importance of time management?											
...talk about peer pressure?											
...address health-related problems?											
...help with behavior problems?											
...aid in explaining test results?											
...help in dealing with feelings of grief and/or loss?											
...give them information on community agencies and/or resources?											
...provide help when they were experiencing academic difficulty?											
...just listen?											
...help deal with stress?											
...coordinate conferences between parents and school staff?											
...help deal with a drug and/or alcohol problem?											
...offer guidance on a personal, private issue?											

6 = All, virtually all   5 = Most   4 = Quite a few   3 = Some; more than just a few   2 = Only a handful, or so   1 = None, virtually none

YOUR CLOSING THOUGHTS: What was the one service or discussion that was *most beneficial or helpful* to the students?

_____

_____

YOUR CLOSING THOUGHTS: Overall, is the high school guidance program meeting your needs?   YES   UNSURE   NO   Why?

_____

_____

3. A LOOK AT THE COUNSELORS FROM THE HIGH SCHOOL TEACHER'S POINT OF VIEW

BACKGROUND INFORMATION:

Campus name: _____

Number of years on this campus (include this year): _____

All the grade levels with which you work: 9   10   11   12

Subject area(s) you teach (mark all that apply):

_____ English   _____ Mathematics   _____ Natural Sciences   _____ Social Sciences

_____ International Languages   _____ Career/Technology Education   _____ Fine Arts

_____ Special Education   _____ Other: _____

SPECIALIZED ROLES: Does your campus have a counselor clearly designated as a (circle one):

. . . Special Education Counselor?	YES	UNSURE	NO
. . . Substance Abuse and Prevention Education Counselor?	YES	UNSURE	NO

Using this coding scheme, circle your observations for each of the following statements. Occurrence: Y = Yes, it occurred. U = Unsure if it occurred. N = No, it never occurred. Helpfulness (If it occurred, did it help the students?):
++ = Very helpful   + = Somewhat helpful   − = Not very helpful   − − = Not at all helpful

	Occurrence	Helpfulness
Counselors (using the Guidance Curriculum) . . .		
. . . assist students in their personal development.	Y U N	++ + − − −
. . . assist students in their social development.	Y U N	++ + − − −
. . . assist students in their career development.	Y U N	++ + − − −
. . . assist students in their educational development.	Y U N	++ + − − −
. . . help students function effectively with others in school.	Y U N	++ + − − −
. . . are an integral part of the school community team.	Y U N	++ + − − −
. . . have favorable interpersonal relations among the school staff.	Y U N	++ + − − −
. . . have adequate physical facilities and equipment.	Y U N	++ + − − −
. . . consult and coordinate with teachers in guidance curriculum delivery.	Y U N	++ + − − −
. . . train teachers in guidance curriculum delivery.	Y U N	++ + − − −
. . . directly teach the guidance curriculum.		
Counselors (using the Individual Planning System) . . .		
. . . conduct group guidance sessions.	Y U N	++ + − − −
. . . ensure accurate and meaningful interpretation of tests and other appraisal results.	Y U N	++ + − − −
. . . consult with those responsible for providing other career and educational information.	Y U N	++ + − − −
. . . collaborate with teachers in the development of individual planning system activities and procedures such as preregistration and testing.	Y U N	++ + − − −

(Continued)

	Occurrence			Helpfulness				
. . . hold new-student orientation seminars.	Y	U	N	+ +	+	−	− −	
. . . disseminate information from special testing (e.g., PSAT, SAT, ASVAB).	Y	U	N	+ +	+	−	− −	
Counselors (using Responsive Services) . . .								
. . . conduct group counseling.	Y	U	N	+ +	+	−	− −	
. . . plan interventions to anticipate recurring problems or situations faced by students due to their developmental stage.	Y	U	N	+ +	+	−	− −	
. . . collaboratively work with mental health specialists as needed.	Y	U	N	+ +	+	−	− −	
. . . maintain appropriate documentation and records as needed.	Y	U	N	+ +	+	−	− −	
. . . provide procedures whereby teachers can make referrals to the counseling office.	Y	U	N	+ +	+	−	− −	
. . . counsel individual students.	Y	U	N	+ +	+	−	− −	
Counselors (providing Support Services to other programs) . . .								
. . . maintain ongoing efforts for better integration of guidance program goals with district goals.	Y	U	N	+ +	+	−	− −	
. . . help in informing the school community of the program mission, purposes, and services available.	Y	U	N	+ +	+	−	− −	
. . . manage the guidance program competently and appropriately.	Y	U	N	+ +	+	−	− −	
. . . demonstrate professionalism.	Y	U	N	+ +	+	−	− −	
. . . guide individuals and groups of students through the development of educational and career plans.	Y	U	N	+ +	+	−	− −	
. . . consult with parents to enhance their relationship with their children.	Y	U	N	+ +	+	−	− −	
. . . consult with teachers to enhance their work with students.	Y	U	N	+ +	+	−	− −	
. . . coordinate with community personnel to bring together resources for students.	Y	U	N	+ +	+	−	− −	
. . . use an effective referral process for assisting students and others to use special programs and services.	Y	U	N	+ +	+	−	− −	
. . . participate in the standardized testing program.	Y	U	N	+ +	+	−	− −	
. . . interpret tests and other appraisal results to students.	Y	U	N	+ +	+	−	− −	
. . . adhere to ethical, legal, and professional standards.	Y	U	N	+ +	+	−	− −	
. . . work cooperatively with campus and district staff members.	Y	U	N	+ +	+	−	− −	

ONE FINAL THOUGHT: If you could make one change that would most improve the guidance program, what would it be? _____

_____

_____

Sample Board of Education Policies for Referrals and for Student Guidance and Counseling Programs

Student Guidance and Counseling Referrals

The FIELD (District Common Name) is focused on the safety and healthy development of its students. The district cannot address all student needs, but will assist students and their families in seeking outside assistance, particularly in situations where a student's life or health is at risk. Staff members are required to refer students for further assessment in accordance with this procedure.

Definitions

Referral Coordinator—Person or persons in the district with specialized training in the assessment of suicide risk who are responsible for receiving and responding to all reports under this procedure.
Suicidal Behavior—An umbrella term that encompasses any behavior that is symptomatic of suicide.
Suicidal Ideation—Thoughts and ideas about committing suicide.
Suicidal Intent—A specific plan and motivation to carry out suicidal ideation.
Suicide Warning Signs—An overt indicator of suicide risk in a particular individual.

Identification of Students for Referral

In general, suicidal behaviors develop over time, allowing for identification of students who become increasingly at risk of suicide before the students actually attempt suicide. Drug and alcohol use and mental health issues are often associated with suicide and attempted suicide. While treatment is a job for mental health professionals, staff members can contribute by identifying certain risk factors and referring students for further assessment.

All staff members who, in the course of their duties, have contact with students on a regular basis will receive annual training that will include:

1. The symptoms of alcohol or drug abuse.
2. The symptoms of mental health problems.
3. Identification of suicidal behavior, including risk factors for suicide, suicide warning signs and familiarity with the assessment process used by mental health professionals.

Reporting

The referral coordinator(s) for the district is (are):

[Title (e.g., High School Counselor)]
[Address]
[Phone]

All reports of drug or alcohol use, suspected mental health issues or suicidal behaviors must be submitted to the referral coordinator in writing. In urgent situations where there is an imminent threat to the health or life of the student, the referral may be made verbally and reduced to writing as soon as possible. Once a report is received, the referral coordinator will:

1. Assess the student.
2. Report drug or alcohol use that violates district policies to the building administrator.
3. Notify parents/guardians of the referral and the results of the assessment.
4. Notify the building administrator of the results of the assessment.
5. If appropriate or if requested, provide information about outside services and identify low- or no-cost services. The referral coordinator will maintain a comprehensive list, including current contact information, of mental health services providers, drug and alcohol counseling and treatment providers, and other appropriate public and private services available to students and their parents/guardians.
6. At the request of the parent/guardian, make a referral to an outside service selected by the parent/guardian.
7. Follow up with the referring staff member by providing information the staff member needs to know to perform his or her duties as they relate to the student.

The referral coordinator will not make recommendations as to which services parents/guardians or the student should use or promise or imply that the district will assume financial responsibility for such services.

Students Identified as Having Suicidal Intent

If a staff member identifies a student with suicidal intent, the staff member will notify the referral coordinator and the building administrator and will stay with the student until the referral coordinator arrives. The following actions should be completed by the referral coordinator, the building administrator or another staff member in the absence of the referral coordinator or building administrator:

1. Do not allow the student to leave school. Call the police if the student attempts to leave.
2. Notify the parents/guardians.
3. Ask the student to turn over any suicide implements, such as pills or weapons, if such a request can be made safely.
4. Make a police report if the student has weapons or drugs.
5. Take the student to a designated safe area.

Confidentiality

It is necessary for counselors to build trusting relationships with students and district staff; however, counselors are not permitted to promise students complete confidentiality.

Counselors may at times be required to disclose information to parents/guardians, to report child abuse or neglect, to convey to district staff information necessary to better serve a student, or to report to supervisors as appropriate.

****

Note: The reader is encouraged to review policies and/or forms for related information in this administrative area.

Implemented: FIELD (Adopt Date)
Revised:
MSIP Refs: 6.9
FIELD (District Location Line)

Student Guidance and Counseling

Definitions

Counselor: For the purposes of this policy, a counselor is a school counselor as defined by the Department of Elementary and Secondary Education (DESE).
Guidance Advisory Committee (GAC): A committee composed of at least one (1) counselor from each grade level, a principal, teachers and others as determined by the superintendent.

General

The FIELD (District Common Name)'s comprehensive guidance program provides important benefits to all students at all grade levels by addressing their personal/social, academic and career development needs. Research indicates that a fully implemented comprehensive guidance program has a positive impact on student achievement and has the potential to increase attendance, reduce discipline referrals and improve Missouri Assessment Program (MAP) scores. In support of the district's efforts to improve student achievement, the Board requires full implementation of the Missouri Comprehensive Guidance Program and will adhere to all of its standards. The program shall be implemented in each attendance area and is considered an integral part of each school's educational program. Guidance program objectives will be aligned with the district's Comprehensive School Improvement Plan (CSIP) and student performance data. The program shall be implemented by certified school counselors with the support of district staff, students and external organizations and agencies.

Guidance Curriculum

Counselors will create and implement a written guidance curriculum that promotes students' academic, career and personal/social development. The Board will provide resources and support activities for implementation of a K–12 guidance curriculum. The guidance curriculum will be systematically reviewed and revised, and modifications to the guidance curriculum will be based on student data, school data and needs-assessment data collected at least every three (3) years.

Individual Planning

Individual planning activities help all students plan, monitor and manage their academic achievement as well as their personal/social and career development. The foundation for individual planning will be established during the elementary school years through guidance activities. Building on this foundation, the individual planning component of the guidance program will assist middle school students as they begin to plan for the future and will continue to support students in their planning endeavors until graduation. A four- to six-year Personal Plan of Study (PPS) will be initiated for students no later than the eighth grade and will minimally include assessment and advisement activities, collaboration with parents/guardians, and identification of long- and short-range educational career goals. The PPS will be reviewed annually and revised as needed.

Responsive Services

Responsive services are referrals and other actions taken by the district in response to the immediate needs and concerns of a particular student or identified needs and concerns of groups of students. The purpose of the responsive services component of the comprehensive guidance program is to work with students whose personal circumstances, concerns or problems are interfering or threatening to interfere with their academic, career or personal/social development. Responsive services will be implemented through individual counseling, small group counseling, consultation and referral.

Referrals shall be made in accordance with Board policies and district procedures. The superintendent, with the assistance of the GAC, will develop procedures for staff to use to identify students who may need a referral for assistance beyond that regularly provided by the counseling staff. All staff members who, in the course of their duties, have contact with students on a regular basis will receive annual training on these procedures.

In the event of a pandemic or other emergency, school counseling staff will assist students with personal and emotional issues. The district's emergency response intervention plan (ERIP) will include methods for continuing counseling support even in the event of a long-term school closure.

System Support

The Board recognizes system support as a crucial component in the full implementation of a comprehensive guidance program. System support of the comprehensive guidance program includes administration and management activities that support the program. The Board directs the administration to implement activities that support the guidance program, such as program management, fair-share responsibilities, professional development, staff–community relations, consultation, committee participation, community outreach, and research and development.

Program Goals

The district will strive to meet the program goals in each of the following areas:

1. *Personal/Social Development*
   - Assist students in gaining an understanding of self as an individual and as a member of diverse local and global communities by emphasizing knowledge that leads

to the recognition and understanding of the interrelationship of thoughts, feelings and actions in students' daily lives.

- Provide students with a solid foundation for interacting with others in ways that respect individual and group differences.
- Aid students in learning to apply physical and psychological safety and promoting the student's ability to advocate for him- or herself.

2. *Academic Development*
- Guide students to apply the skills needed for educational achievement by focusing on self-management, study and test-taking skills.
- Teach students skills to aid them as they transition between grade levels or schools.
- Focus on developing and monitoring personal education plans, emphasizing the understanding, knowledge and skills students need to develop meaningful personal plans of study.

3. *Career Development*
- Enable students to apply career exploration and planning skills in the achievement of life career goals.
- Educate students about where and how to obtain information about the world of work and postsecondary training and education.
- Provide students the opportunity to learn employment readiness skills and skills for on-the-job success, including responsibility, dependability, punctuality, integrity, self-management and effort.

Confidentiality

It is necessary for counselors to build trusting relationships with students and district staff; however, counselors are not permitted to promise students complete confidentiality. Counselors may at times be required to disclose information to parents/guardians, to report child abuse or neglect, to convey to district staff information necessary to better serve a student, or to report to supervisors as appropriate.

Care should be taken in explaining to students, in a developmentally appropriate manner, the limits of confidentiality. Notice of the limits of confidentiality may be made by a variety of methods including classroom lessons, student handbooks, the district website and guidance counseling brochures in addition to oral notification of individual students.

District counselors have the responsibility to protect the confidentiality of student records and only release information in accordance with state and federal law and Board policy. Information transmitted or stored electronically must maintain the same level of confidentiality as traditional paper records. Care shall be taken to send sensitive information by a means that protects student identity.

Guidance Advisory Committee and Evaluation

The GAC will systematically review the district's comprehensive guidance program, including the K–12 guidance curriculum. The comprehensive guidance program will be systematically evaluated through the development and use of a comprehensive evaluation plan. The comprehensive evaluation plan will minimally assess the impact of the comprehensive guidance program on the Missouri School Improvement Plan (MSIP) performance standards and other relevant criteria including, but not limited to, attendance, grades and behaviors.

****

Note. The reader is encouraged to check the index located at the beginning of this section for other pertinent policies and to review administrative procedures and/or forms for related information.

Adopted: FIELD (Adopt Date)
Revised:
Cross Refs: EBCA, Crisis Intervention Plan
              IL, Assessment Program
MSIP Refs: 6.9, 7.7, 8.8
FIELD (District Location Line)

Sample Job Descriptions

High School Counselor

Primary Function: to provide, as a member of the guidance department staff, a comprehensive guidance and counseling program for students in Grades 9–12 and specifically to provide services to meet the special needs of his/her assigned caseload (450); to consult with teachers, staff, and parents to enhance their effectiveness in helping students' educational, career, personal, and social development; and to provide support to other high school educational programs.

Major Job Responsibilities: (1) teach the high school guidance curriculum; (2) guide groups of students and individual students through the development of educational and career plans; (3) counsel small groups and individual students through the development of educational and career plans; (4) counsel small groups and individual students with problems; (5) consult with teachers, staff, and parents regarding meeting the developmental needs of adolescents and regarding specific information about the youths for whom they have responsibility; (6) refer students or their parents with problems to specialists or special programs; (7) participate in, coordinate, or conduct activities that contribute to the effective operation of the school; (8) plan and evaluate the campus guidance program; and (9) pursue continuous professional development.

Illustrative Key Duties:

(1) *teach the high school guidance curriculum:* conduct developmental guidance lessons in classroom settings as planned in conjunction with the instructional departments, or through the advisory system or study halls, or as otherwise devised in conjunction with the school administration; consult with or be a resource person to teachers to facilitate the infusion of guidance content into the regular education curriculum.

(2) *guide groups and individual students through the development of educational and career plans:* provide orientation activities for students new to the school such as brown bag lunch sessions; participate in orientation programs for incoming 9th graders; guide 9th and 10th graders in updating of their "High School 4-Year Plans"; guide 11th and 12th graders to evaluate their current status and plan their achievement of high school graduation; guide 12th graders to develop and take appropriate steps toward implementing their post-high-school educational or career plans; plan/coordinate/assist in preregistration of 9th, 10th, and 11th graders for 10th, 11th, and 12th grades, respectively; collaborate with middle school counselors to effect the preregistration of 8th graders for 9th grade; assist students new to the district with course selection at the time of registration; interpret standardized tests (TAAS [Texas Assessment of Academic Skills], PLAN [a career guidance and pre-ACT tool] results information to students, parents, and teachers; guide groups and individual students in applying the test results information to their educational and career plans; interpret results of college entrance tests or career assessments to groups of students; guide all students to develop tentative career/vocational plans through the conduct or supervision of career education activities such as career center orientations and use

of the DISCOVER system and other career center resources; provide a mechanism for the systematic and efficient dissemination of current, accurate information needed by individual students or parents as they develop their educational or career plans.

(3) *counsel small groups and individual students with problems:* conduct structured, goal-oriented counseling sessions in systematic response to identified needs of individuals or groups of students—recurrent topics at the high school level include academic failure, attendance and behavior problems, peer problems, family issues, child abuse, substance abuse, suicide threats and attempts, and sexuality issues.

(4) *consult with teachers, staff, and parents regarding meeting the developmental needs of adolescents and regarding specific information about the youths for whom they have responsibility:* participate in staffings; conduct in-service programs for faculty as a whole or by departments; conduct/facilitate conferences with teachers, students, or parents; conduct or provide opportunities for parent and education programs; write articles for parent newsletters; assist families with school-related problems.

(5) *refer students or their parents with problems to specialists or special programs:* consult and coordinate with in-district and community specialists such as school nurses, administrators, and psychologists and community-based psychologists, service agencies, and physicians.

(6) *participate in, coordinate, or conduct activities that contribute to the effective operation of the school:* cooperate with administration in planning and implementing preregistration and PREP days; interpret group test results to faculty and staff; contribute to the principal's goals for enhancing education on the campus; cooperate with instructional staff in implementing the "Placement Recommendation Guidelines"; establish effective liaisons with the various instructional departments; provide input to administration as the master schedule is built; act as an advocate for groups or individual students as system decisions are made; supervise the changing of student schedules in accordance with district policies; cooperate with other school staff in placing students with special needs in appropriate programs, including other regular education, special education, and career and technology education opportunities; cooperate with administration/coordinate campus-wide administration of the district testing program (TAAS, PLAN); supervise administration of special group testing (e.g., PSAT, SAT, ACT, AP; the Armed Services Vocational Aptitude Battery [ASVAB]); cooperate with administration/supervise the teacher advisory system.

(7) *plan and evaluate the campus guidance program:* annually design, with other members of the guidance department staff, the campus guidance program based on needs by clearly stating program goals and objectives, establishing the guidance department calendar, and completing the Annual Guidance Program Plan–High School; evaluate strategies as they are implemented; complete the annual Guidance Program Evaluation Report–High School.

(8) *pursue continuous professional growth:* attend district-sponsored staff development offerings; join associations (e.g., Northside Counseling Association, South Texas Counseling Association, Texas Counseling Association, American Counseling Association); read professional journals; attend relevant workshops and conferences sponsored by professionally appropriate organizations (e.g., Region 20, Texas Education Agency, and associations); take postgraduate courses.

Organizational Relationships: is supervised by the head counselor, the principal, and the director of guidance; works collaboratively with other counselors and guidance department staff; and works cooperatively with other campus or district staff.

Performance Standards: A high school counselor's performance is considered satisfactory when (1) the head counselor, principal, and director of guidance concur and the counselor's level of competence is reflected as such on the Northside Independent School District Counselor Evaluation Form; and (2) evaluation of the Annual Guidance Program Plan–High School indicates overall effectiveness of the program.

Director of Guidance

Reports to: Assistant Superintendent for Student Services

Educational and Certification Requirements:
Master's degree in School Counseling from an accredited program. Valid Administrators' certificate for elementary and secondary levels issued by the Texas Education Agency.
At least 5 years' successful experience in school counseling.

Supervises: 1. Comprehensive Guidance Program

Job Performance Statements

I. Instructional Management

1. Administers the efforts of the counselors to provide a guidance program that meets the needs of all students.
2. Plans, designs, implements, and evaluates the guidance program with counselors, principals, and other district administrators.
3. Works cooperatively with others in developing the mission and articulating a vision for the campus's and district's program.
4. Uses knowledge of guidance content and the program development process to facilitate counselor development of appropriate guidance and counseling experiences for students.
5. Works with building principals in creating more effective campus guidance programs.
6. Is aware of the district's curricula and instructional implementation strategies and the ways that the guidance department supports instruction.
7. Facilitates the use of existing technology in the guidance program.
8. Encourages and supports the development and implementation of innovative strategies to meet identified needs of students.
9. Is effective in involving guidance staff in evaluating and selecting materials to meet identified student needs and program goals.

II. School/Organizational Climate

10. Has high expectations and high regard for staff and communicates this perspective to them.
11. Effectively communicates with staff, community, media, and school board on the district's mission, policies, and programs, especially as they relate to the guidance program and the counseling staff.
12. Develops cooperatively with other district staff, long- and short-range plans related to department and division responsibilities.
13. Promotes collegiality, teamwork, and participatory decision making among guidance department staff members.
14. Demonstrates skill in conflict resolution with counselors, administrators, parents, and/or the community.
15. Responds appropriately to situations that could impair the educational environment or could threaten the safety and well-being of students and staff.

16. Adheres and promotes adherence to and interprets appropriately the Codes of Ethics related to school counseling.

III. School/Organizational Improvement

17. Focuses the guidance department's operations toward the accomplishment of the program and the district's mission and attainment of the program's and district's stated goals and objectives.
18. Plans and conducts needs assessments related to department's operations.
19. Applies the findings of research that relate effective guidance and counseling strategies to overall school district and campus program improvement.
20. Develops workable policies and procedures pertinent to the effectiveness of the department.
21. Systematically monitors guidance program implementation.
22. Uses relevant evaluative findings to determine the extent to which goals and objectives are met and to provide the basis for continuous program improvement.
23. Uses and helps others to use student assessment data appropriately in interpreting, reporting, and acting on results.
24. Actively supports the efforts of others to achieve district and campus goals and objectives.

IV. Personnel Management

25. Administers district program for recruitment, selection, orientation, and assignment of counselors.
26. Administers the district's program of counselor evaluation.
27. Administers the preparation and revision of guidance department job descriptions.
28. Maintains a viable application system for counselors that not only represents the district in a positive and professional manner but also facilitates the recruitment and selection process.
29. Administers the Northside Independent School District Counselor Performance Improvement System in collaboration with other responsible administrators.
30. Administers clinical supervision as a means to improve counselor effectiveness in the implementation of the guidance program.
31. Conferences regularly with counselors' supervisors to discuss performance quality.
32. Administers the system by which counselors develop performance improvement objectives and identify professional growth opportunities.
33. Provides guidance program resources and materials to counselors within the limits of available resources.
34. Secures consultants, specialists, and other resources to assist counselors in attaining guidance program objectives.
35. Uses the mission of the school district, program evaluation outcomes, and input from counselors and others to provide effective in-service activities for counselors.

V. Administration and Fiscal/Facilities Management

36. Prepares, recommends, and implements the budget for the guidance program.
37. Administers the process for selecting, evaluating, and purchasing varied materials and equipment to be used in the guidance program.

38. Offers constructive suggestions to ensure that policies and regulations support the educational environment.
39. Analyzes facility and equipment needs for optimum guidance program implementation.
40. Uses information to make necessary changes or adjustments in the guidance program.
41. Demonstrates responsible fiscal control over assigned program budgets.
42. Compiles and maintains written records and reports as required and/or as desirable for continued improvement of the guidance program.

VI. Student Management/Relations

43. Has sufficient understanding of the discipline management system to handle cases brought to his or her attention.
44. Ensures that the guidance program is effective in supporting the educational environment.
45. Supports district and campus rules for conduct.

VII. School/Organizational–Community Relations

46. Cooperates with nondistrict personnel to augment the resources available to students through the guidance program.
47. Articulates appropriately to the general public the school district's overall mission and goals and the ways in which the functions of the guidance department support these directives.
48. Communicates about the district guidance program to parents and the community; solicits their input on relevant issues.
49. Participates in activities of the Northside Council of PTAs to foster rapport and mutual respect between the district and the larger community.
50. Effectively communicates the district's philosophy and guidance program information to the media.
51. Demonstrates a commitment to the mission of the district as it is communicated to the public.

VIII. Professional Growth and Development

52. Actively seeks and uses evaluative feedback from subordinates, peers, and superordinates, using such information to improve performance.
53. Keeps abreast of the profession through participating in a variety of professional development activities.
54. Participation in professional development activities leads to improved job performance.
55. Performs duties in a professional, ethical, and responsible manner, as defined in the Texas Education Agency Code of Ethics for Educators and in the Code of Ethics of the American Counseling Association.

IX. Other

56. Performs other tasks and assumes other responsibilities as may be assigned.

Career Guidance Center Technician

Job Description

The Career Guidance Center Technician, under the supervision of the Head Counselor, operates the High School Career Center and implements portions of the Career Guidance Program.

Duties and Responsibilities

1. Collects and organizes occupational data to provide source materials for Career Center.
2. Teaches portions of the Career Guidance Program to all grade levels of students in class-size groups.
3. Assists teachers and counselors to locate and use career information and materials.
4. Orders, catalogues, maintains files on, and distributes materials relating to job opportunities, careers, vocational programs, schools, colleges, scholarships, grants and loans, armed forces, and other programs.
5. Operates and teaches students to operate audiovisual equipment, the computerized career information system, and personal computers.
6. Coordinates the career guidance speaker program.
7. Assists students to take and score self-administered career interest and other assessments.
8. Makes presentations to teachers and parents to encourage their and students' use of the center.
9. Maintains the Career Center facility and equipment, and schedules their use.
10. Performs some bookkeeping and other general secretarial functions.
11. Assists guidance department as assigned by the Head Counselor.

Minimum Qualifications

High school graduate and one of the following:

- business college certificate
- satisfactory completion of at least one semester of college work, including at least one business course
- enrollment in business college or has completed training in acceptable program leading to proficiency in job assignment
- successful completion of two courses in business college
- successful demonstration of several areas of technical competency, including typing, transcription, filing procedures, and office records management

High School Registrar

Job Description

Under the supervision of the Head Counselor, the High School Registrar maintains students' permanent records and generates related information from the records.

Duties and Responsibilities

1. Register/enroll students new to the district and transfer students within the district.
2. Complete new student records.
3. Input data on Academic Achievement Records.
4. Maintain students' Academic Achievement Records.
5. Maintain files for current and withdrawn students.
6. Coordinate student withdrawals.
7. Send transcripts for active/inactive students upon written request.
8. Request transcripts for new/transfer students.
9. Track graduation progress for all students, consulting with counselors on exceptional cases.
10. Calculate sixth- and seventh-semester ranks and averages.
11. Prepare inactive records for microfilming and destruction according to established schedule.
12. Maintain office equipment and supplies.
13. Do typing and correspondence required in the office.
14. Provide information from the permanent records, in accordance with the Family Educational and Privacy Rights Act (FERPA).
15. Train and supervise student office assistants.
16. Communicate important information as pertains to counselors or administrators.
17. Carry out other duties and responsibilities as assigned by the Head Counselor.

Minimum Qualifications

High school graduate and one of the following:

- Business college certificate
- Appropriate clerical/secretarial skills
- Three years' experience as an educational secretary
- Satisfactory completion of at least one semester of college work, including at least one business course
- Successful demonstration of required technical competency and office records management

Note. From Northside Independent School District, San Antonio, TX. Reprinted with permission.

Procedures for Helping Students Manage Personal Crises

Subject: **Procedures for Helping Students Manage Personal Crises**

To: **All Personnel**

The following procedures have been developed over the past several years and are now being circulated to provide guidance to staff members in applying sound professional judgment when assisting students who are dealing with personal crises. Special reporting requirements, such as those relating to suspected child abuse, are not supplanted by these procedures.

Definition

Students in personal crises are defined as those who are in jeopardy of endangering their own or others' health safety and/or well-being. Students in such crises may be, for example:

- those who threaten to commit suicide, to run away from home, or to otherwise endanger themselves or others;
- those who are or who suspect themselves to be seriously ill, acutely or chronically depressed, grieving, or pregnant;
- those who are using illegal substances, and/or abusing drugs or other substances; or
- those who have engaged in, or are seriously contemplating engaging in, criminal activity (e.g., theft, arson, property damage).

Assumptions and Considerations

There are *constraints to confidentiality*. Students must be informed that some things cannot be kept confidential. School counselors, nurses, administrators, and others must balance their respect for the student's rights and their own responsibilities to the parent(s)/guardian and other authorities by adhering to the following ethical standard:

> Informs parents/guardians or appropriate authorities when the student's condition indicates a clear and imminent danger to the counselee or others. This is to be done after careful deliberation and, where possible, after consultation with other professionals. (ASCA Code of Ethics, 2004)

The school professionals must be careful not to assume the parental role. The student has a right to confidentiality within these limitations; when those limitations are crossed, the parent has the right to know so that appropriate responsibility can be taken to help the student resolve the problem that has precipitated the crisis.

The students must also be helped to feel that the school professionals care about their health, safety, and well-being and will help them resolve their problems within certain boundaries. They must also be helped to understand that their parents have primary responsibility for their health, safety, and well-being and, therefore, must be informed of the crisis and the students' intended plans.

Therefore, a goal of the student-professional interaction in managing a personal crisis situation is for the student's parent/guardian to be informed of the problem in a timely manner. It is preferable in most cases that the student inform the parent(s) and that the professional validate that the student has done so.

Parent/guardian is the person with the responsibility for the student in relationship to the school. For the purposes of this process, the student's having attained age 18 or being legally married does not remove the expectation that a responsible adult (e.g., parent, guardian, or spouse) be notified.

In a timely manner is relative to the situation; the time frame is dictated by the circumstance. The parent(s) or guardian must be informed in time to carry out parental responsibility to help the student. The time frame should also allow the professional(s) involved to provide appropriate consultation to the parent(s) or guardian.

Timeliness is not defined by an arbitrary time frame (e.g., 24 hours, 48 hours) but rather is relative to the situation. For example: the situation of a female student considering terminating a pregnancy within a day or two dictates a very short time frame; the situation of an elementary child planning in February to run away in the summer suggests a longer time frame may be available for resolving the problem.

Note: In some atypical situations, legal statutes, board policy, and/or sound professional judgment dictate that official agencies or other professionals responsible for the student (e.g., department of human services, local law enforcement agencies, probation officer, private therapist) be notified in addition to or instead of the parent/guardian. In making such a decision, it is always wise to consult with the principal.

Procedures

The staff members who typically are involved in helping students resolve personal crisis situations are counselors, nurses, and assistant/vice principals. Teachers and other staff members also need to be aware of those procedures and resources. The school principal is ultimately accountable for the professional management of such cases.

The procedures outlined below rest on the premise that the professionals involved make their decision based on the application of professional judgment to the presenting circumstances and given the information that is available to them.

1. Listen with care, compassion, and sensitivity to the student presenting a problem that may indicate a crisis or an impending crisis.
2. In responding, explain the limits of confidentiality, including clear and imminent danger, goal of informing parents, possibility of consultation and referral.
3. Gather data to make a professional determination about the case (e.g., actuality of the crisis situation, degree of danger, urgency).
4. Develop the plan of action. This step may entail:
   a. Consulting with other professionals, as appropriate, regarding the case and the plan of action.
   b. Referring the student to other professionals who have the expertise to help or who provide the link to community agencies with such expertise (i.e., the counselor

for psychological problems, the nurse for medical problems, the administration for legal problems).

   c. Making the principal aware of the situation.

5. Implement the plan.
6. Counsel the student and ensure that the parents are informed.
7. Monitor the student's progress through to resolution of the problem.
8. Follow up with the student, parent, and/or other professionals after apparent resolution of the problem.

Leadership/Responsibility

The professional who first receives the information from the troubled student must take the leadership in deciding how to handle the situation. This includes deciding which other professionals need to be involved, how, and to what extent. In conversation with the student, it is important to identify other individuals with whom the student has shared the information/problem in order to protect as much as possible the student's right to privacy and confidentiality. Others should be informed of the problem and the relevant details of the situation only on a need-to-know basis.

When more than one professional has received the information/is involved in working with the student to resolve the problem, a team approach is essential. The professionals should jointly decide on the best plan of action, including the time frame, parent notification, the actions to be taken, and the persons responsible. In establishing the plan for helping the student manage the crisis, consideration should be given to such things as the student's age, the family circumstance, the degree of danger, and the urgency of the situation. Relevant Central Office staff—e.g., the Director of Guidance, the Director of Psychological Services, the Coordinator of Health Services— are available for consultation.

If the professionals working with the case are unable to agree on a plan of action, the decision should be deferred to the principal.

Note. From Northside Independent School District, San Antonio, TX. Reprinted with permission.

Impact of Program Balance and Ratio on Program Implementation

Impact of Program Balance on Program Implementation

Alternate Desired Program Balance

	% ES	% MS	% HS
Guidance Curriculum	20	15	10
Individual Student Planning	20	30	40
Responsive Services	50	45	40
System Support	10	10	10
Nonguidance	0	0	0

Activity Slots/Program Component/Week

Elementary School
   Activity Slot = 30 minutes
   School Day = 7 hours
   Activity Slots/Day = 14
   Activity Slots/Week = 70
      Guidance Curriculum   20% (70) = 14
      Individual Student Planning   20% (70) = 14
      Responsive Services   50% (70) = 35
      System Support   10% (70) = 7

Middle School
   Activity Slot = 45 minutes
   School Day = 7 hours
   Activity Slots/Day = 9
   Activity Slots/Week = 45
      Guidance Curriculum   15% (45) = 7
      Individual Student Planning   30% (45) = 14
      Responsive Services   45% (45) = 20
      System Support   10% (45) = 4

High School
   Activity Slot = 55 minutes
   School Day = 7 hours
   Activity Slots/Day = 7
   Activity Slots/Week = 35
      Guidance Curriculum   10% (35) = 4
      Individual Student Planning   40% (35) = 14
      Responsive Services   40% (35) = 14
      System Support   10% (35) = 3

Impact of Ratio on Program Implementation Service Levels/ Program Balance and Counselor-Student Ratio, 1:100

Desired Program Balance

	% ES	% MS	% HS
Guidance Curriculum	40	35	20
Individual Student Planning	10	20	30
Responsive Services	40	35	35
System Support	10	10	15
Nonguidance	0	0	0

Elementary School

Average Class Size: 1:25   Average teacher–student ratio: 1:20
36 weeks per school year

Guidance Curriculum   40% (70) = 28 Activity Slots/Week
    100 counselees/25 students per class   = 4 classes
    28 activity slots/4 classes   = 7 activities/class/week
    252 guidance lessons per year per class

Individual Student Planning   10% (70) = 7 Activity Slots/Week
    7 activity slots × 36 weeks   = 252 slots per year
    252 slots 30 minutes per slot   = 7,560 minutes per year
    7,560 minutes/100 counselees   = 75 minutes per student per year

Responsive Services   40% (70) = 28 Activity Slots/Week
    14 slots for groups (average 6)   = 84 students
    14 slots for individuals   = 14 students
    Total students served at one time   = 98
                       (98 is 98% of the caseload)

System Support   10% (70) = 7 Activity Slots/Week
    100 students/20 students per teacher   = 5 teachers
    7 slots/5 teachers   = 1.4 slots per week per teacher
    7 slots per week × 30 minutes per slot = 210 minutes per week
    210 minutes/5 days   = 42 minutes per day

Elementary School Counselor Potential:
    7 guidance lessons per week
    75 minutes per student per year
    98% receiving responsive services in any one time period
    42 minutes per teacher per week
    42 minutes a day for indirect services to students

Middle School

Average Class Size: 1:25   Average teacher–student ratio: 1:20
36 weeks per school year

Guidance Curriculum   35% (45) = 16 Activity Slots/Week
    100 counselees/25 students per class   = 4 classes
    16 activity slots/4 classes   = 4 activities/class/week
    144 guidance lessons per year per class

Individual Student Planning   20% (45) = 9 Activity Slots/Week
    9 activity slots × 36 weeks   = 324 slots per year
    324 slots × 45 minutes per slot   = 14,580 minutes per year
    14,580 minutes/100 counselees   = 145 minutes per student per year

Responsive Services   35% (45) = 16 Activity Slots/Week
    8 slots for groups (average 9)   = 72 students
    8 slots for individuals   = 8 students
    Total students served at one time   = 80
                       (80 is 80% of the caseload)

System Support   10% (45) = 4 Activity Slots/Week
- 100 students/20 students per teacher   = 5 teachers
- 4 slots/5 teachers   = 4/5 slot per week per teacher
- 4 slots per week × 45 minutes per slot = 180 minutes per week
- 180 minutes/5 days   = 36 minutes per day

Middle School Counselor Potential:
- 4 guidance lessons per week
- 145 minutes per student per year
- 80% receiving responsive services at any one time
- 36 minutes per teacher per week
- 36 minutes a day for indirect services to students

High School

Average Class Size: 1:25   Average teacher–student ratio: 1:20
36 weeks per school year

Guidance Curriculum   20% (35) = 7 Activity Slots/Week
- 100 counselees/25 students per class = 4 classes
- 7 activity slots/4 classes   = 1.75 activities/class/week
- 63 guidance lessons per year per class

Individual Student Planning   30% (35) = 11 Activity Slots/Week
- 11 activity slots = 336 weeks   = 396 slots per year
- 396 slots = 55 minutes per slot   = 21,780 minutes per year
- 21,780 minutes/100 counselees   = 2,178 minutes per student per year

Responsive Services   35% (35) = 12 Activity Slots/Week
- 6 slots for groups (average 10)   = 60 students
- 6 slots for individuals   = _6 students
- Total students served at one time = 66
                                 (66 is 66% of the caseload)

System Support   15% (35) = 5 Activity Slots/Week
- 100 students/20 students per teacher = 5 teachers
- 5 slots/5 teachers   = 1 slot per week per teacher
- 5 slots per week × 55 minutes per slot = 275 minutes per week
- 275 minutes/5 days   = 55 minutes per day

High School Counselor Potential:
- > 1 guidance lesson
- 2,178 minutes per student per year
- 66% receiving responsive services at any one time
- 55 minutes per teacher per week
- 55 minutes a day for indirect services to students

Service Levels/Program Balance and Counselor-Student Ratio, 1:500

Desired Program Balance

	% ES	% MS	% HS
Guidance Curriculum	40	35	20
Individual Student Planning	10	20	30
Responsive Services	40	35	35
System Support	10	10	15
Nonguidance	0	0	0

Elementary School
Average Class Size: 1:25   Average teacher–student ratio: 1:20
36 weeks per school year

Guidance Curriculum   40% (70) = 7 Activity Slots/Week
    500 counselees/25 students per class   = 20 classes
    28 activity slots/20 classes   = 1.4 activities/class/week
    50 + guidance lessons per year per class

Individual Student Planning   10% (70) = 7 Activity Slots/Week
    7 activity slots × 36 weeks   = 252 slots per year
    252 slots × 30 minutes per slot   = 7,560 minutes per year
    7,560 minutes/500 counselees   = 15 minutes per student per year

Responsive Services   40% (70) = 28 Activity Slots/Week
    14 slots for groups (average 6)   = 84 students
    14 slots for individuals   = <u>14</u> students
    Total students served at one time   = 98
               (98 is 19.6% of the caseload)

System Support   10% (70) = 7 Activity Slots/Week
    500 students/20 students per teacher   = 25 teachers
    7 slots/25 teachers   = 1/4 slot per week per teacher
    7 slots per week × 30 minutes per slot   = 210 minutes per week
    210 minutes/5 days   = 42 minutes per day

Elementary School Counselor Potential:
    1+ guidance lessons per week
    15 minutes per student per week
    19.6% receiving responsive services at any one time
    8 minutes per teacher per week, or nearly 4 weeks for all
    42 minutes a day for indirect services to students

Middle School
Average Class Size: 1:25   Average teacher–student ratio: 1:20
36 weeks per school year

Guidance Curriculum   35% (45) = 16 Activity Slots/Week
    500 counselees/25 students per class   = 20 classes
    16 activity slots/20 classes   = 8 activities/class/week
    28+ guidance lessons per year per class

Individual Student Planning   20% (45) = 9 Activity Slots/Week
    9 activity slots × 36 weeks   = 324 slots per year
    324 slots × 45 minutes per slot   = 14,580 minutes per year
    14,580 minutes/500 counselees   = 29+ minutes per student per year

Responsive Services   35% (45) = 16 Activity Slots/Week
    8 slots for groups (average 9)   = 72 students
    8 slots for individuals   = <u>8</u> students
    Total students served at one time   = 80
               (80 is 16% of the caseload)

System Support   10% (45) = 4 Activity Slots/Week
     500 students/20 students per teacher   = 25 teachers
     4 slots/25 teachers   = .16 slot per week per teacher
     4 slots per week × 45 minutes per slot   = 180 minutes per week
     180 minutes/5 days   = 36 minutes per day

Middle School Counselor Potential:
     > 1 guidance lesson per week
     29 minutes per student per year
     16% receiving responsive services at any time
     7 minutes per teacher per week, or 6weeks to consult with all
     36 minutes a day for indirect services to students

High School

Average Class Size: 1:25   Average teacher–student ratio: 1:20
36 weeks per school year

Guidance Curriculum   20% (35) = 7 Activity Slots/Week
     500 counselees/25 students per class   = 20 classes
     7 activity slots/20 classes   = .35 activities/class/week
     12+ guidance lessons per year per class

Individual Student Planning   30% (35) = 11 Activity Slots/Week
     11 activity slots × 36 weeks   = 396 slots per year
     396 slots × 55 minutes per slot   = 21,780 minutes per year
     21,780 minutes/500 counselees   = 43+ minutes per student per year

Responsive Services   35% (35) = 12 Activity Slots/Week
     6 slots for groups (average 10)   = 60 students
     6 slots for individuals   = 6 students
     Total students served at one time   = 66
                                 (66 is 13% of the caseload)

System Support   15% (35) = 5 Activity Slots/Week
     500 students/20 students per teacher   = 25 teachers
     5 slots/25 teachers   = .2 slot per week per teacher
     5 slots per week × 55 minutes per slot   = 275 minutes per week
     275 minutes/5 days   = 55 minutes per day

High School Counselor Potential:
     < 1 guidance lessons per week, or nearly 3 weeks to conduct an activity with each class
     43 minutes per student per year
     13% receiving responsive services at any one time
     11 minutes per teacher per week, or 5 weeks to consult with all
     55 minutes a day for indirect services to students

Service Levels/Program Balance and Counselor-Student Ratio, 1: (Yours)

Desired Program Balance

Level: _____

Guidance Curriculum	_____ %_____	Activity Slots
Individual Student Planning	_____ %_____	Activity Slots
Responsive Services	_____ %_____	Activity Slots
System Support	_____ %_____	Activity Slots
Nonguidance	_____ %_____	Activity Slots

Average Class Size: 1: _____
Average teacher–student ratio: 1: _____
_____ Weeks per School Year
_____ Minutes per Activity Slot _____ # Activity Slots per Week

Guidance Curriculum _____ % (_____) =_____ Activity Slots/Week
        _____ counselees/_____ students per class = _____ classes
        _____ activity slots/_____ classes = _____ activities/class/week
        _____ activities × _____ weeks per year = _____ guidance lessons per year per class

Individual Student Planning _____ % (_____) = _____ Activity Slots/Week
        _____ activity slots × _____ weeks = _____ slots per year
        _____ slots × _____ minutes per slot = _____ minutes per year
        _____ minutes/_____ counselees = _____ minutes per student per year

Responsive Services _____ % (_____) = _____ Activity Slots/Week
        ———— slots for groups = _____ students (average #_____)
        ———— slots for individuals = _____ students
        Total students served at one time = _____
                                        (_____ is _____ % of the caseload)

System Support _____ % (_____) = _____ Activity Slots/Week
        _____ students/_____ students per teacher =_____ teachers
        _____ slots/_____ teachers = _____ slot per week per teacher
        _____ slots per week × _____ minutes per slot = _____ minutes per week
        _____ minutes/5 days = _____ minutes per day

Your School Counselor Potential:
        _____ guidance lessons per week
        _____ % receiving responsive services at any one time
        _____ minutes per teacher per week, or [#] _____ weeks for all
        _____ minutes a day for indirect services to students

Multicultural Counseling Competencies

I. *Counselor Awareness of Own Cultural Values and Biases*

A. Attitudes and Beliefs
  1. Culturally skilled counselors have moved from being culturally unaware to being aware and sensitive to their own cultural heritage and to valuing and respecting differences.
  2. Culturally skilled counselors are aware of how their own cultural backgrounds and experiences and attitudes, values, and biases influence psychological processes.
  3. Culturally skilled counselors are able to recognize the limits of their competencies and expertise.
  4. Culturally skilled counselors are comfortable with differences that exist between themselves and clients in terms of race, ethnicity, culture, and beliefs.

B. Knowledge
  1. Culturally skilled counselors have specific knowledge about their own racial and cultural heritage and how it personally and professionally affects their definitions of normality–abnormality and the process of counseling.
  2. Culturally skilled counselors possess knowledge and understanding about how oppression, racism, discrimination, and stereotyping affects them personally and in their work. This allows them to acknowledge their own racist attitudes, beliefs, and feelings. Although this standard applies to all groups, for White counselors it may mean that they understand how they may have directly or indirectly benefited from individual, institutional, and cultural racism (White identity development models).
  3. Culturally skilled counselors possess knowledge about their social impact on others. They are knowledgeable about communication style differences, how their style may clash or foster the counseling process with minority clients, and how to anticipate the impact it may have on others.

C. Skills
  1. Culturally skilled counselors seek out educational, consultative, and training experience to improve their understanding and effectiveness in working with culturally different populations. Being able to recognize the limits of their competencies, they (a) seek consultation, (b) seek further training or education, (c) refer out to more qualified individuals or resources, or (d) engage in a combination of these.
  2. Culturally skilled counselors are constantly seeking to understand themselves as racial and cultural beings and are actively seeking a nonracist identity.

II. *Counselor Awareness of Client's Worldview*

A. Attitudes and Beliefs
1. Culturally skilled counselors are aware of their negative emotional reactions toward other racial and ethnic groups that may prove detrimental to their clients in counseling. They are willing to contrast their own beliefs and attitudes with those of their culturally different clients in a nonjudgmental fashion.
2. Culturally skilled counselors are aware of their stereotypes and preconceived notions that they may hold toward other racial and ethnic minority groups.

B. Knowledge
1. Culturally skilled counselors possess specific knowledge and information about the particular group they are working with. They are aware of the life experiences, cultural heritage, and historical background of their culturally different clients. This particular competency is strongly linked to the "minority identity development models" available in the literature.
2. Culturally skilled counselors understand how race, culture, ethnicity, and so forth may affect personality formation, vocational choices, manifestation of psychological disorders, help-seeking behavior, and the appropriateness or inappropriateness of counseling approaches.
3. Culturally skilled counselors understand and have knowledge about sociopolitical influences that impinge upon the life of racial and ethnic minorities. Immigration issues, poverty, racism, stereotyping, and powerlessness all leave major scars that may influence the counseling process.

C. Skills
1. Culturally skilled counselors should familiarize themselves with relevant research and the latest findings regarding mental health and mental disorders of various ethnic and racial groups. They should actively seek out educational experiences that foster their knowledge, understanding, and cross-cultural skills.
2. Culturally skilled counselors become actively involved with minority individuals outside of the counseling setting (community events, social and political functions, celebrations, friendships, neighborhood groups, and so forth) so that their perspective of minorities is more than an academic or helping exercise.

III. *Culturally Appropriate Intervention Strategies*

A. Attitudes and Beliefs
1. Culturally skilled counselors respect clients' religious and/or spiritual beliefs and values, including attributions and taboos, because they affect worldview, psychosocial functioning, and expressions of distress.
2. Culturally skilled counselors respect indigenous helping practices and respect minority community intrinsic help-giving networks.
3. Culturally skilled counselors value bilingualism and do not view another language as an impediment to counseling (monolingualism may be the culprit).

B. Knowledge
1. Culturally skilled counselors have a clear and explicit knowledge and understanding of the generic characteristics of counseling and therapy (culture

bound, class bound, and monolingual) and how they may clash with the cultural values of various minority groups.

2. Culturally skilled counselors are aware of institutional barriers that prevent minorities from using mental health services.

3. Culturally skilled counselors have knowledge of the potential bias in assessment instruments and use procedures and interpret findings keeping in mind the cultural and linguistic characteristics of the clients.

4. Culturally skilled counselors have knowledge of minority family structures, hierarchies, values, and beliefs. They are knowledgeable about the community characteristics and the resources in the community as well as the family.

5. Culturally skilled counselors should be aware of relevant discriminatory practices at the social and community level that may be affecting the psychological welfare of the population being served.

C. Skills

1. Culturally skilled counselors are able to engage in a variety of verbal and nonverbal helping responses. They are able to *send* and *receive* both *verbal* and *nonverbal* messages *accurately* and *appropriately*. They are not tied down to only one method or approach to helping but recognize that helping styles and approaches may be culture bound. When they sense that their helping style is limited and potentially inappropriate, they can anticipate and ameliorate its negative impact.

2. Culturally skilled counselors are able to exercise institutional intervention skills on behalf of their clients. They can help clients determine whether a "problem" stems from racism or bias in others (the concept of health paranoia) so that clients do not inappropriately personalize problems.

3. Culturally skilled counselors are not averse to seeking consultation with traditional healers and religious and spiritual leaders and practitioners in the treatment of culturally different clients when appropriate.

4. Culturally skilled counselors take responsibility for interacting in the language requested by the client and, if not feasible, make appropriate referral. A serious problem arises when the linguistic skills of a counselor do not match the language of the client. This being the case, counselors should (a) seek a translator with cultural knowledge and appropriate professional background and (b) refer to a knowledgeable and competent bilingual counselor.

5. Culturally skilled counselors have training and expertise in the use of traditional assessment and testing instruments. They not only understand the technical aspects of the instruments but are also aware of the cultural limitations. This allows them to use test instruments for the welfare of the diverse clients.

6. Culturally skilled counselors should attend to as well as work to eliminate biases, prejudices, and discriminatory practices. They should be cognizant of sociopolitical contexts in conducting evaluation and providing interventions and should develop sensitivity to issues of oppression, sexism, elitism, and racism.

7. Culturally skilled counselors take responsibility in educating their clients to the processes of psychological intervention, such as goals, expectations, legal rights, and the counselor's orientation.

A Procedure for Addressing Parental Concerns

Administrative Regulation

Subject: Response to Parents Expressing Concerns Regarding Developmental Guidance Program

To: Elementary Principals
         Elementary Counselors

Some parents have expressed interest in or concern about the content of the classroom guidance program. Most of these parents, after learning of the actual objectives of and materials used in guidance classes, have become comfortable with their children's participation in those lessons. A few have not.

The district's position is that although parents may choose to allow or not allow their children to participate in counseling, instruction in the guidance curriculum is part of the basic educational program. State-mandated "essential elements" and district-established instructional objectives are taught through the elementary guidance program. Students shall not be excluded from guidance classes solely on the basis of parental request, just as they are not excluded from math classes or physical education classes. In addition to the educational considerations, the logistical problems of supervision of the student during that class time are significant.

In the event of such expression, follow the procedure described below.

1st: When a parent expresses concern about the content of the classroom guidance program, the counselor should meet with the parent to (1) hear the specific concern of the parent and (2) describe the program at the child's grade level, the objectives taught, and the materials used. The Principal or the Director of Guidance may sit in on this initial information-sharing conference if desired.

2nd: If the parent is still uncomfortable with the child's participation in the program, he or she must submit the specific concerns in writing to the Principal. The Principal may have a second conference with the parent to share and gather more information. The parent must be apprised of the problem of supervision of the student if the parent is requesting removal of the child from the guidance classes.

3rd: If the parent continues to request removal of the child from guidance classes, the request is to be forwarded to the Director of Guidance along with any information the counselor and the Principal have gathered.

4th: The Director of Guidance will meet with the parent and, after consultation with the Assistant Superintendent for Student Services, will decide the matter.

Date:
Originated By:

Presenting . . . Your Professional School Counselor

A Vital Link for All Students

- Academic Development
- Career Development
- Personal/Social Development

What Is Guidance and Counseling?

The comprehensive guidance program is an integral part of a school district's total educational program. It is developmental by design and includes sequential activities organized and implemented by professional school counselors with the active support of parents/guardians, teachers, administrators, and the community.

As a developmental program, it addresses the needs of all students by facilitating their academic, personal/social, and career development as well as helping create positive and safe learning climates in schools. At the same time, the program assists students as they face issues and resolve problems that may prevent their healthy development. The program is delivered through the following four program components:

- Guidance Curriculum
- Individual Planning
- Responsive Services
- System Support

What Do Professional School Counselors Do?

Professional school counselors spend 100 percent of their time providing all students with preventative and responsive activities and services delivered through four interrelated program components.

Guidance Curriculum

Professional school counselors work closely with teachers by going into classrooms to present guidance lessons on such topics as:

- self-awareness
- positive mental health
- social skills
- conflict mediation/problem solving
- study habits

- alcohol/drug abuse prevention
- educational and career planning.

Individual Planning

Working closely with parents, professional school counselors provide effective educational and career-planning services that help all students, beginning in middle school, to develop personal plans of study:

- that are organized around personally valued educational and career goals
- that promote participation in relevant co-curricular and community activities
- that provide seamless transition to postsecondary options.

Responsive Services

Professional school counselors assist students who have unique needs (including those who may be experiencing barriers to academic success) through:

- individual counseling
- small-group counseling
- consultation and collaboration with parents, teachers, administrators and community agencies
- school-based referral
- community-based referral.

System Support

Professional school counselors manage the guidance program and support other programs in the school through such activities as:

- guidance program evaluation
- school improvement involvement
- consultation and collaboration
- professional development
- community outreach
- fair-share responsibilities.

How Can Parents Help?

Active parental support of guidance and counseling program activities is essential if students are to make informed choices and achieve success in school. Parents can help by encouraging their children to do their best in school and by staying involved in their children's educational experiences at all levels.

Parents can call their child's professional school counselor at any time to set up a phone conference or a school visit to discuss concerns, ideas, information or requests for assistance.

Who Are Professional Counselors?

Professional school counselors work at elementary, middle/junior high, high school and/or postsecondary levels. They have a master's or higher degree in school counseling from a state-approved school counselor preparation program, and they have been certified as a professional school counselor by the Missouri Department of Elementary and Secondary Education. They are professional educators with specialized training in academic, career, and personal/social development as well as mental health. Their preparation program includes:

- human growth and development
- social and cultural diversity
- assessment
- career development and planning
- helping relationships
- group work
- guidance program development, implementation, evaluation and enhancement
- professional relationships
- legal and ethical standards
- professional orientation, identity and well-being.

For more information regarding your local school guidance and counseling program, contact:

Missouri Department of Elementary and Secondary Education
Division of Career Education Guidance and Placement Section
PO Box 480
Jefferson City, MO 65102-0480
(573) 751-7966
http://dese.mo.gov/divcareered/guidance_placement_index.htm

Missouri Center for Career Education
http://www.mcce.org

Missouri School Counselor Association
3340 American Avenue, Suite F
Jefferson City, MO 65109
(573) 632-6722 or (800) 763-6722
Fax: (573) 632-6724 or (800) 264-6722
http://www.moschoolcounselor.org

The Department of Elementary and Secondary Education does not discriminate on the basis of race, color, national origin, sex, disability, or age in its programs and activities. Inquiries related to Department programs may be directed to the Jefferson State Office Building, Title IX Coordinator, 5th Floor, 205 Jefferson Street, Jefferson City, MO 65102-0480; telephone number 573-751-4212.

Reassignment of Nonguidance Duties

The professional school counselor's time and task analysis has revealed all of the activities that professional school counselors are currently performing. A number of these activities are nonguidance and should not be part of the desired district's guidance program. A few of them are activities that all school staff members, including professional school counselors, take a turn in doing. These activities are fair-share responsibilities for professional school counselors and are included in system support. The nonguidance activities that are assigned to professional school counselors need to be reassigned so that professional school counselors can devote their time to fully implementing the district's comprehensive guidance program.

Budget constraints in many districts may preclude the instantaneous reassignment of nonguidance duties. To ensure that the transition to a fully implemented comprehensive guidance program is made systematically, however, it is critical that a written nonguidance activities displacement plan is developed as a part of the overall implementation plan presented to the board of education. A statewide task force of Missouri administrators and professional school counselors developed the ideas that follow for reassignment consideration. They identified nonguidance duties, grouped them into four categories, and then listed possible ways to handle the reassignment of them.

I. *Supervisory Duties*

A. Coordinating and monitoring school assemblies
- This is an administrative function and is not viewed as a part of guidance program responsibilities.

B. Hall duty, cafeteria supervision, bus loading and unloading supervision, and restroom supervision
- These duties could be shared equally among all staff.
- Teachers could be assigned to some of these duties as a regular part of their schedules.
- Volunteers could assist with some of these tasks.

C. Chaperoning school functions and athletic event supervision
- These duties could be shared among the staff.
- Booster club members could assist staff with some of the athletic events.
- School staff could be paid extra to take on chaperoning duties.

D. Substitute teaching
- Professional school counselors are not substitute teachers. On an occasional basis, however, professional school counselors could conduct guidance learning activities, particularly if teacher absences are known in advance.

II. *Clerical Duties*

A. Selling lunch tickets
  - Office support staff or cafeteria staff should do this.

B. Collecting and mailing out progress reports and deficiency notices
  - Sorting, stuffing, and mailing are clerical/secretarial functions. An individual could be hired on a temporary basis to handle sorting, stuffing, and mailing.
  - Conferences with students regarding progress reports are school staff functions, which includes but should not be limited to professional school counselors.

C. Maintaining permanent records and handling transcripts
  - Posting grades and test labels is a clerical duty. Part-time help could be hired if a full-time person is not available to handle these functions.

D. Monitoring attendance
  - Accounting for daily attendance is not a guidance program's function. However, it is appropriate for professional school counselors to meet with students who have chronic attendance problems.
  - Computer software packages are available to monitor attendance in a very efficient and effective manner.

E. Calculating grade point averages (GPAs), class ranks, or honor rolls
  - Computer software packages are available to efficiently and effectively perform these tasks.

F. Developing and updating the student handbook
  - This is an administrative function that the principal or assistant principal should perform.

G. Developing and updating course guides
  - Department chairpersons (teaching staff) have the responsibility for developing course descriptions and course guides.

H. Completing the paperwork related to changing students' schedules
  - The paperwork involved in changing schedules, balancing class loads, and processing student schedule cards are clerical functions. If full-time clerical assistance is not available, part-time clerical/secretarial assistants should be hired to help at key times during the school year. A wide array of computer software is available to handle the scheduling process including schedule changes and can be purchased to facilitate the completion of these important activities.

III. *Special Programs and Services*

A. Sponsoring class clubs and special programs
  - Sponsorship of these activities is a school staff function usually done on a voluntary basis. Professional school counselors should not be expected to as-

sume any more responsibility for these programs than any other person on the staff.

- Programs such as the Missouri Scholars' Academy should be the responsibility of administrative personnel or a committee of school personnel.

B. Coordinating and administering the school-testing program, which includes individual testing

- The overall coordination and administration of the school-testing program are the responsibilities of the administration.
- Retired teachers could be hired to handle this responsibility.
- School personnel could collaborate to accomplish the coordination and administration of the school-testing program.
- Professional school counselors assist in interpreting test data to teachers, administrators, parents/guardians, and the community; however, they should not be responsible for coordinating and administering the school-testing program.
- Professional school counselors use test data when working with students to help them monitor and manage their academic, personal/social, and career development.
- School psychologists and school psychological examiners are the professionals who are qualified to do individual testing.

C. Completing and managing Individual Education [Programs] (IEPs) and meeting other special education requirements

- Professional school counselors should not function as case managers for students with special needs.
- Professional school counselors could be members of the team involved in the diagnostic aspects of the IEP. However, they should not be responsible for the development, implementation, and monitoring of the IEP or the Individualized Vocational Education Plan unless they are funded by special education or by vocational education funds.
- Professional school counselors could take part in staffing and conferences when appropriate but should not coordinate or chair the staffings, conferences, or IEP meetings.

D. Completing and managing 504 Plans and meeting other 504 Plan requirements.

IV. *Administrative Duties*

A. Developing the master schedule

- This is an administrative function. Administrators can seek input from professional school counselors, but it is their responsibility to plan and develop the master schedule.

B. Acting as the principal of the day

- The professional school counselor should not fill the role of acting principal. Retired school administrators could be hired for this purpose.
- This responsibility could be assigned to teachers who have administrative certification.

- The superintendent or other central office administrators could be called upon to act as principal for the day.

C. Administering discipline
   - Administering discipline and assessing consequences for student actions are administrative functions, not guidance functions. However, it is appropriate for professional school counselors to meet with students who have chronic discipline problems.

D. Managing schedule changes
   - Students who desire or need to have their schedules revised are encouraged to first discuss the changes with the professional school counselor. The mechanics related to this process should be handled through administrative channels. Much of the process is clerical in nature. It is the responsibility of the administration to see that class sizes are appropriate and that sufficient staff members are available to accommodate students' needs.

Note. From *Missouri Comprehensive Guidance Program: A Manual for Program Development, Implementation, Evaluation, and Enhancement* by N. C. Gysbers, L. Kostek-Bunch, C. S. Magnuson, and M. F. Starr, 2002, Columbia, MO: Instructional Materials Laboratory. Reprinted with permission.

Sample Activity Plan Formats

GUIDANCE CURRICULUM COMPONENT
LESSON PLAN

Grade: _____   Lesson Title: _____

Student Need Level: Developmental   Group Size_____
Guidance Curriculum Reference:
    Content Area:
    Goal:
    Competency Indicator:
Instructional Curriculum Reference:
Learning
    Level: Awareness   Skill Development   Application
    Domain: Cognitive   Affective/Attitudinal   Social/Interaction   Behavioral

Expected Result(s)/Activity Objective(s): The student will . . .

Methods/Resources:

   ___Technology   ___Practice   ___Book reading
   ___Internet   ___Role play   ___Worksheet
   ___Demonstration   ___Guest   ___Songs/chants
   ___Discussion   ___Group work   ___Brainstorming
   ___Drawing/artwork ___Lecture   ___Other:_____

Materials:

Procedure Plan:
    Focus:

    Direct Teach/Instruction:

Check for Understanding:

Guided Practice:

Evaluation/Assessment:

___Oral response	___Observation
___Class participation	___Worksheet/written response
___Student response	___Artwork/drawing
___Homework	___Other:_____

Independent Practice:

INDIVIDUAL STUDENT PLANNING COMPONENT
GUIDANCE SESSION PLAN

Grade: _____   Session Title: _____

Student Need Level: Developmental   Remedial   Group Size_____
Guidance Curriculum Reference:
    Content Area:
    Goal:
    Competency Indicator:
Instructional Curriculum Reference:
Learning
    Level: Awareness   Skill Development   Application
    Domain: Cognitive   Affective/Attitudinal   Social/Interaction   Behavioral

Expected Result(s)/Activity Objective(s): The student will . . .

Methods/Resources:

   ___Technology   ___Practice   ___Book reading
   ___Internet   ___Role play   ___Worksheet
   ___Demonstration   ___Guest   ___Songs/chants
   ___Discussion   ___Group work   ___Brainstorming
   ___Drawing/artwork ___Lecture   ___Other:_____

Materials:

Procedure Plan:
    Discussion/Focus:

    Personal Application:

Closure:

Evaluation/Assessment:

   ___Oral response   ___Observation
   ___Class participation   ___Worksheet/written response
   ___Student response   ___Artwork/drawing
   ___Homework   ___Other:_____

RESPONSIVE SERVICES COMPONENT
COUNSELING SESSION PLAN

Topic: _____   Group Size:_____

Student Need Level: Developmental   Preventive   Remedial   Crisis

Guidance Program Curriculum Reference:
    Content Area:
    Goal:
    Competency Indicator:

Instructional Curriculum Reference:

Learning
    Level: Awareness   Skill Development   Application
    Domain: Cognitive   Affective/Attitudinal   Social/Interaction   Behavioral

Expected Result(s)/Activity Objective(s): The student will . . .

Methods/Resources:

    ___Technology   ___Practice   ___Book reading
    ___Internet   ___Role play   ___Worksheet
    ___Demonstration   ___Guest   ___Songs/chants
    ___Discussion   ___Group work   ___Brainstorming
    ___Drawing/artwork ___Lecture   ___Other:_____

Materials:

Resources:

Procedure Plan:
    Opening/Focus:

    Stimulus/Exercise/Approach:

Closure:

Homework:

Follow-Up Plan(s):

SYSTEM SUPPORT COMPONENT
CONSULTATION SESSION PLAN

Topic: _____   Grade: _____   Student Identification:_____

Adult Relationship to Student: _____

Student Need Level: Developmental   Preventive   Remedial   Crisis
Guidance Curriculum Reference:
    Content Area:
    Goal:
    Competency Indicator:
Instructional Curriculum Reference:
Learning
    Level: Awareness   Skill Development   Application
    Domain: Cognitive   Affective/Attitudinal   Social/Interaction   Behavioral

Consultation Purpose/Expected Result(s)/Activity Objective(s):   The consultee will . . .

Relevant Information/Materials Needed:
    Student background information:

    Form(s):
    Resources available:
    Records:
    Agency policy/procedures:

Procedure Plan:
    Statement of Problem:

    Statement of Objective:

    Explanation of Problem:

    Check for Understanding:

    Options:

    Next Step(s) to Be Taken:

    Follow-Up Plan(s):

Evaluation/Assessment:
    ____Observation   ____Participation   ____Written response
    ____Student response   ____Other:_____

☞ Appendix M ☜

Descriptors Related to Evaluation Categories

These descriptors are provided to counselors, their supervisors, and administrators as a means of enhancing communication about the nature of guidance and counseling and the specifics upon which to base sound evaluative judgments as to the proficiency of the school counselor. The specific items were generated by and large by Northside counselors, with some reaffirmation and augmentation from the guidance and counseling literature. They are offered to assist new counselors, experienced counselors, non-guidance-trained administrators, and guidance-trained administrators to have similar definitions for the skills and knowledge expected of our school counselors.

Specifically, the items provide more concrete descriptions for the performance indicators suggested for the areas that counselors are evaluated on. If it were laid out in one document, the format would be as follows:

Category	Performance Indicators	Descriptors
1. Implements guidance curriculum through the use of effective instructional skills	a. appropriate task analysis	1. selection of terminal objective 2. specification of learning increments 3. weeding out of nonessentials 4. instruction at appropriate level of difficulty 5. selection of learning sequence 6. explanation of unfamiliar or specially used terms
	b. effective use of lessons design . . . etc. . . .	1. focus 2. explanation

Still, this list is not all-inclusive, nor are all items necessarily mutually exclusive. It is not meant to be used as a checklist, but rather it is intended to make the school counselor's role more tangible.

1. Implements guidance curriculum through the use of effective instructional skills, including

a. *Appropriate task analysis*
   1. selects terminal objective

    2. specifies learning increments
    3. weeds out nonessentials
    4. instructs at an appropriate level of difficulty
    5. selects learning sequence
    6. explains unfamiliar or specially used terms

b. *Effective use of lesson design*
    1. focus
    2. explanation
    3. checking for understanding
    4. monitoring and adjusting
    5. modeling
    6. guided practice
    7. closure
    8. independent practice
    9. extensions
   10. corrections
   11. evaluation

c. *Active involvement of students in the learning process*
    1. varies activities
    2. interacts with students in appropriate group formats
    3. solicits student participation
    4. extends students' responses/contributions
    5. provides "wait time"
    6. secures and maintains students' attention
    7. gives clear directions
    8. manages students' behavior
    9. uses effective teaching practices
   10. uses strategies to motivate students for learning
   11. maintains supportive environment
   12. provides materials and equipment needed for lessons ready for use at appropriate time

d. *Selection of topics consistent with identified, high-priority student needs and district goals*
    1. implements instruction at appropriate level of difficulty
    2. assesses student needs formally and informally
    3. adheres to district guidance scope and sequence and curriculum

2. *Implements the individual planning system through the effective use of guidance skills, including*

a. *Careful planning of sessions*
    1. performs appropriate task analysis
    2. effectively uses lesson design, with expanded use of guided practice
    3. guided practice
    4. use of variety of guidance techniques
    5. has materials, audiovisual aids, and facilities ready for use
    6. understands/applies theories of vocational choice

b. *Presentation of accurate, relevant, unbiased information*
   1. makes no significant errors
   2. presents information so that students can process/internalize it
      a. uses vocabulary appropriate to students
      b. explains content clearly
      c. presents appropriate amounts of information
   3. stresses important points
   4. clarifies students' misunderstanding
   5. uses accurate language
   6. identifies, selects, organizes, and makes accessible educational and career information systems; makes information resources available to students
   7. uses materials effectively
   8. is knowledgeable about the range of educational and career alternatives and the value of each of these

c. *Involvement of students in personalized educational and career planning*
   1. helps students establish goals and use planning skills
   2. knows students' abilities, achievements, interests, and goals
   3. effectively uses consultation skills as needed
   4. encourages parental input into student planning
   5. correctly assesses students' educational and career aspiration and information needs
   6. makes appropriate and appropriately presented recommendations
   7. conducts activities with groups of sizes conducive to ensure effectiveness and efficiency

d. *Accurate and appropriate test results interpretation*
   1. provides appropriate information to students, parents, and school staff in timely manner
   2. ensures that individuals know how to read reports of interest/use to them
   3. strives to guard against the overinterpretation or other inappropriate use of test results data
   4. in presenting test results interpretation, attends to the confidential and private nature of individual test information
   5. (reference: item 2b above regarding accuracy of information)
   6. understands/applies basic statistical concepts essential in the use of appraisal instruments and data
   7. understands/applies basic concepts and principles of measurement and evaluation
   8. processes appraisal data appropriately for use in guidance and counseling
   9. makes effective use of appraisal data in counseling and guidance

e. *Selection of individual planning activities consistent with identified, high-priority student needs and district goals*
   1. assesses student needs for planning assistance formally and informally
   2. presents needs-identification data to reflect data from follow-up studies of former students' actual educational and career progress
   3. provides information about important dates and tasks to be accomplished
   4. adheres to District Guidance Program Framework time frame and priorities

3. *Implements responsive services through effective use of counseling, consultation, and referral skills, including*

a. *Proper identification of problems/issues to be resolved*
1. uses effective intake procedures to properly discern problems/issues
2. in counseling, assists students to define their problems
3. in consultation, collaborates with consultee in problem definition
4. in referral, understands and articulates the basis for referral

b. *Selection of counseling, consulting, or referral interventions appropriate to students' problems and circumstances*
1. recognizes own personal/professional limitations and organizes caseload appropriately
2. accepts referrals in a competent and professional manner
3. responds appropriately to requests for information

c. *Uses counseling, consulting, or referral skills effectively*

Counseling:
1. uses a variety of techniques and procedures
2. operates from a consistently applied and conscious awareness of own theoretical base
3. is nonjudgmental of students
4. understands the dynamics of individual behavior in the counseling relationship or in a group

Consulting:
1. has expertise to share
2. shares information
3. in problem specification, gathers as much information as needed to consult effectively and efficiently
4. in goal setting, understands consultees' responsibilities and goals
5. establishes credibility by being able to suggest a variety of options, alternatives, resources, or strategies
6. coordinates the development and implementation of the consultees' behavioral plan of action

Referral: (process: problem specification, evaluation of need for referral, resource identification, referral, and follow-up)
1. is knowledgeable about sources for referral
2. seeks out referral sources
3. conducts adequate research about referral sources
4. refers at appropriate time in helping process
5. is able to explain the need for referral and the referral process
6. provides minimum of three referral options to client

d. *Conducts well-planned and goal-oriented sessions*
1. sessions are effective: objectives are established and attained
2. sessions are efficient: objectives are the focus of the sessions; however, sensitivity to divergent needs of the group/individual is imperative also
3. materials, aids, and facilities are ready for use

e. *Use of group and individual techniques that are appropriate to the topic and to students' needs and abilities*
   1. discerns when individual or group counseling would be most facilitative to the problem presented by the counselees
   2. uses group counseling when it is determined to be more effective than or as effective as individual counseling
   3. structures specialized groups as to topic and purpose as well as membership composition
   4. displays working knowledge of developmental tasks and coping behaviors or different age levels and the skills to use group techniques appropriate for client level

f. *Actively involves counselees/consultees/referees in the process*

Counseling:
   1. counseling results in students' acting to solve problems
   2. holds student-oriented sessions
   3. allows students to speak freely about problems
   4. assists students in exploration of affect
   5. assists students in goal setting
   6. assists students in establishing a concrete behavioral plan aimed at problem resolution
   7. ensures that plan is developed at an appropriate level of specificity
   8. avoids premature advice or superficial reassurance
   9. listens effectively

Consulting:
   1. consulting results in consultee acting to solve problem
   2. encourages input from consultee
   3. facilitates communication between participants
   4. avoids premature, superficial advice or reassurance
   5. handles expression of conflict in a constructive manner
   6. is appreciative of ideas expressed by others
   7. promotes a spirit of compromise and cooperation
   8. listens effectively

Referral
   1. exhibits skill in the art of referral such that person needing referral feels comfortable
   2. assistance results in client going to referral source
   3. initiates contacts between referral sources and individuals who have been referred

g. *Timely follow-up*
   1. follows up with students and other clients as to their progress in implementation of the problem-solving action plan
   2. communicates with referral sources
   3. ensures communication between appropriate people
   4. prepares/maintains appropriate documentation, forms, records, etc., relevant to cases

     5. implements follow-up activities as recommended for clients by referral sources

  h. *Provision of services consistent with high-priority, identified student needs and district goals*
     1. conducts formal and informal needs assessments
     2. determines needs and priorities as perceived by students, parents, staff, and administration
     3. recognizes situations that need attention
     4. attends to priorities established in the Guidance Program Framework and in other district memos

4. *Implements system support through providing effective support for other programs and by effectively enlisting support for the guidance program, such as*

  a. *Providing a comprehensive and balanced guidance program*
     1. Uses effective planning skills
       a. assesses program needs and priorities accurately
       b. establishes realistic program goals
       c. uses results of evaluation to improve program
       d. plans program and activities
       e. provides alternative plans
       f. determines suitable and workable time schedule
       g. plans an overview of the year
       h. writes program plan
     2. Uses effective organizational skills
       a. establishes meaningful objectives
       b. sequences activities in a meaningful design
       c. sets time lines and follows them
       d. operates from a program calendar
       e. provides an appropriately balanced and comprehensive program
     3. Uses resources effectively
       a. resources = materials, human, dollars, equipment, facilities
       b. selects and creates sound materials
       c. manages equipment and facilities and budget effectively
       d. takes proper care/makes proper use of equipment
       e. assigns tasks or duties appropriately/delegates effectively
       f. considers strengths of human talent available
       g. seeks assistance if does not have adequate answers
       h. uses administration and other staff as appropriate
       i. uses available resources
       j. provides resource materials and information to students, staff, parents
       k. determines what personal and natural resources are available/needed
     4. Evaluates program effectively
       a. systematically evaluates overall program effectiveness
       b. uses results of evaluation to improve program
  b. *Selecting program activities that meet identified, high-priority student needs and are consistent with campus and district goals*
     1. bases campus program on student and community needs
     2. bases campus program on the district framework

c. *Collecting evidence that students achieve meaningful outcomes from program activities*
1. evaluates effectiveness of activities
2. evaluates quantity and quality of student growth in guidance and counseling activities
3. provides for a system of evaluating programs and activities
4. plans, implements, and accesses systematic evaluation tools
5. uses results of evaluation tools to reassess program goals, objectives, and strategies
6. consistently evaluates program activities

d. *Operating within established procedures, policies, and priorities*
1. complies with letter and intent of regulations, directives, and instructions from superiors
2. administers activities in accordance with district guidelines

e. *Contributing to organizational solutions outside of assigned responsibilities*
1. works as member of team in working to solve organizational problems
2. accepts responsibility for helping others learn their responsibilities and is able to do this without taking over others' roles

f. *Working cooperatively with school administrators to garner support for the guidance program*
1. collaborates with administration in developing the campus guidance program goals and objectives
2. seeks their support on matters of concern

g. *Implementing programs that explain the school guidance program*
1. explains the philosophy, priorities, and practices of the guidance program effectively and articulately
2. has a campus PR plan for helping the parents as well as the students and staff understand the guidance program and its variety of activities
3. uses a variety of strategies to communicate to parents, e.g., newsletters, columns, parent education sessions, open houses

h. *Attending to ideas/concerns expressed regarding the guidance program*
1. listens with an open mind
2. accepts suggestions gracefully
3. is not unnecessarily defensive with parents or community representatives; works to understand their concerns
4. maintains professional detachment in circumstances where patrons are misinformed, mistrusting

i. *Supporting campus administration policies and goals*
1. establishes objectives that contribute to the goals of the campus administration
2. complies with letter and intent of regulations, directives, and instructions from superiors
3. supports administrative directives
4. cooperates with campus administration in addressing campus goals

j. *Supporting district policies and goals*
   1. supports administrative directives, school board goals, and organizational policies
   2. adheres to Guidance Program Framework
   3. cooperates with district administration in guidance program improvement efforts

5. *Establishes effective professional relationships by building rapport with*

a. *Students*
   1. demonstrates knowledge of, interest in, and understanding of the roles and responsibilities of the student
   2. acts as student advocate appropriately and effectively
   3. communicates effectively with and about students
   4. exhibits sensitivity, empathy, and acceptance necessary for establishing rapport
   5. encourages students to have respect for the rights, property, and opinions of others
   6. primary commitment is to the student, yet keeps communications open with others
   7. is student advocate and liaison for students/administrators/faculty/parents
   8. knows the students' backgrounds
   9. encourages students to assume responsibility for own behaviors, choices, and relationships

b. *Staff*
   1. demonstrates knowledge of, interest, in, and understanding of the roles and responsibilities of the teacher and other staff members
   2. works cooperatively as a team member with staff
   3. communicates effectively with and about staff
   4. exhibits sensitivity, empathy, and acceptance necessary for establishing rapport
   5. works as a team member—educator, consultant
   6. respects professional judgments of staff
   7. seeks and respects ideas of others
   8. is receptive to teachers' comments and suggestions
   9. encourages teachers to adjust their programs to individual needs of students

c. *Parents*
   1. demonstrates knowledge of, interest in, and understanding of the roles, responsibilities, and circumstances of the parent
   2. cooperates with parents in problem solving
   3. communicates effectively with and about parents
   4. exhibits sensitivity, empathy, and acceptance necessary for establishing rapport
   5. encourages parents to practice effective parenting skills
   6. communicates effectively with parents regarding students' progress and areas of difficulty and success

d. *Other counselors*
   1. where there is more than one counselor on a campus: operates as a team member; works collaboratively in the development of goals and the implementation of the campus guidance program

2. cooperates with counselors from other campuses in the interest of serving students and the program better

e. *Administrators*
   1. demonstrates knowledge of, interest in, and understanding of the roles and responsibilities of the administrator
   2. works cooperatively as a team member with administrators
   3. communicates effectively with and about administrators
   4. understands and responds appropriately to the different roles/responsibilities of the campus and district administrators
   5. exhibits sensitivity, empathy, and acceptance necessary for establishing rapport
   6. plays the child advocate role appropriately

f. *Other in-school district specialists*
   1. demonstrates knowledge and understanding of the roles and responsibilities of other specialists
   2. communicates effectively with and about other specialists
   3. maintains positive working relationships with other specialists
   4. exhibits sensitivity
   5. seeks specialists' assistance when needed/beneficial to the student or other clients
   6. initiates communication when needed/beneficial to the student or other clients
   7. does not overrely on other specialists

g. *Community representatives*
   1. communicates effectively with referral agency staff
   2. maintains positive working relationships with PTA and other patron groups
   3. is interested in and understands roles/responsibilities of community agency representatives
   4. exhibits sensitivity, warmth, and openness for establishing rapport
   5. establishes harmonious relationships with referral sources commonly used
   6. informs community about total school and guidance programs

6. *Fulfills professional responsibilities by*

a. *Seeking professional development*
   1. has adequate knowledge to be an effective counselor
      a. understands, applies, and can articulate own theoretical framework
      b. understands the organization and operation of the school and the district
      c. is knowledgeable of developmental characteristics of age group served
      d. has basic knowledge of
         —guidance content and theory
         —program model
         —school system organization and operation
      e. can articulate own theoretical framework with respect to guidance and counseling, psychology, and human dynamics
      f. understands and applies basic concepts of psychological theory, measurement and evaluation, group and individual techniques of counseling and guidance
      g. has an internally consistent approach to guidance and counseling

2. plans for and engages in professional development
    a. monitors and evaluates own professional performance
    b. implements own Professional Growth Plan
    c. makes use of opportunities for improving skills and acquiring new and relevant knowledge
    d. has developed and is implementing a personal, professional growth plan
    e. attends professional workshops, conferences, and courses
    f. belongs to professional organization(s)
    g. invests personal time
    h. is selective in choosing programs
    i. participates actively in in-district in-service offerings
    j. assumes responsibilities for own professional growth
    k. seeks opportunities to improve skills and to acquire new knowledge
    l. maintains contact with current research and practice
    m. combines information from various sources to solve problems/to innovate
    n. attempts sound innovative and creative approaches to problems
    o. is open to new learning/is willing to learn
3. demonstrates commitment to the counseling and education professions
    a. invests own resources in professional development—time and money
    b. volunteers to serve on committees or accepts other leadership opportunities as offered
    c. accepts leadership roles in professional associations
    d. shares, joins, serves
    e. encourages others to use new ideas
    f. takes pride in being a member of the counseling profession
    g. understands roles/responsibilities of the school counselor at own and at other levels
    h. applies research knowledge and skills to further the field of guidance and counseling

b. *Keeping records consistent with ethical and legal guidelines*
    1. keeps organized, accurate, legal, and ethically appropriate records
    2. interprets records to others as is consistent with ethical and legal guidelines
    3. keeps records in an organized and consistent fashion
    4. communicates and interprets accurately and openly
    5. monitors overall records procedure
    6. delegates appropriately
    7. supervises paraprofessional staff effectively
    8. ensures security, confidentiality, and legality
    9. is knowledgeable of proper procedures
    10. maintains adequate, differentiated records
    11. documents consultations, referrals, and other guidance and counseling events
    12. completes paperwork in a timely and efficient manner

c. *Maintaining professional work habits*
    1. performs responsibilities in an organized, timely, and dependable manner
    2. complies with district's standards for attendance
    3. is considerate of others' time
    4. completes required forms and reports
    5. attends/participates in required staff meetings

6. exercises professional judgment in absences from work
7. plans and uses time to best advantage
8. complies with established district work hours
9. is task-oriented
10. maintains a positive atmosphere for learning and growing
11. attends to detail

d. *Practicing according to the profession's ethical standards*
1. observes ethical standards of the American School Counselor Association and the American Counseling Association
2. implements counselor's role as defined in the Guidance Program Framework and other district guidelines
3. adheres to district policies and legal guidelines
4. refrains from revealing confidential information inappropriately
5. does not impose personal value judgments on students, their families, or on school staff
6. demonstrates impartiality with respect to sex, ethnicity, or ability of students
7. is aware of own personal/emotional and professional limitations
8. maintains confidentiality within established parameters

e. *Demonstrating appropriate personal characteristics*
1. Demonstrates attitudes conducive to effective guidance and counseling; is:

positive	persevering	accessible/available
pleasant	genuine	supportive
cheerful	open-minded	receptive to change
accepting	future-minded	willing to share
realistic	enthusiastic	information and ideas
cooperative	optimistic	flexible
helpful	personally courageous	has vision

2. demonstrates attributes conducive to effective guidance and counseling:
   a. takes initiative
   b. is caring, kind, warm
   c. has a sense of humor
   d. demonstrates patience
   e. is sensitive to others; has empathy
   f. uses intelligence and creativity
3. holds values conducive to effective guidance and counseling
   a. demonstrates self-acceptance, -understanding, and -confidence
   b. holds positive regard for the worth, dignity, and uniqueness of each individual
   c. demonstrates belief in ability of others to change, grow, and accept responsibility for own actions
   d. demonstrates honesty and loyalty
   e. values own role as model to others
   f. demonstrates belief in the value of learning and schooling
   g. respects individual differences
   h. resists imposing conforming behaviors on individuals
   i. makes a commitment of primary responsibility to students while providing adequate communication to teachers, parents, administrators, and other referral sources without violating confidentiality of the counseling relationship

4. has high professional standards
   a. accepts constructive criticism
   b. adapts to unusual circumstances
   c. tolerates ambiguity
   d. maintains objectivity/professional detachment in problem situations
   e. seems informed and confident in expression
   f. has professional image with students, staff, and parents
   g. models expected social behavior, grooming, and courtesy
   h. maintains poise and emotional stability
   i. strives for excellence
   j. is motivated to achieve
   k. maintains good physical health
   l. provides a good moral example for students
   m. handles decisions of superiors appropriately
   n. recognizes own leadership role on campus and accepts the responsibilities of leadership on the campus

f. *Demonstrating effective use of basic skills, e.g., communication, problem solving, decision making, educational*
   1. uses communication skills
      a. listens actively
      b. builds rapport
      c. is interested in others' messages
      d. uses appropriate vocabulary
      e. maintains a supportive environment
      f. speaks and writes professionally
      g. uses both verbal and nonverbal communication behaviors appropriately
      h. uses appropriate attending behaviors
      i. uses open-ended questions and prompts
      j. reflects feelings of communicator
      k. accurately paraphrases content of communicator's message
      l. uses interpretation skills effectively
      m. responds to verbal and nonverbal communications in meaningful ways
   2. problem solving
      a. diagnoses problems accurately
      b. prescribes appropriate remedies
      c. approaches problems with impartiality
      d. is able to think of multiple options for problem solution
      e. is able to envision consequences of various options
      f. handles dissenting individuals and groups
   3. decision making
      a. recognizes the need for a decision
      b. explores alternative choices
      c. predicts accurately the probable outcome of each choice
      d. assigns personal values to each choice
      e. determines the costs/risks attendant to each choice
      f. applies a variety of decision strategies
      g. makes a plan for decision implementation
      h. evaluates the outcome of decisions

4. educational skills
    a. imparts information effectively
    b. strengthens students' capacity to cope with life situations
    c. allows "wait time"
    d. maintains physical environment appropriate to the session conducted
    e. has materials, aids, and facilities ready for use for various activities
    f. maximizes use of time available for guidance and counseling
    g. manages student behavior, e.g.,
        —specifies expectations
        —uses techniques to prevent, redirect, or stop off-task, inappropriate, or disruptive behavior
        —applies rules consistently and fairly
        —uses reinforcement techniques effectively
    h. uses effective strategies to motivate students to respond to guidance and counseling
    i. displays a working knowledge of group dynamics, e.g.,
        —content and process variables
        —typical stage of group development
        —various leadership styles and their effective use
        —conditions for promoting healthy groups

Note. From *Guide to Counselor Performance Improvement,* by Northside Independent School District, 1987, San Antonio, TX. Reprinted with permission.

Observation Forms for Counseling, Consultation, and Referral Skills

Summary of Counselor Observation: Counseling Skills

Counselor _____ Date of Observation _____

School _____ Observation: From _____ to _____

General Information (theme, screening criteria, etc.)

    Grade level: _____ No. of students: _____

    Session #: _____

    Goal of group: _____

    Objective(s) of session: _____

    Client(s)' descriptions: _____

	Observed? (Circle)		Indicators/ Comments:
I. *Results of Program Plans and Preparation*			
a. Selects group/individual needs appropriately for efficiency and effectiveness	Yes	No	_____
b. Uses appropriate procedures for group member selection	Yes	No	_____
c. Clearly articulates purpose and strategies of session	Yes	No	_____
d. Responds appropriately to requests for information	Yes	No	_____
e. Length of session is appropriate to plans	Yes	No	_____
f. Has materials, etc., ready for use	Yes	No	_____
g. Establishes environment conducive to counseling	Yes	No	_____
h. Selects strategies that are student-centered and appropriate to students' age level and problems	Yes	No	_____
i. Provides services consistent with high-priority student needs and district goals	Yes	No	_____
Comments:			
II. *The Counseling Process*			
a. Provides focus for group	Yes	No	_____
b. Keeps group on task	Yes	No	_____
c. Facilitates students' problem definition and goal setting	Yes	No	_____
d. Gently encourages participation of each member	Yes	No	_____
e. Provides opportunity for student interaction	Yes	No	_____
f. Facilitates communication between participants	Yes	No	_____
g. Listens effectively	Yes	No	_____
h. Avoids premature or superficial advice or reassurance	Yes	No	_____

i. Handles expressions of hostility in a constructive manner	Yes	No	_____
j. Checks for understanding	Yes	No	_____
k. Facilitates "guided practice" (if appropriate)	Yes	No	_____
l. Clearly states follow-up plans	Yes	No	_____
m. States independent practice/"challenges"	Yes	No	_____

Comments:

III. *Personal/Professional*

a. Protects confidentiality	Yes	No	_____
b. Leads without dominating	Yes	No	_____
c. Explains clearly and concisely	Yes	No	_____
d. Is genuine as opposed to "phony"	Yes	No	_____
e. Interrupts destructive interaction appropriately	Yes	No	_____
f. Discloses own feelings and beliefs in a constructive manner	Yes	No	_____
g. Is tolerant of ideas others express	Yes	No	_____
h. Treats individuals with respect	Yes	No	_____
i. Recognizes individuals within group	Yes	No	_____
j. Uses appropriate vocabulary	Yes	No	_____
k. Applies a sound theoretical base	Yes	No	_____
l. Operates within realistic limitations of school counseling services	Yes	No	_____

Comments:

SUMMARY COMMENTS AND RECOMMENDATIONS:
Feedback Conference Date: _____ Time: _____
Observer: _____ Counselor: _____
(Signatures are for the sole purpose of documenting the conference.)

Summary of Counselor Observation: Consultation Skills

Counselor _____ Date of Observation _____
School _____ Observation: From _____ to _____
General Information—(context, participants, objectives, etc.)
    Student grade level: _____
    People involved in session: _____
    Topic: _____

	Observed? (Circle)		Indicators/ Comments:
I. *Planning and Preparation*			
a. Treats individuals with respect	Yes	No	_____
b. Makes objectives of session clear	Yes	No	_____
c. Is prepared for conference (e.g., has relevant information, knows students' background, is focused on the problem/issue)	Yes	No	_____
d. Prepares appropriate documentation, forms, records, etc.	Yes	No	_____
e. Has knowledge of community resources and referral sources	Yes	No	_____
f. Demonstrates knowledge of school district policy	Yes	No	_____
g. Has established that consultation is an appropriate intervention	Yes	No	_____

Comments:

II. *The Consultative Process*

			Yes	No	
a.	Uses effective intake procedures to properly discern problem/issue		Yes	No	_____
b.	Collaborates with consultee in definition of problem and goal setting		Yes	No	_____
c.	Coordinates a specific behavioral plan of action		Yes	No	_____
d.	Listens effectively		Yes	No	_____
e.	Facilitates communication between participants		Yes	No	_____
f.	Suggests various options for problem resolution		Yes	No	_____
g.	Avoids premature, superficial advice or reassurance		Yes	No	_____
h.	Handles expressions of conflict in a constructive manner		Yes	No	_____
i.	Conducts session efficiently and effectively		Yes	No	_____
j.	States plan for follow-up		Yes	No	_____
k.	Summarizes conferences results accurately		Yes	No	_____

Comments:

III. *Personal/Professional*

		Yes	No	
a.	Protects confidentiality	Yes	No	_____
b.	Is genuine as opposed to "phony"	Yes	No	_____
c.	Is appreciative of ideas others express	Yes	No	_____
d.	Recognizes diversity of individuals' perspectives	Yes	No	_____
e.	Promotes a spirit of compromise and cooperation	Yes	No	_____
f.	Establishes professional credibility	Yes	No	_____
g.	Applies a sound theoretical base	Yes	No	_____

Comments:

SUMMARY COMMENTS AND RECOMMENDATIONS:

Feedback Conference Date: _____ Time: _____
Observer: _____ Counselor: _____
(Signatures are for the sole purpose of documenting the conference.)

Summary of Counselor Observation: Referral Skills

Counselor _____ Date of Observation _____
School _____ Observation: From _____ to _____
General Information—(context, participants, objectives, etc.)
    Student grade level: _____
    People involved in session: _____
    Topic: _____

		Observed? (Circle)		Indicators/ Comments:
I. *Plans and Preparation*				
a.	Summarizes conference results accurately	Yes	No	_____
b.	Understands and articulates reason(s) for referral	Yes	No	_____
c.	Is prepared for conference (e.g., has relevant information, knows students' background, is focused on the problem/issue)	Yes	No	_____

d. Prepares appropriate documentation, forms, records, etc.	Yes	No	_____
e. Has knowledge of community resources and referral sources	Yes	No	_____
f. Demonstrates knowledge of school district policy	Yes	No	_____
g. Has established that referral is an appropriate intervention	Yes	No	_____

Comments:

II. *Referral Conference*

a. Uses effective intake procedures to properly discern problem/issue	Yes	No	_____
b. Defines problem clearly	Yes	No	_____
c. Expresses rationale for referral clearly	Yes	No	_____
d. Outlines action steps for referral process	Yes	No	_____
e. Listens effectively	Yes	No	_____
f. Provides minimum of three referral options to client (if referral is nondistrict, program/specialists)	Yes	No	_____
g. Helps individuals referred to have realistic expectations of services available from referral source	Yes	No	_____
h. Helps individuals referred to understand their responsibilities and to make plans for action	Yes	No	_____
i. States own follow-up/coordination plans	Yes	No	_____
j. Summarizes conference results	Yes	No	_____

Comments:

III. *Personal/Professional*

a. Promotes confidentiality	Yes	No	_____
b. Is genuine as opposed to "phony"	Yes	No	_____
c. Recognizes feelings and thoughts of client(s)	Yes	No	_____
d. Promotes a spirit of cooperation and problem solving	Yes	No	_____
e. Establishes professional credibility	Yes	No	_____
f. Assists individual(s) referred to feel comfortable about referral	Yes	No	_____

Comments:

Summary Comments and Recommendations

Feedback Conference Date: _____ Time: _____

Observer: _____ Counselor: _____

(Signatures are for the sole purpose of documenting the conference.)

Note. From Northside Independent School District, San Antonio, TX. Reprinted with permission.

Standards for a Guidance Program Audit

There are eight standards against which a guidance program is audited:

1. The school district is able to demonstrate that all students are provided the opportunity to gain knowledge, skills, values, and attitudes that lead to a self-sufficient, socially responsible life.
2. The school district is able to demonstrate that students have acquired regular and timely information to enable them to make informed decisions.
3. The school district is able to demonstrate that all students have access to assistance in overcoming problems that are impeding their educational, personal, social, and/or career development.
4. The school district is able to demonstrate that a team of educators provides guidance to students within a supportive learning environment.
5. The school district is able to demonstrate implementation of a guidance program that reflects allocation of resources according to students' needs.
6. The school district is able to demonstrate that guidance program staff are used in roles reflective of their training and competence, and relevant staff development opportunities are made available.
7. The school district is able to demonstrate that the guidance program is developmentally sequential, structured comprehensively, designed to ensure appropriate program balance, and is an integral part of the overall educational program.
8. The school district is able to demonstrate that the guidance program is reviewed continually and renewed annually.

STANDARD 1: The school district is able to demonstrate that all students are provided the opportunity to gain knowledge, skills, values, and attitudes that lead to a self-sufficient, socially responsible life.

A school district meeting this standard has defined the content that all students should learn in a systematic, sequential way. The content goals are tied to those defined in the basic mission of the school district and are based on human development theories regarding individuals' personal, social, career, and educational development. The content is further defined in a scope and sequence that outlines the guidance curriculum. The implementation of the guidance curriculum component of a comprehensive guidance program entails teaching lessons and units designed to help students acquire the competencies outlined in the scope and sequence.

What the auditor expects to find:

- A developmentally appropriate guidance curriculum teaches all students the knowledge and skills they need to be self-sufficient and lead socially responsible lives.

- A guidance curriculum is articulated from elementary to middle to high schools.
- Priorities are established for acquisition of competencies and attainment of outcomes by students at each grade level.
- Sufficient curriculum materials support teaching the needed knowledge and skills.
- Yearly schedule incorporates the classroom guidance plan.
- Students in special education and other special programs receive guidance curriculum instruction.

Documentation:

- Guidance curriculum guides
- Guidance curriculum scope and sequence
- Teachers' and counselors' unit and lesson plans
- Yearly master calendar for the guidance program
- Curriculum materials

STANDARD 2: The school district is able to demonstrate that students have acquired regular and timely information to enable them to make informed decisions.

A school district meeting this standard has in place a system for guiding all students as they make and implement plans toward achieving their educational and career goals. In addition, students and their parents are assisted in understanding and monitoring the student's growth and development and in making thoughtful decisions. The individual student planning component of a comprehensive guidance program entails providing accurate and unbiased information at regular and developmentally appropriate times and guiding students and their parents through the use of that information. Activities included in this component include assessment, advisement, and placement assistance.

What the auditor expects to find:

- An individual planning system is in place and assists all students and their parents to understand and monitor the students' growth and development, to problem solve, and to make thoughtful decisions. The system includes assessment, advisement, and placement activities timed to meet students' developmental needs appropriately and effectively for planning, monitoring, and taking next steps in implementing their plans.
- Specific activities include individual and group guidance sessions designed to assist students with their educational and career planning, to assist students in making transitions from one school level to the next, and to assist students and parents to make effective use of standardized test results.
- Information dissemination is conducted systematically and efficiently. Printed information is accurate, complete, and attractive.

Documentation:

- Individual planning system guides
- Guidance session plans
- Career guidance center schedule of activities and bibliography of information sources
- Test results and memos/handouts that indicate efforts addressed at making effective use of these results

- Standardized forms that reflect direct services to students and parent involvement
- Documents distributed through school orientations that provide information on test data interpretation, course content and selection procedures, promotion and graduation requirements, postsecondary educational and career options, financial aid information, and college testing information, requirements, and procedures.
- Individualized Educational Programs (IEPs) and treatment plans that reflect the inclusion of special education students into the activities that meet this standard.

STANDARD 3: The school district is able to demonstrate that all students have access to assistance in overcoming problems that are impeding their educational, personal, social, and/or career development.

A school district meeting this standard provides a variety of services for responding to the special needs and/or problems of students, their families, and teachers. The services that counselors/social workers are specially trained to provide include individual and small-group counseling, crisis counseling and response, consultation with teachers and parents, referral, and individual assessment. The responsive services component of a comprehensive guidance program includes preventive and remedial interventions that are planned in anticipation of recurrent student needs and are responsive when unanticipated needs arise.

Although at any given time all students are not in need of responsive services, these services must be available and accessible to all students. Ensuring equal access to the responsive services component entails guidance staff's outreach efforts and acceptance of students' diverse backgrounds and experiences.

What the auditor expects to find:

- A variety of responsive services—including individual and small-group counseling, crisis counseling, teacher and parent consultation, student assessment, and referral—are provided to students whose problems are interfering with their healthy development. Preventive and remedial interventions are available; services are planned in anticipation of student needs and are responsive when unanticipated needs arise.
- Counselors are readily accessible to students with problems.
- Efforts to reach out to students, teachers, and parents are made to ensure open access for those in need of services. In addition, procedures are in place to systematically identify students at risk and to implement strategies designed to decrease their level of risk.
- Teacher and administrator support teams are in place with counselor representation.
- Interdepartment and interagency linkages are in place to facilitate service delivery. Referral procedures are effective and clear.
- Record-keeping systems ensure confidentiality.
- Counseling staff adequately reflect the diversity in the community.

Documentation:

- Service delivery records that verify equitable service to all students regardless of race, ethnicity, socioeconomic status, ability/achievement level, gender
- Critical documents that are multilingual and interpreter support that is available and provided as needed

- Crisis management plan
- Counseling session plans and notes
- Consultation session plans and notes
- Progress reports and evidence of their use
- Referral documentation forms
- Yearly/monthly/weekly schedules of activities
- Schedule of small-group counseling offerings
- Letters of invitation and explanation; fliers
- Parent permission forms
- Referral source lists
- Case notes
- Multilingual, ethnically diverse staffing guidelines
- Counselor roster

STANDARD 4: The school district is able to demonstrate that a team of educators provides guidance to students within a supportive learning environment.

A school district meeting this standard knows that comprehensive guidance programs feature a team approach. Although professionally certified counselors/social workers provide leadership and are central to the program, all school staff collaborate in guiding students to attain educational success. Guidance staff collaborate with parents and community mental health services providers as well.

For a guidance program to be effective, the learning environment must be supportive and one in which relationships are characterized by mutual respect, trust, and open communication. Clients of the guidance program feel welcome, safe, and assured of their rights. Guidance program staff operate within ethical, legal, and professional standards.

What the auditor expects to find:

- Program delivery is the result of collaborative efforts among counselors, administrators, teachers, parents, and students.
- Building climates promote positive intra- and interpersonal relationships; that is, relationships are characterized by mutual respect, trust, collaboration and cooperation, and open communications.
- To enhance the educational success of students, counselors are in partnership with parents—including parent–teacher association (PTA) members as well as the parents of their counselees; with teachers as part of the educational team; with other school-based specialists as part of the specialist team; and with community mental health workers as part of the community mental health team.
- Communication mechanisms (e.g., staff meetings, case consultations, in-service training) are in place to facilitate these relationships.
- Opportunities are provided and taken for counselors to explain the guidance program to staff, parents, and the community at large.
- Counselors and others working within the context of the guidance program adhere to the American Counseling Association, American School Counselor Association, and other relevant ethical standards, which protect students' and families' rights to privacy, confidentiality, respect, and belief in their integrity, and so forth.
- The guidance program goals and objectives are understood and supported by district and campus administrators, teachers, and parents.
- Students and parents feel invited, welcome, and safe in the counseling office and when receiving counseling services.

Documentation:

- Staff meeting schedules and agendas
- In-service training agendas
- Counselors' meetings, newsletters, and so forth with PTA
- Ethical standards readily accessible to each staff member
- Graduate follow-up information
- Climate studies or results
- School guidance committee philosophy statement/goals and objectives
- Student recognition process
- Natural helpers program plans
- Printed information regarding service offerings
- Documentation supporting parent involvement efforts

STANDARD 5: The school district is able to demonstrate implementation of a guidance program that reflects allocation of resources according to students' needs.

A school district meeting this standard has committed sufficient resources and channeled them to meet the identified, high-priority guidance needs of their students, and established a program implementation plan that focuses on meeting those needs most efficiently and effectively. Students' needs may be identified from the students' perspective as well as from that of the professional staff, the community, and other public policy entities. Consideration must be given to the demographics of the community served. The program's mission is articulated clearly to focus the allocation of resources. Resources include the guidance program staff, administrative support and rules and regulations, and access to students as well as budget, facilities, equipment, and materials.

What the auditor expects to find:

- The guidance program framework/plan is based on sound rationale; that is, an assessment of students' and community's needs is done regularly and leads to the establishment of priorities for program delivery. The campus program is based on accurate information regarding the student body's demographic characteristics (e.g., race, ethnicity, socioeconomic status, parent educational levels, labor market).
- The program is based on a cogent theoretical perspective regarding student (human) growth and development and the contribution that the school-based guidance and counseling program makes to that growth and development.
- The mission of the program—its definition, goals and objectives, and organizational pattern—is stated clearly and is relevant to the district's overall mission.
- The program's implementation plan is clearly tied to the adopted program mission and established priorities and organized to meet these most effectively and efficiently.
- Actual program implementation reflects the plan.
- The resources appropriated are sufficient for the program staff to be held accountable for assisting students to attain high-priority outcomes. Resources include allocation of staff, sufficient access to students, budget appropriations, adequate facilities, equipment and materials, and appropriate regulations and procedures.

Documentation:

- Results of needs assessments
- Campus demographic data reports

- Statements outlining the theoretical basis (philosophy) of the program (the assumptions in the Gysbers model)
- Board policy providing the foundation for the program
- District's strategic plan
- Campus guidance program mission statements
- Written district and campus plans
- Adopted handbook/framework
- Master calendar of activities (planned and completed)
- Calendars and logs of program activities
- Established student ratio guidelines
- Itemized district and campus guidance program budgets
- Facilities standards for counseling offices and rooms, records and storage areas, classroom availability, and so forth.
- Inventory of equipment and materials
- Written procedures and regulations

STANDARD 6: The school district is able to demonstrate that guidance program staff are used in roles reflective of their training and competence, and relevant staff development opportunities are made available.

A school district meeting this standard has defined the appropriate roles various staff members play in the delivery of the comprehensive guidance program. School counselors/social workers are the central guidance program staff; thus, their job descriptions are such that students reap optimum benefit from their special skills (i.e., guidance, counseling, consultation, coordination, referral, assessment). The roles of other guidance program staff are also delineated and appropriate to their training. The relationships among the various staff members are clearly defined. The performance of guidance program staff is nurtured through a relevant and fair performance improvement system, which includes opportunities for supervision, performance evaluation, and professional development.

What the auditor expects to find:

- School counselors provide leadership to the guidance program, and within the program use their special skills—guidance, counseling, consultation, coordination and referral, and case management and assessment—at least 80% of the time. Their involvement in nonguidance tasks is kept to a minimum.
- Professionalism is evidenced in the adherence to professional standards, including the development and implementation of annual professional development plans.
- Other professional and paraprofessional staff with delineated roles in the guidance program are using their special skills; that is, teachers teach, consult, and advise; administrators guide, consult, and advise; registrars maintain records; career guidance center technicians perform resource services; data-entry clerks do data entry.
- Staffing patterns are defined and assignments are based on student-centered rationale.
- A counselor-appropriate performance improvement system is in place that is relevant to effective delivery of the district's guidance program. This system includes supervision and performance evaluation conducted by a trained counselor supervisor/evaluator. Clinical supervision may also be provided by peer supervisors/mentors/ coaches.
- Staff development is provided for regularly and on topics indicated as needed by the counselors and by program priorities.
- Professional induction activities are provided for new counselors.

Documentation:

- Professional certifications
- Staffing pattern/organizational chart
- Program definition with clarification of staff members' roles and responsibilities
- Position-specific job descriptions
- Staff members' professional development plans
- Clinical supervision schedules
- Program improvement goals
- Performance evaluation forms
- Staff development plan
- Staff development agendas and other materials
- New counselor orientation agendas
- Inventories of professional library resources

STANDARD 7: The school district is able to demonstrate that the guidance program is developmentally sequential, structured comprehensively, designed to ensure appropriate program balance, and is an integral part of the overall educational program.

A school district meeting this standard provides activities that are developmentally appropriate, that is, they are based on the theory of human development previously described and are sequenced to ensure student development of prerequisite knowledge and skills. The guidance curriculum and individual student planning components are the basis of the developmental program; however, the responsive services component activities are based on awareness of the knowledge and skills students have/have not acquired.

A characteristic of the comprehensive guidance program is that program activities are organized according to the four delivery system components of guidance curriculum, individual student planning, responsive services, and system support. Between and within these components, priorities are established that direct the appropriate use of guidance program staff time and skills and identify the content to be addressed. In addition to having definitions of its own, the guidance program is integrated with other educational programs to better ensure students' acquisition and application of needed knowledge and skills.

What the auditor expects to find:

- The program is designed to provide students with a developmentally appropriate base of knowledge and skills from which to achieve a self-sufficient and socially responsible life. This basis is delivered to students through the guidance curriculum and individual student planning components.
- The foundation of the program is expressed in the rationale for, assumptions behind, and definition of the program.
- The program activities are organized to ensure implementation of the four delivery system components—guidance curriculum, individual student planning, responsive services, and system support—and of the priorities within each component.
- Priorities are established that direct the program balance, that is, provide the measure of appropriate allocation of resources.
- Fifty to 70% of the activities involve direct contact with students. An exemplary balance might be: (ES = elementary school; MS = middle school; HS = high school)

	% of Counselor's Time		
	ES	MS	HS
Guidance Curriculum	35–45	25–35	15–25
Individual Student Planning	5–10	15–25	25–35
Responsive Services	30–40	30–40	25–35
System Support	10–15	10–15	15–20
Nonguidance	0	0	0

- All staff participate in helping students achieve guidance program goals.
- The guidance program is integrated with other educational programs and has integrity as a separate program.
- Instructional goals are supported by the guidance department through such means as interpretation of standardized test results and other data regarding students' performance to teachers, administrators, and school board members.
- Communication mechanisms exist to ensure integration and understanding of mutual goals and plans—for example, guidance department head meets regularly with instructional department heads; guidance department head meets regularly with administration. Counselors are assigned as liaisons to each department.

Documentation:

- Curricular scope and sequence
- Guidance program framework/handbook, including priority topics by component by grade/school level
- Program balance charts
- Counselors' calendars and logs
- Staff familiarity with guidance program goals and objectives
- Curricular infusion bridge documents
- Staff roles and responsibilities statements
- Guidance program improvement goals and plans correlated to the campus goals and improvement plans
- Staff meeting schedules

STANDARD 8: The school district is able to demonstrate that the guidance program is reviewed continually and renewed annually.

A school district meeting this standard has in place a system for evaluating the effectiveness and efficiency of the comprehensive guidance program. The program is evaluated against the implementation standards that have been adopted (such as this audit). Evaluation is conducted to judge whether program changes are, in fact, program improvements. Finally, assessments are made of students' acquisition of the knowledge and skills taught through the program. The results of evaluations are used to redesign and thereby improve the program and for staff development. Reports of results are shared with appropriate audiences to ensure accountability of the comprehensive guidance program.

What the auditor expects to find:

- An annual process is in place for planning, designing, and evaluating the comprehensive guidance program with time appropriated for these activities and with mechanisms to ensure that evaluation data are considered in replanning the program.

- Evaluation is conducted regarding the effectiveness of program implementation and students' attainment of priority outcomes.
- The process allows the guidance staff some autonomy in designing and implementing the program on the campus. An advisory committee provides meaningful input to the guidance program improvement efforts.

Documentation:

- Annual written evaluation of outcomes students have attained through the program
- Planning forms and evaluation reports
- Yearly, monthly, and weekly calendars
- Written reports analyzing actual versus planned program implementation
- Program improvement plans based on evaluation findings
- Budget expenditures
- Counselor time accountability forms
- Data on effectiveness of program activities
- Advisory committee roster, meeting announcements/agendas, minutes of meetings

☞ Appendix P ☜

Sample Memo Regarding Major Changes and New Program Recommendations

TO: Counselors and Principals
FROM: Director of Guidance
RE: Major Changes and New Recommendations in the Comprehensive Guidance Program Framework
DATE:

Client priorities
- Counselors' priority is students with needs for prevention or intervention services

Priorities for counselors' skill use
- Counseling
- Guidance program management
- Consultation

Guidance as a schoolwide responsibility
- Teamwork and collaboration between counselors, other staff members, and parents emphasized
- Administrators' and teachers' roles outlined
- Student advisory program for all students to extend the individual planning system
- School counselors' responsibilities for the quality of the total guidance program include consultation, support, and supervision

Parents' rights and responsibilities delineated
- Roles outlined
- Responsibilities for parent involvement clarified

Guidance program
- Recommended balance presented in ranges, leaving room for school-based decisions
- Teachers' role in guidance curriculum recognized
- Transition activities emphasized in individual planning system
- Responsive services emphasized for use of counselor time
- Each campus to set topic priorities for responsive services each year on the basis of an assessment of student and community needs
- Counselors' responsive services outlined as a continuum: identification, appraisal, prevention and intervention, follow-up
- New priorities established for the time available to support other programs

- Special elements of the guidance program defined for better coordination with the basic program

Levels of service projected
- Minimum or possible numbers of activities specified for each component
- The number of students possibly served by a counselor in a specific program balance and with a given ratio calculated

Enhanced Performance Improvement System
- Roles related to program components
- Roles, competencies, indicators, and descriptors defined as basis of system
- Roles and responsibilities of specialist counselors detailed
- Supervision system recommended for elementary counselors
- Systematic staff development system implemented

Job descriptions established for guidance department paraprofessionals
- Nonguidance tasks take an undue amount of counselors' time (still)
- Recommendations: building test coordinator responsibilities be shared; 504 coordinator be an administrator; continue to pursue the addition of technical assistants at all three levels

Program management support
- Desired counselor–student ratio established at 1:350; reductions suggested in middle and magnet school head counselors' ratio
- Elementary: guidance classroom; flexible schedule; secretarial time

Index

Figures and tables are indicated by f and t following page numbers. Alphabetization is letter-by-letter (e.g., "Educational" precedes "Education Trust").